11th Edition

Computers
Are Your Future

COMPLETE

Catherine LaBerta

Prentice Hall

Boston Columbus Indianapolis New York San Francisco Upper Saddle River
Amsterdam Cape Town Dubai London Madrid Milan Munich Paris Montréal Toronto
Delhi Mexico City São Paulo Sydney Hong Kong Seoul Singapore Taipei Tokyo

Editor in Chief: *Michael Payne*
Associate VP/Executive Acquisitions Editor,
  Print: *Stephanie Wall*
Product Development Manager: *Eileen Bien Calabro*
Editorial Project Manager: *Virginia Guariglia*
Development Editor: *Linda Harrison*
Editorial Assistant: *Nicole Sam*
Director of Marketing: *Kate Valentine*
Marketing Manager: *Tori Olson Alves*
Marketing Coordinator: *Susan Osterlitz*
Marketing Assistant: *Darshika Vyas*
Senior Managing Editor: *Cynthia Zonneveld*
Associate Managing Editor: *Camille Trentacoste*
Production Project Manager: *Mike Lackey*
Operations Director: *Alexis Heydt*
Senior Operations Specialist: *Diane Peirano*
Art Director: *Anthony Gemmellaro*
Text and Cover Designer: *Anthony Gemmellaro*
Cover Photo: *Shutterstock Images / Stian Iversen*
Manager, Visual Research: *Beth Brenzel*
Photo Researcher: *David Tietz*
Manager, Rights and Permissions: *Zina Arabia*

Image Permission Coordinator:
  Richard Rodrigues
Manager, Cover Visual Research &
  Permissions: *Karen Sanatar*
Rights and Permissions Manager:
  Shannon Barbe
Text Permission Researcher: *Michele Pridmore*
AVP/Director of Online Programs, Media:
  Richard Keaveny
AVP/Director of Product Development, Media:
  Lisa Strite
Product Development Manager, Media:
  Cathi Profitko
Media Project Manager, Editorial: *Alana Coles*
Media Project Manager, Production: *John Cassar*
Supplements Editor: *Tiffany Bottolfson*
Full-Service Project Management:
  MPS Content Services
Composition: *MPS Limited, A Macmillan Company*
Printer/Binder: *Quebecor World Color / Versailles*
Cover Printer: *Lehigh-Phoenix Color / Hagerstown*
Text Font: *New Century Schlbk, 9.5 / 11.5*

CIP Data on file

Prentice Hall
is an imprint of

www.pearsonhighered.com

10 9 8 7 6 5 4 3 2 1
ISBN-10:   0-13-509276-0
ISBN-13: 978-0-13-509276-7

─With **love** ─────────────────

to my parents, Eleanore and Chester, for their unending love and
support; to my son, Michael, for years of laughter and challenges; to my
brother, sister, and brother-in-law for help during the tough times; and to
Stephanie for providing me with an exceptional opportunity.

Acknowledgments

Thanks to the many professionals at Prentice Hall who made this book possible and
assisted with questions and feedback during the writing process. A special thanks to
Stephanie Wall, Associate Vice President and Executive Editor Extraordinaire, for
providing me with this incredible opportunity, and to my project manager, Virginia
Guariglia, for keeping me on schedule and connected to the process. Special thanks
also to Linda Harrison, my developmental editor, for her input, guidance, patience,
and incredible eye for detail throughout the development cycle. I am grateful for the
friends and colleagues that, through the years, have encouraged my professional
growth and energy. Finally, thanks to my family and friends—especially my parents,
Eleanore and Chester, for encouraging me when I was young, and my son, Michael,
for keeping me on my toes. I am sure I forgot to mention someone, but in my heart I
have forgotten no one. Thank you all!

Brief Contents

Contents

Preface

A Reference Tool for Today's Students

Today, students aren't wowed by technology—it is part of their daily lives. This book has been written to match what they already know with what you've told us they should know.

This new edition serves as a reference tool without being overwhelming or intimidating. Today's students want a practical "what it is" and "how it works" approach to computers, with less explanation of "why."

This book is written with this in mind. For example, the Spotlight about Web 2.0 technologies highlights the large variety of newer technologies available that most students aren't aware of.

This text is ready for the challenge of teaching even your most diverse class-without sacrificing quality, integrity, or choice.

This edition has the following new items:

- Scenarios at the start of each chapter to engage students
- New Spotlight on Web 2.0
- New Spotlight on Digital Life
- More on computer ethics by enhancing Spotlight 1
- Microsoft Office Spotlight covers Office 2010
- New end-of-chapter projects
- New Ethics boxes and Green Tech Tips
- Enhanced coverage of social networking and the latest tech products such as the Kindle
- Revised the System Software chapter and File Management Spotlight to cover Windows 7
- Added coverage of Web-based applications
- Added coverage of VPNs
- Enhanced coverage of the costs of identity theft and other security issues.
- Added coverage of approaches to system design— prototyping and joint application development
- Introduction to grid computing and cloud computing
- Enhanced coverage of tactile displays, and simulations in gaming, medicine, and consumer shopping

ABOUT THIS BOOK

Spotlight sections cover the practical, as well as the innovative, in various subject areas. For example, Ethics, File Management, and Buying and Upgrading Your Home Computer System focus on the practical, whereas Microsoft Office, Digital Life, and Emerging Technologies cover innovation in software, hardware, and technology for the future. We've added reinforcing exercises at the end of each Spotlight.

Teamwork exercises are included as an end-of-chapter activity to reinforce chapter concepts by requiring students to work in teams to conduct research and interviews and to create group papers and presentations.

Green Tech Tips provide eco-friendly solutions to living and working with technology. These range from actions students can apply on their own to those that are initiated by companies in an effort to preserve the environment.

Ethics boxes offer an ethical perspective on decisions and situations that involve computers and technology. They raise "what if" type of questions in a "what would you do format" to prompt thoughtful discussion and debate on complicated issues.

INSTRUCTOR'S RESOURCE CENTER CD-ROM

The Prentice Hall Instructor's Resource Center on CD-ROM includes the tools you expect from a Prentice Hall Computer Concepts text, such as:

- Instructor's Manual
- Solutions to all questions and exercises from the book and Web site
- Customizable PowerPoint slide presentations for each chapter
- An image library of all of the figures from the text

TESTGEN SOFTWARE

TestGen is a test generator that lets you view and easily edit test bank questions, transfer them to tests, and print the tests in a variety of formats best suited to your teaching situation. Powerful search and sort functions enable you to easily locate questions and arrange them in the order you prefer.

TOOLS FOR ONLINE LEARNING

Companion Web Site This text is accompanied by a companion Web site at **www.pearsonhighered. com/cayf**. This site offers an interactive study guide, downloadable supplements, additional Internet exercises, Web resource links such as Careers in IT and crossword puzzles.

CourseCompass CourseCompass, available at **www.coursecompass.com**, is a dynamic, interactive online course-management tool powered exclusively for Pearson Education by Blackboard. This exciting product allows you to teach market-leading Pearson Education content in an easy-to-use, customizable format.

Blackboard Prentice Hall's abundant online content, combined with Blackboard's popular tools and interface, results in robust Web-based courses that are easy to implement, manage, and use—taking your courses to new heights in student interaction and learning.

WebCT Course-management tools within WebCT, available at **www.pearsonhighered.com/webct**, include page tracking, progress tracking, class and student management, a grade book, communication tools, a calendar, reporting tools, and more.

Visual Walkthrough

walkthrough walkthrough walkthrough walk

Spotlight

Web 2.0

When was the last time you called a friend or spoke f2f (face-to-face) to ask a question or to tell your friend what you were doing, and when did you send your last e-mail? Today, there are so many ways to keep everyone informed. One of the top choices is using the technologies that have been described in this book and Web 2.0, which has a language all its own. "OMG GTG BRB ur gr8 roflol" is a little shorter than "Oh my gosh, got to go, be right back, you are great, rolling on the floor, laughing out loud." So, what exactly is Web 2.0?

Spotlight

Buying and Upgrading Your Computer System

When buying a computer, you need to know a lot to make a good decision. But buying a computer doesn't have to be intimidating! Many students successfully purchase and maintain their own computers. In fact, at a typical state university, 95 percent of students own a computer.

By having your own PC, you can type term papers, create slide presentations, and in many cases use the high-speed wireless network all over campus. Many schools encourage students to purchase a computer before they arrive on campus. Even though schools still provide computer labs, with your own computer you can work when you want and, in the case of notebooks, where you want. This Spotlight will guide you step by step through the process of buying your own computer. Read on to learn how to choose the equipment you'll need, at the best prices on today's market.

Spotlight sections highlight important ideas about computer-related topics and provide in-depth, useful information to take your learning to the next level.

ETHICS

USB flash drives are incredibly popular, but many experts worry that they pose a great security risk too. Some companies are so concerned about corporate espionage that they disable USB ports to prevent the unauthorized copying of data. Even so, many people carry a lot of critical or personal data on their flash drives. What are the implications if the device is lost? Should USB drive manufacturers be required to provide a means of securing these devices? What actions should individuals take to safeguard their data? Have you ever found a USB drive? What did you do with it?

Ethics Boxes highlight ethical issues for students to think about.

GREEN tech tips

More than 700 million inkjet and laser toner cartridges are sold every year. What happens when they are empty? Although many organizations and retail stores have recycling programs, every second nearly eight used cartridges are thrown away in the United States— approximately 875 million pounds of environmental waste each year! So what can you do? Take advantage of your local recycling program. Some programs even pay you for your old cartridges because they can be recycled and sold again. Keeping them out of the waste stream reduces toxicity levels and saves landfill space. Besides, half a gallon of oil is saved for every toner cartridge you recycle! ●

Green Tech Tips share ways to be aware of the effects of technology on our earth.

Chapter Summary

Computers and You

A computer system is a collection of related components that have been designed to perform the information processing cycle: input, processing, output, and storage. A system includes both hardware—the physical components such as the system unit, keyboard, monitor, and speakers—and software—the programs that run on it. In a typical computer system, a keyboard and a mouse provide input capabilities. Processing is done by the microprocessor (CPU) on programs and data held in RAM (random access memory). You see the results (output) on a monitor or printer, and a hard disk is typically used for long-term storage.

There are two major categories of computers: computers for individuals and those for organizations. Types of computers for individuals include personal computers (PCs), desktop computers, all-in-one computers, notebooks, subnotebooks (ultraportables), tablet PCs, and handheld computers (such as PDAs and smartphones). Types of computers for organizations include professional workstations, servers, minicomputers, mainframes, and supercomputers.

Computers have advantages and disadvantages. Some advantages include speed, memory, storage, hardware reliability, accuracy, and assistance to those with disabilities. Disadvantages include information overload, expense, data inaccuracy, unreliable software, viruses, software piracy, identity theft, loss of jobs to automation, and health problems due to improperly fitting equipment and poorly arranged work environments.

Being a responsible computer user means respecting others when using technology, recycling computer hardware, sharing public computing resources, being aware of computer and Internet overuse, and staying informed about changing technology and its effect on the environment.

Key Terms and Concepts

algorithm 8
all-in-one computer 12
application software 7
automation 22
bug 20
carpal tunnel syndrome 19
central processing unit (CPU), also microprocessor or processor 8
client 14
client/server network 14
communications 9
communications device 9
computer 6
computer ethics 21
computer forensics 17
computer system 6
data 6
desktop computer 11
digital divide 16
digital piracy 21
e-book reader 13
e-learning 22
e-waste 24
ergonomics 19
fat client 14
Google Docs 17
Google Groups 17
handheld computer 13
hardware 6
information 6
information overload 18
information processing cycle 6
input 6
input device 8
instant messaging (IM) 17
integrated peripheral 6
Kindle 2 21
legacy technology 9
mainframe (enterprise server) . . 14
microcomputer 11
microprocessor (processor) 8
minicomputer (midrange server) 14
modem 10
motherboard 6
netbook 13
network 9
network interface card (NIC) . . . 10
notebook computer 12
operating system (OS) 6
output 6
output device 8
outsourcing 23
peripheral device 6
personal computer (PC or microcomputer) 11
personal digital assistant (PDA) 13
petaflop 15
processing 6
professional workstation 14
program 6
random access memory (RAM) 18
server 14
smartphone 13
social network 17
software 6
storage 6
storage device 9
structural unemployment 23
subnotebook 12
supercomputer 15
system software 6
system unit 6
tablet PC 12
terminal 14
thin client 14
tweet 17
Twitter 17
ultraportable 12
USB flash drive 9
virtual keyboard 13
wiki 17

Matching

Match each key term in the left column with the most accurate definition in the right column:

____ 1. program
____ 2. netbook
____ 3. digital piracy
____ 4. bug
____ 5. data
____ 6. tablet PC
____ 7. professional workstation
____ 8. all-in-one computer
____ 9. computer ethics
____ 10. information
____ 11. network interface card
____ 12. ergonomics
____ 13. random access memory
____ 14. communications
____ 15. information processing cycle

a. A portable lightweight computer equipped with wireless technology and used primarily to browse the Web and access e-mail.
b. Facts that have been processed for presentation in a meaningful form.
c. A computer system in which the system unit and monitor are combined to reduce the space needed to hold the system.
d. A high-end computer designed for technical applications requiring powerful processing and output capabilities.
e. A branch of philosophy that deals with computer-related moral dilemmas.
f. A convertible notebook that can be used in two different configurations and accepts handwritten input.
g. Unauthorized reproduction and distribution of computer-based media.
h. A set of instructions that tells a computer how to perform a process.
i. Raw facts.
j. An error in software or hardware that makes a program malfunction.
k. The matching of computer components to fit an individual's posture and body design.
l. The high-speed movement of data within and between computers.
m. Needed to temporarily store data and programs with which the CPU interacts.
n. Four basic operations of a computer system.
o. A hardware component of a computer system that contains the electronics to connect the computer to a network.

Multiple Choice

Circle the correct choice for each of the following:

1. Which of the following is a common input device?
   a. Mouse b. Printer
   c. Disk drive d. Speaker
2. Which of the following is *not* an example of application software?
   a. Word processor b. Spreadsheet
   c. Operating system d. Photo editor
3. What part of the system unit processes the input data?
   a. Read-alone memory
   b. CPU
   c. Random access memory
   d. NIC
4. What component of a computer is located in the system unit and contains the circuitry to connect the computer to a network?
   a. RAM b. Node
   c. CPU d. NIC
5. Which is an example of an e-book reader?
   a. Wiki b. NIC
   c. Kindle 2 d. Tweeter
6. What is the sending of portions of a job to a third party to reduce cost, time, and energy called?
   a. Outsourcing
   b. Automation
   c. Digital piracy
   d. Structural unemployment
7. What is the feeling of anxiety experienced when people are presented with more information than they can handle?
   a. Technology overload b. Technology meltdown
   c. Processing overload d. Information overload
8. Which of the following computers is *not* designed for portability or use while traveling?
   a. All-in-one b. Notebook
   c. Tablet PC d. Ultraportable

End-of-Chapter Material includes updated multiple-choice, matching, fill-in, and short-answer questions, as well as Web research projects so you can prepare for tests.

9. Which of the following is a computer used by government agencies and large corporations like airlines and banks?
   a. Workstation
   b. Mainframe
   c. Supercomputer
   d. All-in-one
10. What is the name given to unemployment caused by technology making an entire job category obsolete?
    a. Technological unemployment
    b. Corporate unemployment
    c. Structural unemployment
    d. Automated unemployment

Fill-In

In the blanks provided, write the correct answer for each of the following:

1. The mouse and keyboard are ________ devices.
2. Monitors, printers, and speakers are ________ devices.
3. Hard drives, DVD drives, and USB drives are examples of ________ devices.
4. The operating system and antivirus software are part of the software group called ________ ________.
5. ________ is a social messaging utility that allows posting of up to 140 characters that take the form of short questions and answers.
6. Obsolete computer equipment is called ________.
7. Facebook and LinkedIn are examples of ________ ________.
8. A(n) ________ ________ is an onscreen touch-activated keyboard.
9. A(n) ________ is a group of two or more connected computer systems that share devices and resources.
10. ________ ________ is a free Web-based word processor and spreadsheet that encourages collaboration by allowing group members to share and edit documents online.
11. A centrally located and operated computer that makes programs and data available to people who are connected to a computer network is a ________.
12. The replacement of human workers by machines is known as ________.
13. The ________ is the circuit board located in the system unit that connects the CPU and other system components.
14. The ________ ________ describes the disparity between groups who own computers and have Internet access and those who do not.
15. The use of computers and computer programs to replace teachers and time-specific learning is ________.

Short Answer

1. Explain the difference between hardware and software.
2. Provide a brief description of the similarities and differences between a desktop computer and an all-in-one computer.
3. What are the differences among a notebook computer, a tablet PC, and a netbook?
4. Define the terms *data* and *information*. Identify the step in the information processing cycle that each is associated with.
5. List three examples of application software found on the computer systems in your home, school, or office.
6. List three advantages and three disadvantages of computer use.
7. List three to five characteristics of a responsible computer user.

Teamwork

1. **Handheld Computers** Your team is to investigate the latest smartphones from at least three manufacturers. Break into three teams with each team researching the features, costs, monthly fees, insurance rates, and accessories for each manufacturer's latest device. Prepare a presentation to make to the rest of the class; and be sure to cite your resources.

2. **"I am a Mac, and I am a PC"** As a team, use a search engine to locate and review at least three of the "I am a Mac, and I am a PC" commercials. These are 30-second commercials that praise the features of the Mac while mocking the PC. Cite the commercials viewed. Create a new 30-second commercial that will reverse the ad: Have the commercial support the PC while mocking the Mac. Your team will have to research both systems to find a PC asset that the Mac lacks. Rehearse your commercial and present it to the class.
3. **Tablet PC or Notebook—You Decide** As a team, determine whether you would purchase a tablet PC or a notebook computer. Use the Internet or contact a local vendor and compare the prices for similarly equipped units. Based on your needs and finances, prepare a report to present to the class explaining which computer you would buy and give reasons that support your decision.
4. **Ergonomics** As a team, use a search engine and locate at least three Web sites that contain information about the ergonomics of setting up computer stations. Prepare a report that covers the following items. First define the term *ergonomics,* and then list at least five items that should be ergonomically designed in a computer station for the user's health and comfort. For at least three of these five items, find two retailers that sell such ergonomic products. Describe the products, explain how they will ergonomically correct or prevent a problem, and note how much the devices cost. Be sure to cite your resources.
5. **Employment** As a team, examine advertisements for jobs in your area. Use online job search sites and your local paper. Make a chart of 10 job categories that require computer knowledge and then review the jobs in each category. In the chart, enter the number of available jobs that were posted or listed for each category. If possible, state the average pay of a position in each category. Present your findings to the class, explaining what you have learned from your research.

On the Web

1. **Green Computers** Go to **www.worldchanging.com/archives/004350.html** and use Google (**www.google.com**) or another search engine to locate sources of information about green computers. List at least three green computer features and their components. Then use the Internet to locate three manufacturers of green computers. State the name of each computer, its price, and the green features that each system possesses. Present this information in a one- or two-page, double-spaced report. Be sure to cite your references.
2. **Digital Divide** Use Google (**www.google.com**) or **www.digitaldivide.org/dd/index.html** to research and obtain background information about the digital divide. Locate three articles with information about the digital divide, its past and present, and actions being taken to reduce it in the future. Cite your references and present your results in a one-page, double-spaced paper.
3. **Robotics** Use your favorite search engine to locate at least three articles about robots in manufacturing. Look for such facts as the number and type of jobs being turned over to robots, the countries buying and producing robotic equipment, and how much a robot costs versus how much a company can save by using a robot. After collecting the data, present your findings in a table, listing at least three advantages and three disadvantages of robot use in manufacturing. Back up each entry in the table with a statistic or fact from your research. Remember to cite your references.
4. **Ethics** Use your favorite search engine and locate the "Ten Commandments of Computer Ethics" published by the Computer Ethics Institute. Read each one, and in a one-page paper indicate at least three commandments with which you agree and three with which you disagree. Give logical and historical reasons for your statement. You might want to reference the Bill of Rights or other historical documents to support your stance. Cite your references and present your reasons in a one- or two-page, double-spaced paper.
5. **Social Networks** Use your favorite search engine to locate a definition of social networking, as well as find articles about the pros and cons of Web sites used to socially network. Visit the social networking sites mentioned in this chapter: Facebook, MySpace, and LinkedIn. Pretend you are going to develop your own social networking site. Use your observations and research to come up with a list of five rules users of the sites will have to follow and five behaviors that will cause a user to be expelled from the site. Define *social networking,* list the pros and cons of social networking you found in your research, and list your five rules and five behaviors that cause expulsion in a one-page, double-spaced paper.

Computers
Are Your Future

chapter 1

Computers and You

Chapter Objectives

- Define the word *computer* and name the four basic operations that a computer performs. (p. 6)

- Describe the two main components of a computer system: hardware and software. (p. 6)

- Provide examples of hardware devices that handle input, processing, output, and storage tasks. (p. 8)

- Give an example of the information processing cycle in action. (p. 10)

- Discuss the two major categories and the various types of computers. (p. 11)

- Explain the advantages and disadvantages of computer use. (p. 17)

- Understand the risks involved in using hardware and software. (p. 19)

- Recognize the ethical and societal impacts of computer use. (p. 20)

- Discuss how computers affect employment. (p. 22)

- List ways to be a responsible computer user. (p. 23)

Hone your imagination—all these products already exist! Prepare yourself to interact successfully with tomorrow's developments by understanding the technology behind today's devices, how to use them, and how to handle the information they provide.

Computers have become so integral to our daily lives that it's difficult to think of a time without them. They're used at home, at work, and in school; they're embedded into our cars, phones, and cameras. You've explored the Web and have used the Internet. You text friends and family or post updates to your Facebook page, take classes online, connect with study group members or coworkers to evaluate information, download music and video files, and burn CDs and DVDs. What more is there to know? You may be able to perform these tasks; but your future isn't about just performing single, unrelated tasks. You must relate the tasks, understand the technology used to perform them, use that technology to collect information, share that information with others locally and globally, and then singularly or collectively use the information to make decisions. What knowledge do you need now to prepare yourself to capitalize on future technological advancements?

Think about the changes that have occurred as a result of technological innovation during the past several decades. When nations were attempting something as complex as sending a person to the moon, there were no telephone answering machines, no cell phones, no handheld calculators, and no personal computers. People wrote letters by hand or with a typewriter, kept track of numbers and data in ledgers, and communicated in person or over the telephone. Those telephones were physically connected: Cordless handsets didn't come onto the market until the late 1970s, and cell phones followed in the 1980s.

In the 1980s only the U.S. government and colleges and universities were able to access the Internet (including e-mail); cell phones were just coming into use; and fax machines were the fastest way for most businesses to share documents across distances. The World Wide Web would not become viable until 1993. Today millions of people use the Internet daily in both their professional and personal lives. Cell phones seem to be a necessary part of everyday life; GPS units guide travelers to their destinations; and retail e-commerce, which didn't begin until 1995 and had sales of $133.6 billion in 2008, is projected to grow to $203 billion by 2013.

To learn more about the development of computers over time, see the "Timeline of Computer History" at **www.computer.org/ portal/cms_docs_computer/computer/ timeline/timeline.pdf**.

Today it's becoming difficult to find an activity that doesn't involve computers, technology, and sharing information (Figure 1.1). It would be advantageous to learn all you can about computers and become comfortable with application programs, the Internet, and the World Wide Web. You'll need computer and Internet skills to succeed in almost any occupational area. Studies consistently show that workers with such skills are in demand and earn salaries significantly above the median personal income level of approximately $30,000 (Figure 1.2). Check out **www.cis. udel.edu/jobs/market** for information about the future of the computer science job market and links to related sites. Another site, **www.ticker.computerjobs.com/ content/ticker.aspx**, lists computer-related jobs and their average salaries.

But isolated skills aren't enough. To be a fully functioning member of today's computerized world, you need to understand the concepts that underlie computer and Internet technologies, such as

FIGURE 1.1 Computers were once considered tools for an information age. Today they are part of our everyday environment.

FIGURE 1.2	Salaries of Workers in Computer and Computer-Related Jobs		
Categories	High ($/yr.)	Low ($/yr.)	Average ($/yr.)
AS/400	$90,000	$51,000	$65,000
Business analyst	$105,000	$40,000	$76,000
Computer operations	$220,000	$23,000	$59,000
Data warehousing	$110,000	$46,000	$81,000
Database systems	$120,000	$30,000	$67,000
E-commerce/Internet	$175,000	$37,000	$79,000
ERP	$120,000	$55,000	$71,000
Executive level	$250,000	$69,000	$118,000
Hardware	$100,000	$30,000	$56,000
Help desk	$110,000	$23,000	$44,000
Legacy systems	$115,000	$48,000	$75,000
Networking	$333,000	$22,000	$69,000
New media	$65,000	$32,000	$43,000
Nontechnical	$80,000	$38,000	$54,000
Project management	$130,000	$34,000	$83,000
Quality assurance	$106,000	$40,000	$72,000
Technical recruiting	$72,000	$30,000	$58,000
Technical sales	$150,000	$60,000	$87,000
Technical writing	$77,000	$45,000	$59,000
Unix	$108,000	$50,000	$79,000
Windows development	$101,000	$40,000	$69,000
Wireless systems	$95,000	$46,000	$66,000

$118,000 is the highest average salary.
Total entries in the survey were 2,145.

Average salary: $70,000 per year.

the distinction between hardware and software and how to manage the plethora of files that are created each day. As computers and the Internet play an increasingly direct and noticeable role in our personal lives, understanding the difference between their appropriate and inappropriate use becomes increasingly difficult. Should you shop on the Internet on company or school time? Are the photos you share with friends on social networking sites like Facebook or MySpace going to turn up when you least expect or cause an employer to disqualify your application because of your Web content? Is your credit card information, Social Security number, or personal communication safe from intrusion or misuse? In the past the only way to shop during work or school was to leave the premises; employers had to call a reference to find personal information about an applicant; and the only time you needed to worry about your personal information was if your wallet or mail had been stolen!

You also need to know enough to choose what types of technology to use in your personal and professional lives (Figure 1.3). How much power and speed do you need for everyday tasks? What will a more powerful and faster computer or smartphone enable you to do better? What types of technology tools do you need? Do you need advanced training? This text provides information and insight into technology, its uses, assets, drawbacks, and the required knowledge and skill set needed to make informed decisions about technology in all areas of your life. When you understand these concepts, you'll be able to

- Decide whether to purchase new equipment or upgrade specific components.
- Judge the likely impact of computer innovations on your personal and business activities.
- Sort through the difficult ethical, moral, and societal challenges that computer use brings.

The more you work with computers, the deeper and richer your understanding of computers and technology will become; you will become quietly confident in your abilities. As your confidence and knowledge grow, you will become more adept in your use of computers and be

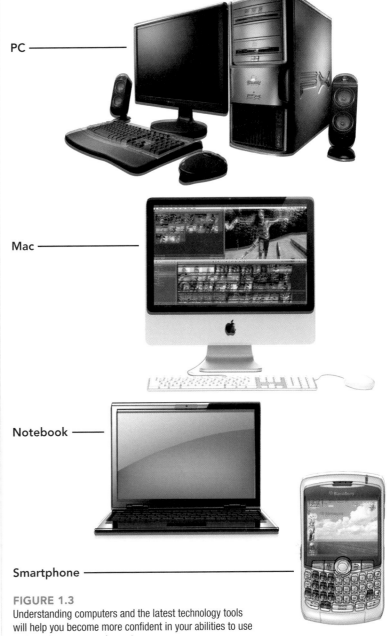

FIGURE 1.3
Understanding computers and the latest technology tools will help you become more confident in your abilities to use and purchase new equipment.

prepared for the changes computer technology brings. Let's start by describing the machine that's at the center of what you need to know.

Computer Fundamentals

Learning computer and Internet concepts is partly about learning new terms. So let's start with the most basic terms.

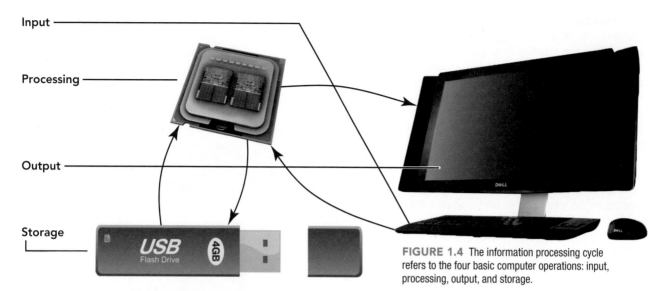

Input

Processing

Output

Storage

USB Flash Drive 4GB

FIGURE 1.4 The information processing cycle refers to the four basic computer operations: input, processing, output, and storage.

UNDERSTANDING THE COMPUTER: BASIC DEFINITIONS

A **computer** is a machine that performs four basic operations: input, processing, output, and storage (Figure 1.4). Together these four operations are called the **information processing cycle**. **Input** is the action of receiving the **data**—raw facts like a list of numbers. **Processing** is the action done on the input to obtain **information**, which is data converted into a meaningful form. Examples of processing could be aligning a letter's return address in a Word document or adding a column of numbers by following a formula that has been entered in an Excel worksheet. **Output** is the actual displaying of the processed data—the viewing of the shifted return address in the Word document or the appearance of the sum for the specified numbers in the Excel worksheet. Finally, **storage** is saving of the output for later use. Because these operations depend on one another, the information processing cycle (sometimes abbreviated as the IPOS cycle) is always performed in this sequence.

You'll often hear the term *computer system,* which is normally shortened to *system.* This term is more inclusive than *computer.* A **computer system** is a collection of related components that have been designed to work together. These components can be placed in two major categories: hardware and software. A computer system's **hardware** includes all the physical components of the computer and its related devices. The components include the **system unit**: the base unit of the computer made up of the plastic or metal enclosure, the motherboard, and the

integrated peripherals. The **motherboard** is the circuit board that connects the central processing unit(s) anchored on the board and other system components. **Integrated peripherals** are the devices embedded within the system unit case and generally include the power supply, cooling fans, memory, CD drive, DVD drive, and internal hard drive. Besides the system unit, the hardware also includes the **peripheral devices**: components located outside the system unit housing that are connected physically or wirelessly to the system unit and motherboard. Examples include keyboards, mice, monitors, speakers, and external storage devices (Figure 1.5).

A computer system's hardware needs programs to function. A **program** is a set of instructions that tells the hardware how to perform the operations in the information processing cycle to accomplish a task. **Software**, a more inclusive term, is the collection of programs that directs the operation of a computer. Software can be divided into two categories: system software and application software. **System software** is the collection of programs written to provide the infrastructure, basic services, and hardware control that let other programs function properly. The most important and well-recognized type of system software is the computer's **operating system (OS)**, which integrates and controls the computer's internal functions and provides a way for the user to interact with the computer. Common operating systems include Microsoft Windows XP, Microsoft Vista, Linux, and the Mac OS X. Operating systems are always being updated to improve performance and accommodate new hardware devices. The

a – Keyboard
b – Monitor
c – Mouse
d – System unit
e – CD or DVD drive
f – Media card reader
g – USB ports
h – Sound connections
i – Speakers
j – Headset with microphone
k – Cable or DSL modem
l – Printer
m – Network interface card

FIGURE 1.5 Get to know your system. A typical computer system includes these hardware components.

most current operating systems are Windows 7, released by Microsoft, and Mac OS X Leopard, released by Apple. Besides operating systems, other examples of system software include system utilities, such as backup and disk cleanup tools and antivirus software. **Application software** can be thought of as sitting on top of the operating system; it uses the computer's capabilities to perform a task for the user. Typical examples of application software include word processing, spreadsheet, database, presentation, e-mail, and Web browser software.

To better understand how computer system components are interrelated, you might compare a computer system to an aquarium. The computer hardware is like the fish tank, the operating system is like the water, and the software applications are like the fish (Figure 1.6). You wouldn't put fish in an empty aquarium. Fish can't survive without water, just as software applications can't function without an operating system to support them. And without the water and fish, an aquarium is an empty box—just as computer hardware

isn't much use without an operating system and applications.

Now that we know the basic terms, let's take a closer look at the operations in the information processing cycle (input, processing, output, and storage) and at the hardware devices involved in each step.

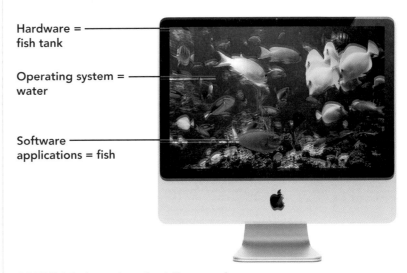

Hardware = fish tank

Operating system = water

Software applications = fish

FIGURE 1.6 A computer system is like an aquarium.

FIGURE 1.7 The most widely used input devices are (**a**) the keyboard and (**b**) the mouse.

INPUT: GETTING DATA INTO THE COMPUTER

During input the computer receives data. The term *data* refers to raw facts, which can be made up of words, numbers, images, sounds, or a combination of these.

Input devices enable you to enter data into the computer for processing. The most common input devices are the keyboard and mouse (Figure 1.7). Microphones, scanners, and devices such as digital cameras and camcorders offer other ways of getting different types of data into the computer.

PROCESSING: TRANSFORMING DATA INTO INFORMATION

Processing transforms data into information. Information is data that have been consolidated and organized in a way that people can use. During processing, the computer's processing circuitry (Figure 1.8), called the **central processing unit (CPU)** or **microprocessor** (or just **processor** for short), performs operations on the input data. The CPU is located within the system unit and is a component on the motherboard.

Even though the CPU is often referred to as the "brain" of the computer, computers don't really think. They are capable of performing only repetitive processing actions organized into an **algorithm**—a series of steps that results in the solution to a problem. After an algorithm is tested for accuracy, it is coded into a language that the computer hardware understands and becomes the program or software that the system uses to solve that problem.

Because the CPU needs to juggle multiple input and output requests at the same time, it uses high-speed memory chips to store program instructions and data so it can move between requests quickly. Memory is essential to the smooth operation of the CPU. A typical computer includes several types of memory; the most important of these is random access memory (RAM), which temporarily stores the programs and data with which the CPU is interacting.

OUTPUT: DISPLAYING INFORMATION

Output commonly uses **output devices**, like monitors and printers, that enable people to see, hear, and—with some newer inventions—feel the results of processing operations (Figure 1.9).

FIGURE 1.8 The CPU (microprocessor or processor) performs operations on the data.

STORAGE: HOLDING PROGRAMS AND DATA FOR FUTURE USE

The storage operation makes use of a hard disk, CD, DVD, or media card to hold all the programs, system and application software, and data that the

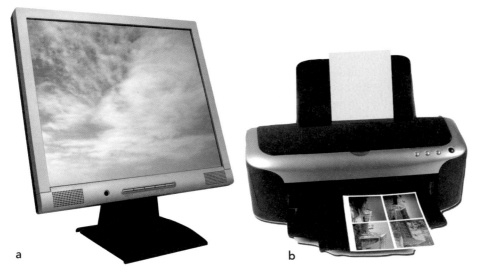

a

b

FIGURE 1.9 The most common output devices are (**a**) monitors and (**b**) printers.

computer system uses (Figure 1.10). These **storage devices** are usually integrated peripherals that are mounted inside the system unit's enclosure and are capable of retaining data even when electrical power is switched off. For additional storage, backup, or portability, these storage devices can also be purchased as nonintegrated peripherals and connected to the system unit through USB cables.

Some older systems may have a floppy disk drive or Zip drive, but such devices are now obsolete and are often referred to as **legacy technology**. The popular **USB flash drive**, an external drive about the size of an adult's thumb, has replaced these legacy devices. Such devices can hold up to 64 GB of data (approximately 180 CDs). USB drives use solid state technology and plug into a computer's USB port, which is usually located on the front or side of the system unit. They are portable, easy to use, rewritable, and inexpensive. Visit **www1.pacific.edu/comp25/ reading/1-InfoProcessingCycle.html**

to find out more about the information processing cycle.

COMMUNICATIONS: MOVING DATA BETWEEN COMPUTERS

Communications, the high-speed movement of data or information within and between computers, have become more important due to our increasingly global and mobile society. Such needs as getting data from your computer to the server hosting your Web site or from a school computer to the one at your house have taken communications technology from the back office and communications department at work to your own desk at home. To communicate, computers have to be connected to a network by a **communications device**, which is a hardware component that moves data into and out of a computer. Two or more connected computers are called a **network**. The primary reason to create a network is to share data, information, input/output devices, and other resources. If sharing is

FIGURE 1.10 The most common storage devices are (**a**) hard disk drives, (**b**) CD and DVD drives, and (**c**) media card readers, which can be used with USB drives and flash memory cards.

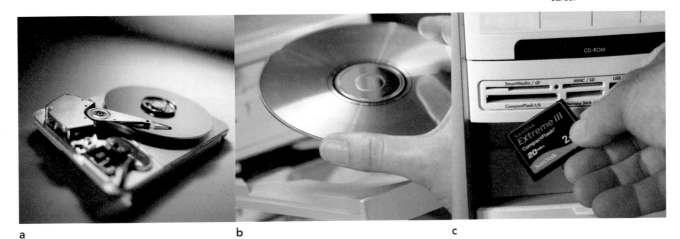

a

b

c

easy, individuals will collaborate more, distribute information more freely, increase their knowledge, expand their scope of reasoning, become more global, and make better individual and group decisions.

Most computers are equipped with a **modem** (short for modulator/demodulator), a communications device that converts data from one form into another. It enables the computer, a digital device, to access data through nondigital media, such as telephone lines, cable, satellite, and cellular connections. Many computers have internal modems that can be used for dial-up Internet access over a standard telephone line. External modems are used for high-speed access to the Internet via cable, DSL, or satellite.

Another important component, a **network interface card**, often referred to as a **NIC**, is a system unit hardware element that houses the electronic components used to connect a computer to a network. Many computers already have a NIC integrated into the motherboard, but external NICs can be plugged into a USB port or inserted into a specially designed slot. NICs can connect to wired or wireless networks.

Now that you understand how hardware and software work in the information processing cycle and where they are located in a typical computer system, let's look at an example of how the computer uses the basic functions of input, processing, output, and storage.

THE INFORMATION PROCESSING CYCLE IN ACTION

Even if you haven't wondered what goes on behind the scenes when you use a computer, the following example illustrates your role and the computer's role in each step of the information-processing cycle (Figure 1.11):

- *Input:* You're writing a research paper for a class. You know it has misspellings and grammatical errors, but you keep typing because you can run your word processing program's spell-checker at any time to help correct the errors. In this example, your entire word-processed document is the input.

- *Processing:* A spell-checker uses the computer's ability to quickly perform simple processing operations. To check your document's spelling, the program constructs a list of all the words in your document. Then it compares these words with a huge list of correctly spelled words. If you've used a word that isn't in this internal dictionary, the program puts that word into a list of apparent misspellings.

Note that the computer isn't really "checking spelling" when it performs this operation. The computer can't check your spelling because it doesn't possess the intelligence to do so. All it

FIGURE 1.11 The Information Processing Cycle in Action

Your role:
Enter word-processed document.

Computer's role:
Receive document.

Your role:
Start spell-checker program.

Computer's role:
Spell-checker program compares words in document to built-in dictionary.

Computer's role:
Display list of misspelled words.

Your role:
Accept or reject suggested misspelled words.

Your role:
Save corrected document.

Computer's role:
Store final document to disk or drive.

Input → Processing → Output → Storage

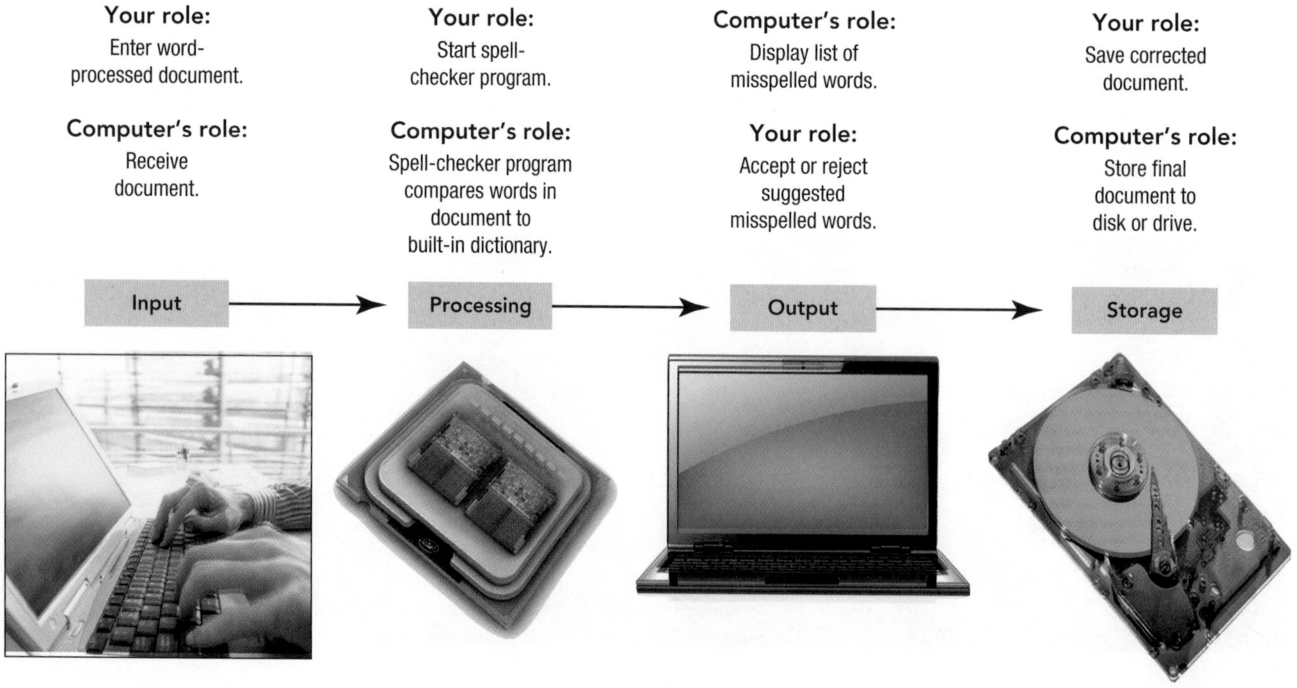

can do is tell you which words you've used do not appear in the dictionary list. Ultimately only you can decide whether a given word is misspelled.

- *Output:* The result of the processing operation is a list of apparent misspellings. The word *apparent* is important here because the program doesn't actually know whether a word is misspelled. It can tell you only that a word isn't in its massive, built-in dictionary. But many correctly spelled words, such as proper nouns and technical terms, aren't likely to be found in the computer's dictionary. For this reason, the program won't make any changes without asking you to confirm them.

- *Storage:* After you've corrected the spelling in your document, you save or store the revised document to disk.

In summary, computers transform data (here a document full of misspellings) into information (a document that is free of misspellings).

Up to this point we've been talking about computers in general. Next let's examine the specific types of computers used in a wide variety of tasks and job situations.

Types of Computers

Computers come in all sizes, from large to small. For discussion it is convenient to divide them into two categories: computers for individuals and computers for organizations. Computers for individuals are designed for one user at a time. They process and store smaller amounts of data and programs, such as a research paper or a personal Web page. In contrast, computers for organizations are designed to meet the needs of many people concurrently. They process and store large amounts of data and more complex programs, such as the database of all students on campus or a school's entire Web site. Computers are further subcategorized by power (their processing speed) and purpose (the tasks they perform).

COMPUTERS FOR INDIVIDUALS

A **personal computer (PC)**, also called a **microcomputer**, is designed to meet the computing needs of an individual. The two most commonly used types of personal computers are Apple's Macintosh (Mac) systems and the more numerous IBM-compatible systems, which are made by manufacturers such as Dell, Gateway, Sony, Hewlett-Packard (HP), and many others. These PCs are called "IBM-compatible" because the first such computer was made by IBM. The acronym *PC*, although originally used to refer to all personal computers, has become more closely aligned with IBM-compatible personal computers, while Apple has coined the term *Mac*. Although PC sales have exceeded those of the Mac, the Mac has a loyal following and has been increasing in popularity. Statistics on the use of the Safari browser, used only on Apple systems, indicate a continuous increase in its use from 2007 to 2009. Apple advocates point to this statistic as an indication of an increase in Apple system sales. Go to **www.w3schools.com/browsers/browsers_stats.asp** and decide for yourself.

Personal computers are subcategorized by size, power, and function. The largest PC is a **desktop computer**: a personal computer designed for use at a desk or in an office environment, running programs to help individuals accomplish their work or gain access to the Internet (Figure 1.12). It has a system unit case

> " Although **PC** sales have exceeded those of the **Mac**, the Mac has a loyal following and has been increasing in **popularity.** "

Desktop computer

FIGURE 1.12 A desktop computer is used by individuals who do not need to take their computers with them and who have desk space to spare.

that is the size of an average printer and is not easily moved. A more compact version of the desktop is the all-in-one computer. **All-in-one computers** (Figure 1.13) combine the system unit and monitor into one unit. The only external peripheral devices required are the mouse and keyboard. From a distance, an all-in-one desktop computer could be mistaken for an LCD television due to its slim design. The Apple iMac, Gateway One, Sony Vaio LT, and Dell XPS One are all major players in the all-in-one market.

All-in-one computer

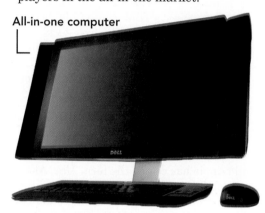

FIGURE 1.13 An all-in-one computer has a compact look but can pack as much power as a desktop.

A **notebook computer** (Figure 1.14), so named because it is roughly the size of a notebook, is small enough to fit into a briefcase or backpack, making it ideal for mobile computing and popular with both students and businesspeople who travel frequently. The original term for this type of computer was *laptop*. Few people, however, actually use notebook computers on their laps because the heat emitted can be uncomfortable, making the name *notebook* more suitable. Many notebook computers today are as powerful as desktop computers and include nearly all of a desktop computer's components, such as speakers, a DVD drive, and a modem. Notebooks

Notebook

FIGURE 1.14 A notebook is designed to provide data processing ability for the mobile user.

range in size from large, desktop-replacement models with displays measuring up to 17 inches to smaller, lighter models with 13-inch screens. Some of the most popular notebook computers are Dell's Inspiron and XPS series, Toshiba's Satellite and Tecra series, Lenovo's Thinkpad, HP's Pavilion, Gateway's MD Series, and for Mac lovers, the MacBook and MacBook Pro.

Subnotebooks, or **ultraportables**, are notebook computers that omit some components (such as a CD or DVD drive) and usually have smaller screens, reducing their size and weight. A significant advantage of subnotebooks is that even though some weigh less than three pounds, they still run a full desktop operating system. For example, the newest Apple MacBook Air weighs only three pounds and is less than one inch thick. One disadvantage of subnotebooks is that users must often carry along external disk drives and their associated wiring. A subnotebook would be used by someone whose specific computing needs do not require all the peripherals and accessories that are available with desktops and notebooks. Subnotebook manufacturers include many familiar names like Apple, Dell, and Sony but also some newer entries like Asus and Everex.

A tablet PC, sometimes called a *convertible notebook,* can be used in two different configurations. **Tablet PCs** (Figure 1.15) typically have a keyboard or a mouse for input and can be used like an ordinary notebook. However, the LCD screen on a tablet PC also swivels to lie flat over the keyboard. In this position, the user can write on it with a special-purpose pen, or stylus. Handwriting recognition software can then convert the

Tablet PC

FIGURE 1.15 A tablet PC will accept both typed and handwritten characters as input.

user's handwriting to digital text, if desired. HP's TX line and Fujitsu's Lifebook are industry leaders; however, the Toshiba Portégé, Lenovo Thinkpad, and Dell Latitude are other popular brands from top manufacturers.

Netbooks have the portability of a notebook but not the functionality. They are designed for wireless Internet access and are used primarily for Web browsing and e-mail. They weigh two to three pounds and are between 5 and 13 inches in size. Netbooks usually run a less intensive operating system (Windows XP or Linux instead of Vista) and do not support full-scale applications. Windows 7 Starter Edition is the least expensive version of the Windows 7 operating system and the one that may enable netbooks to be priced as low as $200. Netbooks are a favorite device for people who use cloud computing, which is an online service that usually charges a user to access resources like business applications over the Internet instead of purchasing the applications and storing them on their own systems. With the cost of netbooks predicted to drop, they are an excellent way to introduce developing nations to the digital world as well as offer busy families a second, less expensive, less powerful PC. Some manufacturers and models are the Acer Aspire one, Dell Mini, and Lenovo IdeaPad.

Our constant need to be connected and have information at our fingertips has pushed technology to create smaller, portable, wireless devices that fit in the palm of the hand. **Handheld computers** (see Figure 1.16), as these pocket-sized units are called, receive input by using a stylus, a **virtual keyboard**—a keyboard shown on a touch screen—or an external corded keyboard. UPS drivers currently record delivery information on such devices. One of the earliest handheld devices was the **personal digital assistant (PDA)**, such as the Palm Pilot from Palm. This small device included software for managing contacts, scheduling appointments, and sending and receiving e-mail.

Over the years, the features of handheld computers have been assimilated into a new generation of cell phones called *smartphones*. **Smartphones** combine the capabilities of a handheld computer with mobile phone capability and Web access. The line between handhelds and smart-

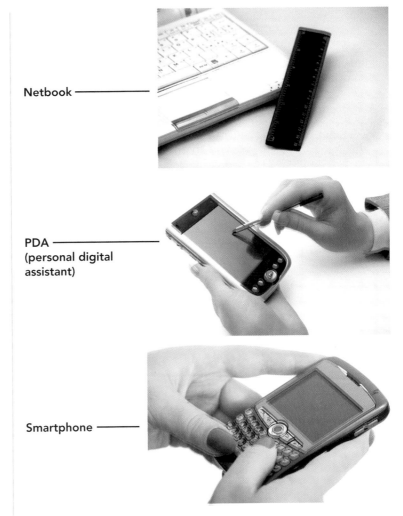

Netbook

PDA (personal digital assistant)

Smartphone

FIGURE 1.16 Handheld Computers for Individuals

phones has blurred as these devices continue to adopt each other's features. In fact, this convergence, or combination of features, has been blamed for the decline of many handheld computer manufacturers. The newest generation of smartphones can read business documents in various formats, play music, browse photos, view video clips, stream live video, handle e-mail, access the Internet, and act as **e-book readers** (electronic book readers). In addition, they can offer nontraditional features such as a traffic and speed trap warning system, a carpenter's level, and driving directions using built-in global positioning systems (GPS). New applications are always being created for these devices. To view some of the newest ones, go to **www.smartphonemag.com**. Some well-known examples of smartphone manufacturers and their products include the Apple iPhone, BlackBerry Curve, Palm Pre, Treo Pro and Centro, and HP iPAQ.

COMPUTERS FOR ORGANIZATIONS

Professional workstations are high-end desktop computers with system units designed for technical or scientific applications, requiring exceptionally powerful processing and output capabilities. Used by engineers, architects, circuit designers, financial analysts, game developers, and other professionals, they are often connected to a network and are equipped with more powerful CPUs, extra RAM, additional graphics power, and multitasking capabilities. For these reasons they are more expensive than desktop PCs. Manufacturers include HP, Dell, and Lenovo.

Servers (Figure 1.17) are computers that use hardware and software to make programs and data available to people who are connected via a network. They are not designed for individual use and are typically centralized or operated from one location. Users connect to a network on **clients**, which can be desktops, notebooks, workstations, or **terminals** (primarily input/output devices consisting of keyboards and video displays, used as an inexpensive means to connect to a server). A **fat client** accesses the server but does most data processing in its own system; a **thin client** relies on the server for its processing ability. This use of client computers and a centralized server is called a **client/server network**. Servers play an important role in today's businesses and can be as small as a personal computer or as large as a computer that runs a banking institution with millions of clients These larger units are typically housed in a secure, temperature-regulated environment to protect them from deliberate or accidental damage. The top three server manufacturers are HP, Dell, and IBM.

Minicomputers or **midrange servers** (Figure 1.18) are midsized servers with the hardware and software to handle the computing needs of 4 to 200 client computers in a smaller corporation or organization. In size and capability, minicomputers fall between workstations and mainframes; but as these markets have evolved and workstations have become more powerful and mainframes less expensive, the demand for minicomputers has decreased. Minicomputers are manufactured by IBM and HP.

Minicomputer

FIGURE 1.18 Minicomputers or midrange servers connect up to 200 users.

Mainframes or **enterprise servers** (Figure 1.19) are powerful servers that are part of a networked system designed to handle hundreds of thousands of clients at the same time. They are usually used in

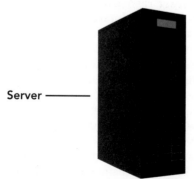

Server

FIGURE 1.17 Servers contain software that enables them to provide services to users connected to it through a network.

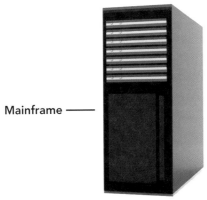

Mainframe ——

FIGURE 1.19 Mainframes or enterprise servers connect thousands of users and are used by large organizations and government agencies.

large corporations or government agencies that handle a high volume of data. For example, an airline might use a mainframe to handle airline reservations, or a bank might manage customer accounts on such a system. Mainframes are usually stored in special secure rooms that have a controlled climate. They are manufactured by firms such as IBM, Fujitsu, and Amdahl.

Supercomputers (Figure 1.20) are ultrafast systems that process large amounts of scientific data, often to search for underlying patterns. A supercomputer can be a single computer or a series of computers working in parallel as a single computer. The main difference between a supercomputer and a mainframe is that a supercomputer focuses on performing a few sets of instruction as fast as possible, whereas a mainframe executes many instructions concurrently.

Supercomputer
⌐

FIGURE 1.20 Supercomputers can perform mathematical calculations at lightning speed and are used in such fields as weather prediction and space travel.

The TOP500 list (**www.top500.org**) tracks the most powerful computer systems worldwide. As of November 2008 the IBM Roadrunner, located at the Department of Energy's Los Alamos National Laboratory, topped the list. Using almost 7,000 dual-core processors, the Roadrunner set a new performance record, reaching a processing speed of over one **petaflop**—over a million billion calculations per second. This equals the combined computing power of over 100,000 of the fastest notebook computers and is twice as fast as the next supercomputer on the list. IBM stated that it would take the entire world population (over 6 billion people) performing one calculation per second with handheld calculators over 46 years to do what the Roadrunner can do in one day!

For more about the various types of computers, go to **www.unm.edu/~tbeach/terms/types.html**. Now that you know about the variety of computers available, let's look at how their use affects you as an individual and society in general.

Computers, Society, and You

A computer, with the appropriate software, can work with all types of data. That is a major reason for the remarkable penetration of computers into almost every occupational area and more than 70 percent of U.S. households today (up from 49 percent in 2001 and 2002). However, although computers are becoming commonplace, computers and the Internet aren't readily accessible in some segments of society. Computer and Internet use cuts across all educational, racial, and economic boundaries; but there are still inequities.

The more educated you are, the more likely you are to own a computer and have Internet access. A study by Pew Internet and American Life Project in December 2008 showed that approximately one-third of people in the United States have a bachelor's degree, and 95 percent of college-educated individuals use the Internet; but only 53 percent of people with a high school education do.

Age, race, and income are also factors in U.S. computer use. The same survey indicated that only 41 percent of adults older than 65 use the Internet, compared with 72 percent of the 50- to 64-year-olds, 82 percent of the 30- to 49-year-olds, and 87 percent of the 18- to 29-year-olds. This report additionally substantiated that 75 percent of whites and English-speaking

Hispanics are online, but less than 60 percent of African Americans are. Similarly, only 60 percent of U.S. households with income levels less than $30,000 have access to the Internet. Internet usage increases as income levels rise, with more than 90 percent of households earning $50,000 or more reporting Internet use. This disparity in computer ownership and Internet access, known as the **digital divide**, isn't limited to the United States. Similar statistics exist for other countries, indicating that this is a global problem. Studies of the expansion or reduction of the digital divide are contradictory; however, government and educational programs are working to bridge this gap by attempting to provide computer access for all (Figure 1.21).

Computers let us collect, organize, evaluate, and communicate information. Although computers are merely tools, requiring humans to write the programs and set up the data, we can use them for a variety of common activities to ease our daily lives. Rather than going to the mall to buy the latest movie on DVD, you can now purchase it or even view it online. To organize your music or movie collection before computers, you would have had to physically sort through and arrange it on your shelf. A computer makes it possible to organize your entire collection and sort it

in a variety of ways, including by title, artist, release date, or genre, making it simple to reorganize and update your collection. And there's no need to wait for reviews to come out in the newspaper—just go online to find the latest reviews from critics and other moviegoers. You can even select your favorite movie and use your smartphone to locate a nearby theater, make dinner reservations before the show, and even display driving directions. To spread the word to family and friends, simply post this information to your Facebook account or Web page. The amount of time we save during a day by using computers or computer-related devices is phenomenal.

Computers also help us be more productive and creative, reducing the amount of time spent on tedious tasks. A good example of this is using a word processing program to create a term paper. The computer gives the student spelling and grammar help as well as formatting suggestions and makes it easy to include graphics. Without a computer, the student would need dictionaries and encyclopedias, not to mention style guides and other special resources, along with extra time to gather and go through all of these sources.

Computers also help us work, teach, and learn together. Computers facilitate

FIGURE 1.21 The global disparity in computer use and ownership, if left unchecked, will continue to create unequal opportunities between the have and have-nots.

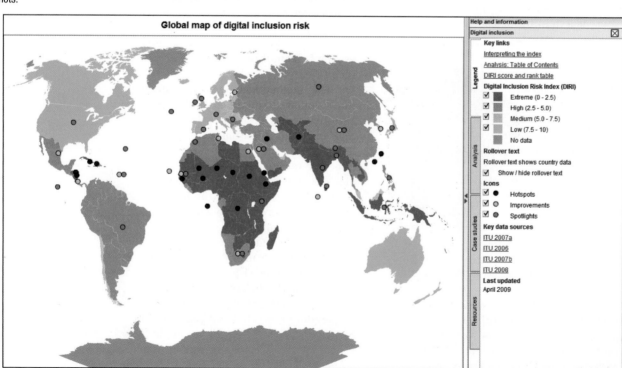

collaboration with others to solve problems (Figure 1.22). For instance, computers are increasingly part of law enforcement activities. They facilitate quick and efficient communication between jurisdictions, enable law enforcement officials to browse criminal databases like the Automated Fingerprint Identification System (AFIS), and allow pertinent data to be shared nationally and globally. Additionally, as cybercrime becomes a bigger concern, police are using the Internet and **computer forensics**, a branch of forensic science that deals with legal evidence found on computers, to find and apprehend these criminals. Collaboration software helps people share ideas, create documents, and conduct meetings, regardless of location or time zone. Whether you're an employee of a multinational firm developing a new product with a group of colleagues located halfway around the globe or a student enrolled in a distance learning course, computers play a big part in making these tasks possible.

With more students studying abroad, the need to stay connected to complete group projects and research has caused a rise in the use of online applications that advance collaboration. **Google Docs**, a free Web-based word processor and spreadsheet, allows project members to share and edit documents online. A **wiki** is a collection of Web pages designed to let anyone with access contribute or modify content. Wikis are often used to create collaborative or community Web sites. The collaborative encyclopedia Wikipedia is one of the best-known wikis. **Google Groups** is a free Web editor that makes it easy for anyone to create and manage simple group Web sites. You can create and publish new pages with the click of a button. After the project is finalized, you can use the computer to produce, print, store, and present it.

More recently the computer has become a place of social interaction. One of the most basic forms of this interaction is **instant messaging (IM)**: a free, real-time connection between two or more parties that uses a buddy list to identify and restrict the users a person wishes to connect with. Many people use online **social network** sites such as Facebook, MySpace, LinkedIn, and Twitter to join groups set up by region, job, interest, or school and communicate with group members. Adult Internet users who have

FIGURE 1.22 Sharing data for professional and personal use is a necessity and privilege in today's fast-paced changing society.

profiles on online social network sites have more than quadrupled in the past four years—from 8 percent in 2005 to 35 percent in 2008, according to the Pew Internet and American Life Project December 2008 report. **Twitter**, the newest phenomenon, is a free, real-time social messaging utility that allows postings of up to 140 characters. The exchanges are short and usually in a question-and-answer mode. People need merely look up the Twitter accounts of their friends and indicate that they want to follow their Twitter posts, which are called **tweets**.

Even though computers offer us many advantages in today's hectic world, the responsible computer user should also be aware of the disadvantages of computer use.

ADVANTAGES AND DISADVANTAGES OF USING COMPUTERS

It seems that for every positive effect an invention provides there is a negative effect. That is also true for computers. A computer system provides certain advantages to its users, such as speed, memory for work in progress, storage for access later, hardware reliability, and accuracy. However, with these advantages come some disadvantages (Figure 1.23), including information overload, the expense of computer equipment,

FIGURE 1.23 Advantages and Disadvantages of Computer Use

Advantages	Disadvantages
Speed	Information overload
Memory	Cost
Storage	Data inaccuracy
Hardware reliability	Software unreliability

data inaccuracy, and an increasing dependence on unreliable software.

Speed is one of the greatest advantages of a computer. It can perform in a minute calculations or tasks that would take a human days. A 2003 study by the University of California at Berkeley's School of Information Management and Systems found that due to the speed at which computers locate information, perform calculations, and transmit communications, the amount of new information generated is increasing by more than 30 percent each year. In fact, people are generating so much information via computers today that they often succumb to **information overload**: a feeling of anxiety and incapacity experienced when people are presented with more information than they can handle. According to research from the firm Bases, which chose information overload as its 2008 problem of the year, constant e-mail messages, phone calls, text messages, and tweets across the U.S. workforce resulted in $650 billion of lost productivity in a single year. That is an estimate of up to eight hours a week per worker. In a 2007 Pew Survey, 49 percent of the workers surveyed indicated that constant connectivity was an annoyance. However, young people do not seem as irritated at the multitasking demands of technology. They listen to music while reading, IM friends while typing a paper, tweet constantly, and do not seem annoyed. It remains to be seen if this ability to handle information overload will produce a future workforce that is better able to handle an overfilled Inbox.

Cost is another drawback that must be weighed against computer performance. A computer's performance is enhanced by the amount of random access memory the system possesses. **Random access memory (RAM)** is high-speed, temporary memory that holds all programs and data currently in use; in other words, it holds our work in progress. The processor accesses programs and data in RAM quickly. The faster the processor receives the data, the faster it returns results. Once we are done with it, the information in RAM must be placed on a storage device so we can retrieve it later. Depending on the quantity of data you process and the number of files you save, you may need to purchase additional RAM and storage devices.

Purchasing more RAM or additional storage can be costly. Most computers are equipped with just enough RAM and storage to hold an average amount of programs and data. If you use many high-end applications, you may experience a slowdown when moving between graphics, see a pause in a long video, or receive a message that one of your storage units is full. If that happens, you need to investigate the reason for the slow down and may need to purchase more RAM or storage. High-end users or intense gamers may also find that when new applications are installed on an older machine, the computer might not have enough CPU power to keep up with the new software speed and graphics. This might require upgrading the CPU or purchasing a new system. Investigate the benefits and drawbacks of either decision on a case-by-case basis.

Reliability and accuracy are two more advantages of computers. Computers show up at school or work every day and almost always respond when turned on. If given a calculation to do several times, they consistently output the same result. A computer can transcribe your speech with an accuracy of 95 percent or more, which is better than most people's typing accuracy. In fact, almost all "computer errors" are actually caused by flaws in software or errors in the data supplied by people. Computers store these mistakes and reuse them on additional data, replicating the errors with amazing speed.

Along with computers' strengths and weaknesses, consider some additional points in your quest to become a responsible user.

BECOME COMFORTABLE WITH HARDWARE

Some people feel threatened by computers because they fear that computers are too complicated. But without humans, computers have no intelligence at all. They process simple repetitive operations. The average insect is a genius compared to a computer. Remember, without a person and a program to tell it what to do, the computer is no more frightening—or useful—than an empty fish tank.

One way to get comfortable with your computer is to learn how to care for it. Read any instructions that accompany your purchase and remember that dust, moisture, static electricity, and magnetic interference may affect your system's performance. Additionally, keeping cords and devices in places that do not interfere with the traffic pattern of the room will avoid unnecessary accidents and make your work environment safe and comfortable. Does your work area look like the one in Figure 1.24?

To maintain a safe working environment for you and your hardware, heed the following advice:

- Use a surge protector and avoid overloads by not plugging too many devices into the same electrical outlet.
- Place computer equipment in a secure position so it won't fall or cause accidents.

- Leave plenty of space around computer equipment for sufficient air circulation to prevent overheating.
- Make sure computer cables, cords, and wires are fastened securely and not strung haphazardly or left lying where you could trip over them or where they could cause a fire.

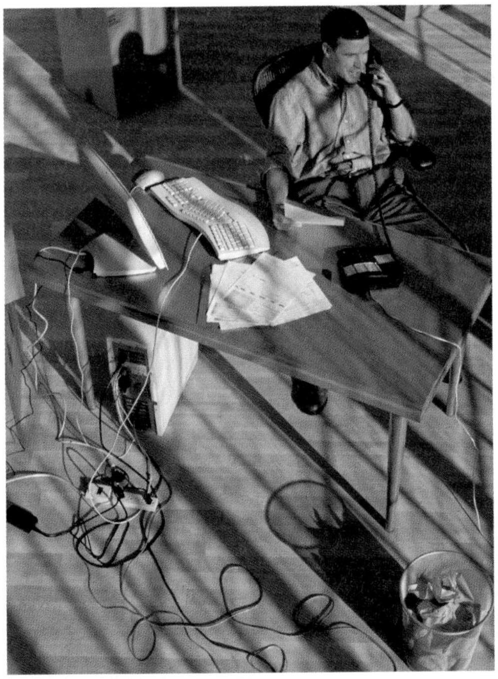

Now that you know how to create a safe computing environment, it is equally important to understand how to avoid eye, back, and wrist strain that can occur from long periods of use. Healthy computing habits combined with ergonomic devices and proper positioning and arrangement of equipment and lighting can make all the difference in your computing environment and physical health.

Ergonomics is the field of study that is concerned with the fit between people, their equipment, and their work. It takes into account worker limitations and capabilities in attempting to ensure that the tasks, equipment, and overall environment suit each worker (Figure 1.25). For example, prolonged keyboard use can cause **carpal tunnel syndrome** (also known as cumulative trauma disorder or repetitive strain injury), which is caused by repeated motions that damage sensitive nerves in the

FIGURE 1.25
Ergonomics is the matching of human posture and functionality with the physical characteristics of various devices.

FIGURE 1.24 A messy computer environment is an unsafe and unproductive one.

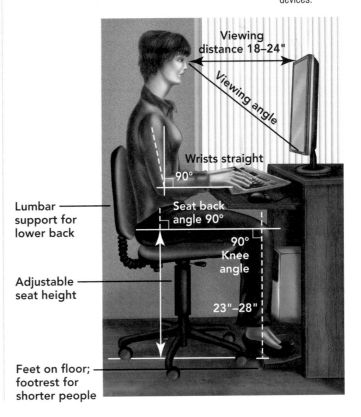

hands, wrists, and arms. Sometimes these injuries are so serious that they require surgery. To help prevent these problems, ergonomic keyboards, such as the Microsoft Natural Keyboard, have been designed to keep your wrists flat, reducing (but not eliminating) your chance of an injury. Many hotel chains try to attract business travelers by promoting their ergonomic desk chairs along with high-speed Internet access. To learn more about ergonomics, go to **http://ergo.human.cornell.edu**.

In addition to using properly designed equipment, you can promote a safe and comfortable computer environment by arranging your chair, lighting, and computer equipment properly and using antiglare computer screens. You should also take periodic breaks from working at your computer to rest your eyes and stretch your legs. For guidance, a workspace planner is provided at **www.ergotron.com/tabid/305/language/en-US/ default.aspx**.

If you purchase devices that fit your body, treat the physical components of your computer with respect, and monitor your work health habits, you will get the most return for your money and promote a healthy work and life style.

RECOGNIZE THE RISKS OF USING FLAWED SOFTWARE

Computer hardware can be amazingly reliable, but software is another matter. Most programs contain some errors or **bugs** as they are called. Many programs contain millions of lines of code (Figure 1.26). In general, each line of program code tells the computer to perform an action, such as adding two numbers or comparing them. Consider this: The program that allows you to withdraw cash from an ATM contains only 90,000 lines of code. But when you file your taxes, the Internal Revenue Service (IRS) program that calculates your refund contains 1,000 times that—100 million lines of code!

With so many lines of code, bugs are inevitable—and they are almost impossible to eradicate completely. On average, commercial programs contain between 14 and 17 errors for every 1,000 lines of code. This means that an ATM is likely to have 1,350 errors in its code, and the IRS program code might have over 1.5 million errors. Fortunately most errors simply cause programs to run slowly or to perform unnecessary tasks; but some errors cause miscalculations or other inconveniences, such as your computer freezing.

These are ample reasons why it's not a good idea to put off writing a paper until the night before your assignment is due. Bugs in a word processing program aren't usually life-threatening, but computers are increasingly being used in mission-critical and safety-critical systems. Mission-critical systems are essential to an organization's viability, such as a company's computerized cash register system. If the system goes down, the organization can't function—and the result is often an expensive fiasco. A safety-critical system is one on which human lives depend, such as an air traffic control system (Figure 1.27) or a computerized signaling system used by high-speed commuter trains. When these systems fail, human lives are at stake. Safety-critical systems are designed to much higher quality standards and have backup systems that kick in if the main computer goes down. For a specific case, do an Internet search on "F-22 software problems."

TAKE ETHICS SERIOUSLY

One disturbing thing about computers isn't the computers themselves—it's what some people do with them. *Ethics* is the behavior associated with your moral beliefs. You have learned what is right and wrong from your parents, teachers, and spiritual leaders. By this stage of your

FIGURE 1.26 Programs often contain millions of lines of code.

Program	Lines of Programming Code
Bank ATM	90,000
Air traffic control	900,000
Microsoft Windows 2000	35 million
Microsoft Windows XP	40 million
Microsoft Office XP	35 million (estimated)
Internal Revenue Service (IRS)	100 million (all programs)

life you know what is right and wrong. However, people's use of computers and the Internet has created ethical situations that we might not have otherwise encountered. **Computer ethics**, a branch of philosophy that continues to evolve, deals with computer-related moral dilemmas and defines ethical principles for computer use.

FIGURE 1.27 Air traffic control, defense, and security systems are referred to as safety-critical software. Code for such systems must be of the highest standards and bug-free.

How many people do you know who have "borrowed" software, downloaded movies from the Web, shared music files with friends, or illegally burned copies of music CDs? If you ask around, you'll find that you're surrounded by people who don't think it's wrong to steal digital data. They view **digital piracy**, the unauthorized reproduction and distribution of computer-based media, differently than photocopying a book or taking a DVD from a store without paying. In reality these forms of theft are similar. Current statistics show that global losses due to digital piracy amount to more than $40 billion annually. This is not just a loss of products, but jobs, retail business, and collected tax dollars. The Business Software Alliance reports that reducing U.S. piracy rates by just 10 percent over the next four years could create more than 32,000 new jobs, generate $6.7 billion in tax revenues, and result in $40 billion in economic growth.

Responsible computing requires that you understand the advantages and disadvantages of using a computer as well as the potential harm from computer misuse. Every day news stories report people misusing computerized data. Names and e-mail addresses are distributed freely without permission or regard for privacy. Viruses are launched against unsuspecting victims. Credit card information is stolen and fraudulently used. Children and women are stalked. Pornography abounds.

Illegitimate copies of software are installed every day. Research papers are bought and sold over the Internet. Homework assignments are copied and then modified to look like original work. The Internet is a hotbed of illicit and sometimes illegal content. Computers are very powerful tools. They can magnify many positive aspects of our lives but can also highlight negative aspects, including unethical behavior.

SOCIETAL IMPACTS OF COMPUTER USE

Computers and the Internet are here to stay, and they have improved the quality of our lives and society as a whole. Almost everyone has been affected by computers and the Internet. Although most people are able-bodied, consider the effect of technologies that support and provide opportunities to the disabled and the disadvantaged (Figure 1.28). To meet the requirements of the Americans with Disabilities Act of 1990, your school must provide computer access to people with disabilities. A college's computing services department must provide special software, such as speech recognition software, to help people with vision impairments use computers. Input and output devices specifically designed for the physically disabled can be installed, or existing devices can be modified, to accommodate users with hearing or motor impairments.

A recent controversy has occurred over a device known as the **Kindle 2**—a portable, wireless, paperback-size e-book reading device onto which people can download books from an immense library of digitized titles. The advantage of the Kindle 2 reader is that a user can scroll through a document instead of flipping pages. Visually impaired users can also increase the font size to make the material more accessible. The digitized titles are sold online; if the books are under copyright, the vendor pays royalties to the authors and publishers. Kindle 2 serves readers and pays writers; this is ethically appropriate, right? But the Kindle 2 is heavily marketed for its text-to-speech function. It can read books aloud. Audio books, previously found on CDs, receive additional royalties. Kindle 2 does not pay for additional audio rights. Kindle 2 was going to remove the text-to-speech function but faced huge protests from the public. The company is currently working on a solution. This technological advancement has a social benefit that seems to have crossed an ethical line.

Computers can also help people with physical disabilities lead more independent lives. From treadmills to muscle stimulators to therapy that involves playing video games, computers give many patients hope of almost full recovery of their former abilities. For instance, the blue-sky research division of the Defense Advance Projects Research Agency (DARPA) is developing a "neutrally" controlled artificial limb that will restore full motor and sensory capability to people who have had their arms amputated. This prosthesis will be controlled, feel, look, and perform like a natural arm. To learn more, go

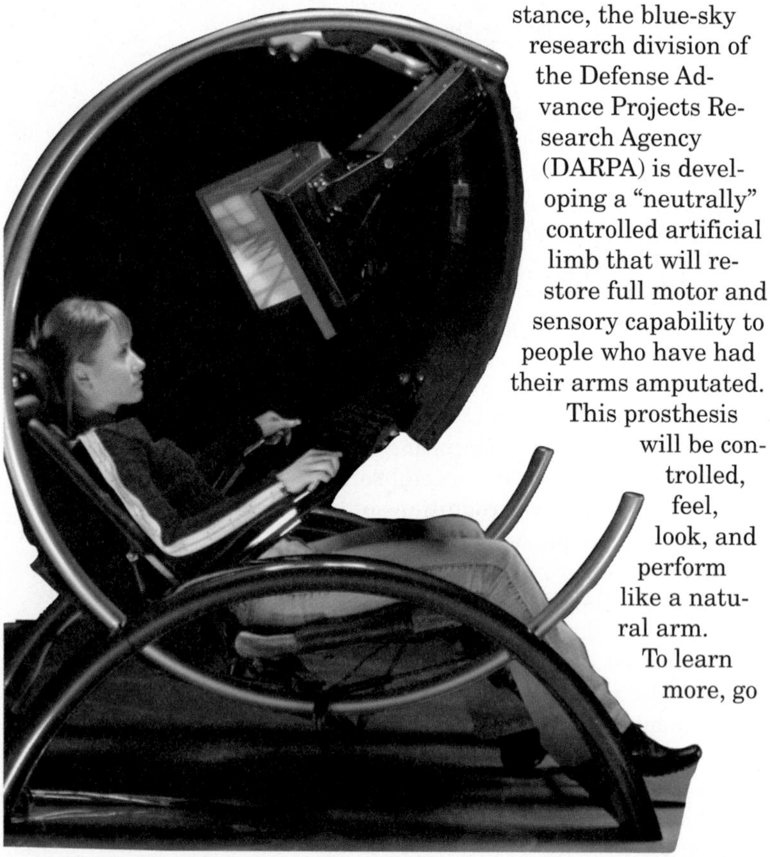

FIGURE 1.28 Continued innovation in computers, software, and related technologies help individuals with myriad disabilities. Shown here, the Alternative Computer Control System (ACCS) manufactured by Gravitonus is designed to provide computer access for severely motor-impaired individuals.

to **www.defensetech.org/archives/001478.html**.

Students can use computers to take advantage of inexpensive training and learning opportunities. **E-learning** is the use of computers and computer programs to replace teachers and the time–place specificity of learning. People also can access computers and the Internet from libraries, Web cafés, and public Internet centers to look for work or find online training, résumé creation tools, and job opportunities.

THE EFFECT OF COMPUTERS ON EMPLOYMENT

Although computers are creating new job opportunities, they're also shifting labor demand toward skilled workers—particularly those who are computer proficient. As a result, these skilled workers are in greater demand and earn higher wages. Computer skills have never been more important to a person's future. A recent ad from an IT (information technology) staffing firm in Providence, RI, announced that the company would host its first RI Young Information Technology Happy Hour. Free food would be provided during the event and free drink tickets given to individuals who signed up to attend before the event. Anyone signing up to attend on the Web site and completing a short survey would also be entered for a chance to win a free ASUS Eee mini laptop computer; registrants had to be present at the event to win. This ad shows the extremes that staffing agencies will go to in hopes of attracting IT and computer-knowledgeable professionals.

As we've pointed out, computers help people complete their work; however, advanced technology can also free people from occupations with hazardous working conditions and ones with repetitive tasks, making workflow safer and more efficient—and increasing productivity. The result is that fewer workers may be required to perform a task, and certain jobs may be eradicated. **Automation**, the replacement of human workers by machines and computer-guided robots, is taking over many manufacturing jobs that people once held (Figure 1.29).

Robots might play a more important role in the future. The robot named ASIMO (Advance Step in Innovative Mobility) is the result of more than two decades of experimentation by Honda engineers. It has humanlike flexibility and endless possibilities. Visitors to the Disneyland park in Anaheim, California, can see ASIMO in action at the Honda ASIMO theater in the Innoventions attractions. ASIMO is still a work in progress.

On a larger scale, more than 1 million robots are in use worldwide, mostly in Japan, though the United States ranks second. In 2007 robotic orders for North American manufacturers totaled over $1 billion in sales—a 24 percent increase from the previous year. Contrary to popular opinion, fewer than half of the robots used in the United States are found in automotive plants. The rest are used in industries such as health care and in locations such as warehouses, laboratories, and energy plants.

The government of South Korea has promised to invest 1 trillion won (about $750 million) in that country's robotics industry in an attempt to accelerate its growth. The goal is to help the global robotics market grow to more than $30 billion by 2013 and to help Korean companies take as much as 10 percent of that market, according to the Director General for Emerging Technologies. This will make Korea one of the top three producers of robotic products by 2013 and the leading producer by 2018.

Globalization of jobs is another effect of technology on employment. No longer is a product made and sold in the same country. More often pieces of a product are produced in several countries, assembled into subunits, and shipped to another location where the subunits are pulled together into the finished product. The term **outsourcing**, the subcontracting of portions of a job to a third party to reduce cost, time, and energy, has become closely related to globalization. Outsourcing is blamed for eliminating many jobs, but studies show that increased productivity is the real cause. Increasing U.S. productivity by as little as 1 percent can eliminate up to 1.3 million jobs a year. In comparison, it is estimated that 250,000 U.S. jobs are lost to outsourcing annually—less than 2 percent of the unemployment total.

Structural unemployment results when advancing technology makes an entire job category obsolete. Structural unemployment differs from the normal economic cycles of layoffs and rehires. People who lose jobs because of structural

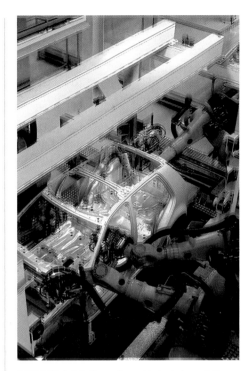

FIGURE 1.29 Computer-guided robots are taking over many manufacturing jobs that people once held.

unemployment are not going to get them back. Their only option is to retrain themselves to work in other careers.

Consider this: Half of all the jobs that will be available in 10 years don't exist today. So who will survive—and flourish—in a computer-driven economy? The answer is simple. The survivors will be people who understand technology, know that education is a lifelong process, and adapt quickly to change.

BEING A RESPONSIBLE COMPUTER USER

You use a computer and the Internet, have a smartphone, and send e-mail, text messages, and tweets throughout the day. All of this seems OK within your own personal space; but how does your usage affect others in your school, office, family, community, and the environment? For starters, don't hog public computer resources. If you are using a computer and Internet connection at a library or in a wireless hot spot, don't download or upload large files; be considerate of others who might be sharing the connection. Recycle paper and printer cartridges to help protect the environment. Don't talk on your phone or text message while driving; many states have enacted laws against using handheld devices while operating a vehicle and impose stringent fines. Be aware of the people near you in the theater; they paid for tickets to watch the show—not to hear your phone or conversation or see your screen light up with a text message.

Another concern is how to dispose of obsolete computer equipment, also called **e-waste**. More than 100 million computers, monitors, and TVs become obsolete each year, and these numbers keep growing. In the first quarter of 2008, 294.3 million mobile phone units were sold, a 13.6 percent increase over the first quarter of 2007. Because monitors, batteries, and other electronic components contain hazardous materials, they can't just be thrown in the trash. Unfortunately only 12.5 percent of this e-waste is properly recycled. At least 24 states either have passed or are considering laws regarding e-waste disposal (Figure 1.30). Responsible users look for computer and electronics equipment disposal and recycling companies in their area or check state and federal Web sites, such as the Environmental Protection Agency site (**www.epa.gov**), for tips on computer disposal.

Private companies are stepping up recycling services. Dell has initiated a program that will recycle anyone's PC, regardless of manufacturer. HP will recycle any manufacturer's computer hardware or printer cartridges and has also set up battery recycling programs in many computer stores. Gateway gives you cash for your old technology; if your product has zero value, Gateway will pay for shipping it and will recycle it free of charge. For more

information go to **www.gateway.com/ about/corp_responsibility/env_ options.php**.

Another way to solve the disposal problem and give back to your community is by donating old computer equipment to local charities that could refurbish it to help new users learn the basics. Perhaps you might consider donating a little of your time to help, too.

Being a responsible technology user also means being aware of how computers and Internet use can affect your own well-being and personal relationships. Researchers at Carnegie Mellon University were surprised to find that people who spent even a few hours a week on the Internet experienced higher levels of depression and loneliness than those who did not. These people interacted with other Internet users online, but this interaction seems to have been much shallower than time spent with friends and family. The result? According to these researchers, Internet use leads to unhealthy social isolation and a deadened, mechanized experience that is lacking in human emotion. Interestingly, other studies show just the opposite; these studies demonstrate that there is no difference in socialization between those who use the Internet and those who

FIGURE 1.30
Responsible computer users and manufacturers recycle old computers, printers, monitors, batteries, and other types of e-waste.

do not. Who is right? It will take years of research to know. But for now, keep in mind that computer and Internet overuse may promote unhealthy behaviors.

STAYING INFORMED ABOUT CHANGING TECHNOLOGY

It is important to stay informed about software and hardware advances in technology. Upgrading the application software on your computer helps you enjoy the most current features the software manufacturer offers. Upgrading your antivirus application helps prevent the latest computer viruses from infecting and harming your system. (A *virus* is a malicious program that enters your computer with or without your permission.) Some viruses are harmless; others slow down performance; and still others delete programs and files. Viruses wreak havoc on computers every day. By knowing all you can about the latest viruses and how they're spread, you can keep your computer from getting infected.

The steady advance of computer hardware has created faster processors, cheaper storage devices, and lighter, thinner, vision-friendly monitors. For the user, this means that next month's computer will be more powerful than this month's computer and will probably cost less. You can stay informed about the latest technology by reading periodicals, visiting Web sites such as CNET (**www.cnet.com**), subscribing to print and online newsletters and publications, and reading technology columns in your local newspaper. Learning about computers and technology will help you be a better consumer, a more productive student and employee, and, in general, a more responsible computer user.

Chapter Summary

Computers and You

A computer system is a collection of related components that have been designed to perform the information processing cycle: input, processing, output, and storage. A system includes both hardware—the physical components such as the system unit, keyboard, monitor, and speakers—and software—the programs that run on it. In a typical computer system, a keyboard and a mouse provide input capabilities. Processing is done by the microprocessor (CPU) on programs and data held in RAM (random access memory). You see the results (output) on a monitor or printer, and a hard disk is typically used for long-term storage.

There are two major categories of computers: computers for individuals and those for organizations. Types of computers for individuals include personal computers (PCs), desktop computers, all-in-one computers, notebooks, subnotebooks (ultraportables), tablet PCs, and handheld computers (such as PDAs and smartphones). Types of computers for organizations include professional workstations, servers, minicomputers, mainframes, and supercomputers.

Computers have advantages and disadvantages. Some advantages include speed, memory, storage, hardware reliability, accuracy, and assistance to those with disabilities. Disadvantages include information overload, expense, data inaccuracy, unreliable software, viruses, software piracy, identity theft, loss of jobs to automation, and health problems due to improperly fitting equipment and poorly arranged work environments.

Being a responsible computer user means respecting others when using technology, recycling computer hardware, sharing public computing resources, being aware of computer and Internet overuse, and staying informed about changing technology and its effect on the environment.

Key Terms and Concepts

Matching

Match each key term in the left column with the most accurate definition in the right column:

_____ 1. program

_____ 2. netbook

_____ 3. digital piracy

_____ 4. bug

_____ 5. data

_____ 6. tablet PC

_____ 7. professional workstation

_____ 8. all-in-one computer

_____ 9. computer ethics

_____ 10. information

_____ 11. network interface card

_____ 12. ergonomics

_____ 13. random access memory

_____ 14. communications

_____ 15. information processing cycle

a. A portable lightweight computer equipped with wireless technology and used primarily to browse the Web and access e-mail.

b. Facts that have been processed for presentation in a meaningful form.

c. A computer system in which the system unit and monitor are combined to reduce the space needed to hold the system.

d. A high-end computer designed for technical applications requiring powerful processing and output capabilities.

e. A branch of philosophy that deals with computer-related moral dilemmas.

f. A convertible notebook that can be used in two different configurations and accepts handwritten input.

g. Unauthorized reproduction and distribution of computer-based media.

h. A set of instructions that tells a computer how to perform a process.

i. Raw facts.

j. An error in software or hardware that makes a program malfunction.

k. The matching of computer components to fit an individual's posture and body design.

l. The high-speed movement of data within and between computers.

m. Needed to temporarily store data and programs with which the CPU interacts.

n. Four basic operations of a computer system.

o. A hardware component of a computer system that contains the electronics to connect the computer to a network.

Multiple Choice

Circle the correct choice for each of the following:

1. Which of the following is a common input device?
   a. Mouse
   b. Printer
   c. Disk drive
   d. Speaker

2. Which of the following is *not* an example of application software?
   a. Word processor
   b. Spreadsheet
   c. Operating system
   d. Photo editor

3. What part of the system unit processes the input data?
   a. Read-alone memory
   b. CPU
   c. Random access memory
   d. NIC

4. What component of a computer is located in the system unit and contains the circuitry to connect the computer to a network?
   a. RAM
   b. Node
   c. CPU
   d. NIC

5. Which is an example of an e-book reader?
   a. Wiki
   b. NIC
   c. Kindle 2
   d. Tweeter

6. What is the sending of portions of a job to a third party to reduce cost, time, and energy called?
   a. Outsourcing
   b. Automation
   c. Digital piracy
   d. Structural unemployment

7. What is the feeling of anxiety experienced when people are presented with more information than they can handle?
   a. Technology overload
   b. Technology meltdown
   c. Processing overload
   d. Information overload

8. Which of the following computers is *not* designed for portability or use while traveling?
   a. All-in-one
   b. Notebook
   c. Tablet PC
   d. Ultraportable

9. Which of the following is a computer used by government agencies and large corporations like airlines and banks?
   a. Workstation
   b. Mainframe
   c. Supercomputer
   d. All-in-one

10. What is the name given to unemployment caused by technology making an entire job category obsolete?
    a. Technological unemployment
    b. Corporate unemployment
    c. Structural unemployment
    d. Automated unemployment

Fill-In

In the blanks provided, write the correct answer for each of the following:

1. The mouse and keyboard are _____ devices.

2. Monitors, printers, and speakers are _____ devices.

3. Hard drives, DVD drives, and USB drives are examples of _____ devices.

4. The operating system and antivirus software are part of the software group called _____ _____.

5. _____ is a social messaging utility that allows posting of up to 140 characters that take the form of short questions and answers.

6. Obsolete computer equipment is called _____.

7. Facebook and LinkedIn are examples of _____ _____.

8. A(n) _____ _____ is an onscreen touch-activated keyboard.

9. A(n) _____ is a group of two or more connected computer systems that share devices and resources.

10. _____ _____ is a free Web-based word processor and spreadsheet that encourages collaboration by allowing group members to share and edit documents online.

11. A centrally located and operated computer that makes programs and data available to people who are connected to a computer network is a _____.

12. The replacement of human workers by machines is known as _____.

13. The _____ is the circuit board located in the system unit that connects the CPU and other system components.

14. The _____ _____ describes the disparity between groups who own computers and have Internet access and those who do not.

15. The use of computers and computer programs to replace teachers and time-specific learning is _____.

Short Answer

1. Explain the difference between hardware and software.

2. Provide a brief description of the similarities and differences between a desktop computer and an all-in-one computer.

3. What are the differences among a notebook computer, a tablet PC, and a netbook?

4. Define the terms *data* and *information*. Identify the step in the information processing cycle that each is associated with.

5. List three examples of application software found on the computer systems in your home, school, or office.

6. List three advantages and three disadvantages of computer use.

7. List three to five characteristics of a responsible computer user.

Teamwork

1. **Handheld Computers** Your team is to investigate the latest smartphones from at least three manufacturers. Break into three teams with each team researching the features, costs, monthly fees, insurance rates, and accessories for each manufacturer's latest device. Prepare a presentation to make to the rest of the class; and be sure to cite your resources.

2. **"I am a Mac, and I am a PC"** As a team, use a search engine to locate and review at least three of the "I am a Mac, and I am a PC" commercials. These are 30-second commercials that praise the features of the Mac while mocking the PC. Cite the commercials viewed. Create a new 30-second commercial that will reverse the ad: Have the commercial support the PC while mocking the Mac. Your team will have to research both systems to find a PC asset that the Mac lacks. Rehearse your commercial and present it to the class.

3. **Tablet PC or Notebook—You Decide** As a team, determine whether you would purchase a tablet PC or a notebook computer. Use the Internet or contact a local vendor and compare the prices for similarly equipped units. Based on your needs and finances, prepare a report to present to the class explaining which computer you would buy and give reasons that support your decision.

4. **Ergonomics** As a team, use a search engine and locate at least three Web sites that contain information about the ergonomics of setting up computer stations. Prepare a report that covers the following items. First define the term *ergonomics,* and then list at least five items that should be ergonomically designed in a computer station for the user's health and comfort. For at least three of these five items, find two retailers that sell such ergonomic products. Describe the products, explain how they will ergonomically correct or prevent a problem, and note how much the devices cost. Be sure to cite your resources.

5. **Employment** As a team, examine advertisements for jobs in your area. Use online job search sites and your local paper. Make a chart of 10 job categories that require computer knowledge and then review the jobs in each category. In the chart, enter the number of available jobs that were posted or listed for each category. If possible, state the average pay of a position in each category. Present your findings to the class, explaining what you have learned from your research.

On the Web

1. **Green Computers** Go to **www.worldchanging. com/archives/004350.html** and use Google (**www. google.com**) or another search engine to locate sources of information about green computers. List at least three green computer features and their components. Then use the Internet to locate three manufacturers of green computers. State the name of each computer, its price, and the green features that each system possesses. Present this information in a one- or two-page, double-spaced report. Be sure to cite your references.

2. **Digital Divide** Use Google (**www.google.com**) or **www.digitaldivide.org/dd/index.html** to research and obtain background information about the digital divide. Locate three articles with information about the digital divide, its past and present, and actions being taken to reduce it in the future. Cite your references and present your results in a one-page, double-spaced paper.

3. **Robotics** Use your favorite search engine to locate at least three articles about robots in manufacturing. Look for such facts as the number and type of jobs being turned over to robots, the countries buying and producing robotic equipment, and how much a robot costs versus how much a company can save by using a robot. After collecting the data, present your findings in a table, listing at least three advantages and three disadvantages of robot use in manufacturing. Back up each entry in the table with a statistic or fact from your research. Remember to cite your references.

4. **Ethics** Use your favorite search engine and locate the "Ten Commandments of Computer Ethics" published by the Computer Ethics Institute. Read each one, and in a one-page paper indicate at least three commandments with which you agree and three with which you disagree. Give logical and historical reasons for your statement. You might want to reference the Bill of Rights or other historical documents to support your stance. Cite your references and present your reasons in a one- or two-page, double-spaced paper.

5. **Social Networks** Use your favorite search engine to locate a definition of social networking, as well as find articles about the pros and cons of Web sites used to socially network. Visit the social networking sites mentioned in this chapter: Facebook, MySpace, and LinkedIn. Pretend you are going to develop your own social networking site. Use your observations and research to come up with a list of five rules users of the sites will have to follow and five behaviors that will cause a user to be expelled from the site. Define *social networking,* list the pros and cons of social networking you found in your research, and list your five rules and five behaviors that cause expulsion in a one-page, double-spaced paper.

Ethics

What's the difference between unethical and illegal? When using computers, and especially the Internet, you may have to face this question daily. Have you downloaded any music recently? Or have you ripped any CDs lately? Have you copied music from a friend? Did you pay for that music? Have you watched a DVD movie or played a video game this weekend? Was the DVD or game a legal purchased copy? Was either overly violent? Have you ever thought about who owns the word processing software you use in your college computer lab? What is your school or company's policy on acceptable computer use? Perhaps you've written a research paper recently that included material you copied from a Web site. Or perhaps you've posted a nasty comment about someone on a discussion board or sent a nasty e-mail. These are some of the ways you can exhibit unacceptable behavior at school or on the job. Ethics is often described as knowing the difference between right and wrong, and choosing to do what is right. In other words, we choose to behave in an ethical way so we can live with our consciences. Ethics is not about whether we'll get caught.

This Spotlight examines some of the most common issues in computer ethics, from ethical dilemmas, where the difference between right and wrong isn't so easy to discern, to legal matters, where right and wrong is determined by law.

Computer Ethics for Computer Users

It isn't always easy to determine the right thing to do. Even when you know what's right, it isn't always easy to act on it. Peer pressure is a tremendous force. Why should you be the one to do the right thing when you believe everyone else is getting away with using copied software and music files?

Computers cause new ethical dilemmas by pushing people into unprecedented situations (Figure 1A). **Computer ethics** uses basic ethical principles to help you make the right decisions in your daily computer use. Ethical principles help you think through your options.

FIGURE 1A Computers cause new ethical dilemmas by pushing people into unprecedented situations.

ETHICAL PRINCIPLES

An **ethical principle** defines the justification for considering an act or a rule to be morally right or wrong. Over the centuries, philosophers have come up with many ethical principles. For many people, it's disconcerting to find that these principles sometimes conflict. An ethical principle is only a tool that you can use to think through a difficult situation. In the end, you must make your choice and live with the consequences.

The Belmont Report from the U.S. Department of Health, Education, and Welfare shows three of the most useful ethical principles:

- *An act is ethical if, were everyone to act the same way, society as a whole would benefit.*
- *An act is ethical if it treats people as an end in themselves rather than as a means to an end.*
- *An act is ethical if impartial observers would judge that it is fair to all parties concerned.*

If you still find yourself in an ethical dilemma related to computer use even after careful consideration of these ethical principles, talk to people you trust. They might be able to help you make the correct decision. Make sure you have all the facts. Think through alternative courses of action based on the different principles. Would you be proud if your parents knew what you had done? What if your actions were mentioned in an article on the front page of your local newspaper? Always strive to find a solution you can be proud of.

FOLLOWING YOUR SCHOOL'S CODE OF CONDUCT

When you use a computer, one of the things you will need to determine is who owns the data, programs, and Internet access you enjoy. If you own your computer system and its software, the work you create is clearly yours, and you are solely responsible for it. However, when you use a computer at school or at work, it is possible that the work you create there might be considered the property of the school or business. In short, you have greater responsibility and less control over content ownership when you use somebody else's system than when you use your own.

Sometimes this question isn't just an ethical one but a legal one as well. How companies and schools enforce computer usage rules tends to vary. So where can you, the college computer user, find guidance when dealing with ethical and legal dilemmas? Your college or place of employment probably has its own code of conduct or **acceptable-use policy** for computer users. You can usually find this policy on your organization's Web site (Figure 1B), in a college or employee handbook, or included in an employment contract. You might call the help desk at your computing center and ask for the Web site address of the policy or request a physical copy of it. Read the policy carefully and follow the rules.

- **Respect yourself.** If you obtain an account and password to use the campus computer system, don't give your password to others. They could do something that gets you in trouble. In addition, don't say or do anything on the Internet that could reflect poorly on you, even if you think no one will ever find out. Internet content has a way of resurfacing.

- **Respect others.** Obviously, you shouldn't use a computer to threaten or harass anyone. You should also avoid using more than your share of computing resources, such as disk space. If you publish a Web page on your college's computers, remember that your page's content affects the college's public image.

- **Respect academic integrity.** Always give credit for text you've copied from the Internet. Obtain permission before you copy pictures. Don't copy or distribute software unless the license specifically states you have permission to do so.

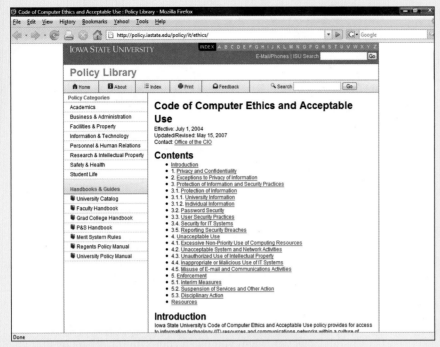

FIGURE 1B Many organizations and schools publish their computer use (or acceptable use) policy on their Web site.

Netiquette is also important in the classroom. At Northern Michigan University you may see the following on the course syllabus:

"Appropriate Classroom Laptop Use . . . Although having a laptop in class opens up new learning possibilities for students, sometimes students utilize it in ways that are inappropriate. Please refrain from instant messaging, e-mailing, surfing the Internet, playing games, writing papers, doing homework, etc., during class time. Acceptable uses include taking notes, following along with the instructor on PowerPoint, with demonstrations, and other whole class activities, as well as working on assigned in-class activities, projects, and discussions that require laptop use. It is easy for your laptop to become a distraction to you and to those around you. Inappropriate uses will be noted and may affect your final grade."

TEN COMMANDMENTS FOR COMPUTER ETHICS

The Computer Ethics Institute of the Brookings Institution, located in Washington, D.C., has developed the following "Ten Commandments for Computer Ethics" for computer users, programmers, and system designers:

1. Thou shalt not use a computer to harm other people.

2. Thou shalt not interfere with other people's computer work.

3. Thou shalt not snoop around in other people's computer files.

4. Thou shalt not use a computer to steal.

5. Thou shalt not use a computer to bear false witness.

6. Thou shalt not copy or use proprietary software for which you have not paid.

7. Thou shalt not use other people's computer resources without authorization or proper compensation.

8. Thou shalt not appropriate other people's intellectual output.

9. Thou shalt think about the social consequences of the program you are writing or the system you are designing.

10. Thou shalt always use a computer in ways that ensure consideration and respect for your fellow humans.

NETIQUETTE

General principles such as the "Ten Commandments for Computer Ethics" are useful for overall guidance, but they don't provide specific help for the special situations you'll run into online—such as how to behave properly in chat rooms or while playing an online game (Figure 1C). As a result, computer and Internet users have developed a lengthy series of specific behavior guidelines called **netiquette** for the various Internet services available (such as e-mail, mailing lists, social networking sites,

FIGURE 1C Netiquette offers guidelines for how to behave properly in chat rooms or while playing an online game.

discussion forums, and online role-playing games) that provide specific pointers on how to show respect for others—and for yourself—while you're online.

Here's a sample, based on Albion.com's Netiquette Home Page (**www.albion.com/netiquette**) and other Internet sources:

- **Discussion forums.** Before posting to a discussion forum, review the forum and various topics to see what kinds of questions are welcomed and how to participate meaningfully. If the forum has a FAQ (frequently asked questions) document posted on the Web, be sure to read it before posting to the forum; your question may already have been answered in the FAQ. Post your message under the appropriate topic or start a new topic if necessary. Your post should be helpful or ask a legitimate question. Bear in mind that some people using the discussion forum may not speak English as their native tongue, so don't belittle people for spelling errors. Don't post inflammatory messages; never post in anger. If you agree with something, don't post a message that says "Me too"—you're just wasting everyone's time. Posting ads for your own business or soliciting answers to obvious homework questions is usually frowned on.

- **E-mail.** Check your e-mail daily and respond promptly to the messages you've been sent. Download or delete messages after you've read them so that you don't exceed your disk-usage quota. Remember that e-mail isn't private; you should never send a message that contains anything you wouldn't want others to read. Always speak of others professionally and courteously; e-mail is easily forwarded, and the person you're describing may eventually see the message. Check your computer frequently for viruses that can propagate via e-mail messages. Keep your messages short and to the point; focus on one subject per message. Don't type in all capital letters; this comes across as SHOUTING. Spell check your e-mail as you would any other written correspondence, especially in professional settings. Watch out for sarcasm and humor in e-mail; it often fails to come across as a joke. Be mindful when you request a return receipt that some people consider this to be an invasion of privacy.

- **Instant messages (IM) and text messages.** IM and text messages are ideal for brief conversations; but complex or lengthy discussions may be better handled in person, by e-mail, or by phone. IM can be easily misinterpreted because tone is difficult to convey. Never share bad news or a major announcement in a text message or send an IM while you are angry or upset. Don't assume that everyone knows what IM acronyms such as BRB (be

right back) and LOL (laughing out loud) mean. Be mindful that some smartphone plans still charge for text messages. Also, remember to set away messages and use other status messages wisely.

Netiquette is important in the classroom. According to an article published in *The Journal of Higher Education*, several colleges have offered guidelines and suggestions for curbing misuse of computers in class and have set netiquette standards, like turning off the computer's volume before class begins.

In addition to respectful use of Internet services, playing computer games is another area in which you might face ethical dilemmas.

COMPUTER GAMES: TOO MUCH VIOLENCE?

Computer gaming isn't universally admired. More than one-third of all games fall into the action category; among these, the most popular are so-called splatter games, which emphasize all-out violence of an especially bloody sort. Parents and politicians are concerned that children who play these games may be learning aggressive behaviors that will prove dysfunctional in real life—and they may be right.

In one study, 210 college students were observed before and after playing an especially violent computer game. Researchers found that the students were more hostile and reacted more aggressively after playing the game. Another study found that young men who played violent computer games during their teenage years were more likely to commit crimes.

> "... young men who played **violent** computer games during their **teenage years** were more likely to commit **crimes.**"

Fears concerning the impact of violent computer games were heightened by the Columbine High School tragedy in 1999, in which two Littleton, Colorado, teenagers opened fire on teachers and fellow students before committing suicide. Subsequently, investigators learned that the boys had been great fans of splatter games such as *Doom* and *Quake* and may have patterned their massacre after their gaming experiences. In 2009, there was a school shooting in Germany that left 15 dead. A neighbor and childhood friend of the shooter was quoted as saying, "He [the shooter] was fascinated by video games, he used to play a shooting game called Tactical Ops and he used to watch horror films like *Alien* and *Predator*."

Still, psychologists disagree on the effect of violent computer games. Some point out that they're little more than an extension of the World War II "combat" games children used to play on street corners before the television—and the computer—came along. Others claim that violent video games provide an outlet for aggression that might otherwise materialize in homes and schools.

One thing is for certain: Computer games are becoming more violent. In the past few years, the video

FIGURE 1D   Some computer games are both engrossing and violent.

game industry has released a slew of new titles that offer a more streamlined gaming experience, particularly when a player is connected to the Internet in multiplayer mode—and of course, much more realistic portrayals of violent acts (Figure 1D).

So who is responsible? Is it the software manufacturers who create the programs? Is it the consumers who purchase and use the programs? Parents certainly have a responsibility over what their children do, but what about you—do you make "good" decisions when it comes to exposure to violence? More importantly, is there anything you can do about it? Refer back to the "Ten Commandments for Computer Ethics," especially numbers 9 and 10.

Now that you know about the ethical issues individuals face, let's take a look at how organizations deal with computer ethics.

Computer Ethics for Organizations

Every day, newspapers carry stories about people getting into trouble by using their computers to conduct personal business while they're at work. In many cases, the offenders use company computers to browse the Web and send personal e-mail on company time or to commit crimes such as cyberstalking or distributing pornography. Although most companies have an acceptable-use policy for computers, you should be aware that using a computer for non-business-related tasks is generally banned within an organization. You should check with your system administrator, supervisor, or human resources department to obtain a copy of the company's acceptable-use policy.

However, those are rules set to control individuals' behavior while at work. What ethical responsibilities do the companies themselves have? To serve its customers and the public effectively, a business or organization must protect its data from loss and damage and from error and misuse.

Protecting data from loss or change is often simply a matter of following proper backup procedures. **Backup procedures** involve making copies of data files to protect against data loss, change, or damage from natural or other disasters. Without backup procedures, an organization may place its customers' information at risk. Moreover, it would be unethical not to keep regular backups, because the loss of the company's data could negatively impact the stakeholders in the business (Figure 1E). What would happen to a bank, for example, if it lost all of its data and didn't have any backups?

Data errors can and do occur. It is the ethical responsibility of any organization that deals with data to ensure that its data is as correct as possible. Data that hasn't been properly maintained can have serious effects on the individual or organization it relates to.

Data misuse occurs when an employee or company fails to keep data confidential. A breach of confidentiality occurs when an employee looks up data about a person in a database and uses that information for

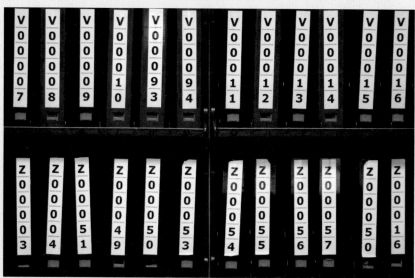

FIGURE 1E   A backup system can help protect a business's information assets. A computer tape library is one way to store backed-up files.

something other than what was intended. For example, U.S. government workers accessed the passport files for 2008 presidential candidates John McCain, Barack Obama, and Hillary Clinton, in addition to more than 100 celebrities. Such actions are grounds for termination.

Companies may punish employees for looking up customer data, but many of them think nothing of selling it to third parties. A mail-order company, for example, can gain needed revenue by selling customer lists to firms marketing related products. Privacy advocates believe that it's unethical to divulge customer data without first asking the customer's permission. These advocates are working to pass tougher privacy laws so the matter would become a legal concern, not an ethical one.

As an employee, what can you do to stop companies from misusing data or to protect your customers' privacy? Often, there's no clear-cut solution. If you believe that the way a company is conducting business poses a danger to the public or appears to be illegal, you can report the company to regulatory agencies or the press, an action called **whistle-blowing**. But what if your whistle-blowing causes your company to shut down, putting not only you but also all of your coworkers out of work? As this example illustrates, codes of ethics don't solve every ethical problem; however, they at least provide solid guidance for most situations.

The Business Software Alliance (BSA) helps to combat software piracy, another ethical and legal issue, by educating the public and businesses about the legal and safety issues regarding commercial software use. You can even fill out a confidential form on their Web site at **https://reporting.bsa.org/usa** to report incidences of piracy. By doing so, you could be eligible for a $1 million reward.

Computer Ethics for Computer Professionals

No profession can stay in business for long without a rigorous (and enforced) code of professional ethics. That's why many different types of professionals subscribe to ethical **codes of conduct**. These codes are developed by professional associations, such as the Association for Computing Machinery (ACM). Figure 1F is an excerpt from the Code of Ethics of the Institute for Certification of Computing Professionals.

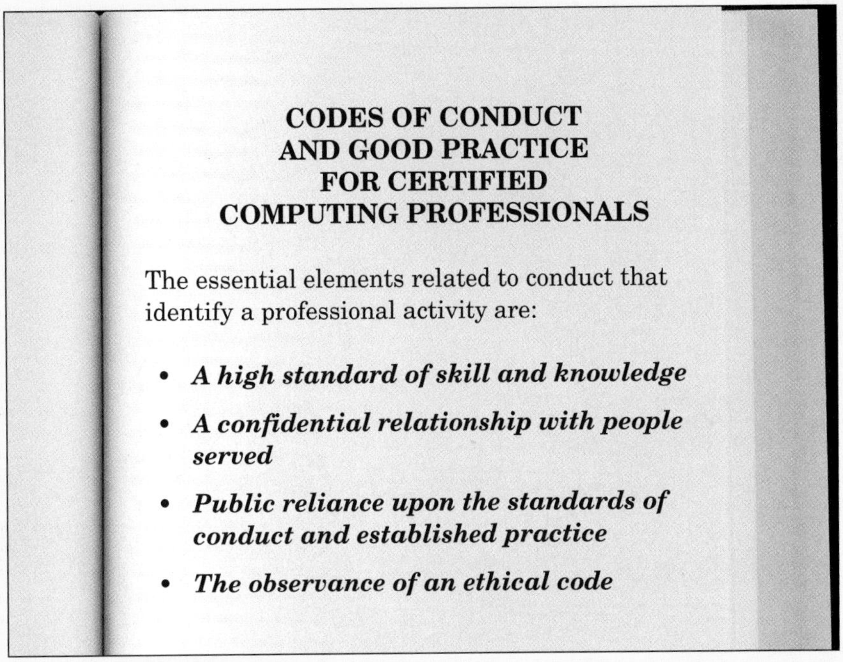

CODES OF CONDUCT AND GOOD PRACTICE FOR CERTIFIED COMPUTING PROFESSIONALS

The essential elements related to conduct that identify a professional activity are:

- *A high standard of skill and knowledge*
- *A confidential relationship with people served*
- *Public reliance upon the standards of conduct and established practice*
- *The observance of an ethical code*

FIGURE 1F Excerpt from the Code of Ethics of the Institute for Certification of Computing Professionals

THE ACM CODE OF CONDUCT

Of all the computing associations' codes of conduct, the one developed by the ACM (**www.acm.org**) is considered the most innovative and far-reaching. According to the ACM code, a computing professional

1. Contributes to society and human well-being
2. Avoids harm to others
3. Is honest and trustworthy
4. Is fair and takes action not to discriminate on the basis of race, sex, religion, age, disability, or national origin
5. Honors property rights, including copyrights and patents
6. Gives proper credit when using the intellectual property of others
7. Respects the right of other individuals to privacy
8. Honors confidentiality

Like other codes of conduct, the ACM code places public safety and well-being at the top of the list.

SAFETY FIRST

Computer professionals create products that affect many people and may even expose them to risk of personal injury or death. Increasingly, computers and computer programs figure prominently in safety-critical systems, including transportation monitoring (such as with air traffic control) and patient monitoring in hospitals (Figure 1G).

Consider the following situation. An airplane pilot flying in poor visibility uses a computer, called an autopilot, to guide the plane. The air traffic control system

FIGURE 1G Patient monitoring in hospitals helps to create a safer environment.

also relies on computers. The plane crashes. The investigation discloses minor bugs in both computer programs. If the plane's computer had been dealing with a person in the tower rather than a computer or if the air traffic control program had been interacting with a human pilot, the crash would not have occurred. Where does the liability lie for the loss of life and property?

Experienced programmers know that programs of any size have bugs. Most complex programs have so many possible combinations of conditions that it isn't feasible to test for every combination. In some cases, the tests would take years; in other cases, no one could think of all the possible conditions. Because bugs are inevitable and programmers can't predict all the different ways programs interact with their environment, most computer experts believe that it's wrong to single out programmers for blame.

Software companies are at fault if they fail to test and document their products. In addition, the organization that buys the software may share part of the blame if it fails to train personnel to use the system properly.

At the core of every computer code of ethics, therefore, is a professional's highest and most important aim: to preserve and protect human life and to avoid harm or injury. If the public is to trust computer professionals, they must have the ethics needed to protect

our safety and welfare—even if doing so means the professional person or the company they work for suffers financially.

Unlike the ethical dilemmas we've discussed up to now, right and wrong are more easily defined when it comes to matters of the law.

It's Not Just Unethical, It's Illegal Too

What else can cause problems for computer users? Let's start with something that gets many college students into serious trouble: plagiarism.

PLAGIARISM

Imagine the following scenario. It's 4 AM, and you have a paper due for your 9 AM class. While searching for sources on the Internet, you find a Web site with an essay on your topic. What's wrong with downloading the text, reworking it a bit, and handing it in? Plenty.

The use of someone else's intellectual property (their ideas or written work) is called **plagiarism**. Plagiarism predates computers; in fact, it has been practiced for thousands of years. But, computers—and especially the Internet—make the temptation and ease

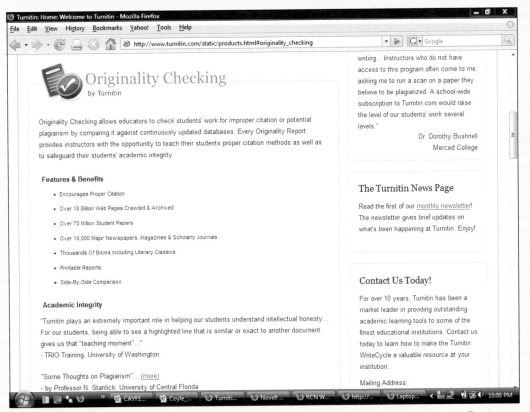

FIGURE 1H Turnitin is one of the popular software packages used by professors at colleges and universities to identify instances of plagiarism.

of plagiarizing even greater. It's not only very easy to copy and paste from the Internet but some sites are actually set up specifically to sell college-level papers to the lazy or desperate. The sites selling the papers aren't guilty of plagiarism, but you are if you turn in the work as your own.

Plagiarism is a serious offense. How serious? At some colleges, even a first offense can get you thrown out of school. You might think it's rare for plagiarizers to be caught, but the truth is that college instructors are often able to detect plagiarism in students' papers without much effort. The tip-off can be a change in the sophistication of phraseology, writing that is a little too polished, or errors in spelling and grammar that are identical in two or more papers. Software programs such as Turnitin are available that can scan text and then compare it against a library of known phrases (Figure 1H). If a paper has one or more recognizable phrases, it is marked for closer inspection. Furthermore, even if your actions are not discovered now, someone could find out later, and the evidence could void your degree and even damage your career.

The more well-known you are, the more you're at risk of your plagiarism being uncovered. Take noted historian and Pulitzer Prize–winning author Doris Kearns Goodwin, for example. In 2002, she was accused of plagiarizing part of her best-selling 1987 book, *The Fitzgeralds and the Kennedys*. Although she claimed her plagiarizing was inadvertent and due to inadequate research methods, she suffered a significant decline in credibility and even felt obligated to leave her position at the PBS news program *NewsHour with Jim Lehrer*." It took 15 years for Goodwin's plagiarism to come to light. Don't think she is alone. You can find a listing of famous plagiarists at **www.famousplagiarists.com**.

Plagiarism is a unique offense because it's both unethical and illegal: The unethical part is the dishonesty of passing someone else's work off as your own. The illegal part is taking the material without permission. Plagiarizing copyrighted material is called **copyright infringement**, and if you're caught, you can be sued and may have to pay damages in addition to compensating your victim for any financial losses due to your theft of the material. Trademarks, products, and patented processes are also protected. If you're tempted to copy anything from the Web, bear in mind that the United States is a signatory to international copyright regulations, which specify that an original author does not need to include an explicit copyright notice to be protected under the law.

Does this mean you can't use the Internet source you found? Of course not. Nevertheless, you must follow certain citation guidelines. In academic writing, you can make use of someone else's effort if you use your own words and give credit where credit is due. If you use a phrase or a few sentences from the source, use quotation marks. Attach a bibliography and list the source. For Internet sources, you should list the Web site's address (or Uniform Resource Locator [URL]), the date the article was published (if available), the date and time you accessed the site, the name of the article, and the author's name. You can usually find a link at the bottom of a Web site's home page that outlines the owner's copyright policy. If not, there is usually a "contact us" link that you can use to contact the owner. You cannot assume that it is legal to copy content from a Web site just because you cannot find a disclaimer. Starting with Microsoft Office 2007, adding citations to a research paper became even easier. One of the features of the software is a tool to help you organize and input the correct reference information in a variety of different referencing styles.

You'll often hear people use the term **fair use** to justify illegal copying. The fair use doctrine justifies *limited* uses of copyrighted material without payment to or permission from the copyright holder. This means that a *brief* selection from a copyrighted work may be excerpted for the purposes of commentary, parody, news reporting, research, and education. Such excerpts are short—generally, no more than 5 percent of the original work—and they shouldn't compromise the commercial value of the work. Of course, you must still cite the source. In general, the reproduction of an entire work is rarely justifiable by means of the fair use doctrine.

As a responsible computer user, you should worry not only about wrongly using someone else's words but also about the content you create yourself. The written word carries a lot of power. If the words you choose are untrue, you could be crossing into dangerous, and illegal, territory.

LIBEL

The power of computers and the Internet as a means of communication makes them ripe for involvement in libel. In the United States, **libel** is the publication of a false statement that injures someone's business or personal reputation. A plaintiff who sues for libel must prove that a false statement caused injury and demonstrate some type of resulting damage. This could include being shunned by friends and associates or the inability to obtain work because potential employers believed the false accusations. Some states allow a jury to assess damages based generally on harm to the person's reputation. It is in your best interest to ensure that any electronic publication statement you make about an individual or a corporation is truthful.

SOFTWARE PIRACY

Here's another common situation. You need to have Microsoft Office 2007 for your computer class. A friend gives you a copy that she got from her mom's office. You've just installed that copy on your computer.

Have you done something wrong? Yes, of course you have! In fact, so has your friend. It is illegal for her to have a copy of the software from her mom's office in the first place.

Just like written works, most computer software (including computer games) is copyrighted, which means that you can't make copies for other people without infringing on the software's copyright. Such infringements are called **software piracy** and are a federal offense in the United States (Figure 1I).

How serious is software piracy? The information technology industry loses billions of dollars a year because of piracy. If you're caught pirating software, you may be charged with a felony. If you're convicted of a felony, you could spend time in jail, lose the right to vote, and ruin your chances for a successful career.

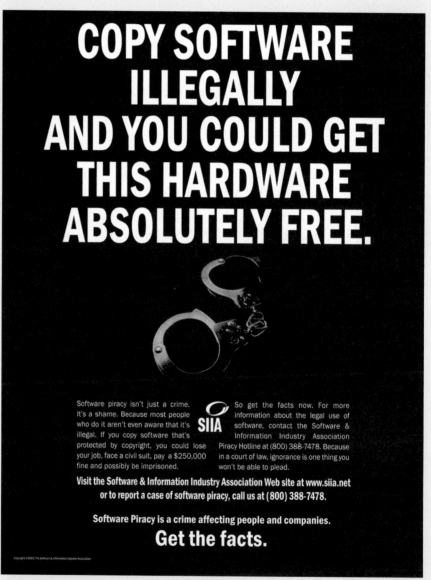

FIGURE 1I The Software & Information Industry Association (SIIA) is trying to raise consciousness about software piracy.

When you purchase commercial software, you're really purchasing a **software license**, which generally grants you the right to make backups of the program disks and install the software. You need to read the license agreement to determine how many machines you can install the software on. Providing the program to others or modifying the program's function is not allowed. A blank sample of a software license can be found at **www.lawsmart.com/documents/ software_license.shtml**. Note that this is a sample, and reading it is *not* a substitute for examining the software license for each program you purchase.

Free programs that users can copy or modify without restriction are called **public domain software**. However, don't assume that a program is public domain unless you see a note (often in the form of a Read Me text file) that explicitly identifies the file as being copyright free.

Unlike public domain software, you can't copy or modify **shareware** programs without permission from the owner. You can usually find the owner and licensing information by accessing the Help menu or by locating and reading a Read Me file that is usually placed in the same directory as the program. You may, however, freely copy trial or evaluation versions of shareware programs. When the evaluation period expires, you must pay a **registration fee** or delete the software from your computer.

Other programs qualify under the provisions of the Free Software Foundation's **General Public License (GPL)**, which specifies that anyone may freely copy, use, and modify the software, but no one can sell it for profit.

Organizations with many computers (including colleges) also have to be concerned about software piracy. A **site license** is a contract with the software publisher that allows an organization to use multiple copies of the software at a reduced price per unit. Taking copies outside the organization usually violates the contract. However, check the license agreement. Some organizations negotiate the agreement to allow employees to load the software on their home computers as well, as long as only one copy is in use at any one time.

Software manufacturers are working very hard to develop **copyright protection schemes** to thwart the illegal use of their programs. Increasingly, software is becoming **machine dependent**. This means that the program captures a machine ID during the installation process and writes that ID back to the software company's server during a mandatory online registration process. If you attempt to install the program on another machine, the code will be checked and the installation will terminate unless your license allows multiple installations. Microsoft checks your computer for a valid copy of its software before it will

permit you to make updates, access templates, or download other add-ons.

How can you tell whether you're guilty of software piracy? All of the following actions are illegal:

- *Continuing to use a shareware program past the evaluation version's expiration date without paying the registration fee.*
- *Violating the terms of a software license, even if you've paid for the program. For example, if you have copies of the same program on your desktop and notebook computers but the license allows only one installation, you are in violation of the license.*
- *Making copies of site-licensed programs that you use at work or school and installing them on your home computer (unless expressly allowed through the license).*
- *Giving or selling copies of commercial software to others.*
- *Incorporating all or part of a GPL program in a commercial program that you offer for sale.*

Do you have pirated programs on your computer? The police aren't likely to storm into your home or dorm room and take you away kicking and screaming. Most software piracy prosecutions target individuals who are trying to distribute or sell infringing copies, or companies that have illegally made multiple copies for their employees. If you have any pirated software, you should remove those programs from your computer right away. In the future, consider whether your actions constitute software piracy before the software is installed on your computer. If you still don't see the need to delete pirated software from your computer, consider this: It's very, very wise to become accustomed to a zero-tolerance approach to pirated software. If you're caught with an infringing program at work, you could lose your job. A company can't risk retaining employees who expose the firm to prosecution. There are software auditing applications that a school or company can purchase to monitor software usage.

Some build-it-yourself computer vendors may load unlicensed (and therefore illegal) software on a system. Ask for original CDs or DVDs. You may also run into this problem with software sold on auction sites.

"If you have any **pirated software**, you should remove those **programs** from your computer **right away.**"

FILE SHARING: MUSIC, MOVIES, AND MORE

You may have heard that it's okay to download a copyrighted MP3 file as long as you keep it for no

FIGURE 1J Sites such as MySpace offer fans the opportunity to learn about their favorite bands.

longer than 24 hours, but that's false. If you upload music copied from a CD you've paid for, you are violating the law. You can't justify spreading a band's copyrighted music around by saying it's "free advertising;" if the group wants advertising, they'll arrange it themselves (Figure 1J). Moreover, don't fall into the trap of thinking that sharing MP3s is legal as long as you don't charge any money for them. Anytime you're taking royalties away from copyright holders, it's illegal.

Several years ago eschoolnews.com reported that more than 400 students were slated to be sued for allegedly using Internet2, a network of academic, business, government, and not-for-profit organizations,

for music and movie piracy. The situation has not improved significantly. A 2008 survey found that the average digital music player contains 842 illegally copied songs. Although many people seem to believe that illegal file sharing is okay because so many others are doing it, the entertainment industry is fighting back. Ohio State University recently led the nation in music piracy—its students received more than 2,300 warning letters about pirated music in just one school year. Students can face fines or even jail time for copyright infringement, but schools may also be penalized. Some colleges are taking steps to reduce their liability, such as limiting bandwidth and providing students with free, legal download service.

Spotlight Exercises

1. What do you do with software you obtain? Do you share it with others, or explain to them the ethics and legality of sharing software. What would you do if your friend only needed to use the software for one semester and never had use for it again? In a small group of three or four people discuss this issue. Summarize your position and supporting arguments in a two- to three-minute oral presentation to the class.

2. You set up a MySpace page and feature your favorite band's music playing in the background. You post photos and explain how to download the music for free. You didn't secure permission from the band. Is your use of the music ethical? Explain your answer in a one-page, double-spaced essay.

3. Locate an online file-sharing source. Are the files copyrighted? Is it okay to download the files? If you download the files, is it okay for you to share them. Defend your position in a one-page, double-spaced report.

4. A computer tech person working at a repair shop finds child pornography on a computer he is repairing. He knows that possession of child pornography is illegal and that he should contact the authorities. However, he also knows that he shouldn't have been looking at the contents of the customer's hard drive so closely and that he may lose his job if his employer finds out he did. He doesn't report his discovery to the police. Instead, he permanently erases all the files containing child pornography from the customer's hard drive. Do you agree with what the computer tech did? What did he do right? What do you think he did wrong? What would you have done if you were put in that position? Summarize your thoughts in a one-page, double-spaced paper.

5. Working with one or more of your classmates, do the following and write a short report: Obtain a copy of your institution's acceptable-use policy for computers and one from another school. What restrictions do the institutions place on computer use that might not apply when using your personal computer or a commercial Internet connection? What are the advantages of connecting to the Internet through an institution or company instead of through a commercial connection? Are there time restrictions? Are there volume restrictions? Are there any content restrictions? Are there ethical concerns when using the school's system that you wouldn't have if you were using your own system? Compare and contrast the two types of policies.

6. You need to use a specific software that is on some of your school's comptuers. When you start the software, you receive a message that all the copies are currently being used by others. Answer the following questions and provide supporting statements in a PowerPoint presentation. Why is this happening? Locate computer auditing software. How does it work? Why would a school or company use this type of software? Do believe it is legal to use? Do you believe it is ethical to use?

chapter 2

Inside the System Unit

Chapter Objectives

- Understand how computers represent data. (p. 44)

- Understand the measurements used to describe data transfer rates and data storage capacity. (p. 45)

- List the components found inside the system unit and explain their use. (p. 48)

- List the components found on the computer's motherboard and explain their role in the computer system. (p. 50)

- Discuss (in general terms) how a CPU processes data. (p. 50)

- Explain the factors that determine a microprocessor's performance. (p. 51)

- List the various types of memory found in a computer system and explain the purpose of each. (p. 57)

- Describe the various physical connectors on the exterior of the system unit and explain their use. (p. 59)

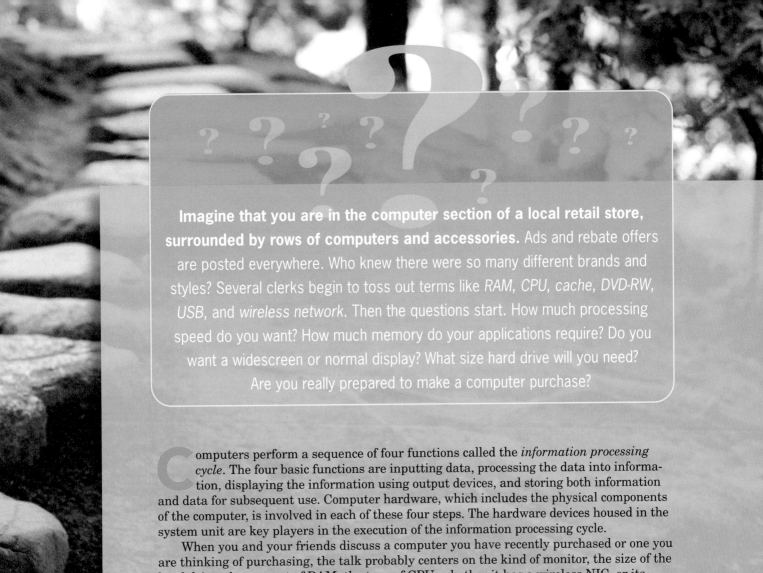

Imagine that you are in the computer section of a local retail store, surrounded by rows of computers and accessories. Ads and rebate offers are posted everywhere. Who knew there were so many different brands and styles? Several clerks begin to toss out terms like *RAM*, *CPU*, *cache*, *DVD-RW*, *USB*, and *wireless network*. Then the questions start. How much processing speed do you want? How much memory do your applications require? Do you want a widescreen or normal display? What size hard drive will you need? Are you really prepared to make a computer purchase?

Computers perform a sequence of four functions called the *information processing cycle*. The four basic functions are inputting data, processing the data into information, displaying the information using output devices, and storing both information and data for subsequent use. Computer hardware, which includes the physical components of the computer, is involved in each of these four steps. The hardware devices housed in the system unit are key players in the execution of the information processing cycle.

When you and your friends discuss a computer you have recently purchased or one you are thinking of purchasing, the talk probably centers on the kind of monitor, the size of the hard drive, the amount of RAM, the type of CPU, whether it has a wireless NIC, or its number of USB ports.

In a nutshell, you are trying to communicate about the power and capability of the computer system—its performance. This is no different than discussing an automobile. You would talk about its cylinders, turbo unit, dual exhaust, power windows, and so on. In both cases you use the equipment, but you are not a maintenance professional.

Our goal here is not to make you a computer maintenance professional. However, to communicate knowledgeably with others about computer hardware capabilities and use your system correctly, you need to understand a little about how a computer represents, transfers, and stores data. Again, this is the equivalent of the knowledge you need to run or discuss a car. For example, you need to know where to put the gas and windshield washer fluid and how to program the GPS.

As with most technology, it is important to understand that all interconnected hardware components in a system need to match in speed and processing capability for that system to run efficiently and error-free. An analogy can be made to replacing just the motor of a four-cylinder car with an eight-cylinder motor. Installing the more powerful engine and leaving all other components of the car unchanged would not work. The car would overheat because the cooling system would be unable to disperse the additional heat emitted by the more powerful motor. Other elements of the car would also fail.

If the hardware components in a computer system do not match, the result is similar: The system will malfunction and fail to perform effectively.

In this chapter we discuss how computers represent data as well as how the components inside and outside the system unit process that data through the four steps of the information processing cycle. This additional knowledge will help you make intelligent decisions when buying a computer system, upgrading a system, or just talking about technology.

How Computers Represent Data

Computers need data to work with, but that data must be represented in a specific way for the computer's hardware to accept and understand them. When you type on a keyboard and the information appears on the monitor, the information passes from the input device to the output device in a manner that is probably not what you expect. The letter Z is not passed inside your system looking anything like a Z; it is represented by units of information called bits. A **bit** (or **binary digit**) is the smallest piece of data a computer can process.

REPRESENTING DATA AS BITS AND BYTES

You are familiar with the decimal system of numbers, which consist of 10 digits (0, 1, 2, 3, 4, 5, 6, 7, 8, 9). Computers do not use the decimal system to represent numbers or characters. Rather, computers use **binary numbers** (also called *binary digits* or *bits* for short), which consist of only two digits, 0 and 1 (Figure 2.1).

To grasp this idea, it might help to think of a bit as acting like a light switch.

Both a light switch and a bit have two possible states. A bit represents its two states with the values of 1 or 0, and a switch is electrically either on or off. If a computer system used one bit (or one switch) to transfer data, your keyboard would have only two keys: a key with the number 0 and a key with the number 1. If the switch was off, that would represent the fact that you pressed 0; if the switch was on, it would represent you pressing the 1 key. If your system had two light switches, you would have four possibilities and thus a keyboard with four keys representing the four options: Both switches are on, both switches are off, the first switch is on and the second switch is off, or the first switch is off and the second switch is on. Three switches allow eight possibilities, and so on (Figure 2.2). The number of possible combinations of on/off patterns is calculated by the formula 2^n, where n is the number of switches. Thus four switches provide 2^4 or 16 possibilities. To represent an entire keyboard with all the letters of the alphabet (both uppercase and lowercase), the numbers 0 through 9, and punctuation marks, a computer system needs approximately 128 to 256 possibilities, which require seven or eight bits (or switches) because $2^7 = 128$ and $2^8 = 256$.

A **byte** is a group of eight bits. Because it takes eight bits (on/off switches) to make

FIGURE 2.1 A bit has two states: on (represented by 1) and off (represented by 0).

Binary digit	○	I
Bit	○	●
Status	Off	On

FIGURE 2.2 Number of Bits versus Number of Possibilities

# of Bits	# of Possibilities
1	$2^1 = 2$
2	$2^2 = 4$
3	$2^3 = 8$
4	$2^4 = 16$
5	$2^5 = 32$
6	$2^6 = 64$
7	$2^7 = 128$
8	$2^8 = 256$

a byte, and eight bits result in 256 possible on/off combinations, you'll see the number 8 and multiples of 8 appearing behind the scenes in many computer functions and applications. A single byte usually represents one character of data, such as the essential numbers (0–9), the basic letters of the alphabet (uppercase and lowercase), and the most common punctuation symbols. For this reason, you can use the byte as a baseline unit to express the amount of information a computer's storage device can hold. For example, a typical college essay contains 250 words per page, and each word contains (on average) 5.5 characters. Therefore, the page contains approximately 1,375 characters. In other words, you need about 1,375 bytes of storage to save one page of a college paper.

While bytes are used to express storage capacity, bits (1s and 0s) are commonly used for measuring the data transfer rate of computer communications devices such as modems. To describe rapid data transfer rates, the measurement units **kilobits per second (Kbps)**, **megabits per second (Mbps)**, and **gigabits per second (Gbps)** are used. These respectively correspond (roughly) to 1 thousand, 1 million, and 1 billion bits per second. Remember that these terms refer to *bits* per second, not *bytes* per second.

Bytes are commonly used to measure data storage. The measurement units **kilobyte (KB)**, **megabyte (MB)**, **gigabyte (GB)**, and **terabyte (TB)** describe the amount of data a computer is managing either in RAM memory or in longer-term storage (hard disk, CD, DVD, or USB drive). Figure 2.3 shows these units and the *approximate* value of text data for each. For these units the

FIGURE 2.3 Units of Data

Unit	Abbreviation	Amount	Text Equivalent
Bit	b	Base unit—represented as either 0 or 1	None
Kilobits per second	Kbps	Transfer rate of 1 thousand bits per second	125 characters
Megabits per second	Mbps	Transfer rate of 1 million bits per second	125 pages
Gigabits per second	Gbps	Transfer rate of 1 billion bits per second	125,000 pages
Byte	B	Stores 8 bits	One character
Kilobyte	KB	Stores 1 thousand bytes	One page
Megabyte	MB	Stores 1 million bytes	1,000 pages
Gigabyte	GB	Stores 1 billion bytes	1,000 books
Terabyte	TB	Stores 1 trillion bytes	1 million books
Petabyte	PB	Stores 1 quadrillion bytes	1 billion books
Exabyte	EB	Stores 1 quintillion bytes	7,500 libraries the size of the Library of Congress
Zettabyte	ZB	Stores 1 sextillion bytes	
Yottabyte	YB	Stores 1 septillion bytes	

equivalents of a thousand, a million, and so on are not exact; rounding numbers has become acceptable. For example, a kilobyte is actually 1,024 bytes.

As the uses of computers escalate and the amount of information we use and save increases, storage devices have had to expand their capacity. Originally storage units held kilobytes and megabytes of data. Today most devices express their capacity in gigabytes and terabytes. In anticipation of a continued increase in data use and storage, terms already exist for representing even larger units. A **petabyte** is 1 quadrillion bytes, an **exabyte** is 1 quintillion bytes, a **zettabyte** is 1 sextillion bytes, and a **yottabyte** is 1 septillion bytes.

Binary numbers are difficult to work with because many digits are required to represent even a small number. For example, when you enter the decimal number 14 into your computer, the binary number representation uses four bits or switches and is represented as 1110. In addition, it's time-consuming for computers to translate binary numbers into their decimal equivalents. For these reasons, computers translate binary numbers into **hexadecimal** (**hex** for short) **numbers**, which use base 16 characters—the numbers 0 through 9 and the letters A through F. For example, the decimal number 100 is represented as the lengthy binary number 01100100 and then quickly translated to 64 in hex notation. Each hex digit represents four binary digits, making it a shorter, faster, and more compact representation of binary numbers (Figure 2.4). You can convert among decimal, binary, and hex by using the converter at **www.mathsisfun .com/binary-decimal-hexadecimal-converter.html**.

REPRESENTING VERY LARGE AND VERY SMALL NUMBERS

To represent and process numbers that have fractional parts (such as 1.25) or are extremely large (in the billions and trillions), computers use **floating-point notation**. The term *floating point* suggests how this notation system works: There is no fixed number of digits before or after the decimal point (thus the word *float*), so the computer can work with very large and very small numbers. Floating-point notation requires special processing circuitry, which is generally provided by the floating-point unit (FPU). Modern computers integrate one or more FPUs with the CPU (processor or microprocessor), but in older computers the FPU was sometimes a separate chip called the *math coprocessor*.

We know that computers process not only numeric data but also character data. Because we communicate with spoken and written text, let's look next at the processing of the character data that compose our daily interaction.

REPRESENTING CHARACTERS: CHARACTER CODE

Character code uses an algorithm as a bridge between the computer's numeric binary world and the letters, numbers, and symbols on our keyboards called **characters** that we're accustomed to using. Computers can convert with one of three different character coding formats: ASCII, EBCDIC, or Unicode.

The most widely used character code is **ASCII** (pronounced "ask-ee"), the **American Standard Code for Information Interchange**, which is used in minicomputers, personal computers, and

FIGURE 2.4	Decimal, Binary, and Hexadecimal Numbers															
Decimal number	0	1	2	3	4	5	6	7	8	9	10	11	12	13	14	15
Binary number	0000	0001	0010	0011	0100	0101	0110	0111	1000	1001	1010	1011	1100	1101	1110	1111
Hexadecimal number	0	1	2	3	4	5	6	7	8	9	A	B	C	D	E	F

FIGURE 2.5   Sample of a Section of Extended ASCII Code

Character	ASCII Code	Character	ASCII Code	Character	ASCII Code
!	00100001	E	01000101	e	01100101
"	00100010	F	01000110	f	01100110
#	00100011	G	01000111	g	01100111
$	00100100	H	01001000	h	01101000
%	00100101	I	01001001	i	01101001

computers that make information available over the Internet. ASCII uses seven bits and can thus represent 128 (2^7 = 128) different characters. A variation of ASCII code, called **Extended ASCII** (see Figures 2.5 and 2.6), uses eight bits and allows 128 additional characters for a total of 256 (2^8 = 256). The code order for ASCII starts with the lowest codes representing punctuation marks and numbers, followed by more punctuation marks, uppercase letters, more punctuation marks, and finally lowercase letters. IBM mainframe computers and some midrange systems use a different eight-bit code system, **EBCDIC** (pronounced "ebb-see-dic"), **Extended Binary Coded Decimal Interchange Code**. EBCDIC code order uses a low-to-high code sequence for punctuation, lowercase letters, uppercase letters, and then numbers.

Although ASCII and EBCDIC provide enough bits to represent all characters used in the English language and some foreign language symbols, neither has enough binary combinations for some Eastern languages that exceed 256 characters. Because computers make international communication and business transactions possible, a new coding system—**Unicode**—is becoming popular. Unicode uses 16 bits, can represent over 65,000 characters, and can symbolize all the world's written languages.

FIGURE 2.6   Hi! Written in Extended ASCII Code

H	i	!
01001000	01101001	00100001

Now that you understand bits, bytes, and how computers represent data, it is important to understand their connection to the rest of the system. Let's take a closer look at the system unit, its components, and how these concepts will come into play.

Introducing the System Unit

The **system unit** is a boxlike case that houses the computer's main hardware components (Figure 2.7). The system unit is actually more than just a case: It provides a sturdy frame for mounting internal components, including storage devices, a power supply, a fan, and connectors for input and output devices; it protects those components from physical damage; and it keeps them cool. A good case also provides room for system upgrades, such as additional disk drives.

System units come in a variety of styles. In some desktop computing systems, the system unit is a separate metal or plastic box. Originally these cases were horizontal and were positioned on top of a desk, often with a monitor sitting on top—thus the name "desktop." To minimize the space it occupied, the case needed a small **footprint**, which was the amount of space used by the device.

a. System unit

b. System unit

c. System unit

d. System unit

FIGURE 2.7 Every kind of computer has a system unit: (a) all-in-one; (b) notebook; (c) smartphone; (d) desktop.

However, a small case didn't allow enough room for add-on components. The **tower case**, a system unit case designed to sit on the floor next to a desk, provided the solution. The tower case has a vertical configuration, being tall and deep. A smaller version is called a **minitower case**.

In a notebook computer or a personal digital assistant (PDA), the system unit contains all the computer's components, including input components, such as a keyboard, and output components, such as the display. Some desktop computers, such as Apple's iMac, contain the display within the system unit, making them all-in-one systems. To ensure access identification and security, biometric authentication devices like fingerprint readers, retina scanners, and face recognition systems are embedded into some individual system units (Figure 2.8).

System units also vary in their form factor. A **form factor** is a specification for how internal components, such as the motherboard, are mounted inside the system unit. Let's take a look!

Inside the System Unit

Most computer users don't need to open their system units; they receive their computers in ready-to-use packages. However, if you ever need to open your system unit, remember that the computer's components are sensitive to static electricity. If you touch certain components while you're charged with static electricity, you could destroy them. To avoid this disaster, always disconnect the power cord before opening your computer's case, and discharge your personal static electricity by touching something that's well grounded or by wearing a grounding bracelet. A **grounding bracelet** is a bracelet that has a cord attached to a grounded object. If it's one of those low-humidity days when you're getting shocked every time you touch a doorknob, don't work on your computer's internal components.

If you open your system unit, you'll see the following components (Figure 2.9):

- *Motherboard:* The motherboard contains the computer's central processing unit (CPU). You'll learn more about the motherboard and the CPU later in the chapter; for now remember that the CPU, referred to as the "brain" of the computer, is the central component of the computer; all other components (such as disk drives, monitors, and printers) exist only to bridge the gap between the user and the CPU.

- *Power supply:* A computer's **power supply** transforms the alternating current (AC) from standard wall outlets into the direct current (DC) needed for the computer's operation. It also steps the voltage down to the low level required by the motherboard. Power supplies are rated according to their peak output in watts. A 350-watt power supply is adequate for most desktop systems, but 500 watts provide sufficient voltage if you plan to add many additional components.

- *Cooling fan:* The computer's components can be damaged if heat accumulates within the system unit. A **cooling fan** keeps the system unit cool. The fan often is part of the power supply, although many systems include auxiliary fans to provide additional cooling.

- *Internal speaker:* The computer's **internal speaker** is useful only for the beeps you hear when the computer starts up or encounters an error. Current computers include sound cards and external speakers for better-quality sound.
- *Drive bays:* **Drive bays** accommodate the computer's disk drives, such as the hard disk drive, CD or DVD drive, and portable drives. Internal drive bays are used for hard disks that are permanently contained in the system unit; therefore they do not enable outside access. External drive bays mount drives that are accessible from the outside (a necessity if you need to insert and remove a CD from the drive). External drive bays vary in size to accommodate different

media devices. Current systems offer 5.25-inch external drive bays to accommodate CD or DVD drives. Older computers were designed to support the legacy technology of 3.5-inch floppy or zip drives.

- *Expansion slots:* The system unit also contains **expansion slots**, which are receptacles that accept additional circuit boards or expansion cards. Examples of expansion cards are memory modules, sound cards, modem cards, network interface cards (NICs), and video cards (Figure 2.10).

Now that you have an overview of the internal components of the system unit, let's look more closely at the most important component: the computer's motherboard.

FIGURE 2.8 Some system units include biometric authentication devices, such as this fingerprint reader, to help ensure access identification and security.

FIGURE 2.9 The motherboard, the power supply, a cooling fan, an internal speaker, internal drive bays, external drive bays, and various expansion cards are located inside the system unit.

Power supply

Cooling fan

Memory cards

Expansion card

Expansion slot

Motherboard

External drive bay

Internal drive bay

Internal speaker (not present)

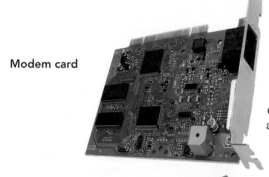

Memory module

Sound card

Modem card

Network
interface card

Video card

FIGURE 2.10 Expansion cards enable you to enhance your system.

What's on the Motherboard?

The **motherboard** is a large flat piece of plastic or fiberglass that contains thousands of electrical circuits etched onto the board's surface (Figure 2.11). The circuits connect numerous plug-in receptacles, which accommodate the computer's most important components (such as the CPU). The motherboard provides the centralized physical and electrical connectivity to enable communication among these critical components. Most of the components on the motherboard are integrated circuits. An **integrated circuit (IC)**, also called a **chip**, carries an electric current and contains millions of transistors. To view a short video about how chips are created, go to **www97.intel.com/en/TheJourneyInside/ExploreTheCurriculum/EC_Microprocessors/MPLesson4**.

A **transistor** is an electronic switch (or gate) that controls the flow of electrical signals to the circuit. A computer uses such electronic switches to route data in different ways, according to the software's instructions.

Encased in black plastic blocks or enclosures, most chips fit specially designed receptacles or slots on the motherboard's surface. What do these chips do? Let's look at some of the most important components you'll see on the motherboard: the CPU (or microprocessor), the system clock, the chipset, input/output buses, and memory.

THE CPU: THE MICROPROCESSOR

The **central processing unit (CPU)** is a **microprocessor** (or **processor** for short)—an integrated circuit chip that is capable of processing electronic signals. It interprets and carries out software instructions by processing data and controlling the rest of the computer's components. Processors are embedded in all kinds of electronic and mechanical devices such as smartphones, calculators, automobile engines, and industrial and medical equipment. They process data so humans can enjoy the information put out by their effective and efficient operation. No single element of a computer determines its overall performance as much as the CPU.

CPUs (microprocessors) are incredibly complex devices. When you're ready to buy a computer, you'll need to understand the capabilities and limitations of current microprocessors.

PROCESSOR SLOTS AND SOCKETS

An integrated circuit of incredible complexity, a CPU plugs into a motherboard in much the same way that other integrated circuits do—through a series of pins that extend out from the bottom of the chip. However, only special slots and sockets can accommodate CPUs. Part of the reason for this is that CPUs are larger and have more pins than most other chips. In addition, CPUs generate so much heat that they could destroy themselves or other system components. The CPU is generally covered by a **heat sink**: a heat-dissipating component that drains heat from the chip. To accomplish this, the heat sink may contain a small auxiliary cooling fan. The latest high-end CPUs include their own built-in refrigeration systems to keep these speedy processors cool.

THE INSTRUCTION SET

Every processor can perform a fixed set of operations, such as retrieving a character from the computer's memory or comparing two numbers to see which is larger. Each of these operations has a unique number, called an *instruction*. A processor's list of instructions is called its **instruction set**. Because each type of processor has a unique instruction set, programs devised for one type of CPU won't necessarily run on another. For example, a program written for an Intel chip may not run on a Motorola chip. A program that can run on a given computer is said to be compatible with that computer's processor. Alternatively, if a program is compatible, it's said to be a **native application** for a given processor design.

cycle (fetch and decode) and the **execution cycle** (execute and store). Today's microprocessors can go through this entire four-step process billions of times per second. The **arithmetic logic unit (ALU)**, as its name implies, can perform arithmetic or logical operations. **Arithmetic operations** include addition, subtraction, multiplication,

Memory slots

Processor chip

Motherboard

Expansion slots

FIGURE 2.11 This typical PC motherboard shows its processor chip and the expansion and memory slots.

THE CONTROL UNIT AND THE ARITHMETIC LOGIC UNIT

A CPU contains two subcomponents: the control unit and the arithmetic logic unit. The **control unit** extracts instructions from memory and then decodes and executes them. Under the direction of a program, the control unit manages four basic operations (Figure 2.12):

- **Fetch:** Retrieves the next program instruction from the computer's memory.
- **Decode:** Determines what the program is telling the computer to do.
- **Execute:** Performs the requested instruction, such as adding two numbers or deciding which one of them is larger.
- **Store:** Stores the results in an internal register (a temporary storage location on the CPU) or in RAM.

This four-step process is called a **machine cycle**, or **processing cycle**, and consists of two phases: the **instruction**

and division. **Logical operations** involve comparing two or more data items. Instead of returning a numeric answer, as would arithmetic operations, a logical operation returns a value of true or false. An example of a logical operation would be to see whether one number is larger than another.

Some operations require the control unit to store data temporarily. **Registers** are temporary storage locations, somewhat like a digital scratch pad, in the microprocessor that are designed for this purpose. There are different types of registers depending on their function. One type of register stores the memory location from which a data element was retrieved; another stores the results of intermediate calculations.

MICROPROCESSOR PERFORMANCE

The number of transistors available has a huge effect on the performance of a processor. The greater their number and proximity to each other, the faster the processing speed. The data bus width and word size,

communicates with the CPU. More technically, the bus is a pathway for the electronic impulses that form bytes. The more lanes this highway has, the faster data can travel. Data bus width is measured in bits (8, 16, 32, or 64).

The width of a CPU's data bus partly determines its **word size**, or the maximum number of bits the CPU can process at once. Data bus width also affects the CPU's overall speed: A CPU with a 32-bit data bus can shuffle data twice as fast as a CPU with a 16-bit data bus. The terms *8-bit CPU*, *16-bit CPU*, *32-bit CPU*, and *64-bit CPU* indicate the maximum number of bits a CPU can handle at a time.

A CPU's word size is important because it determines which operating systems the CPU can use and which software it can run. Figure 2.13 lists the word size requirements of past and current operating systems.

Today's PC market is dominated by 32-bit CPUs and 32-bit operating systems. However, 64-bit CPUs and 64-bit operating systems are taking over the marketplace. Intel's 64-bit Itanium processor, introduced in 2001, brought 64-bit computing to the PC market for the first time. Linux was the first to use the 64-bit technology in 2001. In 2003 Apple released a 64-bit version of Mac OS X, and in 2005 Microsoft released Windows XP Professional ×64. Windows Vista and Windows 7 are available in both 32-bit and 64-bit versions.

To learn more, including whether a 32-bit operating system is adequate for

clock speed, operations per microprocessor cycle, parallel processing, and type of chip are also factors that contribute to microprocessor performance.

Data Bus Width and Word Size The **data bus** is a set of parallel wires that act as an electronic highway on which data travel between computer components. It is the medium by which the entire system

FIGURE 2.12 The control unit manages four basic operations: fetch, decode, execute, and store.

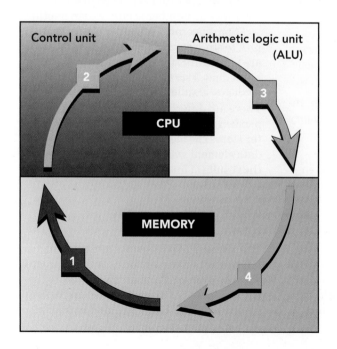

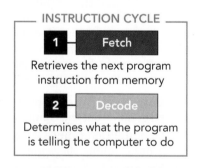

INSTRUCTION CYCLE

1 — Fetch
Retrieves the next program instruction from memory

2 — Decode
Determines what the program is telling the computer to do

EXECUTION CYCLE

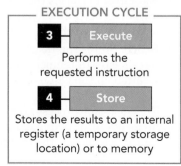

3 — Execute
Performs the requested instruction

4 — Store
Stores the results to an internal register (a temporary storage location) or to memory

your needs, visit **www.microsoft.com/ windows/products/windowsvista/ editions/64bit.mspx**.

Clock Speed Within a computer, events happen at a pace controlled by a tiny electronic "drummer" on the motherboard: The **system clock** is an electronic circuit that generates rapid pulses to synchronize the computer's internal activities. These electrical pulses are measured in **gigahertz (GHz)**, or billions of cycles per second, and are referred to as a processor's **clock speed**. Any new computer will have a clock speed of 3 GHz or higher; a 3-GHz processor is capable of processing 3 billion cycles in 1 second. In general, the higher a processor's clock speed, the faster the computer. For editorial reviews of the latest products, such as the fastest processors, memory, graphics chips, and more go to **www.geek.com/chips**.

Operations per Cycle The number of *operations* per clock tick (one pulse of the system clock) also affects microprocessor performance. You might think that a

GREEN tech tips

Keeping computers turned on all the time drains the community power supply, stresses the computers' internal components, and wastes energy. The Environmental Protection Agency (EPA), technology manufacturers, and non-profit organizations are working on ways to keep you connected 24/7 with reduced environmental consequences. If you purchase a computer with the EPA's Energy Star Logo, it can go to sleep during intervals of inactivity, thus boosting its energy efficiency.

Experts at Intel, working with the Natural Resources Defense Council and several power supply manufacturers, have developed new specifications for computer power supplies that will reduce their electrical consumption by 25 percent or more. This reduction would save the United States an estimated 16 billion kilowatts per year, shrink electric bills by $1.25 billion annually, and reduce carbon emissions by 10 million tons. For the individual PC owner this translates to a savings of $50 over three years. ●

FIGURE 2.13 Word Size Capacity (in Bits) of Popular Operating Systems

Operating System	Word Size	When Used
MS-DOS	8	Past
Windows 3.1	16	Past
Windows 95/98/NT/2000/XP	32	Past
Windows Vista (all editions except Starter)	64	Current
Linux	64	Current
Mac OS X (with Velocity Engine chip)	64	Current
Windows 7	64	Current

CPU can't perform more than one instruction per clock tick, but thanks to new technologies that's no longer the case. **Superscalar architecture** refers to the design of any CPU that can execute more than one instruction per clock cycle; today's fastest CPUs use superscalar architectures. Superscalar architectures often use **pipelining**, a processing technique that feeds a new instruction into the CPU at every step of the processing cycle so that four or more instructions are worked on simultaneously (Figure 2.14).

Pipelining resembles an auto assembly line in which more than one car is being worked on at once. Before the first instruction is finished, the next one is started. If the CPU needs the results of a completed instruction to process the next one, that condition is called **data dependency**. It can cause a pipeline stall in which the assembly line is held up until the results are known. To cope with this problem, advanced CPUs use a technique called **speculative execution**, in which the processor executes and temporarily stores the next instruction in case it proves useful. CPUs also use a technique called **branch prediction**, in which the processor tries to predict what will happen (with a surprisingly high degree of accuracy).

Parallel Processing Another way to improve CPU performance is by using **parallel processing**, a technique that uses more than one processor running

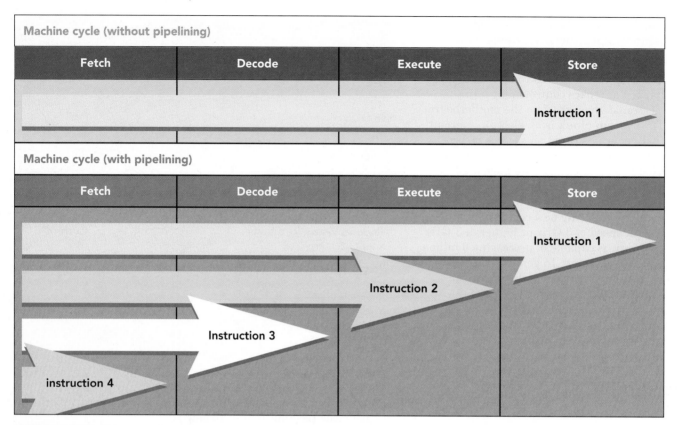

Machine cycle (without pipelining)			
Fetch	**Decode**	**Execute**	**Store**

Instruction 1

Machine cycle (with pipelining)			
Fetch	**Decode**	**Execute**	**Store**

Instruction 1

Instruction 2

Instruction 3

instruction 4

FIGURE 2.14 Pipelining greatly increases the efficiency of the processor.

simultaneously in parallel (Figure 2.15). The idea is to speed up the execution of a program by dividing the program into multiple fragments that can execute simultaneously, each on its own processor. A program will execute faster across multiple processors than with a single processor.

POPULAR MICROPROCESSORS

The most commonly used microprocessors are those found in IBM-compatible

computers and Macs. Most PCs are powered by chips produced by Intel, although AMD also makes IBM-compatible chips. Figure 2.16 shows how popular microprocessors for PCs have improved since the days of the first PC. In 2008 Intel released a version of the Core 2 Extreme microprocessor with a clock speed of 3.20 GHz—the first commercially available chip to attain that speed (Figure 2.17). Since 2003 Intel has been

FIGURE 2.15 Parallel processing computers have multiple processors that run simultaneously.

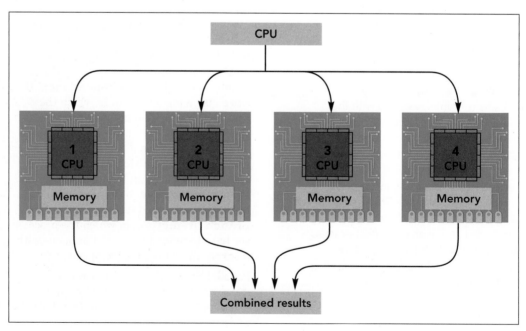

CPU

1 CPU — Memory

2 CPU — Memory

3 CPU — Memory

4 CPU — Memory

Combined results

FIGURE 2.16 The Evolution of Intel Microprocessors				
Year	Chip	Bus Width	Clock Speed	Transistors
1971	4004	4 bits	108 KHz	2,300
1974	8080	8 bits	2 MHz	6,000
1979	8088	8 bits	Up to 8 MHz	29,000
1982	80286	16 bits	Up to 12 MHz	134,000
1985	80386	32 bits	Up to 33 MHz	275,000
1989	Intel 486	32 bits	Up to 50 MHz	1.2 million
1993	Pentium	32 bits	Up to 66 MHz	3.1 million
1995	Pentium Pro	32 bits	Up to 200 MHz	5.5 million
1996	Pentium MMX	32 bits	Up to 200 MHz	4.5 million
1997	Pentium II	32 bits	Up to 300 MHz	7.5 million
1998	Xeon	32 bits	Up to 450 MHz	7.5 million
1998	Celeron	32 bits	Up to 300 MHz	7.5 million–19 million
1999	Pentium III	32 bits	Up to 600 MHz	9.5 million–28 million
2000	Pentium 4	32 bits	Up to 2 GHz	42 million
2001	Itanium	64 bits	Up to 800 MHz	25 million
2003	Pentium M	32 bits	Up to 1.7 GHz	77 million
2006	Core Duo	32 bits	Up to 2 GHz	151 million
2006	Dual Core Itanium 2	64 bits	Up to 1.60 GHz	1.72 billion
2006	Core 2 Duo	64 bits	Up to 2.66 GHz	291 million
2007	Core 2 Quad	64 bits	Up to 2.4 GHz	582 million
2008	Core 2 Extreme, Quad Processor	64 bits	3.2 GHz	820 million

concentrating on producing processors that are suited to certain computing needs—such as the Centrino processor for mobile computing or the Core 2 Extreme for multimedia and gaming. Intel now rates its processors not only by cycles per second, but also by features such as architecture, cache, and bus type. The rating, then, is the power and usefulness of the processor—not just the clock speed. To view a detailed timeline of the history of Intel processors go to **http://download .intel.com/pressroom/kits/ IntelProcessorHistory.pdf**.

Normally faster is better; however, the cost of microprocessor speed can keep it out of reach. When deciding on a processor, list the activities you plan to use your system for over the next few years. Then match the processor capabilities to those activities. For example, the Intel Celeron is a processor geared to users who perform basic tasks such as word processing, Web surfing, and listening to and buying music. The Intel Pentium Core 2 family of processors is geared toward advanced applications such as gaming, video editing, and advanced digital photography.

Some additional processors, including specialized CPUs, are not included in Figure 2.16. As an example, the Intel Atom is specifically designed for handheld devices and mobile Internet devices.

After you match your needs with the processors that can manage them, you can address the processor's speed. For most users an increase of .4 GHz in speed would not perceptibly change performance, but it would make a noticeable difference in cost. For articles, videos, forums, and charts that provide detailed information about a large variety of processors and other hardware elements, go to **www.tomshardware.com/cpu**.

For years Motorola Corporation and IBM made the chips for Apple computers, producing the 68000 series and the PowerPC series. Apple gave its own name

FIGURE 2.17 The Core 2 Extreme quad-core processor (**a**) uses two pairs of co-processor cores (**b**) for parallel processing.

to the PowerPC chips: Motorola's 750 was the same chip as Apple's G3, Motorola's 7400 was the G4, and the 64-bit IBM chip was the G5. In January 2006 Apple began transitioning to Intel processors for the Mac, with all new Macs using Intel processors by August of that year.

THE CHIPSET AND THE INPUT/OUTPUT BUS

Another important motherboard component is the **chipset**, which is a collection of chips that work together to provide the switching circuitry needed by the microprocessor to move data throughout the computer. One of the jobs handled by the chipset is linking the microprocessor with the computer's input/output buses.

An **input/output (I/O) bus** refers specifically to the pathway that extends beyond the microprocessor to communicate with input and output devices. Typically an I/O bus contains expansion slots to accommodate plug-in expansion cards.

Today's PCs use the **PCI (peripheral component interconnect) bus**. Many motherboards still contain an industry standard architecture (ISA) bus and have one or two ISA slots available. The accelerated graphics port (AGP) is a bus designed for video and graphics display.

The microprocessor is just one of several chips on the computer's motherboard. Among the others are those that provide the computer with various types of memory.

MEMORY

Memory refers to the chips that enable the computer to retain information. Memory chips store program instructions and data so the CPU can access them quickly. As you'll see in this section, the computer's motherboard contains several different types of memory, each optimized for its intended use.

RAM

The large, rectangular memory modules housed on the computer's motherboard contain the computer's **random access memory (RAM)**. RAM stores information temporarily so it's directly and speedily available to the microprocessor. This information includes all work in progress—program instructions as well as the data to be processed by the program. RAM is volatile memory, which means it is not permanent and its contents are erased when the computer's power is switched off.

Why is it called *random access memory*? RAM is called *random access* because any storage location can be accessed directly without having to go from the first location to the last in sequential order. Perhaps it should have been called *nonsequential memory* because RAM access is hardly random. RAM is organized and controlled in a way that can be compared to post office boxes (Figure 2.18). Each location has a **memory address** (in binary form) that enables the location to be found and the content within to be accessed directly. IBM preferred the term *direct access storage*. Note that other forms of storage such as the hard disk and

CD-ROM are also accessed directly or randomly (meaning out of sequential order), but the term *random access* is never applied to these forms of storage.

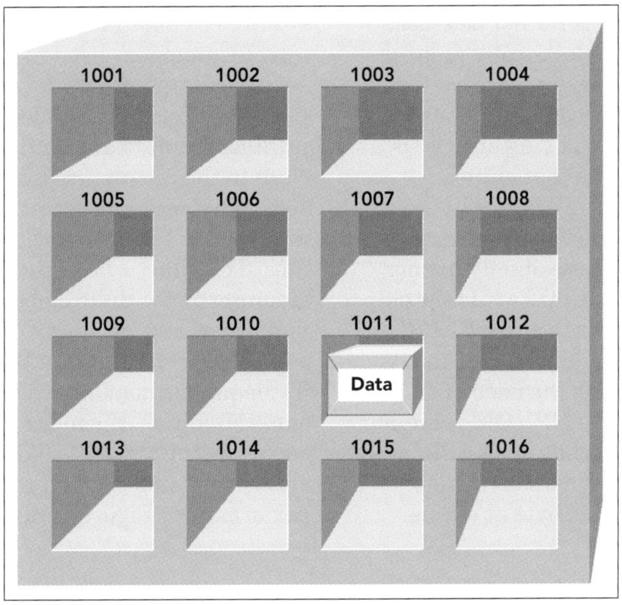

Of the various types of RAM available, today's newest and fastest PCs contain either DDR2-SDRAM (double-data-rate two synchronous dynamic RAM) or DDR3-SDRAM. These types of RAM must have a constant power supply or they lose their contents.

How much RAM does a computer need? In general, the more memory the better. Windows Vista and Mac OS X theoretically require only 512 MB of RAM, but neither system functions well with so little. For today's Microsoft Windows, Linux, and Macintosh operating systems, 1 GB of RAM is a practical working minimum.

Windows 7 is touting a new reduced **memory footprint**, the amount of RAM the program uses while it operates. In the past, each successive Windows OS required larger amounts of system resources like RAM. Thus Microsoft's claim that Windows 7 is going to buck that trend is giving people hope that OS RAM requirements might stabilize.

Frequently operating systems use **virtual memory** in addition to RAM. With virtual memory, the computer looks at RAM to identify data that have not been used recently and copies those data onto the hard disk. This frees up space in RAM to load a new application or increase the space needed by a program currently in use. The computer uses virtual memory when RAM gets full (which can easily happen if you run two or more programs at once). Accessing data on a disk drive is much slower than using RAM, so when virtual memory kicks in, the computer may seem to slow to a crawl. To avoid using

> " For **today's** Microsoft Windows, Linux, and Macintosh **operating systems**, 1 GB of RAM is a practical working **minimum**. "

FIGURE 2.18 RAM stores data in specific addressed locations for easy access and retrieval.

virtual memory, choose a system with at least 2 GB of RAM. Many new systems are being advertised with 3 to 4 GB of RAM.

ROM

If everything in RAM is erased when the power is turned off, how does the computer start up again? The answer is **read-only memory (ROM)**, a type of memory in which instructions have been prerecorded. The instructions to start the computer are stored in read-only memory chips located on the motherboard. When a computer is turned on, the instructions in ROM are read; they cannot be erased. In contrast with RAM, ROM is nonvolatile memory, meaning it retains information even when the power is switched off.

There are several variations of ROM memory; knowing the differences is important if you intend to install a new hard drive or upgrade your start-up program. **PROM**, programmable read-only memory, can be written on only once but requires a special writing device. It cannot be erased and reused. **EPROM**, electrically programmable read-only memory, is erasable PROM that can be reused many times. Erasure is accomplished using an UV (ultraviolet) light source that shines through a quartz erasing window in the EPROM package. **EEPROM**, electrically erasable programmable read-only memory, can be rewritten many times while the chip is in the computer. You can erase EEPROM by using an electric field instead of an UV light source, eliminating the need of an erasing window. A **flash EPROM** is similar to an EEPROM except that flash EPROMs are erased all at once, whereas regular EEPROMs can erase one byte at a time.

CACHE MEMORY

RAM is fast, but it isn't fast enough to support the processing speeds of today's superfast microprocessors, such as the Intel Core 2 Extreme or the AMD Phenom X4. These microprocessors use cache memory to function at maximum speed. **Cache memory** is a small unit of ultrafast memory built into the processor that stores frequently or recently accessed program instructions and data. Cache (pronounced "cash") memory is much faster than RAM, but it's also more expensive. Although relatively small compared with RAM (up to 12 MB), cache memory greatly improves the computer system's overall performance.

Two types of cache memory are available. The first type, called **primary cache** or **level 1 (L1) cache**, is a unit of 8 KB to 64 KB of ultrafast memory included in the microprocessor chip that runs at the same speed as the microprocessor. Primary cache is the fastest memory. The second type, called **secondary cache** or **level 2 (L2) cache**, is a small unit of 256 KB to 2 MB of ultrafast memory used to store frequently accessed data and improve overall system performance. It is included on a separate printed circuit board on the motherboard close to the microprocessor. To improve secondary cache performance, the latest microprocessors are housed in plastic modules. This plastic housing includes the microprocessor (with its embedded L1 cache) and a special type of secondary cache called **backside cache**. Backside cache is in the plastic housing with, but not on the same circuit as, the microprocessor and L1 cache. Keeping the secondary cache as close as possible to the processor improves performance (Figure 2.19).

FIGURE 2.19 Primary cache is included in the microprocessor chip. Secondary cache is included on a separate printed circuit board. Keeping the secondary cache as close as possible to the processor improves performance.

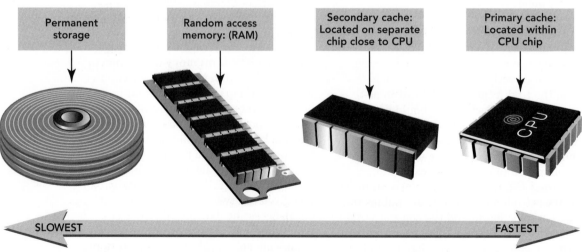

| Permanent storage | Random access memory: (RAM) | Secondary cache: Located on separate chip close to CPU | Primary cache: Located within CPU chip |

SLOWEST ←→ FASTEST

The following sections explore what can be found on the outside of the system unit of a typical desktop computer.

What's on the Outside of the Box?

You'll find the following features on the outside of a typical desktop computer's system unit:

- The front panel with various buttons and lights.
- The power switch.
- Connectors and ports for plugging in keyboards, mice, monitors, and other peripheral devices.

THE FRONT PANEL

On the front panel of some system units, you'll find a **drive activity light**, which indicates your hard disk is accessing data, and a **power-on light**, which indicates whether the power is on.

The **power switch** is usually on the front of the system unit. In earlier days it was placed on the back of the unit because of fears that users would accidentally press it and inadvertently shut down their systems. Computers don't handle sudden power losses well. For example, a power outage could scramble the data on your hard drive. Likewise, just turning off your computer instead of shutting it down properly can leave the system unstable and possibly unable to restart. You should always follow the appropriate shutdown procedure to shut off your computer.

If your computer freezes up or won't respond to any key or mouse commands, first try pressing the Ctrl, Alt, and Del keys simultaneously to activate the Windows Task Manager and attempt to shut down your system normally. This is a last resort because using the Ctrl, Alt, Del action will cause any unsaved work to be lost.

CONNECTORS AND PORTS

A **connector** is a physical receptacle located on the system unit or an expansion card that is visible on the outside of the unit. Each connector is designed for a specific type of plug. Plugs are sometimes secured by **thumbscrews**—small screws that are usually attached to the plug and are used to secure the plug to the

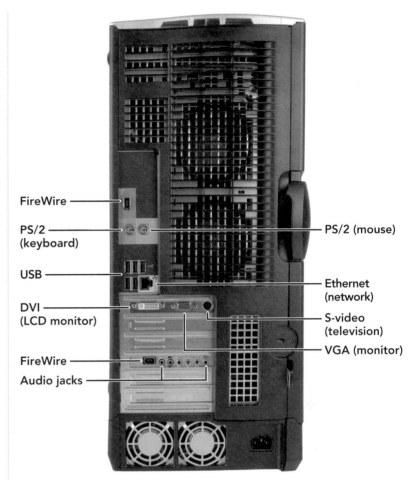

FireWire

PS/2 (keyboard)

USB

DVI (LCD monitor)

FireWire

Audio jacks

PS/2 (mouse)

Ethernet (network)

S-video (television)

VGA (monitor)

FIGURE 2.20 The connectors on the outside of a system unit enable you to connect peripherals such as a printer, keyboard, or mouse.

system unit or expansion card extender to prevent an accidental disconnect. **Expansion cards** (also called **expansion boards**, **adapter cards**, or **adapters**) are plug-in adapters that fit into slots on the motherboard and connect the computer with various peripherals. The connectors on these cards are located on extender pieces that are visible through slots on the outside of the system case, enabling you to connect peripheral devices such as a printer, keyboard, or mouse. Connectors (Figure 2.20) are described as being *male* (those with external pins) or *female* (those with receptacles for external pins).

Figure 2.21 summarizes the connectors you may find on the computer's case. Most of these connectors are on the back of the case, but on desktop computers it's now common to find several on the front, providing easier access for many different peripheral devices.

It's important to remember that a connector isn't the same thing as a port. A **port** is an electronically defined pathway

FIGURE 2.21 Most connectors are on the back of the computer's case, but some may be on the front.

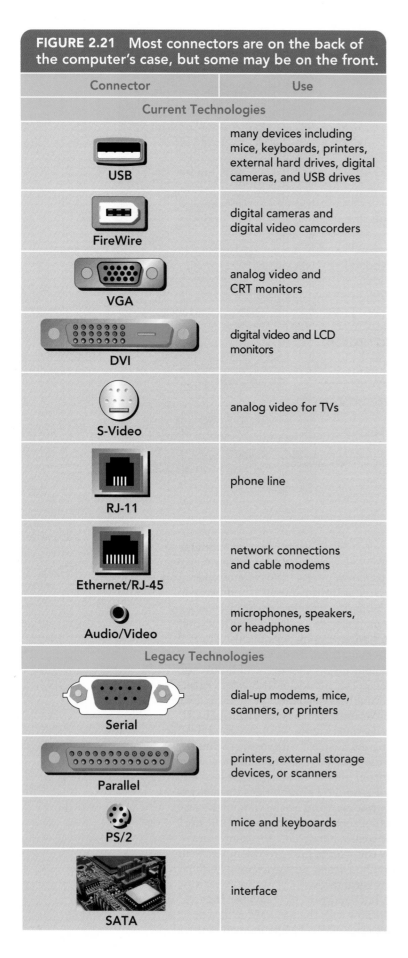

Connector	Use
Current Technologies	
USB	many devices including mice, keyboards, printers, external hard drives, digital cameras, and USB drives
FireWire	digital cameras and digital video camcorders
VGA	analog video and CRT monitors
DVI	digital video and LCD monitors
S-Video	analog video for TVs
RJ-11	phone line
Ethernet/RJ-45	network connections and cable modems
Audio/Video	microphones, speakers, or headphones
Legacy Technologies	
Serial	dial-up modems, mice, scanners, or printers
Parallel	printers, external storage devices, or scanners
PS/2	mice and keyboards
SATA	interface

or interface for getting information into and out of the computer. A connector is a physical device—a plug-in. A port is an interface—the matching of input and output flows. A port almost always uses a connector, but a connector isn't always a port. For example, a telephone jack is just a connector—not a port. To function, a port must be linked to a specific receptacle. This linking is done by the computer system's start-up and configuration software located in ROM memory. For more information about connectors and ports, their location on the system unit, and the devices that connect to each, go to **www .howstuffworks.com** and type "connectors and ports" in the search box located near the top of the screen.

The following section uses *port* as if it were synonymous with *connector*, in line with everyday usage; however, keep the distinction in mind. Let's look next at the types of ports found on the exterior of a typical computer system's case.

USB PORTS

USB (universal serial bus) ports can connect a variety of devices, including keyboards, mice, printers, and digital cameras, and were designed to replace older parallel and serial ports. A single USB port can connect up to 127 peripheral devices, eliminating the need for special ports that work only with specific devices (Figure 2.22). Although introduced in 1995, USB ports didn't become widespread until the 1998 release of the best-selling iMac. The current standard, USB 2.0 (high-speed USB), replaced USB 1.1 and was released in April 2000. USB 2.0 is fully compatible with USB 1.1 products, cables, and connectors.

FIGURE 2.22 USB ports and connectors will be the standard for years to come.

USB 2.0 ports use an external bus standard that supports data transfer rates of 480 Mbps (480 million bits per second) between the computer and its peripheral devices; they do not transfer data between devices within the system. Some advantages include **hot swapping** and support for **plug-and-play (PnP)**. Hot swapping is the ability to connect and disconnect devices without shutting down your computer. This is convenient when you're using portable devices that you want to disconnect often, such as a digital camera. PnP refers to a set of standards, jointly developed by Intel Corporation and Microsoft, that enable a computer to automatically detect the brand, model, and characteristics of a device when you plug it in and configure the system accordingly.

Computer manufacturers have been installing increasing numbers of USB ports because of their convenience and versatility; many systems now have six or more. Ports on the back of a computer are typically used for peripherals that won't be removed often, like a printer or keyboard, whereas front ports are ideal for syncing a handheld device or MP3 player. If your computer doesn't have enough USB ports, it is possible to obtain a **USB hub**—a device that plugs into an existing USB port and contains four or more additional ports (Figure 2.23).

Up next on the horizon is USB 3.0, known as *SuperSpeed USB*. USB 3.0 is expected to use a fiber optic link to attain a data transfer rate of 4.8 Gbps—up to 10 times faster than USB 2.0. Additionally, USB 3.0 will be compatible with older versions, providing the same benefits while consuming less power.

FIGURE 2.23 If your computer needs more USB ports, a USB hub can expand your options.

1394 PORTS (FIREWIRE)

In 1995 Apple introduced **FireWire**, an interface Apple created and standardized as the IEEE 1394 High Performance Serial Bus specification. It is also known as Sony i.Link or IEEE 1394, the official name for the standard. FireWire is similar to USB in that it offers a high-speed connection for dozens of peripheral devices (up to 63 of them). It is especially well suited for transmitting digital video and audio data (Figure 2.24).

On non-Apple systems a FireWire port is called a **1394 port** after the international standard that defines it. Like USB, FireWire enables hot swapping and PnP. However, it is more expensive than USB and is used only for certain high-speed peripherals, such as digital video cameras, that need greater throughput (data transfer capacity) than USB provides.

FireWire 400 has a data transfer rate of 400 Mbps; FireWire 800 offers 800 Mbps. The next generation, FireWire S3200, is expected to transfer data at 3.2 Gbps. Although some experts consider FireWire technologically superior to USB, the popularity and affordability of USB 2.0, coupled with the promise of an even faster USB interface in the future, lead most to believe that the 1394 FireWire standard may fade away.

VIDEO CONNECTORS

Most computers use a video adapter (also called a video card) to generate the output that is displayed on the computer's screen or monitor. On the back of the adapter you'll find a standard **VGA (video graphics array) connector**, a 15-pin male connector that works with standard monitor cables. VGA connectors transmit analog video signals and are used for legacy technology cathode ray tube (CRT) monitors.

Many liquid crystal display (LCD) monitors can receive analog or digital video signals. A **DVI (digital visual interface) port** lets LCD monitors use digital signals. However, unless you have a keen eye or are doing professional video editing, the difference between analog and video signals may not be noticeable.

On some computers the video circuitry is built into the motherboard. This type of video circuitry is called **onboard video**. On such systems the video connector is on the back of the system unit case.

ADDITIONAL PORTS AND CONNECTORS

You may find the following additional ports and connectors on the exterior of a computer's case or on one of the computer's expansion cards:

- *Telephone connector:* The typical modem interface, a telephone connector (called RJ-11), is a standard modular telephone jack that will work with an ordinary telephone cord.

- *Network connector:* Provided with networking adapters, the network connector (called an RJ-45 or Ethernet port) looks like a standard telephone jack but is bigger and capable of much faster data transfer.

- *PC card slots:* Notebook computers provide one or more PC card slots for plugging in PC cards or ExpressCards. Like USB devices, these cards can be inserted or removed while the computer is running.

- *Sound card connectors:* PCs equipped with sound cards (adapters that provide stereo sound and sound synthesis), as well as Macs with built-in sound, offer two or more sound connectors. These connectors, also called jacks, accept the same stereo miniplug used by portable CD players. Most sound cards provide four connectors: Mic (microphone input), Line In (accepts input from other audio devices), Line Out (sends output to other audio devices), and Speaker (sends output to external speakers).

- *Game card:* Game cards provide connectors for high-speed access to the CPU and RAM for graphics-intensive interaction.

- *TV/sound capture board connectors:* If your computer is equipped with TV and video capabilities, you'll see additional connectors that look like those found on a television monitor. These include a connector for a coaxial cable, which can be connected to a video camera or cable TV system.

- *ExpressCard:* This is the newest standard for the PC card, originally known as the PCMCIA card (short for Personal Computer Memory Card International Association). Mostly designed for and used in notebook computers, the ExpressCard can also be found in desktops. The **ExpressCard** is a credit-card-sized adapter that fits into a designated slot to provide expanded capabilities such as wireless communication, additional memory, multimedia, or security features.

FIGURE 2.24 FireWire cables are used with FireWire ports to transmit digital video or audio files at high rates of speed.

Some legacy ports are being replaced by technologies like **SATA (serial advance technology attachment)**. The Serial ATA International Organization (SATA IO) is responsible for developing, managing, and pushing the adoption of the serial ATA specifications. Users of the SATA interface benefit from greater speed, simpler upgradable storage devices, and easier configuration. The interface greatly increases the data transfer rate between the motherboard and hard drive.

LEGACY TECHNOLOGY

Legacy technology is an older technology, device, or application that is being phased out in favor of new advances in technology. Although legacy technology may still work, it may not be available on newer computer systems. The following types of ports are all considered legacy technology.

Parallel ports were commonly used to connect a PC to a printer but have been replaced by USB ports and Ethernet ports. Many new computers no longer include parallel ports. Parallel ports could send and receive data eight bits at a time over eight separate wires. Data transfer was fast, but the eight-wire cable was bulky. Later versions were capable of two-way communication between the printer and computer, allowing the printer to send information, such as error messages, back to the computer.

Serial ports were one of the earliest types of ports and were often used with dial-up modems to achieve two-way communication. Although they are still in use on servers, many new computers no longer include serial ports, opting to use USB ports instead. Serial ports sent and received data one bit at a time using three separate wires—one to send, one to receive, and a signal ground wire. A serial port took eight times as long as a parallel port to transfer data, but the cables were smaller and less expensive.

SCSI (pronounced "scuzzy"; short for **small computer system interface**) **ports** were a type of parallel interface. Unlike a standard parallel port, a SCSI port enabled users to connect up to 15 SCSI- compatible devices, such as printers, scanners, and digital cameras, in a daisy-chain series.

PS/2 ports were typically used for mice and keyboards but were not interchangeable. Only one port could be used by each device, and ports were often color-coded to prevent users from plugging in the wrong device. USB ports don't have these limitations.

These legacy ports are becoming obsolete because newer ports, such as USB, FireWire, and SATA, provide greater flexibility and faster data transfer rates.

Chapter Summary

Inside the System Unit

The basic unit of information in a computer is the bit—a single digit (either 0 or 1). A sequence of eight bits, called a byte, is sufficient to represent the basic letters, numbers, and punctuation marks of most languages.

The system unit contains the motherboard, memory, circuits, power supply, cooling fan(s), internal speakers, drive bays for storage devices, and expansion cards. The computer's motherboard contains the microprocessor, the system clock, the chipset, memory modules, and expansion slots. The computer's central processing unit (CPU) processes data in a four-step machine cycle using two components: the control unit and the arithmetic

logic unit (ALU). The control unit follows a program's instructions and manages four basic operations: fetch, decode, execute, and store. The ALU performs arithmetic and logical operations.

The computer's main memory, random access memory (RAM), holds programs, data, and instructions for quick use by the processor. Read-only memory (ROM) holds prerecorded start-up operating instructions. Primary and secondary cache memory operate at very high speeds and keep frequently accessed data available to the processor.

A variety of ports and connectors enable peripheral devices to function effectively.

Key Terms and Concepts

Matching

Match each key term in the left column with the most accurate definition in the right column:

_____ 1. bit

_____ 2. instruction cycle

_____ 3. port

_____ 4. ASCII

_____ 5. byte

_____ 6. connector

_____ 7. Unicode

_____ 8. arithmetic logic unit

_____ 9. cache

_____ 10. control unit

_____ 11. register

_____ 12. Extended ASCII

_____ 13. ROM

_____ 14. execution cycle

_____ 15. hot swapping

a. A character coding system that uses seven bits and can represent 128 characters.

b. Connecting and disconnecting peripherals while the computer is running.

c. The portion of the CPU that performs mathematical computations and logical functions.

d. Memory that cannot be erased and contains start-up instructions.

e. The execute and store steps of the machine cycle.

f. The smallest unit of information a computer can work with.

g. A temporary storage location used by the control unit.

h. Character coding system that uses eight bits and can represent 256 characters.

i. The fetch and decode steps of the machine cycle.

j. A physical receptacle designed for a plug.

k. An electronically defined pathway for getting information into or out of a computer.

l. A small unit of very high-speed memory that works closely with the microprocessor and is either located in the microprocessor or in close proximity.

m. Used to represent one character of data.

n. A character coding system that uses 16 bits and can represent 65,000 characters.

o. The portion of the CPU that obtains program instructions and sends out the signals to carry them out.

Multiple Choice

Circle the correct choice for each of the following:

1. What is the term used to refer to the amount of memory that a program uses while running?
   a. Form factor
   b. Memory footprint
   c. Capacity
   d. Speculative execution

2. RAM is an example of which of the following?
   a. Nonvolatile memory
   b. Cache memory
   c. Volatile memory
   d. Virtual memory

3. Which of the following is listed in order from smallest to largest?
   a. KB, GB, MB, TB
   b. KB, MB, TB, GB
   c. MB, KB, GB, TB
   d. KB, MB, GB, TB

4. Which of the following is an example of a binary number?
   a. 5GA1   b. 0101
   c. 003   d. ABC

5. Which of the following is a new port that provides greater speed, simpler upgradable storage devices, easier configuration, and an increased data transfer rate between the motherboard and hard drive?
   a. USB drives   b. PS/2
   c. Ethernet   d. SATA

6. Which of the following character codes uses 16 bits and can represent many languages?
   a. Unicode   b. ASCII
   c. PCI   d. EBCDIC

7. Which number would never describe a computer's word size?
   a. 32   b. 64
   c. 60   d. 16

8. What is plug-and-play (PnP)?
   a. The connecting and disconnecting of a periph-
      eral while the system is running
   b. A feature that automatically detects new
      compatible peripherals connected to a system
   c. Hard drive storage that is used as RAM when
      RAM is filled
   d. The name of a new CPU for systems used by
      gamers

9. Which of the following would *not* be added by an
   expansion card?
   a. Additional RAM   b. Sound card
   c. Video card   d. Additional cache

10. What is the freeway of parallel connections that
    allows components within and connected to the
    system unit to communicate?
    a. Bus   b. Port
    c. ALU   d. Register

Fill-In

In the blanks provided, write the correct answer for each of the following:

1. The name, coined by Apple, for a high-speed 1394
   port that best transfers digital video and audio data
   is _____.

2. The port to which a flash or jump drive connects is
   a(n) _____ port.

3. Besides SCSI and PS/2 ports, two more examples of
   legacy hardware are _____ and _____.

4. A process used by the CPU to predict what will happen and thus prevent a pipeline stall is _____
   _____.

5. The _____ step of the machine cycle retrieves
   the next program instruction from memory.

6. The two subcomponents of the CPU are the
   _____ _____ and the _____ _____
   _____.

7. The word size of a CPU is important because it
   determines the _____ _____ and _____
   the CPU can run.

8. Video circuitry built into the motherboard is called
   _____ _____.

9. The network connector called RJ-45 that looks like a
   standard phone jack but is bigger and capable of
   faster data transfer is also called a(n) _____ port.

10. The _____ _____ of a computer converts AC
    to DC.

11. A PC card that is the size of a credit card, fits into a
    designated slot, and provides capabilities such as
    additional memory or wireless communication is
    a(n) _____.

12. _____ _____ is a processor specifically for
    handheld devices and mobile Internet devices.

13. If your computer system freezes, pressing Ctrl, Alt,
    and Delete will access the _____ _____
    _____.

14. _____ _____ improves CPU performance by
    running more than one processor at the same time.

15. The two types of operations performed by the ALU
    are _____ and _____ operations.

Short Answer

1. List the four operations of the processing cycle and
   provide a brief description of their function.

2. What is the difference between pipelining and parallel processing?

3. List three to five factors that affect the performance and speed of a computer.

4. What is the difference between registers and
   primary cache?

5. What is the difference between a USB port and a
   FireWire port? What devices connect to each?
   Which one is more cost-effective?

Teamwork

1. **Hardware Jeopardy** For this exercise it will help if
   everyone on your team has watched the game show
   Jeopardy. Your team is to create a game board, similar
   to that on the TV show, from index cards. Use at least
   four columns for the categories and four rows for the

questions. First create the four categories relative to
the hardware discussed in this chapter. Some categories might be memory, system unit components,
ports, or processing. After you have determined the categories, break the team into two groups and assign two

categories to each group. The group members are to come up with four answers to hardware questions for each of their assigned categories. Recall that in this game the players have to come up with the question for the answer. Rank the answers in difficulty, and assign values of 100 to the lowest and 400 to the highest. When both groups are done, assemble the game board and have the rest of the class play Hardware Jeopardy.

2. **Hardware Components for a New Lab** As a team, use a word processing program to create a questionnaire with options for possible computer systems to be placed in a hypothetical new computer lab on campus. Use the hardware and system information in this chapter to help create the checklist on the questionnaire. Distribute the questionnaire to at least 30 students on campus. Collect the data, and using prices from local vendors or Internet retail sites, generate a spreadsheet. The spreadsheet should list the most popular components chosen by the survey participants and their cost from at least two different vendors. Use the cost of the least expensive units to estimate the cost for 20 units. If time allows, add to the spreadsheet the cost of 20 desks and 20 chairs for a more comprehensive lab cost estimate. Turn in the questionnaire distributed, the responses to the questionnaire, the spreadsheet with the cost comparisons of at least two vendors, and your final lab estimate.

3. **Step into the Game** Your team is to research the newest and best video cards for gaming systems on the market. Research and locate at least three video cards that are placed in computer systems designed for gaming. In a one-page, double-spaced report, identify the video cards, the systems that use these cards, and what they bring to the game.

4. **Ports of Call** Your team is to locate three different computers. Create a log of the type and manufacturer of each system. If possible, photograph each system's ports. Using the textbook and other resources, add the names of each port on the systems, the purposes of the ports, and any peripheral devices connected to the ports. If you take photos, label the ports on the photos and include them in your log.

5. **Buy New or Upgrade?** Whether to buy a new computer or upgrade is a question that every computer owner faces at some time. Your team members should locate several references on this topic. In a one-page, double-spaced report, summarize and compare the reasons you would use to justify a decision to buy a new system or to upgrade. Remember to cite your references.

On the Web

1. **Processors on the Go** Use your favorite search engine to locate information about CPUs for mobile devices. Locate several Web sites that either give you information about the new ARM processors or direct you to articles about this topic. In a one-page, double-spaced report, provide information about the competition in this mobile market. Who are the key players? Which devices use which processors? What are the capabilities of competing processors? Remember to cite your Web references.

2. **Let the Games Begin!** Computer gaming has created a use for computer systems that demands more speed and graphic capabilities than are available from most systems in a business environment. Go to **www.cyberpowerpc.com**. On the menu across the top of the page, select the Intel desktop and AMD desktop options. From each of these two choices, additional choices appear. Select an option under each that contains the word *gaming*. After reviewing several gaming systems, pick two from Intel and two from AMD. In a spreadsheet or table list the following information: name of each system, price, CPU name and speed, amount of RAM, name and number of video cards, size of hard drive, and any additional fans or cooling systems. When you have researched all four systems, indicate the one you favor and the reasons for your choice.

3. **Binary Code Converter** Use your favorite search engine to locate a Web site that displays the "ASCII code binary table." Use that table to code the message here into binary form. Once it's converted, use the converter calculator in the chapter, or any other such calculator located on the Web, to convert the binary code into hexadecimal.

Message to convert: Singing in the rain!

4. **All Aboard the Motherboard** Go to **http://computer.howstuffworks.com/motherboard.htm** and watch the video about the components found on the motherboard. In a one-page, double-spaced report list the seven items the video reviews that are found on the motherboard, plus five additional pieces of information that the video covers that are not in this chapter.

5. **Processors for Speed** As this book is being written, the current fastest processor made by Intel is the Core 2 Extreme with a clock speed of 3.2 GHz; the fastest AMD processor is the Phenom X4 with a clock speed of 2.5 GHz. Because technology changes rapidly, newer and faster processors may already have been produced by these two manufacturers. Go to **www.intel.com** and **www.AMD.com**; using the search box on each home page, enter "processor." Find additional information about these processors and any more powerful processors made by these two companies. Summarize your results in a one-page, double-spaced report.

chapter 3

Input/ Output and Storage

Chapter Objectives

- Explain the purpose of the special keys on the keyboard and list the most frequently used pointing devices. (p. 69)

- List the types of monitors and the characteristics that determine a monitor's quality. (p. 78)

- Identify the two major types of printers and indicate the advantages and disadvantages of each. (p. 80)

- Distinguish between memory and storage. (p. 82)

- Discuss how storage media and devices are categorized and how data is stored on a hard drive. (p. 84)

- List factors that affect hard disk performance. (p. 85)

- Explain how data is stored on flash drives. (p. 86)

- List and compare the various optical storage media and devices available for personal computers. (p. 87)

- Describe solid-state storage devices and compare them with other types of storage devices. (p. 89)

Have you ever left a family event and felt like you should go for a physical? With the increased use of computers in every aspect of our lives, constant talk about carpel tunnel syndrome, headaches from poor screen resolution, stress from equipment failure and data loss, and vision problems at ever younger ages seem to be topics at many gatherings. These discussions should provoke you to research the devices you use to enter input, view results, and store important data.

Do you know about the various keyboard and mouse options? How about monitor resolution and glare reduction preferences? Do you know about Internet data storage sites and portable storage media?

Hardware comes in different forms. Some is hidden in the system unit; other hardware is considered to be peripheral to the computer. Let's take a closer look at those components of the computer system that you manage daily: the equipment that facilitates inputting data and commands, emits audio and visual output, and stores your work.

Input Devices: Giving Commands

Input refers to providing data and instructions into the computer for processing. This section discusses **input devices**, the hardware components that make it possible for you to get data and instructions into RAM, where it is held while in use (Figure 3.1).

KEYBOARDS

Despite all of the high-tech input devices on the market, the keyboard is still the most common. A **keyboard** is an input device that uses switches and circuits to translate keystrokes into a signal a computer understands. With a keyboard, a user can enter a document, access menus, use keyboard shortcuts, control game settings and characters, and perform many other actions, depending on the application being run. The 80 keys (or keycaps) on most keyboards are the same and include letters of the alphabet, numbers, punctuation marks, function keys, and control keys. Additional keys may exist depending on the operating system for which the keyboard was designed and whether it is used in a desktop or notebook unit (Figure 3.2).

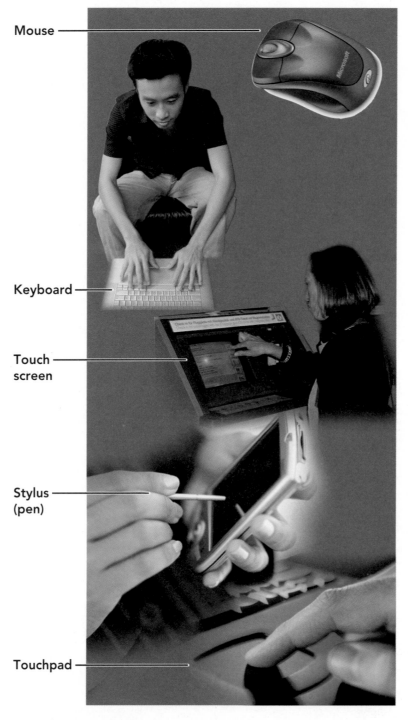

Mouse

Keyboard

Touch screen

Stylus (pen)

Touchpad

map is a comparison chart or lookup table that tells the processor what key is being pressed. For example, the character map lets the processor know that pressing the z key by itself corresponds to a small letter z, but the Shift and z keys pressed together correspond to a capital Z.

The character then appears onscreen at the location of the **cursor** (also called the **insertion point**). The cursor indicates where text will appear when you type and may take the shape of a blinking vertical line, a blinking underscore, or a highlighted box.

How do the impulses get from the keyboard to the monitor? Many keyboards are connected to the computer through a cable with a USB (Universal Serial Bus) connector. Some older computers may use a PS/2 cable. Notebooks use internal connectors. Regardless of the type of connector, the cable must carry power into the keyboard and signals from the keyboard out to the computer.

Wireless keyboards, on the other hand, connect to the computer through infrared (IR), radio frequency (RF), or Bluetooth connections. IR and RF connections are similar to what you'd find in a television remote control. Regardless of which sort of signal they use, wireless keyboards require either a built-in

How Do Keyboards Work? There is a **key matrix**, a grid of circuits, located under the keys. When you press a key, it presses a switch, completing the circuit and allowing a tiny amount of current to flow. When the processor finds a circuit that is complete, also referred to as closed, it compares the location of that circuit on the key matrix to the character map, located in its read-only memory (ROM) on the motherboard. A **character**

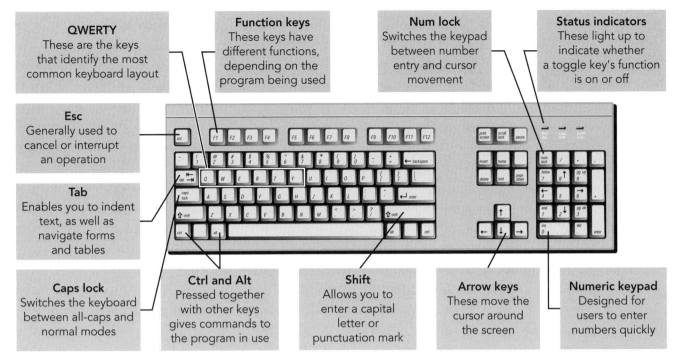

QWERTY
These are the keys that identify the most common keyboard layout

Function keys
These keys have different functions, depending on the program being used

Num lock
Switches the keypad between number entry and cursor movement

Status indicators
These light up to indicate whether a toggle key's function is on or off

Esc
Generally used to cancel or interrupt an operation

Tab
Enables you to indent text, as well as navigate forms and tables

Caps lock
Switches the keyboard between all-caps and normal modes

Ctrl and Alt
Pressed together with other keys gives commands to the program in use

Shift
Allows you to enter a capital letter or punctuation mark

Arrow keys
These move the cursor around the screen

Numeric keypad
Designed for users to enter numbers quickly

FIGURE 3.2 Most computers use the standard QWERTY keyboard layout. (QWERTY layout is named after the first six letters at the upper left of the letter area.) This enhanced QWERTY keyboard also includes a number of special keys and a numeric keypad.

receiver or one that is plugged into the USB port to communicate with the computer. Because they aren't physically connected to the computer, to obtain power wireless keyboards have an AC power connection or use batteries.

Using Special Keyboard Keys In addition to numeric and alphanumeric characters, a computer keyboard has several special keys that facilitate scrolling and cursor movement and thus increase productivity (Figure 3.3).

To reposition the cursor, you use the mouse or the appropriate **cursor-movement keys** (also called **arrow keys**) to move it to the desired location.

A **toggle key** is a key named after a type of electrical switch that has only two positions: on and off. For example, the Caps Lock key functions as a toggle key. When the Caps Lock mode is engaged, or on, you don't have to press the Shift key to enter uppercase letters. To turn off the Caps Lock mode, just press the Caps Lock key again. When Caps Lock is off, letters typed without holding down the Shift key are entered as lowercase letters.

Above the letters and numbers on the keyboard, you'll find function keys (labeled F1 through F12 or F15). The action a **function key** performs depends on the program in use. Near the function keys,

you'll also notice the Esc (short for Escape) key. The Esc key's function also depends on which program you're using, but it's generally used to interrupt or cancel an operation.

Some keys, like Shift, Alt, and Ctrl, have no effect unless you hold them down and press a second key. These are called **modifier keys**, because they modify the meaning of the next key you press. Modifier keys are frequently used to execute keyboard shortcuts, which provide quick keyboard access to menu commands. For example, if you are using a Microsoft Office application, pressing Ctrl + S (the + notation means to hold down the Ctrl key while pressing the s key) saves a file, and Windows + L locks the screen quickly. Links to shortcut keys for many of Microsoft's products are listed at **www.microsoft.com/enable/products/keyboard.aspx.** For a list of Mac shortcut keys and unique control, command, and option keys (that do not appear on a PC keyboard), go to **http://support.apple .com/kb/HT1343**.

Using Alternative Keyboards A **soft keyboard**, or **virtual keyboard**, is a keyboard that appears on a touch-sensitive screen. With such keyboards, tapping the key on the screen with a stylus or finger is the same as pressing a key on a traditional keyboard.

FIGURE 3.3 Special Keys on the PC Enhanced Keyboard

Key Name	Typical Function
Alt	In combination with another key, enters a command (example: Alt + F = file menu).
Backspace	Deletes the character to the left of the cursor.
Caps Lock	Toggles Caps Lock mode on or off.
Ctrl	In combination with another key, enters a command (example: Ctrl + C = copy).
Delete	Deletes the character to the right of the cursor.
Down arrow	Moves the cursor down, one line at a time.
End	Moves the cursor to the end of the current line.
Esc	Cancels the current operation or closes a dialog box.
F1	Displays on-screen help.
Home	Moves the cursor to the beginning of the current line.
Insert	Toggles between insert and overwrite mode, if these modes are available in the program you're using.
Left arrow	Moves the cursor to the left, one character at a time.
Num Lock	Toggles the numeric keypad's Num Lock mode between number entry and cursor movement.
Page Down	Moves down one full screen or one page.
Page Up	Moves up one full screen or one page.
Pause/Break	Suspends a program. (This key is not used by most applications.)
Menu key	Displays context-sensitive menu (instead of right-clicking).
Print Screen	Captures the screen image and places it in memory.
Right arrow	Moves the cursor to the right, one character at a time.
Up arrow	Moves the cursor up, one line at a time.
Windows key	Displays the Start menu in Microsoft Windows.

A **virtual laser keyboard** is generated by a device about the size of a small cellular phone and enables users to type texts or e-mails as easily as with an ordinary keyboard. It displays a light projection of a full-sized computer keyboard on almost any surface. Used with PDAs and smartphones, it provides a practical way to do e-mail, word processing, and spreadsheet tasks, enabling users to leave laptops and computers at home.

Virtual keyboard adaptable technology studies the user's finger movements to interpret and record keystrokes. Because the virtual keyboard is an image projected by light, it disappears completely when not in use. The settings to control this keyboard can be changed either via your laptop, PC, or compatible smartphone and PDA (Figure 3.4).

A **flexible keyboard** is a very adaptable foldable keyboard that weighs just 250 grams. The size and layout are the same as a standard PC keyboard. The keyboard is completely sealed, so it is spill and dust resistant. Its light weight makes it a perfect computer travel accessory, while its durability makes it the perfect choice for use in factories, wet areas, and retail environments. The characters on

FIGURE 3.5 A flexible keyboard is foldable, lightweight, and completely sealed.

the keys will not rub off; they are printed under the protective flexible membrane (Figure 3.5).

Media center PCs are becoming more and more popular. These all-in-one entertainment devices provide easy access to photos, TV, movies, and the latest in online media—all from the comfort of the couch, by using a remote control. These additional features and placement of the units in family rooms have generated the need for a remote keyboard that is stylish and unobtrusive. The small, wireless keyboards that accompany media center PCs combine a cursor control pad with a miniature keyboard to allow you to manage your unit and entertainment viewing experience with your fingertips (Figure 3.6).

Now that we've discussed the basics of using keyboards, let's move on to another piece of equipment commonly used for input: pointing devices.

FIGURE 3.4 A virtual laser keyboard projects a full-sized keyboard onto almost any surface.

FIGURE 3.6 Keyboards for PC home entertainment systems, such as the Logitech DiNovo Mini, are compact and allow users to control various media components by keyboard or touchpad.

THE MOUSE AND OTHER POINTING DEVICES

A **pointing device** (see Figure 3.7) is an input device that allows you to control the movements of the on-screen pointer. The **pointer** is an on-screen symbol, usually an arrow, that shows the current location of on-the-screen activity. The shape of the on-screen symbol also signifies the type of command, input, or response a user gives. If the pointer is an arrow with the head pointing to the upper-left corner of the screen, the mouse is set to accept the item clicked on as input, or the user's choice. If the arrow head is pointing to the upper right, the mouse is a text selection tool and will highlight a portion of text. Some applications allow the user to substitute other shapes for the familiar arrow; however, most users keep the arrow, as it is the most familiar. The behavior of a pointing device is related to the software program used. The most common actions performed by these devices—clicking, double-clicking, selecting, and dragging—are actually means of giving commands and responses to the program. Pointing devices are also used to provide input. For example, they're used in graphics programs to draw and paint on the screen, just as if they were a pencil or brush.

The most widely used pointing device is the mouse. A standard piece of equipment on most computer systems, a **mouse** is a palm-sized device designed to move about on a clean, flat surface. Although older roller-ball mice needed a mouse pad for traction, newer optical mice do not unless the surface that supports them is reflective or the wrong texture. As you move the mouse, its movements are mirrored by the on-screen pointer. You initiate actions by using the mouse buttons. Users of notebooks may like the **travel mouse**, a pointing device half the size of a normal mouse but with all the same capabilities. Developed by Microsoft, the **wheel mouse** includes a rotating wheel that is used to scroll text vertically within a document or on a Web page (Figure 3.8). Another type of mouse, the **wireless mouse** (also called a **cordless mouse**), transmits infrared or radio signals (RF) to a base station receiver on the computer. Wireless mice eliminate the cord tangling associated with the corded variety. The infrared mouse requires line of sight to the receiver, whereas the RF variety uses radio waves that transmit in a wider pattern, eliminating the line of site requirement.

Mouse Alternatives Although the mouse is by far the most popular pointing device, there are some alternatives such as trackballs, pointing sticks, or touch pads. These alternatives work well when desktop space is limited or nonexistent (as is often the case when using a notebook or netbook computer). Other devices, such as joysticks, touch screens, and styluses, are popular for playing games, using ATMs, and managing handheld devices.

FIGURE 3.7 Pointing devices come in a variety of shapes and styles.

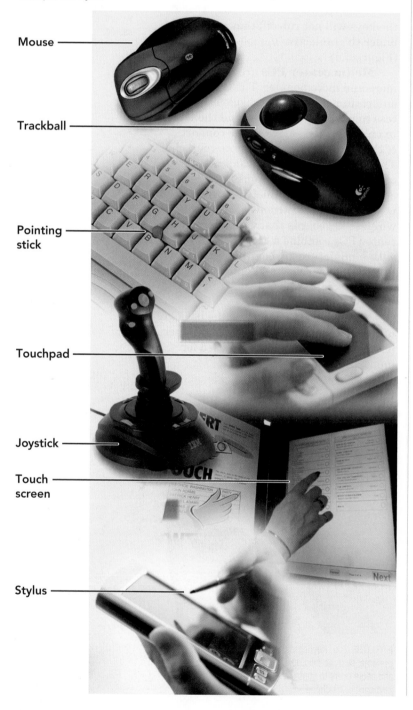

Mouse

Trackball

Pointing stick

Touchpad

Joystick

Touch screen

Stylus

A **trackball** is a stationary pointing device that contains a movable ball held in a cradle. The on-screen cursor is moved by rotating the ball with one's fingers or palm. From one to three keys are located in various positions, depending on the unit.

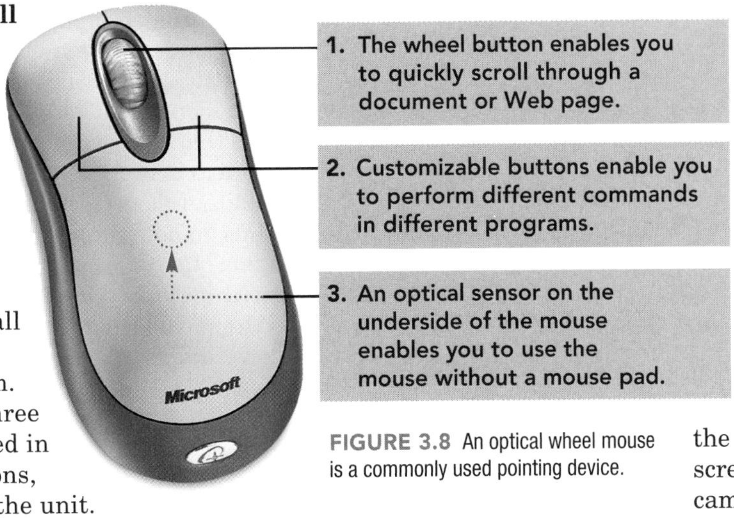

1. The wheel button enables you to quickly scroll through a document or Web page.

2. Customizable buttons enable you to perform different commands in different programs.

3. An optical sensor on the underside of the mouse enables you to use the mouse without a mouse pad.

FIGURE 3.8 An optical wheel mouse is a commonly used pointing device.

A **pointing stick** is a pointing device that looks like a pencil eraser between the G, H, and B keys. It is pressure sensitive and is pressed and moved in various directions with the forefinger. IBM popularized this device by introducing the TrackPoint on its ThinkPad notebooks.

Today, most notebook computers use a touchpad as a pointing device. A **touchpad** (also called a **trackpad**) is a small, stationary, pressure-sensitive, flat surface located on the notebook on which you slide your finger using the same movements as you would a mouse. You issue commands through one of the touchpad keys located near the edge of the pad or by tapping on the pad's surface. **Scrolling TrackPad** is the name of Apple Inc.'s patent-pending trackpad. It enables users to scroll in an arbitrary direction by touching the pad with two fingers instead of one, and then moving their fingers across the pad in the direction toward which they wish to scroll. Current MacBooks, MacBook Pros, and MacBook Airs have a Scrolling Multi-Touch pad. In comparison, most PC notebook touchpads set aside an area along the right and bottom edges of the pad to accommodate vertical or horizontal scroll operations, respectively.

A **joystick** is a pointing device used to easily move objects in any direction on-screen. It employs a vertical rod mounted on a base with one or two buttons. Although you can use joysticks as pointing devices, they're most often used to control the motion of an on-screen object in computer games, training simulators, or CAD (Computer Aided Design) systems.

A **touch screen** is a display screen that is sensitive to the touch of a finger or stylus. Used on ATM machines, airport kiosks, retail point-of-sale terminals, car navigation systems, medical monitors, and industrial control panels, the touch screen became wildly popular on handhelds after Apple introduced the iPhone with its improved user-friendly interface in 2007. The primary advantage of a touch screen is the unlimited ways the user display can be designed for input compared to a fixed set of physical keys or buttons. If there is no hardware keyboard on the unit, a soft keyboard can be displayed on screen whenever there is a need to input text. Touch screens also accept hand printing, handwriting, graphics, and finger movements (Figure 3.9).

Because human fingers are much bigger than an on-screen pointer, software designers must provide fewer options and larger on-screen buttons on touch screens. These characteristics of touch screens make them best suited to simple, special-purpose programs.

A **stylus**, which looks like an ordinary pen except that the tip is dry and semi-blunt, is commonly used as an alternative to fingers on touch-screen devices.

FIGURE 3.9 Self-service kiosks using touch-screen technology are found in many locations.

Styluses are often used with pressure-sensitive graphics tablets, a drawing tablet used for sketching, in CAD applications and other graphics applications to create designs or draw objects such as cars, buildings, medical devices, and robots. You may have also used a stylus to create your digital signature when using your credit card or accepting a package from a delivery person.

ADDITIONAL INPUT DEVICES

Though keyboards and pointing devices are most commonly used to input data, specialized input devices are also available. This section introduces some of these alternative input devices and their uses.

Speech recognition, also called **voice recognition**, is the conversion of spoken words into computer text. The spoken word is first digitized and then matched against a dictionary of coded voice waves. The matches are converted into text as if the words were typed on the keyboard. This method of input is favored by individuals for whom traditional input devices are not an option (for example, those with limited hand movement) and by those who want to significantly limit their use of the mouse and keyboard while maintaining or increasing their overall productivity (for example, writers). To accept speech, a computer must have a

microphone, an input device that converts sound waves into electrical signals that the computer is able to process. Speaker-dependent recognition systems require that users speak sample words into the system in order to adjust it to their individual voices. Speaker-independent systems do not require tuning and can recognize limited vocabularies such as numeric digits and a handful of words. It is the speaker-independent system that replaces human operators for telephone services.

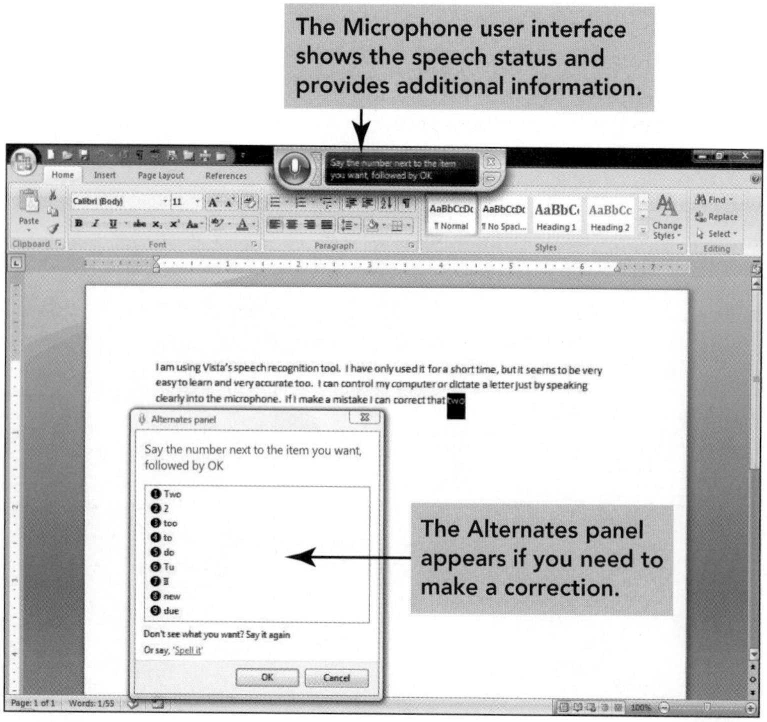

There are three types of voice recognition systems. Command systems recognize only a few hundred words and eliminate using the mouse or keyboard for repetitive commands like open file or close file. This is the least taxing on the computer. Discrete Voice recognition systems are used for dictation, but require a pause between each word. Continuous Voice recognition understands natural speech without pauses and is the most process intensive. Speaker-independent continuous systems that handle large vocabularies are quickly becoming popular.

Dragon NaturallySpeaking is a speech recognition software package developed by Dragon Systems. It was among the first programs to make speech recognition practical on a PC. NaturallySpeaking uses a simple visual interface. Dictated words appear in a floating tooltip as they are spoken; when the speaker pauses, the program writes the words in the active window at the location of the cursor. Like other speech recognition software, early versions of the software had to be trained to recognize the user's voice, a process that took approximately 10 minutes. With the release of version 9, training the software is no longer necessary.

A speech recognition system that works with Microsoft's mainstream applications is included in the Microsoft Vista and Windows 7 operating systems. It is a speaker-independent continuous system that allows the user to dictate documents and e-mails, use voice commands to start and switch between applications, control the operating system, and even fill out forms on the Web (Figure 3.10).

Windows 7 has improved speech recognition by extending it to additional Windows applications. When using this feature with a program that Microsoft considers incompatible, the spoken text is placed into a text box rather than directly into the document. After finishing a sentence or paragraph, the user clicks the

FIGURE 3.10 Speech-recognition technology enables users to issue commands and enter text.

The Microphone user interface shows the speech status and provides additional information.

The Alternates panel appears if you need to make a correction.

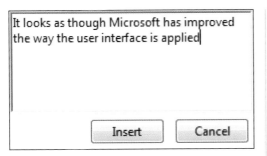

Insert   Cancel

FIGURE 3.11 Depicted here is the text box for the updated speech recognition program that works with applications that are normally not compatible.

Insert or Cancel button (Figure 3.11). If inserted, the text is placed in the document at the location of the cursor. This feature does not work with all applications, so the user must confirm its compatibility.

The Apple speech recognition program, MacSpeech Dictate 1.5, is up to 20 percent more accurate than previous versions, recognizes 13 English dialect variations, and is optimized for performance with key Macintosh productivity applications.

Speech recognition systems have improved over the years, but are still not perfect. Read about some of the weaknesses and flaws of these systems at **http://electronics.howstuffworks .com/speech-recognition3.htm**.

A **scanner** copies anything that's printed on a sheet of paper, including artwork, handwriting, and typed or printed text, and converts the input into a graphics image for the computer. The scanner does not recognize or differentiate the type of material it is scanning. Everything is converted into a graphic **bitmapped image**, a representation of an image as a matrix of dots called picture elements (pixels). All images acquired by digital cameras and camcorders, scanners, and screen capture programs are bitmapped images. Most scanners use **optical character recognition (OCR)** software to automatically convert scanned text into a text file instead of a bit mapped image. Even though this technology has greatly improved, foreign characters and poor quality of the original document will increase the errors in the final file.

There are several types of scanners. Flatbed scanners copy items placed on a stationary glass surface (Figure 3.12a). They are good for books or other bulky objects and are also useful for photos and other documents that shouldn't be bent. Sheet-fed scanners use a roller mechanism to draw in multiple sheets of paper, one sheet at a time, and are useful for high-volume scanning. Handheld scanners are similar to sheet-fed scanners, in that the item to be copied must pass through the scanner, but they are smaller and portable. They are often used to copy business cards, magazine articles, small photos, or business documents (Figure 3.12b).

In many retail and grocery stores, employees use a **bar code reader**, a handheld or desktop-mounted scanning device that reads an item's Universal Product Code (UPC). The UPC is a pattern of bars printed on merchandise that the store's computer system uses to retrieve information about an item and its price. Today, bar codes are used to update inventory and ensure correct pricing. For example, FedEx uses a bar code system to identify and track packages.

You may recognize the Scantron form. This is the grid-like form you fill in with a no. 2 pencil when taking a computer-scored test. Your marked paper is scanned by an **optical mark reader (OMR)**, a scanning device that senses the magnetized marks from your no. 2 pencil, to

FIGURE 3.12 (a) Flatbed scanners scan a single piece of paper at a time. **(b)** Handheld scanners are more portable and flexible, and are often used to scan business cards, small photos, or documents.

a   b

determine which responses you marked. Almost any type of questionnaire can be designed for OMR devices, making it helpful to researchers who need to tabulate responses to large surveys.

Now that we know how to get our data into a computer system, let's look at how output devices are used to send the data and processed information back to us.

Output Devices: Engaging Our Senses

Output devices enable people to see, hear, and even feel the results of processing operations. The most widely used output devices are monitors and printers.

MONITORS

Monitors (also called **displays**) are screens that display data and processed information called **output**. It's important to remember that the screen display isn't a permanent record. To drive home this point, screen output is sometimes called **soft copy**, as opposed to **hard copy** (printed output). To make permanent copies of your work, you should save it to a storage device or print it.

There are two basic types of monitors. The big, bulky cathode-ray tube (CRT) monitors that look like traditional televisions and are usually connected to older desktop computers and the thin, popular liquid crystal display (LCD) monitors like those that accompany new desktops and all-in-one units, and are incorporated

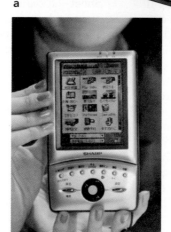

a

b

c

FIGURE 3.13 LCD monitors are ideal for small portable devices such as (**a**) notebooks, (**b**) PDAs, and (**c**) smartphones.

into notebooks, handheld computers, and smartphones (Figure 3.13)

A **CRT monitor** screen is a grid of millions of dots called pixels. Each pixel is composed of three smaller elements (one red, one green, and one blue) called phosphors. An electron gun passes over the grid emitting an electron beam that excites the phosphors in various intensities and creates the viewable colors. The beam moves continuously across the screen at a **refresh rate** of 75 to 85 times a second. This refresh action can sometimes causes a visually irritating flicker effect.

Liquid crystal displays (LCDs), or **flat-panel displays**, are rapidly replacing CRT monitors. An LCD screen is also a grid of pixels. A florescent panel at the back of the system generates light waves to make the images and colors. These waves pass through a layer of crystal solution. The electric current moves the crystals and either blocks the light or lets it through, thus creating the images and colors viewable on the display. The least expensive LCDs are called **passive-matrix** LCDs (also called **dual scans**). In these units, the electrical current drives the display by charging groups of pixels, either in a row or column, at once. The screen brightens and fades as the current moves from group to group. Appliances, toys, remote controls, and home medical products use this type of display. Passive-matrix LCD displays are usually not as sharp as active-matrix displays, have less of a viewing angle, and are too slow for full-motion video.

Active-matrix, or **Thin Film Transistor (TFT)**, technology drives the display by charging each pixel individually as needed. As the price of active-matrix displays drops,

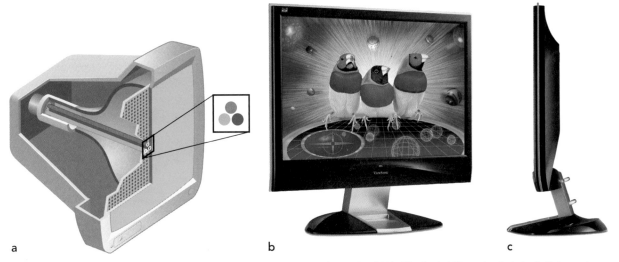

a   b   c

FIGURE 3.14 (**a**) Cathode-ray tube (CRT) monitors are used with older desktop units. (**b**) The ViewSonic LCD monitor includes built-in speakers and HDMI (high-definition multimedia interface) input for high-definition video, and (**c**) has an incredibly thin profile.

passive-matrix displays may become obsolete (Figure 3.14).

Other flat-panel display technologies include field-emission displays (FEDs), which look and operate in much the same way as an LCD monitor, except that tiny stationary carbon nanotubes illuminate each on-screen pixel. Although FEDs are considered more rugged and are better for harsh environments, they have not seen any mass-market adoption.

Screen Size The size of a monitor is determined by measuring it diagonally. This is fairly straightforward for LCD monitors. However, for CRT monitors it's a bit trickier because there are two different measurements. The **quoted size** is the diagonal measurement of the CRT screen, but because part of the screen is obscured by its housing, the actual **viewable area** is somewhat smaller. Both of these sizes must be disclosed by the manufacturer.

Typical desktop PC monitors range from 17 to 21 inches, whereas notebook computers measure 12 to 17 inches. Larger monitors, such as the 28-inch ViewSonic monitor shown in Figure 3.14, are popular with gamers, graphic designers, and others who have to display two documents side by side. In fact, a recent study commissioned by Apple looked at the productivity impact of using a 30-inch monitor as compared to a 20-inch or 17-inch monitor. The results indicated that a user on a 30-inch monitor would save about 1.3 hours per week over a person using a 17-inch monitor. The

report is based on what they consider to be normal usage. Depending on your work, the savings in productivity could be much greater.

Resolution The term **resolution** generally refers to the sharpness of an image and is controlled by the number of pixels on the screen. The higher the resolution, the sharper the image. Units of resolution are written as 1024 × 786. This notation means the display has 1,024 distinct dots on each of 768 lines. Figure 3.15 lists common PC monitor resolutions.

For color graphics displays, **Video Graphics Array (VGA)** is the lowest-resolution standard (640 × 480). Most of today's monitors can be adjusted to resolutions up to **Extended Graphics Array** (**XGA**, 1024 × 768). The newest models sport Super and Ultra Extended Graphics Array video adapters—allowing for an

FIGURE 3.15	**Common PC Monitor Resolutions**	
640 x 480	VGA	Video Graphics Array
800 x 600	SVGA	Super Video Graphics Array
1024 x 768	XGA	Extended Graphics Array
1280 x 1024	SXGA	Super Extended Graphics Array
1600 x 1200	UXGA	Ultra Extended Graphics Array

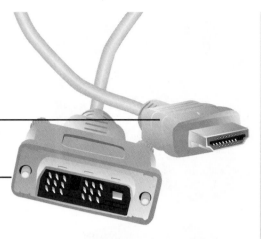

The HDMI end of the cable plugs into the TV.

The DVI end of the cable plugs into the PC.

FIGURE 3.16 If your PC doesn't have an HDMI port, an HDMI-DVI cable can be used to connect the PC to the TV.

FIGURE 3.17 Inkjet printers produce high-quality color output.

amazing 1600 pixels per line and 1200 lines of pixels per screen!

Televisions as Monitors The resolution on older TVs was much lower than PCs, so the viewing results were less than optimal. However, newer **high-definition televisions (HDTVs)** have higher resolutions, typically 1920 × 1080 or better, making this less of a problem. So, to the casual observer, there doesn't seem to be much difference between an LCD monitor and an LCD TV, so why not hook up your PC to your TV for an even bigger computer screen? HDTV, a digital television standard that provides extremely high-quality video and audio, makes this a possibility. HDTV displays include direct-view, plasma, rear screen, and front screen projection. These units require an HDTV tuner to view HDTV-formatted programs. You'll need a video card with a DVI (digital video interface) or HDMI (high-definition multimedia interface) port on your PC and the corresponding input on the TV (Figure 3.16).

If you'd rather watch live TV on your PC, you can do that too. Install a TV tuner card in your PC and get ready to watch or record your favorite shows.

Now that we've discussed monitors and soft copy, let's move on to devices that produce hard-copy output: printers.

PRINTERS

Printers produce a permanent version, or hard copy, of the output on the computer's display screen. Some of the most popular printers are inkjet printers and laser printers.

Inkjet printers are relatively inexpensive nonimpact printers that produce excellent color output, making them popular choices for home users (Figure 3.17). They spray ionized ink from a series of small jets onto a sheet of paper, creating the desired character shapes. Today, inkjet printers are capable of producing high-quality print approaching that produced by laser printers. A typical inkjet printer provides a resolution of 300 dots per inch, although some newer models offer higher resolutions. One drawback of an inkjet printer is that it is relatively slow compared with its laser competitor.

FIGURE 3.18 Black and white laser printers provide quick output at affordable prices.

A **laser printer** is a high-resolution nonimpact printer that uses an electrostatic reproductive technology similar to that used by copiers (Figure 3.18). Under the printer's computerized control, a laser beam creates electrical charges on a rotating print drum. These charges attract toner, which is transferred to the paper and fused to its surface by a heat process. Laser printers print faster than inkjets; some laser printers can crank out 60 or more pages per minute. Black and white laser printers are becoming more affordable and generally have a lower per-page print cost than inkjet printers; however, color laser printers are still more expensive to buy and maintain.

Dot-matrix printers (also known as **impact printers**) were once the most popular type of printer but are declining in use. Such printers create characters by striking pins against an ink ribbon. Each pin makes a dot, and combinations of dots form characters and illustrations. Although they are capable of printing 3000 lines per minute, their print quality is lower than other printers and they are noisy. Dot-matrix printers are used for printing backup copies and, because they physically strike the paper, for printing multipart forms such as invoices or purchase orders.

Thermal-transfer printers use a heat process to transfer an impression onto paper. There are two types of thermal printers. Thermal-wax transfer printers adhere a wax-based ink onto paper, whereas direct thermal printers burn dots onto coated paper when the paper passes over a line of heating elements. The best thermal-wax transfer printers are called **dye sublimation printers**. These printers are slow and expensive, but they produce results that are difficult to distinguish from high-quality color photographs. Thermal printers are becoming popular for mobile and portable printing. These are the printers used by car rental agencies to generate an instant receipt or by a traffic officer to print out a traffic ticket.

Photo printers are either inkjet or laser printers and use special inks and good-quality photo paper to produce pictures that are as good as those generated by commercial photo processors. Many allow you to bypass your computer to print directly from a digital camera or memory card.

A **plotter** is a printer that produces high-quality images by physically moving ink pens over the surface of the paper. A continuous-curve plotter draws maps from stored data (Figure 3.19).

FIGURE 3.19 Plotters are useful for printing oversized output such as maps, charts, and blueprints.

GREEN tech tips

More than 700 million inkjet and laser toner cartridges are sold every year. What happens when they are empty? Although many organizations and retail stores have recycling programs, every second nearly eight used cartridges are thrown away in the United States— approximately 875 million pounds of environmental waste each year! So what can you do? Take advantage of your local recycling program. Some programs even pay you for your old cartridges because they can be recycled and sold again. Keeping them out of the waste stream reduces toxicity levels and saves landfill space. Besides, half a gallon of oil is saved for every toner cartridge you recycle! ●

Computer-generated maps, such as those used by cartographers and weather analysts, can be retrieved and plotted or used to show changes over time.

ADDITIONAL OUTPUT DEVICES

All systems include basic built-in speakers to transmit the beeps normally made during processing. These speakers, however, are not designed for playing CDs. You'll have to purchase **speakers** to listen to computer-generated sound, such as music and synthesized speech, unless higher-end speakers were included with your system. Like microphones, speakers require a sound card to function. Sound cards play the contents of digitized recordings, such as music recorded in WAV (short for waveform) and MP3 sound file formats. Some sound cards do this job better than others. Quality is most noticeably a consideration when the sound card reproduces MIDI (musical instrument digital interface) files. MIDI files play over **synthesizers**, electronic devices that produce music by generating musical tones. Sound cards have built-in synthesizers. Better sound cards use wavetable synthesis, whereby the sound card generates sounds using ROM-based recordings of actual musical instruments. The latest sound cards may include surround sound (systems set up so that they surround you with sound as in a theatre) and subwoofer (speakers that produce only low bass sounds) effects.

Data projectors display a computer's video output on a screen for an audience to view. They range from small, lightweight

a

b

c

FIGURE 3.20 The View-Sonic PJ260D (**a**) is a powerful portable DLP projector. A fax machine (**b**) performs both input and output functions. A multifunction device (**c**) combines an inkjet or laser printer with a scanner, a fax machine, and a copier.

devices used for business or class presentations and home theaters, to larger, more expensive models suitable for use in auditoriums or stadiums. Individuals and businesses often use LCD or DLP projectors. In an **LCD projector**, an image is formed by light passing through three colored panels—red, green, and blue. LCD projectors produce sharp, accurate color images; however, they are subject to pixilation and have less contrast than a DLP projector. **DLP (digital light-processing) projectors** project light onto a chip made up of millions of microscopic mirrors. DLP projectors (Figure 3.20a) are often smaller and lighter than LCD projectors and have better contrast; but in some models, the reflected light can create a rainbow effect that causes eyestrain for some people.

Computers equipped with a fax modem and fax software can receive incoming faxes. The incoming document is displayed on the screen, and it can be printed or saved.

Computers also send faxes as output. To send a fax using your computer, you must save your document using a special format that is compatible with the fax program. The fax program then sends the document through the telephone system to a traditional distant fax machine. This output function is helpful because you don't have to print the document to send it as a fax (Figure 3.20b).

Multifunction devices combine inkjet or laser printers with a scanner, a fax machine, and a copier, enabling home

office users to obtain all of these devices without spending a great deal of money (Figure 3.20c).

Now that you've learned about a variety of output devices, let's look at how you can store data for later use.

Storage: Holding Data for Future Use

Storage (also called **mass storage**, **auxiliary storage**, or **secondary storage**) refers to the ways a computer system retains software and data for future use. Storage relies on two components—recording media and storage devices. **Recording media** are hardware components, such as hard disks, floppy disks, flash memory, CDs, and DVDs, on which data is held. The **storage device** is the computer hardware that facilitates embedding data onto recording media. In other words, storage devices are the actual drives (hard drive, floppy drive, USB flash drive, and so on) that contain the tools to place the data on the recording media. For photos and descriptions of current storage devices, go to **www.worldstart.com/tips/tips.php/3769**. Organizations increasingly turn to computer storage systems to store all of their computer software, data, and information. The reason? Storing information on paper is expensive and offers no opportunity for electronic manipulation and sharing. A simple storage device can store the amount of information that would cost $10,000 to store on paper for less than $10 per gigabyte (1 billion characters). In fact, storage devices are increasing in capacity to the point that they can hold an entire library's worth of information. Read on to learn why storage is necessary, what kinds of storage devices and media are out there, and which best fit your computing needs.

MEMORY VERSUS STORAGE

To understand the distinction between memory and storage, think of the last time you worked at your desk. In your file drawer, you store all your personal items and papers, such as your checking account statements. The file drawer is good for long-term storage. When you decide to work on one or more of these items, you take it out of storage and put it on your desk. The desktop is a good place to keep the items you're working with (work in progress); they're close at hand and available for use right away. Your desktop can be thought of as memory—the place where you temporarily put things that you are using or working on.

Computers work the same way. When you want to work with the contents of a file, the computer transfers the file to a temporary workplace: the computer's memory—technically called RAM (random access memory) or primary memory. This memory is a form of storage—a holding area for items in use—but it is temporary. Why don't computers just use RAM to hold all of a user's files, regardless of whether or not they are in use? Here are some reasons:

- **Recording media retain data when the current is switched off.** The computer's RAM is volatile. This means that when you switch off the computer's power, all of the information in RAM is irretrievably lost. So, if your work in progress has not been saved onto a recording medium by a storage device, it is no longer retrievable unless the application you were running has an auto save feature for emergency rescue. In contrast, recording media are nonvolatile; they will not lose data when the power goes off or when they are removed from the system.
- **Storage devices are cheaper than memory.** RAM operates very quickly to keep up with the computer's CPU. For this reason, RAM is expensive—much more expensive than storage. In fact, most computers are equipped with just enough RAM to accommodate all of the programs a user wants to run at once. In contrast, a computer system's storage devices hold much more data and software than the computer's memory does. Today, you can buy a storage device capable of storing more than 300 GB of software and data for about the same amount you would pay for 2 GB of RAM.
- **Storage devices play an essential role in system start-up operations.** When you start your computer, the operating system appears on the monitor. Actually, a copy of the operating system software is transferred from the hard disk, where it is permanently stored, into the

computer's RAM—making it available and ready for use.
- **Storage devices are needed for output.** When you've finished working, you use the computer's storage system as an output device to save a file. When you save a file, the computer transfers your work from the computer's RAM to recording media via a storage device. If you forget to save your work, it will be lost when you switch off the computer's power. Remember, the computer's RAM is volatile! (Figure 3.21)

For all of these reasons, demand for storage capacity is soaring. Storage capacity is measured in bytes (KB, MB, GB, TB, and PB). A report presented in January 2009 by Coughlin Associates at the Storage Visions Conference cites a 12-fold increase in required storage media (what we have termed recording media here) between 2008 and 2014 and, for the same time span, a total increase in revenue related to storage media from $387 M to $807 M. Now that you understand the importance of storage, let's look at the devices and media used to hold data.

HARD DISK DRIVES

On almost all computers, the hard disk drive is by far the most important storage device. A **hard disk drive** (or simply **hard disk**) is a high-capacity, high-speed storage device, usually housed in the system unit, that consists of several rapidly rotating disks called **platters** on which programs, data, and processed results are stored. To communicate with the CPU, hard disks require a hard disk controller.

FIGURE 3.21   Memory versus Storage

		Access Speed	Cost per MB	Storage Capacity
Memory	Cache memory	Fastest	Highest	2 MB
	RAM	Fast	High	4 GB
Storage	Hard disk	Medium	Medium	1 TB
	CD-R disc	Slow	Low	700 MB

A **hard disk controller** is an electronic circuit board that provides an interface between the CPU and the hard disk's electronics. The controller may be located on the computer's motherboard, on an expansion card, or within the hard disk.

The computer's hard disk, also referred to as **secondary**, or **fixed**, **storage**, consists of the storage devices that are actively available to the computer system and that do not require any action on the part of the user. Hard disks can also be categorized as both random access and magnetic storage devices. A **random access storage device** can go directly to the requested data without having to go through a linear search sequence. **Magnetic storage devices** use disks that are coated with magnetically sensitive material.

Magnetic storage devices use an electromagnet called a **read/write head** that moves across the surface of a disk and records information by transforming electrical impulses into a varying magnetic field. As the magnetic materials pass beneath the read/write head, this varying field forces the particles to be rearranged in a meaningful pattern of positive and negative magnetic indicators that represents the data. This operation is called *writing*. When *reading*, the read/write head senses the recorded pattern and transforms this pattern into electrical impulses that are decoded into text characters. A hard disk contains two or more vertically stacked platters, each with two read/write heads (one for each side of the disk). The platters spin so rapidly that the read/write head floats on a thin cushion of air, at a distance 1/300th the width of a human hair. To protect the platter's surface, hard disks are enclosed in a sealed container.

How does the read/write head know where to look for data in order to access it randomly? To answer this question, you need to know a little about how stored data is organized on a disk. Like a vinyl record, disks are formatted, physically laid out, in circular bands called **tracks**. Each track is divided into pie-shaped wedges called **sectors**. Two or more sectors combine to form a **cluster** (Figure 3.22).

To keep track of where specific files are located, the computer's operating system records a table of information on the disk. This table contains the name of each file and the file's exact location on the disk. Older versions of Microsoft Windows called this the **file allocation table**, or **FAT**. The current system for Windows NT, 2000, XP, Vista, and Windows 7 is known as **NTFS (new technology file system)** and is more advanced and powerful. It improves performance and is required to implement numerous security and administrative features in the operating system. Hard disks can be divided into partitions. A **partition** is a section of a hard disk set aside as if it were a physically separate disk. Partitions are required if a system is going to give the user an option of running more than one operating system. The average user won't need to partition the hard disk, but some individuals like to create one partition for Linux and another for Microsoft Windows. In this way, they work with programs developed for either operating system.

FIGURE 3.22 Disks contain circular bands called tracks, which are divided into sectors. Two or more sectors combine to form a cluster.

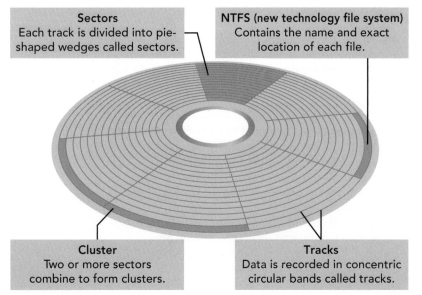

Sectors
Each track is divided into pie-shaped wedges called sectors.

NTFS (new technology file system)
Contains the name and exact location of each file.

Cluster
Two or more sectors combine to form clusters.

Tracks
Data is recorded in concentric circular bands called tracks.

Filename	Track	Sector
lettrz.wp	2	3
sales.wks	14	2
memo.doc	10	6
dpt.cht	deleted	
logo.art	18	2
forecast.wks	13	6
agenda.doc	21	4

Factors Affecting Hard Disk Performance
If a hard disk develops a defect or a read/write head encounters an obstacle, such as a dust or smoke particle, the head bounces on the disk surface, preventing the computer from reading or writing data to one or more sectors of the disk. Hard disks absorb minor jostling without suffering damage, but a major jolt—such as one caused by dropping the computer while the drive is running—could cause a head crash to occur. Head crashes are one of the causes of **bad sectors**, areas of the disk that have become damaged and can no longer reliably hold data. If you see an on-screen message indicating that a disk has a bad sector, try to copy the data off the disk and don't use it to store new data.

A hard drive's most important performance characteristic is the speed at which it retrieves desired data. The amount of time it takes a device from the request for the information to the delivery of that information is its **access time**. Access time includes the **seek time**, the time it takes the read/write head to locate the data before reading begins. **Positioning performance** refers to the time that elapses from the initiation of drive activity until the hard disk has positioned the read/write head so that it can begin transferring data.

Transfer performance refers to how quickly the read/write head transfers data from the disk to random access memory. One way disk manufacturers improve transfer performance is to increase the speed at which the disk spins, which makes data available more quickly to the read/write heads. Another way is to improve the spacing of data on the disk so that the heads can retrieve several blocks of data on each revolution.

Hard disk performance can also be improved with a type of cache memory called disk cache (Figure 3.23). **Disk cache**, usually incorporated in the hard drive, is a type of RAM that holds recently used data and instructions and the data and instructions it anticipates you will use in the near future. When the CPU needs to get information, it looks in the disk cache first. If it doesn't find the information it needs, it retrieves the information from the hard disk.

Network Attached Storage (NAS) As demands for data storage have increased, **network attached storage (NAS)** devices are becoming more popular. NAS devices are comprised primarily of hard drives or other media used for data storage and are attached directly to a network. The network connection permits each computer on the network to access the NAS to save or retrieve data.

Some external hard drives sold for the home market can function as NAS devices. The advantage is that one device can be

FIGURE 3.23 Disk cache, a type of RAM, dramatically improves hard disk performance. When the CPU needs to get information, it looks in the disk cache first.

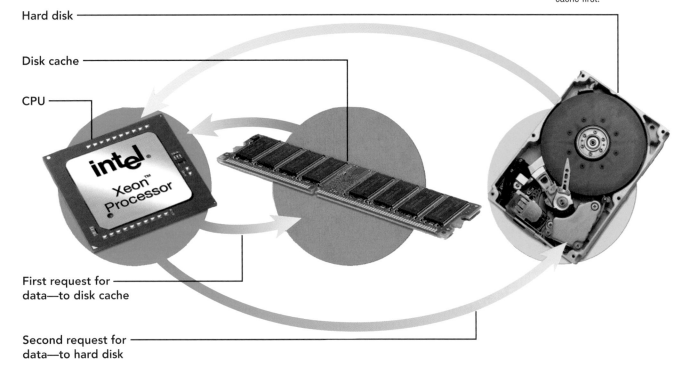

Hard disk

Disk cache

CPU

First request for data—to disk cache

Second request for data—to hard disk

used to coordinate and store backup files for all PCs connected to the home network.

Remote Storage **Remote storage**, sometimes referred to as an **Internet hard drive**, is storage space on a server that is accessible from the Internet. In most cases, a computer user subscribes to the storage service and agrees to rent a block of storage space for a specific period of time. Instead of sending e-mail attachments to share with family and friends, you might simply post the files to the remote storage site and then allow them to be viewed or retrieved by others. You might save backup copies of critical files or all the data on your hard disk to your Internet hard drive.

The key advantage of this type of remote storage is the ability to access data from multiple locations. You can access your files from any device that connects with the Internet, so everything you store on the site is available to you at any time. Some disadvantages are that your data may not be secure; the storage device might become corrupt, causing you to lose your data; and the company offering the Internet storage may go out of business.

FLASH DRIVES AND STORAGE

Although hard disks are currently the most important storage media, the disks explored in this section are examples of portable storage, which means that you can remove a disk from one computer and insert it into another. A **flash drive** is a type of storage device that uses solid-state circuitry and has no moving parts (Figure 3.24). Flash drives are also known as **solid-state drives (SSDs)** and use flash memory, which is nonvolatile, electronic memory. **Flash memory** stores data electronically on a chip in sections known as **blocks**. Rather than erasing data byte by byte, flash memory uses an electrical charge to delete all of the data on the chip or just the data contained in a specific block, which is a much quicker method than other types of storage use. Flash memory is limited to 100,000 write cycles. This means

information can be written and erased 100,000 times to each block, which could conceivably take years to occur. Because of their lack of moving parts, lower power consumption, and lighter weight, flash drives are becoming an alternative to hard disk drives, especially in notebook computing. Flash drives are also found in some MP3 players, smartphones, and digital cameras. Although flash drives are more expensive and have less storage capacity than hard disk drives, these differences are expected to erode over time. Additionally, some hard disk drives are incorporating flash technology, creating **hybrid hard drives (HHDs)** that use flash memory to speed up the boot process.

FIGURE 3.24 Flash drives provide a durable, lightweight alternative to hard disks.

Another form of flash storage is the USB flash drive. **USB flash drives**, also known as **memory sticks**, **thumb drives**, or **jump drives**, are popular **portable**, or **removable**, **storage** devices. Because of their small size and universal ease of use, they have supplanted floppy disks and Zip disks as the removable storage medium of choice. Both floppy disks and Zip disks are now considered legacy technologies. USB flash drives work with both the PC and the Mac. No device driver is required—just plug it into a USB port and it's ready to read and write. USB flash drives are made of plastic and are shock-proof, moisture-proof, and magnetization-proof. Many USB flash drives include security and encryption software to help protect your data in case you lose it. Some devices have a retractable USB connector, eliminating the need for a protective cap, which is often misplaced. Others are available in different colors and novelty shapes (Figure 3.25).

a

One interesting characteristic is that the drives get their power supply from the device they are plugged into. Capacities range from 1 GB to 64 GB, and they are able to read and write at speeds up to 30 Mbps. Watch for capacities to go up and prices to come down.

Because your USB drive has no moving parts, it can be difficult to tell when it is working. Usually, if the contents of a USB drive are being accessed, a small LED light on the drive flashes. It is very important not to disconnect the flash drive when a file is being saved or accessed, because this can corrupt the data. Make sure any files on your USB drive are closed, then look for the Safely Remove Hardware icon in the system tray on the bottom right side of the screen. Double-click the icon to open the dialog box, then select USB Mass Storage Device and click the Stop button. Another box may appear with a list of USB devices—if it does, click the device name that matches the USB flash drive, then click OK. Unplug the flash drive when the message appears indicating that it is safe to do so.

CD AND DVD TECHNOLOGIES

Software, music, and movies used to be distributed primarily on CDs and DVDs, however today direct downloads from the Internet have caused some manufacturers to make these drives an optional component of the system unit. If a unit does not come with a CD or DVD drive, you can purchase an external unit and connect it via the USB port. **CD-ROM** (short for **compact disc read-only memory**) and **DVD-ROM (digital video** [or **versatile**] **disc read-only memory)** are the most

popular and least expensive types of optical disc standards and are referred to as optical storage devices. These discs are read-only discs, which means that the data recorded on them can be read many times, but it cannot be changed or erased. Notice that when the storage medium is optical, the correct spelling is *disc*. Magnetic storage media are spelled with a *k—disk*.

A **CD drive** and a **DVD drive** (Figure 3.26) are read-only disk drives that read data encoded on CDs and DVDs and transfer this data to a computer. These drives are referred to as optical

b

storage devices. **Optical storage devices** use tightly focused laser beams to read microscopic patterns of data encoded on the surface of plastic discs (Figure 3.27). The format of a CD or DVD includes microscopic indentations called **pits** that scatter the laser's light in certain areas. The drive's light-sensing device receives no light from these areas, so it sends a signal to the computer that corresponds to a 0 in the computer's binary numbering system. Flat reflective areas called **lands** bounce the light back to a light-sensing

FIGURE 3.25 Many USB flash drives retract to protect the USB connector (**a**), whereas others (**b**) take a more unique approach to data storage.

FIGURE 3.26 CD and DVD drives use popular and inexpensive optical discs.

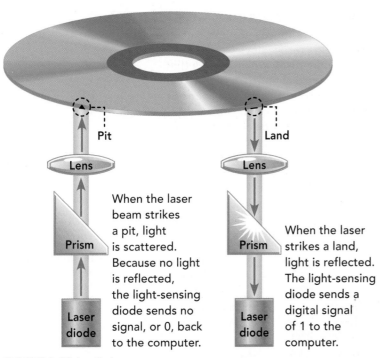

When the laser beam strikes a pit, light is scattered. Because no light is reflected, the light-sensing diode sends no signal, or 0, back to the computer.

When the laser strikes a land, light is reflected. The light-sensing diode sends a digital signal of 1 to the computer.

FIGURE 3.27 In optical storage devices such as CD and DVD drives, a tightly focused laser beam reads data encoded on the disc's surface. Some optical devices write data as well as read it.

device, which sends a signal equivalent to a binary 1.

CD-ROMs can store up to 700 MB of data. They are a different format than the audio CDs, from which they evolved, in that some space is used for an additional level of error detecting and correcting code. This is necessary because data CDs cannot tolerate the loss of a handful of bits now and then, the way audio CDs can. DVD-ROMs store up to 17 GB of data—enough for an entire digitized movie. Whereas CD drives transfer data at speeds of up to 150 Kbps, DVD drives transfer data at even higher speeds (up to 12 Mbps; comparable to the data transfer rates of hard drives). DVD drives read CD-ROMs as well as DVD-ROMs.

FIGURE 3.28 ExpressCards are about the size of a credit card and fit into ExpressCard slots, which are standard in most notebooks.

CD-R, CD-RW, DVD-R, and DVD+RW Discs and Recorders Several types of optical read/write media and devices are available. Many PCs now include a combination drive that read and write CDs and DVDs. For this reason, these read/write discs are a popular,

cost-effective alternative medium for archival and storage purposes.

CD-R (short for **compact disc–recordable**) is a "write-once" technology. After you've saved data to the disc, you can't erase or write over it. An advantage of CD-Rs is that they are relatively inexpensive. **CD-RW** (short for **compact disc–rewritable**), which is more expensive than CD-R, allows data that has been saved to be erased and rewritten. **CD-RW drives**, also known as **burners** or **CD burners**, provide full read/write capabilities.

DVDs come in two standards. The first (newer) format is the DVD+ (DVD plus) standard. This standard employs two types of discs, DVD+R and the DVD+RW. **DVD+R** is a recordable format that enables the disc to be written to one time and read many times. The **DVD+RW** is a recordable format that enables the disc to be rewritten to many times.

The second format, which is older and more compatible, is the DVD– (DVD dash) standard. **DVD-R** operates the same way as CD-R; you can write to the disc once and read from it many times. With **DVD-RW**, you can write to, erase, and read from the disc many times.

One of the newest forms of optical storage, Blu-ray, also known as Blu-ray Disc, is the name of a next-generation optical disc format jointly developed by the Blu-ray Disc Association (BDA, a group of the world's leading consumer electronics, personal computer, and media manufacturers, including Apple, Dell, Hitachi, HP, JVC, LG, Mitsubishi, Panasonic, Pioneer, Philips, Samsung, Sharp, Sony, TDK, and Thomson). The name is derived from the blue-violet laser beams (blue rays) used to read and write data. The **Blu-ray Disc (BD)** format was developed to enable recording, rewriting, and playing back of high-definition video (HD), as well as storing large amounts of data. The format offers more than five times the storage capacity of traditional DVDs and can hold up to 25 GB on a single-layer disc and 50 GB on a dual-layer disc—the equivalent of 9 hours of high-definition video or 23 hours of standard definition (SD) video. This extra capacity combined with the use of advanced video and audio features offers consumers an unprecedented HD experience.

Multilayer discs capable of even more storage are under development. **BD-ROM** discs are a read-only format used for video or data distribution. **BD-R** is a recordable disc useful for HD video or PC data storage, and **BD-RE** is the rewritable format, allowing data or video to be recorded and erased as needed. Currently, a dedicated Blu-ray player or recorder is required to use this new technology; however, there are plans to create a hybrid Blu-ray Disc/DVD that can be used in Blu-ray or DVD players. It is expected that Blu-ray will eventually replace DVDs, especially when HDTVs become more commonplace.

Protecting the Data on Your Discs As with magnetic disks, it's important that you handle CDs and DVDs carefully. The following are a few things to remember when caring for discs:

- Do not expose discs to excessive heat or sunlight.
- Do not touch the underside of discs. Hold them by their edges.
- Do not write on the label side of discs with a hard instrument, such as a ballpoint pen.
- To avoid scratches, do not stack discs.
- Store discs in jewel boxes (plastic protective cases) or paper-like sleeves when not being used.

SOLID-STATE STORAGE DEVICES

A **solid-state storage device** consists of nonvolatile memory chips, which retain the data stored in them even if the chips are disconnected from a computer or power source. The term *solid state* indicates that these devices have no moving parts; they consist only of semiconductors. Solid-state storage devices have important advantages over mechanical storage devices such as hard disk drives: They are small, lightweight, highly reliable, and portable. In addition to the flash drives discussed earlier, some solid-state storage devices in common use are ExpressCards, flash memory cards, and smart cards.

An **ExpressCard** is a credit card–sized accessory typically used with notebook computers (Figure 3.28). Previous versions were known as **PC cards** or **PCMCIA cards**. ExpressCards can serve a variety of functions. For example, some Express-Cards are modems, others are network adapters, and still others provide additional memory or storage capacity.

When used as storage devices, ExpressCards are most commonly used to transfer data from one computer to another. (However, each computer must have an ExpressCard slot.) For example, a notebook computer user can store documents created on a business trip on a solid-state memory card and then transfer the documents to a desktop computer.

ExpressCards follow standards set by the Personal Computer Memory Card International Association (PCMCIA), a consortium of industry vendors. As a result, a notebook computer equipped with an ExpressCard slot can use ExpressCards from any ExpressCard vendor.

Flash memory cards (Figure 3.29), which use nonvolatile flash memory chips, are becoming increasingly popular. **Flash memory cards** are wafer-thin, highly portable solid-state storage systems

FIGURE 3.29 Flash memory cards are thin, portable solid-state storage systems.

FIGURE 3.30 A flash memory reader can be used to transfer the contents of a memory card to your PC.

that are capable of storing as much as 64 GB of data. They are also used with smartphones, MP3 players, digital video cameras, and other portable digital devices. To use a flash memory card, the device must have a compatible **flash memory reader**—a slot or compartment into which the flash memory card is inserted (Figure 3.30).

The SmartMedia flash memory card was one of the first examples of this technology. Many others, in various sizes and storage capacities, soon followed, including CompactFlash, Secure Digital, Memory Stick, miniSD, and microSD. It is important to know what type of memory card a specific device requires, because they are not interchangeable.

A **smart card**, also known as a **chip card** or an **integrated circuit card (ICC)**, is a credit card–sized device that combines flash memory with a tiny microprocessor, enabling the card to process as well as store information. It is viewed as a replacement for magnetic stripe cards, from which data is eventually lost. Smart cards, not being magnetic, provide an additional longevity and may include a hologram to help prevent counterfeiting. Smart cards also promote quicker transactions with little need for personal interaction. If you've ever waved your card at the gas pump to pay for your gas or used a specially encoded student ID card to pay for your meal in the dining hall or unlock your dorm room, you may have used a smart card (Figure 3.31).

More smart card applications exist or are on the way. For example, **digital cash systems**, which are widespread in Europe and Asia, enable users to purchase a prepaid amount of electronically stored money to pay the small amounts required for parking, bridge tolls, transport fares, museum entrance fees, and similar charges.

STORAGE HORIZONS

In response to the explosive demand for more storage capacity, designers are creating storage media and devices that store larger amounts of data and retrieve it more quickly. Exemplifying these trends are holographic storage and wireless flash memory cards.

Holographic Storage **Holographic storage** uses two laser beams to create a pattern on photosensitive media, resulting in a three-dimensional image similar to the holograms you can buy in a novelty shop. It is anticipated that this 3-D approach will enable much higher-density storage capacities and is being promoted for its archiving capabilities. Although still under development, experts predict that holographic storage may enable us to store terabytes of data in a space no thicker than the width of several CDs. Or to put it another way, imagine storing 50,000 music files on an object the size of a postage stamp!

Wireless Memory Cards The Eye-Fi **wireless memory card** takes all the storage features of a regular flash memory

FIGURE 3.31 Smart cards can be used for quick transactions, to identify the user, or to access electronically controlled doors.

card and combines it with wireless circuitry so it can connect with your PC via a wireless network or send pictures directly from your digital camera to your favorite online photo site. The Eye-Fi card can store up to 2 GB of pictures and works like a traditional memory card if you are out of wireless range. Digital photography is the only application this wireless memory card is currently marketed for, but new uses are being explored.

Racetrack Memory Flash memory and hard drives are the main storage devices in today's computing devices. But the designers of storage devices constantly face these challenges: making data storage more cost effective, reducing the size of storage devices, and decreasing the power consumption of storage devices. These issues are extremely critical for mobile devices. Hard drives and flash memory may eventually be replaced by a new technology called "racetrack" memory, which is under development by Stuart Parkin and his colleagues at IBM's Almaden Research Center.

Racetrack memory uses the spin of electrons to store information. This allows the memory to operate at much higher speeds than today's storage media, which is a boon for transferring and retrieving data. In addition, it is anticipated that racetrack memory will consume much less power and that mobile devices may be able to run for as long as several weeks on a single charge. After the memory is rolled out for the mass market, it should be even cheaper to produce than flash memory.

A current limitation of flash memory is that it can only be written to (store data) several thousand times before it wears out. Racetrack memory will not suffer from this limitation and will have no moving parts, making it much less susceptible to breakage than conventional hard drives. The capacity of racetrack memory could allow iPods to store 500,000 songs instead of the 40,000 that the largest units can handle today.

Use Secondary Storage Devices and Media to Back up Your Data Data on any secondary storage device, like a USB drive or a hard drive, will at some point get damaged or "lost" and be unretrievable. A wise computer user has a backup strategy in place and uses it. A **backup** is a copy of programs, data, and information created in one secondary storage medium that duplicated to another. Ask yourself the following questions to determine the best backup strategy:

- How much data do you have to backup?
- Do you need to back up every program and all data files at every backup or just those data files that were recently modified?
- How large are the files? Is there enough room on the backup media for all of the files?
- Should you use a remote service?
- How frequently will you perform a backup?
- What is the capacity of the backup storage media?
- Will you backup manually by using the copy and paste command or purchase a backup program that can be set up to automatically backup certain folders at certain intervals (Figure 3.32)?
- Have you located a secure remote location to keep your backup copies?

Do not take backing up your data lightly. If you don't backup on a regular schedule, you could permanently lose critical data and information, resulting in frustration, time wasted on recreating the data, and loss of revenue.

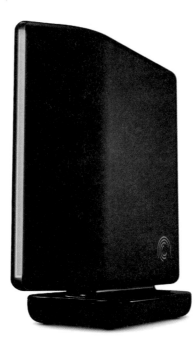

FIGURE 3.32 Products such as the Seagate FreeAgent Pro external hard drive include software that allows you to back up files as you create them.

Chapter Summary

Input/Output and Storage

The computer's main input devices are the keyboard and mouse. Other pointing devices include trackballs, pointing sticks, touchpads, joysticks, touch screens, and styluses.

Outputs devices that produce soft copy (not permanent) are monitors and speakers. The two main types of monitors are liquid crystal displays (LCD) and cathode-ray tube (CRT), which is now considered a legacy technology.

Printers are output devices that produce hard copy. The most popular printers use inkjet or laser technology. Inkjet printers produce excellent-quality text and images for a reasonable price. However, they are slow and ink cartridges may be expensive. Laser printers are faster and produce excellent-quality text and graphics, but color models are expensive.

Storage devices save programs, data, and information on nonvolatile storage media. These types of media retain information even when the power is switched off. Storage media and devices can be categorized as read only or read/write; random access; magnetic, flash, or optical; and secondary (online or fixed), external, or portable (or removable). Examples of storage media are CD-R, DVD-R, and DVD+R, which are read-only technologies. Such discs can record once. Hard disks, CD-RW, DVD-RW, and DVD+RW, flash drives, USB flash drives, and memory cards can be rewritten to multiple times.

Key Terms and Concepts

Matching

Match each key term in the left column with the most accurate definition in the right column.

_____ 1. plotter

_____ 2. access time

_____ 3. laser printer

_____ 4. virtual laser keyboard

_____ 5. FAT

_____ 6. resolution

_____ 7. seek time

_____ 8. NTFS

_____ 9. trackball

_____ 10. hybrid hard drive

_____ 11. inkjet printer

_____ 12. stylus

_____ 13. touchpad

_____ 14. soft keyboard

_____ 15. transfer performance

a. Measure of image sharpness.

b. The time from the request for the information to the delivery of the information.

c. A stationary pointing device that contains a movable ball in a cradle.

d. An input device that appears as a keyboard on a touch-sensitive screen.

e. A table hidden on a disk that keeps records concerning the storage location of files on older Windows operating systems.

f. The time it takes the read/write head to move data from the hard disk to random access memory.

g. A nonimpact printer that forms characters by spraying ink from a series of small nozzles.

h. A magnetic storage device that uses flash memory to improve the time it takes to boot up.

i. An input device that looks like a pen and is used as an alternative to fingers on a touch-screen device.

j. A keyboard projected onto almost any surface by a small device, approximately the size of a cell phone. The movement of the user's fingers are interpreted into key strokes.

k. A stationary, pressure-sensitive pointing device that has a small flat surface on which you slide your finger to activate mouse movement.

l. The time it takes for the read/write head to locate the information on the disk.

m. A file allocation system for newer operating systems like Vista and Windows 7.

n. A nonimpact printer that uses the electrostatic reproduction technology of copying machines.

o. A printer that produces high-quality output by moving pens over the surface of papers.

Multiple Choice

Circle the correct choice for each of the following.

1. Which storage media uses laser beams to create three-dimensioned storage images?
   a. CD   b. Flash
   c. DVD   d. Holographic

2. Which of the following is an output device?
   a. Speaker   b. Microphone
   c. Internet hard drive   d. Smart card

3. A flash drive is an example of _____ storage.
   a. Optical   b. Magnetic
   c. Solid-state   d. Cache

4. Which is *not* an action performed using a pointing device?
   a. Selecting   b. Tagging
   c. Clicking   d. Double-clicking

5. What is a unit of memory on a flash drive called?
   a. Platter   b. Cluster
   c. Block   d. Sector

6. Which term describes what you create in order to compartmentalize a hard drive so that it is capable of storing two operating systems and allowing you to select one at start-up?
   a. Sector   b. Tag
   c. Cluster   d. Partition

7. What is the name of the grid of circuits located under the keys of a keyboard?
   a. Express grid   b. Soft keyboard
   c. Key matrix   d. Character map

8. In a hard disk drive, the two or more rapidly rotating disks used as storage media are called _____.
   a. Platters   b. Cache
   c. Sectors   d. FATs

9. Which is *not* an example of secondary storage?_____
   a. USB drive   b. RAM
   c. DVD-ROM   d. Hard drive

10. Which of the following statements about flash storage is true?
    a. Flash storage is not portable.
    b. Flash storage does not require an installed device driver.
    c. The largest flash storage device is 8 gigabytes.
    d. Flash storage is also called Internet storage.

Fill-In

In the blanks provided, write the correct answer for each of the following.

1. Making an exact copy of programs and data from one storage device to another is called making a(n) _____.

2. Keys like Ctrl and Shift that change the meaning of the next key pressed are called a(n) _____ keys.

3. A(n) _____ _____ - _____ projector is an output device that projects a computer's monitor display on a screen by using millions of microscopic mirrors.

4. A(n) _____ device often combines a printer, scanner, and copier.

5. A(n) _____ is an output device that comes with OCR software installed.

6. _____ _____ is the conversion of spoken words to computer text.

7. _____ is a form of optical storage media that holds up to 17 GB of information and can be written on, read from, and erased many times.

8. Hard disks are a form of _____ storage media.

9. An input device found at ATMs and airport check-ins is a(n) _____ _____.

10. Optical storage devices use laser beams to read data patterns formed by indented _____ and flat _____.

11. _____ _____ is memory that uses the spin of electrons to store information.

12. Remove a USB drive by using the Remove Hardware icon located in the _____ _____.

13. Trackballs, joysticks, and scanners are all examples of _____ devices.

14. Flash, jump, or thumb drives connect to a computer system through _____ ports.

15. The keys located at the top of the keyboard and labeled F1 through F12 are called _____ keys.

Short Answer

1. Today there are the three types of optical storage devices. State the name of each and specify the amount and type of data each can hold.

2. Define *remote storage* and cite three reasons for using remote storage to back up your programs and data.

3. Define the term *solid state* and give three examples of solid-state storage devices.

4. Name the two most common types of printers and briefly explain how they operate.

5. What are three things that a user can do to protect data from being damaged on a CD or DVD?

Teamwork

1. **Input Device Usage** Have all team members make a list of the input devices they use every day for a week. Indicate the type of input device, the location or transaction it was used for, and the time of day. (For example: GPS in the car, 8:00 AM; touch screen at the bank, 1:00 PM.) At the end of the week, combine your lists into one and see whether any devices, uses, or times of day are related. Present the combined list and any conclusions in a report no longer than two double-spaced pages.

2. **Output, Output, and More Output** Have each team member keep a list for one week of the methods by which he or she received output (a response to input) throughout each day. Indicate whether the output was audio (a phone message or verbal reply), printed (a sales receipt), or visual (a display); the location; transaction the output was received for; and the time of day. (For example: phone message at 10:00 AM Monday about meeting on Friday, a paper receipt from the bank at 3:00 PM on Thursday.) At the end of the week, combine your lists into a team list and see whether you can detect any trends. Present the combined list and any conclusions in a report no longer than two double-spaced pages.

3. **RAM Memory and Secondary Storage over Time** The amount of RAM memory and hard drive storage vary from system to system. Break your team into two groups and locate a minimum of eight computer systems. Be sure to include some desktop models and some notebooks. Ask the system owner or use the control panel to determine the year purchased (or operating system version), amount of RAM on the system, and size of the internal hard drive. Combine your team's data into one chart or table. Draw at least three conclusions from the data collected about desktops versus notebooks and the changes in RAM amount and hard disk size over the years. If you see a trend, let a team member with some math skills determine what the RAM amount and hard drive size will be in 5 years. Present your results in a one-page, double-spaced report containing your table and conclusions.

4. **The Relationship between Applications and Storage** Have your team select five software application programs that members are familiar with. Some common programs are Word, Excel, Access, and PowerPoint, but team members will likely have experience with others. Research the programs and find out how much hard disk space each requires in order to be installed on a system. Then create files, or locate files created in each program, and check their file size in the My Computer window. Make a list of the elements in each file (number of words, records or rows; number of pictures or animations; amount of sound; and so on) and the size of the file. From your data, draw a conclusion about the file sizes and their relation to the type of elements found in the file. Combine all of the data and your conclusions into a one-page, double-spaced report.

5. **Portable Memory Choices** As a team, research portable memory devices. Include memory sticks, memory cards (used in digital cameras), and USB flash drives. As a group, list each device in a table with its current manufacturer, and compare each device's cost per megabyte and maximum storage capacity. Include a picture of each device, if possible. Come to a group consensus as to which portable device the team prefers. Present the table, your conclusion, and the reasons for your decision in a one-page, double-spaced report.

On the Web

1. **Adaptive Technologies** Visit **www.indiana.edu/~iuadapts/technology/index.html** and **www.maltron.com/** to begin research on alternative software and hardware devices to aid individuals with disabilities. Using these sites and at least two other Web sites, find four hardware devices and/or software programs that interest you. In a one- to two-page, double-spaced report, describe each device or program, list the manufacturer, describe the population it would service, list the cost, provide a picture of the device or a screen capture of the program, and cite your references.

2. **Storage Forever?** The amount of data that must be stored and retained is increasing yearly. Keeping all data records forever is impractical. Use the Web to research the length different types of data should be retained. Use at least three to five Web sites and make a list of the data type and the recommendations for storage time. Cite your references and summarize your results in a one-page, double-spaced paper.

3. **Internet Storage** If your hard drive is running out of room, one method for increasing your storage capacity is to use an Internet hard drive. Visit the Mozy site at **www.mozy.com** and the flip drive site at **www.flipdrive.com** to learn more about Internet storage sites. Perform a Web search to determine which two major ISPs also offer Internet storage. List at least two advantages and two disadvantages of using Internet storage. Compare a site that offers free storage and one that charges. For each site, describe the following:

   • The registration process

   • The amount of free storage space or the cost of storage

   • Additional services provided

   Would you consider using this site? Explain why or why not. Write a one- to two-page, double-spaced paper that cites your references and discusses your findings.

4. **Talk, Talk, Talk** One of the features of Windows 7 and Microsoft Vista is the embedded speech recognition feature. Go to your favorite search engine and type in the keywords "Windows 7 Speech Recognition" and "Vista Speech Recognition" to learn about this method of entering input. Go to the Microsoft site (**www.microsoft.com**) and enter the same keywords in the search box there. On the basis of your research, what three actions can speech recognition help users perform? What types of users will benefit from this technology? What are two suggestions for minimizing speech-recognition errors? Cite your references and present your findings in a one-page, double-spaced paper.

5. **Hear the Sound** Use your favorite browser and search engine to find information on surround sound and subwoofer systems for PCs. What is the range of costs for such systems? What components are required? Is it acceptable to buy at the low end, or is there a mid-range point that will ensure a good result? Is there much to install? Can a non-technical person install a surround sound system? Based on your research, which system would you recommend? (Include a list of the components and the cost.) Why? Construct a one-page summary of these questions aimed at the novice user. The paper should help the reader understand surround-sound systems.

File Management

You've just finished your term paper—where should you save it?

You never know when you may need a writing sample for a graduate school or job application, so you'll want to keep it someplace safe. The secret to finding what you're looking for in the future is good file management now. Managing computer files is an essential skill for any computer user.

For most people, managing files is intuitive; it's simple once they learn the basics. You can think of managing computer files as being similar to the way you organize and store paper files and folders in a file cabinet (Figure 2A). You start with a storage device (the filing cabinet), divide it into definable sections (folders), and then fill the sections with specific items (documents) that fit the defined sections. Most people tend to organize the things in their lives, and the organizational principles used are the same ones used when managing computer files.

The Big Picture: Files, Folders, and Paths

A **file** is a named unit of related data stored in a computer system. Your data and the programs installed on your computer are stored in files. Files store Word documents, music, photo images, Excel spreadsheets, applications, and a variety of other digital compilations.

FIGURE 2A You can organize files on your computer the same way you would organize documents in a filing cabinet.

Every file that is stored has certain properties. A **property** is a setting that provides information such as the file's date of creation, its size, and the date it was last modified.

You use **folders** (also called **directories**) to organize groups of files that have something in common. Many folders have **subfolders**—folders within folders—that enable you to organize your files even further. For example, you might create a folder called "Classes," and then create subfolders for each school term, and then subfolders within each school term for your individual courses (Figure 2B).

All of the files and folders you create must reside on a storage device called a **drive**. The primary storage devices on desktop computers are the hard drive, the CD and DVD drives, the external hard drives, and USB flash drives. Older computers may also have a floppy disk drive. On PCs, these storage devices are designated by drive letters. A **drive letter** is simply a letter of the

alphabet followed by a colon and a backslash character. If your computer has a floppy disk drive, it is typically referred to as A:\. The hard drive is generally referred to as C:\. The CD or DVD drive might be labeled drive D (D:\), and other drives are often labeled sequentially, so a USB flash drive might be labeled drive E (E:\). (On the Mac, drives are not labeled with letters. You'll see them as icons appearing on your screen.)

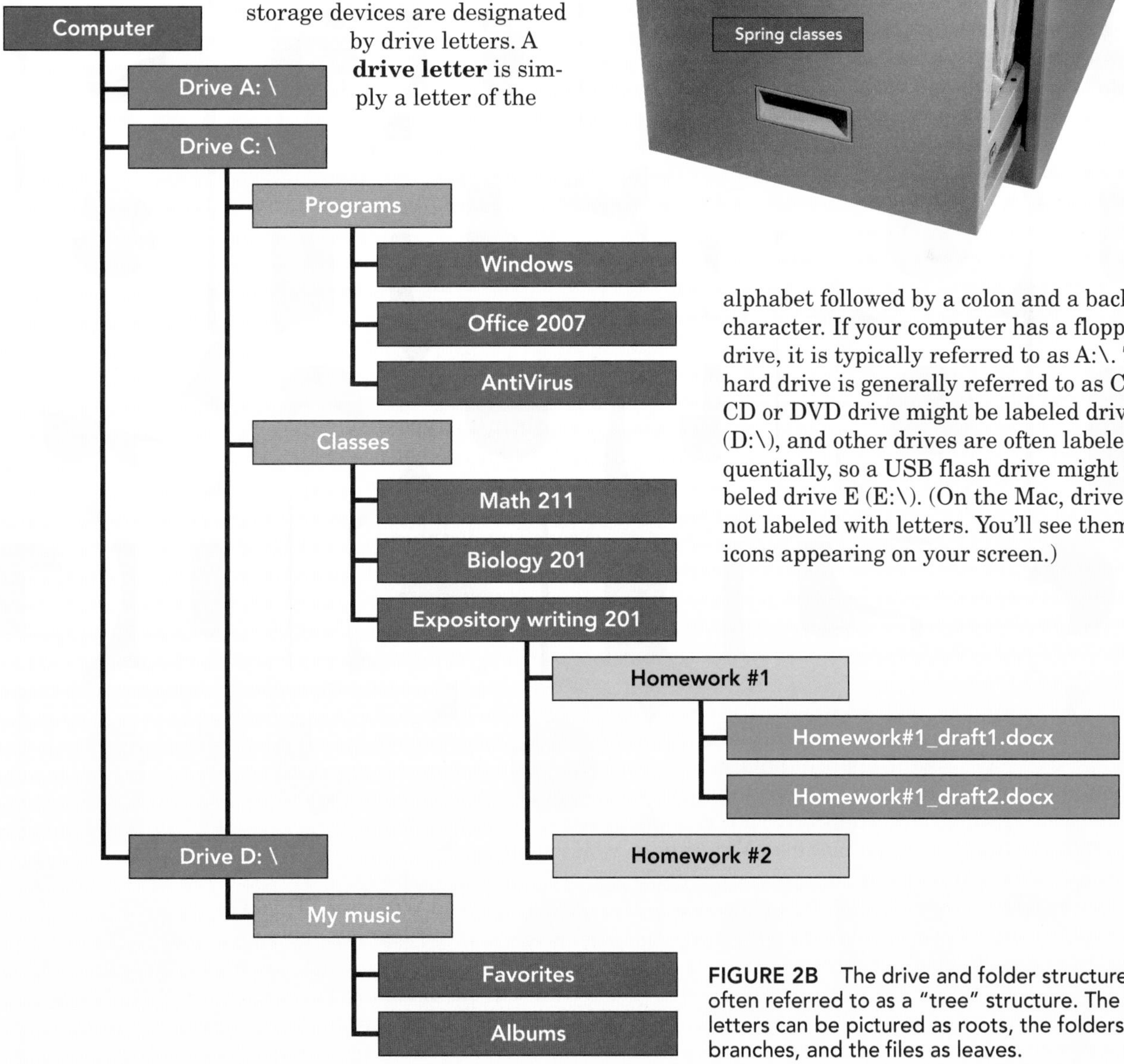

FIGURE 2B The drive and folder structure is often referred to as a "tree" structure. The drive letters can be pictured as roots, the folders as branches, and the files as leaves.

For the computer to access a particular file, it needs to know the path it should take to get to the file. A **path** is the sequence of directories that the computer must follow to locate a file. A typical path might look like this:

C:\Classes\ Expository Writing 201\
Homework#1_draft1.docx

In this case, the C:\ in the path indicates that the file is located on the C:\ drive. The **top-level folder**, "Classes," contains, as the name indicates, things that have to do with classes. The subfolder named "Expository Writing 201" is the subfolder for your writing class. The file at the end of the path, "Homework#1_draft1.docx," is the first draft of your first homework assignment. The .docx extension indicates that the file is a Microsoft Word 2007 document. We'll discuss file names in greater depth shortly. Figure 2B illustrates what a hierarchical drive, folder, and file structure might look like.

FILE-NAMING CONVENTIONS

To save a file, you need to know where you're going to store it—in other words, on which storage device and in which folder. In addition, each file needs a specific file name. The **file name** is the name that the storage device uses to identify each unique file, so the name must differ from all other file names used within the same folder or directory. You may use the same name for different files, but they must exist on different drives or in different folders. Be careful to include enough detail in naming a file so that you will be able to recognize the file name when you need the file later. The name you use when you create a file is usually very obvious to you at the time—but the name may elude you when you try to remember it in the future.

Every file name on a PC has two parts that are separated by a period (read as "dot"). The first part, the part you're probably most familiar with, is called the **name**. The second part is called the **extension**, an addition to the file name, typically three to five characters in length. In a file called "Homework#1_draft1.docx," Homework#1_draft1 is the name and .docx is the extension; together they make up the file name.

Typically, an extension is used to identify the type of data that the file contains (or the format it is stored in). Sometimes it indicates the application used to create the file. In Microsoft Windows, each application automatically assigns an extension to a file when you save it for the first time. For example, Microsoft Word 2007 automatically assigns the .docx extension. Workbooks created in Microsoft Excel 2007 use the .xlsx extension. When naming files, you never need to be concerned about typing in an extension, because all programs attach their extension to the file name by default.

FIGURE 2C Commonly Used File Name Extensions

Extension	File Type
.exe	Program or application
.docx	Microsoft Word 2007
.xlsx	Microsoft Excel 2007
.pptx	Microsoft PowerPoint 2007
.accdb	Microsoft Access 2007
.pdf	Adobe Acrobat
.txt	ASCII text
.htm or .html	Web pages
.rtf	Files in rich text format
.jpeg or .jpg	Picture or image format

Program files, also called application files, usually use the .exe extension, which stands for executable. The term *executable* is used because when you use an application, you execute, or run, the file. Figure 2C lists several of the most commonly used extensions and their file types. Note that when using Mac OS, extensions are not needed because Macintosh files contain a code representing the name of the application that created the file. However, it is generally recommended that Mac users add the appropriate extension to their file names so that they can more easily exchange them with PC users and avoid conversion problems.

In Microsoft Windows 7, you can use up to 260 characters in a file name, including spaces. However, this length restriction includes the entire file path name; therefore, file names actually need to be shorter than 260 characters to be valid. Windows file names cannot include any of the following characters: forward slash (/), backslash (\), greater than sign (>), less than sign (<), asterisk (*), question mark (?), quotation mark ("), pipe symbol (|), colon (:), or semicolon (;). In Mac OS and Windows XP, you can use up to 255 characters in a filename, including spaces, and all characters except the colon. Although you can use a large number of characters to create a file name, it is still best to keep file names concise and meaningful.

Longer file names may be subject to automatic truncation (shortening), which can create file management difficulties.

Now that you understand the basics of paths, folders, and file-naming conventions, let's turn our attention to the business of managing files.

Managing Files

Files can be managed in two ways: (1) with a file management utility such as Windows Explorer or (2) from within the programs that create them. In the following sections, we'll explore both methods.

FILE MANAGEMENT UTILITIES

Microsoft Windows uses the Windows Explorer program for file management. There are a number of ways that you can launch this program. The Start, All Programs, Accessories menu sequence is one method. Another method is to click Start and select one of the options shown on the top right side of the Start menu to view the contents of a specific folder (Figure 2D). The Start menu can also be used to access the Computer folder, which lets you view the disk drives and other hardware connected to your computer (Figure 2E).

The Windows Explorer program in Windows 7 has a number of new features that make file management easier and more versatile. The Windows Explorer window includes navigation buttons, an address bar (also known as a breadcrumb bar), a search box, and a toolbar at the top of the window. The main body of the window is split into two panes—a navigation pane and

FIGURE 2D   The Start menu provides various options for viewing commonly accessed files and programs.

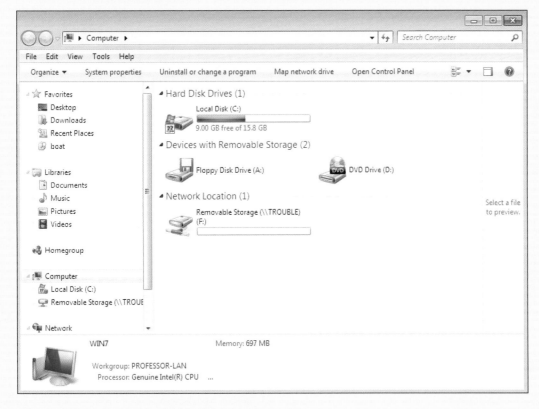

FIGURE 2E   The Computer window provides quick access to information about the disk drives and other hardware that are connected to your computer.

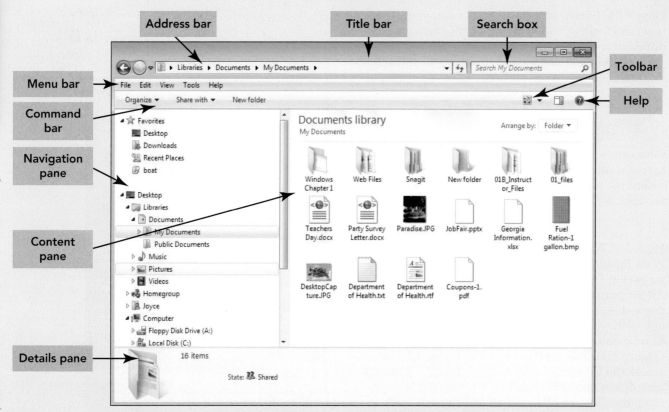

Address bar

Title bar

Search box

Menu bar

Command bar

Navigation pane

Content pane

Details pane

Toolbar

Help

FIGURE 2F Windows Explorer is a useful and versatile file management tool.

a content pane—and a detail pane is displayed at the bottom of the window (Figure 2F). The **navigation pane** on the left allows you to navigate directly to specific folders listed in the Favorite Links area or access a prior search that you have saved by clicking on a desired folder. You can also add a shortcut to a frequently used folder by dragging the folder into the Favorite Links area of the navigation pane. At the bottom

FIGURE 2G The drop-down list on the Date Modified heading provides a way to group files and folders by date.

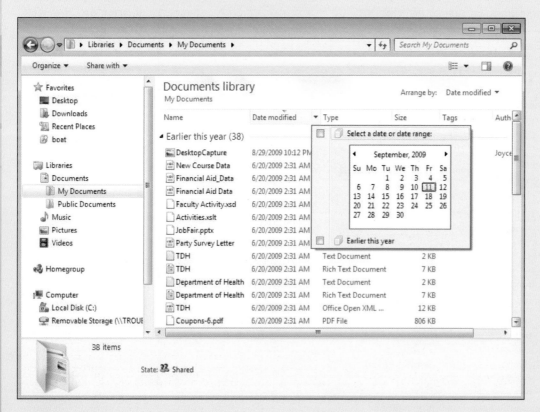

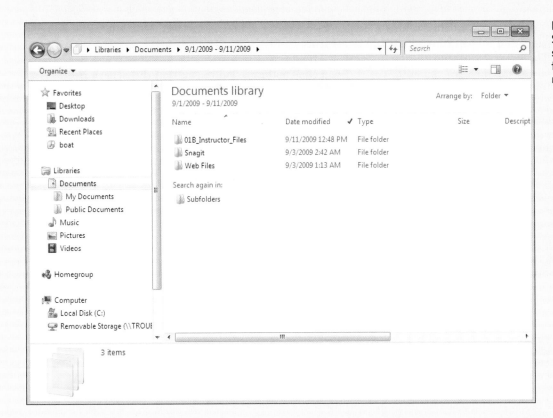

FIGURE 2H   The Select by date range shows only files and folders created or modified in that range.

of the navigation pane is a Folders bar. Expanding this bar displays a hierarchical list of all folders and drives on the computer and also provides access to areas such as the Desktop, Control Panel, Computer, Libraries, and Network.

The right pane, or **content pane**, sometimes called a **file list**, displays subfolders and files located within the selected folder. The column headings at the top of the file list can be used to change how the files are organized. New column headings can be added by right-clicking a heading and selecting one or more from the shortcut menu. You can also delete column headings by selecting the heading that is checked. As in previous versions of Windows Explorer, it is possible to sort the contents of a folder, but users can now also group, stack, and filter the items displayed in the right pane. To sort, simply click a column heading; click the column heading a second time to reverse the sort order. A sorted column displays a small triangle in the column heading; the direction of the triangle indicates whether the column has been sorted in ascending or descending order. If a folder contains subfolders and files, the subfolders are sorted separately from the files.

To access the group options, click the drop-down arrow beside the column heading to reveal the submenu. The group option arranges files and folders within specified groups, depending on the column heading you've selected. You can select how you want to group files and folders (Figure 2G). It is possible to select files and folders by the date they were modified (Figure 2H).

The **address bar** has also been updated. It is now possible to use it for breadcrumb navigation. The address bar displays the route you've taken to get to the current location. It may or may not correspond with a file's path name. To view the actual path name, click the icon on the left side of the address bar. The breadcrumbs can be used to easily move from one location to another—simply click the drop-down arrow to reveal a list of destinations (Figure 2I).

FIGURE 2I   The address bar lets users navigate by breadcrumbs. Click the drop-down arrow to reveal a list of possible destinations.

The **details pane** at the bottom of the window provides a thumbnail view and information about the selected file or folder. The details vary depending on the object that has been selected. Users can edit many of these items. Just click the item you wish to change, revise it, and press the Save button.

You can view the contents of the right pane in several ways. Seven different view options are accessible from the View menu or from the Views button on the Standard toolbar. You can click the Views button to cycle through the choices or click the drop-down arrow next to the button to make a selection. The Tile view and various icon views are particularly helpful if you're searching through pictures and photographs, because they show you a small copy of the images you have in the folder—before you open them. The List view simply lists the names of the files, whereas the Details view offers you information regarding file size, file type, and the date a file was last modified.

Locating Files and Folders Despite your best efforts, it's possible to forget where you've saved a file. The **Search box** in Windows Explorer can make this process less painful. Select one of the main folders, such as Documents and begin typing a search term in the box. As you type, Windows Explorer searches the contents of the folder and subfolders, immediately filtering the view to display any files that match the search term. Windows Explorer searches file names, file properties, and file contents for the search term. If the search returns too many results, or you need to

create a more complex search, the Advanced Search feature can help.

If you can't locate the file or folder using Search, you can customize your search in the Search Documents window by adding a filter (Figure 2J). If you find that you are often searching for the same files, click the Save Search button on the toolbar. Assign a name for your search and, by default, the results will be stored in the Searches folder. Searches are **dynamic**, which means that the next time you open a saved search, the results are automatically refreshed—new files are added and files that no longer meet the search criteria are not included.

In this example, the folder's contents have been filtered to display only those files that were modified within the current week.

Creating Folders Another way to manage your files effectively is to create a **folder**, or directory, **structure** (the terms *folder* and *directory* are synonymous)—an organized set of folders in which to save your files. The process of creating a folder structure is accomplished in two steps:

Step 1. Decide which drive, such as a USB flash drive, hard drive, or CD drive, you will create your folder on. To create a folder on your computer's hard disk drive, click the Start menu and select your personal folder—typically, this folder will use your name and will appear at the top of the Start menu. Windows Explorer will open with a number of commonly used folders,

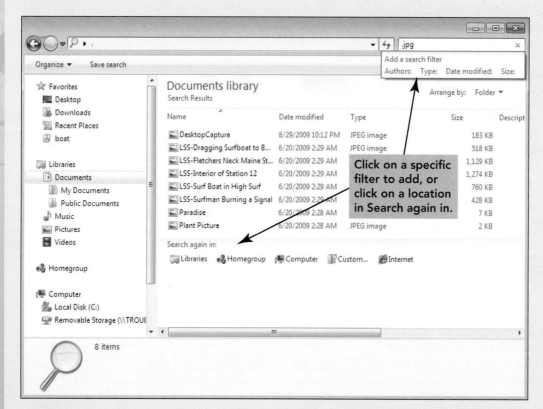

FIGURE 2J You can add a search filter or, if you do not see the file you need, you can search other locations.

such as Documents, Pictures, and Music, displayed in the right pane. If you prefer to create your folder on a removable storage device, instead choose Computer from the Start menu and double-click the storage device you wish to use.

Step 2. Select a folder, such as Documents, and double-click it. While pointing to the right pane, right-click and choose "New" and then "Folder" from the shortcut menus to create a folder within the selected folder. In other words, if you have selected the Documents library, the new folder will be placed at the top level. See Figure 2K for an example of a new folder that has been created within the Documents library.

You can repeat this process as many times as is necessary to create your desired folder structure. For example, if you're taking three classes, you might want to create three separate subfolders with the appropriate class names under a top-level folder called "Classes." That way, you'll know exactly where to save a file each time you create one, and you'll avoid having a cluttered and disorganized storage space.

Of course, creating a well-organized folder structure requires that you add, rename, and move folders as your needs change. For example, if you add a class to your schedule, you'll want to create a new subfolder in your top-level "Classes" folder. Next term, you'll create new subfolders for each of your classes.

One Windows method that is effective for managing, modifying, and creating folders, subfolders, and files is the use of the right-click mouse action. Right-clicking within the right pane of Windows Explorer, in a blank space, will cause a pop-up context-sensitive menu to appear. Right-clicking on a folder or file will provide a menu with different choices.

Transferring Files When you've created a useful folder structure, you're ready to transfer files and folders that already exist. Whether you're working with files or folders, the same rules apply. Files and folders can be transferred in two ways: You can copy them or you can move them. The easiest way to accomplish these tasks is to *right-drag* the files you want to transfer to the new location. Press the right mouse button and drag to new location. When you release the right mouse button, a context-sensitive menu appears, allowing you to choose the result of your right-drag. The choices on this menu are Copy Here, Move Here, Create Shortcuts Here, and Cancel.

- **Copying** creates a duplicate file at the new location and leaves the existing file as is.
- **Moving** is similar to cutting and pasting; the file is moved from its original location to the new location.
- **Creating a shortcut** leaves the original file in place and creates a pointer that will take you to the file for which you've created the shortcut. This action is handy for files that you access often.

If you *left-drag* a file *within the same drive*, the file is automatically moved to the new location on the

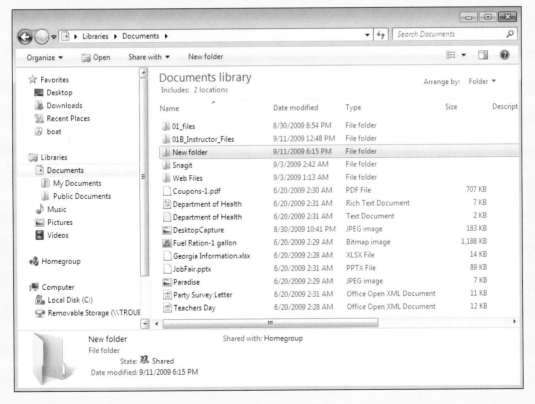

FIGURE 2K The New folder was created within the Documents library on the hard disk drive.

FIGURE 2L The context menu that appears when you right-click provides you with a shortcut to common tasks.

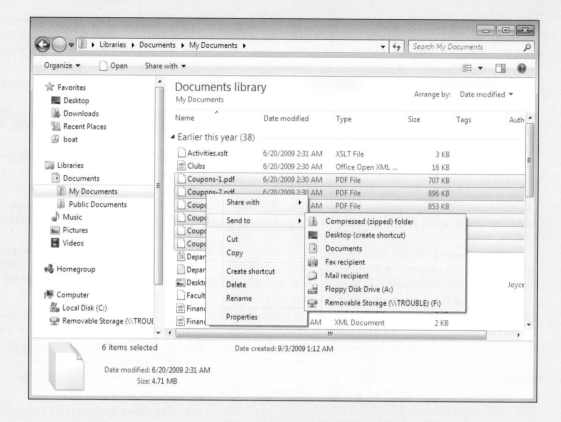

drive. Left-dragging by pressing the left mouse button and dragging file *between drives* creates a copy of the file in the new location.

Right-clicking a file invokes a context-sensitive menu that enables you to choose among many common tasks, such as copying, deleting, and renaming files and creating shortcuts (Figure 2L). You may also use the toolbar to accomplish these and other file management tasks.

Backing Up You can create a backup copy of your files in several ways. The first, and easiest, way is to create intermediate copies as you work. You can do this by using the Save As menu sequence every 15 or 20 minutes. Name your intermediate copies by appending a number or letter to the file name. For example, "Writing121_homework.docx" would become "Writing121_homework1.docx," then "Writing121_homework2.docx," and so forth.

Additionally, you can use the Windows Explorer program to drag a copy of your file to a USB flash drive or CD/DVD drive. Backing up files to the same drive that the original copy is on risks losing both copies in a disk failure or other disaster, so you should always use a remote or portable medium for your backups.

A third way to be sure that you don't lose your work is to use backup software that is specifically designed to back up files.

Getting Help If you need help when working within the Windows Explorer program, click the Get help button on the right side of the toolbar and then type "managing files" into the Search box of the Windows Help and Support dialog box. This will bring up a variety of links to topics that will help you to further understand file management practices.

MANAGING FILES FROM WITHIN PROGRAMS

As mentioned earlier, all software applications use program-specific file name extensions. The advantage of using a default file extension is that both you and your computer will be able to easily associate the file with the program with which it was created. By using appropriate extensions, you can double-click a file in a file management utility such as Windows Explorer and the program used to create the file will be launched.

You can use an application to open a file or use a file to launch the application that created it. Let's say you create a document in Microsoft Word. You give the file the name "Letter Home," and Word 2007 assigns the extension ".docx" by default. Later, you use Windows Explorer to locate the file and then double-click the file name. The file will open in Word. Alternately, you could launch Word and then click the Office button and choose Open to locate the file and open it. The Open dialog box includes a button that allows you to decide which files to display—there are a number of options to choose from. Selecting All Files from the drop-down list will display all files in the current location, no matter what the file type might be. Choosing All Word Documents displays files created in any version of Word, whereas selecting Word Documents will show only Word 2007 files.

Choosing the File, Open menu sequence in many programs, or clicking the Office button and then choosing Open in Microsoft Office 2007 applications, also enables you to manage files. There are icons for creating new folders and for changing the current view, and there is an icon called Organize that enables you to copy, rename, and create shortcuts to files. Pointing to a file and pressing the right mouse button within the Open menu also invokes a file management menu with various tasks.

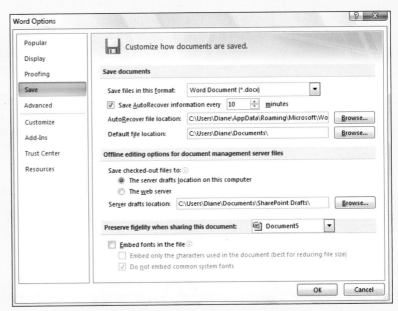

FIGURE 2M To change the default location for saved files in Microsoft Office 2007, click the Office button, then click the Options button to access the dialog box.

SAVING FILES

Saving refers to the process of transferring a file from the computer's temporary memory, or RAM, to a permanent storage device, such as a hard disk. In Microsoft Windows, documents are saved by default to a folder called Documents unless you specify another folder from within the Tools, Options menu or, for Office 2007 applications, from within the program's Word Options menu, which can be found by clicking the Office button (Figure 2M). A critical decision you'll make when managing files is whether to use the Save or Save As command to save files.

Save or Save As? Many computer users never figure out the difference between Save and Save As. It is actually quite simple. When you choose the Save command under the Office button, the program takes what you've created or modified in memory and writes over, or replaces, it to the same storage device and folder, with the same file name that it had when it was opened in the application. When you first save a file, the initial Save menu sequence always invokes the Save As dialog box, because the drive, path, and file name must be designated the first time a file is saved. You can select any folder by using the navigate pane. But when you're working with a previously saved file, you need to be more careful. The Save command doesn't allow you to designate a different drive, folder, or file name; it simply replaces what is stored with the contents of memory.

The Save As command, however, brings up a dialog box that offers all of the choices you had when you first saved a file. You may choose a different drive or a different folder or a different file name. Modifying the file name is a good way to save various versions of your work, just in case something happens to what is in memory and you need to go back to a previous version.

Once you've successfully saved a file, you can always save another copy elsewhere by using the Save As command, which enables you to save the file using a new location, a new file name, or both. You might also use the Save As command to save a copy of your finished work on a USB flash drive, CD, or DVD or in an alternate folder as backup, just in case something happens to your original work. Once you use Save As, all subsequent saves of that file will now be saved in that location.

Managing E-mail

Many e-mail users quickly become overwhelmed by the number of messages they receive. It's not unusual to get dozens, or even hundreds, of messages every day. You can handle the deluge by organizing your messages into folders.

Most e-mail programs enable you to create your own mail folders. For example, you could create folders for each of the classes you're taking. In each folder, you can store mail from the teacher as well as from other students in the same class. You could create another folder to store mail from your family. In many e-mail programs you can create a rule to send e-mail to a specific folder or send an auto reply.

If you're trying to find a message in a lengthy message list, remember that you can sort the mail in different ways. By default, your e-mail program probably sorts mail in the order the messages were received. You can also sort by sender or recipient; some programs give you more ways to sort. With Microsoft Outlook you can quickly sort messages by clicking one of the buttons at the top of the message list. For example, to sort messages by date, click the Received button. Click it again to sort the list in the opposite order.

Still can't find a message? Most e-mail programs provide a Find or Search command, which enables you to search for information in the message header. The best programs enable you to search for text in the message body as well. To search for a message within Outlook, enter a search term in the Search box. Results begin to display as soon as you begin typing.

A Few Last Reminders

Good file management is the hallmark of a competent computer user. File management should not be an intimidating or frustrating task. Computers are tremendously complex and powerful devices, but the principles of managing your work are simple. Plan and construct folder structures that make sense to you. Name your files in such a way that you can easily find them. Always begin at the beginning. If something doesn't work, go back to when it did. Read the manual. Follow directions carefully. Make backup copies of your work. And if all else fails, don't be afraid to ask for help.

Spotlight Exercises

1. Launch Windows Explorer. Select a folder from the navigation pane. Sort the contents in the content pane, using the column headings. Sort it several different ways. Write a brief paper that answers the following questions. Why is sorting beneficial? Which sort would you use most often? Why? List the sorts you tried and how you would use them.

2. In this exercise, you will use the Windows Explorer program to use the group, stack, and filter options. Select a folder from the navigation pane. Using the drop-down arrow next to the sorted column, choose one of the options. Experiment with how it works and how it can be used. Repeat for the other options available. Write a one-page paper on the different options and how they can be used to help you in your courses.

3. Being able to locate your files and folders is very important. To locate files and folders we create a folder (directory) structure. In this exercise, you will use the Windows Explorer program to build a folder structure within the Documents folder. Create a top-level folder named with your name that contains three subfolders and then right-drag two or more files from some other source into one of the three subfolders (make sure you copy these files and do not move them). Click the new folder that has your name in the address bar and then double-click on the subfolder that contains the files. Now press the Print Screen key that is at the top of the right side of your keyboard. Open a Word document and press Ctrl+v. Type your name below the picture on your screen and follow your instructor's instructions to send it to him or her. When you are finished with all your exercises, you may want to delete the new folder structure you created if it is not on your personal computer.

4. Open your e-mail program. Create a new folder using the File, New, Folder menu sequence (in Outlook—other mail readers will have a similar method). For the folder name, use the name and year of the term you are in now, such as Fall2010. Open your new folder and create a folder for each of your classes. Now practice dragging messages back and forth between your deleted files folder and your new folders. Feel free to delete these folders when you are through; make sure any e-mails in the folders can be deleted, or drag them back to their original locations. Write a paragraph describing your experience.

5. It is a very sad day when you go to open a document and either it is not there or the content is incorrect. One way to help prevent this horror is to make backups of your files. Open Word and create a short document stating why you should do backups. Save the file with the name "backup1.docx." You can use the folder structure you created earlier. After the file has been saved, make some changes to the document. Use Save As to save the document with the name "backup2.docx." Make a few more changes to the document, explaining what you did. Save the document one more time as "backup3.docx." Be prepared to hand in your work.

6. Create a simple folder structure on your hard drive that consists of three folders named draft_1, draft_2, and draft_3. Using the documents from Exercise 5 or others you may have on your computer, practice moving and copying the files to different folders. Use a flash drive to copy and move files. Write a short paper on the benefits of moving and copying files. When and why would you move a file? When and why would you copy a file?

chapter 4

System Software

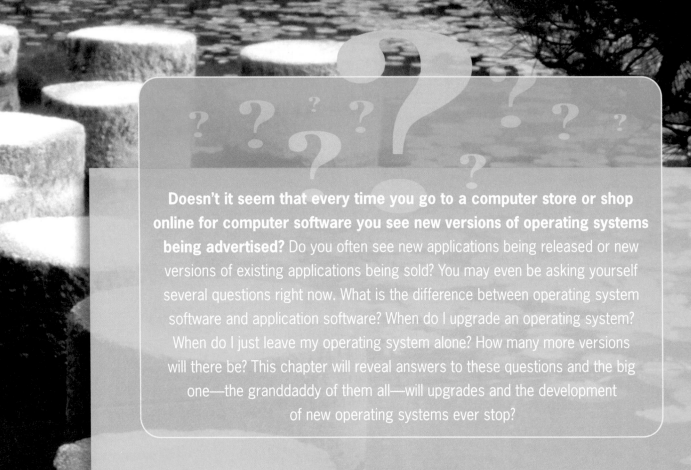

Doesn't it seem that every time you go to a computer store or shop online for computer software you see new versions of operating systems being advertised? Do you often see new applications being released or new versions of existing applications being sold? You may even be asking yourself several questions right now. What is the difference between operating system software and application software? When do I upgrade an operating system? When do I just leave my operating system alone? How many more versions will there be? This chapter will reveal answers to these questions and the big one—the granddaddy of them all—will upgrades and the development of new operating systems ever stop?

Without software—the set of instructions that tells the computer what to do—a computer is just an expensive collection of wires and components. You're probably familiar with one type of software: application software. Application software helps you accomplish a task such as writing a college essay or creating a presentation. The other major type of software is system software. **System software** includes all the programs that provide the infrastructure and hardware control needed for a computer, its peripheral devices, and other programs to function smoothly. Although some system software works behind the scenes, some requires your guidance and control.

System software has two major components: (1) the operating system and (2) system utilities that provide various maintenance functions. Learning how to use an operating system and system utilities is the first step you should take toward mastering any computer system. Mastering a computer system is not unlike understanding the fundamentals of any type of system. The more you know about managing the water, filters, plants, and water temperature in your aquarium, the healthier and happier your fish will be. It's the same with computers; the more you know about and understand the operating system, the better your computer will function. In this chapter, you'll learn what operating systems do, look at the most popular operating systems, and learn which utilities you should use to ensure that your computing experience is safe and enjoyable.

The Operating System

The **operating system (OS)** is a set of programs designed to manage the resources of a computer. Its most important role lies in coordinating the various functions of the computer's hardware. The OS also coordinates interaction between application software and the computer hardware. An OS performs five basic functions (Figure 4.1): It starts the computer, manages applications, manages memory, handles messages from input and output

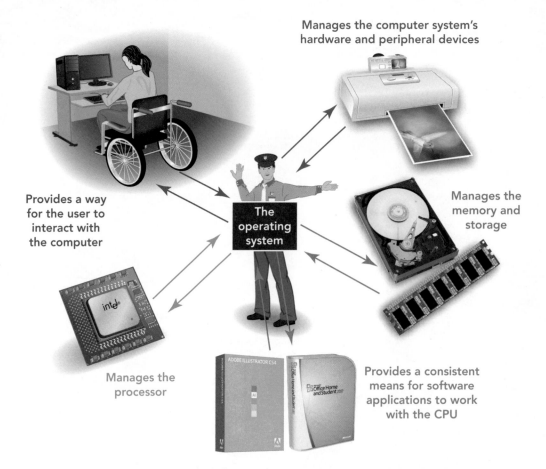

FIGURE 4.1 The operating system works at the intersection of application software, the user, and the computer's hardware. It starts the computer, manages applications and memory, handles messages from input and output devices, and provides a means of communicating with the user.

Manages the computer system's hardware and peripheral devices

Provides a way for the user to interact with the computer

The operating system

Manages the memory and storage

Manages the processor

Provides a consistent means for software applications to work with the CPU

devices, and provides the user interface (a means of communicating with the user). The OS is most often found on a hard disk, although it can be stored and loaded from a USB drive, CD, or DVD. On some small handheld computers, it is held on a memory chip.

Imagine the traffic at a downtown New York City intersection at rush hour and you'll have a good idea of what it's like inside a computer. Bits of information are whizzing around at incredible speeds, sent this way and that by the OS, the electronic equivalent of a harried traffic officer. Impatient peripherals and programs are honking electronic "horns," trying to get the officer's attention. As if the scene weren't chaotic enough, the "mayor" (the user) wants to come through right now. Just like a traffic officer, the computer's OS, standing at the intersection of the computer's hardware, application programs, and user, keeps traffic running smoothly.

Let's examine the five functions of an OS more closely.

STARTING THE COMPUTER

The first function of the operating system is to start the computer. When you start a computer, it loads the OS into the computer's RAM. (To **load** means to transfer something from a storage device, such as the hard disk, to memory.) RAM is a form of volatile memory. **Volatile memory** is storage that is very fast but that is erased when the power goes off. RAM memory is located on the motherboard and holds all programs in use and all documents in progress. The process of loading the OS to memory is called **booting**. This term has been used in computing circles since the very early days. It comes from an old saying that people can pull themselves up by their boot straps, or in other words, get started on their own. With a **cold boot**, you start a computer that is not already on. With a **warm boot**, you restart a computer that is already on. Warm boots are often necessary after installing new software or after an application crashes or stops working. In Windows, you can initiate a warm boot by simultaneously pressing the Ctrl+Alt+Del keys and then choosing the Restart option from the Shut Down menu. (On the Mac, the system will restart when you press the Control, Command, and Eject keys at the same time.) A warm boot, sometimes referred to as restart, can also be initiated through the

Start button in Windows and the Apple menu on the Mac.

With both types of booting, the computer copies the kernel along with other essential portions of the OS from the hard disk into the computer's memory, where it remains while the computer is powered on and functioning. The **kernel** is the central part of the OS that consists of the instructions that control the actions the OS uses most frequently, for example, starting applications and managing hardware devices and memory. The kernel resides in RAM memory at all times, so it must be kept as small as possible. Less frequently used portions of the OS are stored on the hard disk and retrieved as needed. Such portions are called *nonresident* because they do not reside in memory.

A cold or warm boot is a step-by-step process (Figure 4.2). The following sections discuss the steps followed by the computer during the boot-up process.

Step 1: The BIOS and Setup Program

When you first turn on or reset a PC, electricity flows from the power supply through the system. When the CPU receives the signal that the power level is sufficient for the system to run, the CPU will start executing. The CPU can be said

to have amnesia at this time; it has absolutely nothing at all in memory to execute or work on. So the processor makers have programmed it to always look in the same place in the system, the BIOS ROM, for the start of the system's BIOS boot program. The **BIOS (basic input/output system)** is the part of the system software that equips the computer with the instructions needed to accept keyboard input and display information on the screen. The BIOS is encoded, or permanently written, in the computer's ROM. **ROM**, or **read-only memory**, is **nonvolatile memory**—memory that is permanent and unchanging. Programs, such as the BIOS, that are encoded in ROM are meant to be reliably used over and over again. After the BIOS is located, you may briefly see the BIOS screen, a text-only screen that provides information about the BIOS (Figure 4.3).

While the BIOS information is visible, you can access the computer's setup program by pressing a special key, such as Del or F8. (During the boot process, you'll see an on-screen message indicating which key to press to access the setup program.) The **setup program** includes settings that control the computer's hardware. You should *not* alter or change *any* of these settings without understanding the purpose of each setting and the problems that arise from incorrect selections. We'll look more closely at the setup program in "Step 3: Loading the Operating System."

FIGURE 4.2 The Six Sequential Steps Involved in Starting a Computer

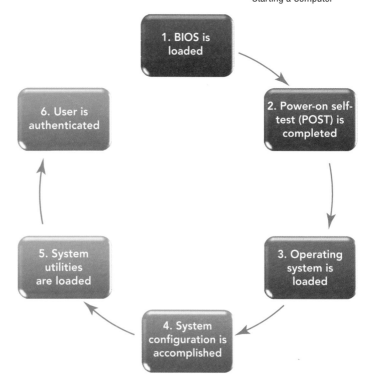

Step 2: The Power-On Self-Test After the BIOS instructions are loaded into memory, a series of tests are conducted to make sure that the computer and associated peripherals are operating correctly. Collectively, these tests are known as the **power-on self-test (POST)**. Among the components tested are the computer's main memory (RAM), the keyboard and mouse, disk drives, and the hard disk. If any of the power-on self-tests fail, you'll hear a beep, see an on-screen error message, and the computer will stop. You often can correct such problems by making sure that components, such as keyboards, are plugged in securely.

However, some failures are so serious that the computer cannot display an error message; instead, it sounds a certain number of beeps. If this happens, it's time to call for technical support. To help the technician repair the computer, write down any error messages you see and try to remember how many beeps you heard.

Step 3: Loading the Operating System Once the power-on self-test is successfully completed, the BIOS initiates a search for the operating system. Options (or settings) in the setup program determine where the BIOS looks for the OS. If multiple possible locations exist (such as an optical drive, a floppy drive, a hard disk), the settings also specify the search order. If no OS is found in the first location, the BIOS moves on to the next location. The user can modify these options.

On most PCs, the BIOS first looks for the OS on the computer's hard disk. When the BIOS finds the OS, it loads the OS's kernel into memory. At that point, the OS takes control of the computer and begins loading system configuration information.

Step 4: System Configuration In Microsoft Windows, configuration information about installed peripherals and software is stored in a database called the registry. The registry also contains information about your system configuration choices, such as background graphics and mouse settings.

Once the operating system's kernel has been loaded, it checks the system's configuration to determine which drivers and other utility programs are needed. A **driver** is a utility program that contains instructions to make a peripheral device addressable or usable by an OS. If a peripheral device that is already installed on the system requires a driver to operate, that peripheral's driver will be installed and loaded automatically. If the driver is missing or has become corrupted, you may be prompted to insert a CD or download the needed driver from the manufacturer's Web site.

Windows and Mac operating systems are equipped with **plug-and-play (PnP)** capabilities, which automatically detect new PnP-compatible peripherals that you might have installed while the power was switched off, load the necessary drivers, and check for conflicts with other devices. Peripheral devices equipped with PnP features identify themselves to the OS and require no action on the part of the user.

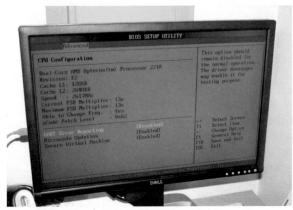

FIGURE 4.3 The BIOS screen provides information about your computer's default input and output settings.

Step 5: Loading System Utilities After the operating system has detected and configured all of the system's hardware, it loads system utilities such as speaker volume control, antivirus software, and power management options. In Microsoft Windows, you can view available custom configuration choices by right-clicking one of the small icons in the System Tray, which is located on the right side of the Windows taskbar. You can access additional system-configuration choices in the Control Panel (Figure 4.4).

Step 6: Authenticating Users When the operating system finishes loading, you may see a dialog box asking you to type a user name and password. Through this process, called **authentication** (or **login**),

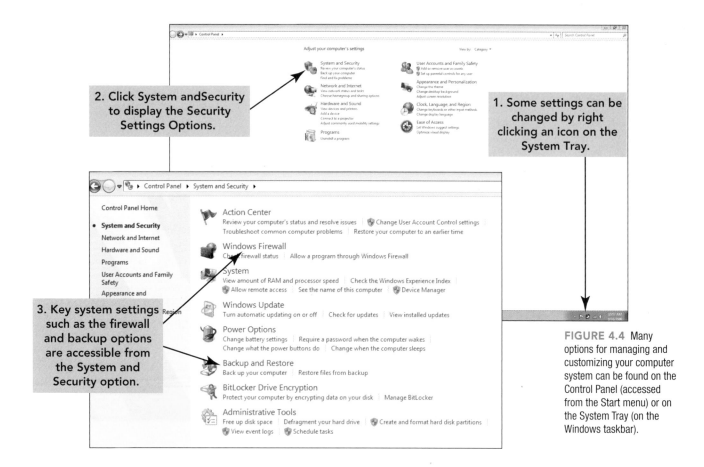

2. Click System andSecurity to display the Security Settings Options.

1. Some settings can be changed by right clicking an icon on the System Tray.

3. Key system settings such as the firewall and backup options are accessible from the System and Security option.

FIGURE 4.4 Many options for managing and customizing your computer system can be found on the Control Panel (accessed from the Start menu) or on the System Tray (on the Windows taskbar).

you verify that you are indeed the person who is authorized to use the computer.

Today, most consumer-oriented operating systems such as Microsoft Windows and Mac OS require or highly recommend that you supply a user name and password to use the computer. Associated with a user name is a **profile**, a record of a specific user's preferences for the desktop theme, icons, and menu styles. If you set up a profile for yourself, your preferences will appear on the screen after you log on. You can enable other users to create profiles that are associated to their user names and passwords so that when they log in they'll see their preferences without disturbing yours.

On multiuser computer systems such as in a university lab or a corporate office environment, you must have an account to access a computer. Your **account** consists of your user name, your password, and your storage space, which is called a *user folder* or *user directory*. The account is usually created by a server/computer administrator, who is a person responsible for managing the accounts.

Now that the OS is loaded and running, let's look at another important task that the OS handles: managing applications.

MANAGING APPLICATIONS

The operating system function that most dramatically affects overall quality of the system is the ability to run and manage applications. When you start an application, the CPU loads the application from storage into RAM. In the early days of personal computing, **single-tasking operating systems** could run only one application at a time, which was often inconvenient. To switch between applications, you had to quit one application before you could start the second.

Today, multitasking operating systems are the norm. **Multitasking operating systems** enable more than one application to run at the same time. With multitasking operating systems, the computer may not actually run two applications at once but switches between them as needed. For example, a user might be running two applications, such as Word and Excel, simultaneously. From the user's perspective, one application (the **foreground application**) is active, whereas the other (the **background application**) appears

FIGURE 4.5 Multitasking operating systems allow more than one application to run at the same time. A user can switch between applications by clicking the desired application or its corresponding button on the taskbar.

The Word document is the active window.

Clicking the Excel document will make it the active window.

Buttons on the taskbar will change their background shading to indicate the active or inactive window.

inactive, as indicated by its appearance on the desktop (Figure 4.5).

A clear measure of the operating system's stability is the technique it uses to handle multitasking. If one of the running applications invades another's memory space, one or both of the applications will become unstable or, at the extreme, crash.

Most current operating systems use a more recent, improved type of multitasking called **preemptive multitasking**, an environment in which programs that are running receive a recurring slice of time from the CPU. Depending on the operating system, the time slice may be the same for all programs or it may be adjustable to meet the various program and user demands. This method of multitasking ensures that all applications have fair access to the CPU and prevents one program from monopolizing it at the expense of the others. Even if one program becomes unstable or stops working, the OS and other applications will continue to run. Although you may lose unsaved work in the application that has crashed, chances are good that everything else will be fine.

Now that you understand how the OS manages individual and multiple applications, let's take a look at how it manages RAM, its primary memory.

MANAGING MEMORY

If the operating system had to constantly access program instructions from their storage location on your computer's hard disk, programs would run very slowly. A **buffer**, an area that temporarily holds data and instructions, is needed to make the processing of instructions more fluid. Computers use RAM memory, a temporary storage medium, to function as this buffer. The computer's OS is responsible for managing this memory. The OS gives each running program its own portion of RAM memory and attempts to keep the programs from interfering with each other's use of memory (Figure 4.6).

Today's operating systems can make the computer's RAM seem larger than it really is. This trick is accomplished by means of **virtual memory**, a method of using the computer's hard disk as an extension of RAM. In virtual memory, program instructions and data are divided into units of fixed size called **pages**. If memory is full, the OS starts storing copies of pages in a hard disk file called the **swap file**. This file is not an application but a temporary storage space for bits and bytes that the OS will access as you do your work. When the pages are needed, they are copied back into RAM (Figure 4.7).

The transferring of files from the hard disk to RAM and back is called **paging**.

Although virtual memory enables users to work with more memory than the amount of RAM installed on the computer, paging slows the computer. Accessing data from a hard disk is much slower than accessing it from RAM. For this reason, adding more RAM to your computer is often the best way to improve its performance. With sufficient RAM, the OS makes minimal use of virtual memory.

Once the computer's OS is running and managing applications and memory, it needs to be able to accept data and commands and to represent the results of processing operations.

HANDLING INPUT AND OUTPUT

How does your computer "know" that you want it to do something? How does it show you the results of its work? Another operating system function is handling input and output, as well as enabling communication with input and output devices.

Most operating systems come with drivers for popular input and output devices. Device drivers are programs that contain specific instructions to allow a particular brand and model of input or output device to function properly. The driver enables communication between the OS and the input and output devices connected to a computer system. Printers, scanners,

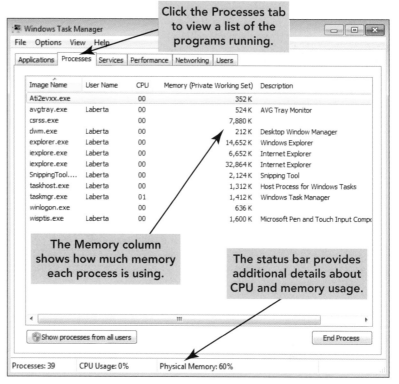

FIGURE 4.6 Use the Windows Task Manager (press Ctrl+Alt+Del, and select Start Task Manager) to get information about programs that are currently running.

monitors, speakers, and the mouse all have drivers (Figure 4.8). Hardware manufacturers usually update their drivers when they develop a new operating system. You can obtain updated drivers from the manufacturer if they are not already included with the OS. For many devices,

FIGURE 4.7 In virtual memory, the OS makes use of a hard disk as an extension of RAM. Instructions and data are divided into units of fixed size called pages and are swapped back and forth between RAM and the hard disk as needed.

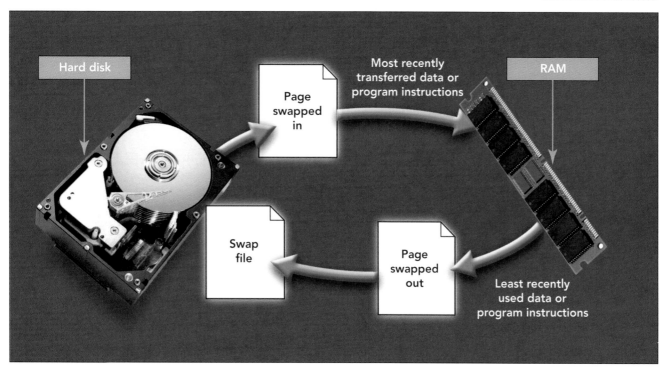

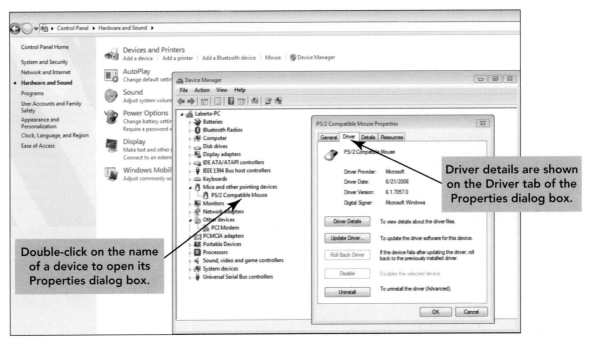

Double-click on the name of a device to open its Properties dialog box.

Driver details are shown on the Driver tab of the Properties dialog box.

FIGURE 4.8 The Device Manager is accessible from the Hardware and Sound option in the Control Panel and provides information on the devices connected to your computer and the drivers they are using.

the Windows operating system can automatically detect new hardware and install the required driver in less than one minute. Microsoft's Windows Update also handles the retrieval and installation of new drivers as they are needed. But new drivers aren't always needed. If your device is working properly, you may not need to upgrade the driver. A good rule of thumb is: If it's not broken, don't fix it.

Hardware, such as input and output devices, as well as software can generate **interrupts**, signals that inform the OS that an event has occurred. For hardware, this can be the user pressing a key, the mouse moved to a new position, or a notice that a document has finished printing. A software event that generates an interrupt would be an attempt to divide by zero. This operation is undefined and throws the system into an interrupt to prevent the processor from attempting something that cannot be done. Software interrupts are handled mostly by the processor, whereas hardware interrupts are handled by the OS. Our discussion will focus on hardware interrupts.

The OS provides **interrupt handlers**, also called **interrupt service routines**, which are miniprograms that immediately respond when an interrupt occurs. The type of response or action the handler initiates depends on the type and source of the interrupt. The actual interrupting of an event by an interrupt signal is called an **interrupt request (IRQ)**. These

requests are handled by **interrupt request (IRQ) lines**. Most PCs have 16 IRQs lines, numbered 0 through 15. If two devices are configured to use the same IRQ line but aren't designed to share that IRQ line, the result is a serious system failure called an **IRQ conflict**. In most cases, an IRQ conflict makes the system so unstable that it cannot function. To remedy an IRQ conflict, you may need to shut down the computer and remove peripheral devices, one by one, until you determine which one is causing the conflict. Happily, PnP-compatible operating systems and peripherals have made IRQ conflicts much less common. Still, this phenomenon is worth mentioning because it may help you solve a problem your computer might encounter.

Now we will explore the different interfaces that the OS provides to interact with you, the user.

PROVIDING THE USER INTERFACE

From the user's perspective, the most important function of an operating system is providing the **user interface**, the part of the OS that you see, interact with, and use to communicate with programs.

User Interface Functions User interfaces typically enable you to do the following:

- Start (launch) application programs.
- Manage storage devices, such as hard disks, optical drives, and USB drives,

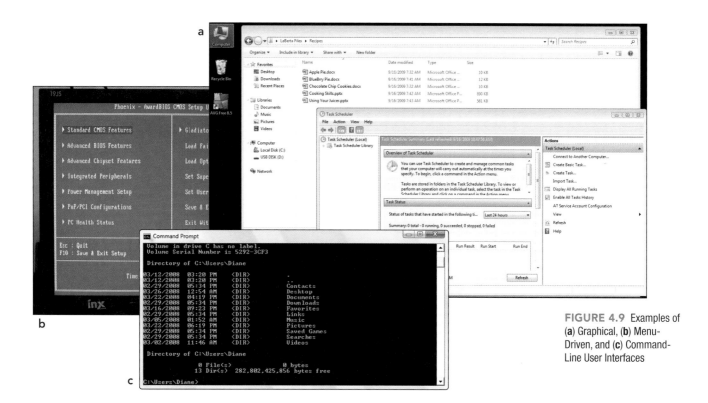

FIGURE 4.9 Examples of (**a**) Graphical, (**b**) Menu-Driven, and (**c**) Command-Line User Interfaces

and organize files. The user interface provides options to copy files from one storage device to another, rename files, and delete files.

- Shut down the computer safely by following an orderly shutdown procedure.

Types of User Interfaces The three types of user interfaces are graphical, menu-driven, and command-line interfaces (Figure 4.9).

By far the most popular user interface, a **graphical user interface** (**GUI**; pronounced "goo-ee") takes advantage of the computer's graphics capabilities to make the operating system and programs easier to use. On most of today's computers, GUIs are used to create the **desktop**, the screen image that appears after the OS finishes loading into memory (RAM), replicating the view of work available. The desktop image can change with the OS or OS version. If someone were to ask you about your desktop, you can say that you are running Linux, or Mac OS, or Windows. A typical desktop on most personal computers consists of several **icons**, small images that represent computer resources such as programs, data files, and network connections, a Start button, task bar, and other user selected options. Clicking an icon causes the associated program to run within resizable on-screen windows,

making it easy to switch from one program to another (Figure 4.10). Within programs, you can give commands by choosing items from pull-down menus, some of which display dialog boxes. In a **dialog box**, you can supply additional information that the program needs (Figure 4.11).

Menu-driven user interfaces enable you to avoid memorizing keywords (such as *copy* and *paste*) and syntax (a set of rules for entering commands). On-screen, text-based menus show all the options available at a given point. With most systems, you select an option with the arrow keys and then press Enter. Some systems enable you to click the desired option with the mouse or to choose a letter with the keyboard.

Command-line user interfaces require you to type commands using keywords that tell the OS what to do (such as *format* or *copy*) one line at a time. You must observe complicated rules of syntax that specify exactly what you can type in a given place. For example, the following command copies a file from the hard disk drive C to a removable USB drive identified as drive F:

```
copy C:\myfile.txt F:\myfile.txt
```

Command-line user interfaces aren't popular with most users because they

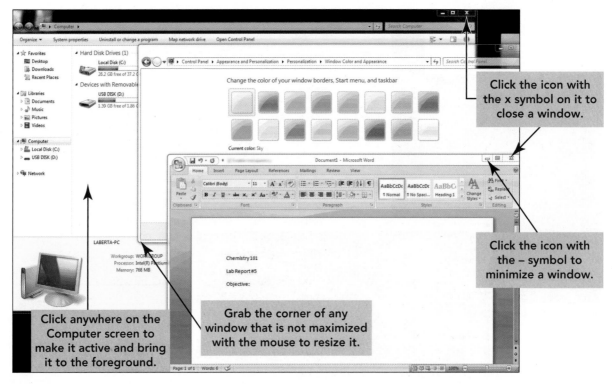

Click the icon with the x symbol on it to close a window.

Click the icon with the − symbol to minimize a window.

Click anywhere on the Computer screen to make it active and bring it to the foreground.

Grab the corner of any window that is not maximized with the mouse to resize it.

FIGURE 4.10 Programs run within resizable on-screen windows, making it easy to switch from one program to another.

require memorization, and it's easy to make a typing mistake. Although the commands are usually very simple, such as *copy* and *paste*, others are more cryptic. However, some experienced users actually prefer command-line interfaces because they can operate the computer quickly after memorizing the keywords and syntax.

Now that you've seen how the OS makes itself available to you, let's explore the most popular OSs in depth.

Exploring Popular Operating Systems

We will begin with Microsoft Windows and then look at the Mac OS, UNIX, Linux, embedded operating systems, and DOS. Although your choice of operating system might be limited by the computer you have, you should know how the various systems have evolved over time and what their strengths and weaknesses are.

FIGURE 4.11 A dialog box enables you to provide additional information that a program needs. This is the print dialog box.

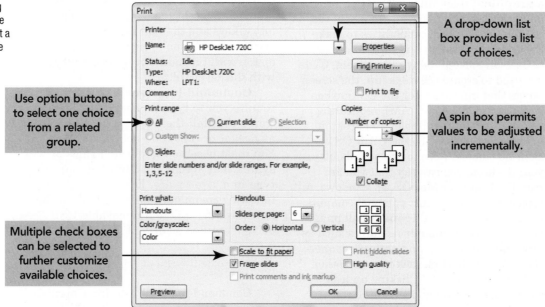

A drop-down list box provides a list of choices.

Use option buttons to select one choice from a related group.

A spin box permits values to be adjusted incrementally.

Multiple check boxes can be selected to further customize available choices.

FIGURE 4.12 Windows Time Line	
Year Released	Version
2009	Windows 7
2007	Windows Vista
2001	Windows XP
2000	Windows 2000/ME
1998	Windows 98
1995	Windows 95
1993	Windows NT
1992	Windows 3.1
1990	Windows 3.0
1987	Windows 2.0
1985	Windows 1

MICROSOFT WINDOWS

Microsoft Windows is by far the most popular operating system. Over the years, it has gone through several iterations (Figure 4.12), and it is now considered *the* operating system of PCs worldwide. When you purchase a computer, it usually comes with an OS already installed. Microsoft has agreements with the major computer manufacturers to provide Windows on almost all of the personal computers that are made today. Some manufacturers offer a choice of operating systems, but Windows is expected to remain the standard for years to come.

Let's start by looking at the most recent version, Windows 7, and then we'll look at the other operating systems you might encounter on today's personal and corporate computers.

Microsoft Windows 7

Microsoft Windows 7 is the latest version of the Microsoft Windows operating system, released in late 2009, and is available in six different versions: Starter, Home Basic, Home Premium, Professional, Enterprise, and Ultimate. All versions of Windows 7 promise to be more efficient than its predecessor, performing equally or better on the same hardware, and claim to have resolved the compatibility issues that existed between applications (Figure 4.13). Home Premium, Professional, and Ultimate are the versions designed for use by the home user, college student, or small business.

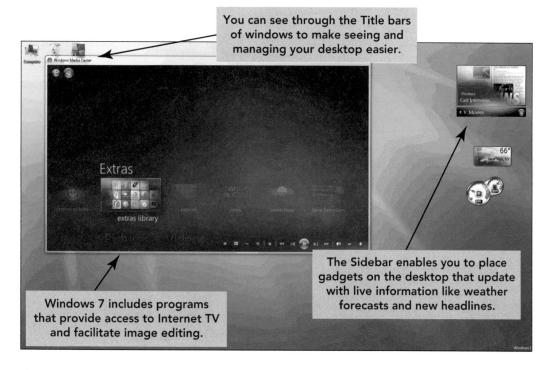

You can see through the Title bars of windows to make seeing and managing your desktop easier.

Windows 7 includes programs that provide access to Internet TV and facilitate image editing.

The Sidebar enables you to place gadgets on the desktop that update with live information like weather forecasts and new headlines.

FIGURE 4.13 Windows 7 focuses on ease of use, multimedia, application compatibility, and increased security.

FIGURE 4.14 Windows 7 Features That Make Using a Notebook PC Simple

Feature	Description
Jump list	A feature activated by right-clicking an icon on the taskbar or the Start menu. The jump list that appears will display, depending on the icon selected, documents, pictures, songs, or Web sites you turn to each day.
Pin	A method of attaching your favorite program anywhere on the taskbar for easy access.
Snap	A quick (and fun) new way to resize open windows by dragging them to the edges of your screen.
Windows Search	A feature activated by simply typing in the Start menu search box. You'll see a list of relevant documents, pictures, music, and e-mail on your PC. Because most users store data on several devices, Windows 7 is designed to search external hard drives, networked PCs, and libraries (a Windows 7 feature that groups related files together regardless of their storage location).

The Starter edition is designed for small notebook PCs and has to be installed by the OEM (original equipment manufacturer). It professes to give the user less waiting, less clicking, and fewer hassles while adding new devices or connecting to a network. Such new Windows 7 features as jump lists, pin, snap, and Windows Search have been added to make the use of a PC notebook easier (Figure 4.14).

Windows 7 Home Basic is a version designed by Microsoft for emerging markets. Its features are slightly superior to those included in the Starter version but not as encompassing as those in the Home Premium Edition. Windows 7 Enterprise has the same feature set as Windows 7 Ultimate. The only difference is that the Enterprise edition is reserved for large companies.

The features found in the three most commonly installed versions of Windows 7 are best presented in the comparison chart displayed in Figure 4.15. Explore the features of Microsoft's latest Windows offerings at the Windows home page at **www.microsoft.com/windows/default. aspx**.

Microsoft Windows Vista Released to the general public in January 2007, **Microsoft Windows Vista** replaced the popular Windows XP operating system

and is designed for home and professional use. Vista is available in five different versions—Basic, Home Premium, Business, Ultimate, and Enterprise. Vista features a slick new interface called Windows Aero (unavailable in the Basic version) that features translucent windows, three-dimensional animation, and live taskbar thumbnails—just hover the mouse over a button on the taskbar to get a preview of its contents. Vista also addresses the growing popularity of mobile computing. Previously, tablet PCs required the Windows XP Tablet PC Edition OS, but Vista supports tablet PCs and other mobile devices through the Windows Mobility Center. Responding to concerns about security, the Windows Security Center integrates programs and tools like Windows Defender, Windows Firewall, and Windows Updates for ease of access and also includes user-installed security programs. Implementing the User Account Control feature can prevent unauthorized users from installing unwanted or malicious programs. However, Windows Vista isn't all work. Windows Media Center, available in the Home Premium and Ultimate versions, allows you to enjoy your audio and video files, including recorded TV shows and DVDs, whenever you want. Watch on your PC, TV, or Xbox, or sync your files to a portable media device. This

FIGURE 4.15 Comparison of Windows 7 Features in Popular Installations

Feature	Versions		
	Home Premium	Professional	Ultimate
Improved desktop navigation, including Windows Touch, a feature that enables touch screen input	X	X	X
Starts programs faster; finds documents quicker	X	X	X
Web experiences are faster, easier, and safer	X	X	X
Watch, pause, and rewind TV on your PC	X	X	X
Create a home network with HomeGroup	X	X	X
Run Windows XP productivity programs in XP Mode		X	X
Connect to company networks more easily and with more security with Domain Join		X	X
Back up to a home or business network		X	X
Protect data on your PC and portable storage devices against loss or theft with BitLocker			X
Work in the language of your choice and switch between any of 35 languages			X

version differentiates itself from previous ones by its improved search features and networking tools, integrated speech recognition capabilities, and new multimedia tools such as **gadgets**, applications that appear as active icons in the Windows Sidebar. Gadgets are selected or downloaded by the user and display photos, current weather conditions, control a multimedia player, or monitor the CPU's performance.

Microsoft Windows Server 2008
Microsoft Windows Server 2008 is a sophisticated operating system specifically designed to support client/server computing systems in a corporate environment. Servers are special computers used to manage various resources on a network, including printers and other devices, file

storage, and Web sites. Windows Server 2008 shares many similarities in architecture and functionality with Windows Vista because the underlying code is closely related. Benefits include the following:

- **Security.** New technologies help prevent unauthorized access to corporate networks, data, and user accounts.
- **Web Server.** Enhanced capabilities are available for developing and hosting Web applications and services.
- **Administration.** All configuration and maintenance is done through the command-line interface or through remote administration.
- **Virtualization.** Multiple servers can be consolidated as separate virtual

FIGURE 4.16 Although Windows Mobile can look slightly different depending upon the phone vendor, it still brings Windows functionality to mobile devices.

machines on a single physical server, and multiple operating systems can run in parallel.

Microsoft Windows Mobile Designed for smartphones and PDAs, **Microsoft Windows Mobile** provides a user interface for simplified versions of Windows programs, such as Microsoft's own Office applications. Users can create documents on the go and then transfer them to a desktop computer for further processing and printing. Personal information-management tools, such as a calendar and address book, along with an e-mail client and a Web browser are also included (Figure 4.16). Windows Mobile supports handwriting recognition and voice recording. Users can quickly synchronize their mobile devices with corresponding programs on their desktop computers.

MAC OS

Mac OS was the first OS to successfully bring the GUI to the world. The original Macintosh operating system was released in 1984. Although Apple eventually lost market share to Microsoft, it has a diehard fan base. Many prefer the Mac OS for its stability, and ease of use (Figure 4.17). Operating systems for the MAC were numbered as Mac OS 8, Mac OS 9, and Mac OS X (X for the Roman numeral 10). Newer versions of Mac OS X

have, in addition to their numeric identification, been given names associated with large cats. Mac OS v10.0 is called Cheetah and Mac OS V10.6 is labeled Snow Leopard. For a detailed explanation on what Mac OS X is, go to **www.apple.com/macosx/what-is-macosx/**.

Mac OS X Snow Leopard, the current version of Mac OS X, has a smaller footprint (taking up to 50 percent less storage space than the previous version). It includes a more responsive and snappier Finder, a Put Back option to return deleted items to their original location, more reliable ejection of external drives, faster shut down and wake up, four new fonts, 80 percent faster Time Machine backup, increased Airport signal strength for wireless networks, and built-in support for Microsoft Exchange Server 2007. For a detailed review of the new features incorporated into Snow Leopard, visit **www.apple.com/macosx/refinements/enhancements-refinements.html**. Mac support has been gaining ground, especially with folks who are dissatisfied with their Windows experience. At the beginning of 2008, Macs held an 8 percent market share, reflecting a 28 percent growth in one year.

UNIX

Developed at AT&T's Bell Laboratories in 1969, UNIX is a pioneering operating

FIGURE 4.17 The Mac OS X interface is similar to the one used by Microsoft Windows.

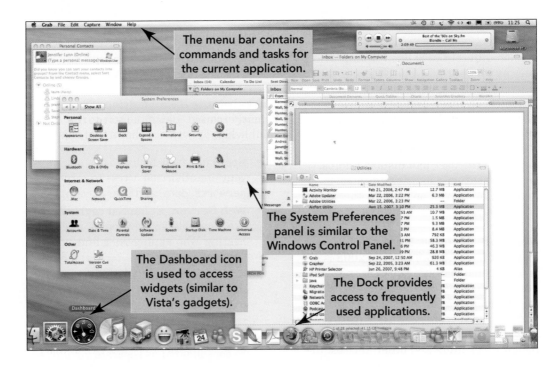

The menu bar contains commands and tasks for the current application.

The System Preferences panel is similar to the Windows Control Panel.

The Dashboard icon is used to access widgets (similar to Vista's gadgets).

The Dock provides access to frequently used applications.

FIGURE 4.18 GUI interfaces developed for UNIX have made this OS more user friendly.

system that continues to define what an OS should do and how it should work. **UNIX** (pronounced "you-nix") was the first OS written in the C language. It is a free OS installed primarily on workstations and features preemptive multitasking.

If UNIX is so great, why didn't it take over the computer world? One reason is the lack of compatibility among the many different versions of UNIX. Another reason is that it's difficult to use. UNIX defaults to a command-line user interface, which is challenging for new computer users. An online tutorial on UNIX is available at **www.ee.surrey.ac.uk/Teaching/ Unix**.

In the past few years, a number of GUI interfaces have been developed for UNIX, improving its usability (Figure 4.18). In fact, the Mac OS X is based on UNIX!

LINUX

In 1991, Finnish university student Linus Torvalds introduced **Linux**, his new freeware operating system for personal computers (Figure 4.19). He hoped Linux would offer users a free alternative to UNIX. Linux has since been further developed by thousands of programmers, who have willingly donated their time to make

sure that Linux is a very good version of UNIX. The community approach to Linux has made it a marvel of the computer world and has made Torvalds a folk legend.

Linux is **open source software**, meaning that its source code (the code of the program itself) is available for all to see and use. Unlike most other commercial software, which hide the program's code and prohibit users from analyzing it to see how the program was written, users of open-source software are invited to scrutinize the source code for errors and to share their discoveries with the software's publisher. Experience shows that this approach is often a very effective measure against software defects.

What makes Linux so attractive? Two things: It's powerful and it's free. Linux brings many features similar to those found in commercial versions of UNIX, including multitasking, virtual memory, Internet support, and a GUI, to the PC. (Versions of Linux have also been created for the Mac.)

Although Linux is powerful and free, there are some versions that are proprietary or are available for a fee. Because Linux isn't a commercial product with a

FIGURE 4.19 Ubuntu, a popular version of Linux, features a very Windows-like GUI interface and includes programs such as a media player, image editor, and the Firefox Web browser.

single stable company behind it, many corporate chief information officers shy away from its adoption. When someone needs technical support, they have to find a Web site such as **www.redhat.com** or someone who knows more about Linux than they do—this is not the same as calling technical support when your Mac OS X is on the fritz. Also, Linux can't run the popular Microsoft Office applications, which most corporate users prefer. But Linux is gaining acceptance, especially for use with Web servers.

The beauty of Linux, and its development model, is that it doesn't run on any particular type of computer: It runs on them all. Linux has been translated to run on systems as small as iPods and as large as homegrown supercomputers. For the latest in Linux news and developments, visit Linux Today at **www.linuxtoday. com**. Linux beginners can get assistance at **www.justlinux.com** and at **www. linux.org**.

EMBEDDED OPERATING SYSTEMS

Embedded operating systems are specialized operating systems designed for specific applications. They are usually very compact and efficient. They also eliminate many features that nonembedded computer operating systems provide because the specialized application has no need for them. PDAs, cell phones, point-of-sale devices, VCRs, industrial robot control, and even modern toasters that control the temperature based on bread type and the settings for the attached egg poacher, are examples of devices that contain embedded systems. Some of the more common embedded operating systems that are installed on our handheld devices are Windows CE, Palm OS, Symbian OS, and Android.

Windows CE, one of the early embedded operating systems, was first introduced in 1996, with a significant upgrade made available in 1997. It consists of a low overhead device driver and built-in power manager. Windows CE is used by consumer electronic devices like handheld PCs, video game players, and digital cameras, and by industrial products like barcode readers. The Palm OS was initially developed by Palm Inc. for personal digital assistants (PDAs) in 1996. It was designed for use with a touch screen using graphical user interfaces and comes with a suite of personal information management applications. The most current versions power smartphones like the Palm Pixi that runs on the Palm webOS platform and responds to a multitouch screen and natural gestures (Figure 4.20). The Symbian OS is an open industry standard operating system for data-enabled mobile phones. Open standard guarantees that the OS must be freely and publicly available (e.g., from a stable Web site) under royalty-free terms at reasonable cost. Symbian promoters insist that it will continue to power devices at the lower end of the smartphone price spectrum because of its reasonable cost, ample suppliers of add-on devices, and the operating system's reduced demand on the processor and memory. Android is the operating system for mobile devices created by Google. The latest version, Android 1.6 (known as Donut), was released in late 2009 and adds support for CDMA (Code Division Multiple Access) and more screen resolutions. Supporting CDMA will allow operators like Verizon to add Android phones to their portfolios.

MS-DOS

MS-DOS (or **DOS**, which is short for Microsoft *disk operating system*) is an operating system for IBM and IBM-compatible PCs that uses a command-line user interface. Developed by Bill Gates and Paul Allen's fledgling Microsoft Corporation for the original IBM PC in 1981, MS-DOS was marketed by IBM in a virtually identical version called PC-DOS. The command-line interface is difficult to learn, and the syntax and commands are not easy for the casual user to remember. It is unlikely that you will ever encounter a command-line interface on a modern personal computer.

PC VERSUS MAC VERSUS LINUX

Traditionally, computer users have had two major platforms to choose from. A **platform** is determined by the

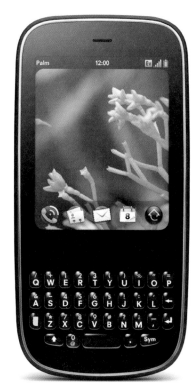

FIGURE 4.20 The Palm Pixi offers the ability to combine online conversations into a single chat style, link multiple social network sites into one contact, and layer calendars from various sources like Outlook, Google, and Facebook.

combination of microprocessor chip and operating system used by a distinct type of computer, such as a Mac or a PC. Previously, Macs used a Motorola or IBM chip and the Mac OS, and PCs have used an Intel or AMD chip and the Windows OS. Macs have since switched to Intel chips, which has blurred the platform lines a bit because they can now run the Windows OS too. Depending on which OS is loaded on a computer, it is simply referred to as a Mac or a PC. As the Linux OS becomes more popular, some people may want to consider a third alternative.

The debate over which platform is best has raged for years, and if market power is anything, PCs are winning by a landslide. But Apple hangs in there with its slew of adherents who choose to "think different." What's the difference between the platforms? Although you'd never know from listening to people who love or hate Macs, there's really not much difference, at least not in terms of power. Still, the debate goes on.

On the one side, Mac lovers say their machines are easier to set up and use. Macs come with everything you need built right in—simply plug them in and you're on your way. Mac lovers also point out that Apple has developed some incredibly advanced technology. (Even PC users will agree to that.)

It's not just the system and the software Mac users love. Most Macophiles love their one-button mice as well as their many shortcut keys. In addition, certain professions, especially creative fields such as graphic design, rely almost exclusively on Macs.

Linux offers another option. Linux can be installed on a Mac or a PC, and because it is open source software, cost isn't an issue. Security is another benefit. Few types of malware are targeted at Linux machines. Experts disagree on whether

FIGURE 4.21 Windows operating systems dominate the market, with Mac OS X and Linux quite a distance behind.

	Operating Systems	
1	Windows XP	60.55%
2	Windows Vista	22.64%
3	Mac OS X	7.11%
4	Linux	1.97%
5	Windows 7	1.69%
6	Windows 2000	0.78%
7	Windows 2003	0.65%
8	iPhone OSX	0.40%
9	Windows 98	0.13%
10	WAP	0.07%

this is due to the security of the Linux OS or the fact that there are so few systems that hackers can't create the chain reaction they can easily muster using Windows. The casual user cites the lack of structured computer support and the level of computer knowledge required to set up a Linux system as the main deterrent.

However, PCs still dominate, and the race isn't even close. PCs claim the largest chunk of the marketplace and are the choice of corporate America. They tend to be cheaper in terms of both their hardware and software, with a much larger selection of software products to choose from than their Mac or Linux counterparts. In recent years, Apple, through its humorous "I am a Mac, I am a PC" commercials, has tried to woo PC users by playing on the idea that Macs are easier to use. However, software products developed for Windows greatly outnumber those written for Macs, one reason PCs have led the marketplace. But now that Mac OS X can run Windows, Mac users are able to run existing Windows software. Unfortunately, as Apple moves into the PC market with its recent innovations, it may make itself more vulnerable to the viruses that have been, until now, mostly a PC headache. In any case, both Macs and Linux have a long way to go to catch PCs—and few experts see that happening any time soon. It is only fair to mention that although slow to

catch on in the PC market, the growth of Linux in the area of server installations has been exponential.

For a look at a humorous spin on the familiar "I am a Mac, I am a PC" commercial that includes the arrival of Linux, watch the clip at **www.youtube.com/ watch?v=cldeHjFig_c**. For a more serious comparison between the use of the big three and other operating systems, review the statistics in Figure 4.21 published by W3Counter in August 2009.

The cost of software and frequent upgrades is a source of concern for all users, regardless of the platform they are using. Open source software seems to be a viable solution for this problem; however, some warning is needed. Arguments can be presented to support the fact that although the software is free, you pay for quality support or the courses to learn to support the OS yourself.

OPEN SOURCE SOFTWARE

The open source model is revolutionizing the software world. Because the basic code is free, you can find pieces of it running iPods, supercomputers, smartphones, and many other computer systems. Need Linux in Hungarian, Thai, or Zulu? Don't worry: Volunteers have translated versions of Linux into dozens of languages, giving computer users of all types—individuals, government organizations, and research groups—a free alternative to buying traditional operating systems. You can even download free open source programs for applications such as word processing and database management.

Although Linux remains free, adapting it to the needs of corporations and other large-scale users has become big business. For example, IBM will customize Linux for corporate customers; Red Hat offers a Linux version, as well as consulting, development, and training services to Linux users. With assistance and customization so readily available (for a fee), it's not surprising that Linux's popularity with large-scale users is growing.

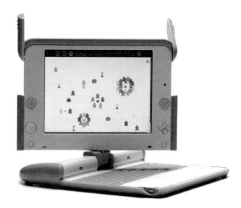

FIGURE 4.22 Open source operating systems are installed on many systems to reduce the initial purchase price.

Although Linux held almost 25 percent of the Web server market in 2007, it had less than 2 percent of the desktop market. There are, however, signs that this may be changing. For instance, France's police force, the National Gendarmerie, has switched 70,000 desktop computers from Windows to Linux. And low-cost computers like the OLPC XO, Everex CloudBook, Classmate PC, and the Asus Eee PC are being offered with the Linux OS (Figure 4.22). Linux is also making inroads in mobile computing, holding approximately 13 percent of the global smartphone market share. Motorola expects to offer Linux on 60 percent of their phones within the next few years. Other devices, such as TiVo and Amazon Kindle, also use Linux-based operating systems.

Linux usage is especially strong in the Asia-Pacific market. However, reports indicate that some worldwide purchasers are ordering thousands of new PCs with the Linux OS installed (because it is free) and are then installing illegal copies of the Microsoft Windows OS. They do this to lower the cost of the PC package. The effect is that the statistics for PCs shipping with Linux are overstating the adoption of Linux as an OS and reporting an equal decline in the reported use of Windows when, in fact, illegal copies of Windows are being installed on those very machines. This does not detract from the attractiveness of Linux to its adopters, but it does show that reports of its adoption may be inflated.

No matter what operating system you or your company are running, you need to work with associated programs, called utilities, that help maintain the smooth operability of your system.

System Utilities: Housekeeping Tools

Providing a necessary addition to an operating system, **system utilities** (also called **utility programs**) are programs that work in tandem with the operating system and perform services that keep the computer system running smoothly. Sometimes these programs are included in the OS; sometimes you must purchase them from other software vendors. System utility programs are considered essential to the effective management of a computer system by backing up system and application files, providing antivirus protection, searching for and managing files, scanning and defragmenting disks and files, and compressing files so that they take up less space.

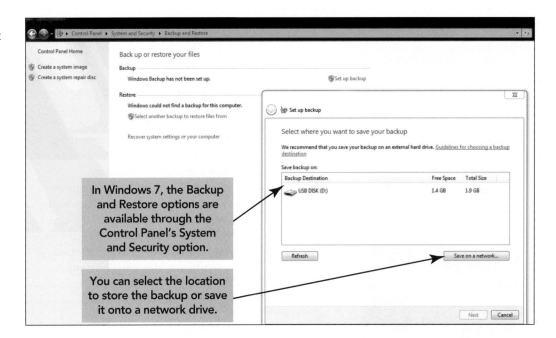

FIGURE 4.23 Backup software is an essential part of computing and can avoid the loss of essential data.

In Windows 7, the Backup and Restore options are available through the Control Panel's System and Security option.

You can select the location to store the backup or save it onto a network drive.

BACKUP SOFTWARE

An essential part of safe, efficient computer usage, **backup software** copies data from the computer's hard disk to backup devices, such as CDs or DVDs, an external hard drive, or an online storage location. Should the hard disk fail, you can recover your data from the backup disk (Figure 4.23).

Backup software can run a **full backup**, which includes all files and data on the entire hard disk or an incremental backup. In an **incremental backup**, the backup software copies only those files that have been created or changed since the last backup occurred. In this way, the backup disk always contains an up-to-date copy of all data. Full backups should be made at least once each month. Incremental backups should also be made on a regular basis. In a business environment, that can be as frequently as one or more times a day.

Drive imaging software creates a mirror image of the entire hard disk—including the OS and applications, as well as all files and data. In the event of a hard disk or computer system failure, the drive image can be used to restore the system. This avoids the individual reinstallation of each program and can save an incredible amount of time.

Even if you don't have backup software, you can still make backup copies of your important files: Just copy them to an alternative storage device. Don't ever rely on a hard disk to keep the only copies of

your work. Backups should be stored away from the computer system, usually in a different building that can withstand natural disasters and is located in a geologically stable region, so that, in the event of a fire or flood, they don't suffer the system's fate.

Windows Vista and Windows 7 include a backup utility that you can access from the Backup and Restore Center on the Control Panel. The Complete PC Backup will create an exact image of your computer—backing up all files and data, plus the OS and applications, but is only available on the Business, Ultimate, and Enterprise editions. Windows Automatic Backup option backs up files and data and is available for most versions of Vista, including Home Basic and Home Premium. Although many people know that backing up their files is important, most don't regularly do so. The Automatic Backup option solves that problem with the File Backup Scheduling Wizard. Choose the time and backup location you prefer and Vista will do the rest! You can also obtain stand-alone backup or imaging software from local or online retailers, or check for user reviews and find free utility programs on sites like Download.com (**www.download.com**).

ANTIVIRUS SOFTWARE

Antivirus software protects a computer from computer viruses (Figure 4.24).

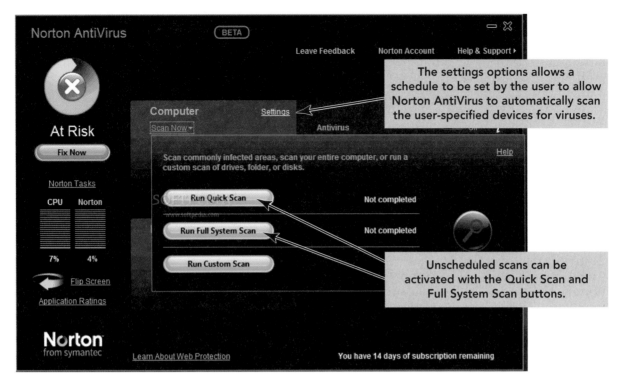

FIGURE 4.24 Norton Internet Security includes an antivirus program that allows the user to run both scheduled and unscheduled checks for viruses. Special editions of this program exist for gamers, with options to turn off advanced protection and intrusion protection.

Such software uses a pattern-matching technique that examines all of the files on a disk, looking for telltale virus code "signatures." One limitation of such programs is that they can detect only those viruses whose signatures are in their databases, and there are plenty of those. As of this writing, one antivirus program, Webroot, scans for over 1,358,000 viruses and adds more each day. Most antivirus programs enable you to automatically update the software. However, new viruses appear every day. If your system becomes infected by a virus that's not in the system's database, it may not be detected. Because of this shortcoming, many antivirus programs also include programs that monitor system functions to detect and stop the destructive activities of unknown viruses.

Norton AntiVirus, McAfee VirusScan Plus, and AVG are three of the most popular antivirus applications in use today. All three programs provide users with frequent updates for the term of a license. Licenses are typically issued for a year. Additionally, many ISPs now offer free antivirus protection and other security tools to help keep their customers safe online.

Some viruses do their damage immediately, whereas others hide on your hard disk waiting for a trigger before doing their work. Regardless of when they do their damage, viruses spread quickly and can affect thousands, even millions, of users in a short time if the malware can locate targeted hosts. Some argue that the resistance to viruses is more a function of market share and concentration than security advances. This might be true; however, it takes only one nasty virus to cause you a lot of grief. So, install and use antivirus software to avoid possible hours of aggravation and data loss.

SEARCHING FOR AND MANAGING FILES

Another important system utility is the **file manager**, a program that helps you organize and manage the data stored on your disk. The file manager enables you to perform various operations on the files and folders created on your computer's storage devices. You can use file managers to make copies of your files, manage how and where they are stored, and delete unwanted files. Windows 7 and Vista use Explorer, Mac OS X uses Finder, and Linux has various file management utilities. Explorer has been enhanced considerably in the latest Window operating systems and includes many new features (Figure 4.25).

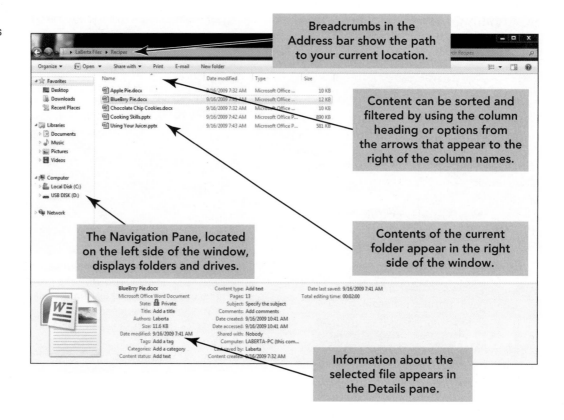

Breadcrumbs in the Address bar show the path to your current location.

Content can be sorted and filtered by using the column heading or options from the arrows that appear to the right of the column names.

The Navigation Pane, located on the left side of the window, displays folders and drives.

Contents of the current folder appear in the right side of the window.

Information about the selected file appears in the Details pane.

On a large hard disk with thousands of files, the task of finding a needed file can be time-consuming and frustrating if you try to do it manually. For this reason, most operating systems include a **search utility**, which enables you to search an entire hard disk or any indexed network storage device for a file. In Microsoft Windows, Instant Search is integrated into every Explorer window, and you can query for files in a number of ways, including by name, date, and size (Figure 4.26). The Spotlight utility in the Mac OS performs similar tasks.

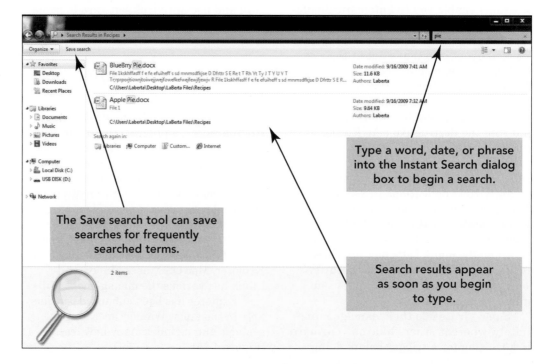

Type a word, date, or phrase into the Instant Search dialog box to begin a search.

The Save search tool can save searches for frequently searched terms.

Search results appear as soon as you begin to type.

SCANNING AND DEFRAGMENTING DISKS

A **disk scanning program**, or error checking program, can detect and resolve a number of physical and logical problems that may occur when your computer stores files on a disk. The error-checking and defragmenting utilities in Windows are found by clicking the Computer option in the Start menu, then right-clicking the drive to be checked, and choosing Properties. Select the Tools tab in the Properties dialog box to access the utilities. The Mac OS X scanning utility is called Disk Utility. You can find commercial products that perform this function, but the one that comes with your operating system is usually adequate and best suited for managing your hard disk.

A physical problem that a scanning program might detect involves an irregularity on the disk's surface that results in a **bad sector**, a portion of the disk that is unable to store data reliably. The scanning program can fix the problem by locking out the bad sector so that it's no longer used.

Logical problems are usually caused by a power outage that occurs before the computer is able to finish writing data to the disk. In this situation, the system is unable to place an end of file marker (eof), and there is some confusion as to where the file actually terminates. Logical errors are more complex to correct than physical ones.

A **disk cleanup utility** differs from a disk scanning program in that it doesn't rectify any problems. Instead, it improves system performance and increases storage space by removing files that you no longer need. Without your knowledge, some programs create temporary files on the hard drive to perform actions that improve their performance. These files are automatically removed when the program is properly closed. A power outage can cause these files to remain on your hard drive and waste valuable storage space. A disk cleanup utility will search for and delete these unusable files along with any files in the Recycle Bin.

As you use a computer, it creates and erases files on the hard disk. The result is

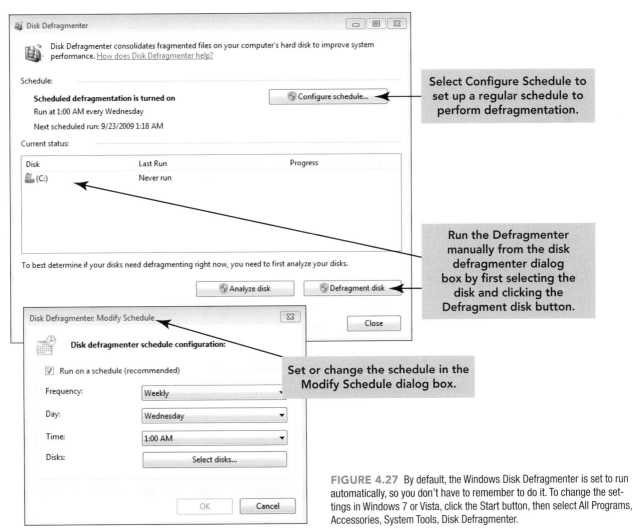

Select Configure Schedule to set up a regular schedule to perform defragmentation.

Run the Defragmenter manually from the disk defragmenter dialog box by first selecting the disk and clicking the Defragment disk button.

Set or change the schedule in the Modify Schedule dialog box.

FIGURE 4.27 By default, the Windows Disk Defragmenter is set to run automatically, so you don't have to remember to do it. To change the settings in Windows 7 or Vista, click the Start button, then select All Programs, Accessories, System Tools, Disk Defragmenter.

that the disk soon becomes a patchwork of files, with portions of files scattered here and there. This slows disk access because the system must look in several locations to find all of a file's segments. A disk with data scattered around in this way is referred to as being **fragmented**. A fragmented disk isn't dangerous—the locations of all the data are known, thanks to the operating system's tracking mechanisms—but periodic maintenance is required to restore the disk's performance. **Disk defragmentation programs** are utility programs used to reorganize data on the disk so that file pieces are reassembled as one chunk of disk space (decreasing disk search time), storage is made more efficient (by clustering files into structures more efficiently searched), and the time needed to access files decreased (Figure 4.27). Scanning and defragmentation utilities should be run anywhere from once every three or four months for the light computer user to as much as once every three to four weeks for the power user.

FILE COMPRESSION UTILITIES

Most downloadable software is compressed. To exchange programs and data efficiently, particularly over the Internet, a **file compression utility** (Figure 4.28) is a program that can reduce the size of a file by as much as 80 percent without harming the data. Most file compression utilities work by searching the file for frequently repeated but lengthy data patterns and then substituting short codes for these

patterns. Compression enables faster downloads, but you must decompress a file after downloading it. When the file is decompressed, the utility restores the lengthier pattern where each short code is encountered. Both compressed and decompressed files can be saved on a computer system, but a file needs to be decompressed prior to use if changes that are made to that file are to be saved.

Most compression utilities also can create archives. An **archive** is a single file that contains two or more files stored in a compressed format. Archives are handy for storage as well as file-exchange purposes because as many as several hundred separate files can be stored in a single, easily handled unit. The most basic archiving programs sequentially attach or pack files into the archive including some additional information about each file, for example, the name and lengths of each original file, so that proper reconstruction or unpacking is possible. To edit and save the changes to any file in the archived packet, the packet must first be restored to its original format.

To compress, or zip, a file in Windows 7 or Vista, right-click it and choose Send To Compressed (zipped) Folder. This creates a new zipped file with the same file name. There are several ways to decompress, or unzip, a zipped file. One way is to double-click the file and use the Extract all files button. Another way is to right-click the zipped file and choose Extract All.

FIGURE 4.28 A file compression utility enables you to create archives and compressed files.

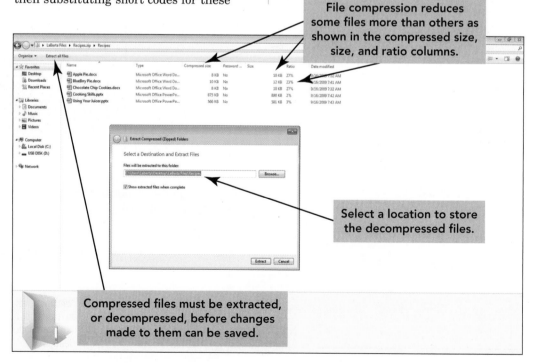

File compression reduces some files more than others as shown in the compressed size, size, and ratio columns.

Select a location to store the decompressed files.

Compressed files must be extracted, or decompressed, before changes made to them can be saved.

SYSTEM UPDATE

Because the world of computers is rapidly changing, Microsoft provides an operating system update service called **Windows Update** that is meant to keep your operating system up to date with fixes (service patches) or protections against external environment changes. If you are using Windows 7 or Vista, you can ensure that your OS is current by going to the Security area of your Control Panel and setting Windows Update to automatically download and install updates at a time of your choosing (Figure 4.29). You can also get more information at Microsoft's Security at Home page (**www.microsoft.com/protect**).

Updates may include service packs, version upgrades, and security updates. They are designed to maintain your computer's security and reliability and to help protect against malicious software and exploits. Mac users have access to a similar software update service.

Besides system utilities, there are additional ways to safeguard your data or take care of operating problems.

TROUBLESHOOTING

Almost every user of a computer system experiences trouble from time to time. Whether the trouble stems from starting the computer, running programs, or adding hardware or software, users need troubleshooting tips to get them through a crisis.

If your computer fails to start normally, you may be able to get it running by inserting a **boot disk** (also called an **emergency disk**). The boot disk is a storage device, like a USB drive, CD, DVD, or network device, that in case of an emergency or boot failure can load a reduced version of the OS that can be used for troubleshooting purposes. Sometimes the boot disk comes with a new computer, but often you need to create it yourself. Consult the

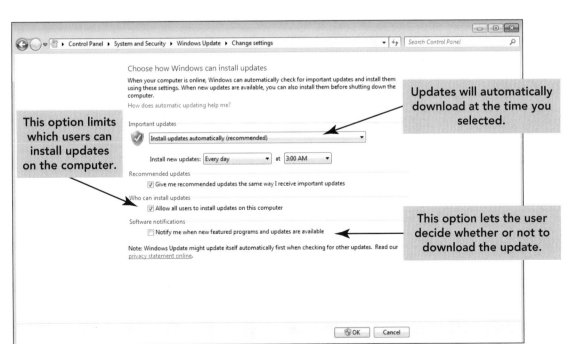

FIGURE 4.29
Setting the appropriate Windows Update options ensures your system will receive the latest software patches and protection.

documentation that came with your computer or choose Help and Support from the Windows Start menu to learn about this process.

In Microsoft Windows, configuration problems can occur after adding a new peripheral device such as an external hard drive or new printer to your system. Conflicts can often be resolved by starting the computer in Windows **safe mode**, an operating mode in which Windows loads a minimal set of drivers that are known to function correctly. Within safe mode, you can use the Control Panel to determine which devices are causing the problem. You access safe mode by pressing the F8 key repeatedly during the start-up process (before the Windows splash screen with the logo appears). Safe mode will reset or report any conflicting programs or device drivers. Shut down the system, boot up normally, and then correct any conflicts that were not reset in safe mode.

System slowdown can sometimes occur because something has changed gradually over time to cause performance to degrade or there has been a hardware or software change. The Windows operating system has a tool to help diagnose these problems—the Reliability and Performance Monitor. The quickest way to access this tool is to open the Start menu and type "Reliability" in the Start Search text box. The Reliability and Performance Monitor will appear in the top of the list. The Resource Overview page provides real-time usage and performance data for four key resources: CPU, Disk, Network, and Memory. An expandable module for each resource provides additional details. There are also two monitoring tools. The Performance Monitor can be customized to display various performance counters. The Reliability Monitor generates a System Stability Chart that includes a graph and a report showing potential causes of reduced stability, such as botched software installations or hardware failures (Figure 4.30). You can easily check to see when your system's performance began to degrade and get details about individual events that might have caused the problem. The best way to ensure that your system runs optimally is never to change more than one thing at a time. That way, if the system has problems, you can undo your last action or installation and see whether the problem goes away.

Help and Support Sometimes the best place to look for troubleshooting guidance is right on your own computer. Microsoft Windows includes a Help and Support utility. You can explore its contents by clicking the Start button and then clicking Help and Support. The Windows Help and Support Center includes several ways to manage and maintain your computer. For example, selecting an option that appears in the initial Windows Help and Support window will provide a list of related topics from which to choose. Click the desired topic and your information will appear.

FIGURE 4.30 Windows Reliability Monitor can help you identify problems with your system's performance.

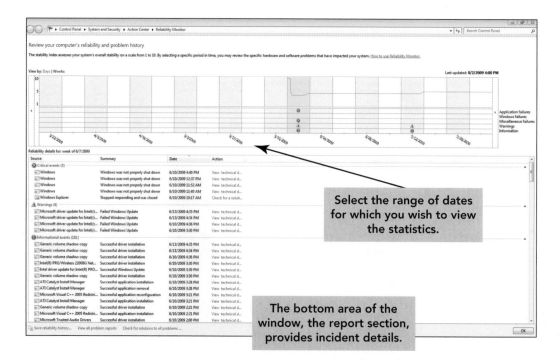

Another useful feature is the Help and Support Search box located at the top of the window. Take the time to explore some of these topics; you may be surprised at the confidence you will gain by interacting with your operating system.

You can find all sorts of troubleshooting sites for both PCs and Macs on the Web. Some offer free advice and user forums, whereas others, such as Ask Dr. Tech, offer support packages for a price. Type "troubleshooting" into your favorite search engine or visit sites such as **www.macfixit.com** or **www.askdrtech.com** to find out more.

> " **Don't** just **switch** off the power without going through the full **shutdown procedure**.... If you switch the **power off** without **shutting down**, the operating system may **fail** to write certain **system files** to the hard disk. "

Shutting Down Your System When you've finished using the computer, be sure to shut it down properly. Don't just switch off the power without going through the full shutdown procedure. In Microsoft Windows 7, click Start and then click the Shut Down button. In Windows Vista, click start, then click the arrow to the right of the Lock button, and click Shut Down. In Mac OS, choose Shut Down from the Apple menu. If you switch the power off without shutting down, the operating system may fail to write certain system files to the hard disk. File fragments that result from improper shutdown could result in permanent damage to the OS or to personal files.

An alternative to completely shutting down your system is to put it in **sleep** mode, a low-power state that enables you to restore your system to full power quickly without going through the lengthy boot process. Sleep mode is available in both Windows and Mac OS. In Windows 7, you can initiate sleep mode from the Start menu by clicking the arrow to the right of the Shut Down button. In Windows Vista, it is activated when you click Start and then click the Power button.

Chapter Summary

System Software

System software has two major components: (1) the operating system (OS) and (2) system utilities that provide various maintenance functions. The programs that comprise the OS coordinate the various functions of the computer's hardware and provide support for running application software.

An operating system acts as an interface between the user and the computer's hardware. Its five basic functions are starting the computer, managing applications, managing memory, handling internal messages from input and output devices, and providing a means of communicating with the user.

When you start or restart a computer, it reloads the operating system into the computer's memory. A computer goes through six steps at start-up: loading the BIOS, performing the power-on self-test, loading the OS, configuring the system, loading system utilities, and authenticating users.

The three major types of user interfaces are graphical user interfaces (GUIs), menu-driven user interfaces, and command-line user interfaces. Most users prefer to use graphical user interfaces that make use of small images, called icons, to identify the linked program.

The two major operating systems for the personal computer are Microsoft Windows and Mac OS X. The major strength of Windows is that it has dominated the market for more than 15 years and is installed and maintained on more than 90 percent of the personal computers in the world. The major strength of OS X is that it has been modified and upgraded for more than 20 years and is the most stable graphical OS. The biggest weakness of Windows is that Microsoft continues to bring new versions to market before all of the bugs and security holes have been resolved. The main disadvantage of OS X is that it is used on only approximately 8 percent of the computers in the world and thus does not support as many applications as Windows does.

Essential system utilities include backup software, antivirus software, file managers, search tools, file compression utilities, disk scanning programs, and disk defragmentation programs. Additionally, features like Windows Update and its Mac equivalent keep your OS up to date with fixes (service patches) or protections against external environment changes.

Key Terms and Concepts

Matching

Match each key term in the left column with the most accurate definition in the right column.

_____ 1. virtual memory

_____ 2. driver

_____ 3. registry

_____ 4. archive

_____ 5. gadget

_____ 6. booting

_____ 7. graphical user interface (GUI)

_____ 8. profile

_____ 9. loading

_____ 10. bad sector

_____ 11. incremental backup

_____ 12. menu driven

_____ 13. authentication

_____ 14. command line

_____ 15. full backup

a. A single file containing two or more files in compressed format.

b. A method of interacting with a program or OS by selecting choices from on-screen, text-based options.

c. A record of a specific user's preferences for the desktop theme, icons, and menu styles.

d. An unusable portion of the hard disk surface.

e. Only new or changed files are copied during this process.

f. Stores configuration information for installed peripherals and software.

g. A method of interacting with a program or OS by typing instruction one line at a time, using correct syntax.

h. The use of a computer's hard disk as an extension of RAM.

i. The process of loading the operating system into RAM.

j. A process that copies all files and data.

k. A utility program used by a peripheral device to function properly.

l. Requesting a user to enter a user name and password to verify identity.

m. The process of transferring a file from storage to memory.

n. The use of small images to activate choices, making a program or OS easier to use.

o. An application that appears as an icon in the Windows Sidebar.

Multiple Choice

Circle the correct choice for each of the following.

1. Which OS is specially designed for smartphones and PDAs?
   a. Windows XP   b. Windows Vista
   c. Mac OS X   d. Windows Mobile

2. What utility program reduces a file size by as much as 80 percent by substituting short codes for lengthy data patterns?
   a. Defragmentation b. Compression
   c. Interrupt   d. Cleanup

3. Which of the following is not an OS function?
   a. Creating documents and spreadsheets
   b. Managing memory
   c. Starting the computer
   d. Providing the user interface

4. Which OS is least likely to be used on a home computer?
   a. Windows Vista   b. Windows CE
   c. Linux   d. Mac OS X

5. Virtual memory is used when:
   a. booting fails.
   b. an IRQ conflict occurs.
   c. RAM is full.
   d. a power-on self-test fails.

6. What happens when a warm boot is performed?
   a. A computer that is already on restarts.
   b. A swap file is created.
   c. A computer that is not already on starts up.
   d. Preemptive multitasking occurs.

7. In virtual memory, what are program instructions and data divided into?
   a. Drivers   b. Pages
   c. IRQs   d. Archives

8. Which system utility creates duplicates of the files and programs on a system?
   a. Compression   b. Defragmentation
   c. Backup   d. Driver

9. Which term describes all of the programs needed for a computer and its peripheral devices to function properly?
   a. Operating system b. BIOS
   c. System utilities d. System software

10. Which tool creates a System Stability Chart to help diagnose performance problems in Windows 7?
    a. Windows Update
    b. Disk defragmentation tool
    c. Reliability Monitor
    d. Performance Monitor

Fill-In

In the blanks provided, write the correct answer for each of the following.

1. _____ _____ automatically installs fixes and service patches to maintain a computer's security and reliability.

2. Windows Explorer and Mac Finder are both examples of a(n) _____ _____ utility.

3. _____ - _____ is an example of a Microsoft OS that uses a command-line user interface.

4. _____ _____ is an environment in which programs that are running receive a recurring slice of time from the CPU.

5. A device _____ is a program that enables communication between the operating system and a peripheral device.

6. In a graphical user interface, a(n) _____ is used to represent computer resources such as programs and files.

7. _____ mode is a low-power alternative to shutting down a computer.

8. The _____, or login, process verifies that the user is authorized to use the computer.

9. The first step in starting a computer is to load the _____ _____.

10. The POST, or _____-_____ _____-_____, makes sure the computer and its peripherals are working correctly during the start-up process.

11. _____ _____ is the name of the most current Windows operating system for a PC.

12. A(n) _____ operating system permits users to work with more than one program at the same time.

13. A(n) _____ is determined by the combination of microprocessor chip and operating system used by a computer.

14. Linux makes its source code available for everyone to see and use. This is an example of _____ _____ software.

15. _____ _____ is an operating mode in which a minimal set of drivers is loaded, usually to help resolve configuration problems.

Short Answer

1. Explain the difference between performing a cold and warm boot. How is a warm boot executed? What activities are not performed during a warm boot?

2. List at least three improvements that Windows 7 offers its customers over Windows Vista.

3. What is the difference between shutting down your computer and putting it into sleep mode? What are the advantages to sleep mode? Are there any disadvantages?

4. List three utilities that are installed with the Windows 7 operating system. Provide a brief description of what each utility does and how it is activated.

5. Explain the differences between a full backup and an incremental backup. Have you ever lost important files because you did not back them up? If you have done a backup, did you copy the entire disk or just selected files? When was the last time you performed a backup?

Teamwork

1. **Operating Systems** Your team is to research three of the operating systems presented in this chapter. In a table created in Microsoft Word or Excel, compare the basic functions performed by each. What future improvements in each OS can you envision or do you see as essential? If you have used several versions of the same OS, what improvements have been incorporated into new versions? Present your comparison table and answers to the questions above in a one-page, double-spaced paper.

2. **Mac OS versus Windows OS** Your team is to locate one or more labs on campus that have PCs running a Windows operating system and Macs. Experiment with both a Mac and a PC and determine the answers to the following questions. What version of each OS did you use? Is it the latest release of the OS? How are the two OSs similar? Can you determine the strengths of each system? Which OS do you prefer? Why? Present your findings in a one-page, double-spaced paper or a PowerPoint presentation of 7 to 10 slides.

3. **Exploring Linux, Mac OS X, and Windows with Humor** Review the humorous spin on the familiar "I am a Mac, I am a PC" commercial that includes the arrival of Linux at **www.youtube.com/watch?v=cldeHjFig_c**. As a team, research the difference between these three systems. Create a short commercial, under 90 seconds, that actually provides some information (and humor) to the viewer on the strengths, differences, or shortcomings of each. Cite your references in a Word document.

4. **Using System Tools** As a team, create a survey with questions relative to the backup procedures that an individual or company might use. Reference the text or Internet sources if you need some additional information on the backup process or types of backups that can be performed. Ask questions about the type of backup performed, the frequency with which it is performed, the medium used for the backup, and other questions that the team finds relevant. Give the survey to at least 20 individuals. Collect and analyze your responses. In a one-page, double-spaced paper, present a summary of your findings and a conclusive statement on the use or lack of use of backup procedures.

5. **Buying a Smartphone** You and your teammates are to consider the purchase of a smartphone. Split into groups and visit local mobile device stores. What companies manufacture smartphones? What operating system and applications are installed on the phones that you are researching? Obtain literature and try out several models. Specifically, try out the operating system. What OS and version of that OS does each use? How does this OS compare with those on desktop and notebook computers? How does it differ? What phone would you recommend and why? Collate your findings and present a summary in a one-page, double-spaced paper.

On the Web

1. **File Compression** Examine a compression program introduced in this text or any other you locate on the Internet. Write a one-page, double-spaced paper that summarizes your answers to these questions.

   - How easy was the program to download?

   - Was the file compression program simple or complicated to use?

   - Perform the compression on several files of different types. Create some files that have all text and no pictures. Create some files with more images than text. What was the size of the file before compression and after?

   - Can you draw any conclusions on the effect of compression and file content?

   - Would you purchase one of these products? Explain why or why not.

2. **Antivirus Programs** In this exercise, you'll examine antivirus software. Write a one-page, double-spaced paper that summarizes your answers to the following questions. Have you ever had to disinfect a file that was infected by a virus?

   - If you have, identify the brand name and version of the antivirus application you used and which operating system you were using. Were you able to disinfect the file successfully? Was the antivirus program simple or complicated to use? Would you recommend this product to someone else? Why or why not?

   - If you have not, visit the sites of the two most popular antivirus applications, Norton AntiVirus at **www.symantec.com/norton/index.jsp** and McAfee VirusScan Plus at **www.mcafee.com/**. With which operating systems does each work? What are the current versions and suggested retail prices of each? Are free or evaluation versions available? Would you purchase one of these products? Explain why or why not.

3. **Windows 7 versus Mac OS X Snow Leopard** Using the Internet and a search engine of your choice, research the features of each of the two top operating systems, Windows 7 and Mac OS X Snow Leopard. In a Word table or Excel spreadsheet, list the features and make a chart that clearly displays which features each OS supports. Indicate the various versions of each system and the cost of each.

4. **Google Android** Use the Internet and search engine of your choice to research the most current version of Android, the embedded operating system developed by Google. Using a table in Word or a spreadsheet in Excel, make a list of its features and locate some of the devices that use this OS. Are there any companies that use this OS exclusively, or countries that use it more than others?

5. **Exploring Linux** Using the Internet and a search engine of your choice, research the Linux operating system. In a one-page, double-spaced paper or PowerPoint presentation, provide a short history of the development of this OS. Indicate where it is primarily used and what applications it is used for. Locate several versions of this system, and indicate the official URL of each product and the features of each. Describe the interface and desktop features of each version. Specify which version you prefer, and explain why.

Buying and Upgrading Your Computer System

When buying a computer, you need to know a lot to make a good decision. But buying a computer doesn't have to be intimidating! Many students successfully purchase and maintain their own computers. In fact, at a typical state university, 95 percent of students own a computer.

By having your own PC, you can type term papers, create slide presentations, and in many cases use the high-speed wireless network all over campus. Many schools encourage students to purchase a computer before they arrive on campus. Even though schools still provide computer labs, with your own computer you can work when you want and, in the case of notebooks, where you want. This Spotlight will guide you step by step through the process of buying your own computer. Read on to learn how to choose the equipment you'll need, at the best prices on today's market.

Getting Started the Right Way

There's a right way and a wrong way to select a computer system. The right way involves understanding the terminology and the relative value of computer system components. You then determine your software needs and choose the computer that runs this software in the most robust way. What's the wrong way? Buying a computer system based only on price, being influenced by sales hype, or purchasing a system you know nothing about. First, we'll discuss how to select the best type of computer for your needs.

Notebook, Netbook, or Desktop?

Deciding whether to buy a notebook (also referred to as a laptop), a notebook, or a desktop computer is often one of the hardest decisions you'll have to make when considering which computer to buy (Figure 3A). Today's notebook computers rival the power of desktop machines. The best of them are truly awesome machines, with big (17-inch or larger) displays and fast processors.

Notebook

    The main advantages of a notebook computer are portability and size. Because notebooks are portable, you can take them to class in a specially designed carrying case (Figure 3B). In class, a notebook fits easily on your desk so you can type notes. As you're probably well aware, campus housing or shared rental units often have a limited amount of desk space, which makes notebooks even more appealing. Although desktops are not as portable as notebooks and netbooks, they can have more processing speed and more RAM. This makes them quite powerful. They can also have a larger internal hard drive.

Netbook

Desktop

FIGURE 3A Which one is right for you? Desktop? Notebook? Netbook?

On the downside, notebook computers cost more than comparable desktop models. You should also consider that notebooks are easily lost or stolen. And if your notebook goes missing, your precious data will go along with it. More than 12,000 notebooks are lost every week in U.S. airports, and the FBI reports that every 53 seconds a notebook is stolen. Sadly, 97 percent of these notebooks are never recovered. Thieves also target college campuses, making safety another important factor when considering a notebook.

    Netbooks are even smaller, making them easier to carry with you. The downside to them is they do not have internal CD/DVD drives, and they have smaller hard drives. Still, if you want something very portable to take to class, a netbook might be the answer. If you want to listen to music, view a DVD, or install software you will need an external device or need to be connected to a network.

    In the end, the decision most often hinges on convenience versus expense. It's a good idea to speak with friends, family, and instructors about their experiences with different computers. Additionally, many computer sites like **www.pcmag.com** or **www.cnet.com** regularly review and rate products from many different manufacturers. Besides choosing

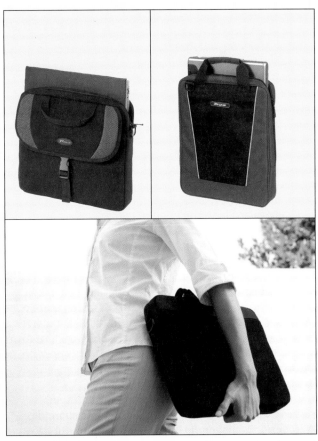

FIGURE 3B Notebook computer bags come in a variety of sizes and styles designed to protect your computer and hold your work too.

a notebook or desktop model, another decision you'll need to make is which platform you want to work on: Mac or PC.

MAC or PC?

There are two main computer system platforms: Windows (PC) and Mac (Figure 3C). If you ask around, you'll find that some users prefer the Mac, whereas others prefer Windows. Each thinks their platform is the best, and rarely do they cross platforms. How do you know which platform is best for you?

Today's top-of-the-line Macs and PCs are virtually indistinguishable in terms of features and performance. Although the market share for Macs is only about 9.6 percent, they have been gaining on PCs in recent years. This has been attributed to Macs now using Intel processors and being capable of running the Microsoft Windows operating system and Windows-based software. In addition, the dissatisfaction that many people have expressed regarding the Windows Vista operating system has helped the Mac's market share grow. So how do you decide? First, you need to know some of the differences between Macs and PCs that can become major issues for some people.

One difference between Macs and PCs is software availability. More than 90 percent of the computers in use today are PCs, and developers are more inclined to develop software for the broadest market. The most noticeable gap is within the gaming software industry, which is primarily Windows based. With the advent of VMware, you can create a virtual Windows PC on your MAC and run Windows based-software. Although play is possible, performance will not be the same as running the application with the Windows operating system because the resources are being shared.

Some software publishers have discontinued some of their Mac products altogether. For example, Autodesk, publisher of the top-selling computer-aided design (CAD) program AutoCAD, dropped its sluggish-selling Mac version to focus on its Windows products,

but it still produces other applications for Macs. Even software publishers that continue to support the Mac typically bring out the Mac versions later and may not include as many features. However, many of the most popular software packages, including Microsoft Office, are available for Macs as well as PCs. Microsoft Office file formats are compatible between the Mac and the PC. You can also choose to run Windows on your Mac using VMware. If you do, you will be able to use Windows-based software too. This, however, adds to the cost of the system because you have to purchase VMware.

In the past, file compatibility between Macs and PCs was a problem, but that's no longer true. Not only can users easily share files between Macs and PCs, they can attach both types of computers to a network and share printers, Internet access, and other resources.

So does software availability really make a difference? If you're planning to use your computer only for basic applications, such as word processing, spreadsheets, databases, presentation graphics, e-mail, and Web browsing, the Mac-versus-PC issue really isn't important. Because many of the formats are compatible (particularly if you use Microsoft Office), you can often move files from the PC to the Mac and back again using a flash drive. Excellent software for all of these important applications is available for both platforms. But look down the road. What if you declare a major a couple of years from now, only to find that your professors want you to use special-purpose programs that run on the platform that you don't have?

Thus, when deciding whether to buy a PC or a Mac, it's important that you anticipate your future software needs. Find out which programs students in your major field of study are using, as well as which programs are used by graduates working in the career you're planning to pursue. To find out what type of computer is preferred by people working in your chosen career, interview appropriate professionals. PCs

FIGURE 3C (a) PCs figure prominently on the desktops of engineers and businesspeople. (b) Macs have a strong niche market in artistic fields, such as music, graphic design, and illustration.

figure prominently on the desktops of engineers and businesspeople. The classic stereotype is that the successful artist has a Mac, but her accountant uses a PC. But like all stereotypes, this is not always the case. For example, you might think that scientists would use PCs, but that's not necessarily true. In the "wet" sciences (chemistry and biology), Macs have many adherents, because these sciences involve visual representation, an area in which Macs excel.

If you're on a budget, consider cost too. Although the price gap is narrowing, Macs and Mac peripherals and software are somewhat more expensive than comparable PC equipment. Macs used to be easier to set up and use, but thanks to improvements in Microsoft Windows, Macs and PCs are now about even.

Now that you've determined whether your computer will be a Mac or a PC, we'll discuss how to select the right hardware.

Choosing the Right Hardware

You'll need to understand and evaluate the following hardware components when buying your computer:

- Processors
- Memory
- Hard disks
- Internal and external drives
- Monitors and video cards
- Printers
- Speakers and sound cards
- Modems and network cards
- Keyboards and mice
- Uninterruptible power supplies
- Notebook cooling pads

The following sections examine each of these components.

PROCESSORS

One of the most important choices you'll make when buying a computer is the microprocessor (also known as the processor or CPU). This decision may seem overwhelming. Not only do you have to compare brands—Intel versus AMD—and each brand's models, you also have to consider features such as clock speed, number of cores, and power consumption. With the advent of multicore processing, a processor's performance isn't defined solely by its clock speed (typically measured in GHz). In most modern applications, a dual-core CPU can outperform a single-core CPU, even if the single-core has a higher clock speed. Using this reasoning, you might think that a quad-core CPU would be even better, but many applications are unable to take advantage of the quad-core's power. Using a quad-core processor for ordinary computer tasks such as word processing and surfing the Internet is a bit like taking a Formula One race car around the block to the minimarket! When it comes to measuring performance, a dual-core processor is about 50 percent faster than a single-core processor. A quad-core processor is only about 25 percent faster than a dual-core processor. Visit the Intel (**www.intel.com**) and AMD (**www.amd.com**) sites to compare the different types of processors each company manufactures. Many sites, such as PassMark Software (**www.cpubenchmark.net**), rigorously test processors. Known as benchmarking, these tests provide a good way to compare overall processor performance results (Figure 3D). Keep these results in mind as you compare computer systems. Each system will have its

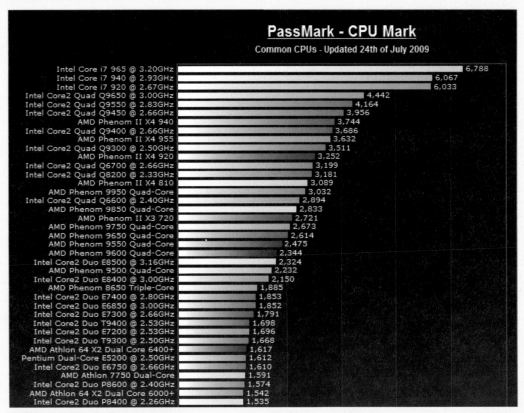

FIGURE 3D PassMark Software (**www.cpubenchmark.net**) provides benchmark test results for more than 300 CPU models and updates its results daily.

strengths and weaknesses; however, the processor is the brain of the machine and often dictates the robustness of the rest of the components. It's important that the processor be a good match for the rest of the system. You don't want to put a high-performance processor on a low-end machine or use an underperforming processor on a high-end system.

When researching different processors, keep in mind that you'll pay a premium if you buy the newest, most powerful processor available. One approach is to buy the second-best processor on the market. That way you'll get plenty of processing power without paying a penalty for being the first to have the most. You only need enough processing power to handle the work or play you intend to accomplish. If you're a heavy game user, you may need a lot of processing power, but if you will use your computer only to surf the Web, play audio files, access social networking sites, and communicate using e-mail and instant messaging, a mid-speed processor should suit your needs just fine.

> "A good **rule** of thumb is never to use more than **75 percent** of available disk space."

MEMORY

The next item to consider when buying a computer is how much memory you need. Two important issues are the amount of RAM and whether the system has cache memory. You really can't have too much memory; a good rule of thumb is to buy as much as you can afford.

RAM To maximize your computer's performance, you should seriously consider purchasing as much RAM as you can. You need to check the operating system's requirements and any applications you will be running. If you are purchasing a new computer and a new operating system is being released, you will want to make sure your computer's RAM can handle the requirements or better yet, the recommendation for RAM, especially if you plan to use a virtual environment or play games. The operating system and applications use RAM for temporary storage. Increasing the amount of available memory allows the CPU to process more instructions and permits more applications to be run simultaneously. Computers with sufficient amounts of RAM are quicker and more responsive than computers with inadequate amounts.

When purchasing a new computer, ask whether the memory can be upgraded and what the maximum amount of memory is for the system. You never know what your future use will demand. You may find that you already own a perfectly good system that just needs more memory to be effective and efficient.

Secondary Cache When researching cache memory, keep in mind that systems with cache memory tend to be faster than systems without it. Secondary cache,

also known as L2 cache, provides an additional location for memory storage that can be quickly accessed by the processor. It may be located on the processor's architecture or very close to it. If a CPU already includes L2 cache, another level, known as L3 cache, may be located close to the processor on the motherboard.

HARD DISKS

A common mistake made by first-time buyers is underestimating the amount of disk storage they'll need. Today, a 500 GB hard drive may sound like quite a lot, but you won't believe how easy it is to fill it up. (For example, 500 high-resolution photos take up approximately 1 GB of storage.) A good rule of thumb is never to use more than 75 percent of available disk space. Many entry-level systems on the market today come with a hard drive that store anywhere from 160 GB to more than 1 TB. Yes, that's correct—1 trillion bytes! Storage has become very inexpensive, so purchase as much as you can.

INTERNAL AND EXTERNAL DRIVES

A **drive** is a connected storage device. Drives can be internal (installed within the system unit) or external (attached to the system unit by a cable connected to a port). For instance, to install new software from a DVD or CD, you'll need a drive that is capable of reading these discs. Although it is possible to have individual DVD and CD drives installed internally or attached as standalone devices, most new computers include a combination DVD±RW/CD-RW drive that is capable of reading and writing both DVDs and CDs. Not only will you be able to read CDs, you'll also be able to view movies on DVDs and save files to either storage medium. The latest optical disc format is Blu-ray Disc, which was developed to enable recording and viewing of high-definition video (Figure 3E).

FIGURE 3E Blu-ray Disc drives are used for recording and playing high-definition video and storing large quantities of data.

Blu-ray also enables you to store large amounts of data. Up to 25 GB of data can be stored on a single-layer disc and up to 50 GB can be stored on a dual-layer disc. Currently only available on high-end systems or as an external drive, Blu-ray is expected to become more popular as high-definition material becomes more prevalent.

Flash drives, also known as thumb drives or USB drives, are an excellent supplement to your hard drive. They came in many different sizes from 128 MB to 64 GB and higher. You can also purchase external hard drives that can be as big as 1 TB. These drives are great for backing up your system or storing your digital photos and videos.

MONITORS AND VIDEO CARDS

Monitors are categorized by the technology used to generate images, the colors they display, their screen size, and additional performance characteristics.

In the past few years, as LCD monitor pricing has dropped, CRT monitors have become obsolete and are now considered legacy technology. LCD monitors have become popular because they consume less electricity, have a slimmer design, and weigh less than older CRT monitors. LCD monitors are sometimes referred to as flat-screen or flat-panel monitors because they are very thin, usually no more than 2 inches deep. The flat screen also causes less distortion, resulting in decreased eyestrain—which is critical for people who spend long stretches of time working on a computer.

The quality and resolution of the display you see on your monitor is determined by the computer's **video card**. Display standards vary depending on whether you have a standard monitor with a 4:3 aspect ratio or a widescreen monitor with a 16:10 aspect ratio. Aspect ratios are determined by dividing a monitor's width by its height. Standard 17- and 19-inch monitors typically use **Super Extended Graphics Array (SXGA)** with a resolution of 1280 × 1024. Widescreen standards include **Widescreen Extended Graphics Array plus (WXGA+)** for 19-inch monitors with a 1440 × 900 resolution, **Widescreen Super Extended Graphics Array plus (WSXGA+)** for 20-inch monitors with a 1680 × 1050 resolution, and **Widescreen Ultra Extended Graphics Array (WUXGA)** for

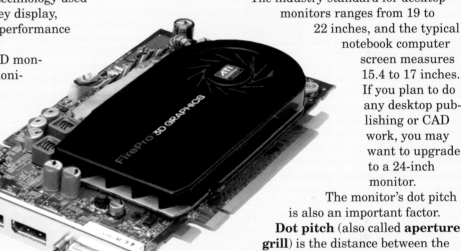

FIGURE 3F Current video graphics cards use PCI Express Base 2.0 technology for improved performance.

24-inch monitors with a 1920 × 1200 resolution. The higher the resolution, the more memory required. Generally, video cards made before 2006 are unable to support widescreen monitors and standard monitors larger than 19 inches.

To increase performance speed, video data is transferred directly from the video graphics card to the motherboard. The interface used by the graphics card is determined by the motherboard. Older systems used the **Accelerated Graphics Port (AGP)** interface; however, AGP is being phased out in favor of the faster **PCI Express** and **PCI Express Base 2.0** interface. Most current video cards from manufacturers like ATI and NVIDIA use PCI Express (Figure 3F).

Monitors are available in different sizes. You can purchase anything from a 17-inch to a 26-inch monitor, but the larger the monitor, the higher the cost. The industry standard for desktop monitors ranges from 19 to 22 inches, and the typical notebook computer screen measures 15.4 to 17 inches. If you plan to do any desktop publishing or CAD work, you may want to upgrade to a 24-inch monitor.

The monitor's dot pitch is also an important factor. **Dot pitch** (also called **aperture grill**) is the distance between the dots (pixels) on a CRT monitor. The lower the dot pitch, the closer the dots are to each other—and the sharper the image produced. Don't buy a monitor with a dot pitch larger than 0.28 mm—the smaller the dot pitch, the better your display.

PRINTERS

Printers fall into four basic categories: color inkjet printers, monochrome laser printers, color laser printers, and multifunction devices that fax and scan as well as print. The difference in print quality between inkjets and laser printers is virtually indistinguishable. Color inkjets and monochrome laser printers are popular and affordable choices for college students. However, the pricing for color lasers and multifunction devices is becoming more competitive, making these viable options too.

You should also consider the cost of supplies such as ink or toner for your printer. Toner for laser printers is often more expensive than the ink used by inkjet printers, but it also lasts longer. When shopping for a new printer, be sure to research a printer's cost per page, not just the purchase price.

Speed matters, too. The slowest laser printers are faster than the fastest inkjet printers, and the slowest inkjet printers operate at a glacial pace. High-end laser printers can print as many as 60 ppm (pages per minute). Still, the best inkjet printers churn out black-and-white pages at a peppy pace—as many as 35 ppm. If you go the inkjet route, look for a printer that can print at least 15 ppm.

If you have a notebook you may not want to be encumbered by wires. One option is a wireless printer. It can be across the room from you and still print. The speed of wireless printers is about the same as for their wired relatives. You also have the option of choosing a laserjet, inkjet, or multifunction printers.

Stay with a major brand name, and you'll be served well. It's always a good idea to purchase an extra print cartridge and stash it away with 30 or 40 sheets of paper. This way, Murphy's Law won't catch you at 2 AM trying to finish an assignment without ink or paper.

SPEAKERS AND SOUND CARDS

To take full advantage of the Internet's multimedia capabilities, you will need speakers and a sound card. The sound card is built into the motherboard; however, you'll need external speakers to hear stereo sound. For the richest sound, equip your system with a subwoofer, which realistically reproduces bass notes.

Be aware that many computers, especially the lowest-priced systems, come with cheap speakers. If sound matters a lot to you—and it does to many college students—consider upgrading to a higher-quality, name-brand speaker system.

If you are taking your notebook to class or have a roommate, be considerate and purchase a good set of headphones.

MODEMS AND NETWORK CARDS

If you plan to log on to the campus network, you'll need a **Network Interface Card (NIC)**, consider wired or wireless or both. Check with your campus computer center to find out how to connect to your school's system and what kind of network card you need. Most colleges run 100-Mbps (100Base-T) Ethernet networks, but some require you to get a 1000-Mbps (1000Base-T) network card.

Macs and PCs have built-in support for Ethernet networks. If you have purchased a computer without a wireless NIC, you can buy one and install it in your PC, or you can purchase a USB wireless NIC.

KEYBOARDS AND MICE

Most computers come with standard keyboards. If you use your computer keyboard a lot and you're worried about carpal tunnel syndrome, consider upgrading to an ergonomic keyboard, such as the Microsoft Natural Keyboard.

Most systems also come with a basic mouse, but you can ask for an upgrade. With Windows PCs, there's good reason to do so, thanks to the improved mouse support built into the Windows operating system. Any mouse that supports Microsoft's IntelliMouse standard includes a wheel that enables you to scroll through documents with ease. Wheel mice also include programmable buttons to tailor your mouse usage to the software application you're using (Figure 3G).

There is also an option for using a wireless mouse and keyboard with your desktop system. Many of the new notebooks use Bluetooth for the mouse and external keyboards.

To choose a good keyboard and mouse, go to a local store that sells computers and try some out. The button placement and action vary from model to model. You'll be using these input devices a lot, so be sure to make an informed decision.

FIGURE 3G An ergonomic keyboard (a) may be for you if you have pain when typing on a standard keyboard. A wheel mouse (b) includes a scrolling wheel and programmable buttons.

UNINTERRUPTIBLE POWER SUPPLIES

"I'm sorry I don't have my paper. I finished it, and then a power outage wiped out my work." If this excuse sounds familiar, you may want to purchase an **uninterruptible power supply (UPS)**, a device that provides power to a computer system for a short time if electrical power is lost (Figure 3H). With the comparatively low price of today's UPSs—you can get one with surge protection for less than $200—consider buying one for your campus computer, especially if you experience frequent power outages where you live or work. A UPS gives you enough time to save your work and shut down your computer properly until the power is back on. Many UPS devices act as surge protectors to help against power spikes and may have multiple outlets so you can protect more than one piece of computer equipment.

NOTEBOOK COOLING PADS

Due to the amount of processing and memory in today's notebooks, they run very hot. To safeguard your notebook, it is wise to purchase a cooling pad (Figure 3I). The prices vary depending on the features you select. Some are adjustable to variable heights, some have extra USB ports, some have multiple fans, some are plastic, and some are aluminum. It doesn't matter which one you get, but it is strongly recommended that you get one. They are lightweight and can add years to the life of your notebook. Check to see whether your notebook has vents on the bottom. If it does, a cooling pad will be beneficial. Even though notebooks are often called laptops, do not place notebooks with vents on the bottom on your lap. It will block the cooling ability of the internal fan.

A few other items you might consider are a backup system and locks for your desktop and notebook. Now that you know what to look for when choosing hardware for your computer system, let's examine how to choose between a notebook and a desktop model.

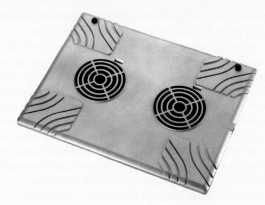

FIGURE 3I A Cooling Pad for Notebooks

FIGURE 3H A UPS device can easily justify its purchase price by saving your data in an unexpected power outage.

Shopping Wisely

When you buy a computer, it's important to shop wisely. Should you buy a top-of-the-line model or a bargain-bin special? Is it better to buy at a local store or through a mail-order company? What about refurbished or used computers or a name-brand versus a generic PC? Let's take a look at some of these issues.

TOP-OF-THE-LINE MODELS VERSUS BARGAIN-BIN SPECIALS

A good argument for getting the best system you can afford is that you don't want it to become obsolete before you graduate. Inexpensive systems often cut corners by using less powerful CPUs, providing the bare minimum of RAM, and including an operating system with fewer features and capabilities. For example, if the word *home* is part of the name of your operating system, it may not be as robust as what you might need for your studies; however, it will be great for writing papers and sending email. In your senior year, do you want to spend time upgrading your hardware and software when you should be focusing on your studies? In addition, every time you open the computer's cover and change something, you risk damaging one of the internal components.

The most important consideration is the type of software you plan to run. If you'll be using basic applications such as word processing, you don't need the most powerful computer available. In this situation, a bargain-bin special may be okay, as long as you exercise caution when making such a purchase. But what if you decide to declare a major in mechanical engineering? You might want to run a CAD package, which demands a fast system with lots of memory. In that case, you'd be better off paying extra to get the memory you need up front, rather than settling for a bargain-bin special that may end up being inadequate later.

LOCAL STORES VERSUS MAIL-ORDER AND ONLINE COMPANIES

Whether you're looking for a Windows PC or a Mac, you need to consider whether to purchase your system locally or from a mail-order or online company. If you buy locally, you can resolve problems quickly by going back to the store (Figure 3J). With a system from a mail-order or online company, you'll have to call the company's technical support line.

If you are considering ordering through the mail or online, look for companies that have been in business a long time—particularly those that offer a no-questions-asked return policy for the first 30 days. Without such a policy, you could get stuck with a lemon that even the manufacturer won't be able to repair. Be aware that the lowest price isn't always the best deal—particularly if the item isn't in stock and will take weeks to reach you. Also, don't forget about shipping and handling charges, which could add considerably to the price of a system purchased online or through the mail.

In addition, make sure you're not comparing apples and oranges. Some quoted prices include accessories such as modems and monitors; others do not. To establish a level playing field for comparison, use the shopping comparison worksheet in Figure 3K. For the system's actual price, get a quote that includes all of the accessories you want, such as a printer, a monitor, and a UPS.

You should also consider warranties and service agreements. Most computers come with a one-year warranty for parts and service. Some companies offer service agreements for varying lengths of time that will cover anything that goes wrong with your system—for a price. In the vast majority of cases, a computer will fail within the first few weeks or months. You should feel comfortable with the amount of coverage you have during the first year. Be aware, though, that extra warranty coverage and service contracts can add significantly to the cost of your system. You may also want to check to see where repairs need to be completed. Do you have to take the system back to where you purchased it? Do you have to mail it back to the manufacturer? Will a service technician come to your house or dorm? What happens if a component goes bad? Do you have to replace it yourself or take it

into a shop? These are all things to consider when purchasing a computer and extended warranty.

BUYING USED OR REFURBISHED

What about buying a used system? It's risky. If you're buying from an individual, chances are the system is priced too high. People just can't believe how quickly computers lose their value. They think their systems are worth a lot more than they actually are. Try finding some ads for used computers in your local newspaper and then see how much it would cost to buy the same system new, right now, if it's still on the market. Chances are the new system is cheaper than the used one.

FIGURE 3J If you buy a computer at a local retail store, you can evaluate different models and speak with a salesperson to obtain additional information.

A number of computer manufacturers and reputable businesses refurbish and upgrade systems for resale. National chains such as TigerDirect.com or Newegg.com have standards to ensure that their systems are "as good as new" when you make a purchase. As always, check out the storefront and stay away from establishments that don't look or feel right. And most important, your refurbished machine should come with a warranty and should include software that has a valid license.

NAME-BRAND VERSUS GENERIC PCS

Name-brand PC manufacturers, such as Hewlett-Packard, Dell, and Gateway, offer high-quality systems at competitive prices. You can buy some of these systems from retail or mail-order stores, but some are available only by directly contacting the vendor.

If you're buying extended warranty protection that includes on-site service, make sure the on-site service really is available where you live; you may find out that the service is available only in major metropolitan areas. Make sure you get 24-hour technical support; sometimes your problems don't occur between 8 AM and 5 PM.

If something breaks down, you might have only one repair option: Go back to the manufacturer. And after the warranty has expired, you may end up paying a premium price for parts and repairs. Fortunately, this is becoming less of an issue. Almost all of today's name-brand computers run well right out of the box, and in-service failure rates are declining.

What about generic PCs? In most cities, you'll find local computer stores that assemble their own systems using off-the-shelf components. These systems are

Shopping Comparison Worksheet

VENDOR _____ Date _____

    Brand Name _____

    Model _____

    Real Price _____ (including selected components)

PROCESSOR

    Brand _____

    Model _____

    Speed _____ MHz

RAM

    Type _____

    Amount _____ MB

HARD DRIVE

    Capacity _____ GB   Seek time _____ ns

    Speed _____ rpm   Interface _____

MONITOR

    Size _____ x _____ pixels   Dot pitch _____ mm

VIDEO CARD

    Memory _____ MB   Max. resolution _____ x _____ pixels

    Accelerated? .... ☐ yes ☐ no

REMOVABLE DRIVE

    Type _____

    Location .... ☐ internal ☐ external

DVD DRIVE

    Speed _____

DVD BURNER

    Included? .... ☐ yes ☐ no

BLU-RAY DISC DRIVE

    Included? .... ☐ yes ☐ no

SPEAKERS

    Included? .... ☐ yes ☐ no

    Upgraded? .... ☐ yes ☐ no

SUBWOOFER

    Included? .... ☐ yes ☐ no

NETWORK CARD

    Included? .... ☐ yes ☐ no

    Wireless? .... ☐ yes ☐ no

    Speed (100/1000) _____

KEYBOARD

    Upgraded? .... ☐ yes ☐ no

    External for laptop? .... ☐ yes ☐ no

    Wireless? .... ☐ yes ☐ no

    Model _____

MOUSE

    Included? .... ☐ yes ☐ no

    Wireless? .... ☐ yes ☐ no

    Upgraded? .... ☐ yes ☐ no

UPS

    Included? .... ☐ yes ☐ no

SOFTWARE

_____

_____

WARRANTY _____

    Service location _____

    Typical service turnaround time _____

FIGURE 3K   Shopping Comparison Worksheet

often just as fast (and just as reliable) as name-brand systems. You save because you don't pay for the name-brand company's marketing and distribution costs. Because of their smaller client base, the staff at local computer stores has a better chance of knowing their customers personally and thus may provide more personalized service. Their phones are not nearly as busy, and if something goes wrong with your computer, you won't have to ship it halfway across the country. Ask the technician about his or her training background and experience. Another thing to consider is that the industry's profit margin is razor thin; if the local company goes bankrupt, your warranty may not mean much.

What if you don't need an entire new computer system, but just want to improve your current system's performance? That's when you should consider upgrading.

Upgrading Your System

You may want to upgrade your system for a variety of reasons. You may have purchased new software that requires more memory to run properly. You may decide to add a game controller. You could decide that a new monitor and printer will enhance your computing experience. Many computer owners improve their system's performance and utility by adding new hardware, such as RAM, sound cards, and additional memory. This section discusses the two most common hardware upgrades: adding expansion boards and adding memory.

Some upgrades, such as upgrading the hard drive, can be accomplished by using an external device. Some thumb drives or flash drives can be used to supplement the RAM on your computer. However, many enhancements require more invasive actions. Before you decide to upgrade your computer on your own, be aware that doing so may violate your computer's warranty. Read the warranty to find out. You may need to take your computer to an authorized service center to get an upgrade. Although it can be relatively simple to install new components, it can be risky. If you have a notebook or a netbook, you may want to take your computer to a trained technician. Upgrading a notebook is not an easy task. If you aren't absolutely certain of what you're doing—don't do it! Also, before you start any upgrade, consider whether it may be more cost effective to purchase a new computer than to upgrade your existing one.

REMOVING THE COVER

If you have a desktop computer, begin upgrading your computer by unplugging the power cord and removing all the cables attached to the back of the system unit. Make a note of which cable went where so that you can plug the cables back in correctly. With most systems, you can remove the cover by removing the screws on the back of the case. If you don't know how to remove the cover, consult your computer manual. Keep the screws in a cup or bowl so they'll be handy when you reassemble the computer.

ADDING EXPANSION BOARDS

To add an expansion board to your system, identify the correct type of expansion slot (ISA [Industry Standard Architecture], PCI [Peripheral Component Interconnect], or AGP [Accelerated Graphics Port]) and unscrew the metal insert that blocks the slot's access hole. Save the screw, but discard the insert. Gently but firmly press the board into the slot. Don't try to force it, though, and stop pressing if the motherboard flexes. If the motherboard flexes, it is not properly supported, and you should take your computer to the dealer to have it inspected. When you've pressed the new expansion board fully into place, screw it down using the screw you removed from the metal insert. Before replacing the cover, carefully check that the board is fully inserted.

FIGURE 3L SDRAM Chip Showing Both Sides

UPGRADING MEMORY

Many users find that their systems run faster when they add more memory. With additional memory, it's less likely that the operating system will need to use virtual memory, which slows the computer down. To successfully upgrade your computer's memory, visit a leading memory site like Kingston (**www.kingston.com**) or Crucial (**www.crucial.com**). There are several different kinds of memory, but only one type will work with your computer. Both of these sites include tools to help you determine what type of memory your computer requires (Figure 3L). Crucial also includes a system scanner that will tell you how much memory is currently installed in your computer. Both sites will tell you the maximum amount of memory your system can use, what type of memory is compatible with your system, and whether you need to buy the memory modules singly or in pairs. You can purchase the specified memory directly from the site or use this information to check pricing and shop around.

When you purchase memory modules, a knowledgeable salesperson might help you determine which type of module you need and how much memory you can install. But in most cases, the salesperson won't know any more about installing memory than you do.

Before you install memory modules, be aware that memory chips are easily destroyed by static electricity. Do not attempt to install memory chips without wearing a **grounding strap**, a wrist-attached device that grounds your body so that you can't zap the chips. Remember, don't try to force the memory modules into their receptacles; they're supposed to snap in gently. If they won't go in, you don't have the module aligned correctly or you may have the wrong type of module.

REPLACING THE COVER

When you have checked your work and you're satisfied that the new hardware is correctly installed, replace the cover and screw it down firmly. Replace the cables and then restart your system. If you added PnP devices, you'll see on-screen instructions that will help you configure your computer to use your new hardware.

If you're thinking about upgrading your system or if you want to understand what a particular component does, the Internet is a great resource. Sites like CNET (**www.cnet.com**) and PCMag.com (**www.pcmag.com**) can be used to learn about the newest products and read expert reviews. Other sites like HowStuffWorks (**www.howstuffworks.com**) can provide details and explanations for various components. Using a search engine for specific questions can also turn up valuable information.

Whether your computer system is brand new or merely upgraded, you need to know how to properly maintain your system's components.

Caring for Your Computer System

After your computer is running smoothly, chances are it will run flawlessly for years if you take a few precautions:

- Equip your system with a surge protector, a device that will protect all system components from power surges caused by lightning or other power irregularities (Figure 3M). Remember a power strip is not necessarily a surge protector. Most surge protectors come with a guarantee. APC, one of the largest makers of UPSs and surge protectors, has a lifetime Equipment Protection Policy on most of its equipment.
- Consider purchasing a UPS. These devices protect your system if the computer loses power.
- Don't plug your dorm refrigerator into the same outlet as your computer. A refrigerator can cause fluctuations in power, and a consistent power

supply is critical to the performance and longevity of your computer.

- There should be sufficient air circulation around the components. Don't block air intake grilles by pushing them flush against walls or other barriers. Heat and humidity can harm your equipment. Your computer should not be in direct sunlight or too close to a source of moisture.
- Before connecting or disconnecting any cables, make sure your computer is turned off.
- Cables shouldn't be stretched or mashed by furniture. If your cables become damaged, your peripherals and computer might not communicate effectively.
- Clean your computer and printer with a damp, soft, lint-free cloth.
- To clean your monitor, use a soft, lint-free cloth and gently wipe the surface clean. If the monitor is very dirty, unplug it and wipe with a cloth slightly dampened with distilled water. Never apply any liquids directly to the surface, and don't press too hard on it.
- Avoid eating or drinking near your computer. Crumbs can gum up your mouse or keyboard, and spilled liquids (even small amounts) can ruin an entire system.
- To clean your keyboard, disconnect it from the system unit and gently shake out any dust or crumbs. You can also use cans of compressed air to clear dust or crumbs from underneath the keys. Vacuums specially designed for keyboards also are on the market. Never use a regular vacuum cleaner on your keyboard. The suction is too strong and may damage the keys.
- To keep your hard disk running smoothly, run a disk defragmentation program regularly. This program ensures that related data is stored as a unit, increasing retrieval speed.

FIGURE 3M Surge protectors prevent costly damage to delicate circuitry and components.

- Get antivirus and antispyware software and run it frequently. Don't install and run any software or open any file that you receive from anyone until you check it for viruses and spyware. Be sure to update your antivirus and antispyware software. They won't be beneficial to you if you do not keep them updated.

Some Final Advice

Conducting research before you buy a computer is fairly painless and very powerful. To prepare for buying a computer, peruse newspaper and magazine ads listing computer systems for sale. Another great source is the Web, which makes side-by-side comparison easy. For instance, typing "PC comparison shopping" (without the quotes) into the Google search engine returns close to 12 million links. It's also a good idea to visit a comparison site, such as CNET, PCMag.com, Yahoo!, AOL, or PCWorld. To research particular computer manufacturers (such as Apple, Dell, Sony, Toshiba, Lenovo, Gateway, and so on), simply type the manufacturer's name in the address bar of your Web browser and add the .com extension. Use as many resources as you can when you shop for a computer, and then remember that no matter how happy or unhappy you are with your end purchase, you'll most likely be doing it all again within three to five years.

Spotlight Exercises

1. Have you considered purchasing a used or refurbished computer? You can purchase a computer from a company or from an individual. What are some of the advantages and disadvantages of purchasing a used or refurbished computer from a company or individual? Visit **www.tigerdirect.com** or **www.newegg.com** and search for refurbished computers. Select a specific notebook computer. Identify the computer, its specifications, and its cost. Where would you search to buy a used notebook computer from an individual? Write a short paper on where you would purchase the computer and its specifications. The paper should show that you understand at least six terms from the Spotlight as they apply to purchasing a used computer.

2. You need to upgrade your computer because the new computer game you just purchased needs more RAM than you have in your system. Go to **www.crucial.com** or **www.kingston.com** and see how much RAM your computer has and how much more you can add. Once you determine how much RAM you need to add to max out your system, go shopping for that specific configuration on three Web sites, including the one you used to obtain the information. Use your word processor or spreadsheet program to create a table of the costs. Remember to add the shipping cost if that is not included in the purchase price.

3. Use your favorite browser to go to **www.shopping .com/xPP-laptops**. Locate and compare two notebooks (laptops)—one less than $500, the other above $1,500. Use the "Choosing the Right Hardware" section of this Spotlight as a basis for comparing the two. Write a paper that includes a table that compares the computers on at least four points and that explains why you would purchase one over the other.

4. If you purchase a computer that does not have enough storage space and you need more, what would you purchase? Research different types of external drives that you could use. Create a chart that lists at least four different types of drives, their specifications, and price. Then indicate which of the options you would choose and explain your choice.

5. Today, we all need to be savvy consumers. The Internet has made shopping and comparing items much easier than driving to many different stores. Compare online shopping with in-store shopping for purchasing a computer. Pick any online computer sales vendor and build a system of your choice. Write down or print out the details and specifications of the computer you've built, including the price and shipping costs. Visit a store that sells computers, such as Staples, Office Depot, Wal-Mart, Best Buy, or a local shop. Duplicate what you selected online. (If you do not have a computer store in your area, use newspaper or magazine advertisements). Write at least two paragraphs about each experience. Which did you prefer? What are the advantages and disadvantages of each? Would you rather buy online or in person? Why?

6. It is important to know what is in your computer if you plan to upgrade or purchase a new computer. Windows provides a utility to check your computer. System Information is the utility that shows the hardware that is in your system, regardless of whether it is a notebook or desktop. Use the Start, All Programs, Accessories, System Tools menu sequence to access the System Information utility. If you use Control Panel in the classic view and select System, you will get an experience rating and suggestions of how to improve performance by selecting the Windows Experience Index. Write a short paper that includes a table with the values for the following components: the operating system, processor, total physical memory, available physical memory, total virtual memory, and available virtual memory. Using what you learned in the sections on processing, memory, and RAM, is your system current with today's standards? Should you upgrade your computer? Why or why not?

chapter 5

Application Software: Tools for Productivity

Chapter Objectives

- Understand how system software supports application software. (p. 157)

- List the most popular types of general-purpose applications. (p. 157)

- Discuss the advantages of Web-hosted technology and file compatibility. (p. 166)

- Discuss the advantages and disadvantages of standalone programs, integrated programs, and software suites. (p. 171)

- Explain the concept of software versions and software upgrades. (p. 173)

- Understand how commercial software, shareware, freeware, and public domain software differ. (p. 175)

- Describe the essential concepts of application software and the skills needed to use it. (p. 176)

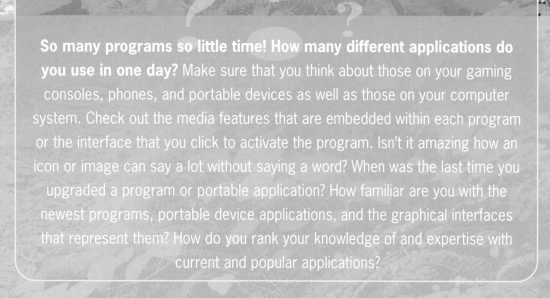

So many programs so little time! How many different applications do you use in one day? Make sure that you think about those on your gaming consoles, phones, and portable devices as well as those on your computer system. Check out the media features that are embedded within each program or the interface that you click to activate the program. Isn't it amazing how an icon or image can say a lot without saying a word? When was the last time you upgraded a program or portable application? How familiar are you with the newest programs, portable device applications, and the graphical interfaces that represent them? How do you rank your knowledge of and expertise with current and popular applications?

Application software refers to all of the programs that enable you to use the computer to perform tasks and accomplish work. In this sense, application software differs from system software, the programs that provide the infrastructure and hardware control so other programs can function properly. You use application software to work efficiently with the documents that are created in almost any line of work, such as invoices, letters, reports, proposals, presentations, customer lists, newsletters, tables, and flyers. Recall our aquarium analogy. In that analogy, applications are the fish that swim in the water (the operating system). The operating system provides the environment in which the applications run. It supports the functions of input, processing, output, and storage, whereas the applications enable users to accomplish specific tasks. People use applications to create products, communicate with others, store and find information, and derive entertainment.

In this chapter, you'll learn how to make sense of the world of application software. You'll read about the various types of application software and learn how to install, maintain, and upgrade the programs that you use each day.

General-Purpose Applications

General-purpose applications are programs used by many people to accomplish frequently performed tasks. These tasks include writing documents (word processing), working with numbers (spreadsheets), keeping track of information (databases), developing multimedia and graphic content, facilitating Internet usage, and a variety of other tasks handled by home and educational programs. These applications are found on home and

FIGURE 5.1 General-Purpose Application Software

Personal Productivity Programs	Multimedia and Graphics Software	Internet Programs	Home and Educational Programs
Word processing	Desktop publishing and multimedia authoring programs	E-mail programs	Personal finance software
Spreadsheet	Paint, drawing, and animation programs	Web browsers	Tax preparation software
Database	Image-editing programs	Instant messaging software	Home design and landscaping software
Presentation graphics	3-D rendering programs	Videoconferencing software and IP telephony	Computer-assisted tutorials
Personal information management	Audio software	Web-hosted applications	Computerized reference information (e.g., encyclopedias, street maps)
	Video-editing software	Spyware, adware, pop-ups	Games

business computers as well as mobile devices and media-specific technology such as iPods. Figure 5.1 lists the various types of general-purpose application software, including some applications that work through and run from the Internet.

Personal Productivity Programs

The most popular general-purpose applications are **personal productivity programs**, which, as the name implies, help individuals do their work more effectively and efficiently. Productivity programs include word processors, spreadsheets, and presentation software (Figure 5.2). Their value is that they perform their functions regardless of the subject matter. For instance, a word processor is equally valuable for typing a term paper for your writing class or for typing one for your marketing class.

Using the appropriate application for the appropriate purpose further facilitates tasks. Excel can be used for a presentation, but it is much better to use Power-Point and embed Excel spreadsheets and charts in it. In Word, you can use tables to add numbers together, but Excel is much better suited to this task. One maxim you may have heard is, "You can drive a screw with a hammer—but a hammer is best used for driving nails and a screw should be set with a screwdriver." The same rule applies to using the right productivity program for the right job. You can increase your productivity by choosing an application such as Excel to manage numbers and an application such as Word to manage text.

Programs that act as personal information managers (PIMs) offer electronic address books, scheduling tools, and database programs, that enable you to manage, track, report, and share information. Such programs are also considered personal productivity software. Outlook is an example of a personal information management program (Figure 5.3).

Multimedia and Graphics Software

What exactly is **multimedia**? The standard definition is that it is any application that involves two or more media, such as

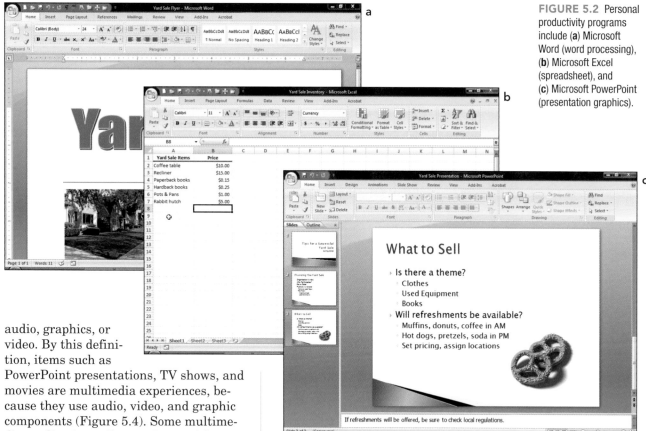

FIGURE 5.2 Personal productivity programs include (**a**) Microsoft Word (word processing), (**b**) Microsoft Excel (spreadsheet), and (**c**) Microsoft PowerPoint (presentation graphics).

audio, graphics, or video. By this definition, items such as PowerPoint presentations, TV shows, and movies are multimedia experiences, because they use audio, video, and graphic components (Figure 5.4). Some multimedia applications offer another exciting characteristic: interactivity. For example, in an interactive multimedia presentation, users can choose their own path through the presentation. The interactive dimension makes computer-based multimedia a non-couch-potato technology; instead of sitting back and letting someone else determine the presentation's flow, you're in control.

Interactivity is a big factor in the popularity of the Web. In fact, the Web could be viewed as a gigantic multimedia presentation. Most Web pages include graphics along with the text, and many also offer animations, videos, and sounds. On some Web pages, you can click parts of a graphic to access different pages or other sections of the same page.

Computer applications use multimedia features where text alone would not be

effective. Graphics, sounds, animations, and video can often do a more effective job of involving the user (and conveying information) than text alone. These features, which once were considered entertainment or amusement, have become standard components of business and educational programs.

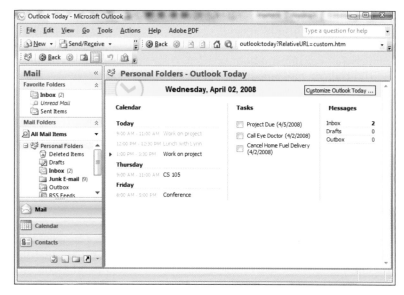

FIGURE 5.3 Outlook helps you manage your e-mail, contacts, calendar, and tasks.

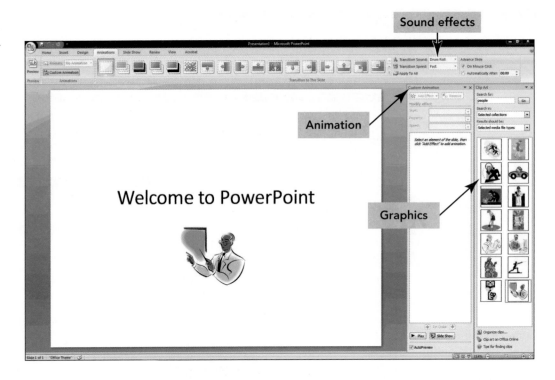

FIGURE 5.4 Multimedia presentations involve two or more media. Such presentations are now the norm in professional settings.

Sound effects

Animation

Graphics

Multimedia and graphics software includes professional desktop publishing programs (such as QuarkXPress) and multimedia authoring programs; paint, drawing, and animation programs; image-editing programs (such as Photoshop); three-dimensional (3-D) rendering programs (such as computer-aided design [CAD] programs); audio software; and video-editing programs.

A multimedia presentation typically involves some or all of the following: bitmapped graphics, vector graphics, edited photographs, rendered 3-D images, edited videos, and synthesized sound. In the following sections, we'll discuss each of these and look briefly at some of the software used to create multimedia productions. For information, articles, and tutorials on multimedia products and current industry trends visit **http://graphicssoft.about.com**.

Compression and Decompression

Computers can work with art, photographs, videos, and sounds only when these multimedia resources are stored in digitized files, which require huge amounts of storage space. To use the space on your hard disk more efficiently and improve file transfer speeds over the Internet, most multimedia software programs reduce file size by using compression/decompression algorithms called **codecs**.

Codecs use two different approaches to compression: lossless compression and lossy compression. With **lossless compression**, the original file is compressed so that it can be completely restored, without flaw, when it is decompressed. With **lossy compression**, the original file is processed so that some information is permanently removed from the file. Lossy compression techniques eliminate information that isn't perceived when people see pictures or hear sounds, such as frames from a video that are above the number needed to eliminate the flicker effect and very high musical notes. In the area of medical imaging, a hybrid technique is being used for CTs and MRIs that combines both compression schemes in one image. The dilemma in this field is to keep high image quality in the region of interest (ROI). Therefore, a very lossy compression scheme is suitable in non-ROI regions to give a global picture to the user, while a lossless compression scheme is necessary for ROI regions.

Paint Programs Paint programs are used to create **bitmapped graphics** (also called **raster graphics**), which are composed of tiny dots, each corresponding to one pixel on the computer's display (Figure 5.5). You can use a professional paint program such as Corel Painter to create beautiful effects. Although paint programs enable artists to create pictures easily, the resulting bitmapped image is difficult to edit. To do so, you must zoom the picture so that you can edit the individual pixels, and enlargement may produce an unattractive distortion called the *jaggies* (Figure 5.6).

It is possible, in some graphic applications, to convert a graphic in bitmapped graphic format (.bmp) to jpeg format through the Save As option. Once the Save As dialog box appears, select jpeg in the Save As type input box.

Paint programs can save your work to the following standard formats:

- **Graphics Interchange Format (GIF;** pronounced "jiff" or "giff"**).** GIF is a 256-color file format that uses lossless compression to reduce file size. It's best for simple images with large areas of solid color. Because this file format is a Web standard, it's often used for Web pages.

- **Joint Photographic Experts Group (JPEG;** pronounced "jay-peg"**).** JPEG files can store up to 16.7 million colors and are best for complex images, such as photographs. This image format is also a Web standard. The JPEG file format uses lossy compression to reduce file size.

- **Portable Network Graphics (PNG;** pronounced "ping"**).** A patent-free alternative to GIF, PNG produces images that use lossless compression and are best suited to Web use only.

- **Windows Bitmap (BMP).** BMP is a standard bitmapped graphics format developed for Microsoft Windows. Compression is optional, so BMP files tend to be very large.

- **Tag Image File Format (TIFF).** A TIFF file can be identified as a file with a ".tiff" or ".tif" file name suffix. This format, used in publishing, allows very specific instructions to be attached to an image and captures as much detail as possible. In fact, most of the images in this book were submitted in TIFF file format.

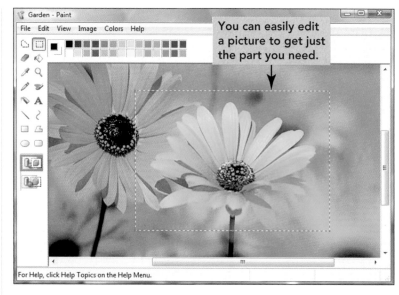

You can easily edit a picture to get just the part you need.

FIGURE 5.5 The program Paint is included in Microsoft Windows. Although not as full-featured as professional paint programs, it is possible to create your own bitmapped graphics or edit existing images.

- **Drawing Programs.** Drawing programs are used to create **vector graphics**, images generated by the use of points, lines, curves, polygons, and basically any shape that can be generated by a mathematical description (equation). What this means, in practice, is that the final product in a vector graphic can be independently edited and resized, by a change in an equation, without introducing edge distortion, the curse of bitmapped graphics (Figure 5.7). To compose an image with a drawing program, you create independent lines and shapes; you can then add colors and textures to these shapes. Because the resulting image has no inherent resolution, it

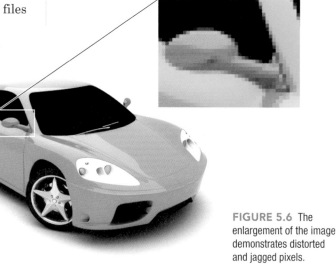

FIGURE 5.6 The enlargement of the image demonstrates distorted and jagged pixels.

FIGURE 5.7 The
elephant is a vector image
generated by points, lines,
and curves.

are saved to the Encapsulated PostScript
(EPS) format, which combines the original
PostScript document in a file that also
contains a bitmapped thumbnail
image of the enclosed graphic.
(The thumbnail image enables
you to see the graphic on the
screen.)

Drawing programs have
been optimized to create art for
the Web and mobile devices.
Adobe Illustrator is tightly integrated with Adobe Flash, a
program commonly used to create
animated Web graphics.

can
be any
size you
want. The
picture will be
printed using the
output device's
highest resolution.
See Figure 5.8 for a comparison in the
enlargement of a vector image versus
a bitmapped image.

Professional drawing programs, such
as CorelDRAW and Adobe Illustrator,
save files by outputting instructions in
PostScript, which is an automated page-
description language (PDL), a language
designed to precisely describe the appearance of a printed page including fonts
and graphics. PostScript graphic files

FIGURE 5.8 The
enlargement of the image
demonstrates distorted and
jagged pixels.

Vector

Bitmap

Three-Dimensional Rendering
Programs A 3-D rendering program
adds three-dimensional effects to graphic
objects. The results are strikingly realistic.
Objects can be rotated in any direction
to achieve just the result the artist is
looking for.

In the past, rendering software
required a high-powered engineering
workstation, but today's top desktop computers are up to the task. One rendering
technique, **ray tracing**, adds amazing
realism to a simulated three-dimensional
object by manipulating variations in
color intensity that would be produced
by light falling on the object from multiple
directions, which is the norm in the real
world (Figure 5.9). Detailed steps to create
night lighting using ray tracing can be
found at **www.cgdigest.com/index.php/
night-rendering-tutorial-vray/**.

For a list of available programs, issues,
and general information on 3-D graphics
go to **www.google.com/Top/Computers/
Software/Graphics/3D/Rendering_
and_Modelling**. To view a brief video
on the capabilities of AutoCAD, a three
dimensional rendering program, check
out **http://download.autodesk.com/
us/autocad/interactiveoverview/
autodesk.htm**. Click on Explore,
then select Watch Video.

Image editors are sophisticated versions of paint programs that are used to
edit and transform—but not create—
complex bitmapped images, such as photographs. Programs like Picasa and Gimp
make use of automated image-processing
algorithms to add a variety of special effects, remove blemishes, crop portions, and
adjust coloring to photographic images.
They also enable skilled users to doctor
photographs in ways that leave few traces
behind. After using image editors to

improve your photos, you can share them with friends and family at Web sites such as Flickr (**www.flickr.com**; Figure 5.10).

Professional design studios have used image editors such as Adobe Photoshop for years (Figure 5.11), but image editors have captured a wider market because of the popularity of digital cameras. Programs such as Adobe's Photoshop Elements are designed for beginners who want to perform the most common image-enhancement tasks quickly and easily and then print their pictures on a color printer. These programs can be used to remove red-eye from flash snapshots and adjust a picture's overall color cast.

Animation Programs When you see a movie at a theater, you're actually looking at still images shown at a frame rate (images per second) that is sufficiently high to trick the eye into seeing continuous motion. Like a movie, computer animation consists of the same thing: images that appear to move. Computer animators create each of the still images separately in its own frame with the help of computer programs that contain tools to facilitate the image creation as well as animation.

It's relatively easy to create a simple animation using GIF, which enables programs to store more than one image in a GIF file. The file also stores a brief script that tells the application to play the images in a certain sequence and to display each image for a set time. Because Web browsers can read GIF files and play the animations, GIF animations are common on the Web (Figure 5.12).

Professional animation programs provide more sophisticated tools for creating and controlling animations, but they create **proprietary files**, files whose format is patented or copyright protected and controlled by a single company. The extent of restriction depends on the company and its policies. To view these files on the Web, you need a special plug-in program such as the Shockwave Player or Flash Player from Adobe (Figure 5.13).

FIGURE 5.9 Ray tracing is a technique that adds realism to an image by adding the appearance of natural light.

Audio Software A variety of programs are available for capturing and processing sound for multimedia presentations, including sound mixers, compression software, bass enhancers, synthesized stereo, and even on-screen music composition programs. You won't see any tape recorders in today's recording studios—just computers!

Sound files contain digitized data in the form of digital audio waveforms (recorded live sounds or music), which are saved in one of several standardized sound formats. These formats specify how sounds should be digitally represented and generally include some type of data compression that reduces the size of the file:

- **MP3.** MP3 is a patented audio sound file format that enables you to compress CD-quality digital audio by a

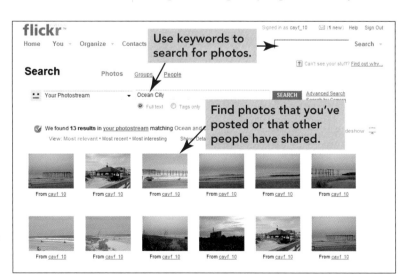

FIGURE 5.10 You can use Web-based photo communities such as Flickr (**www.flickr.com**) to upload photos and make them available to your friends and family at no charge.

FIGURE 5.11 Adobe Photoshop is an image editor that has been used by professional design studios for years.

FIGURE 5.12 Advanced GIF Animator (**www.gif-animator.com**) is an example of Web animation software.

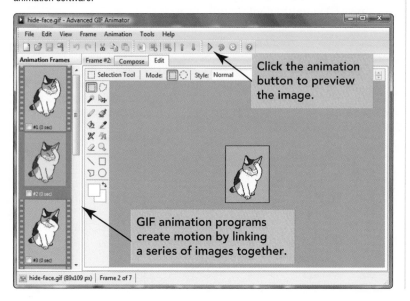

Click the animation button to preview the image.

GIF animation programs create motion by linking a series of images together.

ratio of 12:1 using lossy compression format. The compression greatly reduces the file size with no perceptible loss in sound quality (Figure 5.14).

- **Windows Media Audio (WMA).** The WMA is a Microsoft proprietary data compression file format that is similar to the MP3 format. This proprietary format produces files smaller in size that require less processing power than the MP3 format but still maintain the same audio quality. WMA is one of the most popular audio file

formats and currently has four variations: Windows Media Audio, Windows Media Audio Professional, Windows Media Audio Lossless, and Windows Media Audio Voice.

- **WAV.** The default Microsoft Windows sound file format uses the .wav extension (short for "Wave Sounds"). It can be saved with a variety of quality levels, from low-fidelity mono to CD-quality stereo. WAV sounds usually aren't compressed, so they tend to take up a lot of disk space.

- **Ogg Vorbis.** An open source format that is an even faster format than MP3, Ogg files are also about 20 percent smaller than MP3 files. You can fit more of them on your hard disk or MP3 player. See **www.vorbis.com**.

- **Musical Instrument Digital Interface (MIDI).** MIDI files don't contain waveforms. They are text files that contain a text-based description that tells a synthesizer when and how to play individual musical notes.

Streaming audio formats are available that enable Internet-accessed sounds to play almost immediately after the user clicks an audio link. To hear some popular snips of commercials, movies, TV series, and special sound effects visit **http://wavcentral.com**.

Video Editors Video editors are programs that enable you to modify digitized videos. With a video editor, you can cut segments, resequence frames, add transitions, compress a file, and determine a video's frame rate (the number of still images displayed per second). To view a list of video editing programs and a brief description of some of their capabilities go to **www.google.com/Top/Arts/Video/ Video_Editing/Equipment_and_ Software/Professional**.

Video editors also enable you to save video files to some or all of the following video file formats:

- **Moving Picture Experts Group (MPEG).** A family of video file formats and lossy compression standards for full-motion video, MPEG includes MPEG-2, the video format used by DVD-ROMs. MPEG-2 videos offer CD- and DVD-quality audio. MPEG-4 absorbs many of the features of MPEG-1 and MPEG-2 and other related standards but includes new features as (extended) virtual reality modeling language (VRML) support for 3D rendering, object-oriented composite files (including audio, video and VRML objects), and supports various types of interactivity.

- **QuickTime.** A video file format developed by Apple Computer, Quick-Time 7 Pro is the latest version. It plays full-screen, broadcast-quality video as well as CD- and DVD-quality audio. It is widely used in multimedia CD-ROM productions.

- **Video for Windows.** The native (or original format a program uses internally) video file format for Microsoft Windows, Video for Windows is often called AVI (Audio Video Interleave). This format is still widely used but is inferior to the new MPEG-4 standard.

Because a huge amount of data must be stored to create realistic-looking video on a computer, all video file formats use codec techniques. For the best playback, special video adapters are required. These adapters have hardware that decodes videos at high speed.

To make video available on the Internet, streaming video formats have been developed. These formats enable the video picture to start playing almost immediately after the user clicks the video link. (With nonstreaming video, users have to wait for the entire file to be transferred to their computer before it begins to play.) Streaming video formats rely on compression, low frame rates, and small image size to deliver video over the Internet, which does not have sufficient bandwidth (signal-carrying capacity) to disseminate broadcast-quality video. Other, competing streaming video formats are available; the most popular is RealNetwork's RealVideo format.

Multimedia Authoring Systems

Authoring tools are used to create multimedia presentations. These tools enable you to specify which multimedia objects to use (such as text, pictures, videos, or animations), how to display them in relation to each other, how long to display them, and how to enable the user to interact with the presentation (Figure 5.15). To take full advantage of an authoring tool's capabilities, it's often necessary to learn a scripting language (a simple programming language). Leading authoring packages include iMovie, part of Apple iLife suite, and Adobe Director.

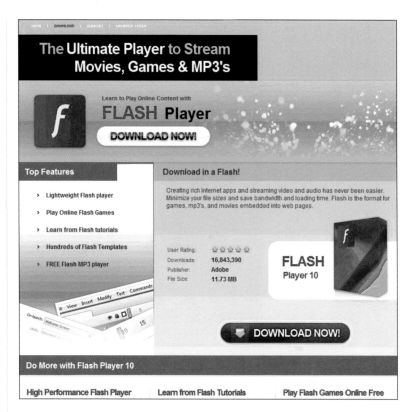

Many commercial authoring tools, such as Adobe Director, save output in proprietary file formats. To view Adobe presentations on a Web site, it's necessary to download and install a plug-in program (software that extends another program's capabilities). Some users do not like to download viewers, so the organization that sets Web standards, the World Wide Web Consortium (W3C), recently approved **Synchronized Multimedia Integration Language (SMIL)**, a simple multimedia scripting language designed for Web pages. SMIL enables Internet users to view multimedia without having to

FIGURE 5.13 To view animations on the Web, you need a special plug-in program such as Adobe's Flash Player or Shockwave Player.

FIGURE 5.14 The Windows Media Player is handy for ripping (also known as burning) CDs and for creating MP3 files.

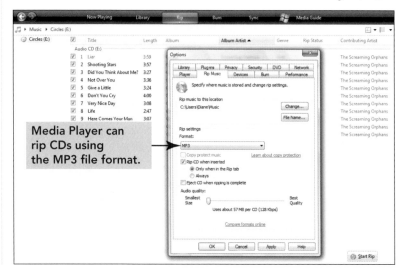

FIGURE 5.15 You can easily build your own multimedia by using iMovie (part of Apple iLife) to combine audio, images, and video.

download plug-ins. However, multimedia that use plug-ins (like Shockwave) are still more widely used.

The Adobe Creative Suite media development kit is a powerful tool for developing multimedia Internet applications. If you are a Mac user, you'll most likely be interested in visiting **www.apple.com/ilife** to learn about Apple's multimedia iLife suite. With the iLife package, you can create music with GarageBand; integrate and organize your music, photos, and home videos with iTunes, iPhoto, and iMovie; and pull it all together on your own DVD with iDVD.

One thing to keep in mind is that multimedia authoring programs tend to use lots of disk space and often require extra memory to run efficiently. Additionally, due to the intensive computational processes needed, it is advisable not to run other applications while rendering video. Be sure to read the program's system requirements and usage recommendations, which are usually listed on the packaging or in the documentation. Realize that the hardware requirements stated are truly minimum requirements.

APPLICATIONS THAT WORK THROUGH AND RUN FROM THE INTERNET

There are a many types of Internet applications. Some work through the Internet, using it as the transport medium. Others actually run from the Internet, using programs that reside there.

Applications That Work through the Internet A variety of applications work through the Internet, meaning that they use the Internet as their transport medium. Such applications include e-mail clients, instant messaging programs, Web browsers, and videoconferencing software, which will be discussed in detail elsewhere in this book. For now, simply note that they are general-purpose applications because they help us to communicate, learn, and interact.

Applications That Run from the Internet: Web-Hosted Technology The new wave in office suites is **Web-hosted technology,** which for application software means the capability to upload files to an online site so they can be viewed and edited from another location. It is also possible to share your files with others, making group collaboration easier. Windows Office Live (**http://workspace.officelive.com**) and Google Docs (**http://docs.google.com**) are two examples of sites that offer these capabilities. Most of these services are free to use, but you do need to create an account and sign in.

Office Live provides storage space for your files and enables you to create separate areas called workspaces, some of which have themes and include sample files (Figure 5.16). You can share an individual document, an entire workspace, or even the screen you're currently working on by sending an e-mail invitation to one or more people. You can also set a person's access level by assigning viewing or editing rights. You can access and view all files online, even on computers that don't have Microsoft Office. However, to revise a file, you will have to download it, edit it using Microsoft Office, and then upload it back to the site.

Google Docs also provides file storage space and enables you to share your files with others. One advantage of Google Docs is the ability to open files directly within your Web browser and make basic editing and formatting changes—no additional software is required. It is also possible for more than one person to work on the same document at the same time, making real-time collaboration possible.

Web-hosted technology can help avoid file incompatibility problems that may arise when using traditional file-sharing methods. Proprietary file formats can limit file usage to a specific vendor's software or computer model. For instance, if Microsoft Word is not installed on your system, you can't view a Word file unless you use a conversion program or a free display/reader program, which you can download from the Internet. Such problems can also arise when software publishers introduce new file formats in new versions to support new features. The ability to save a file to a Web-hosted software suite can eliminate file conversion costs, because the file can be read by anyone with a Web browser, not just those users who have installed the actual software. A word of caution: Due to this global accessibility, passwords should be complex in design and carefully guarded.

Undesirable Internet Software: Spyware, Adware, and Pop-Ups Right now, your hard drive probably holds some programs that you don't know about, didn't mean to install, and don't really want—and they're not viruses. **Spyware** is Internet software that is installed on your computer without your knowledge or consent. It may monitor your computer or online activity, relay information about you to the spyware's source, or allow others to take control of your computer. Spyware usually enters your system through the Internet, sometimes when you open seemingly innocent e-mails and sometimes when you download software—especially shareware and freeware. Some types of spyware, known as keyloggers, can

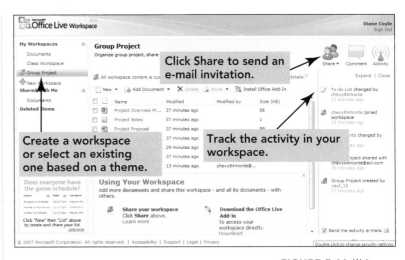

record every keystroke you type and every Internet address you visit. It can capture your login name and password, your credit card numbers, and anything else you input while the spyware is active. Other spyware programs look only at your Web browsing habits so they can arrange for ads keyed to your interests.

If you've ever downloaded software and then seen a banner or **pop-up**, a small window, that suddenly appears ("pops up") in the foreground of the current window, you've downloaded a form of adware. **Adware** is like spyware, only it's created specifically by an advertising agency to collect information about your Internet habits, or encourage you to purchase a product. Although the practice is ethically questionable, shareware and freeware creators sometimes allow advertisers to tag along invisibly by bundling adware with their software.

No matter how they get into your system, spyware and adware invade your privacy and present a serious security threat. How can you get rid of them? First, find out whether your ISP can help. Many ISPs provide built-in clean-up utilities that find and remove spyware and adware. Second, look into utilities from antivirus companies such as Symantec's Norton (**www.symantec.com**) and spyware specialists such as PC Tools Spyware Doctor (**www.pctools.com**), Spybot Search and Destroy (**www.safer-networking.org**), and Webroot

FIGURE 5.16 Web-hosted software suites like Microsoft's Office Live allow users to view and share documents over the Web.

"Web-hosted **technology** can help avoid file **incompatibility** problems that may arise when using **traditional** file-sharing methods."

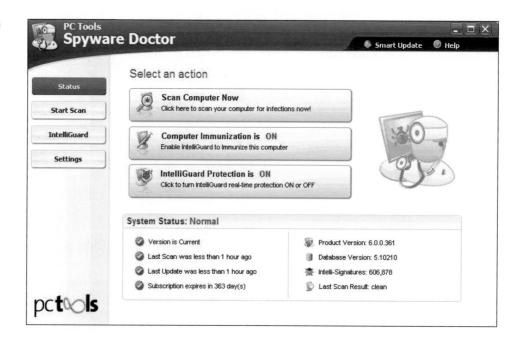

(**www.webroot.com**). These utilities scan your computer's memory, registry, and hard drive for known spyware and then safely eliminate these sneaky programs (Figure 5.17). Because new spyware is created all the time, remember to scan your system frequently (experts recommend at least once a week) so you can root out hidden programs.

HOME AND EDUCATIONAL PROGRAMS

General-purpose software also includes **home and educational programs**, such as personal finance and tax preparation software, home design and landscaping software, computerized reference information (such as encyclopedias, street maps, and computer-assisted tutorials), and games.

Hot sellers in the reference CD/DVD-ROM market include multimedia versions of dictionaries (which include recordings that tell you how to pronounce difficult words), encyclopedias (complete with sound and video clips from famous moments in history), and how-to guides (which use multimedia to show you how to do just about anything around the home; Figure 5.18).

Computer Games By any standard, computer games are big business. The worldwide video game industry has predicted that the video game boom will continue, with total sales soaring to $68.4 billion by 2012 (Figure 5.19). This highly profitable industry got its start in the 1970s, when the earliest computer video games (such as Pong) appeared in

bars and gaming arcades. Video games then entered the living room with the advent of Atari, Nintendo, and Sega console game players, which are special-purpose computers designed to display their output on a TV screen. Games soon migrated to personal computers—and from there, to the Internet.

Multiplayer online gaming enables players to interact with characters who are controlled by other players rather than by the computer. Combining a rich graphical virtual environment with multiplayer thrills, these types of games are attracting increasing numbers of users. Role-playing games are a natural for Internet-connected

ETHICS

Virtual Life versus Real Life

Some people get so involved with online games that their real life begins to suffer. People buy and sell virtual items on eBay, develop online relationships that supersede face-to-face relationships, and become increasingly isolated. When does online gaming stop being a game and become a way of life? How much is too much? Have you or someone you know gotten so involved online that your real-world activities suffered because of it?

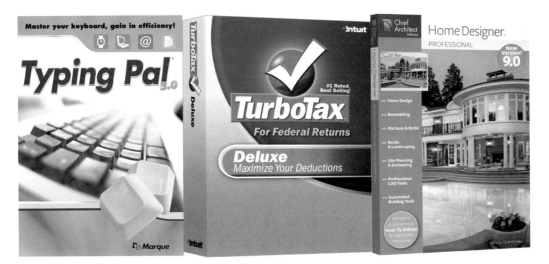

FIGURE 5.18 These typing software, personal finance, and home design applications represent just a few of the home and educational programs on the market today.

computers, which enable players to participate even if they're not physically present in the same room. Originally, online role-playing games were known as **MUDs**, an acronym for **multiuser dungeons** (or **dimensions**). The name *MUD* is based on the noncomputerized Dungeons and Dragons role-playing game. Early MUDs and their various offshoots took place in a text-only environment, and players used their imaginations to construct a persona and build their environment. They interacted with other players by means of text chatting, similar to talking in a chat room.

As the Internet and the Web have evolved over the years, Internet gaming has changed as well. Currently, **graphical MUDS (gMUDs)** bring the virtual environment to life in 3-D graphical environments, and **massively multiplayer online role-playing games (MMORPGs)** permit increasingly larger numbers of players to interact with one another in virtual worlds. These virtual worlds are often hosted and maintained by the software publisher, unlike other environments that end when the game is over. MMORPGs also encourage team-building—to progress to higher levels, it is frequently necessary to band with others whose skills and abilities complement those of your character.

Some MMORPGs are directly accessible online and do not require any special equipment other than a Web browser, whereas others require a locally installed game package to speed up processing. Examples of such games include *EverQuest* and *World of Warcraft* (Figure 5.20).

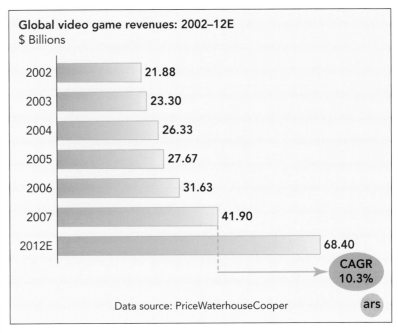

Global video game revenues: 2002–12E
$ Billions

Year	$ Billions
2002	21.88
2003	23.30
2004	26.33
2005	27.67
2006	31.63
2007	41.90
2012E	68.40

CAGR 10.3%

Data source: PriceWaterhouseCooper

ars

FIGURE 5.19 The video gaming industry pattern of continual growth is displayed in this chart of industry revenue along with estimated revenues for 2012.

FIGURE 5.20 MMORPGs such as *World of Warcraft* bring the virtual world to life with 3-D graphical environments.

Application Software: Tools for Productivity **169**

Players purchase the locally installed software and pay a monthly fee for online access.

Recent statistics on gaming popularity, sales, age group usage, and international comparisons can be obtained at **www.theesa.com/facts/pdfs/ESA_EF_2008.pdf** and **http://arstechnica.com/gaming/news/2009/02/in-2008-game-sales-the-uk-trumps-japan-for-first-time.ars**.

If you can't find general-purpose applications to meet your computing needs, you might consider tailor-made applications.

Tailor-Made Applications

Tailor-made applications are designed for specialized fields or the business market. For example, programs are available to handle the billing needs of medical offices, manage restaurants, and track occupational injuries (Figure 5.21).

Tailor-made applications designed for professional and business use often cost much more than general-purpose applications. In fact, some of these programs cost $10,000 or more. The high price is due to the costs of developing the programs and the small size of most markets.

If the right application isn't available, programmers can create custom software to meet your specific needs.

CUSTOM VERSUS PACKAGED SOFTWARE

In the world of application software, a distinction can be made between custom software and packaged software. **Custom software** is developed by programmers and software engineers to meet the specific needs of an organization. Custom software can be quite expensive, but sometimes an organization's needs are so specialized that no alternative exists. An example of a custom software package might be the grade-tracking software that has been programmed to meet the needs of your college registrar's office. Custom software is almost always a tailor-made application.

Packaged software, in contrast, is aimed at a mass market that includes both home and business users. Although packaged software can be customized, it is designed to be immediately useful in a wide variety of contexts. An example of packaged software is the presentation software program your instructor may use to create class presentations. The payoff comes with the price: Packaged software is much cheaper than custom software.

In addition to the choices of custom or packaged software, users have three other options when purchasing software: stand-alone programs, integrated programs, and software suites.

FIGURE 5.21 Medical and dental offices often use tailor-made applications to manage their scheduling and billing. Color coding is a common feature with these applications.

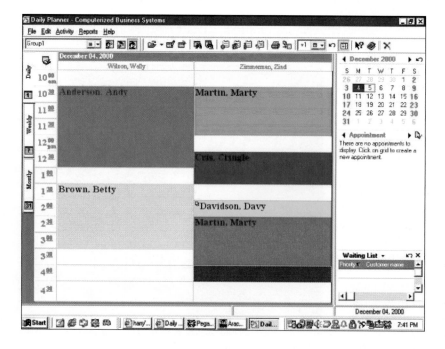

Standalone Programs, Integrated Programs, and Software Suites

A **standalone program** is a program that is fully self-contained. Microsoft Word and Excel are examples of standalone programs. You can purchase and install them separately, and they function perfectly well all by themselves. However, standalone programs require a lot of storage space. For example, if you purchase Word and install it and then purchase Excel and install it, neither program would know about the other, nor would they share any resources, such as menus, drivers, graphics libraries, or tools. Obviously, this is a very inefficient way to install and use software when the programs have so many resources they could share.

An **integrated program** is a single program that manages an entire business or set of related tasks. It combines the most commonly used functions of many productivity software programs, like word processing, database management, spreadsheet, accounting, and customer service into one single application. Integrated programs such as Microsoft Works offer easy-to-learn and easy-to-use versions of basic productivity software (Figure 5.22). All of the functions, called **modules**, share the same interface, and you can switch among them quickly. In some cases, the individual modules may be short on features compared with standalone programs. The lack of features may make these easy programs seem deficient when you start exploring the program's more advanced capabilities.

Microsoft Works contains a word processor that is very similar to Word, a spreadsheet program that is very similar to Excel, a database program, a calendar, and other productivity tools. The modules of an integrated program are not available as standalone programs—you cannot purchase the spreadsheet program in Works as a standalone product.

A **software suite** (sometimes called an **office suite**) is a collection of individual, full-featured, standalone programs, usually possessing a similar interface and a common command structure, that are bundled and sold together. The cost of purchasing a suite is usually less than buying each program individually. If Microsoft Windows is your operating system, then Microsoft Office is the set of tools that you typically use at work. A suite may include as many as five or more productivity applications. Today, most personal productivity software is sold in

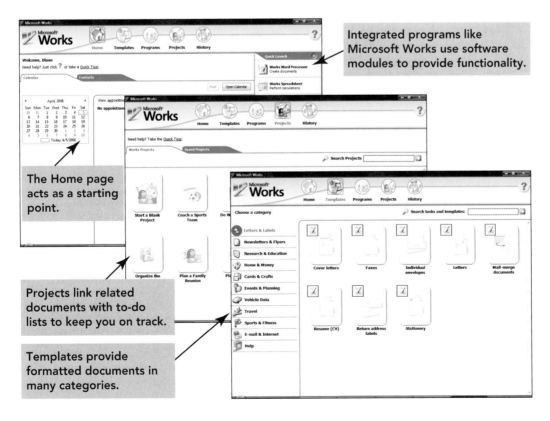

Integrated programs like Microsoft Works use software modules to provide functionality.

The Home page acts as a starting point.

Projects link related documents with to-do lists to keep you on track.

Templates provide formatted documents in many categories.

FIGURE 5.22 Microsoft Works modules provide basic productivity tools that are helpful for new users.

office suites, such as Corel WordPerfect Office, IBM Lotus SmartSuite, and the market leader, Microsoft Office. Sun's StarOffice is another personal productivity software suite that has a small but loyal following.

The advantage of a software suite is that the individual applications share common program code, interface tools, drivers, and graphics libraries. For instance, if you purchased Word and Excel as standalone applications, each would require you to install a printer. Each would have its own dictionary, thesaurus, toolbars, and graphics library. When you use Word and Excel as a part of Microsoft Office, all of these features are shared.

Office suites typically include a full-featured version of leading word processing, spreadsheet, presentation graphics, database, and personal-information-manager programs (Figure 5.23).

- **Word processing programs** enable you to create, edit, and print your written work. They also offer commands that enable you to format your documents so that they have an attractive appearance. Although some people still prefer to use other writing tools, word processing programs are the most often used office suite software.
- **Spreadsheet programs** present users with a grid of rows and columns, the computer equivalent of an accountant's worksheet. By embedding

formulas within the cells, you can create "live" worksheets, in which changing one of the values forces the entire spreadsheet to be recalculated. Spreadsheets are indispensable tools for anyone who works with numbers.

- **Presentation graphics programs** enable you to create transparencies, slides, and handouts for presentations.

FIGURE 5.23 Office Suites Available for Microsoft Windows

	Microsoft Office	WordPerfect Office	IBM Lotus SmartSuite
Word processing	Word	WordPerfect	Word Pro
Spreadsheet	Excel	Quattro Pro	Lotus 1-2-3
Database	Access	Paradox	Approach
Presentation graphics	PowerPoint	Presentations	Freelance Graphics
Personal information manager	Outlook	WordPerfect MAIL	Lotus Organizer

- **Database programs** give you the tools to store data in an organized form and retrieve the data in such a way that it can be meaningfully summarized and displayed.
- **Personal information managers (PIMs)** provide calendars, contact managers, task reminders, and e-mail capabilities.

To learn more about other office suites that offer Web integration, visit **www.wordperfect.com**, **www.openoffice.org**, and **www.sun.com/software/star/staroffice**.

System Requirements and Software Versions

When you buy software, your computer system will need to meet the program's **system requirements**, the minimal level of equipment that a program needs in order to run. For example, a given program may be designed to run on a PC with a Pentium-class microprocessor, a CD or DVD drive, at least 512 MB of RAM, and 2 GB of free hard disk space. If you're shopping for software, you'll find the system requirements printed somewhere on the outside of the box or online through a link that is usually called "system requirements." Although a program will run on a system that meets the minimum requirements, it's better if your system exceeds them, especially when it comes to memory and disk space.

You've no doubt noticed that most program names include a number, such as 6.0, or a year, such as 2010. Software publishers often bring out new versions of their programs, and these numbers help you determine whether you have the latest version. In a version number, the whole number (such as 6 in 6.0) indicates a major program revision. A decimal number indicates a **maintenance release** (a minor revision that corrects bugs or adds minor features). The year 2010 would

> " Although a **program** will run on a system that meets the **minimum requirements**, it's better if your system **exceeds** **them,** especially when it comes to **memory** and **disk space.** "

indicate the year that the software was published; however, it does not indicate how many versions of the software there were previously. For example, Office 2003 is technically Office 11, whereas Office 2007 is Office 12.

Software publishers sometimes offer **time-limited trial versions** of commercial programs on the Internet, which expire or stop working when a set trial period (such as 60 or 90 days) ends. You can download, install, and use these programs for free, but after the time limit is up, you can no longer use them.

Beta versions of forthcoming programs are sometimes available for free. A **beta version** is a preliminary version of a program in the final phases of testing. Beta software is known to contain bugs (errors); it should be installed and used with caution. Users try out these preliminary versions and tell the publisher about any major bugs so they can be fixed before the applications are officially released. But there's more to it than just finding and fixing bugs. As users talk up the program to friends and colleagues, the publisher hopes more people will like what they hear and buy the program themselves.

Beta testers like trying out new applications for four main reasons. First, many are power users who are extremely involved with a certain program and interested in seeing (and influencing) how it evolves. Second, testers want their voices to be heard when they give the publisher feedback about bugs, features, and functionality. Third, they really enjoy being on the cutting edge, being among the first people to try new versions. And finally, they may get the software for free or at a discount.

SOFTWARE UPGRADES

Software upgrading describes the process of keeping your version of an application current with the marketplace. Some upgrades are small changes called *patches*; sometimes they are major fixes called *service releases* or *service packs*. Service releases keep the current version up to date. The ultimate upgrade is when you purchase and install the next version or release of a program. For instance, you might have recently upgraded from Microsoft Office 2003 to Microsoft Office 2007.

So how do you know whether you should purchase the next version of a software application or whether there is a patch or fix available that will make your current version perform better? Well, when it comes to upgrading you should look at two things: Is your current version so out of date hat you are having compatibility or security problems? Are there features in the newer version that you find attractive? Consider the fact that newer versions provide more compatibility options and include security built to withstand the vulnerabilities of the Internet. As for patches, you should occasionally visit the software manufacturer's Web site to see if there are any service releases or patches. Microsoft software has a built-in capability to automatically check with Microsoft's Web site to determine whether updates are available.

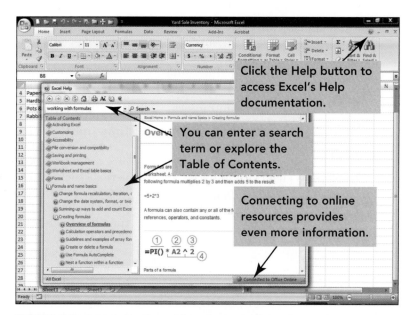

FIGURE 5.24 Instead of looking up information in a printed user's manual, you can use a program's Help feature to read documentation right on the computer.

DISTRIBUTION AND DOCUMENTATION

Before the Internet came along, most software was available only in shrink-wrapped packages that included floppy disks or CD-ROMs containing the program installation files. Now, many software publishers use the Internet to distribute programs and program updates. Doing so, rather than physically delivering a program in a box, is much cheaper for the company and often more convenient for the consumer.

If you buy software in a shrink-wrapped package, you typically get at least some printed documentation in the form of a brief tutorial to help you get started. Downloaded software contains Read Me files and help files. A Read Me file is a plain-text document that is readable by any text-reading program. It contains information the software manufacturer thinks you'll find helpful. Many programs also have help screens that enable you to consult all or part of the documentation on screen (Figure 5.24). At a software publisher's Web site you may also find additional information and possibly the actual manual itself in PDF file format. Collectively these items are considered **documentation**.

Now that you've chosen the right application software version, considered upgrades, and looked over the documentation, let's look at some other considerations you might have when using application software.

Software Licenses and Registration

A **software license** is a contract distributed with a program that gives you the right to install and use the program on one computer (Figure 5.25). Typically, to install a program on more than one computer, you must purchase additional

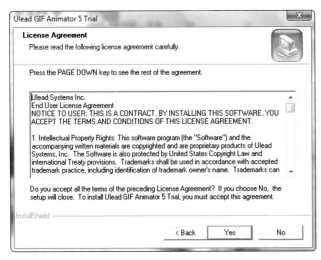

FIGURE 5.25 A software license gives you the right to install and use a program on a specified number of computers. If you want to install the program on additional computers, you must purchase additional licenses.

licenses. However, some programs allow home users to install software on one or two additional computers. Always read the license to be sure.

Organizations such as colleges and universities often purchase **site licenses**, which are contracts with a software publisher that enable an organization to install copies of a program on a specified number of computers. Site licenses offer large organizations multiple software licenses at a slightly reduced cost.

In addition, when you own an original and legitimate copy of a program, you're entitled to certain warranties and guarantees. With regard to warranties, most software publishers will be happy to replace a defective CD or DVD, but that's it. The software license expressly denies any liability on the publisher's part for any damages or losses suffered through the use of the software. If you buy a program that has bugs and if these bugs wipe out your data, it's your tough luck. At least that's what software companies would like you to believe. In the past, these licenses haven't stood up in court; judges and juries have agreed that the products were sold with an implied warranty of fitness for a particular use. Some unethical publishers may bundle spyware with their programs and actually include this information in their license. If you accept the license, they may claim you have no right to complain about the spyware! You should always carefully read any licensing agreement before installing software.

Every day, customers worldwide are victims of counterfeit programs, especially Windows and Office applications. Often a user does not realize the program is an unofficial or invalid copy until he or she attempts to upgrade from a valid site or invoke a warranty. When you purchase a program, you may need to **validate** your software by providing a special code or product key before you can use it. Validation proves that you are using a legal copy, not a pirated version. You may also be asked to register your software. Doing so may provide you with product news or notifications about software upgrades. You may get the chance to upgrade to new versions at a lower price than the one offered to the general public. Registration may also qualify you for technical assistance or other forms of support. To learn more about software validation, visit the Genuine Microsoft Software site at **www.microsoft.com/genuine**.

COMMERCIAL SOFTWARE, SHAREWARE, FREEWARE, AND PUBLIC DOMAIN SOFTWARE

The three types of copyrighted software are commercial software, shareware, and freeware. **Commercial software** is copyrighted software that must be purchased. The current trend is to make programs available as an online download or initially as shareware, to give the potential customer a trial period. Once the trial period is over, the user can pay for the program directly on the Web site and download an official copy. Microsoft Office, Adobe Acrobat, and Mac OS X are examples of commercial software. **Shareware** refers to software that you can use on a "try before you buy" basis (Figure 5.26). If you like the program after using it for a specified trial period, you must pay a registration fee or you violate the copyright. **Freeware** refers to software given away for free, with the understanding that you can't turn around and sell it for profit. Included in the freeware category are programs distributed under the Free

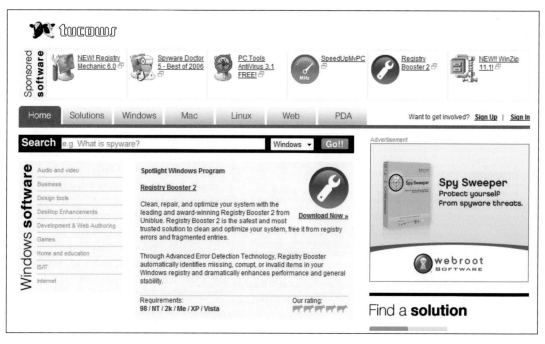

FIGURE 5.26 Shareware is copyrighted software that you can use on a "try before you buy" basis. Tucows, launched in 1993, is renowned for its large library of shareware.

Software Foundation's General Public License (GPL). There is one type of software that is not copyrighted. **Public domain software** is expressly free from copyright, and you can do anything you want with it, including modify it or sell it to others.

When a program includes some mechanism to ensure that you don't make or run unauthorized copies of it, it is called **copy-protected software**. Examples of such software include the Microsoft Windows operating system and some CDs and DVDs. Copy-protected software isn't popular with users because it often requires extra steps to install and usually requires a call to technical support if any program

files become corrupted. Perhaps the loudest objection to copy-protected software, though, is that the copy-protection schemes are beginning to work. It is becoming difficult to "share" a copy of major software programs with friends and family.

Copyright or not, you're always better off owning a legitimate copy of the software you're using. It's the right thing to do, and it offers you the greatest opportunity to derive benefits from the software. You're entitled to full customer support services should anything go wrong and to add-ons or enhancements the company offers. You should also be sure that any shareware or freeware is from a reliable source.

Now that you know what to look for when you purchase application software, let's look at what to do with that software once you have it.

ETHICS

You download a piece of shareware software that has a free preview period of 30 days. After that time frame, you realize the software still works. Is it OK to continue using the software even though you haven't paid for it? Is it "legal" to continue using the software? Is it "ethical" to continue to use the software? What would you do?

Installing and Managing Application Software

To use your computer successfully, you'll find it useful to understand the essential concepts and acquire the skills of using application software, including installing applications, launching and exiting applications, and choosing options. The following sections briefly outline these concepts and skills.

INSTALLING APPLICATIONS

Before you can use an application, you must install it on your computer. After you've purchased software, read the directions both before and during installation. When you purchase the right to use a software program, you are usually provided with CDs or DVDs that contain the program and an installation or setup utility. If you purchase software online as a download, it is a good practice to make a CD or DVD of the loaded software for backup purposes. **Installing** an application involves more than transferring the software to your computer's hard disk. The program must also be configured properly to run on your system. Installation software makes sure that this configuration is performed properly.

To install an application on a computer running the Windows operating system, you insert the disk into the appropriate drive. The operating system automatically senses the insertion and attempts to locate and run an install or start-up file. You are then prompted for any necessary input as the program installs.

Should inserting the disk not invoke the installation program, you will need to click the Windows Start button and then type the drive letter designation for the drive (such as E:\) in the Start Search box. A list of the files on the disk will appear in the Start pane. Click the installation or start-up file to begin the installation.

If the software was obtained from the Internet, you may first have to decompress it, although some decompression occurs automatically when opened. Most programs are installed using a wizard. The installation wizard is a step-by-step process that installs the program in the correct location and may also provide some customization options. After the program has been installed, you will see its name in menus or on the desktop, and you can start using it.

You should know where the program is being installed, how to access it, and whether shortcuts have been created on the desktop. Shortcuts usually carry the name of the program and use the company logo for an icon. If you don't want these shortcuts on your desktop, delete them by right-clicking the icons and choosing Delete. This doesn't affect the program in any way, because a shortcut is just a pointer to a program or file. The program will still be available via the Start, Programs menu sequence.

If you later decide that you don't want to use an application, you shouldn't just delete it from your hard disk. The proper way to remove, or uninstall, a program from your computer is to use the Windows Programs and Features utility located on the Control Panel, which is listed on the Start menu (Figure 5.27). **Uninstalling** removes the application's files from your hard disk. Choose the program that you wish to uninstall from the list of installed programs and then provide any input the uninstaller asks you for. Because most programs create library files and ancillary files in various directories, all of the files will not be removed if you simply delete the program icon or delete the program files from within the file management utility. If you don't remove all of the program files correctly, the operating system may not run efficiently. Always use the Programs and Features utility to remove unwanted programs.

LAUNCHING APPLICATIONS

After you have installed an application, you can launch it. **Launching** an

> " Because most **programs** create library files and ancillary files in **various directories**, all of the files will not be **removed** if you simply delete the program icon or delete the **program files** from within the **file management** utility. "

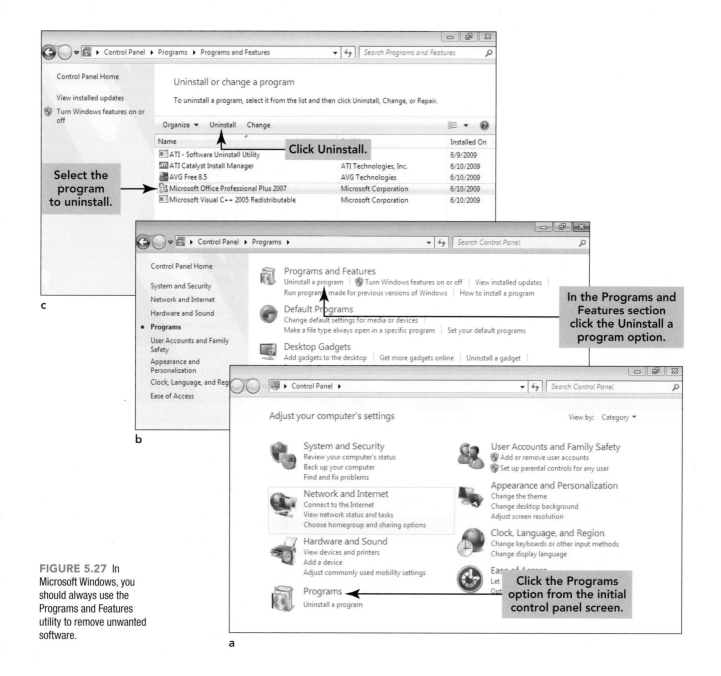

FIGURE 5.27 In Microsoft Windows, you should always use the Programs and Features utility to remove unwanted software.

application transfers the program code from your computer's hard disk to memory, and the application then appears on the screen. Programs can be launched in a number of ways. The two most reliable ways in Microsoft Windows are to click the Start menu, point to All Programs, and choose the application you want to launch or to type the program name in the Start Search text box (Figure 5.28). In Mac OS, you locate the application's folder and double-click the application's icon. Application icons are also often available on the desktop, in the System Tray on the taskbar, or on the Quick Launch toolbar.

CHOOSING OPTIONS

Applications typically enable you to choose **options** that specify how you want the program to operate. Your choices can change the program's **defaults**, which are the settings that are in effect unless you deliberately override them. For example, in Microsoft Word you can choose an option for displaying formatting marks on the screen—such as tabs, paragraph marks, and object anchors.

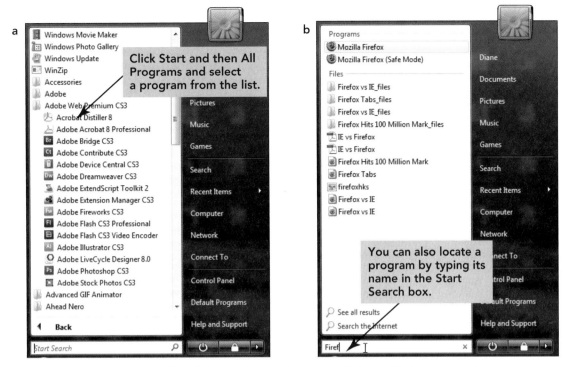

FIGURE 5.28 In Windows, choose Start, All Programs to access the programs that are installed on your computer.

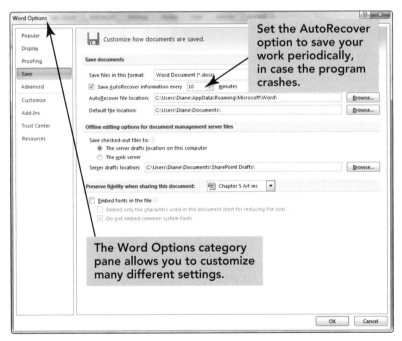

FIGURE 5.29 Most Microsoft applications enable you to choose options for program defaults by using the Office button at the top left corner of the application window.

When you start working with a newly installed application, check the options menu for a setting—usually called **autosave** or **autorecover**—that automatically saves your work at a specified interval (Figure 5.29). With this option enabled, you'll ensure that you won't lose more than a few minutes' worth of work should the program fail for some reason.

EXITING APPLICATIONS

When you've finished using an application, don't just switch off the computer. **Exiting** an application refers to quitting, or closing down, the program. You exit an application by choosing the Exit command from the File menu or by clicking the x icon in the upper right most corner of the application window. By doing so, you ensure that the application will warn you if you've failed to save some of your work. In addition, you'll save any options you set while using the program.

Chapter Summary

Application Software: Tools for Productivity

System software provides the environment in which application software performs tasks. Application software enables users to create, communicate, and be entertained. The most popular general-purpose applications are personal productivity programs, multimedia and graphics software, Internet programs, and home and educational programs.

A standalone program provides just the software tool that you need, but it is often nearly as expensive as a complete office suite. Integrated programs are aimed at beginning users and may not include features that some users will want as they become more comfortable with the software. Most people who need personal productivity software purchase an office suite because they can save money by doing so. Publishers often bring out new or updated versions of their software. In a version number, the whole number (such as 6 in 6.0) indicates a major program revision. A decimal number indicates a maintenance release. Software upgrades enable you to keep your version of an application current with the marketplace by downloading and installing small changes called *patches* or major fixes called *service releases* or *service packs*.

Commercial software, like Microsoft Office, is copyrighted software that must be purchased. The current trend is to make such programs available as an online download or initially as shareware, to give the potential customer a trial period. Once the trial period is over, the user can pay for the program directly on the Web site and download their official copy. Shareware is copyrighted but distributed on a "try before you buy" basis. You may use the program for a specified trial period without paying. Freeware is copyrighted but available for free, as long as you don't turn around and sell it. Public domain software is not copyrighted. You can do anything you want with it, including modify it or sell it to others.

Key Terms and Concepts

Matching

Match each key term in the left column with the most accurate definition in the right column.

_____ 1. beta version

_____ 2. commercial

_____ 3. lossless

_____ 4. site license

_____ 5. uninstallling

_____ 6. video editing

_____ 7. proprietary

_____ 8. freeware

_____ 9. launching

_____ 10. maintenance release

_____ 11. lossy

_____ 12. validate

_____ 13. codec

_____ 14. shareware

_____ 15. defaults

a. A process that proves you have the right to run a program.

b. A type of software that can be used for free but never sold for profit.

c. A minor revision, indicated by a decimal number.

d. A type of software you must pay for before using.

e. A compression technique that allows a file to be completely restored without any flaws.

f. The software settings that are in effect until changed by a user.

g. The removal of an application's files from your hard disk.

h. A type of software that can be used for a specified trial period without payment.

i. A file format that is patented or copyright protected and controlled by a single company.

j. A type of software used to cut segments, sequence frames, add transitions, compress files, and determine frame rate.

k. A compression/decompression algorithm.

l. A preliminary version of a software program in the final testing phase.

m. A contract between an organization and a software publisher permitting multiple installations.

n. A compression technique that permanently removes some data from the file.

o. The transfer of a program's code from a computer's hard drive to memory.

Multiple Choice

Circle the correct choice for each of the following.

1. Which file format is best used for images placed in documents to be published in paper form?
   a. JPEG
   b. TIFF
   c. BMP
   d. PNG

2. What type of programs are Picasa 3 and Gimp 2?
   a. 3-D rendering programs
   b. Animation programs
   c. Sound capturing and processing programs
   d. Image editors

3. Which is *not* a format for saving an image created in a paint program?
   a. JPEG
   b. PNG
   c. PDS
   d. BMP

4. Read Me files and help files are examples of which of the following?
   a. Freeware
   b. Documentation
   c. Codecs
   d. Packaged software

5. Which of the following is *not* a sound file format?
   a. WAV
   b. MPEG
   c. MP3
   d. WMA

6. Which of the following images can be edited and resized without edge distortion?
   a. Bitmapped graphic
   b. AVI file
   c. Raster graphic
   d. Vector graphic

7. Which of the following are examples of personal productivity software?
   a. Word-processing and personal information management programs
   b. Spreadsheets and Web browsers
   c. Audio software and e-mail programs
   d. Personal finance software and database programs

8. What is the technique that adds realism to an image by what appears to be the addition of natural light?
   a. MUD
   b. Codecs
   c. Light animation
   d. Ray tracing

9. What application software category would include tax preparation and landscape programs?
   a. Personal productivity programs
   b. Multimedia and graphics software
   c. Internet programs
   d. Home and educational programs

10. Adobe Director and iLife are examples of which of the following?
    a. Internet programs
    b. Multimedia authoring systems
    c. Validation tools
    d. Ray tracing software

Fill-In

In the blanks provided, write the correct answer for each of the following.

1. _____ _____ is a data compression method that reduces the size of multimedia files by eliminating information that is not normally perceived by human beings.

2. _____ permit large numbers of individuals to interact in an online virtual world.

3. A(n) _____ application is any application that involves two or more types of media, such as audio, video, or graphics.

4. A(n) _____ is a small or minor software update.

5. The autorecover feature is also known as _____ .

6. Bitmapped graphics are also called _____ _____ .

7. _____ _____ represent the minimal level of equipment a computer needs for an application to run properly.

8. _____ is an undesirable program written by an advertising agency to collect information on your Internet habits and installed, without your permission over the Internet.

9. _____ is a file format best suited for simple images with large areas of solid color.

10. An interconnected bundle of programs that share resources is known as a(n) _____ _____ .

11. _____ - _____ programs include a mechanism to prevent users from making or running unauthorized copies.

12. _____ _____ are programs sold individually and are not part of a package of related applications.

13. Noncopyrighted software that anyone may copy and use without charge and without acknowledging the source is _____ _____ _____ .

14. _____ _____ are images generated by the use of points, lines, curves, polygons, and basically any shape that can be generated by a mathematical description.

15. _____ is the process of confirming that a program is not counterfeit.

Short Answer

1. Explain the difference between application software and system software. Give a specific example of each.

2. Explain the difference between lossy and lossless compression schemes. Explain why a hybrid of these was developed and what field makes use of the hybrid scheme.

3. How do shareware, freeware, and public domain software differ?

4. Explain the difference between a maintenance release, patch, service pack, and an upgrade.

5. Define the acronyms MUD and MMORPGS as they relate to gaming applications. Provide an example of a popular game that falls into each category.

Teamwork

1. **Categorizing your Software** As a team, make a list of 10 to 15 programs that are installed on your systems at school or at home. For each program, indicate whether it is a commercial, shareware, or freeware program. Use a table or spreadsheet to present your final list.

2. **Rate your School's Web Site** As a team, make a list of five to eight multimedia and graphic features that can be incorporated into a Web site (sound, animation, video clips, jpg images). Create a ranking system (for example, a scale of 1 to 5, where 1 = does not exist, 5 = exists five or more times in the site). Examine your school's Web site and rank it for each of the features in your list. Locate the Web site of another local educational institution and rank it in the same manner. Present the rankings of both schools in a table or spreadsheet. Include a paragraph with suggestions on what multimedia features should be included or excluded to make the site more dynamic and appealing.

3. **Investigate Career-Specific Applications** For this exercise, each team member will interview a faculty member from his or her major or intended major department to find out what career-specific applications are used by professionals in that discipline and what they are specifically used for. Additionally, use the Web to support your interview findings. Regroup, pull all of the interview material together into a consolidated and presentable format, and give a class presentation of your findings.

4. **Start the Game** As a team, develop a survey to determine the gaming behavior of individuals. Make a

list of the popular computer games that exist today. Include Internet-based games like *Halo* and *World of Warcraft* along with games designed for specific game platforms like Wii, Xbox, and PlayStation. Have the survey respondents select the game or games they play most frequently. Ask respondents how many hours a week they spend gaming. Are they members of a gaming club (either local or online)? Do other members of their family game? Give the survey to at least 15 individuals. Collect the data and present your results in a table, slide show, or one-page, double-spaced summary report.

5. **Site Licenses** Businesses and institutions frequently use site licenses to purchase multiple copies of software applications. Your team is to contact your computing services center to find out whether your school uses this method to purchase software. If it does, identify the applications for which site licenses have been purchased. Is student and faculty home use of software applications included in the license? If home use is permitted, is there an associated fee? If permitted, how is the software made available to students and faculty (online or purchased on CD)? What, if any, limitations are placed on these student or faculty extensions of the site license? What is the primary advantage of purchasing site licenses for an application? If your university or college does not subscribe to site-licensed software, do research on the Web to see what you can learn about site licensing. Write a one-page, double-spaced report based on your findings.

On the Web

1. **Check It Out** Using the Internet and your favorite search engine, locate and compare at least three antispyware utilities. Use a table to create a checklist of features each possesses. In a one-page, double-spaced report, include the name of each program, the URL at which each was located, the cost of each, and the program that you recommend to purchase along with the reasons for your choice.

2. **Why Uninstall?** Using a search engine, locate information on the process to uninstall software. Locate the steps to follow to uninstall an application and the reasons it is important to use the uninstall process to remove applications, as opposed to simply deleting the program file. Using the Web, research at least three uninstall programs. For each program, list its features, cost (unless freeware), and approval ratings (if provided). Present your findings in a one-page, double-spaced report.

3. **Finding Freeware Paint Programs** Do you want some free or inexpensive software? The Internet is frequently used to distribute shareware and freeware applications. Go to **www.yahoo.com** and type "freeware" in the Search box at the top of the window. Browse some of the more than 242 million sites returned by your search. Perform a more limited search to zero in on free paint programs. Download two programs. Use both and critically compare their interface, use of brush editing features, layers, and other paint features. Include the product names, the URLs from which you downloaded the product, the file size, comparisons of the interfaces, and your assessment of functionality in a one-page, double-spaced summary report.

4. **Software Upgrades** Using a search engine, find out how a user can tell what upgrades, patches, or service packs have been installed on their operating system or are available for application software on their system. Check a Vista and Windows XP machine (if possible). Find out who is eligible for patches, service packs, and upgrades. How can a user get notified of such offerings? Are there ever fees associated with these activities? List at least five products that currently have upgrades, patches, or service packs available. Present the answers to these questions and any other relevant information on this topic in a one-page, double-spaced report.

5. **Competitive Office Suites** The major competitors of Microsoft Office are Corel's WordPerfect Office, IBM's Lotus SmartSuite, and Sun's StarOffice.

   - Visit the Corel Web site at **www.corel.com**. Identify the application areas and product names that are included in the professional version of Corel's office suite. What are the suggested full and upgrade prices? Are there different prices for digital and boxed versions? Is a free trial version available?

   - Visit the IBM Lotus Software Web site at **www.lotus.com**. Identify the application areas and product names that are included in the professional version of the Lotus office suite. What are the suggested full and upgrade prices? Is a free trial version available?

   - Visit the StarOffice site at **www.sun.com/ software/star/staroffice/**. Identify the application areas and product names that are included in the professional version of the Sun office suite. What are the suggested full and upgrade prices? Are there different prices for digital and boxed versions? Is a free trial version available?

   Present the results of your research in a one-page, double-spaced report or a PowerPoint presentation. Conclude with a brief statement as to why you would or would not purchase these products.

Microsoft Office

Your boss asks you to create a presentation that she can deliver at the annual stockholders' meeting in two days. Although you know creating a professional presentation is a challenge, this is the opportunity you've been waiting for—you were hired, in part, because of your abilities to use productivity software programs.

You get started right away by using Microsoft Access to generate reports that are based on data that provides you with important information about your company's activities throughout the year. You then import some of the data from Access into Microsoft Excel so that you can perform some statistical analyses and produce key charts and graphs for the stockholders. Now that you have the background materials covered, you open Microsoft Word. You paste the Excel charts and use the Report Merge feature to export reports from Access to Word using Access 2007's Word (Export to RTF file) button on the External Data tab in the Export group. You also type and format a meeting agenda that your boss will distribute to the attendees. Now comes the fun part: You open Microsoft PowerPoint and create a professional, visually appealing presentation using the Word, Excel, and Access documents you've already created. As you put the finishing touches on your presentation—embedding an MP3 file in the introduction slide—you realize you've finally been able to use the skills you worked so hard to acquire.

FIGURE 4A   Knowing how to use software programs, such as those in Microsoft Office, will help you gain a competitive edge in whatever career you choose.

All of the programs you've used to create your presentation are components of a suite of software programs called Microsoft Office. This Spotlight explores the various programs, features, and uses of Microsoft Office (Figure 4A).

Introducing Microsoft Office

If you intend to use a Microsoft operating system, then you will probably use the tools in the Microsoft Office suite to manage documents, spreadsheets, databases, presentations, and communications. Microsoft Office 2007 is available in eight versions. You are most likely going to use either the Home and Student edition, which includes Word, Excel, PowerPoint, and OneNote, or the Professional version, which also includes Access, Publisher, Outlook, and Accounting Express but omits OneNote. Released in early 2007, Office 2007 is the most recent version of Office for the PC on the market (Figure 4B). Office 2008 for Mac is the most current version for the Mac OS X operating environment.

In the following sections, we'll look more closely at how Office components can help you represent your thoughts, ideas, and solutions in a professional way.

THE SHARED OFFICE INTERFACE AND TOOLS

Office applications use many interfaces that are similar to those of Windows. When an application is opened, you'll see some or all of the following features within the **application window**, the area that encloses and displays the application (Figure 4C).

The **application workspace** displays the document you are currently working on. In computing, a **document** is any type of product you create with the computer, including typewritten work, an electronic spreadsheet, or a graphic.

The topmost area of each program interface is called the **title bar**. It includes the program icon, the name of the application, and the name of the file you are working on. If you haven't yet saved the file, you'll see a generic file name, such as Untitled, Document1, Book 1, or another such name. Within the title bar, you'll also find three **window control** buttons, a group of window management tools located in the upper right corner of each window that enable the user to minimize, maximize, restore, or close the window. The left button enables you to **minimize** the window so that it is cleared from the screen and reduced down to a button on the task bar. Simply click the task bar button to retrieve the document. The right button is used to close the window once you finish with the document. The middle button toggles between two functions, depending on whether the program is occupying the entire screen (known as full screen) or is a smaller size. If the window is full screen, the button is in the **restore down** mode, which means clicking it will cause the window to revert to a smaller size. If the window is not full screen, clicking this button enables you to **maximize**, or enlarge, the window so that it fills the whole screen.

FIGURE 4B   Microsoft Office 2007 is the result of many generations of Office.

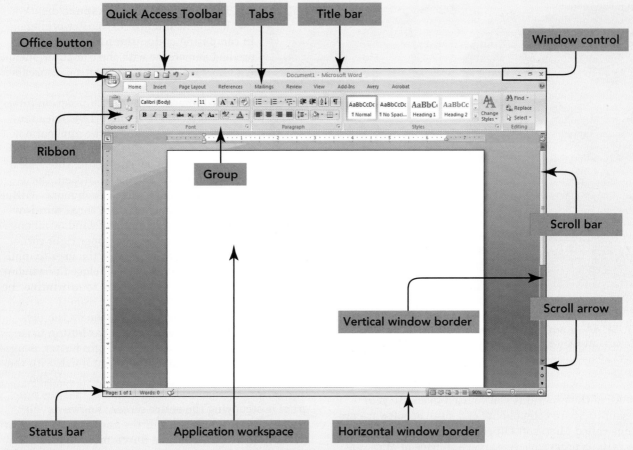

FIGURE 4C These components are found in most Microsoft Office 2007 applications.

In Microsoft applications, you can change the size of a window by dragging a vertical **window border** left or right or a horizontal border up or down. The window border is a thick line that encloses the window. If you click and drag a window corner, you can size the window horizontally and vertically at the same time. Note that this process will work only if a window is not maximized.

The bottom part of the application interface, called the **status bar**, displays information about the application and the document, such as the current page number and the total number of pages.

Scroll bars are located at the right and bottom of a document. They allow you to see different parts of a document without moving your cursor or selection. You can use scroll bars and **scroll arrows**, the arrows that appear on the scroll bar, to move (scroll) through the document. Typically, you can click the scroll arrows to move line by line or drag the scroll bar to move longer distances faster.

At the top left of the application window is the **Office button**, which contains choices for creating new documents; opening existing documents; and printing, saving, and closing documents. The **Quick Access Toolbar** appears just to the right of the Office button. The Quick Access Toolbar displays a series of buttons used to perform common tasks, such as saving a document and undoing or redoing the last action.

The Quick Access Toolbar is customizable, so you can add some of your favorite shortcuts to it. It remains available at all times, no matter which tab on the Ribbon is selected.

The shared interface also includes the **Ribbon** with tabs containing groups, which are positioned beneath the title bar. A **tab** contains categories of tasks you can accomplish within an application. The Ribbon enables you to manage and modify your documents. For instance, you might choose the Home tab and then in the Font group select the button for changing the font color.

Each application in Office has its own customized Ribbon of tabs. Office also has several advanced tabs, such as Add-Ins and Developer, which are not visible by default and can be turned on by clicking the Office button and then the Options button for that particular application at the bottom of the window. Some third-party programs, such as Adobe Acrobat, may also add helpful tabs to the Ribbon. However, the Ribbon in Word 2007 is representative of the Ribbons in the others:

- **Home.** The Home tab includes many of the most frequently used features and is the default tab that appears when you open an Office program. On it you'll find groups for the clipboard, font management, paragraph settings, styles, and editing (find and replace, go to, etc).

- **Insert.** On the Insert tab, you'll find groups for working with pages, tables, illustrations, managing links, working with headers and footers, manipulating text, and inserting symbols.
- **Page Layout.** The Page Layout tab contains groups for document themes, page setup, page background and borders, paragraph alignment, and object arrangement.
- **References.** The References tab contains groups for table of contents, footnotes, citations and bibliography, captions, indexing, and table of authorities.
- **Mailings.** The Mailings tab features groups for creating envelopes and labels, performing a mail merge, working with fields, previewing results, and finishing the merge.
- **Review.** The Review tab has groups for proofing a document, commenting, tracking changes, accepting or rejecting changes to tracking, comparing documents, and protecting documents.
- **View.** The View tab features groups for viewing a document in different ways, showing or hiding rulers and gridlines, zooming in to see different parts of a document, and window choices that allow you to work on more than one document simultaneously.

The Ribbon is a dynamic tool. Depending on what you are doing, other tabs may be displayed. For instance, if you insert a photo in a document, whenever the image is selected, a Picture Tools tab appears. Such tabs are said to be **contextual tabs** (Figure 4D).

Groups, which are located within the tabs, contain buttons and commands. The icon on each button provides a visual clue to the button's purpose. Clicking on a button causes the named action to occur. For instance, in Word, if you highlight any text and then select the Home tab, the Font group, and the Bold button (letter **B**), the highlighted text will be bolded (Figure 4E). Some groups also contain a dialog launcher icon, which looks like a small arrow, in the bottom right corner. Clicking this icon will open a dialog box so you can make additional choices.

Office applications share a number of other resources, including the Clip Organizer and the Office Clipboard. The **Clip Organizer** is a repository of clip art and images that can be inserted into a document or presentation (Figure 4F). You can access the Clip Organizer by selecting the Insert tab and then choosing the Clip Art button from the Illustrations group.

Office applications also share the Clipboard. The **Office Clipboard** temporarily stores in memory whatever you've cut or copied from a document and makes that cut or copied item available for use within any Office application. For example, you can create a financial summary in Excel, copy it to the Clipboard, and then paste it into Word.

Most Office applications also have smart tags. A **smart tag** is associated with text or data that has been entered in a document. Depending on the type of data, it may appear as a purple dotted underline or as a small icon or button. A smart tag is displayed when the program recognizes the location as a place where you might want to perform an additional task. When you click on a smart tag, an options menu appears (Figure 4G). For example, when you copy text from one place in a Word document and paste it to another location, a Paste Options smart tag appears listing options for how the pasted text should be treated.

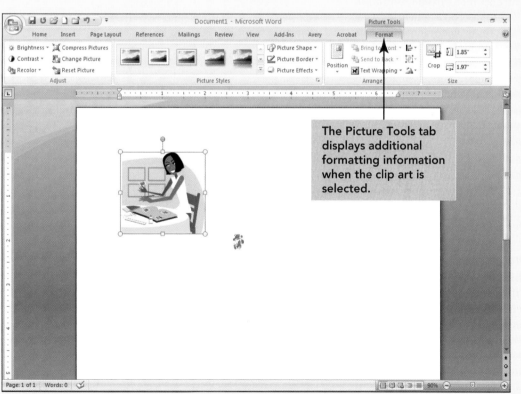

The Picture Tools tab displays additional formatting information when the clip art is selected.

FIGURE 4D Contextual tabs appear on the Ribbon to provide additional functionality when an object is inserted or selected.

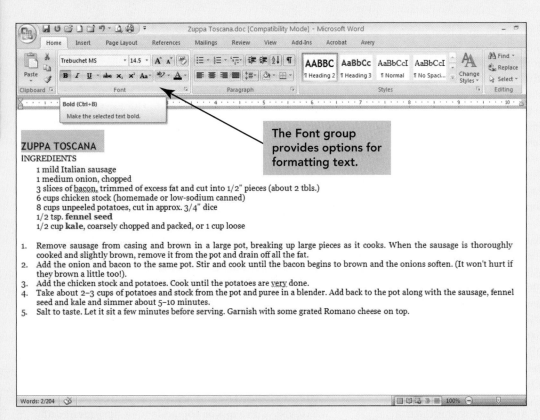

FIGURE 4E Each group within a tab contains buttons and commands used to perform specific tasks.

The AutoCorrect Options smart tag lets you modify the program's AutoCorrect feature, and other tags such as those for dates, times, names, and addresses provide options for working with specific data.

Another feature common to Office applications is the ability to create a new document from a template. The templates vary depending on the application you are using. When you create a new document, you can start with a new blank document or a template (Figure 4H). **Templates** are document frameworks that are created once and then used many times. For example, word processing programs typically include templates for faxes, letters, memos, reports, resumes, brochures, and many more types of documents. The template may include text, formatting, graphics, and many other features.

To locate and use a template, click the Office button and select New. A New Document dialog box appears with three panes. The Template pane on the left shows the various types of template categories, including Blank and recent, Installed Templates, My templates, and New from existing. Below that is a list of categories for templates that can be downloaded from Microsoft Office Online. The middle pane displays the list of available templates within the category selected in the Template pane. The right pane shows a thumbnail view of the template selected in the middle pane. Once you've chosen the template you wish to use, click Create to open the template in a new document window. You can make any necessary changes to this document and save it. The original template will remain unchanged and will be available for use again later. Depending on the Windows operating system you use, your copy of Office may be automatically

validated by Microsoft when you seek to download a template or access other online features. You can learn whether you have a valid copy of Office or Windows by visiting **www.microsoft.com/genuine/default.aspx?displaylang=en**.

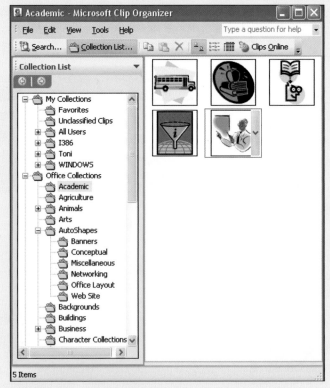

FIGURE 4F The Clip Organizer is an efficient way to insert images into documents and presentations.

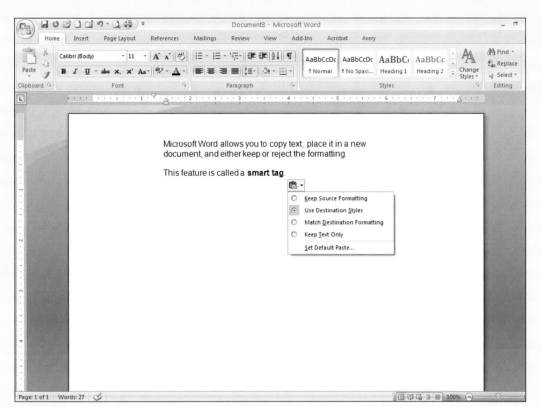

FIGURE 4G Smart tags offer choices for completing common Office tasks and provide additional options.

To **open** an existing document, you need to locate the document and load it into the application workspace. Essentially, you are transferring an existing document from storage to memory. You can do this through the Open dialog box. Figure 4I shows the typical appearance of an Open dialog box. To open a document, select the folder that contains the document. Next, highlight the document's name. Click Open to transfer the document to the application workspace.

Now that you've gotten an overview of Office, let's explore each of the applications individually.

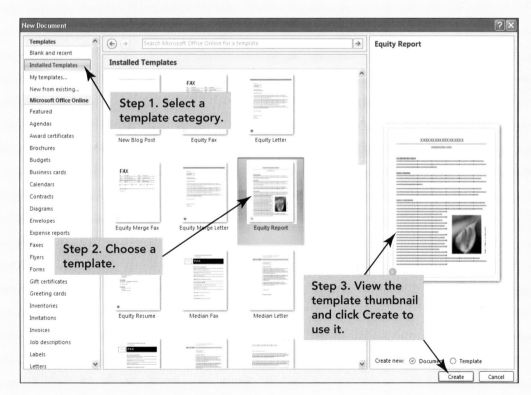

FIGURE 4H Templates provide consistent background content and formatting for multiple documents.

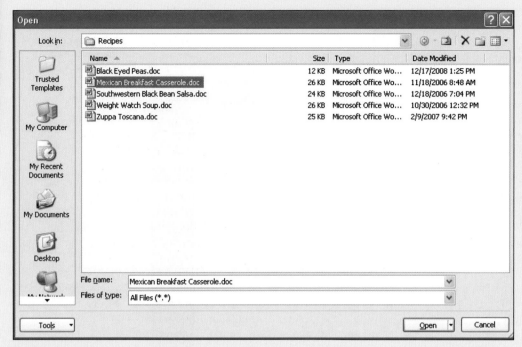

FIGURE 4I To open a document, select the folder that contains the document, highlight the document's name, and then click Open.

other features that can enhance your ability to present your thoughts in a formal way. For example, you can create lengthy reports and books that incorporate embedded pictures, graphics, charts, tables, and other objects. You can work with columns and set tabs to align text. You can print your document in portrait (vertical) or landscape (horizontal) orientation. It's almost true that if you can imagine it, you can do it in Word.

If you're using a PC, the files that you create in Word 2007 include the .docx extension by default. Word can also save your documents as plain text (.txt), HTML (.htm), Rich Text Format (.rtf), or formats that can be read by previous versions of Word or by competing products, such as WordPerfect. You will learn about other Office program extensions as you continue reading this Spotlight.

Microsoft Word

Microsoft Word is a very powerful word processing program. As with other Office applications, its interface includes the title bar, the Office button, the Quick Access Toolbar, the Ribbon, and the groups of tasks that can be executed. The remainder of the screen is basically a blank sheet of paper on which you can create your documents.

Using Word at its most basic level to create short letters, memos, and faxes is extraordinarily simple; you just type text into the Word document, click the Office button, and click Print from the menu to send your document to the printer (Figure 4J). Word features automatic text wrapping, a Find and Replace utility, and the ability to cut, copy, and paste both within the document and between documents or other programs. To improve the presentation of your documents, you can use editing and formatting tools to insert headers and footers, page breaks, page numbers, and dates. Word also includes

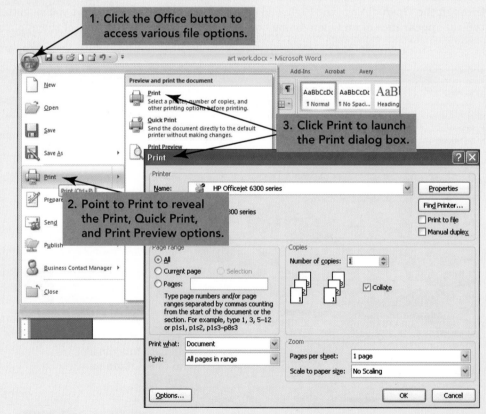

1. Click the Office button to access various file options.

2. Point to Print to reveal the Print, Quick Print, and Print Preview options.

3. Click Print to launch the Print dialog box.

FIGURE 4J Use the Office button to view file options, including saving and printing documents.

Now that you have a basic understanding of what Word can do for you, you're ready to move on to other Office applications. The following section will introduce you to Excel.

Microsoft Excel

Microsoft Excel is the leading spreadsheet program for business and personal use. The primary function of a spreadsheet program is to store and manipulate numbers. You use a spreadsheet either to record things that have actually happened or to predict things that might happen through a method called **modeling**, or **what-if analysis**. Projected income statements are a good example of spreadsheet modeling. You plug in your assumed values, and the model provides the prediction. If your assumptions are correct, the model will closely match the actual outcome. If your assumptions are faulty, then you can learn from your experience and perhaps make better assumptions in the future.

Excel's user interface is very similar to that of Word. Like Word, Excel has a status bar at the bottom of the screen and scroll bars that enable you to move your view vertically and horizontally.

In Excel, each file is called a **workbook**. A workbook is made up of **worksheets**. Each worksheet is composed of **columns**, vertical lines of data, and **rows**, horizontal lines of data, the intersections of which are called **cells** (Figure 4K).

A cell is identified by its column letter and its row number—known as the **cell address**. The columns in a spreadsheet are identified by the letters of the alphabet; rows are represented by numbers. For example, A1, B3, and AC342 each represent an individual cell in column A, row 1; column B, row 3; and column AC, row 342, respectively.

A **range** of cells consists of two or more cells selected at the same time, and is identified by the addresses of the top-left and bottom-right cells separated by a colon. For example, the range from cell A1 to cell D5 would be represented as A1:D5.

Cells store text, numbers, and formulas. Text entries, also referred to as **labels**, are used to identify numeric entries. For example, you might type the label "First month's rent" in cell A5 and then place the value "$650" next to it in cell B5. Labels are also used to identify typed-in numbers and the results of formulas.

A **formula** is a combination of numeric constants, cell references, arithmetic operators, or functions that display the result of a calculation. Excel interprets a cell entry as a formula if the entry starts with an equal sign (=). Formulas may be mathematical expressions or functions. In a **mathematical formula**, the mathematical order of operations is followed; that is, values in parentheses are acted on first, followed by exponentiation, multiplication and division, and then addition and subtraction. (You can remember this order of operations through the mnemonic Please Excuse My Dear Aunt Sally, or PEMDAS.) It is important to note that with PEMDAS order multiplication and division are the same rank, and addition and subtraction are also the same rank. You must evaluate from left to right for operations that are the same rank. For example, the formula $=6 * (4 - 2)/3 + 2$ is equal to 6, because 4 minus 2 is 2, 6 times 2 is 12, 12 divided by 3 is 4, and 4 plus 2 is 6.

The other type of a formula is called a function. A **function** is a very powerful type of formula because it allows you to perform operations on multiple inputs. As an example, the payment function is able to take the rate of interest, time period, and amount borrowed to produce the payment amount on a loan. Like mathematical formulas, a function begins with the equal sign. However, it then lists the name of the function (such as PMT for calculating payments on a loan) and an argument set, which is

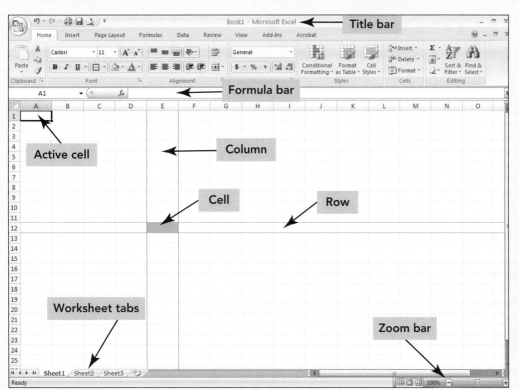

FIGURE 4K By default, the Excel workbook includes three worksheets. Each worksheet is made up of columns and rows, the intersections of which are cells in which data can be entered.

placed within parentheses. An **argument set** contains the passable parameters or variables in a function. For example, when calculating loan payments, the argument set contains the rate of interest (6% divided by 12 monthly periods), the time period of the loan (4 years times 12 payments per year), and the amount borrowed ($18,000). For example, =PMT(6%/12,48,18000) would return the payment for a loan of $18,000 at an interest rate of 6 percent for 4 years.

Excel also has features for creating **charts**, which are a graphical representation of data (Figure 4L). Charts are based on data sets and the labels that identify the data. There are 11 different categories of charts in Excel, and each category includes several different chart styles. The most commonly used charts are bar, column, pie, and area. Bar charts show the value of two or more items horizontally. They are good for depicting dramatic differences between positive and negative values. Column charts show two or more values side by side and are a vertical display. Pie charts represent data as a percentage of the total. Area charts are good for depicting magnitude of change over time.

It's possible to create other types of useful charts with Excel too. Line charts illustrate trends over time. Doughnut charts have the appearance of a pie but display more than one series. Radar charts depict frequency and change relative to a central point. Scatter charts depict two values and show relationships, usually independent of time. Surface charts present a 3D surface that shows trends in values across two dimensions in a continuous curve. Stock charts require three series of values in the order of high, low, close. Bubble charts compare three sets of values. They are similar to scatter charts with the third value displayed as the size of a bubble. Various chart subtypes are available within each chart category. Depending on the type of chart selected, you may have the option to create 3D charts or exploded charts, or to display data as cylinders, cones, or pyramids. Although these options can make your chart appear more interesting, it is important to make sure that your chart remains easy to read and that your data's perspective is not distorted.

Several other tools are also available for developing, managing, and assessing data. You can create pivot tables and charts (designed so that your data "pivots" about one field of interest) or sorted reports with subtotals, and you can use the database feature to extract information from your data set.

The files that you create in Excel 2007 include the .xlsx extension by default. Excel can also save your documents as plain text (.txt), HTML (.htm), eXtensible Markup Language (.xml), or in formats that can be read by previous versions of Excel.

To learn more about creating charts and reports in Excel, consult the online help at **www.microsoft.com** or use the Excel Help feature.

Next, we'll take a look at the Office application for managing databases.

Microsoft Access

Microsoft Access is a database management system (DBMS), which is a software application designed to capture, store, manipulate, and report data and information.

The opening Access interface offers choices for opening an existing database, using a template to create a new database, or beginning a new blank database from scratch (Figure 4M). In Access, you must always work on an existing database or on a new database that you've named and saved to disk. Access does not offer a default blank database screen like the blank document in Word or the blank worksheet in Excel. Access must

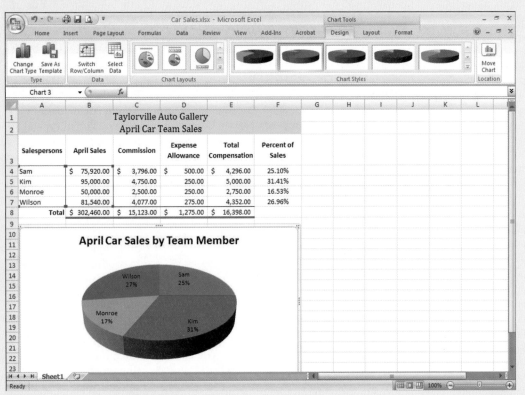

FIGURE 4L An Excel chart can add color and visual interest to your reports.

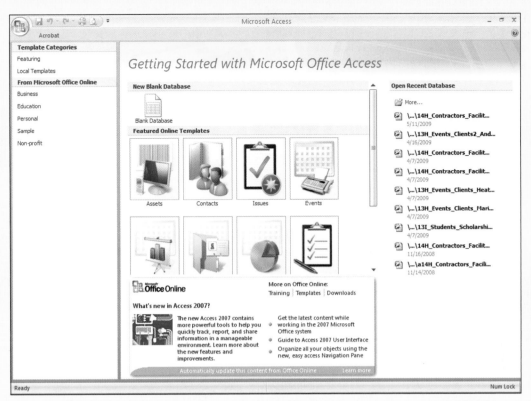

FIGURE 4M The Access opening interface provides options for opening an existing database or creating a new database from scratch or from a selection of templates.

always work between storage and memory—you cannot work within the program without first establishing a file on disk.

Access uses objects to manage and present data. In Access, an **object** is a subprogram that manages one aspect of database management. For instance, you use the **Form object** to collect data, the **Table object** to store data, the **Query object** to ask questions of the database, and the **Report object** to present your data (Figure 4N). The functions of these four objects match your computer's input, storage, processing, and output functions. (The order is usually input, processing, output, and storage, but in a database management system, the input has to be stored before it can be processed.)

Access is capable of importing data from many sources, including Microsoft Excel. If data is not imported from an outside source, it can be entered directly into a table or by using a form. Entering data into a table is useful when you wish to see multiple records at one time. A **form** is a template with blank fields in which users input data one record at a time. You have filled out physical and electronic forms many times in your life. Forms should be organized so that the person who is typing in the data can easily move from one field to the next in a logical order.

To be useful, the data usually must be processed using the Query object. You can use the Query object to ask questions of a data set. A **data set** describes the contents of a table. Let's say you have a data set that includes the names and addresses of family, friends, and

business associates. You want to send a mailing to your family to let them know how school has been going. To find the names and addresses of just your family members, you would run a query on your data set and set the filtering parameter to include only those names that have a field entry under the field name "family."

A **filter** uses one or more criteria to establish conditions an item must meet. Only the data that meets the conditions that have been set is allowed to pass through the filter. In this case, you are asking the Query object to provide you with your family members and no one else. The filtering parameter is that the query will return only records where the field for "family" is checked.

When you use Access, you need to present the results of your query in a manner that is not only useful but also professional in appearance—in short, you must design a report. We receive reports from databases all the time. Junk mail, utility bills, and credit card solicitations all come from reports that have been generated from massive data sets.

Access 2007, which uses the .accdb file extension by default, has a host of wizards available for the user. These wizards help users create tables, queries, forms, and reports with ease. Access has long been seen as a program that is difficult to use. Not only is Access 2007 dramatically improved over the last few versions, but the new and upgraded wizards are a giant leap forward.

To learn more about how to use Access, visit the online help provided at **www.microsoft.com**. Let's

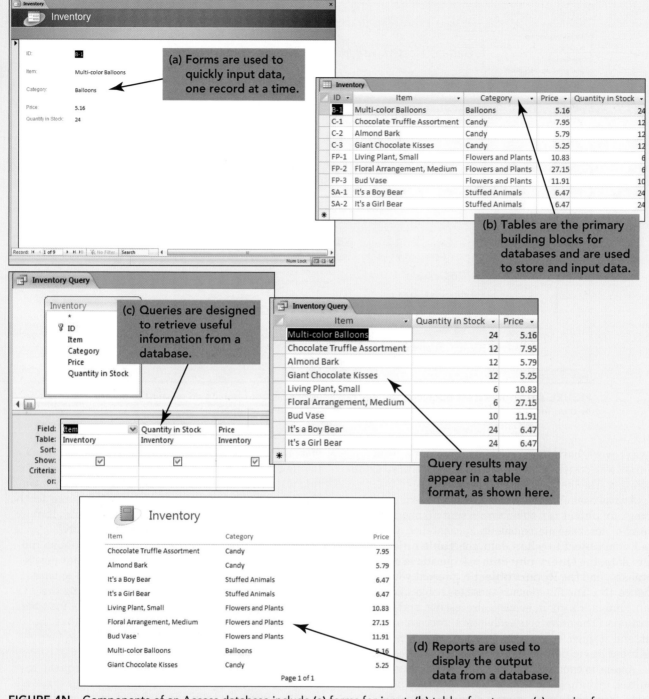

FIGURE 4N Components of an Access database include **(a)** forms for input, **(b)** tables for storage, **(c)** queries for processing, and **(d)** reports for output.

now look at a program that's a favorite among many college students: PowerPoint.

Microsoft Powerpoint

Microsoft PowerPoint is a popular program used to create and deliver presentations. When you open PowerPoint, you are presented with a blank slide that is in the Title slide format (Figure 4O). A **slide** is the canvas on which you organize text boxes and graphics to represent your ideas or points. PowerPoint offers nine slide layouts. All layouts with the exception of the Blank Layout slide format have text boxes for inserting text or graphics boxes for embedding graphics. These boxes are often referred to as placeholders. The various boxes are in a set position on the slide canvas, but you can modify the size or position of the placeholders by using your mouse or by selecting one and

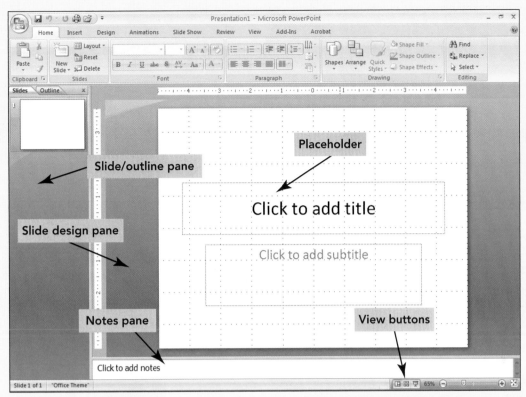

FIGURE 4O The PowerPoint screen features the slides or outline pane on the left, the slide design pane in the center, a notes pane across the bottom, and the buttons used to switch between Normal, Slide Sorter, and Slide Show views.

using the appropriate tools on the Ribbon. There are different layouts to choose from for each slide. For example, a Title slide has two text boxes. The top box is for the title of your presentation, and the bottom box is for a subtitle or your name. You might choose Title and Text as the layout for your second slide, because it has a text box for the title at the top of the slide and a bulleted list text box for the major presentation points on the lower portion of the slide.

A PowerPoint template contains preformatted fonts, locations for text and graphics, and color schemes. **Design templates** are professionally created slide designs that can be applied to a presentation. You might create your slides in the blank presentation (black and white, with no special fonts or effects) and then apply various design templates until you achieve the desired effect (Figure 4P). Some of the templates are casual or festive, whereas others are appropriate for business purposes. As you create your presentation, keep in mind that the design template used should match the purpose and content of the presentation.

Click the Office button and then click New to open the New Presentation window. In the left pane, Microsoft Office Online includes presentation categories for home and business projects.

It is often helpful to create an outline for your topic (either by hand or with Word) before starting

PowerPoint. Once you've done so, you are ready to create your presentation. The easiest way is to begin with a blank presentation. If you begin with a blank presentation, you will perform an iterative process of typing in your text, choosing whether to include graphics, inserting a new slide that is based on a slide layout template, and then repeating.

It's very easy to get caught up in all the bells and whistles available in PowerPoint. Ultimately, though, *you* are the presenter, and therefore *you* must command your audience. A good PowerPoint slideshow should serve as a backdrop to your presentation; it shouldn't be the main feature.

Be forewarned: Presentations on a video projector almost never look the same as they do on your computer screen. With this in mind, it's a good idea to try out your presentation in the room where you'll give it. If you allow yourself plenty of time, you'll be able to change the design template to colors that will work best in the room.

PowerPoint 2007 applies the .pptx extension by default. PowerPoint can also save your documents as HTML (.htm); in various graphics formats, such as .jpg and .gif; or in formats that can be read by previous versions of PowerPoint.

Let's now move on to a program that will help you communicate with others and manage your busy schedule: Microsoft Outlook.

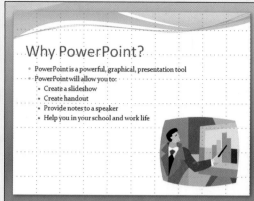

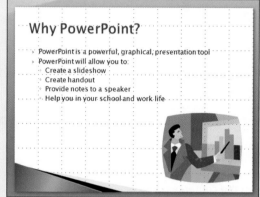
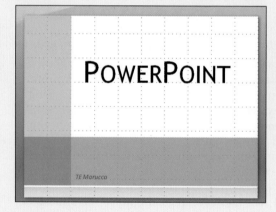
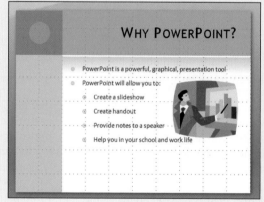

FIGURE 4P Design templates provide a way to change the look and feel of your presentation to suit your audience.

Microsoft Outlook

Microsoft Outlook is an e-mail and organizational communications tool that you can use to send and receive mail, maintain a personal calendar, schedule meetings with coworkers, and store information about your personal contacts. Figure 4Q shows two aspects of the Outlook interface.

When you use the e-mail function of Outlook, you obviously need to know the recipient's e-mail address. For example, an e-mail address might look like student@college.edu. Outlook has an autocomplete feature that suggests the completion of an address you've previously used as you type on the To: line. For example, if you begin typing the address myfriend@yahoo.com, the autocomplete feature suggests the complete address when you type the first letter, *m*, in myfriend. If the

suggestion is correct, press the Enter key to insert the address. If the suggestion is not the address you intend, then simply keep typing the correct address.

One feature of Outlook that is very helpful is the ability to create folders, which you can use to organize your saved e-mail messages. For example, you could create a Family folder for family mail, a separate folder for each of your classes, and perhaps a Friends folder for personal messages you've received from friends. Placing mail that you've read in these folders will then help you keep your inbox uncluttered.

You may find the Outlook calendar helpful in managing all of the activities associated with school, work, and socializing. The calendar is very easy to use and even includes an alarm to alert you 5, 10, 15, or 30 minutes or some specified number of hours or days before a scheduled event.

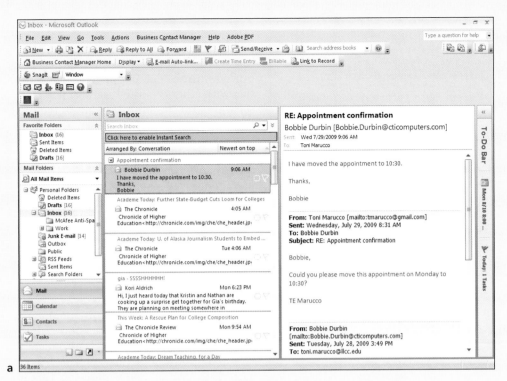

a

FIGURE 4Q Outlook helps you organize and manage your e-mail **(a)**, and the Outlook calendar **(b)** is a good way to keep track of your college schedule and personal activities.

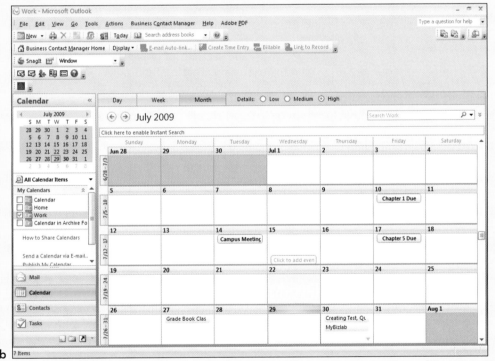

b

The best way to learn how to use Outlook is to experiment with it. Also remember that you can use the Help program to learn how to use the various features Outlook includes. You'll be surprised at just how easy it is to manage Outlook.

Introduction to Microsoft Office 2010

Microsoft continually seeks to improve their software by upgrading and updating their product line. This is evident by their recent announcement of the soon-to-be-released Microsoft Office 2010, which will feature many new enhancements, with special attention to collaboration among users (Figure 4R).

The new Office 2010 release promises to improve your computing experience with powerful new tools within the applications. Across the suite of products, the cut and paste functionality will be improved to allow users to preview paste formats before clicking Paste. You will also be able to edit video, photos, and graphics from within an application and share them with others. Office 2010 provides Office Web Apps, a

FIGURE 4R The new Office 2010 Suite will offer a variety of improved software products.

mechanism for users to access their files from virtually any PC or smartphone. Overall, the new suite of products promises that users will be able to work faster and more intuitively whether they are on the road, in the office, or at home. The new product will also be easy for IT staff members and solo users to install, integrate, and support.

MICROSOFT WORD 2010

Microsoft Word 2010 will allow you to create and organize professional documents in less time with less effort and share them more easily with others. Upgrades include an improved Navigation Pane, improved Ribbon, improved picture-editing capabilities, improved SmartArt capabilities, and more. New features will allow you to store documents online and access them from practically any Web browser.

MICROSOFT EXCEL 2010

The excellent data analysis features of Microsoft Excel will be dramatically improved in Excel 2010 with the addition of collaboration capability, which will enable multiple people to edit an Excel worksheet simultaneously while working over the Internet. Data analysis will also be more visual, highlighting important data trends, through the use of the new sparklines tool. Other improvements include new search filters, improved conditional formatting, improved charting, and additional SmartArt graphics.

MICROSOFT ACCESS 2010

Access 2010, like the other components of the Microsoft Office 2010 suite, has been improved with the enhancement of collaboration with others via the Internet. The software provides multiple built-in templates that are easy to use. In addition, the application's powerful tools will enable users to become productive much more quickly. Some of the enhancements include reusable database parts, improved macro design capabilities, an improved Ribbon, and improved trend analysis through conditional formatting.

MICROSOFT POWERPOINT 2010

PowerPoint 2010 allows you to create visuals that are professional looking. The update allows you to embed, edit, and manage videos from within the application, using a variety of different formats. It also includes new and improved picture-editing effects, such as saturation and watercolor. This release improves the PowerPoint experience by offering an Animation Painter, improved transitions, and enhanced capabilities to add sections of presentations; it even allows you to get tips on creating high-powered presentations from an award-winning design firm.

MICROSOFT OUTLOOK 2010

Microsoft Outlook 2010 improves the tracking and managing of e-mail conversations, while saving valuable Inbox space. Users will be able to compress long e-mail threads into a few conversations that can be categorized, filed, ignored, or cleaned up within a few clicks, using Conversation View. Other key enhancements include an improved Ribbon and a new scheduling view.

MICROSOFT OFFICE WEB APPS

Office Web Apps offers the advantage of greater flexibility when working in Microsoft Word, Excel, PowerPoint and OneNote. You will be able to access your work at any time from a smartphone or computer with an Internet connection. You will be able to post your work online and share it with others from across town or around the world. It's convenient and easy. This feature is not available out of the box. To take advantage of it, you will need a Windows Live account, which is fairly easy to obtain, or access to Microsoft SharePoint 2010.

MICROSOFT OFFICE BACKSTAGE

Microsoft Office Backstage view replaces the traditional file menu, helping users get to operations such as save, share, print, and publish with just a few clicks. An enhanced Ribbon will be available across all Office applications so you can access more commands quickly and create custom work flows.

Spotlight Exercises

1. Open Microsoft Excel from the Start, All Programs, Microsoft Office menu sequence. You are going to create a simple budget. Click any cell to select it, type in "Rent," and then press the Enter key. Next, type in "Utilities," press Enter, and then type "Food" and press Enter. Next, type a number next to each expense type. Select the Rent cell and hold down the left mouse button as you drag down through the expenses and then over to the bottom right number. Choose the Insert tab and then in the Charts group choose the column button to create a column chart. Use the mouse to move the chart around and resize it by clicking and dragging the sizing handles. Print the chart so that your professor can see what you've accomplished.

2. Open PowerPoint from the Start, All Programs, Microsoft Office menu sequence. Click the Office button, and then click New to open the New Presentation window. In the left pane, choose a category under Microsoft Office Online. Choose a subcategory in the middle pane, if necessary, and then double-click a template to download it. Create a presentation about yourself. It must have at least 6 slides. Have some fun with this—see whether you can change the backgrounds or patterns. (*Hint:* Click the Design tab.) When you are through creating your slides, click the Office button, point to the arrow to the right of the Print button, and then click Print. In the "Print what" dropdown list, select **Handouts**. In the Slides per page dropdown list, select **6**. Print your handout, mark it with your name, and submit it to your instructor as directed.

3. You can customize the Quick Access Toolbar by choosing the down-pointing arrow at the right side of the toolbar. Choose two additional buttons you want to add to the Quick Access Toolbar. Move the toolbar below the Ribbon by clicking on the down arrow next to the toolbar and selecting Show Below the Ribbon. Write a short memo to your instructor that explains why you chose the buttons you did to add to the Quick Access Toolbar and which position you prefer for the location of the Quick Access Toolbar. Be sure to include your thoughts about how many icons you think would be enough and how many would be too many. Explain your reasoning.

4. Office 2010 promises to enhance your productivity. Visit **www.microsoft.com/presspass/presskits/2010office/materials.aspx**. Read about what's new with Office 2010 and read the Fact Sheet for Office 2010. Which items do you think will be most beneficial to you? Which are less likely to be helpful? Explain your choices in a short paper and be ready to defend your decisions.

5. Visit the sites given below and add a site from your own research. Based upon what you have read, give at least five rules you think make an effective PowerPoint presentation. List your rules and explain what they mean. Also give your site reference.

   - http://sbinfocanada.about.com/cs/management/qt/powerptpres.htm
   - http://desktoppub.about.com/od/microsoft/bb/powerpointrules.htm

chapter 6

The Internet and the World Wide Web

Chapter Objectives

Are you a little overwhelmed, confused, and irritated with all of the data, links, spam, and advertising you see on the Web every time you connect to the Internet? Join the club. Obtaining the skills to locate accurate information quickly, with little irritation and rekeying of information, seems to be a necessity, and not just for personal use, but for business as well. How do your Internet search skills, data evaluation techniques, and overall patience stack up with what is needed to succeed in today's online world?

The **Internet** is a global computer network made up of thousands of privately and publicly owned computers and networks that grew and interlinked, over time, into one giant network. Through a powerful combination of surveys, comScore, a global leader in measuring the digital world, released data in December 2008 estimating the global Internet audience (defined as users ages 15 and older) using home and work computers surpassed 1 billion unique visitors. Based on their data, comScore, Inc., believes that while hitting the billion user mark signifies the growth of a unified global community, the leap to the second and third billion will come more quickly and represent a truly global network of connected people and ideas that transcend cultural and physical borders.

The Internet was originally planned to be nothing more than a communication and file-exchange network for academics and government agencies. However, it has become a medium for discovering and exploring information, marketing products, shopping, taking classes, and socializing (Figure 6.1). To learn more about the history of the Internet and how it evolved into the media giant it is today, start with the Internet Society's "Histories of the Internet" page located at **www.isoc.org/internet/history**. The Internet Society is an organization for professionals who are interested in supporting the technical development of the Internet.

Today, we're witnessing the birth of the first major mass medium since television; more than 70 percent of U.S. residents are Internet users, and the number of users from regions around the globe keeps increasing (Figure 6.2). What's more, the Internet isn't simply a new mass medium; it's the first mass medium that involves computers and uses digitized data. It's more interactive than TV, radio, and newspapers, which limit a user to a noninteractive consumption role. With the Internet, people can create information as well as consume it. With the growing popularity of Web 2.0 applications such as wikis and blogs, it's the first truly democratic mass medium, allowing anyone to add content to the growing mass of information available online.

Most college students have used the Internet—it's hard to imagine students these days not having heard of a Web page, a URL, or a Web link. But no matter how familiar you think you are with this part of the Internet, this chapter will help you fully understand the concepts behind the Web and Web browsers. In addition, this chapter will show you how to use the Web effectively for research and evaluate the quality of the information you

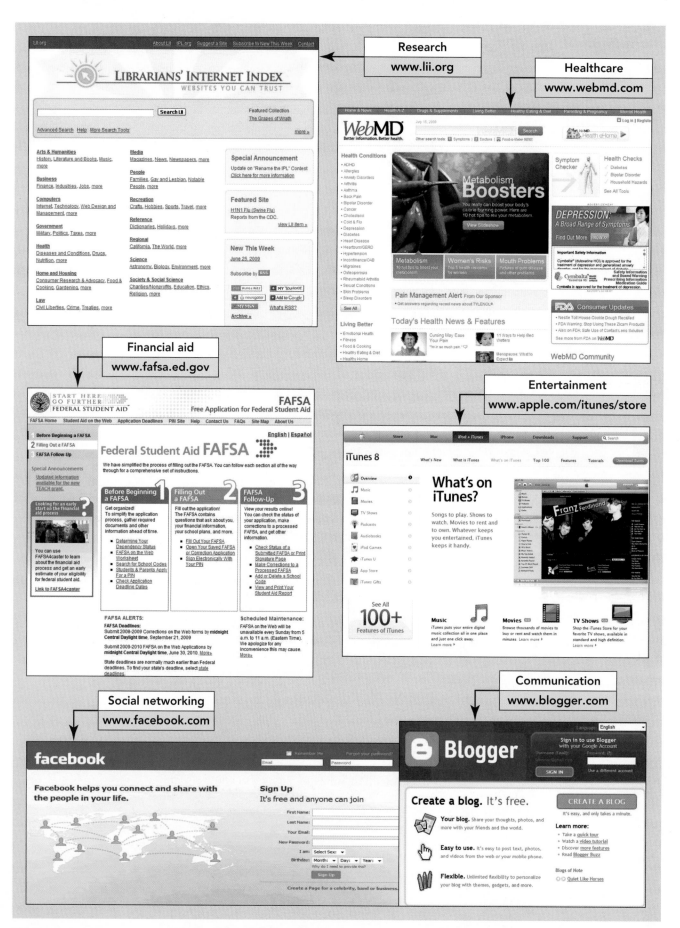

FIGURE 6.1 The Internet is rich with informative and entertaining sites.

FIGURE 6.2 World Internet Usage and Population by Regions

World Region	Population (est. 2008)	Internet Usage (Dec. 31, 2000)	Internet Usage (Mar. 31, 2009)
Africa	975,330,899	4,514,400	54,171,500
Asia	3,780,819,792	114,304,000	657,170,816
Europe	803,903,540	105,096,093	393,373,398
Middle East	196,767,614	3,284,800	45,861,346
North America	337,572,949	108,096,800	251,290,489
Latin America/Caribbean	581,249,892	18,068,919	173,619,140
Oceania, Australia	34,384,384	7,620,480	20,783,419
World Total	6,710,029,070	360,985,492	1,596,270,108

retrieve. It will examine the expansion of the Web into the area of e-commerce, review the benefits and hazards that e-commerce has brought about, and explore how to surf the Web safely.

Now that you know what the Internet is, let's explore how it works and how it is used.

How the Internet Works

The Internet is best thought of as *the* over-arching network of networks. In this network of networks, theoretically every connected computer can exchange data with any other computer on the network. The Internet is also referred to as **cyberspace**—a term used to refer to the intangible, nonphysical territory that encompasses the unlimited span of world-wide computer networks that use the same method to exchange data. The networks that make up the Internet are not maintained by one company or organization. Believe it or not, the Internet is maintained by a conglomerate of volunteers across the world. Some governing bodies restrict control and/or provide equipment. But the majority of network servers and connectivity equipment are provided by universities, telecommunications companies, businesses, corporations, and services that sell Internet access (Figure 6.3). It really is amazing that it all works!

The **Internet backbone**, the main high-speed routes through which data travels, are maintained by **network service providers (NSPs)** such as AT&T, NCI, Sprint, BBN, and UUNET. The equipment of these providers is linked at **network access points (NAPs)** so that data may, for example, begin its journey on a segment maintained by AT&T but cross over to a Sprint segment in order to reach its destination. Visit **www.internet2.edu** for information on a nonprofit consortium of universities, government agencies, and computer and telecommunication companies in over 50 countries that develop and deploy advanced networking applications and technologies. For information on the structure of the Internet and a visual representation of its complex nature go to "An Atlas of Cyberspaces," at **www.cybergeography.org/atlas/ atlas.html**, and use the cybermaps to

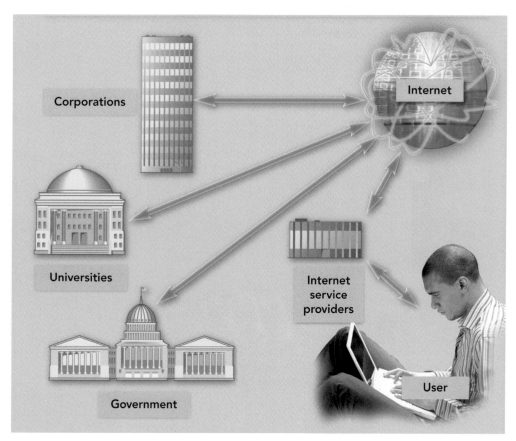

Corporations

Universities

Government

Internet

Internet service providers

User

FIGURE 6.3 The networks that make up the Internet's infrastructure are maintained by government agencies, universities, telecommunication companies, businesses, corporations, and Internet service providers. Users interact with them all through their Internet service provider.

communications and browsing devices. The Internet enables these computers and devices to exchange data and even control each other's operations, regardless of the system being used, allowing greater flexibility for communication and collaboration. The reason for this interoperability is the **TCP/IP (Transmission Control Protocol/Internet Protocol)** suite of protocols, which supply the standard methods of packaging and transmitting information on the Internet. When you obtain direct access to the Internet, usually through an Internet service provider, your computer is provided with a copy of the TCP/IP programs just as every other computer that is connected to the Internet. The TCP/IP suite employs a two-layer communication design. The TCP layer, **Transmission Control Protocol**, manages the assembling of a message or file into smaller packets that are transmitted over the Internet and received by a TCP layer on the destination computer that reassembles the packets into the original message. The lower layer, the **Internet Protocol**, handles the address part of each packet so that it gets to the right destination.

Now that you've learned about how the Internet works, the next section explores how you go about getting online.

navigate the digital landscape. This project by Martin Dodge of the University of Manchester's School of Environment and Development ran from 1997 through 2004. It was updated through February 2007.

INTEROPERABILITY

The Internet does more than merely allow any one of millions of computers to exchange data with any other. One key to the Internet's success is called **interoperability**, the ability to work with a computer even if it is a different brand and model. This remarkable characteristic of the Internet comes into play every time you use the network. When you access the Internet using a Mac, for example, you contact a variety of machines that may include other Macs, Windows PCs, UNIX machines, and even mainframe computers. You don't know what type of computer you're accessing, however, and it doesn't make any difference (Figure 6.4).

The Internet's interoperability helps explain the network's popularity. No network could match the Internet's success if it forced people to use just one or two types of computers. Many home computer users have IBM-compatible PCs, but others have Macs or other types of computers or

> "One key to the **Internet's** success is called **interoperability**, the ability to work with a computer even if it is a different **brand** and model."

FIGURE 6.4 The interoperability of the Internet allows people to interact and communicate with one another, no matter which type of computer or operating system they use.

Accessing the Internet: Going Online

When you access the Internet, it is referred to as *going online*. You usually do not connect directly to the Internet backbone. Instead, you usually connect to an Internet service provider (ISP) that in turn connects you to the backbone.

INTERNET SERVICE PROVIDERS AND ONLINE SERVICES

Internet service providers (ISPs) are companies that provide access to the Internet and no additional services. An **online service** is a for-profit firm that provides a proprietary network offering special services that are available only to subscribers. Members may participate in chat rooms and discussions and take advantage of fee-based content, such as magazines and newspapers. When they began, online services provided a large amount of content that was accessible only by those who subscribed to that online service, whereas ISPs predominantly served to provide access to the Internet and generally provided little, if any, exclusive content of their own. The distinction between these two services has become less defined as online services

today offer Internet access in an attempt to keep existing customers and attract new ones. While retaining their proprietary network and custom content, they have, in effect, become ISPs. Verizon, Comcast, and AOL are examples of current ISPs (Figure 6.5).

To access the Internet backbone, ISPs distribute software that runs on users' computers that enable the connection. Essentially, the ISP provides an access ramp to an expressway; in this case, the expressway is the Internet backbone. These various providers usually charge a monthly fee for Internet access, again like the fee to use some expressways, but you can sometimes obtain free trial accounts for a certain number of days or hours.

ISPs have several roles and responsibilities. They are responsible for providing and maintaining a connection to the Internet. ISPs must also support the hardware and software needed to service that connection. They need to protect their site and network from external threats such as viruses, hacker attacks, and other illegal activities. And finally, they should provide 24-hour customer service and technical support. If you are looking for an ISP, you might want to start with "The List" at **www.thelist.com**. This is a buyer's guide to ISPs and can be searched by area or country.

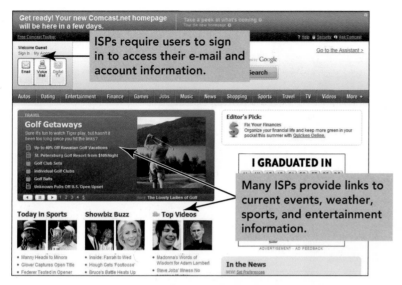

ISPs require users to sign in to access their e-mail and account information.

Many ISPs provide links to current events, weather, sports, and entertainment information.

FIGURE 6.5 Internet service providers, such as Comcast, provide Internet access to individuals and businesses.

In addition to obtaining an Internet account, you have to decide how you will access the Internet (Figure 6.6). Be aware that the speed of access advertised by a service provider is often a maximum. Few users actually find their usage reaching these advertised numbers. Your access choices typically include the following options:

- **Dial-up access.** If you are searching for an affordable ISP solution and speed is not a high priority, then the dial-up Internet service providers will likely meet your needs. Dial-up Internet service does not require any special

hardware; it uses your existing phone jack and dial-up modem configurations. The downside of this type of access is the speed; it is the slowest of all Internet services. Dial-up Internet pricing has come down to record low levels, and for the occasional Web surfer it's a great way to spend less and surf more. Moreover, many people still use a dial-up ISP as a backup for their existing broadband service.

- **Digital subscriber line (DSL).** DSL connections offer faster access speeds than dial-up, while making use of ordinary phone lines with the addition of a special external modem. One drawback of DSL is that service doesn't extend more than a few miles from a telephone switching station or central office (CO). Although this distance is being extended, DSL service may be unavailable in some rural areas.

- **Cable access.** Many cable TV companies provide permanent online connections and offer high-speed Internet access, comparable to—and sometimes surpassing—DSL speeds. No phone line is needed, but a cable modem is required.

- **Satellite access.** If your geographical area has been overlooked by DSL and cable providers, go outside. If you have a clear view of the sky, then you can most likely get high-speed

FIGURE 6.6	Types of Internet Access			
Type	Price Range per Month	Speed of Access (receiving data)	Advantages	Disadvantages
Dial-up	$5 to $20	Slow: 56 kilobits per second (Kbps)	Availability Low user cost	Slow speed
DSL	$10 to $30	Average: 1.5 megabits per second (Mbps) Maximum: 7+ Mbps	Speed Reliability	Availability High user cost
Cable	$30 to $60	Average: 3 Mbps Maximum: 30+ Mbps	Speed Reliability	Availability High user cost
Satellite	$60 to $100	Average: 700 Kbps Maximum: 1.5 Mbps	Availability Speed	High user cost Reliability
FiOS	$40 to $180	Average: 15 Mbps Maximum: 50+ Mbps	Speed	Availability High user cost

satellite Internet service! The connection to your high-speed satellite Internet service is comprised of both indoor and outdoor equipment. Outside, there is an antenna and transmit-and-receive electronics, along with a connection to a small, unobtrusive dish. This equipment connects to an Indoor Receive Unit (IRU) and Indoor Transmit Unit (ITU) that connect to your computer through a simple USB connector. Satellite is more costly than cable or DSL, but if you live in a rural area, it might be a viable alternative to dial-up.

- **Fiber-optic service (FiOS).** Fiber-optic lines running directly to the home provide users with incredibly fast Internet access, easily surpassing other methods. With more than 1.5 million customers (with a goal of 3 to 4 million by 2010) in at least 16 states, **fiber-optic service** is rapidly becoming a challenger to DSL and cable providers, especially in the suburbs. However, this service is still unavailable in many cities and rural areas and is only provided by Verizon. No modem is needed, but fiber-optic cable may need to be run to and within your home.

If you don't need a constant, daily connection, many ISPs provide direct connections on special leased lines for businesses, educational institutions, and large organizations. Internet access is attained through the organization's network and is usually free to the users, because the company or institution pays the bill.

Now that you understand the various ways to access the Internet, let's differentiate the Internet from its most popular entity, the World Wide Web.

FIGURE 6.7 The Internet provides the infrastructure used to transport the ideas, queries, and information available on the World Wide Web to and from users.

The Internet and the Web: What's the Difference?

What's the difference between saying, "I'm on the Internet" versus "I'm on the Web"? Although many people talk as if the Internet and the Web were the same thing, they are not. Recall, the Internet is a network of hardware (computers, cables, and routers) through which any computer can directly access other computers and exchange data. The **World Wide Web** (or **Web** or **WWW**) is a portion of the Internet that contains billions of documents. The Web *uses* the Internet as its transport mechanism, but it's a separate entity (Figure 6.7). The Internet is the physical connection of millions of networks, whereas the Web is one of many applications that run on the top of the Internet architecture.

Who owns or controls the Web? As with the Internet, no one. Both involve thousands of publicly and privately owned computers and networks, all of which agree to follow certain standards and guidelines and share resources on the network. A variety of organizations are responsible for different aspects of the network (Figure 6.8). For example, the World Wide Web Consortium (W3C), based in Cambridge, Massachusetts, issues standards related to all aspects of the Web.

A **Web page** is a document or resource of information on a Web site suitable for the World Wide Web that is accessed by a browser. The information on the page is in HTML or XHTML format and can include text, graphics, sound, animation, video, and hypertext links to other Web pages. A **Web browser** is a program on your computer that displays a Web document

FIGURE 6.8 Internet Management Organizations

Name	Purpose
ICANN—Internet Corporation for Assigned Names and Numbers **www.icann.org**	Nonprofit, international organization responsible for keeping the Internet secure, stable, and interoperable by coordinating the Internet's Domain Name System and assigning IP addresses.
IETF—Internet Engineering Task Force **www.ietf.org**	International community of information technology (IT) professionals, including network designers, operators, vendors, and researchers, responsible for improving the operation of the Internet by developing Internet standards, best current practices, and informational documents.
ISOC—Internet Society **www.icoc.org**	Nonprofit, international association consisting of over 80 organizations and 28,000 individual members, formed to provide leadership in Internet-related standards, education, and policy and to ensure the open development, evolution, and use of the Internet for the benefit of people throughout the world.
IAB—Internet Architecture Board **www.iab.org**	Advisory body to the ISOC, this international committee of the IETF is comprised of 13 volunteers from the IT community who oversee the development of Internet architecture, protocols, procedures, and standards.
IRTF—Internet Research Task Force **www.irtf.org**	A task force of individual contributors from the research community working together in small, long-term research groups that report to the IAB and explore important topics related to the evolution of the Internet.
Network Solutions **www.networksolutions.com**	Organization responsible for managing the central domain name database. Network Solutions was the first and only public domain name registrar until 1999, when the registration process was opened to competition.
W3C—World Wide Web Consortium **www.w3.org**	An international consortium of over 440 organizations in more than 40 countries responsible for ensuring long-term growth for the World Wide Web and promoting Web interoperability through the publication of open standards for Web languages and protocols.

by interpreting the HTML or XHTML format, enabling you to access Web pages and linked documents. A **Web site** is a collection of related Web pages. A Web site typically contains a **home page** (also called an **index page**), which is a default page that's displayed automatically when you enter a site at its top level.

It's amazing to think that the Web's billions of documents are almost instantly accessible by means of the computer sitting on your desk. Tens of thousands of new Web pages appear every day. The Web is also appealing because of its graphical richness, which is made possible by the integration of text and images.

In the following section, you'll learn how all of these pieces work together on the Web, starting with the concept of hypertext.

THE HYPERTEXT CONCEPT

Hypertext is a system in which objects (text, pictures, music, programs, and so on) can be creatively linked to each other. It works by means of **hyperlinks** (also called **links**), elements in an electronic document that act as the connector to another place in the same document or to an entirely different document. Typically, you click on the hyperlink to bring another object into view. Hyperlinks are the most essential ingredient of the World Wide Web (Figure 6.9).

This system of hypertext is created by a special code called **Hypertext Markup Language (HTML)** or **Extensible Hypertext Markup Language (XHTML)**. HTML is a language that uses a tag system of code to create Web pages. This language is interpreted by browsers, which display the page according to the directions specified by the HTML language. XHTML combines the flexibility of HTML with the extensibility of **Extensible Markup Language (XML)**, a language designed to reduce the complexity of HTML. But what does this mean? Some HTML tags are only viewable in one browser or another. The only solutions that an HTML writer has are to avoid using those tags, use those tags and state that the page is meant for one browser or another, or write multiple pages and direct readers to the appropriate pages. With XHTML, however, if you need to define a tag for clarity across different browsers or create a new markup tag, you simply define it in an XHTML module and use it in your page as you would any other HTML tag. This feature makes a page truly compatible with all browsers. The agency responsible for standardizing HTML and XHTML is the World Wide Web Consortium (W3C).

In addition to being a global hypertext system, the Web is a distributed hypermedia system. A **distributed hypermedia system** is a network-based content development system that uses multimedia resources, such as sound, video, and text, as a means of navigation or illustration. In this system, the responsibility for creating content is distributed among many people. The next generation of the Web, known as **Web 2.0**, provides even more opportunities for individuals to collaborate, interact with one another, and create new content by using applications such as blogs, wikis, and podcasts. The more people who create content, the easier information creation and dissemination becomes. For example,

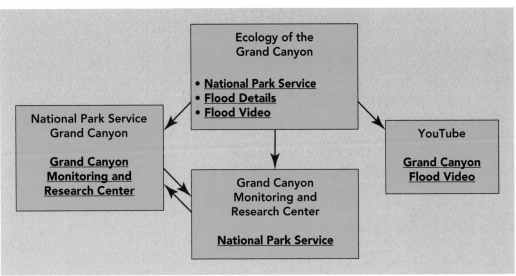

if you are researching the ecology of the Grand Canyon, you might link to the National Park Service for a general overview, link to the Grand Canyon Monitoring and Research Center for details on the flood dam operators released in 2008 to improve the canyon's ecosystem, and link to a site such as YouTube for a video of the event.

The Web's distribution of content creation responsibilities does have a drawback: You can link to any page you want, but you can't guarantee that the page's author will keep the page on the Web. The author can delete it or move it at any time without notice. For this reason, **dead links** (also called **broken links**), which are links to documents that have disappeared, are common on the Web.

Now that you understand hypertext, let's move on to what enables us to use it: browsers and servers.

WEB BROWSERS AND WEB SERVERS

The first graphical Web browsers, programs that display Web pages and make hypertext become "live" on your computer

FIGURE 6.9 In hypertext, you follow the links to related information. The links are the underlined text and are usually blue.

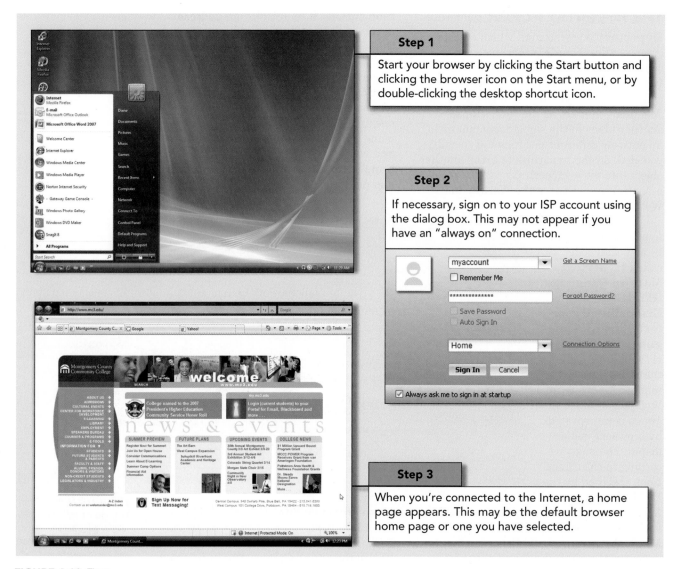

Step 1

Start your browser by clicking the Start button and clicking the browser icon on the Start menu, or by double-clicking the desktop shortcut icon.

Step 2

If necessary, sign on to your ISP account using the dialog box. This may not appear if you have an "always on" connection.

Step 3

When you're connected to the Internet, a home page appears. This may be the default browser home page or one you have selected.

FIGURE 6.10 These steps show how to connect to the Web via your browser icon.

screen, were developed in 1993. Figure 6.10 illustrates how to connect to the Web via your browser.

The first successful graphical browser, called Mosaic, helped launch the Web on the road to popularity. Developed by the National Center for Supercomputing Applications at the University of Illinois, Mosaic was followed by two commercial products, Netscape Navigator and Microsoft Internet Explorer. Initially, Netscape was extremely successful, but it eventually lost ground to Internet Explorer. The last version of Netscape was released in 2008. However, Mozilla Firefox, a new browser built using the Netscape model, began to challenge the popularity of Internet Explorer in 2004. Firefox is now ranked as the most frequently used browser.

Recently, Google has joined the Internet browser competition full force with a very impressive entry, Chrome. Google Chrome takes a unique approach to browsing the Web by making complex features easy to use. In Google Chrome, every time you open a new tab, you'll see a visual sampling of your most visited sites, most used search engines, recently bookmarked pages, and closed tabs. You can drag tabs out of the browser to create new windows, gather multiple tabs into one window, or rearrange them. Every tab you use is run independently in the browser; so if one application crashes, it won't take anything else down. Even bookmarking is easy, just click the star icon at the left edge of the address bar and you're done.

Another browser, Opera, originated in 1994 as a research project. Within a year, it branched out into an independent company named Opera Software ASA. Today Opera is a high-quality product for navigating the Internet that is compatible with a wide range of operating systems. Safari is no longer exclusively an Apple browser; the top-notch browser is now available for PCs as well. Safari provides the Mac look and feel in the Internet environment. It is lightweight, nonobtrusive, and enables tabbed browsing, spell

tion buttons, a search box, an address toolbar, and a status bar, as shown in Figure 6.11. When you first launch a browser, it may default to a preset home page from your ISP or the publisher of the browser software. You can either keep this as your home page, which will be displayed each time you start your browser,

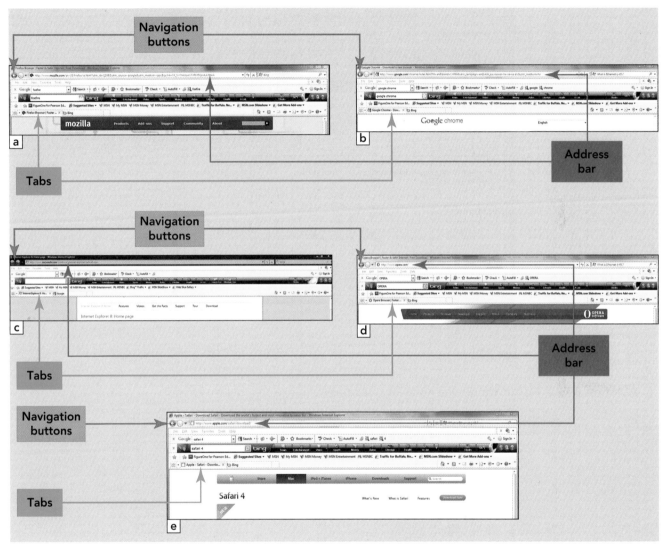

FIGURE 6.11 (a) Mozilla Firefox (b) Google Chrome (c) Explorer (d) Opera and (e) Safari are the five most popular graphical Web browsers. They use similar features, such as tabbed browsing, navigation buttons, and an address bar.

checking for all fields, and snapback—a temporary marker that allows a user to return to a Web page even after he or she has wandered off the beaten path. Safari competes with the top browsers but lacks some features like parental controls and antiphishing controls. Current browser rankings and a detailed list of the features that each possesses can be viewed at **http://internet-browser-review .toptenreviews.com/**.

All five browser programs use similar features, such as tabbed browsing, naviga-

or you can change the browser's default home page, also referred to as customizing your browser. You can find the default home page settings in Internet Explorer under the Tools, Internet Options menu (Figure 6.12).

Browsers display and act on documents that are created using hypertext. It is the browser that allows the text and graphics on a hypertext document to be active. In short, browsers are meant to work with Web pages. Sometimes you need to upgrade your browser to the latest

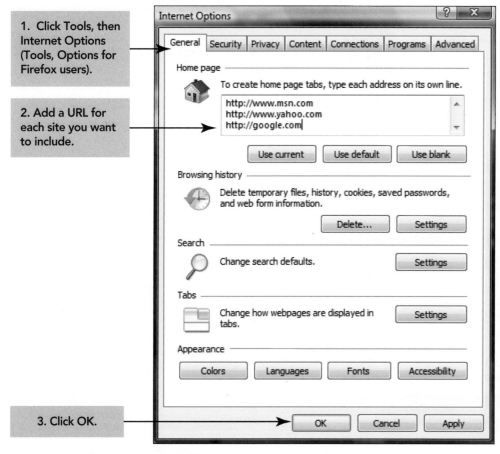

1. Click Tools, then Internet Options (Tools, Options for Firefox users).

2. Add a URL for each site you want to include.

3. Click OK.

FIGURE 6.12 You can customize the Internet Explorer browser by changing the default home page.

version so that you can fully enjoy the features of a Web site. New Web page creation software is being developed all the time, and eventually older browsers don't have the capability of displaying the newest features or animations. Browsers use **plug-ins**, which are software programs that allow you to derive the full benefits of a Web site, such as sound or video. If a Web site requires a plug-in to function properly, a pop-up message will appear in newer browsers, indicating which plug-in is needed, with an option to install the plug-in or cancel the installation.

Another feature that browsers share is the ability to cache, or store, Web page files and graphics on your computer. When you browse a Web page the first time, it is stored on your hard drive in a specially assigned storage space. This allows Web pages to be retrieved faster the next time you want to browse them because they don't have to be transferred across the Internet. The positive aspect of this feature is that it appears that you retrieved the Web pages faster; the downside is that you really retrieved the stored copy from your hard disk, and it may not be the most

current version. This does not happen often, but if it does, simply click the Refresh button on your browser's toolbar to obtain the latest content.

Web sites and their affiliated materials are housed on **Web servers**, a computer running server software that returns requested information or accepts inputted information. Millions of Web servers are located all over the world. When you click a hyperlink on a Web page, you either request information from a server (a list of sweatshirts available in size medium) or ask the server to accept your information (your order for three size medium sweatshirts in blue). Your browser sends a message to a Web server, asking the server to retrieve or accept the information. The server either sends the information or a confirmation back to the initiating browser through the network. If the file isn't found, the server sends an error message.

WEB ADDRESSES

To locate a resource on the Web, you have to know how to find the Web server on which it resides. Every host, computer, server, device, and application that communicates over the Internet is assigned an **Internet Protocol address (IP address)**, a numerical identification and logical address that is assigned to devices participating in a computer network. The IP address consists of four groups of numbers, separated by periods. The value in each group ranges from 0 to 255. As a example, 128.30.52.38 is the IP address, using Internet Protocol Version 4 (IPv4), for the W3C Web site. IP addresses are either static or dynamic. A static IP address never changes. It's the type used by most major Web sites. A dynamic IP address is automatically assigned to a computer when you log on to a network. Internet service providers (ISPs) assign dynamic IP addresses to their customers. Although this numeric system works well for computers, it doesn't work as well for people. You could type the numeric address into your browser, but most of us find that it's much easier to use text names, such as those found in a URL. A **URL (Uniform Resource Locator)** is a string of characters that precisely identifies an Internet resource's type and location. It is much easier to access the W3C Web site by typing the URL, **www.w3.org**, than it is to remember *128.30.52.38*.

At times, keying in a URL can seem tedious. A complete URL actually has four distinct parts: protocol, domain name, path, and resource name. Each component provides a piece of data needed to locate the site (Figure 6.13).

Protocol The first part of a complete URL specifies the **Hypertext Transfer Protocol (HTTP)**, the Internet standard that supports the exchange of information on the Web. Most browsers can also access information using other protocols like FTP (File Transfer Protocol), used to transfer files from one computer on the Internet to another, and POP protocols, used to receive e-mail. The protocol name is followed by a colon and two forward slash marks (//). You can generally omit the http:// protocol designation when you're accessing a Web page, because the browser assumes that you are browsing an unsecured hypertext Web page. For example, you can access **http://www.pearsonhighered.com/cayf** by typing **www.pearsonhighered.com/cayf**.

Domain Name The second part of a complete URL specifies the Web site's **domain name**, which correlates to the Web server's IP address. The domain name has two parts: a host name and a top-level domain name. Some domain names also include a prefix, the most common of which is "www." Early Web servers adopted the name "WWW," but this has become less common. The **host name** is usually the name of the group or institution hosting the site. The **top-level domain (TLD) name** is the extension (such as .com or .edu) following the host name and indicates the type of group or institution to which the site belongs.

The Domain Name System The Internet uses a system called the **Domain Name System (DNS)** to link domain names with their corresponding IP addresses, func-

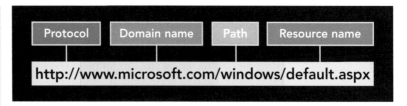

FIGURE 6.13 A complete URL has four parts: protocol, domain name, path, and resource name. This is the URL for the default Microsoft Windows home page.

tioning like a phone book for the Internet. The Domain Name System enables users to type an address that includes letters as well as numbers. A process called **domain name registration** enables individuals and organizations to register a domain name with a service organization, such as InterNIC, and link this name to a specific Internet address (IP address). You can use your favorite search engine to search for domain name registrars to find other sites that provide this service.

Domain names can tell you a great deal about where a computer is located. For Web sites hosted in the United States, top-level domain names (the *last* part of the domain name) indicate the type of organization in which the computer is located (Figure 6.14). Outside the United States, the top-level domain indicates the name of the country where the computer hosting the Web site is located, such as .ca (Canada), .uk (United Kingdom), and .jp (Japan). For more information on domain names visit the Internet Corporation for Assigned Names and Numbers (ICANN) at **www.icann.org**.

Path The third part of a complete URL specifies the location of the document on the server. It contains the document's location on the computer, including the names of subfolders (if any). In the example in Figure 6.13, the path to the default.aspx file on the

FIGURE 6.14 Common Top-Level Domain Names

Top-Level Domain Name	Used By
.com	Commercial businesses
.biz	Businesses
.edu	Educational institutions
.info	Information
.gov	Government agencies
.pro	Professionals
.mil	Military
.aero	Aviation
.net	Network organizations (such as ISPs)
.coop	Cooperatives
.org	Nonprofit organizations
.museum	Museums
.name	Names

Web server at **www.microsoft.com** is **/windows/default.aspx**.

Resource Name The last part of a complete URL gives the file name of the resource you're accessing. A resource is a file, such as an HTML file, a sound file, a video file, or a graphics file. The resource's extension (the part of the file name after the period) indicates the type of resource it is. For example, HTML documents have the .html or .htm extension.

Many URLs don't include a resource name because they reference the server's default home page. If no resource name is specified, the browser looks for a file named *default* or *index*—a default page that's displayed automatically when you enter the site at its top level. If it finds such a file, it loads it automatically. For example, **www.microsoft.com/windows** displays the default Microsoft Windows home page. Other URLs omit both the path name and the resource name. These URLs reference the Web site's home page. For example, while entering **www.microsoft.com** into a browser's address bar displays Microsoft's home page, its actual URL is **http://www.microsoft.com/en/us/default.aspx**.

BROWSING THE WEB

When you have installed browser software and are connected to the Internet, you're ready to browse the Web. To access a Web page, you can do any of the following (Figure 6.15):

- **Type a URL in the Address bar.** You don't need to type http://. Watch for spelling errors, and don't insert spaces. A common mistake is typing a comma instead of a period to separate the components of a URL.

- **Click a tab in the browser window.** Both major browsers offer **tabbed browsing**, which enables a user to switch quickly between Web sites. You can customize your home page by adding tabs for sites that you frequently access.

- **Click a hyperlink.** Hyperlinks are usually underlined, but sometimes they're embedded in graphics or highlighted in other ways, such as with shading or colors. To tell whether a given portion of a Web page contains a hyperlink, position your mouse pointer over it and watch for a change in the pointer's shape. Most browsers indicate the presence of a hyperlink by changing the on-screen pointer to a hand shape.

As you browse the Web, your browser keeps a list of the Web pages you've accessed called the **history list**. If you'd like to return to a previously viewed site and

FIGURE 6.15 There are many ways to access a typical Web page.

Enter the URL carefully to reach the correct destination.

Click a tab to switch from one site to another.

Click a hyperlink, which may be underlined or appear like normal text until the mouse pointer changes to a hand.

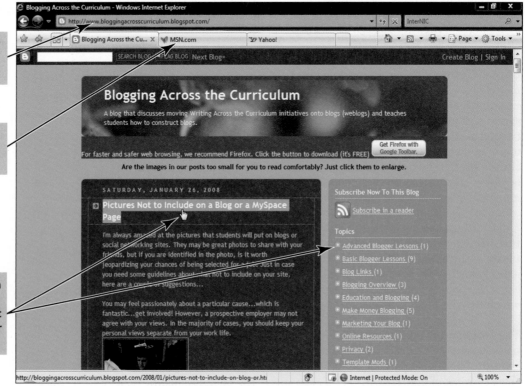

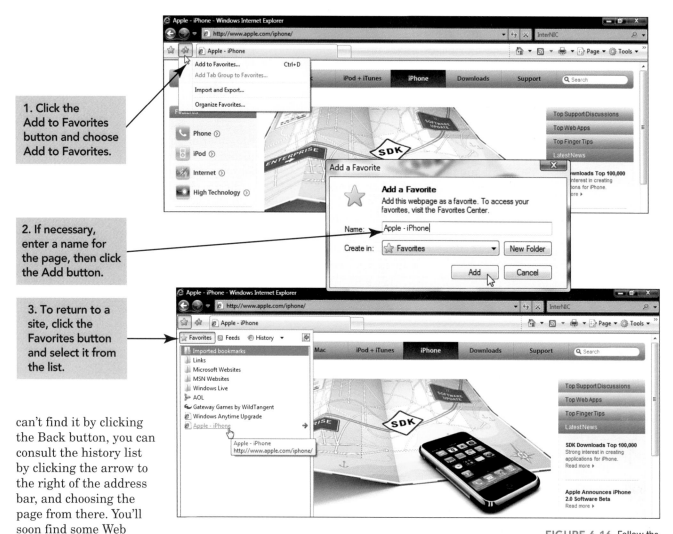

1. Click the Add to Favorites button and choose Add to Favorites.

2. If necessary, enter a name for the page, then click the Add button.

3. To return to a site, click the Favorites button and select it from the list.

can't find it by clicking the Back button, you can consult the history list by clicking the arrow to the right of the address bar, and choosing the page from there. You'll soon find some Web pages you'll want to return to frequently. To return easily, you can save these pages as Favorites (Internet Explorer) or Bookmarks (Mozilla Firefox), as illustrated in Figure 6.16. After you've saved these pages as Favorites or Bookmarks, you'll see the names of these pages in the Favorites or Bookmarks menu.

Uploading and Downloading After you have browsed the Web and accessed various Web pages, you may want to try downloading or uploading data. With **downloading**, a document or file is transferred from another computer to your computer. With **uploading**, you transfer files from your computer to another computer.

You should exercise caution when downloading files of unknown origin from the Web. If you download software from a site that doesn't inspect files using up-to-date antivirus software, you could infect your computer with a virus. Most Internet users believe that it's safe to download software from Web sites maintained by software companies. However, be aware

that some viruses are spread in the data files of popular programs, such as Microsoft Word or Excel. Be sure to use an antivirus program to check any software or data files that you download. Now that you understand the basics of the Internet and Web, let's examine how to conduct research on the Web.

SHARING INFORMATION FAST: WIKIS, BLOGS, AND PODCASTS

Want to share information fast through the Web for either personal or professional reasons? A wiki, a blog, or a podcast might be just what you need. A **wiki** (short for wiki-wiki, the Hawaiian word for "fast") is a simple Web page on which any visitor can post text or images, read previous posts, change posted information, and track earlier changes. No elaborate coding needed—just click to post, click to refresh the page, and you're done. If a visitor changes what you've posted and you don't like the change, just click to revert to an earlier version. Next time you're online,

FIGURE 6.16 Follow the steps shown to save a Web page to your Favorites in Internet Explorer. Creating Bookmarks in Mozilla Firefox is very similar.

surf over to **www.wikimusicguide.com**, an open-content music guide. Fans can create new pages, share information about their favorite songs or artists, and edit the entries others have created.

Wikis can be public or restricted to specific members. Besides its use in the entertainment industry, business and educational institutions are making use of this information-sharing feature to reduce e-mail and increase collaboration.

Another way to share information online is via a **blog** (short for Weblog). A blog is the Internet equivalent of a journal or diary. Bloggers post their thoughts and opinions, along with photos or links to interesting Web sites, for the entire world to see. Of the 1 million blogs posted daily on the Web, some are meant for family and friends, some offer running commentary

means of Web syndication, a delivery method that makes use of **podcatchers** (applications such as Apple Inc.'s iTunes or Nullsoft's Winamp) that can automatically identify and retrieve new files in a given series and make them available through a centrally maintained Web site.

You can listen to podcasts on your computer or on an MP3 player. You can go to sites that provide podcasts or sign up for one using an RSS feed. Imagine taking a physics class at Massachusetts Institute of Technology or catching the radio interview with your favorite musician that you missed last week. Podcasts can make it happen. Check the Podcast Directory at **http://podcast.com** and hear what's new!

Through the simplicity of wikis, blogs, and podcasts, the Web has been expanded into a means of interactive communication.

FIGURE 6.17 Blogs like this one from Microsoft can be entertaining and provide information on a wide variety of subjects.

Use RSS or Atom to subscribe to a blog.

Recent blog posts appear first, followed by older posts.

Tags are categories visitors create for blog posts. A tag's size increases as it is used.

Links lead to recent posts and archived material too.

on politics and other timely topics, and others are written by employees about their employers and other subjects. Blogs by Microsoft employees (see **http://blogs.msdn.com**) have a loyal following because of their insightful observations and tech know-how (Figure 6.17). Visit **www.blogsearchengine.com** to search for blogs by subject and for FAQs about blogging. If you are interested in creating a blog, **www.blogger.com/start** is a great place to get started.

If you'd rather get your information in an audio or video format, podcasts may be just what you need! Despite the name, and its link to music, **podcasts** have evolved from containing just sound to including any kind of audio as well as images and video. Podcasts files are released periodically by

Finding Information on the Web

Although browsing by means of hyperlinks is easy and fun, it falls short as a means of information research. Web users soon find themselves clicking link after link, searching for information that they never find. If you can't find the information you're looking for after a bit of browsing, try searching the Web. You've no doubt heard of Google, Yahoo!, Bing, and Ask. Although these and other Web search tools are far from perfect, knowing how to use them effectively (and knowing their limitations) can greatly increase your chances of finding the information you want. Computer programs, referred

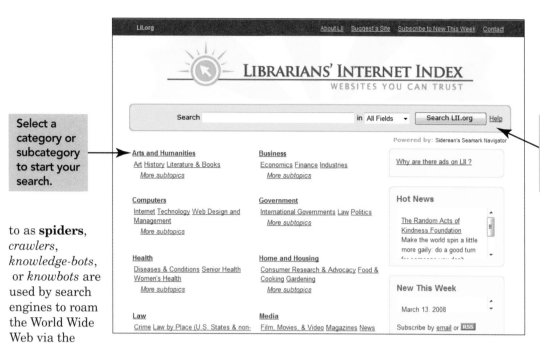

FIGURE 6.18 Subject guides can help you quickly find the information you seek.

Select a category or subcategory to start your search.

Many subject guides include a search tool for searching their site.

to as **spiders**, *crawlers*, *knowledge-bots*, or *knowbots* are used by search engines to roam the World Wide Web via the Internet, visit sites and databases, and keep the search engine database of Web pages up to date. They obtain new pages, update known pages, and delete obsolete ones. Their findings are then integrated into the search engine's database. Most large search engines operate several robots all the time. Even so, the Web is so enormous that it can take six months for spiders to cover it, resulting in a certain degree of "out-of-datedness," or **link rot**, in all the search engines.

Some search sites offer a **subject guide** to the Web, grouping Web pages under headings such as business, news, or travel (Figure 6.18). These guides don't try to include every Web page on the World Wide Web. Instead, they offer a selection of high-quality pages that the search site believes represent some of the more useful Web pages in a given category. If you're just beginning your search for information, a subject guide is an excellent place to start.

USING SEARCH ENGINES

If you can't find what you're looking for in a Web subject guide, you can try searching databases that claim to index the full Web, but with more than 110 million Web sites—and billions of Web pages—in

existence, that's a pretty daunting task. These **search engines** maintain databases of the Web pages they've indexed, but it is estimated that more than 75 percent of the Internet is yet to be mined.

More than 10 billion searches were conducted just in June 2009! Of the five core search engines used that month, Google was used more often than all of the other search engines combined, with Yahoo! a distant second (Figure 6.19).

Although an enormous pool of information is available on the Web, chances are that by using these search engines you'll find information relevant to the subject you're researching. A side effect of your clicking from site to site on the Web is the clickstream you leave in your wake. A **clickstream** is the trail of Web links that you have followed to get to a particular site. Internet merchants are quite interested in analyzing clickstream activity so they can do a better job of targeting

FIGURE 6.19 Google's search tool is used more than all of the others combined, according to a June 2009 report by hitwise and comScore

Top Search Engines for 2009

* Search.MSN.com 301 redirects to Bing.com aka Live.com

2009	Google	Yahoo!	Bing	Ask	Total
2009 06	74.04%	16.19%	4.99%*	3.15%	98.37%
2009 05	73.66%	15.55%	5.64%	3.81%	98.66%
2009 04	72.68%	16.29%	5.67%	3.96%	98.60%
2009 03	72.13%	16.56%	5.50%	4.02%	98.21%
2009 02	72.11%	17.52%	5.55%	3.47%	98.65%

advertisements and tailoring Web pages to potential customers.

Feel like you're stuck in a rut? Try using a different search engine. Visit sites like Mahalo (**www.mahalo.com**), KartOO (**www.kartoo.com**), Dogpile (**www.dogpile.com**), FindSounds (**www.findsounds.com**), or SurfWax (**www.surfwax.com**) and see what you find!

To use a search engine, type one or more words that describe the subject you're looking for into the search text box and click Search (or press Enter). Generally, it's a good idea to type several words (four or five) rather than just one or two. If you use only one or two words, the Web search will produce far more results than you can use.

Why do search engines sometimes produce unsatisfactory results? The problem lies in the ambiguity of the English language. Suppose you're searching for

specialized search engines include Indeed, a database of more than 1 million jobs, and Infoplease, which contains the full text of an encyclopedia and an almanac (Figure 6.20).

You can save the results of your searches—the Web pages you visit by following the results links of a search engine—to your hard drive by using your browser's Page (or File), Save As menu sequence. If you don't want or need the entire Web page, you can right-click the various elements of the page and choose from a variety of options (Save, Print, Copy). You can also use your mouse and cursor to highlight and then copy text on a Web page for pasting into a word-processing file or other document. Sometimes you might want to view a Web page that you've saved *offline*, that is, without connecting to the Internet. This is easily accomplished by opening your browser and then choosing the File, Open menu

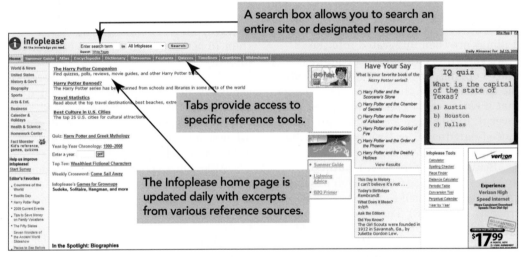

FIGURE 6.20 Specialized search engines, like Infoplease, provide access to selected reference tools and resources.

information on the Great Wall of China. You'll find some information on the ancient Chinese defensive installation, but you may also get the menu of the Great Wall of China, a Chinese restaurant; information on the Great Wall hotel in Beijing; and the lyrics of "Great Wall of China," a song by Billy Joel.

Specialized Search Engines Full Web search engines generally don't index specialized information such as names and addresses, job advertisements, quotations, or newspaper articles. To find such information, you need to use **specialized search engines**. Examples of such

sequence. Simply browse through your folders and files to locate the file and then open it.

Search engines are not the only way to find information on the Web. Sites such as MSN, AOL, and Yahoo! offer many services, including search features, on their home pages. These sites are also referred to as portals. A **portal** is a gateway that provides a conveniently organized subject guide to Internet content, fast-breaking news, local weather, stock quotes, sports scores, and e-mail (Figure 6.21). Portal sites usually use indexes and lists of links to provide you with a jumping-off place for your search.

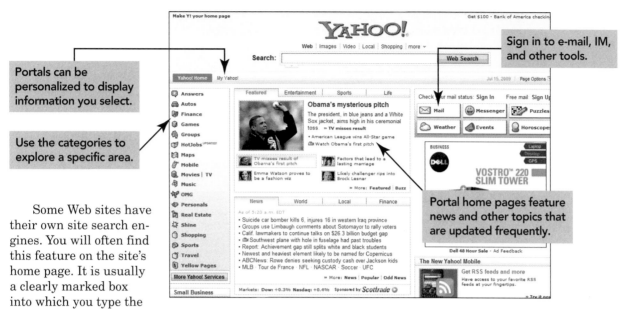

Portals can be personalized to display information you select.

Use the categories to explore a specific area.

Sign in to e-mail, IM, and other tools.

Portal home pages feature news and other topics that are updated frequently.

Some Web sites have their own site search engines. You will often find this feature on the site's home page. It is usually a clearly marked box into which you type the keywords of what you are looking for. Some home pages will have a Search icon or button that will take you to the site's search page.

Aggregators, Web sites at which headlines are collected, either manually, such as the Drudge Report, or through the use of algorithms, as is done by Google News, are gaining in popularity. These sites can be be narrow or wide in scope and provide quick access to information from many sources in one location.

For the socially conscious Web searcher, there are search sites that will make donations to your favorite charity. Check out **www.goodsearch.com** and begin to donate to the charity of your choice.

USING SEARCH TECHNIQUES

By learning a few search techniques, you can greatly increase the accuracy of your Web searches. **Search operators**, which are symbols or words used for advanced searches, can be helpful. Most search engines include a link for advanced searches or provide search tips to explain which search operators you can use. Although specific methods may vary, some or all of the following techniques will work with most search engines.

INCLUSION AND EXCLUSION

With many search engines, you can improve search performance by specifying an **inclusion operator**, which is generally a plus (+) sign (Figure 6.22). This operator states that you only want a page retrieved if it contains the specified word. By listing several key terms with this search operator,

you can zero in on pages that only contain one or more of the essential terms.

If the list of retrieved documents contains many items that you don't want, you can use the **exclusion operator**, which is generally a minus (−) sign. You can exclude the undesired term by prefacing it with the exclusion operator.

Environmental concerns generate a lot of interest. Now there's even a "green" search engine—Green Maven (**www.greenmaven.com**). Use it to find environmentally conscious Web sites and news.

You can also find a variety of ecologically and socially conscious search engines that donate to various causes based on the searches people run. Two such engines are Ecosearch (**www.ecosearch.org**) powered by Google and GoodSearch (**www.goodsearch.com**) powered by Yahoo. There are, however, plenty of other such sites. Use them as you would your normal search engine, and you'll get great results. Don't just click to donate. Without attempting a legitimate search, you'll jeopardize the relationships that enable such sites to fund their initiatives. ●

FIGURE 6.21 The Yahoo! portal to the Web provides a conveniently organized subject guide to Internet content, news, local weather, stock quotes, and much more.

FIGURE 6.22 Improving Your Search Results

Search Operators		
Symbol	Example	Result
Plus sign (+)	CD+Aerosmith	Web pages that contain all search terms listed, in any order. In this case, pages would include *both* the word **CD** *and* the word **AEROSMITH**.
CD+Aerosmith	CD+Aerosmith−eBay	Web pages that contain all included search terms listed, but not the excluded term. In this case, pages would include *both* the word **CD** *and* the word **AEROSMITH** but *not* the word **EBAY**.
Wildcards (*)	CD*	Web pages that include variations of the search term or additional words. For example, pages could include the terms **CD**, **CDs**, **CD Ripping**, **CD Files**, etc.
Quotation Marks (" ")	"Aerosmith Just Push Play CD"	Web pages that contain the exact phrase in the order listed.
Boolean Search Terms		
Terms	Examples	Result
AND	CD **AND** Aerosmith	Returns the same result as using the plus sign (+)
OR	CD **OR** Aerosmith	Web pages that include either or both of the search terms listed, usually providing a large number of hits. For this example, results would include *either* the word **CD** *or* the word **AEROSMITH** or *both*.
NOT	CD **AND** Aerosmith **NOT** eBay	Returns the same results as using the minus sign (−)
Parenthesis ( )	(CD **OR** MP3 **OR** Record) **AND** Aerosmith	Search terms in parenthesis are located first, using the search operator provided. In this case, results would include pages that included any combinationof **CD**, **MP3**, or **RECORD** *and* the word **AEROSMITH**

Wildcards Many search engines enable you to use wildcards. **Wildcards** are symbols such as * and ? that take the place of zero or more characters in the position in which they are used. The use of wildcards, also called **truncation symbols**, to search for various word endings and spellings simultaneously is a technique called **truncation**.

Wildcards help you improve the accuracy of your searches and are useful if you are unsure of the exact spelling of a word. Wildcards may be handled differently, depending upon the search engine used. So the search term *bank** might return *bank, banks, banking, bankruptcy, bank account*, and so forth.

Phrase Searches Another way to improve the accuracy of your searches is through **phrase searching**, which is generally performed by typing a phrase within quotation marks. This tells the search engine to retrieve only those documents that contain the exact phrase (rather than some or all of the words anywhere in the document).

Boolean Searches Some search engines enable you to perform Boolean searches. **Boolean searches** use logical operators (AND, OR, and NOT) to link the words you're searching for. By using Boolean operators, you can gain more precise control over your searches. Let's look at a few examples.

The AND, OR, and NOT Operators. When used to link two search words, the AND operator tells the search engine to return only those documents that contain both words (just as the plus sign does). You can use the AND operator to narrow your search so that it retrieves fewer documents.

If your search retrieves too few documents, try the OR operator. This may be helpful when a topic has several common synonyms, such as car, auto, automobile, and vehicle. Using the OR operator usually retrieves a larger quantity of documents.

To exclude unwanted documents, use the NOT operator. This operator tells the search engine to omit any documents containing the word preceded by NOT (just as the minus sign does).

Using Parentheses. Many search engines that support Boolean operators allow you to use parentheses, a process called **nesting**. When you nest an expression, the search engine evaluates the expression from left to right and searches for the content within the parentheses first. Such expressions enable you to conduct a search with unmatched accuracy. To learn more about search engines, their specialized capabilities, and specific examples go to **www.internettutorials.net/**.

> " Although you can find excellent and **reliable information** on the Web, you can also find pages that are **biased** or blatantly incorrect. "

EVALUATING INFORMATION

After you've found information on the Web, you'll need to evaluate it critically. Anyone can publish information on the Web; many Web pages are not subject to the fact-checking standards of newspapers or magazines, let alone the peer-review process that safeguards the quality of scholarly and scientific publications. Although you can find excellent and reliable information on the Web, you can also find pages that are biased or blatantly incorrect.

Rules for Critically Evaluating Web Pages As you're evaluating a Web page, carefully note the following:

- Who is the author of this page? Is the author affiliated with a recognized institution, such as a university or a well-known company? Is there any evidence that the author is qualified with respect to this topic? A page that isn't signed may signal an attempt to disguise the author's lack of qualifications.

- Does the author cite his or her sources? If so, do they appear to be from recognized and respected publications?

- Who provides the server for publishing this Web page? Who pays for this page?

- Does the presentation seem balanced and objective, or is it one sided?

- Is the language objective and dispassionate, or is it strident and argumentative?

- What is the purpose of this page? Is the author trying to sell something or promote a biased idea? Who would profit if this page's information were accepted as true? Does the site include links to external information, or does it reference only itself?

- Does the information appear to be accurate? Is the page free of sweeping generalizations or other signs of shoddy thinking? Do you see many misspellings or grammatical errors that would indicate a poor educational background?

- Is this page up to date? When was it last updated?

In the next section, you will explore the practical applications of Web research to both the work and school environments.

USING THE WEB FOR SCHOOLWORK

Finding information on the Web can help you as a consumer. But how can it help you as a student? The following sections provide some helpful hints.

Authoritative Online Sources Many respected magazines and journals have established Web sites where you can search back issues, giving you the best of both worlds—the power and convenience of the Internet, plus material that is more reliable than the average Web page.

Locating Material in Published Works Remember that the Web is only one of several sources you can and should use for research. Many high-level research tools can be found in your institution's library. Additionally, librarians are trained research professionals who are there to assist you. As institutions have begun to offer distance-learning courses, student access to library materials has become a critical issue. To meet the needs of distance-learning students, many college libraries now provide online access to their services. Check your library's home page to find out what Internet services are available. In addition to standard card-catalog information—such as author, title, and publication date—you can often access full-text versions of books and periodicals online. Some libraries provide these materials directly, whereas others use a third party to provide these services. You can almost certainly access and search your library's inventory of books and can often order them online. The library's books and articles search engine will allow you to search by author, title, or key term. Your library may also provide access to valuable search tools such as EBSCOhost, LexisNexis, and other professional databases. Sometimes you can access these online materials from off campus as well as on campus. Materials may be accessible only to faculty and students, or they may also be available to the general public.

Also, visit Google Scholar (**http://scholar.google.com**) to search for scholarly literature from many academic disciplines. You can use advanced search methods and even personalize

> " . . . the **Web** is only **one** of several **sources** you can and should use for research. "

your searches to have Google Scholar indicate when materials are held by your local library. Google Scholar can help you locate peer-reviewed papers, theses, books, abstracts, and articles from academic publishers and professional sources (Figure 6.23).

Citing Online and Offline References Including citations in your work is an important way to honor copyright and avoid accusations of plagiarism. Because citing Internet-based sources is not the same as citing traditional references, visit University of California Berkeley's General Guides site at **www.lib .berkeley.edu/Help/guides .html** to learn how to properly cite online and electronic resources. You should know how to cite Web sites, e-mail messages, and online databases. When citing electronic resources, it is important to include the date the site was last accessed. Even more than the written and published sites, electronic sites are time sensitive.

Now that you're familiar with how to find and evaluate information on the Web, let's look at some of the Internet's most useful services.

Exploring Internet Services

An **Internet service** is best understood as a set of standards (protocols) that define how two types of programs—a client, such as a Web browser that runs on the

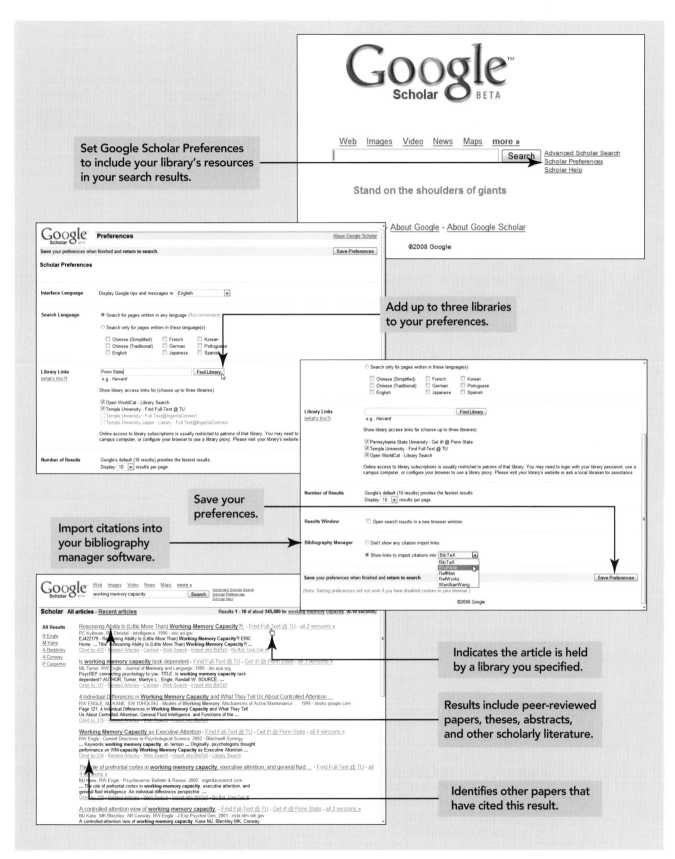

Set Google Scholar Preferences to include your library's resources in your search results.

Add up to three libraries to your preferences.

Save your preferences.

Import citations into your bibliography manager software.

Indicates the article is held by a library you specified.

Results include peer-reviewed papers, theses, abstracts, and other scholarly literature.

Identifies other papers that have cited this result.

FIGURE 6.23 Google Scholar uses the power of Google to search scholarly literature and provide high-quality results for academic research.

user's computer, and a server—can communicate with each other through the Internet. By using the service's protocols, the client requests information from a server program that is located on some other computer on the Internet.

At one time, some browsers, such as Netscape Navigator and the Mozilla Suite, were distributed as software suites that included client programs to handle e-mail, newsgroups, and chat services, as well as browsing. However, most current browsers, including Internet Explorer, Firefox, and Safari (for Macs), operate as stand-alone programs. Although it's still possible to obtain client software for some of these services, many of them are Web based and don't require any special software to use, but you may need to install a plug-in to ensure full functionality. Figure 6.24 lists a selection of commonly used services and plug-ins.

E-MAIL: STAYING IN TOUCH

The most popular Internet service is e-mail (Figure 6.25). **E-mail** (short for electronic mail) is a software application that enables you to send and receive messages via networks. E-mail has become an indispensable tool for businesses and individuals due to its speed and convenience. However, many younger people report a strong preference for text messaging over e-mail. Both of these communications tools have become media of choice for interpersonal written communication, far outpacing the postal system.

When you receive an e-mail, you can reply to the message, forward it to someone else, store it for later action, or delete it. In addition to the text message, you can include an e-mail attachment. An **e-mail attachment** can be any type of computer file—document, photo, audio, or video—that is included with an e-mail message. If you receive an e-mail message containing an attachment, your e-mail program displays a distinctive icon, such as a paper clip, to notify you. E-mail usually arrives at the destination server in a few seconds. It is then stored on the server until the recipient logs on to the server and downloads the message.

> " Perhaps the worst thing that can happen with e-mail is that you **hastily** send a message that you later wished you hadn't or you use the **Reply All** or Forward feature to send inappropriate or irrelevant messages. . . "

To send an e-mail, you need to know the recipient's e-mail address. An **e-mail address** is a unique cyberspace identity for a particular recipient that follows the form myname@somedomain.com. The components of an e-mail address are the user name or other identifier, the name of the domain that is hosting the e-mail service, and the top-level domain that identifies the provider's type of institution. For instance, you can send mail to the president of the United States at the e-mail address president@whitehouse.gov. In this instance, the user name is "president," the domain is "whitehouse," and the top-level domain is ".gov" (for government). You can often tell quite a bit about someone just by seeing his or her e-mail address!

E-mail has many benefits. It is inexpensive, fast, and easy to access from almost any Internet-connected computer. People use e-mail to collaborate with others quickly and efficiently. It also creates an electronic paper trail that documents both the timeliness and content of past communications.

The benefits of e-mail are tempered by some potential problems that you should be aware of. Sometimes e-mail systems fail to properly send or receive mail. Attachments may not be delivered or they may be blocked by e-mail system administrators as potentially unsafe. Messages can become corrupted and may not display properly. Sometimes, if you don't regularly check your mail, your inbox may overflow, which causes messages received past the overflow point to be bounced out of the box and never delivered. Perhaps the worst thing that can happen with e-mail is that you hastily send a message that you later wished you hadn't or you use the Reply All or Forward feature to send inappropriate or irrelevant messages that can embarrass you or that inconvenience the receiver.

SPAM: CAN IT BE STOPPED?

Many e-mail users receive unsolicited e-mail advertising called **spam**. In fact, according to estimates, as much as 92 percent of all e-mail was spam during the

Service	Client	Web-Based	Comments
E-mail			
AOL Mail	X	X	Available with AOL Desktop installation or as Web-based service
Google Mail		X	
Microsoft Outlook	X		Part of the Microsoft Office suite
Microsoft Windows Mail	X		Replaced Outlook Express in Windows Vista
Mozilla Thunderbird	X		Coordinates with Mozilla Firefox
Windows Live Hotmail		X	Replaced MSN Hotmail
Yahoo! Ail		X	
Instant Message			
AOL AIM	X	X	Available with AOL Desktop installation or as a Web-based service
Google Talk	X	X	Available for download or as Web-based service
meebo.com		X	Users can access other IM clients on the meebo site
ICQ	X	X	Available for download or as Web-based service
Yahoo! Messenger		X	
Windows Live Messenger		X	Formerly MSN Messenger
Internet Relay Chat (IRC)			
mIRC	X		
Mozilla ChatZilla	X		Runs only in Mozilla Firefox browser
Trillian	X		Also supports instant message clients
Plug-ins			
Adobe Reader	X		Viewer for Adobe PDF files
Adobe Flash Player	X		Viewer for Web animation (Flash) files
Adobe Shockwave Player	X		Used for interactive games, multimedia, graphics, and streaming audio and video
Apple QuickTime Player	X		Used for animation, music, MIDI, audio, and video files
RealPlayer	X		Used for streaming audio, video, animation, and multimedia presentations
Windows Media Player	X		Used for MP3 and WAV files, live audio, movies, and live video broadcasts

FIGURE 6.24 Commonly Used Internet Services and Plug-ins

first quarter of 2008, which amounts to approximately 62 trillion messages a year. This mail is sent by spammers, businesses or individuals that specialize in sending such mail. Spammers believe that they're doing only what direct-marketing mail firms do: sending legitimate advertising. But they don't acknowledge a crucial difference between unsolicited postal advertising and spam. With postal advertising, the advertiser pays for the postage. With spam, the recipient pays the postage in the form of lost time and productivity for individuals and businesses. A 2007 study estimated that managing spam costs U.S. businesses more than $71 billion annually. That's $712 per employee!

Most Internet users detest spam but feel helpless to prevent it. For businesses,

anything from the Web pages a user visits to personal information, such as credit card numbers.

Can you filter out spam? You can try. It's often possible to set up a spam or bulk mail folder in your e-mail account. Check your mail options for how to enable this service (Figure 6.26). Spam can originate from a new account, which is almost immediately closed down after the service provider receives hundreds of thousands of outraged complaints. The spammer just moves on to a new account. A more modern way to send spam is through a **botnet**, a set of computers infected with a malicious program that places the computers under the control of a **bot herder**. Vulnerable systems are ones without current security patches or antispam protection. Once

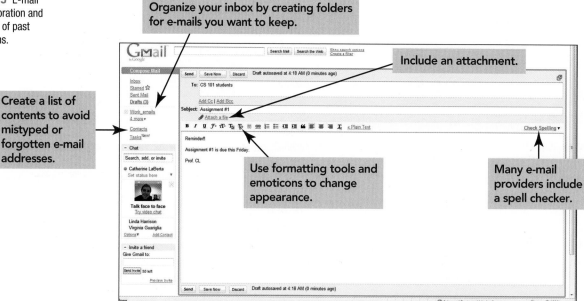

FIGURE 6.25 E-mail enables collaboration and keeps a record of past communications.

Organize your inbox by creating folders for e-mails you want to keep.

Include an attachment.

Create a list of contents to avoid mistyped or forgotten e-mail addresses.

Use formatting tools and emoticons to change appearance.

Many e-mail providers include a spell checker.

spam is a costly nuisance. It's not unusual for a massive amount of spam messages to overwhelm mail servers, resulting in impaired service for legitimate, paying customers.

In most cases, little or nothing of worth is being peddled: pornographic Web sites, get-rich-quick scams, bogus stock deals, rip-off work-at-home schemes, health and diet scams, and merchandise of questionable quality. Some spam can contain **malware**, malicious software, that places a computer in the spammer's control. This type of software can wreak havoc on a user's system by deleting files and directory entries; it can also act as **spyware**, gathering data from a user's system without the user knowing it. This can include

infected, a machine becomes one of many zombies in a botnet and responds to commands given by the bot herder.

One thing you can do to help prevent spam is to avoid posting your e-mail address in any public place. In fact, you should be very selective when providing your e-mail address to anyone. Companies like Cloudmark and ChoiceMail provide businesses with enterprise-level protection from spam. Antivirus software manufacturers like Symantec and McAfee incorporate antispam features in their products to help home users recognize and avoid opening spam. Free or low-cost alternatives such as SpamBully and MailWasher attempt to clear spam out of your Inbox. Some e-mail providers offer on-site spam-filtering services that try to filter out spam before it is even sent to your mailbox, but so far there is no way to get rid of spam entirely.

Don't reply to spam or request to be removed from a spammer's mailing list. All that does is verify to the spammer that your e-mail address is valid. If possible, you should also modify your e-mail account to disable graphics, because some graphics, known as **Web beacons**, alert the sender that the message has been opened. Your address will be added to a list of validated addresses, so all that will happen is that you'll get even more spam.

Increasingly, state and federal legislatures are attempting to pass laws against

Although it's no fun, most of us have learned to live with spam—just don't open it! For more information and tips on how to avoid spam, recent law enforcement actions against deceptive commercial e-mail and spammers, and a location to file a complaint, check out the Federal Trade Commission's spam site at **www.ftc.gov/spam**.

INSTANT MESSAGING: E-MAIL MADE FASTER

What's faster than e-mail and more convenient than picking up the phone? **Instant messaging (IM) systems** alert you when a friend or business associate who also uses the IM system (a buddy or

Use the settings option to divert unwanted e-mail to a trash or spam folder.

Avoid e-mails from specific individuals by blocking their addresses.

Be sure to check the spam and trash folder. Legitimate mail can be misrouted.

FIGURE 6.26 Check your e-mail account's mail settings to set spam filters.

spam. Bills have been introduced in Congress, and the Senate's CAN-SPAM Act of 2003 is aimed at deceptive e-mails, unsolicited pornography, and marketing. The Direct Marketing Association (DMA), an advocacy group for both online and offline direct marketers, counters that the appropriate solution is an opt-out system, in which spam recipients request that the sender of spam remove their names from the mailing list—but that's just what e-mail users have been trained not to do because of fear that they'll receive even more spam. In addition, efforts to outlaw spam run afoul of free-speech guarantees under the U.S. Constitution's First Amendment, which applies to businesses as well as individuals. Furthermore, many spammers operate outside the United States, making effective legislation even more difficult. One solution under consideration is a congressional measure that would give ISPs the right to sue spammers for violating their spam policies.

contact) is online (connected to the Internet). You can then contact this person and exchange messages and attachments, including multimedia (Figure 6.27).

To use IM, you need to install instant messenger software from an instant messenger service, such as AOL's AIM or Microsoft's Windows Live Messenger, on your computer. You can use IM systems on any type of computer, including handhelds. Many IM services also give you access to information such as daily news, stock prices, sports scores, and the weather, and you can keep track of your appointments. There is no standard IM protocol, which means that you can send messages only to people who are using the same IM service that you are.

An increasing number of businesses and institutions are trying out IM services, with mixed results. On the one hand, IM is a novel and convenient way to communicate. On the other hand, voice communication is faster and richer. Additionally, the tone of an instant message can easily be misinterpreted, and privacy and security concerns also exist.

Another threat to the use of IM is a phenomenon known as *spimming*. **Spimming** is spam that targets users of instant messaging. Spimming is to IM as spam is to e-mail. Be very careful about opening files or clicking on a link sent in an instant message by an unknown sender.

Facebook or MySpace? Why not start your own social network? Ning (**www.ning.com**) is a free site that encourages people to start their own social networking community (Figure 6.28). Artists, hobbyists, educators, athletes . . . , the list continues to grow. Find a community to join or start your own!

Many privacy and security concerns surround social networking sites. A 2008

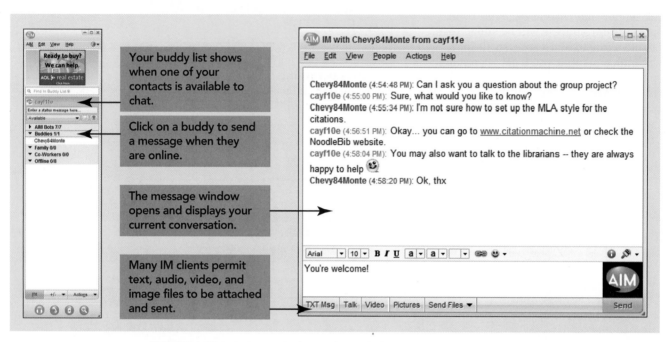

Your buddy list shows when one of your contacts is available to chat.

Click on a buddy to send a message when they are online.

The message window opens and displays your current conversation.

Many IM clients permit text, audio, video, and image files to be attached and sent.

FIGURE 6.27 Instant messaging is a popular way for Internet users to exchange near real-time messages.

INTERNET RELAY CHAT: TEXT CHATTING IN REAL TIME

Internet relay chat (IRC) is an Internet service that enables you to join chat groups, called **channels**, and participate in real-time, text-based conversations. Popular in the early days of the Internet, IRC has been replaced by tools like IM. Today it is mostly the province of specialized communities, such as gamers or programmers.

SOCIAL NETWORKING: HELPING PEOPLE CONNECT

Social networking is a way to build expanding online communities. On a social networking site like Facebook or MySpace, you can create an online profile, invite friends and acquaintances to join your network, and invite their friends to join too. Some sites, like LinkedIn, are used by business professionals to expand their network of business contacts. Tired of

Pew Internet report revealed that more than 68 percent of 18- to 29-year-olds use these sites. Once posted, pictures and content are easily shared and distributed to others, sometimes with detrimental effects. Users should give thought to the information they publicly display and consider the possible consequences. If you are searching for employment, make sure that your social networking site is not offensive. Employers are researching candidates' Facebook or MySpace sites to gain insight into a potential employee's personality and behavior.

USENET: JOINING ONLINE DISCUSSIONS

Usenet is a worldwide computer-based discussion system accessible through the Internet. It consists of thousands of topically named **newsgroups**, which are discussion groups devoted to a single topic. Each newsgroup contains articles that users have posted for all to see. Users can respond to specific articles by posting follow-up articles. Over time, a discussion thread develops as people reply to the replies. A **thread** is a series of articles that offer a continuing commentary on the same specific subject.

Usenet newsgroups are organized into the following main categories:

- **Standard newsgroups.** You're most likely to find rewarding, high-quality discussions in the standard newsgroups (also called world newsgroups). Figure 6.29 lists the standard newsgroup subcategories.

- **Alt newsgroups.** The alt category is much more freewheeling. Anyone can create an alt newsgroup (which explains why so many of them have silly or offensive names).

- **Biz newsgroups.** These newsgroups are devoted to the commercial uses of the Internet.

The easiest way to access Usenet is through Google Groups (**http://groups .google.com**). You can read and post messages, but be careful what you post on Usenet. When you post an article, you're publishing in the public domain. Sometimes articles are stored for long periods in Web-accessible archives.

Also be aware that you'll be expected to follow the rules of **netiquette**, guidelines for good manners when you're communicating through Usenet (or any Internet service). To avoid errors, check the group's FAQs to see how they operate. If you violate netiquette rules, you may receive **flames** (angry, critical messages) from other newsgroup subscribers.

ELECTRONIC MAILING LISTS

Electronic mailing lists of e-mail addresses are similar in many ways to newsgroups and forums, but they automatically broadcast messages to all individuals on a mailing list. Because the messages are transmitted as e-mail, only individuals who are subscribers to the mailing list receive and view the messages. Some colleges and universities host electronic mailing

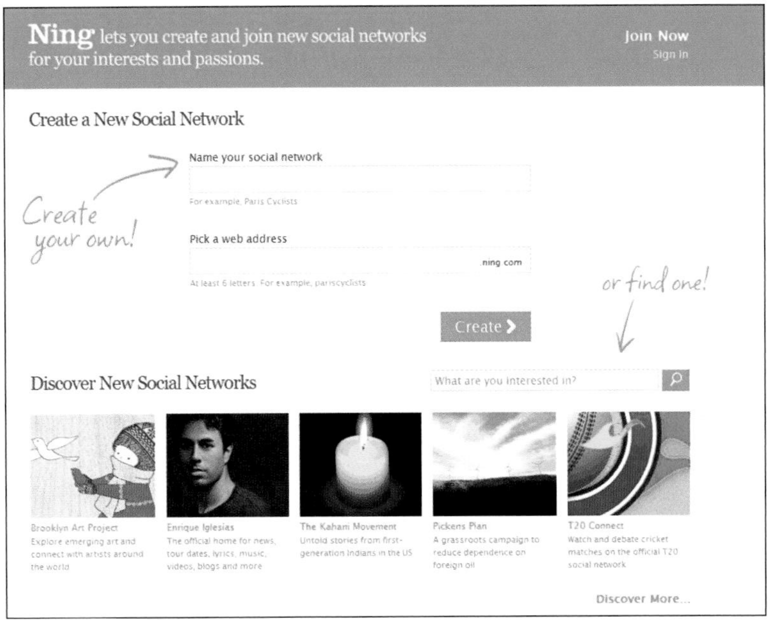

FIGURE 6.28 Social networking sites like Ning.com allow users to create their own social network communities.

lists. Eric Thomas developed the first electronic mailing list program, Listserv, in 1986 for BITNET. The most common freeware version of an electronic mailing list manager program is Majordomo.

FIGURE 6.29	Standard Newsgroup Subcategories
Subcategory Name	**Description of Topics Covered**
Comp	Everything related to computers and computer networks, including applications, compression, databases, multimedia, and programming
Misc	Subjects that do not fit in other standard newsgroup hierarchies, including activism, books, business, consumer issues, health, investing, jobs, and law
Sci	The sciences and social sciences, including anthropology, archaeology, chemistry, economics, math, physics, and statistics
Soc	Social issues, including adoption, college-related issues, feminism, human rights, and world cultures
Talk	Debate on controversial subjects, including abortion, atheism, euthanasia, gun control, and religion
News	Usenet itself, including announcements and materials for new users
Rec	All aspects of recreation, including aviation, backcountry sports, bicycles, boats, gardening, and scouting

FILE TRANSFER PROTOCOL: TRANSFERRING FILES

File Transfer Protocol (FTP) is one way that files can be transferred over the Internet, and it is especially useful for transferring files that are too large to send by e-mail. Although you can use special FTP client software, such as WS_FTP Home, you can also transfer files to and from an FTP server simply by using your browser or Windows Explorer. FTP can transfer two types of files: ASCII (text files) and binary (program files, graphics, or documents saved in proprietary file formats).

In most cases, you need a user name and a password to access an FTP server. However, with **anonymous FTP**, files are publicly available for downloading. A word of warning, due to the lack of security on an anonymous FTP site, do not use it to send sensitive information such as financial account numbers and passwords. FTP sites are structured hierarchically—that is, they use a folder and file structure similar to that used on your own computer. Depending on how you access the site, downloadable files may appear as hyperlinks. Just click the link to download the file. If you access the site using Windows Explorer, you can use the same file management techniques you use to organize your own files.

FTP is also used to upload Web pages from your computer to the ISP or hosting service's Web server, making your Web site available to other Internet users.

E-Commerce

A large portion of Internet traffic and Web sites are associated with e-commerce. **Commerce** is the selling of goods or services with the expectation of making a reasonable profit. **E-commerce (electronic commerce)** is the use of networks or the Internet to carry out business of any type. Many **e-tailers** (Web-based retailers) hope that while you are surfing the Web, you will stop and make a purchase. Online merchants sell books, CDs, clothes, and just about anything else you might want to buy. If you've ever made a purchase online, you're one of millions engaging in e-commerce.

E-commerce supports many types of traditional business transactions, including buying, selling, renting, borrowing, and lending. E-commerce isn't new; companies have used networks to do business with suppliers for years. What is new is that, thanks to the Internet and inexpensive PCs, e-commerce has become accessible to anyone with an Internet connection and a Web browser (Figure 6.30).

The U.S. Census Bureau reported that total retail e-commerce sales for the first quarter of 2009 was $31.7 billion, an

FIGURE 6.30 E-commerce has become accessible to anyone with an Internet connection and a Web browser.

increase of 0.7 percent ($\pm1.1\%$) from the fourth quarter of 2008. For the first quarter of 2009, e-commerce sales accounted for 3.5 percent of total sales. There are three types of e-commerce: business-to-business (B2B), consumer-to-consumer (C2C), and business-to-consumer (B2C).

BUSINESS-TO-BUSINESS E-COMMERCE (B2B)

When a business uses the Internet to provide another business with the materials, services, and/or supplies it needs to conduct its operations, they are engaging in **business-to-business (B2B) e-commerce**. Even though you might not personally engage in B2B, you'll probably recognize many of the industries and companies that do, for example, companies in the health care, aerospace and defense, real estate, automotive, and construction industries, and familiar computer and software companies such as Dell, IBM, and Microsoft.

In addition, many traditional and online retailers have special B2B units. For instance, the popular office supplies chain Staples has a B2B division that operates the Web site **www.staplescentral.com** for mid-size and Fortune 1000 companies. The Staples Contract division has experienced double-digit growth for the last seven years and launched the office supply industry's first online B2B catalog in 2007.

Unlike B2B, you may have engaged in the next type of e-commerce: consumer-to-consumer.

CONSUMER-TO-CONSUMER E-COMMERCE (C2C)

The online exchange or trade of goods, services, or information between individual consumers is **consumer-to-consumer (C2C) e-commerce**. Often C2C e-commerce involves the use of an intermediate site, such as the popular online auction destination eBay. eBay has more than 84 million active users in more than 39 global markets with 10 million items for sale on the site at any one time. In 2007, eBay reported that more than $59 billion in merchandise was auctioned. At least $2,000 worth of goods changes hands every second (Figure 6.31). Other C2C sites include craigslist and Amazon Marketplace.

BUSINESS-TO-CONSUMER E-COMMERCE (B2C)

When a business uses the Internet to supply consumers with services, information, or products, they are engaging in **business-to-consumer (B2C) e-commerce**. B2C is essentially the same as shopping at a physical store—you have a need or want, and the online marketplace offers products and solutions. The primary difference is that B2C e-commerce is not place or time specific, which means that you don't have to be in any particular place at any particular time to participate. This freedom of time and place enables you to shop whenever you wish and to choose from more products and services than could ever be assembled in any one physical location.

ONLINE SHOPPING

The trend is for more Web users to purchase merchandise online. In addition,

FIGURE 6.31 eBay is the most well-known C2C trading site.

many more people use the Web to research purchases from brick-and-mortar stores.

Getting Good Deals Online Have you ever tried to comparison shop on the Web? After surfing at 10 different sites (or more!), it can be daunting to keep track of where you saw the best price on that new digital camera you want. You might want to turn to shopping portals such as PriceGrabber.com, Shopzilla, NexTag, and others. These sites help you conduct price and product comparisons. They also offer reviews on just about any product you can imagine (Figure 6.32).

FIGURE 6.32 Shopping comparison sites can help users locate items, compare prices, view consumer feedback, and buy products.

You can search and sort by brand, price range, or product rating. To save even more, you can also check sites that offer coupons and rebates, such as The Bargainist and eCoupons.

THE DOT-COM PHENOMENON

Much e-commerce occurs in the *dot-com world*, the universe of Web sites with the suffix *.com* appended to their names. This unique world has been in existence only since 1995. Before 1995, companies were not able to sell over the Internet. But in 1995, the government eliminated all taxpayer funding of the Internet and opened it up to commercial development. The period between 1995 and 2000 is referred to as the *dot-com boom*. As the dot-com crash of 2000 made painfully clear, not every online business is able to succeed.

A dot-com company that has held its ground and become profitable is Amazon.com (Figure 6.33). Amazon

to take it home the same day, but many sellers are adopting creative solutions to these issues by offering online chats with live customer service representatives, various ways to view products, and a wide array of shipping options. One of the hallmarks of a successful online business is good customer service. Customers are reassured by sites that clearly post their contact information, offer pages of frequently asked questions, and respond quickly to customer inquiries.

BUILDING YOUR OWN ONLINE BUSINESS

One of the tremendous advantages of B2C e-commerce is the low capital investment needed to start an online business. For less than $50, a person can open a Web storefront and start selling products online. In contrast, a brick-and-mortar business requires land, a building, utilities, display shelving, and salespeople. A Web-based storefront requires only an

FIGURE 6.33 Amazon.com provides both breadth and depth of products and services.

quickly discovered that books are a commodity well-suited for online trade, but it didn't stop there. Its offerings have grown to include music, videos, groceries, tools, jewelry, and clothing. Amazon entices buyers to access, shop, and complete their sales online by offering professional and peer product reviews; author, artist, and subject matching; and book excerpts and music samples. Shoppers can choose from a variety of shipping options and track their purchases.

There are some drawbacks to B2C e-commerce. Buyers might miss speaking with a real sales clerk, being able to touch and feel the merchandise, and being able

ISP, a Web site, and the ability to ship goods or services to customers.

The first thing you need to do when starting any business is to develop a business plan (Figure 6.34). You must decide what products to offer, determine your target market, select how many items you plan to sell and at what price. Who will pay for shipping? Will there be service provided after the sale? Who are your competitors? What profit margin do you expect to achieve?

All businesses need to have a name, and an online business is no different, except that the online business's name is almost always the same as its Web site or domain name. So, after you've completed your business plan, you will need to shop for a domain name and a Web hosting service. Many Web hosting companies, such as 1&1 (**www.1and1.com**), offer domain name search and registration services as part of their package. You will most likely want a name with a .com extension. Try to pick a name that will be easy for your customers to remember.

You may also wish to employ an electronic shopping cart. This feature is much like the physical shopping cart you'd use at a grocery store. It remembers your customer's order items and provides the results to the summary order page. Your Web site should project a professional image and be structured to meet your customers' needs to encourage their confidence in your product or service. Go to GoodPractices (**www.goodpractices.com**) for some Web site development guidelines.

You will also need to make arrangements for Web hosting, if you haven't already done so. Web hosting services provide server space, make your site available to the public, and offer site management utilities such as preprogrammed shopping cart services. There are thousands of Web hosting companies. Many Web hosting services offer templates and other tools to make it simple to build a professional-looking site. Sites such as 1&1, GoDaddy, and Yahoo! offer a variety of pricing plans for personal and commercial sites. Expect to pay a start-up fee as well as a monthly amount that is usually based on a one-year contract.

You can ensure that your site gets listed with search engines by visiting each engine's Web site (**www.google.com**, **www.yahoo.com**, **www.msn.com**, and so on) and searching for "submitting my site." Provide the information requested, and then when someone searches for keywords that match your site, it will be one of the sites that are provided in the search results answer screen.

To operate a business, you need a way to receive payments. Just like in a traditional retail business, perhaps the best option may be to take credit cards. You should be aware that there are many costs involved with setting up and maintaining a credit card acceptance account—but the benefits may well outweigh the costs. Customers are comfortable using their

FIGURE 6.34 Sites such as Bplans.com can help get your small business plan off to a good start.

credit cards online, and many feel more secure knowing that the credit card company is there in case of a dispute or fraudulent use.

One of the best and quickest ways to accept credit cards is to use a PayPal merchant account (Figure 6.35). PayPal

FIGURE 6.35 PayPal accounts make online purchases easier and more secure.

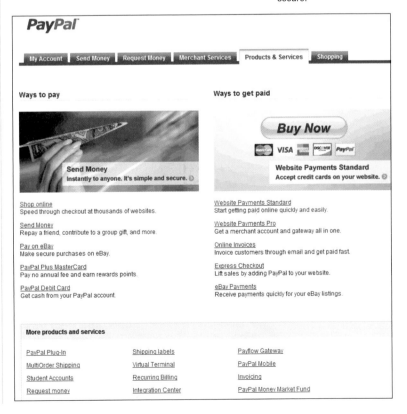

also acts as a secure intermediary, offering users the ability to make payments from their bank account, credit card, or PayPal account without revealing their personal financial information to the seller. PayPal manages more than 40 million accounts worldwide. Transaction fees range from 2 to 3 percent, and there is a per-transaction fee of about 30 cents per transaction.

OTHER AREAS OF E-COMMERCE GROWTH

Making travel reservations is an area of e-commerce experiencing rapid growth. Sites such as Travelocity, Expedia, and CheapTickets enable leisure travelers to

by the end of 2011. By that time, some 76 percent of Americans (72 million households) will be using online banking services. Currently, banks that offer online banking gain a competitive advantage over those that do not because most customers now consider it a necessary and expected service, like ATMs. What else is in it for banks? Plenty. Online banking helps banks cut down on the expenses of maintaining bank branches and paying tellers and also allows them to provide advanced levels of electronic customer service.

The sale of stock through the Internet has only been possible since 1996; however, online stock trading now accounts for one out of every six stock trades,

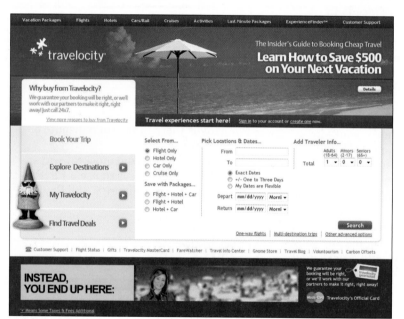

FIGURE 6.36 Sites such as Travelocity (**www.travelocity.com**) are popular because they help travelers find the cheapest fares and reservations available.

easily making it the fastest-growing application in B2C e-commerce. Offering secure connections through the customer's Web browser, online stock trading sites enable investors to buy and sell stocks online without the aid of a broker.

The attraction of online stock trading can be summed up in one word: cost. Traditional, full-service brokerages charge up to $100 per trade; discount brokerages charge about $50. But the most aggressive e-traders have

book flights, hotels, and car rentals online, as well as find the cheapest fares based on their trip parameters (Figure 6.36). Most travel sites provide e-tickets so that you can quickly check in at airport terminals by using small self-service kiosks.

Another rapidly growing online activity is banking. Access to your banking accounts enables you to use a Web browser to check account balances, balance your checkbook, transfer funds, and even pay bills online (Figure 6.37). In fact, 40 million Americans used online banking services by the end of 2005. The use of online banking is expected to grow by 55 percent

cut the charges to $10 per trade or less. E-traders, such as E*TRADE and Ameritrade, can offer such low prices because the trading is automatic—no human broker is involved.

Nonretail online services have spiked in activity in the last few years. These activities include dating services; credit reports; health and medical advice; news, weather, and sports information; real estate listings (for homes and apartments); and insurance products. These sites offer various levels of access and services for members and nonmembers. Some services, such as insurance quotes, up-to-the-minute news reports, and severe-weather alerts, are free. You can also post dating profiles or receive diet and other health-related profiles as well as trial passes for sports subscriptions.

SAFE SURFING GUIDELINES

By taking some simple precautions, you can keep your Internet activities safe. You'll avoid malware, unscrupulous vendors, identity theft, and threats to you and your family.

AVOIDING MALWARE

Short for "malicious software," malware refers to software programs designed and written to damage a computer system. Examples of malware events range from deleting files on a hard drive or removing directory information to gathering data from a user's system that can include Web sites the user visited and account numbers or passwords that were keyed in. It is unfortunate that there are individuals out there with malicious intent, but there are—and you must be prepared. You can keep your system free of malware by installing antivirus and antispyware utilities on your computer. These utility programs will seek and destroy the malware programs they find on your computer.

AVOIDING E-COMMERCE HAZARDS

Although there are many benefits to engaging in e-commerce, it also entails risks. These risks include identity theft, personal information exposure, money loss, and being ripped off by unscrupulous charlatans. To protect yourself, carefully create user names and passwords, particularly at sites where you must pay for goods or services. It is also wise to avoid e-commerce with little-known companies, at least until you've taken the opportunity to check their legitimacy. Checking

shopping portals or other review sites to locate feedback from other users or conducting an online search combining the company's name with keywords such as *problem*, *fraud*, or *scam* can help you be better informed.

Even though you are most likely protected from monetary losses by your credit card company, you should always be careful when giving out your credit card information—and do so only on secure sites. Never share credit card numbers, account numbers, user name, or password information with others, even if you receive an e-mail requesting that information from what seems to be a legitimate source.

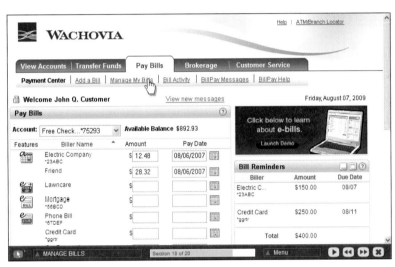

FIGURE 6.37 Online banking enables customers to access their accounts, balance checkbooks, and even pay bills online.

Some of the things you should look for on a secure site (one that is protected from intrusion of your personal business by others) include:

- *https://* in the address of the site instead of the usual *http://* (The added "s" stands for "secure site.")
- The VeriSign logo
- A locked padlock symbol
- The logo from other site-security entities such as Verified by Visa
- A message box that notifies you when you are leaving (or entering) a secure site

Sometimes you will find that the seller is a person just like you—that the seller doesn't have the ability to take credit cards and that he or she has set up an account with an online transaction processing system such as PayPal. It is the seller who decides which vendor to use for the payment. For instance, if you see the Pay-Pal logo on an eBay auction item site, it means that you can use PayPal as a payment option. In fact, sometimes this is the only option available. The PayPal Web site even offers a tool to help you manage your buying experience. The PayPal Auction-Finder searches eBay for items you've recently won and prefills your payment form with details taken straight from the item listing. With AuctionFinder, you can eliminate errors and pay for your items instantly. Always use extra care and caution whenever you conduct financial transactions on the Internet.

PROTECTING YOUR IDENTITY

More than half a million people find themselves victims of identity theft each year. Nothing is more frustrating than having to spend the time and energy to straighten the mess created by a loss of identification. And, nothing is more difficult than restoring your credit after an identity theft has destroyed your credit rating.

> "Always use **extra care** and caution whenever you conduct **financial transactions** on the Internet."

There are steps you can take to greatly reduce your risk of having your identity stolen or a portion of it pilfered. Try to avoid shoulder-surfers, these are individuals at ATMs and phone booths who stand close enough to see PIN numbers keyed in by users. When shopping with an e-merchant for the first time, look for the secure Web site features before entering any personal or credit card information. Also check out any feedback provided by previous purchasers or any comments by the Better Business Bureau. Only shop on Web sites that offer a privacy policy. Make it a habit to print out privacy policies, warranties, price guarantees, and other important information. Most importantly, *never* include any financial account numbers or passwords in an e-mail or respond in any way to spam. And, be sure to change the passwords on your accounts frequently.

Simply being watchful and careful with your personal information, completing transactions only on validated Web sites, and knowing the signs of a secure site will help you use the Web to its full potential safely.

PROTECTING CHILDREN IN CYBERSPACE

With statistics supporting the use of social networks, chat rooms, and other forms of anonymous communication by minors, there have been some creative protective responses to insulate youth from cyberstalkers, cyberbullies, and other unhealthy contact. A couple in Fanwood, New Jersey, contacted CyberAngels (**www.cyberangels .org**), a volunteer organization of thousands of Internet users worldwide, after their computer-addicted 13-year-old daughter ran away from home. The group's purpose: to protect children in cyberspace.

CyberAngels was founded in 1995 by Curtis Sliwa, who also started the Guardian Angels (the volunteer organization whose members wear red berets as they patrol inner-city streets). Today, CyberAngels volunteers scour the Internet for online predators, cyberstalkers, and child pornographers, and they've been responsible for a number of arrests. Their Web site and newsletter provide many useful articles about practical safety measures to keep you and your loved ones safe and has brought their Children's Internet Safety Program to thousands of schoolchildren across the United States.

The Internet can be a dangerous place for young children, and older ones too! **Cyberbullying** occurs when one individual targets another for some form of torment or abuse through digital tools. The term used to apply to children acting against other children. However the recent suicide death of a teen in Missouri due to the cyberbullying by a parent who masqueraded as another youth has shed light on the intensity of this problem. Online stalkers and sexual predators haunt social networking sites. **Cyberstalkers** use e-mail, instant messaging, chat rooms, pagers, cell phones, or other forms of information technology to make repeated, credible threats of violence against another individual or family members of an individual.

Speaking with children about Internet safety practices, being aware of where and when they surf, and knowing who their cyberfriends are should be a top priority. Concerned parents can implement the parental controls that are provided by their ISPs or included in safety and security software. Web site blocking and content-filtering software and monitoring programs like Net Nanny (**www .netnanny.com**), and bsecure (**www.bsecure.com**) can add another level of security.

And, what about the New Jersey couple? Their daughter is home and safe thanks to the CyberAngels who successfully used their network to identify the child's online contact.

To learn more about how to protect yourself or the children in your household, visit Stop Cyberbullying (**www.stopcyberbullying.org**), SocialSafety.org (**www.socialsafety.org**), and the Family Online Safety Institute (**www.fosi.org/resources/parents**). Also, Ken Leebow's blog, Crossing the Digital Divide (**http://crossingthedigitaldivide .blogspot.com**), tries to keep adults up to date on the cyber activities of their children.

Chapter Summary

The Internet and the World Wide Web

The Internet is the network of networks. The Internet allows every connected computer to directly exchange data with any other computer on the network. The Internet is able to work this way because of interoperability, the ability to work with a computer even if it is a different brand and model. Users access the Internet by way of a public or private Internet service provider (ISP). You can connect to your ISP by way of a telephone modem, a digital service line (DSL), a cable modem, a satellite, or a fiber-optic cable.

Whereas the Internet is a global computer network that connects millions of smaller networks, the World Wide Web is a global system that contains billions of hypertext documents and uses the Internet as its transport mechanism. Millions of users turn to the Web to research current events, obtain general information, locate product information, investigate scientific developments, access e-commerce sites, communicate, and much more.

A Web browser is a program that displays a Web document and enables you to access linked documents. A Web server is a computer that retrieves documents requested by browsers. Web pages are requested most often by entering the URL of the page, clicking a hyperlink in a document already open, or using a tab in a browser window.

Popular Internet services include e-mail and instant messaging (IM) for sending messages, Internet relay chat (IRC) for text chatting, social networking sites for online communities, Usenet for joining discussion groups, electronic mailing list managers for broadcasting content to subscribers, File Transfer Protocol (FTP) for file exchange, and e-commerce. There are three types of e-commerce, business-to-business (B2B), consumer-to-consumer (C2C), and business-to-consumer (B2C).

When using the Web, use the following safe surfing guidelines. Avoid malware by installing antivirus and antispam spoftware. Conduct your e-commerce transactions only on secured sites. Make sure you change your passwords frequently, and never enter your account number unless you are on a secured site. Make sure you watch the computer usage of your children and install software to protect your children from cyberstalkers, cyberbullies, and undesirable Web sites.

Key Terms and Concepts

Matching

Match each key term in the left column with the most accurate definition in the right column.

_____ 1. e-commerce

_____ 2. aggregator

_____ 3. Boolean search

_____ 4. dead link

_____ 5. netiquette

_____ 6. exclusion operator

_____ 7. spam

_____ 8. truncation

_____ 9. Domain Name System

_____ 10. spider

_____ 11. link rot

_____ 12. thread

_____ 13. clickstream

_____ 14. interoperability

_____ 15. blog

a. Unsolicited advertising or offers for services or products.

b. The action of using wildcards to search the Web for a word with various endings.

c. An online equivalent to a journal or diary.

d. The selling of goods and services online with the expectation of making a profit.

e. Keywords include AND, OR, and NOT.

f. Results from a Web page that is not found at the location reported.

g. Out-of-datedness due to delay in spiders accumulating data.

h. Web sites where headlines are collected, either manually or through the use of algorithms.

i. A continuing commentary on a specific subject.

j. Describes the Internet's ability to work with computers and applications of different brands and models, through the use of a common protocol.

k. Rules or guidelines for good Internet behavior.

l. The set of Web links that indicate a user's Web session activity trail.

m. A symbol or word used to indicate that the content that follows is to be eliminated from the search.

n. A program that roams the Web and updates the database of a search engine.

o. Used by the Internet to link a domain name with its corresponding IP address.

Multiple Choice

Circle the correct choice for each of the following.

1. Which of the following is an example of a wildcard in a search?
   a. (
   b. +
   c. *
   d. @

2. Which of the following is an example of a top-level domain?
   a. .asp
   b. .hub
   c. .corp
   d. .gov

3. Which action can be used as a tool to decrease spam?
   a. Enable graphics.
   b. Reply to all spam messages, the sender will get tired and stop.
   c. Avoid posting your e-mail.
   d. Remove your postings from a social network.

4. What is the name given to nonphysical space that is accessible through a network of computers?
   a. Chatroom
   b. URL
   c. XHTML
   d. Cyberspace

5. What is the name of the next generation of the Web that provides increased opportunities for collaboration?
   a. URL
   b. Web 2.0
   c. HyperWeb
   d. Usenet

6. What is the term for an organization or institution that makes Web sites available?
   a. Usenet
   b. Host
   c. Newsgroup
   d. Protocol

7. Which of the following is the term for transferring files from your computer to another computer?
   a. Downloading
   b. Flaming
   c. Blogging
   d. Uploading

8. Which of the following is *not* part of the process to create an online business?
   a. Create and register a domain name
   b. Create a default or index page
   c. Purchase display shelves
   d. Find a host for your Web site

9. What is the name of the opening page of a Web site?
   a. Main page
   b. Index page
   c. Host page
   d. Target page

10. Which of the following automatically broadcasts messages to subscribers?
    a. Instant messenger service
    b. Wiki
    c. Newsgroup
    d. Electronic mailing list

Fill-In

In the blanks provided, write the correct answer for each of the following.

1. _____ _____ _____ is the Internet standard that supports the exchange of information on the Web.

2. A(n) _____ _____ alerts a sender that a message has been opened.

3. A Web-based retailer is called a(n) _____.

4. A URL consists of a protocol, _____ _____, path, and resource name.

5. Domain names must be _____ in order to link the name to its numeric IP address.

6. _____ _____ is the online exchange or trade of goods, services, or information between two businesses.

7. A(n) _____ _____ _____ provides individuals and businesses with access to the Internet via phone, DSL, cable, satellite, or fiber-optic lines for a fee.

8. _____ is the action of transferring a file from another computer to your computer by means of a computer network.

9. _____ is the use of e-mail, instant messaging, chat rooms, pagers, cell phones, or other forms of information technology to make repeated, credible threats of violence against another individual.

10. A(n) _____ networking site allows the user to create a profile and invite friends to join.

11. Surrounding a series of search terms with quotation marks is known as _____ _____.

12. Every computer, server, or device connected to the Internet has a numeric address known as a(n) _____ _____, which uniquely identifies it to the network.

13. A(n) _____ _____ displays Web pages and enables users to access linked documents.

14. _____ _____ is the of "out-of-datedness" that occurs in a search due to the amount of time it takes for spiders to accumulate data from the Web.

15. _____ occurs when one child targets another for some form of torment or abuse through digital tool.

Short Answer

1. List three to four of the responsibilities of an Internet service provider.

2. List and explain five rules for critically evaluating Web pages.

3. State the three ways to access a Web page.

4. What are the four parts of a Uniform Resource Locator (URL).

5. Explain the difference between a wiki, blog, and podcast.

Teamwork

1. **Internet Access and ISPs** Make a list of at least five Internet service providers your team member's use or are familiar with and categorize them by type of provider (dial-up, DSL, cable, satellite, or FiOS). Have each team member research a different type of provider. List the fees associated with each, the number of account names each allows, the free services provided, and the services that add additional cost. See whether the team can agree on one that is more user- or student-friendly than another. Present your findings in table format listing each provider and your research results.

2. **Social Networks: The Pros and Cons** Ask at least 20 students whether they are on a social network, the name of the network, how often they access it, and type and content of their postings. Then split you team into two groups. One group will research the pros of social networking and the other the cons. Present your survey and research results in a one-page, double-spaced paper. Remember to cite your research sources.

3. **Using a Search Engine** As a team, evaluate each of search statements below and describe the result that each will achieve. Use **www.internettutorials.net** for help with symbols you might not understand. Then create the search string to meet the specified change. Take a screen capture of the results from each search. Complete the table that follows and turn in the completed table and the screen capture from each one of the five searches.

   To create a screen capture, first press the PrtScrn key on the keyboard while the search result is on the screen. Open the Word file you plan to submit for this question. Position the cursor in the location you want the capture to appear, and from the contextual menu in the Word window select Edit then select Paste. The PrintScrn image captured earlier will appear in the Word document. Then simply print the document.

Search String	Purpose	Change to Be Made	Search String with Change
Sports +Sabres +Penguins		exclude the Penguins	
"To be or not to be"		include Shakespeare	
logo brown		include Cleveland	
clothing +Sabres +women		remove women and add men	
HR*		Remove human resources	

4. **Internet Usage** Have each team member keep a journal of their Internet use for three to five days. Record such data as the number of hours used in a session, the number of Web pages visited in a session, the types of Web pages visited (educational, finance, news). Regroup and make a combined list of your findings. Using **www.hitwise.com/datacenter/main/dashboard-10133.html**, or any other online source for Internet usage statistics, compare the usage patterns of your team to national or global statistics. Present your team data compared to the statistics you found on the Internet in both tabular and graphical form. Include a summary that indicates where your team statistics ranked in comparison to the national or global average. Turn in your team data and summary statement. Be sure to cite your references.

5. **Build Your Own Online Business** As a team, come up with a creative online business. Follow the steps in the text and use the Internet as a resource tool to develop a step-by-step business plan. Include specifics on products, goods, or services your online business will sell and the cost of each. Then shop for a domain name and attempt to register it (note the cost). Determine the features you want your business to have (a shopping cart, payment by PayPal, etc.), and locate a hosting service and record its fees.

Create and submit an outline of your business plan clearly explaining each step and listing its associated costs. Be sure to compile an estimate of the total investment needed to start your business.

On the Web

1. **Searching Ebay** Visit eBay at **www.ebay.com** and track the sale of an item. Select and describe an item that you wish to purchase. There are two methods for finding your item.

   - You can select a general category and then refine your search by selecting successive subcategories.
   - You can enter a description of the item in the search textbox and then click the Search button.

   Try both methods. Which method do you prefer? How many items met your criteria? If the number is too large, refine your criteria. View the list of items and sellers, and select a specific item. Identify the item, the seller, the first bid, the current bid, the bid increment, the number of bids, and the amount of time left in the auction. Click the bid history link, and identify the bidders and how many bids they have submitted. Click the "See detailed feedback" link to see the seller's rating. What is the seller's overall number of positive, neutral, and negative ratings? Based on buyer activity and the seller's profile, determine the amount of money that you would initially bid for this item. Track the bidding of this item until the auction closes, increasing your imagined bid as necessary. When the auction ends, determine whether you would have been the successful bidder. If not, what was your maximum bid? What was the final bid? Would you consider actually bidding for items in an online auction? Explain why you would or would not use an Internet auction to sell or purchase an item. Substantiate your choice by using specific incidents from your overall experience.

2. **Netiquette** Using your favorite search engine, find several Web sources on the topic of netiquette.

Make a list of ten netiquette practices and their purposes. Then go to **http://www.albion.com/netiquette/netiquiz.html** and take the online netiquette quiz. When you have finished, make a screen capture of the screen displaying your score. Turn in a Word document containing your list of netiquette practices, a list of your references, and the screen capture of your quiz score. To create a screen capture and then print the screen containing your score, first press the PrtScrn key on the keyboard while the score is on the screen. Open the Word file you plan to submit for this question. Position the cursor in the location you want the score to appear, and from the contextual menu in the Word window select Edit then select Paste. The PrintScrn image captured earlier will appear in the Word document and will print when you print the document.

3. **Check Domain Names for Availability** Have you ever thought about getting your own domain name in order to start a Web site? What would you like it to be? Visit **www.register.com** and try different top-level domain names (.com, .net, .org, and so on) to see if they're available. If they are, what is the annual registration cost? If the domain names are already taken, who owns them, when did they acquire them, and when do they expire? What are some of the other activities offered by register.com besides indicating URL availability? In a one-page, double-spaced report or PowerPoint presentation, present a summary of the results of your domain name search, a list of some of the domain names that were taken, their prices and expiration dates, and a short description of the other activities offered by register.com.

4. **Security Indicators** Using the Internet and your favorite browser, research the security issues of online transactions. What are at least three ways that a user can tell whether a Web site is secure? What is a security certificate? Locate a site that has a security certificate. How can a security certificate be viewed? View a certificate. What information is on a security certificate? What is encryption? In a one-page, double-spaced paper, present the results of your research and the answers to the questions above. Remember to cite the Web site you referenced.

5. **Browser versus Browser versus Browser** Use the search techniques discussed in this chapter to locate the home pages for each of the three main browsers, Internet Explorer 8, Firefox 3.5, and Opera 9.6. Using a table, compare at least eight features of each. Be sure to address the following questions: Which ones use tabbed browsing? Which ones can identify old Web pages and make them compatible with the new versions and technology? Which ones permit the easy sharing of information between users and across platforms? Present your results in a clear and easy to read table.

Web 2.0

When was the last time you called a friend or spoke f2f (face-to-face) to ask a question or to tell your friend what you were doing, and when did you send your last e-mail? Today, there are so many ways to keep everyone informed. One of the top choices is using the technologies that have been described in this book and Web 2.0, which has a language all its own. "OMG GTG BRB ur gr8 roflol" is a little shorter than "Oh my gosh, got to go, be right back, you are great, rolling on the floor, laughing out loud." So, what exactly is Web 2.0?

What Is Web 2.0?

No one recognized the Web as Web 1.0 until after Web 2.0 was named, which makes sense because Web 1.0 was the precursor to the type of Web experience we now are able to create. **Web 1.0** consisted of static Web pages with no interactivity other than hyperlinks. The links allowed a user to move around a Web site from page to page or item to item. There was no other interaction of the type that would come with Web 2.0.

WEB 1.0

Web 1.0 has the following characteristics:

- **Web 1.0 sites are static.** They contain information that might be useful, but there's no reason for a visitor to return to the site later. An example might be a personal Web page that gives information about the site's owner, but never changes. A Web 2.0 version might be a blog or MySpace account that owners can update frequently.

- **Web 1.0 sites aren't interactive.** Visitors can only visit these sites; they can't impact or contribute to the sites. Most organizations have profile pages that visitors can look at but not impact or alter, whereas a wiki allows anyone to visit and make changes.

- **Web 1.0 applications are proprietary.** Under the Web 1.0 philosophy, companies develop software applications that users can download, but they can't see how the application works or change it. A Web 2.0 application is an open source program, which means the source code for the program is freely available. Users can see how the application works and make modifications or even build new applications based on earlier programs. For example, Netscape Navigator was a proprietary Web browser of the Web 1.0 era. Firefox follows the Web 2.0 philosophy and provides developers with all the tools they need to create new Firefox applications.

WEB 2.0

There are so many definitions of Web 2.0; it could make your head spin. **Web 2.0** is a set of techniques that collectively provide an upgraded presentation and usefulness for the World Wide Web.

The term *Web 2.0* was coined by Tim O'Reilly. His philosophy of Web 2.0 included these ideas:

- Using the Web as an applications platform
- Democratizing the Web
- Employing new methods to distribute information

Because Web 2.0 has so many meanings, many people refer to it by the particular facet they are using, for example, social networking. The Web 2.0 toolbox includes such applications as:

- Blogs and vlogs
- Wikis
- Podcasts and vodcasts
- Social networking
- Photosharing
- Communication
- Collaboration
- Content sharing

Let's take a look at how we use those Web 2.0 technologies.

Blogs and Vlogs

Many of us were taught to keep journals. At one point, they were very private. Some of us even kept them under lock and key hidden somewhere in our rooms. Today, many people want to share the thoughts they write. To share with the most readers at any time, the media of choice is the World Wide Web.

WHY BLOG?

The journals people create on the Web are called **blogs** (short for **Web log**). The Merriam-Webster dictionary defines a *blog* as a Web site that contains an online personal journal with reflections, comments, and often hyperlinks provided by the writer. If you want to create a blog, you can access many free sites that provide helpful instructions and tutorials to guide you as you set up your blog. One of the most popular is **www.blogger.com** (Figure 5A). Another is iGoogle

FIGURE 5A Blogger is one of the more popular blogging Web sites.

(**http://googleblog.blogspot.com/**). If you do not like one of these, just search for free blogging sites and you find over 270,000,000 possibilities. Hopefully, there will be one that works for you.

Today we are all concerned about identity theft and privacy. We'll discuss the issues related to Web 2.0 and security more throughout this spotlight. The Web 2.0 tools can be safe if you take the necessary precautions. With regard to blogs, you may want to share your thoughts with friends but not strangers. If so, you can restrict who has access to your blog by protecting it with a password.

If you don't want to blog, but want to see what others have written, you can locate a blog on just about any subject in any language. Google has a blog search engine. Visit **http://blogsearch.google.com** and you can search for a blog by subject. If you go to the advanced search on blogsearch, you can search by author and date. While using blogsearch and the advanced search capability, select the Filter using safe search option, and you can screen for sites that contain explicit sexual content and delete them from your search results. If you are taking this course online or have access to your school's Learning Management System, there may be a blog component that will permit you to create a blog for your classmates.

WHY VLOG?

When written blogs are just not enough, some journalers turn to video logs. A **vlog** (short for **video log**) is a series of personal reflective videos that are usually created simply by talking to a Web cam and uploading the video. Many vloggers post their vlogs on YouTube, even though the video postings can only be 10 minutes long and up to 2GB in size. The stoutest vloggers update their vlogs daily. If you are reporting from a conference or are a personality, you might update your vlog on a regular basis.

There aren't as many sites for posting your vlog as there are blogging sites. The one that turns up at the top of the lists generated by most search engines is **www.freevlog.org/**. Depending on the site you use to post your vlog, you can password protect it, which is really a good idea. Just remember that what you post is out there for the world to view. If you only want to view vlogs, use the same Google blog search to search for vlogs.

Wikis

Wiki, which means "quick" in Hawaiian, was created by Ward Cunningham in 1995. A **wiki** is an online information source that allows anyone to edit, delete, or modify content that has been added to the Web site. Wikis are said to be self-correcting—if you add content that is incorrect, someone will correct it for you. Although wikis are a good source for information, they should not be a primary source for research or academic assignments because they are not always created by content experts and there may be errors in the text. They can, however, be used for confirmation of other sources.

There are many sites that have wikis. Wikipedia is one of the popular Web sites for information. It lists itself as the free encyclopedia. You can visit the site (**www.wikipedia.com**) and search on terms to gain insight into a variety of different topics. Even though it is a free site, it is important to cite your source if you use information you find on Wikipedia. If you'd like to participate in the community that keeps Wikipedia updated, you have to create an account. Once you have an account, you can correct the entries you find.

To create your own wiki, **www.wikispaces.com/** has different levels of space for business, higher education, nonprofit organizations, and K–12 education. You can create an account, then start working on your wiki. PBworks.com is another popular wiki site. You can make your wiki private or public by assigning who can see or edit it.

You can edit a wiki in several different ways. You can use plain text editing, which we are all familiar with, or simple markup language, which is a variation of hypertext markup language. Figure 5B is an example of input and output using markup language.

CoffeeCup (Figure 5C) is an HTML wiki software. This software gives you a sophisticated way to do HTML editing using a graphic user interface (GUI). You can preview the text before it is posted. Of course, you don't *have* to edit a wiki; you can just read it. Many wikis are private to small groups, such as a class.

FIGURE 5B Editing a Wiki Using HTML

HTML Text	Rendered Output

`<p>"Take some more`
`<a href="/wiki/Tea"`
`title="Tea">tea</a>," the`
`March Hare said to Alice,`
`very earnestly.</p>`
	"Take some more tea," the March Hare said to Alice, very earnestly.

`<p>"I've had nothing yet,"`
`Alice replied in an`
`offended tone: "so I can't`
`take more."</p>`
	"I've had nothing yet," Alice replied in an offended tone: "so I can't take more."

`<p>"You mean you can't`
`take <i>less</i>," said`
`the Hatter: "it's very`
`easy to take <i>more</i>`
`than nothing."</p>`
	"You mean you can't take *less*," said the Hatter: "it's very easy to take *more* than nothing."

FIGURE 5C   CoffeeCup is a free software download.

Podcasts and Vodcasts

Do you like to listen to lectures while working out? Do you want to watch the world's funniest commercials on your time schedule, not when they are scheduled on TV? If so, consider a podcast or a vodcast.

PODCASTS

A **podcast** is a blend of the words *iPod* and *broadcast*. It has come to mean a program (music or talk) that is made available in digital format for automatic download over the Internet. Although, podcasts were originally for Apple's iPod, you can listen to them on other media players. You can also download podcasts to a computer and upload them to a handheld device such as an iPod or MP3 player.

There are many sources for podcasts in many different subjects. One of the premier sources of podcasts is iTunes (Figure 5D). Most podcasts are free; others have nominal charges. Want to listen to a book? Try **www.openculture .com/2006/10/audio_book_ podc.html**. In additon to iTunes (**www.itunes.com**) which you need to download before you can see the available podcasts, **www.podcastdirectory.com/** and **www.podcastalley.com/**

are two sites where you can get a directory of podcasts on a variety of subjects.

To create your own podcast you can use software such as Audacity, which is available as a free download at **http://audacity .sourceforge.net/download/**. You will also need a microphone that will work with your computer to record the podcast. Once completed, you can save and upload your own podcasts to the podcast directory sites, but you must be a registered user todo so.

VODCASTS

A **vodcast** or **video podcast** is a term used for the online delivery of a video clip on demand. Over the past few years, creating such videos has become very popular.

YouTube   YouTube (**www.youtube. com**) is a popular video-sharing Web site at which users can upload vodcasts and vlogs. As previously mentioned, you are limited to the size and length of the video or vlog you can upload, and you must be registered to upload videos, but anybody can watch them. The site warns users that they must have permission before they can upload any material that has been copyrighted. An excellent video on YouTube, created by mwesch and entitled *Information R/evolution,* explores the changes in the way we find, store, create, critique, and share information

FIGURE 5D   Podcasts Home Page on Apple.com

(www.youtube.com/watch?v=-4CV05HyAbM). This video was created as a conversation starter. Watch it and see what you think!

You can locate short videos on a multitude of topics on YouTube. Do you like to watch mints explode in carbonated beverages? If so, you can find about 27,000 videos on the site. YouTube is also being used by colleges and universities as a recruiting tool.

iTunes iTunes is another source of short videos. Yes, iTunes is a proprietary digital media player application used for playing and organizing digital music and video files, but it is also an interface you can use to manage the files on Apple's popular iPod digital media players as well as the iPhone and iTouch. The iTunes application must be downloaded and installed.

In addition to using iTunes on your devices to download podcasts and vodcasts, you can also install it on your computer and use it to manage your playlist. Or just listen or watch the videos through your computer. There are versions for Windows and Macs. iTunes will allow you to play music, movies, TV shows, podcasts, audio books, and applications. These can all be purchased at the iTunes store. There is a nominal charge for most, but some are free. You can create a playlist on your computer and upload it to your iPod or MP3 player. You just need to be aware of which type of device the downloads will play on. Some devices play only MP3s.

iTunes Higher Education Many professors also use iTunes as a place to post lecture supplements and other pertinent information for their courses. Similarly, some colleges and universities have set up a virtual campus in iTunes. These include some of the Ivy League schools (Figure 5E). Such campuswide storehouses of course content were very popular in 2007 and 2008. Many schools have left their content online but have not updated it because they have set up in-house access and created their own Learning Management Systems. There may be a page on your school's Web site that provides access to a number of podcasts.

Social Networking

Social networking is a group of individuals creating a community. Social networking sites include Facebook, MySpace, LinkedIn, Twitter, Ning, and Digg, to name a few. Social networking provides a way for you to share pictures, what you are doing, and some of your thoughts with friends and family. And, it is relatively easy to share your common interests with people around the world. Rather than call or e-mail each person, all you have to do is post once, and all your friends can see what you wrote.

However, social networking is not without risks. Due to the popularity of social networking sites, there have been breaches in security. In October 2005, the infamous "Samy" MySpace XSS worm effectively shut that site down for a few days. Identity theft is also an issue with respect to safety on social networking sites due to the amount of information available at these sites. Features that invite user participation—messages, invitations, photos, open platform applications, and so on—are often the avenues less scrupulous individuals use to gain access to private information. This is especially true in the case of Facebook because of its popularity and the amount of information some people include. The problems plaguing social network security and privacy issues, for now, can only be resolved if users take a more careful approach to what and how much they share.

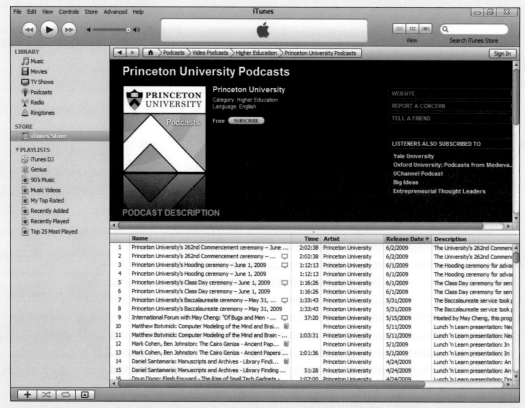

FIGURE 5E Princeton University is one of many colleges that post podcasts or coursework on iTunes.

Network World Panorama presented a podcast on how social networks can help recruiters in their search for quality employees. The podcast references how companies can benefit by looking at sites like Facebook and Twitter in order to find the best possible employee. It stresses that potential employees should use their social networking sites and skills to find out more about companies to help them land jobs. The following sections list several of the most popular social networking sites.

SECOND LIFE

Second Life defines itself as a free online virtual world imagined and created by its residents. From the moment you enter Second Life, you'll discover a fast-growing digital world filled with people, entertainment, experiences, and opportunity. Philip Rosedale founded Linden Lab in 1999. He created a revolutionary new form of shared experience (Figure 5F). It provides a venue where individuals jointly inhabit a 3D landscape and build the world around them. The monetary unit is called Linden dollars. These dollars can be used in the virtual world in the same way that "real" dollars can be used in the "real world," to purchase goods and services. Many businesses and schools have purchased land and built a virtual complex where you can learn about their products or attend classes. If you are studying Edgar Allen Poe, you can go and visit his house. Second Life has its own blog and wiki. Second Life was featured on an episode of CSI: NY in Season 4, Episode 5: "Down the Rabbit Hole."

To get started, go to **http://secondlife.com/** and download the software to build your avatar. An **avatar** is a virtual representation of the player in a game, in this case, Second Life. Creating a basic avatar is free. If you don't like the standard choices, however, you can purchase hair and clothes using Linden dollars. Don't have any Linden dollars? You can use your credit card to buy some. Once you have chosen your name and are logged in, there is an excellent tutorial to get you flying. Then visit the virtual world.

FACEBOOK

The Facebook mission is "Giving people the power to share and make the world more open and connected." There are over 250 million people signed up on Facebook—you, movie stars, rock groups, the President, and me just to name a few. President Barack Obama embraced Facebook during his run for office. He uses it now for town hall meetings. You can visit the White House page to join discussions. People are using Facebook (**www.facebook.com**) to stay updated on what's happening around them and share their experiences with the people in their lives.

Facebook has limitless possibilities. You can join groups, start groups, become a fan, start a fan club, get updates, send updates, and connect with friends you haven't seen in a while or those you see every day. You can upload photos, share your position or political thoughts, or let folks know just how you feel at the moment. You can play games and share the score or play games against your friends, or find your horoscope or what kind of sandwich you are in a Facebook quiz.

Remember, however, on this social networking site and others, be sure to protect your personal information. Don't post those party pictures or anything else that may present you in a less than favorable light. Some potential employers are looking at these social networking sites. And, in any instance, keep in mind that the more information you post, the more help you give to identity thieves.

TWITTER

Twitter (**www.twitter.com**) is a service for friends, family, and coworkers to communicate and stay connected through the exchange of quick, frequent

FIGURE 5F The possibilities in Second Life are endless. Get set to enjoy the ride and meet some interesting people (avatars) along the way.

answers to one simple question: What are you doing? With Twitter, you can stay hyperconnected to your friends and always know what they're doing. On the other hand, you can stop following them any time. You can even set quiet times on Twitter so you're not interrupted. Twitter puts you in control and becomes a modern antidote to information overload. You can follow your favorite person or movie star. Among the notables listed you can follow are Oprah, Tiger Woods, and the latest movie or album. There have been unofficial contests about who can get the most followers. Ashton Kutcher challenged CNN to a Twitter popularity contest—and won. The potential is staggering. You can tweet from your mobile device or your computer. Staying connected is what it's all about (Figure 5G).

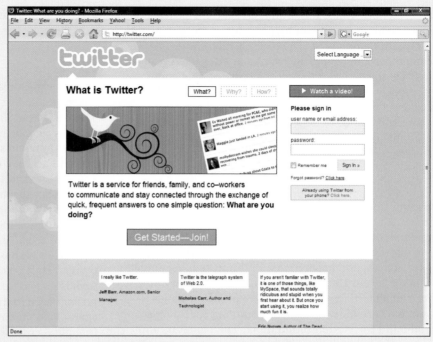

FIGURE 5G Sign up for Twitter. It doesn't cost anything and will keep you connected.

FLICKR

Flickr (**www.flickr.com**) is an online service that allows users to store and share photos. It is a way to get your photos and videos to the people who matter to you. You can:

- Upload from your desktop, send by e-mail, or use your camera phone.

- Edit to get rid of red eye, crop a photo, or get creative with fonts and effects!
- Organize your photos by setting up collections, sets, and tags.
- Share photos and videos using group and privacy controls.
- Map where your photos and videos were taken.
- See photos and videos taken near you.
- Make stuff such as cards, photo books, framed prints, DVDs, and so on.
  - Send photos to a vendor for printing and pickup.
  - Keep in touch by getting updates from family and friends.

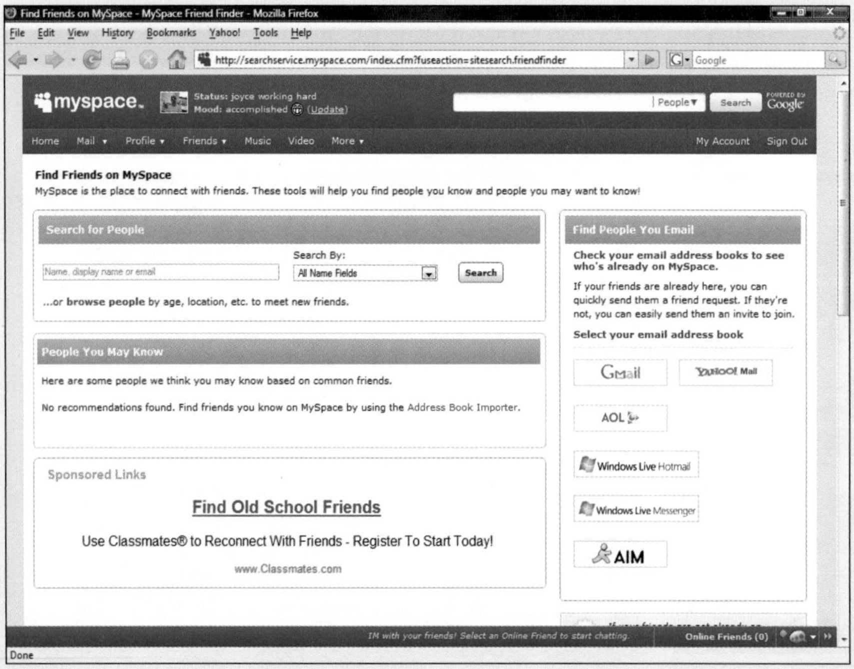

MYSPACE

MySpace (**www.myspace.com**) permits users to view profiles, connect with others, blog, rank music, and much more! MySpace is the application that started the big push to social networking. When you set up your page, you can change the wallpaper, layout, and add music. Many sites specialize in writing the scripts you can use to change your background or make other design-related changes. Just search on "MySpace backgrounds" in any search engine. Use MySpace to find friends and classmates (Figure 5H), meet new people,

FIGURE 5H Find your friends on MySpace.

listen to free music and build playlists, share photos, and watch videos. You can also blog and join forums.

LINKEDIN

Professionals use LinkedIn (**www.linkedin.com**) as a social networking site to exchange information, ideas, and opportunities. As of August 2009, it had more than 40 million registered users spanning 170 industries. On this site, your network consists of your connections, your connections' connections, and the people those connections know, linking you to a vast number of qualified professionals and experts. Through your network you can:

- Manage the information that's publicly available about you as a professional.
- Find and be introduced to potential clients, service providers, and subject experts who come recommended.
- Create and collaborate on projects, gather data, share files, and solve problems.
- Find potential business partners with whom to collaborate.
- Be invited by others to become involved in a business venture.
- Gain new insights from discussions with like-minded professionals in private group settings.
- Discover inside connections that can help you land jobs and close deals.
- Post and distribute job listings to find the best talent for your company.
- Start discussions and dialogues on topics of interest or questions you have.

Many employers are using this site to help screen potential employees. Many professionals are recommending others. It is a way to interface in a professional manner.

NING

Ning (**www.ning.com**) allows you to create and join new social networks related to your interests and passions. If Facebook and MySpace are not enough for you, you can have your own social network. With over 1.3 million social networks created and more than 30 million registered members, millions of people everyday are coming together across Ning Networks to explore and express their interests, discover new passions, and meet new people around shared pursuits.

Ning also enables artists, brands, and organizations to simplify and control their online presence with their own unique social network that beautifully integrates with other social media services while providing the most direct, unique, and lucrative relationship with fans, consumers, and members.

DIGG

Digg is a place for people to discover and share content from anywhere on the Web. A disclosure on the Digg site (**www.digg.com**) states: "The person who associated a work with this document has dedicated this work to the Commons by waiving all of his or her rights to the work under copyright law and all related or neighboring legal rights he or she had in the work, to the extent allowable by law." This means that you no longer have ownership to what you post here. It can be copied and used anywhere without your permission. As with most social networking sites, you can link Digg with Facebook and Twitter.

RSS FEEDS

In the good old days when you needed updates on information, you looked it up. Today, it looks you up. **RSS (Really Simple Syndication or Rich Site Summary)** will publish information to you and let you know when Web content has been updated or news events are taking place (Figure 5I). Does this symbol look familiar to you? You have seen it on numerous Web sites. You click on this icon to select the feed you want. Once you request a feed, it can be sent to your computer, personal digital assistant (PDA), or any mobile device that has Web access. Want to find out what RSS feeds are available to

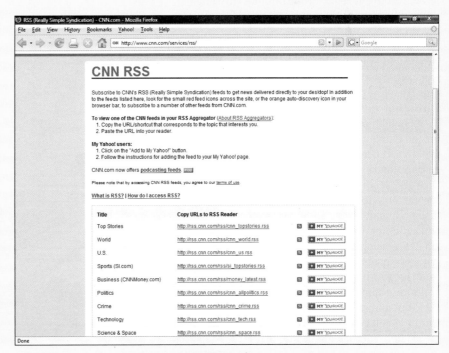

FIGURE 5I A Popular Site to Get RSS Feeds

you? Go to your favorite search engine and search for "RSS feed directory." In a recent search, over 90,000,000 were listed.

As with any Web 2.0 application, security can be an issue with RSS. There are two principal approaches for hackers to take advantage of RSS. In the first situation, the feed owner is malicious and injects malicious code into the feed directly. That's not the most popular way RSS feeds are hacked. The more common approach is for a hacker to inject an attack into an RSS feed instead of defacing a Web site. In such a scenario, the attacker would then "own" all of the site's subscribers. So, before you sign up for an RSS feed, make sure you know where your feeds are coming from. Check source Web sites for authenticity. Request RSS feeds only from Web sites with which you are familiar. Check the copyright information or learn more about the company to see whether they are who they say they are.

Instant Messaging

Instant messaging (IM) is a quick way of chatting with your buddies. There are several popular IM software packages you can download. AOL Instant Messenger (AIM) **www.aim.com**, Microsoft's Live Messenger **www.download.live.com/messenger**, and Yahoo! **http://messenger.yahoo.com/** are just a few. If you are mobile, most IMs have Web versions or mobile versions. Using IM, you never have to be too far from your buddies. The problem is that not all your friends may be on the same IM network, and individual IM networks don't play well together. If you have friends on different IM networks, there are a few programs that allow you to aggregate your buddies into one list. To use them, you also need to be a member of that platform. Two examples are Trillian (**www.trillian.com**) and Gaim (**www.gaim.com**). Many social networking sites have their own chat features. For example, you can have a live chat with your friends on Facebook or while you're playing an online game.

Instant messaging has become so popular that many colleges and universities have an IM presence for various departments: Admissions, Registration, and even Counseling. Some businesses and software applications have live help (chat) to assist you rather than making you look up a response or send an e-mail to explain a problem. It's a great way to provide customer service in the digital world.

When you are chatting with someone, you have to do a lot of typing. So, maybe you'd like to chat by voice. Add a Webcam, microphone, and speakers to your system along with a service such as Skype, and you can talk your way through a conversation (Figure 5J). Chatting is a **synchronous communication** activity, where you and your buddy are both online at the time and have a coherent conversation. Texting, however, is **asynchronous communication**—you are not necessarily both online at the same time. And only one of you can send a message at a time.

Texting

Court reporters have a language all their own. Gregg shorthand is a language all its own. Well, so is texting. Usually accomplished using a mobile phone, **texting** provides quick communication. Texting has been extended to include messages containing image, video, and sound content. Messages are referred to as *text messages* or *texts*.

Most texts are person-to-person, but many schools have automated systems for alerts or weather closings. Advertisers and service providers may use texting for promotions. Internet Service Providers (ISPs) have plans for texting or charge a fee for each text message you send or receive.

Because texting is usually done on a small keyboard and because they are short messages, typing full words is not efficient. Instead, text messages have their own language. Having trouble translating? Try the Lingo2word Web site (**www.lingo2word.com/translate.php**). This Web site allows you to translate Lingo to plain English or from plain English to lingo.

FIGURE 5J Chatting Online

Figure 5K is a short list of some of the favorite text abbreviations:

FIGURE 5K Favorite Text Abbreviations	
Lingo Expression	English Translation
@TEOTD	at the end of the day
ur gr8	you are great
Adip	another day in paradise
ILU	I love you
JAS	just a second
TTFN	ta-ta for now
np	no problem
BFF	best friend forever

You can locate a full list if you search the Web.

SEXTING

Sexting is a combination of sex and texting—the sending of sexually explicit messages or photos electronically, primarily between cell phones. In 2009, *ABC News* did a story about the consequences of sexting. Several students who thought the sexually explicit message was just for each other were shocked when they discovered the message had been shared. A 17-year-old was arrested for child pornography after he uploaded pictures of his 16-year-old girlfriend online. Reuter's News Service published an article in 2009 entitled "Safe 'Sexting?' No Such Thing, Teens Warned." The article states, "In the United States, a survey last fall (2008) found one in five teenagers said they had sent or posted online nude or semi-nude pictures of themselves and 39 percent said they had sent or posted sexually suggestive messages, according to the National Campaign to Prevent Teen and Unplanned Pregnancy."

Several states have proposed legislation to prevent sexting. The legislation is designed to help young Internet users avoid sexual predators, bullies, stalkers, and other dangerous contacts while interacting with friends through electronic devices. Sexting and related behaviors are also receiving attention at the federal level.

Once compromising photos are transmitted, they will never go away. Once something has been put into cyberspace, it is there forever. Just because it has been deleted from your phone doesn't mean it has been deleted from your service provider's servers or their backups. Those photos can (and sometimes do) come back to haunt those whose pictures were taken and those who transmitted them. So, stay away from questionable practices and practice safe texting.

SAFE TEXTING

WiredSafety (**www.wiredsafety.org**/), the world's largest Internet safety, help, and education resource, is a great source for information and resources on protecting yourself and others online. It provides guidance on creating a safe online presence, protecting yourself against cybercrime, and understanding cyberlaw.

Texting while driving is an international issue, and according to an article in the TimesOnline, it is more dangerous than driving under the influence of alcohol or drugs (Figure 5L). The reaction times for texters deteriorated by 35 percent, whereas the performance of those who drank alcohol at the legal limit decreased by only 12 percent. These statistics are not presented to suggest that you drink and drive. Rather, they suggest that you pay attention to the road. Avoid texting when you are:

- In motion: walking, running, jogging, riding a bike, skateboarding, skiing
- Sitting alone in a remote public place (where you could be surprised, robbed, or attacked by someone coming up behind you)
- Walking in crowds (where someone could come up behind you and either attack you or grab your purse or wallet)
- Driving

FIGURE 5L Texting and driving are a dangerous combination. Don't mix them!

Here are three more ways to make sure texting doesn't send you to the hospital:

- Always put your phone in an easily accessible place.
- If you need to text right away, stop what you're doing or pull off the road.
- Turn off your phone when you're doing something that requires your full attention.

Texting safely is not just avoiding texting while you are moving; it also includes protecting yourself. To guard yourself, don't send text messages to people you don't know. If you receive a text from a stranger, don't even open it. Delete it immediately. In addition, don't give out any personal information in a text message. Following these guidelines will start you on the road to safe texting.

Tagging

A **tag** is any user-generated word or phrase that helps organize Web content and label it in a more human way. You use tags when you want someone to find your Web page or blog. In Web development, they are called *metatags*. Using tags can bring your Web site to the top of the list when people are searching for specific content. For example, if you want someone to locate your blog on the latest way to fold napkins, you might use the tags: napkins, folding, napkin folding, and napkin folding techniques. This will help insure that your blog will show up on the list. In another meaning of the word, you may have been tagged in a photo posted on Facebook. Someone picks a photo and assigns names to the people or objects in the photo. Sometimes it is a real photo of your group and sometimes, for the novelty, it is a gag photo. You might see a lamppost tagged with the name of a friend. To tag a photo on Facebook, click on a person's face in the photo and then select their name in the box that pops up. If their name is not already in the box, you can provide it. Repeat this process for everyone in the photo. If you need to tag yourself, select "me."

A note about tagging: When you tag a friend in a photo, that photo will appear in their profile. If they don't want the photo in their profile, they can simply click "remove" next to their name. There are many Web sites where you can find group pictures and photos you can use for this purpose. Just remember turnabout is fair play.

Collaboration Tools

Web 2.0 has opened up a new world for online collaboration. **Collaboration tools** help you work in partnership with team members online. Working on a project is hard enough, but what happens when you need to share a document or idea? These tools provide a way to work together without having to physically meet. Virtual worlds are everywhere. There are many different types of collaboration tools. Some are free and some have a cost associated with them. Some are for a specific type of application such as project management, and some are a suite of applications.

One of the first of its kind is Google Apps, a suite that combines Gmail, Google Docs, Google Calendar, and other Web applications. Google hosts it all, providing space on its servers for you to save documents and collaborate. You can edit your documents from any device in the world as long as it has Internet access and can access Google Apps. Many companies and colleges are switching or have switched to these applications. For personal use, Google Apps includes:

- Gmail—Send and receive fast, searchable e-mail with less spam.
- Google Talk—IM and call your friends through your computer.
- Google Calendar—Organize your schedule and share events with friends.
- Google Docs—Share online documents, presentations, and spreadsheets.
- Google Sites—Create Web sites and secure group wikis.

Google Docs is a free, Web-based word processor, spreadsheet, presentation, and form application offered by Google (**http://docs.google.com**). This URL for Google Docs has information and a tour you can take to see how these applications can help you collaborate. Google Docs allows users to create and edit documents online while collaborating in real time with other users. You can create, edit, and upload the documents quickly. One handy feature is that you can import your existing documents, spreadsheets, and presentations, or create new ones from scratch. Many of the popular document extensions are accepted. With this software, you can access and edit your files from anywhere; all you need is a Web browser. Your documents, spreadsheets, and presentations are stored securely online. The collaboration feature is that you can share changes in real-time and invite people to view your documents and make changes together, at the same time.

"Web 2.0 has opened up a **new world** for online collaboration.**"**

Web 2.0 in the Classroom

Web 2.0 has many uses in the classroom. Forums and discussion boards are very, very useful. There has been some debate about the differences between these tools, but the commonality wins. They differ from a blog or a wiki because forums and discussion boards are threaded discussions in which someone asks a question or expresses an idea and others can add their thoughts or answers. Discussion boards are common on Learning Management Systems such as ANGEL or Blackboard, where the class meets in a virtual classroom instead of face-to-face. Some are formal discussions started by the professor; some are informal and are started by a classmate.

Forums and discussion boards can be monitored or unmonitored. When you post a comment to an article on a Web site, you may not see it posted until it has been cleared for content. If you have a hobby, you will probably be able to find a forum on that topic. Having a problem with something, such as your car not starting? You can find a forum on that. You name it, and there is most likely a forum on that topic. To locate a forum or discussion board directory, use your favorite search engine. If you were working on a team project and you sent an e-mail to each member, you would receive individual responses. Then you would have to take the time to put it all together. If you had taken advantage of a discussion board, all the responses would be in one place, where each of the team members can immediately read and respond to what the other members had to say.

Collaboration is very important in courses that have you doing team projects. You can use many tools for this. Podcasts on iTunes, videos on YouTube, and Web searches are all very relevant to today's classroom. To locate podcasts that can be used in the classroom, check the section on podcasts. And, don't forget blogs and wikis. Some professors are even exploring using Twitter in the classroom. They believe it has made the student and the classroom more productive; some disagree and have banned all computer and mobile access in the classroom.

The use of digital devices in the classroom is something that will be debated for years. Remember netiquette is applicable in the classroom. It is rude to have someone clicking keys while a serious discussion is going on, as is the sound you hear when you receive an IM. If you need to listen to something that is on your computer, be courteous and use headphones. Web 2.0 can enhance a classroom or subject, but be careful not to make it the only way you communicate in the classroom.

When the search engines online are not enough, along comes Rollyo. Do you have a group of Web sites that are your favorites? Or a set of online resources that you use frequently to answer homework or reference questions? Well, Rollyo (**www.rollyo.com/**) may be the tool for you. Rollyo allows you to create your own search tool for the just the Web sites you know and trust. It is a perfect application to help with your research papers.

> " To **locate** a forum or discussion board **directory**, use your favorite search engine. "

> " Some **professors** are even exploring using **Twitter** in the classroom. They believe it has made the student and the **classroom** more **productive**. "

Web 2.0 in Business

An article in *PC World* magazine states that more and more employers are checking social networking sites of potential employees. Careerbuilder.com has researched this and noted that although 24 percent of employers had hired a staff member based on his or her social networking profile, 33 percent had also decided *not* to make a job offer after reviewing the content on a profile. Use of drugs or drinking and the posting of photographs deemed inappropriate or provocative were identified as the most popular reasons why employers eliminated a candidate after viewing his or her social networking profile. So, be careful what you post on your social networking sites. Having a proper profile on Facebook or MySpace can be beneficial in your job search, as can having a professional LinkedIn page.

Similarly, many businesses are embracing Web 2.0 technologies for their Web sites. Consider Amazon.com. When you visit a book page on Amazon.com, a list of prices for that book on other sites pops up. This shows you, the buyer, other options.

Did you ever wonder who is looking at where you are traveling on the Internet? Those top five lists you do on Facebook—who really reads them? According to *Network World* magazine, LivingSocial, the company behind the application that lets you create the lists, is selling your Top 5 data to major entertainment outfits. When asked what LivingSocial does with all the data they collect from the Top 5 applications on Facebook, The CEO of LivingSocial said, "We go to marketers and say, 'Here are a couple million people into music, and here are a couple million into movies.' We're working with *American Idol*, Green Day, TNT, a lot of large brands." So not only are you sharing your Top 5 movies and books with your friends, you are potentially sharing that data with producers, rock bands, TV stations, and who knows what else. Businesses love this stuff and use the information in formulating marketing strategies.

Safety and Privacy

Here are some tips for safe social networking to help you have a good experience. After all, participating in online social networking sites leaves a trail of personal information that can make stealing your identity a whole lot easier.

- Beware of giving out too much information. You never want to share your social security number (including just the last four digits), your birth date, home address, or phone number. Protect all your passwords, PINs, bank account numbers, and credit card information.

- Use the privacy options. Don't let people who you do not know see your information.
- Don't trust, just verify. Verify the page belongs to who it says it does. For URLs and domain names, you can do this by going to **www.whois.com** and doing a WHOIS lookup. That will tell you who owns a domain name.
- Control comments. You can set comments so they can't be left anonymously. However, this will not stop people from using false names. Therefore, you may not want comments to post until you approve them.
- Avoid sharing personal details accidentally. Be careful about what information you list.
- Search yourself. It is a good idea to search your name on several search engines and to check your profile as others see it on the social networking sites.
- Don't violate your school or company's social networking policies. Be aware of the acceptable use policies (AUP) of your school or company, and follow them.

"The Web 3.0 browser will act like a personal assistant, learning what you are interested in as you browse."

- Learn how Web sites can use your information. Read the privacy statement.
- Don't play the popularity contest. There is no race to see who has the most friends. Do not invite strangers into your networks.
- Create smaller social networks. You may be better served by creating a smaller, more personal network using Ning.

Web 2.0 is an exciting concept. Use it, but be careful about abusing it. Protect yourself from fraud and you will be able to enjoy the benefits. So, what's next?

Web 3.0?

Some experts believe the next generation of the Web, **Web 3.0**, will make tasks like your search for movies and food faster and easier. Many of these experts believe that the Web 3.0 browser will act like a personal assistant, learning what you are interested in as you browse. The more you use the Web, the more your browser learns about you and the less specific you'll need to be with your questions.

Spotlight Exercises

1. With your instructor's permission, set up a classroom discussion board. Use it to discuss Web 2.0 and how you use it now and how you would use it once you are in the business world. Send the link to your instructor so he or she can follow the discussion. Write a one-page paper on the advantages and disadvantages of discussion boards.

2. In small groups of three or four, create a Ning page for your group. Each person in the classroom should set up an ID. Everyone should be invited to join each group. Take time to post to the page and share ideas. Add an event, chat with a classmate. Write a one-page paper on how you could use Ning in all your classes. How did you like the opportunity to set up your own social network?

3. To gain experience in setting up a community, create a blog related to a computer topic that interests you on one of the blogging sites and share the address with the class. If you created a Ning page, use it to share the address. Write a one-page paper detailing your blogging experience. What did you like and/or dislike? Be sure to comment on two of your classmates' blogs.

4. Google apps is not the only collaboration tool. For this exercise, take a look at a Web-based word processing tool called Zoho Writer (**www.zohowriter .com/**). Create a simple document and then document your discoveries in your blog. If you're up to the challenge, you might even export your document as an HTML file or publish it through Zoho to your blog.

   - Create a free account for yourself in Zoho Writer.
   - Explore the site and create a few test documents.
   - Try out Zoho Writer's features and create a blog post about your discoveries.

   Be sure to give your instructor your blog address or submit the document as directed.
   Optional: If you're up for the challenge, try using Zoho's "publish" options to post to your blog.

5. Using the Rollyo Web site, create an account for yourself. Explore the site. Then create a search roll for a project you need to complete in either this course or another. Create a post in your blog and link to your search roll. Can you see a potential use for tools like this? Write a one-page paper with your thoughts.

6. With RSS feeds becoming more popular, create and share your feeds. Create a free online Bloglines account (**www.bloglines.com/**) for yourself and subscribe to at least 10 newsfeeds to your reader using Bloglines tutorial steps 1 through 3 for instructions. You can search for the tutorial on Google videos. Once you have created your account, subscribe to several of your classmates' feeds. This is as easy as typing the blog URL into the subscribe field in Bloglines. Try it—it's easy! Then try adding a few other types of news feeds from news sources.

chapter 7

Networks: Communicating and Sharing Resources

Chapter Objectives

- Understand basic networking concepts. (p. 259)

- Discuss the advantages and disadvantages of networks. (p. 263)

- Distinguish between peer-to-peer and client/server local area networks (LANs). (p. 265)

- Define topology and understand how the three LAN topologies differ. (p. 266)

- Explain the importance of network protocols. (p. 268)

- Name the most widely used LAN protocol and its versions. (p. 270)

- Identify the special components of a wide area network (WAN) that differentiate it from a LAN. (p. 273)

- Contrast circuit-switching and packet-switching networks and explain their respective strengths and weaknesses. (p. 276)

- Identifying the options, components, configuration, and maintenance of a home area network (HAN). (p. 278)

Networking was a concept associated with the future or sci-fi movies, where everyone seemed to be able to communicate with each other by the use of simple portable devices. Well, it seems like sci-fi technology is here and here to stay. How do you communicate with your family members and friends? How do you communicate with your instructors? Are you aware of the technology involved when you communicate or transfer information to others by dialing a number or clicking a mouse? Understanding the technology that enables you to communicate with ease can be the link to being comfortable with the technology of the future. Do you overlook understanding the technology you use because it seems so simple to use?

Fast forward a few years and imagine that you are building a house. Everyone in your five-person family wants a computer, a printer, and an Internet connection. You could pay for five computers, five printers, and five Internet accounts. Or you could pay for five computers, one really good printer, one Internet account, and inexpensive network hardware so that everyone can share the printer and the Internet connection. If you think the second option makes sense, you've just joined the huge and growing number of people who've discovered the benefits of networking.

Businesses of all sizes are already convinced that networking is a great idea. They're spending billions of dollars annually on networking equipment. The benefits of networking go far beyond saving money on shared peripherals. Networks enable organizations to create massive, centralized pools of information, which are vital to performing their mission. In addition, networks enable people to communicate and collaborate in ways that were not possible before computers could be connected to each other (Figure 7.1).

As an informed and literate computer user, you need to know enough about networking to understand the benefits and possibilities of connecting computers. In addition, learning about networking is a good idea for anyone looking for a job these days; employers like to hire workers who understand basic networking concepts. This chapter presents essential networking concepts and explains the basic networking terms you'll need to know to discuss the subject intelligently.

Network Fundamentals

Computer networking is essential to businesses and has become popular with many home users too. The concepts behind computer networking are easy to understand: Computer networking is all about getting connected.

A **network** is a group of two or more computer systems linked together to exchange data and share resources, including expensive peripherals such as high performance laser printers (Figure 7.2).

Computer networks for business and organizations fall into two categories: local area networks and wide area networks. A **local area network (LAN)** uses cables, radio waves, or infrared signals to link computers or peripherals, such as printers, within a small geographic area, such as a building or a group of buildings. A **wide area network (WAN)** uses long-distance transmission media to link computers separated by a few miles or even thousands of miles. The Internet is the largest WAN—it connects millions of LANs all over the globe.

A network needs communications devices to convert data into signals that can travel over a physical (wired) or wireless medium. **Communications devices**

FIGURE 7.2 People use networks to share data and resources.

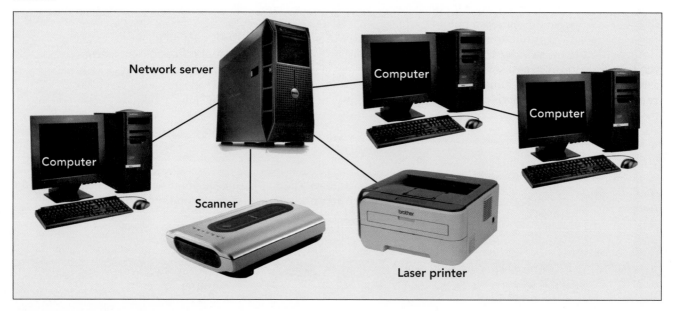

Network server

Computer

Computer

Computer

Scanner

Laser printer

include computers, modems, routers, switches, wireless access points, and network interface cards. These devices transform data from analog to digital signals and back again, determine efficient data-transfer pathways, boost signal strength, and facilitate digital communication (Figure 7.3).

Any device connected to a network is referred to as a **node**. A node can be any computer, peripheral (such as a printer or scanner), or communication device (such as a modem). Each node on the network has a unique **logical address**, or name, assigned by the software in use, as well as a unique numeric or **physical address**, called the Data Link Control address, Data Link Control identifier (DLCI), or Media Access Control (MAC) address, which is built into the hardware. Depending on the format of the network, the DLCI, MAC address, or logical address can be used to identify the node.

A computer needs a network interface card to connect to a network. **Network interface cards (NICs)** are expansion boards that fit into a computer's expansion slots, or adaptors built into the motherboard. They provide the electronic components to make the connection between a computer and the network (Figure 7.4). Today's desktop computers usually include NICs, and most notebook computers have wireless NICs.

In addition to your data passing through a NIC card to get to and from a network, there is a high probability it has also passed through such devices as routers, switches, and wireless access points on its network journey from source to destination. A **router** is a complex device, or in some cases software, that is used to connect two or more networks. Routers have the capability to determine the best path to route data and locate alternative pathways so that the data reaches its destination. **Switches** are devices that filter and forward data between computers, printers, and other network nodes, enabling them to talk to each other. Switches are similar to routers but are used only to move data between nodes within a single network. A **wireless access point**, also known as an **AP** or **WAP**, is a node on a network that acts as a receiver and transmitter of wireless radio signals between other nodes on a network. A WAP can also act as a joint or bridge connecting wireless nodes to a wired network (Figure 7.5).

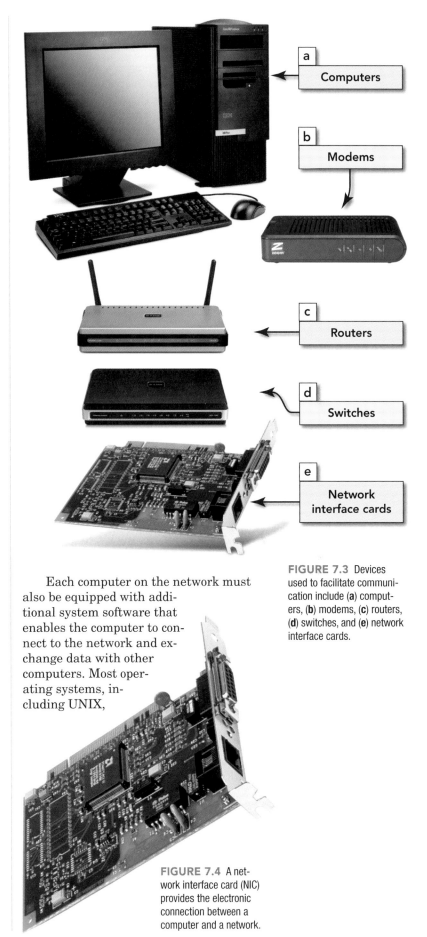

FIGURE 7.3 Devices used to facilitate communication include (**a**) computers, (**b**) modems, (**c**) routers, (**d**) switches, and (**e**) network interface cards.

Each computer on the network must also be equipped with additional system software that enables the computer to connect to the network and exchange data with other computers. Most operating systems, including UNIX,

FIGURE 7.4 A network interface card (NIC) provides the electronic connection between a computer and a network.

Networks: Communicating and Sharing Resources **261**

Linux, Windows, and Mac OS, now include such software in their standard installations. Most business networks also typically include one or more **servers**, a computer or device with software that manages network resources like files, e-mails, printers, and databases. The most common type of server is the **file server**, a high-capacity, high-speed computer with a large hard disk. A file server is set aside (dedicated) to make program and data files available to users on a network that have been granted access permission. The file server also contains the **network operating system (NOS)**, an operating system designed to enable data transfer and application usage between computers and other devices connected to a local area network. A network operating system, such as Novell SUSE or Microsoft Windows Server 2008, is a complex program that requires skilled technicians to install and manage it. A network operating system provides the following:

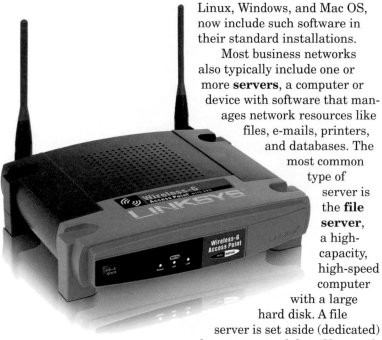

FIGURE 7.5 A wireless access point is commonly used as a bridge between a wireless and a wired network.

- File directories that make it easy to locate files and resources on the LAN
- Automated distribution of software updates to the desktop computers on the LAN
- Support for Internet services such as access to the World Wide Web and e-mail
- Protection of services and data located on the network
- Access to connected hardware by authorized network users

In addition to a network's special hardware and software, people are also necessary for the proper functioning of a network. **Network administrators** (sometimes called *network engineers*) install, maintain, and support computer networks (Figure 7.6). They interact with users, handle security, and troubleshoot problems.

FIGURE 7.6 Network administrators are essential to the efficient management of networks.

A network administrator's most important task is granting access to the network. In most cases, a network user logs into a network by providing a user name and a password. When logged in, the user has access to his or her folders that reside on the server and possibly other people's folders and files. The user may also have the right to use peripheral devices on the network, such as printers, and the Internet. The network administrator sets permissions for which files, folders, and network devices a user has the right to use based on such items as the division of the organization the user is employed, the level of security clearance the user holds, and the confidentiality of the data itself.

As you read through this chapter, note that some of the concepts discussed apply to local networking, in which all of the computers and peripherals are locally connected, whereas others apply to networks that are made up of computers and peripherals that may be tens or hundreds of miles apart. For some additional information on LANs, WANs, and networks in general visit **http://compnetworking. about.com/cs/basicnetworking/f/ whatsnetworking.htm**.

What's the point of having a computer network instead of many standalone computers and peripherals? Let's look at some of the benefits as well as the risks of networking.

Advantages and Disadvantages of Networking

When you connect two or more computers, you see gains in every aspect of computing, especially with regard to efficiency and costs:

- **Reduced hardware costs.** Networks reduce costs because users can share expensive equipment. For example, dozens of users on a network can share a high-capacity printer, storage devices, and a common connection to the Internet.
- **Application sharing.** Networks enable users to share software. Network versions of applications installed on a file server can be used by more than one user at a time. For example, companies that have implemented server-based order-tracking programs that enable their sales representatives to upload orders from their notebook computers have found that the salespeople gained up to 20 percent more time to focus on their customers' needs.
- **Sharing information resources.** Organizations can use networks to create common pools of data that employees can access. At publisher Pearson Education, for example, book designers can use the network to access a vast archive of illustrations, greatly reducing the amount of time spent tracking down appropriate photographs for textbooks and other publishing projects.
- **Centralized data management.** Data stored on a network can be accessed by multiple users. Organizations can ensure the security and integrity of the data on the network with security software and password protection. Centralized storage also makes it easier to maintain consistent backup procedures and develop disaster recovery strategies.
- **Connecting people.** Networks create powerful new ways for people to work together. For example, workers can use groupware applications to create a shared calendar for scheduling purposes. Team members can instantly see who's available at a given day and time. What's more, these people don't have to work in the same building. They can be located at various places around the world and still function effectively as a team.

The advantages of networks are offset by some disadvantages:

- **Loss of autonomy.** When you become a part of a network, you become a part of a community of users. Sometimes this means that you have to give up personal freedoms for the good of the group. For example, a network administrator may impose restrictions on what software you can load onto network computers.
- **Lack of privacy.** Network membership can threaten your privacy. Network administrators can access your files and may monitor your network and Internet activities.
- **Security threats.** Because some personal information is inevitably stored on network servers, it is possible that others may gain unauthorized access to your files, user names, and even your passwords.
- **Loss of productivity.** As powerful as networks are, they still fail. Access to resources is sometimes restricted or unavailable because of viruses, hacking, sabotage, or a simple breakdown. Data loss can be minimized by good backup practices, but waiting for your data to be restored is an inconvenience or, worse yet, a direct threat to your ability to produce work on time.

> "When you **connect** two or more computers, you see **gains** in every aspect of **computing**, especially with regard to **efficiency** and **costs**."

Now that you know the benefits and risks of using networks, let's look at the specific types of networks.

Local Area Networks

Have you ever walked into your dorm, your school's computer lab, or your office at work and wondered how all of the separate computers in each room, seat, or office are able to work at the same time? The answer is through a local area network. A home network is also an example of a LAN. It comprises two or more computers that communicate with each other and with peripheral devices such as a printer or cable modem (Figure 7.7).

LANs transform individual hardware devices into what appears to be one gigantic computer system. From any computer on the LAN, you can access any data, software, or peripherals (such as fax machines, printers, or scanners) that are on the network.

With a **wireless LAN**, users access and connect to other nodes on the network through radio waves instead of wires. Wireless LANs come in handy when users need to move around in or near a building. In Veterans Administration hospitals, for example, wireless LANs help hospital personnel track the distribution of controlled substances, a job that's both time-consuming and prone to error without a computer's help. Nurses use bedside computers that are connected to the network through wireless signals to track the administration and dosage of these controlled substances. This form of data sharing on the network protects the patient from receiving an unauthorized drug or unsuitable quantity of an authorized drug. Most colleges have installed wireless LANs to serve students seamlessly as they move around the campus. These campus networks enable students to receive e-mail and access the Internet while having lunch or lounging in the common room of a dorm. A student does not have to be at a desk in his or her own room to have use of these features.

Many wireless LANs ensure security with a radio transmission technique that spreads signals over a seemingly random series of frequencies. Only the receiving device knows the series, so it isn't easy to eavesdrop on the signals. A conscientious user should still look into using encryption software to guarantee a higher level of protection. Radio-based wireless LAN signals have an effective range of between 125 and 300 feet.

FIGURE 7.7 Setting up a LAN for the home enables everyone to use the available resources.

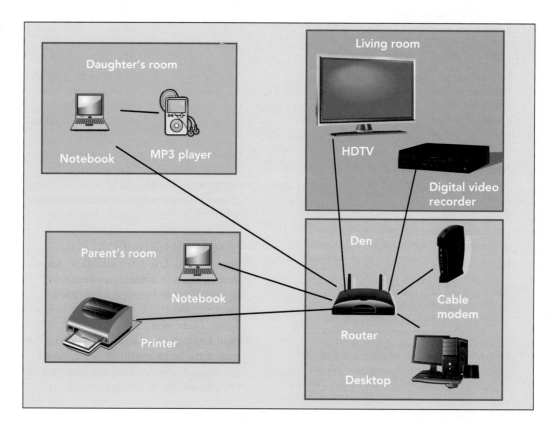

Whether wired or wireless, LANs can be differentiated by the networking model they use: peer-to-peer or client/server.

PEER-TO-PEER NETWORKS

In a **peer-to-peer (P2P) network**, all of the computers on the network are equals, or peers—that's where the term *peer-to-peer* comes from—and there's no file server. But there is file sharing, in which each computer user decides which, if any, files will be accessible to other users on the network. Users also may choose to share entire directories or even entire disks. They also can choose to share peripherals, such as printers and scanners.

P2P networks are easy to set up; people who aren't networking experts do it all the time, generally to share an expensive laser printer or to provide Internet access to all of the computers on the LAN (Figure 7.8). P2P networks are often used for home networks or small businesses. They do not require a NOS (network operating system) and can be set up with most operating systems in use today. They tend to slow down as the number of users increases, and keeping track of all of the shared files and peripherals can quickly become confusing. Most importantly, security is not strong due to the lack of hierarchy among the participants. For this reason, peer-to-peer LANs are best used for simple networks connecting no more than 10 computers.

P2P networking gained notoriety when Napster, a peer-to-peer music file-sharing site, was sued for copyright infringement. Since then, other sites, like Kazaa and LimeWire, that claim their P2P network is just like sharing a music or movie CD with a friend, have also lost similar battles with the entertainment industry. Current proposed legislation is seeking to hold colleges and universities responsible for monitoring students' downloads, and ISPs are in contention with sites like BitTorrent because of the large amount of bandwidth taken up by users sharing videos.

However, not everybody wants to stop P2P music swapping. Some artists offer free downloads in hopes that fans will share the files with friends and buy more songs. Some companies are even sponsoring music downloads that link their products with promising new groups and build goodwill as the groups' music files move from computer to computer. P2P networks are good for sharing more than

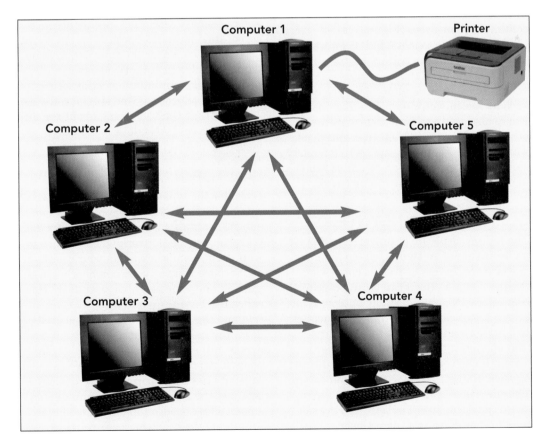

FIGURE 7.8 Peer-to-peer networks enable users to share resources equally.

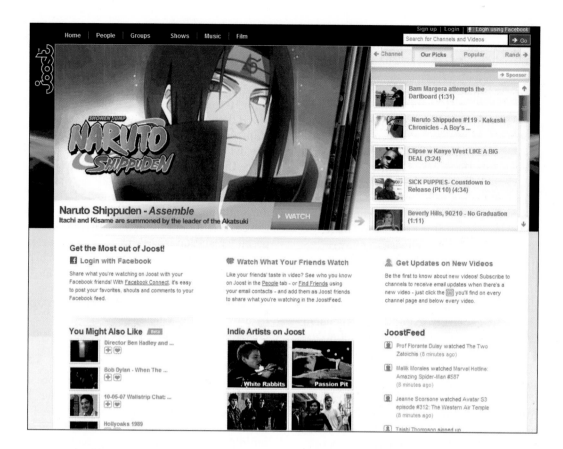

music. Legitimate companies such as Skype (**www.skype.com**) or Joost (**www.joost.com**) use the power of P2P technology to provide Voice over IP (VoIP) phone service and streaming television content to their users (Figure 7.9).

If you decide to join a P2P network, give some thought to privacy and security. Unless you read all the fine print before you download free versions of programs such as Kazaa, you may not realize that you're also getting adware, spyware, and other files. Be sure to keep your antivirus software up-to-date to avoid getting a nasty surprise in the form of infected files from another computer on the P2P network.

CLIENT/SERVER NETWORKS

The typical corporate or university LAN is a **client/server network**, which includes one or more servers as well as clients (Figure 7.10). A **client** can be any type of computer—PC, Mac, desktop, notebook, or even a handheld device—that is connected to a network and contains the software that enables it to send requests to the server. It can connect via modem, dedicated physical connection, or wireless connection. The client/server model works with any size or physical layout of LAN and doesn't tend to slow down with heavy use.

VIRTUAL PRIVATE NETWORK (VPN)

Many businesses use a **virtual private network (VPN)** to provide their employees and customers with quick, secure access to corporate information. A VPN operates as a private network over the Internet, making data accessible to authorized users in remote locations through the use of secure, encrypted connections and special software.

Now that you've learned about the different types of LANs, let's look at their various physical layouts.

LAN TOPOLOGIES

Consider the typical college dorm or corporate office. Each separate room, office, or cubicle contains a computer. How does data travel across the network when you are in your dorm room working on your computer at the same time as your neighbor across the hall and your neighbor next door? How can you all use the same Internet connection and the printer in the common area down the hall at the same time? It all depends on the type of network topology in place. The physical layout of a LAN is called its **network topology**. A topology isn't just the arrangement of computers in a particular space; a topology provides a solution to the problem of **contention**,

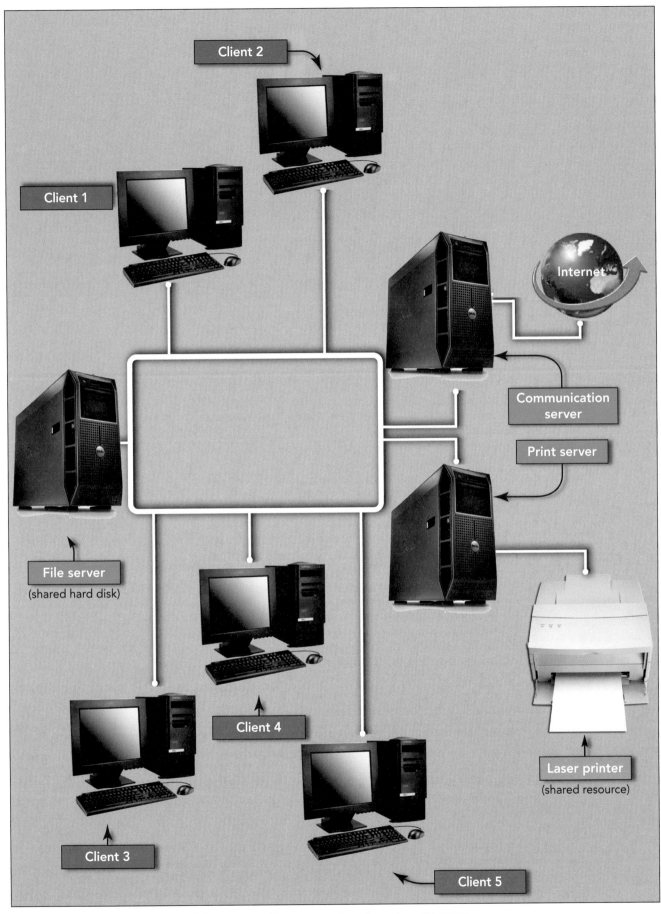

Client 2

Client 1

Internet

Communication
server

Print server

File server
(shared hard disk)

Client 4

Laser printer
(shared resource)

Client 3

Client 5

FIGURE 7.10 A client/server network includes one or more file servers as well as other nodes on the network.

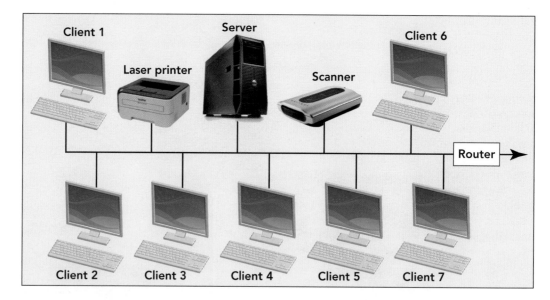

which occurs when two computers try to access the LAN at the same time. Contention sometimes results in **collisions**, the corruption of network data caused when two computers transmit simultaneously.

With a **bus topology**, the network cable is a single conduit that forms a bus, or line; every node, whether it is a computer or peripheral device, is attached to that bus (Figure 7.11). At the ends of the bus, special connectors called **terminators** signify the end of the circuit. With a bus topology, only one node can transmit at a time. If more than one node tries to send data at the same time, each node waits a small, random amount of time and then attempts to retransmit the data. Other limitations of a bus topology include length restrictions because of the loss of signal strength and practical limits as to the number of nodes attached because of increases in contention caused by each added node. On the plus side, bus networks are simple, reliable, and easy to expand. The bus topology is practical in a relatively small environment such as a home or small office.

To resolve the contention problem, bus networks use some type of **contention management**, a technique that specifies what happens when a collision occurs. A common contention-management technique is to abandon any data that could have been corrupted by a collision.

A **star topology** solves the expansion problems of the bus topology with a central wiring device, which can be a **hub** (simple broadcast device that does not manage traffic and usually results in frequent collisions), switch, or computer (Figure 7.12). Adding users is simple; you just run a cable to the hub or switch and

plug the new user into a vacant connector. Star networks also generally use contention management to deal with collisions. The star topology is ideal for office buildings, computer labs, and WANs. The down side of a star topology is that the loss of the hub, switch, or central computer, caused by a power outage or virus invasion, can bring down the entire network.

With a **ring topology**, all of the nodes are attached in a circular wiring arrangement. This topology, not in common use today, provides a unique way to prevent collisions (Figure 7.13). A special unit of data called a **token** travels around the ring. A node can transmit only when it possesses the token. Although ring networks are circular in that the token travels a circular path, they look more like star networks because all of the wiring is routed to a central switch. The ring topology is well suited for use within a division of a company or on one floor of a multifloor office building.

LAN PROTOCOLS

In addition to the physical or wireless transmission media that carry the network's signals, a network also uses **protocols** (standards or rules) that enable network-connected devices to communicate with each other. Protocols may be implemented by hardware, software, or a combination of the two.

Protocols can be compared to the manners you were taught when you were a child. When you were growing up, you were taught to use appropriate comments, such as "It's nice to meet you," when you met someone in a social situation. The other person was taught to reply, "It's nice to meet you, too." Such exchanges serve to get communication going. Network protocols are similar. They are fixed, formalized exchanges that specify how two dissimilar network components can establish a communication.

All of the communications devices in a network conform to different protocols. Take modems, for example. To establish communications, modems must conform to standards called **modulation protocols**, which ensure that your modem can communicate with an-other modem even if the second modem was made by a different manufacturer.

Several modulation protocols are in common use. Each protocol specifies all of the necessary details of communication, including the data transfer rate, or the rate at which two modems can exchange data. The protocol also includes standards for data compression and error checking.

Two modems can communicate only if both follow the same modulation protocol. When a modem attempts to establish a con-nection, it automatically negotiates with the modem on the other end. The two modems try to establish which protocols they share and the fastest data transfer rate that each is capable of. When that is established, data will be transferred at the fastest speed the slower modem is capable of.

A single network may use dozens of protocols. The complete package of proto-cols that specify how a specific network functions is called the network's **protocol suite**. Collectively, a protocol suite specifies how the network functions, or its **network architecture**. The term *architecture* may sound daunting, but in the next section you'll learn that the basic idea isn't much more complicated than a layer cake.

Network Layers Because they're complex systems, networks use a network architec-ture that is divided into separate **network** **layers**. Each network layer has a function that can be isolated and treated separately from other layers. Because each layer's protocols precisely define how each layer passes data to another layer, it's possible

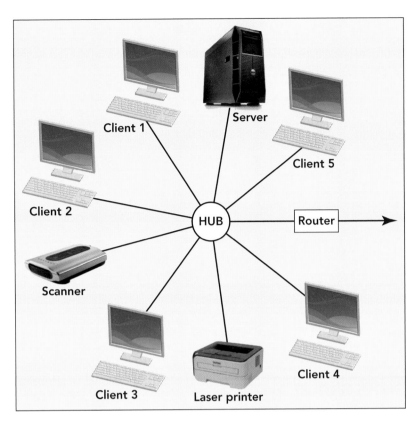

FIGURE 7.12 A central wiring design makes it easy to connect a new user in a star topology.

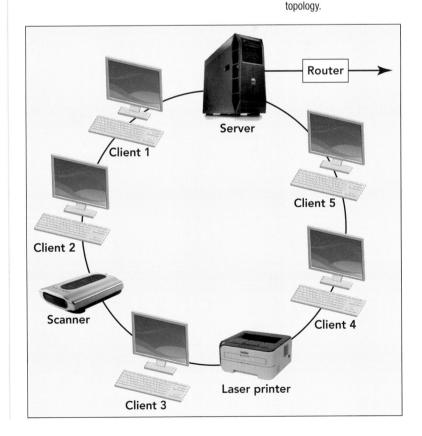

FIGURE 7.13 All nodes are attached in a circular wiring arrangement in a ring topology.

to make changes within a layer without having to rebuild the entire network.

How do layers work? To understand the layer concept, it's helpful to remember that protocols are like manners, which enable people to get communication going. Let's look at an example.

Suppose you're sending an e-mail message. Now imagine that each protocol is a person, and each person has an office on a separate floor of a multistory office building. You're on the top floor, and the network connection is in the basement. When you send your message, your e-mail client software calls the person on the next floor down: "Excuse me, but would you please translate this message into a form the server can process?" The person on the floor below replies, "Sure, no problem." That person then calls the person on the next floor down: "If it isn't too much trouble, would you please put this translated message in an envelope and address it to such-and-such computer?" And so it goes, until the message finally reaches the physical transmission medium, the hardware layer, which connects the computers in the network.

At the receiving computer, precisely the opposite happens. The message is received by the hardware in the basement and is sent up. It's taken out of its envelope, translated, and handed up to the top floor, where it's acted on.

To summarize, a network message starts at the top of a stack of layers and moves down through the various layers

until it reaches the bottom (the physical medium). Because the layers are arranged vertically like the floors in an office building, and because each is governed by its own protocols, the layers are called a **protocol stack**. On the receiving end, the process is reversed: The received message goes up the protocol stack. First, the network's data envelope is opened, and the data is translated until it can be used by the receiving application. Figure 7.14 illustrates this concept.

LAN Technologies By far the most popular LAN standard for large and small businesses is **Ethernet**. The various versions of Ethernet are used by approximately 90 percent of all LANs.

Ethernet uses a protocol called Carrier Sense Multiple Access/Collision Detection, or CSMA/CD. Using the CSMA/CD protocol, a computer looks for an opportunity to place a data unit of a fixed size, called a **packet**, onto the network and then sends it on

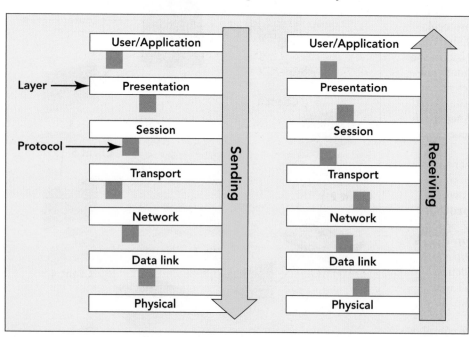

FIGURE 7.14 Open System Interconnection (OSI) model defines a networking framework for implementing protocols in seven layers.

its way. Each packet contains a header that indicates the address of the origin and destination of the data being transmitted. Every time a packet reaches its destination, the sender gets confirmation, and the computer waits for a gap to open to shoot off another packet. Devices along the way read the address and pass the packet along to the next device, routing it toward its destination. Occasionally, two devices send a packet into the same gap at the same time, resulting in a collision and the loss of both packets, but only for the moment. When packets collide, the computers that sent them are instantly notified, and each chooses a random interval to wait before it resends the packet. This approach helps prevent network gridlock.

Although early versions of Ethernet (called 10Base2 and 10Base5) used coaxial cable in bus networks, the most popular versions today are Ethernet star networks that use switches and twisted-pair wire. Currently, three versions of Ethernet are in use: 10Base-T (10 Mbps), Fast Ethernet (100 Mbps, also called 100Base-T), and Gigabit Ethernet. The hardware needed to create a 10Base-T Ethernet for five PCs can cost as little as $200. The newest version, 10 Gigabit Ethernet, is making possible next-generation applications such as

"Ten Gigabit **Ethernet** is making possible next-generation applications such as **cloud computing**, server **virtualization**, **network convergence**, and **multicasting**."

cloud computing, server virtualization, network convergence, and multicasting.

These superfast connections are often used to create large metropolitan and regional networks because they prevent data bottlenecks. To learn more about Ethernet, check out Charles Spurgeon's Ethernet Web site at **www.ethermanage. com/ethernet/ ethernet.html**. The site covers all of the Ethernet technologies in use today and includes a practical guide for do-it-yourselfers. Figure 7.15 provides a comparison of several popular LAN protocols.

Wi-Fi Wi-Fi is a wireless LAN standard that offers Ethernet speeds through the use of radio waves instead of wires. Wi-Fi networks, even though wireless, still need a central server, or access point. In other words, with Wi-Fi technology computers can communicate with each other, but to access the Internet or to communicate across distances, a central access point is required. Wireless routers sold for home use contain a wireless access point inside the router. The router also has an omnidirectional antenna to receive the data transmitted by wireless transceivers. External Wi-Fi transceivers connect to desktop computers through USB connections, whereas most notebooks are equipped with built-in wireless network adapters.

FIGURE 7.15 Popular LAN Protocols

Protocol Name	Data Transfer Rate	Physical Media	Topology
Ethernet (10Base-T)	10 Mbps	Twisted-pair cable	Star
Fast Ethernet (100Base-T)	100 Mbps	Twisted-pair or fiber-optic cable	Star
Gigabit Ethernet	1,000 Mbps	Fiber-optic cable	Star
10 Gigabyte Ethernet	6.375 Gbps	Fiber-optic cable	Star
IBM Token Ring Network	4–16 Mbps	Twisted-pair cable	Ring

FIGURE 7.16 Popular Wireless Networking Standards

Standard	Frequency	Transmission Speed	Comments
802.11a	5 GHz	Up to 54 Mbps	Fast, low interference, short range, doesn't work well indoors
802.11b	2.4 GHz	Up to 11 Mbps	Low cost, replaced by faster standards
802.11g	2.4 GHz	Up to 54 Mbps	Fast, backward compatible with 802.11b
802.11n (draft)	2.4 GHz and/ or 5 GHZ	Up to 540 Mbps	Improved speed and range, operates on both frequencies, backward compatible with 802.11a/b/g standards
802.11r	2.4 GHZ and/ or 5 GHz	Up to 540 Mbps	An amendment to the 802.11 standard that governs the way roaming mobile clients communicate with access points. It will speed up the handoff of data between access points or cells in a wireless LAN to less than 50 ms (milliseconds), greatly improving VOIP or Internet-based telephony.
802.15	2.4 GHz	Up to 50 Mbps	Used for Bluetooth technology, very short range (up to 10 meters)
802.16	2–11 GHz	Up to 70 Mbps	WiMax provides high-speed wireless Internet access over long distances (more than 30 miles)

Wi-Fi uses the 802.11 wireless networking standard and transmits on the 2.4-GHz or 5-GHz radio frequency band. There are currently five 802.11 standards (Figure 7.16). The 802.11g standard is the most common, with 802.11n and 802.11r being the newest standards.

Although Wi-Fi is convenient, there are some security risks. Wired networks require a computer or other device to be physically connected, but wireless networks broadcast radio waves that can be picked up by anyone using the correct configuration. These signals can extend beyond the walls of your home or office, so it is important to properly secure your network and data. To safeguard your network do the following:

- Always use a firewall and updated antivirus and antispyware software.
- Change the router's default network name, also known as an SSID, and the default password.
- If possible, turn off SSID broadcasting to avoid detection by hackers.
- Ensure your router's software has been upgraded to the most recent version.

- Turn on WPA (Wi-Fi Protected Access) to enable encryption.
- Turn on MAC (Media Access Control) address filtering so only authorized devices can obtain access.

Similarly, when using a public wireless access location, known as a **hot spot**, you should take the following precautions:

- Be aware of your surroundings—ensure no one is watching over your shoulder for logon and password information.
- Be sure to log on to the correct wireless network, not a look-alike or so-called evil twin network.
- Disable file and printer sharing.
- Don't transmit confidential data—if you must, be sure to use encryption.
- Turn off your wireless access when it is not in use.

Whether wired or wireless, LANs enable an organization to share computing resources in a single building or across a group of buildings. However, a LAN's geographic limitations pose a problem.

Today, many organizations need to share computing resources with distant branch offices, employees who are traveling, and even people outside the organization, including suppliers and customers. This is what wide area networks (WANs) are used for—to link computers separated by even thousands of miles.

Wide Area Networks

Like LANs, WANs have all of the basic network components—cabling, protocols, and devices—for routing information to the correct destination. WANs are like long-distance telephone systems. In fact, much WAN traffic is carried by long-distance voice communication providers and cable companies. So you can picture a WAN as a LAN that has long-distance communications needs among its servers, computers, and peripherals. Let's look at the special components of WANs that differentiate them from LANs: a point of presence and backbones.

POINT OF PRESENCE

To carry computer data over the long haul, a WAN must be locally accessible. Like long-distance phone carriers or ISPs, WANs have what amounts to a local access number, called a point of presence. A **point of presence (POP)** is a wired or wireless WAN network connection point that enables users to access the WAN. To provide availability to it users, WANs have a POP in as many towns and cities as needed. However, in many rural areas, POPs may still not be available, reducing a potential subscriber's choices and ability to connect.

BACKBONES

The LANs and WANs that make up the Internet are connected to the Internet backbone. **Backbones** are the high-capacity transmission lines that carry WAN traffic. A variety of physical media are used for backbone services, including microwave relays, satellites, and dedicated telephone lines. Some backbones are regional, connecting towns and cities in a region such as Southern California or New England. Others are continental, or even transcontinental, in scope (Figure 7.17).

A **gigaPoP (gigabits per second points of presence)** is a POP that provides access to a backbone service capable of data transfer rates exceeding 1 Gbps (1 billion bits per second). These network connection points link to high-speed networks that have been developed by federal agencies. Whatever their scope, backbones are designed to carry huge amounts of data traffic. Cross-country Internet backbones, for example, can handle up to 13 Gbps, and much higher speeds are on the way.

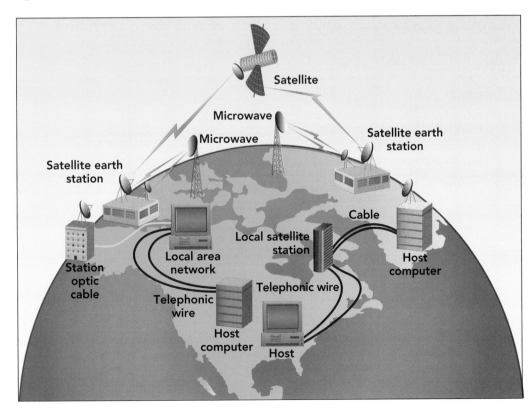

FIGURE 7.17
Backbones can connect local regions, continents, and even expand in scope to connect transcontinental destinations.

Make a Difference: Lend Your Computer to Science

You can help save the planet, save lives, or find new life in space by offering your computer's idle time to science. Distributed computing, in which networked computers work on small pieces of large complex tasks, is revolutionizing research in a number of areas. Nearly 5 million computer users are already lending their computing power to a variety of diverse projects. Climateprediction.net (**http://climateprediction.net**) is attempting to forecast the climate for the 21st century (Figure 7.18). The Folding@home (**http://folding.stanford.edu**) project studies the behavior of human proteins, and SETI@home (**http://setiathome.berkeley.edu**) analyzes radio signals in the search for extraterrestrial life. The combined power of these networked computers is equivalent to years of supercomputer time—an enormous help to nonprofits with limited resources but ambitious goals. If you volunteer your computing power to any of these causes, be sure to take the necessary security precautions to safeguard your system.

To volunteer your computer, you will need to download and install a special screen saver program. If this software detects that your computer is on and not busy with something else, it uses your Internet connection to reach the research center's server, downloads numbers to crunch or data to sift, and then submits the results to the server. At the other end, the research center's computer assembles all of these bite-size answers to complete one task and then parcels out pieces of the next task. Your computer's spare computing power may be used dozen of times daily or just a few days a week, depending on what the scientists are working on at that time. To see how much computing time your computer has contributed, you can check the screensaver or the project's Web site.

Many of these research projects use the Berkeley Open Infrastructure for Network Computing (BOINC; **http://boinc.berkeley.edu**) as their software platform, which means that your computer can work on multiple

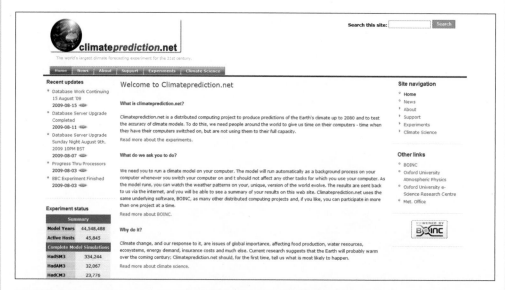

FIGURE 7.18 Volunteer your computer's spare time to help predict the Earth's climate up to the year 2080.

(Continued)

projects by using just a single screen saver. Current statistics on users and the percentage of computing power being donated to a project are displayed in the upper right corner of the Web site's home page

(Figure 7.19). If you decide to get involved, you will need to update your security program regularly to protect against hackers. Is distributed computing in your future? ●

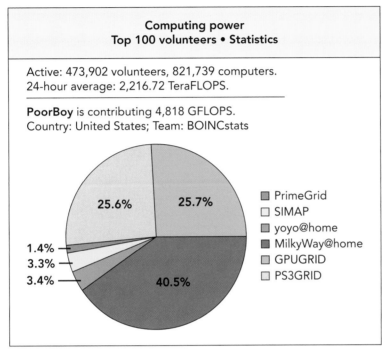

Computing power
Top 100 volunteers • Statistics

Active: 473,902 volunteers, 821,739 computers.
24-hour average: 2,216.72 TeraFLOPS.

PoorBoy is contributing 4,818 GFLOPS.
Country: United States; Team: BOINCstats

- PrimeGrid
- SIMAP
- yoyo@home
- MilkyWay@home
- GPUGRID
- PS3GRID

25.6% 25.7% 1.4% 3.3% 3.4% 40.5%

FIGURE 7.19 Statistics on distribution of the computing power donated by the top 100 volunteers are continuously updated and displayed on the Boinc home page.

To understand how data travels over a WAN, it helps to understand how data travels over the largest WAN, the Internet. This journey can be compared to an interstate car trip. When you connect to the Internet and request access to a Web page, your request travels by local connections—the city streets—to your ISP's local POP. From there, your ISP relays your request to the regional backbone—a highway. Your request then goes to a network access point—a highway on-ramp—where regional backbones connect with national backbone networks. And from there, the message gets on the national backbone network—the interstate. When your request nears its destination, your message gets off the national backbone network and travels regional and local networks until it reaches its destination.

WAN PROTOCOLS

Like any computer network, WANs use protocols. For example, the Internet uses more than 100 protocols that specify every aspect of Internet usage, such as how to retrieve documents through the Web or send e-mail to a distant computer. Internet data can travel over any type of WAN because of Internet protocols.

The Internet Protocols The Internet protocols, collectively called **TCP/IP**, are open protocols that define how the Internet works. TCP/IP is an abbreviation for Transmission Control Protocol (TCP)/ Internet Protocol (IP). However, more than 100 protocols make up the entire Internet protocol suite.

Of all of the Internet protocols, the most fundamental one is the **Internet**

Protocol (IP) because it defines the Internet's addressing scheme, which enables any Internet-connected computer to be uniquely identified. IP is a connectionless protocol. This means that with IP, two computers don't have to be online at the same time to exchange data. The sending computer just keeps trying until the message gets through.

Because IP enables direct and immediate contact with any other computer on the network, the Internet bears some similarity to the telephone system (although the Internet works on different principles). Every computer on the Internet has an **Internet address**, or **IP address** (similar to a phone number). A computer can exchange data with any other Internet-connected computer by "dialing" the other computer's address. An IP address has four parts, which are separated by periods (such as 128.254.108.7).

The **Transmission Control Protocol (TCP)** defines how one Internet-connected computer can contact another to exchange control and confirmation messages. You can see TCP in action when you use the Web; just watch your browser's status bar. You'll see messages such as "Contacting server," "Receiving data," and "Closing connection."

Circuit and Packet Switching WAN protocols are based on either circuit- or packet-switching network technology, but most use packet switching. The Internet uses packet switching, whereas the public switched telephone network (PSTN) uses circuit switching. Still, the Internet does for computers what the telephone system does for phones: It enables any Internet-connected computer to connect almost instantly and effortlessly with any other Internet-connected computer anywhere in the world.

With **circuit switching**, the method used in the public switched telephone system, there is a direct connection between the communicating devices. Data is sent over a physical end-to-end circuit between the sending and receiving computers. Circuit switching works best when

> **"Packet switching** is more **efficient** and less expensive than circuit switching. What's more, packet-switching networks are more **reliable.**"

avoiding delivery delays is essential. In a circuit-switching network, high-speed electronic switches handle the job of establishing and maintaining the connection.

With **packet switching**, the method used for computer communication, no effort is made to create a single direct connection between the two communicating devices. The sending computer's outgoing message is divided into packets (Figure 7.20). Each packet is numbered and addressed to the destination computer. The packets then travel to a router, which examines each packet it detects. After reading the packet's address, the router consults a table of possible pathways that the packet can take to get to its destination. If more than one path exists, the router sends the packet along the path that is most free of congestion. The packets may not all take the same path or arrive in the order they were sent, but that's not a problem. On the receiving computer, protocols put the packets in the correct order and decode the message they contain. If any packets are missing, the receiving computer sends a message requesting retransmission of the missing packet.

So which type of switching is best? Compared with circuit switching, packet switching has many advantages. It's more efficient and less expensive than circuit switching. What's more, packet-switching networks are more reliable. A packet-switching network can function even if portions of the network aren't working.

However, packet switching does have some drawbacks. When a router examines a packet, it delays the packet's progress by a tiny fraction of a second. In a huge packet-switching network—such as the Internet—a given packet may be examined by many routers, which introduces a noticeable delay called **latency**. If the network experiences **congestion** (overloading), some of the packets may be further delayed, and the message can't be decoded until all of its packets are received. For these reasons, packet switching is not well suited to the delivery of real-time voice and video.

FIGURE 7.20 Packet Switching

1 An outgoing message is divided into data units of a fixed size called packets.

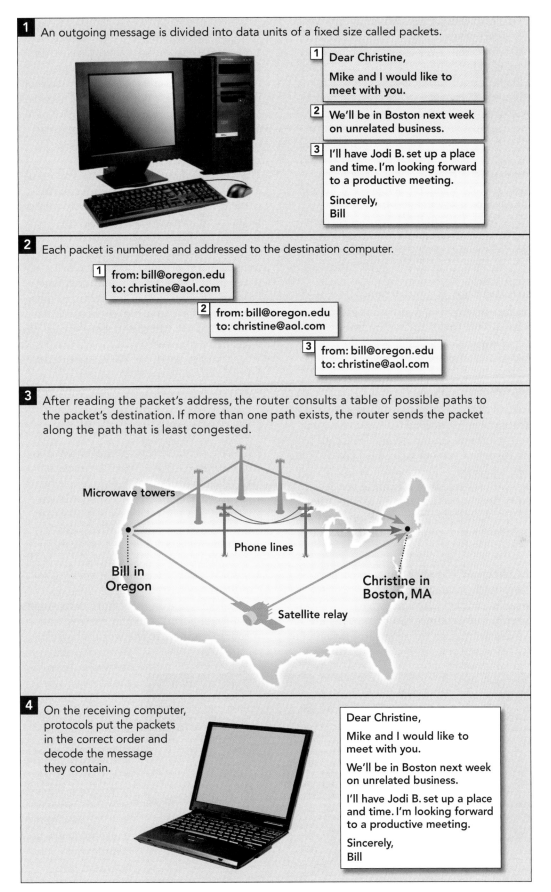

1 Dear Christine,

Mike and I would like to meet with you.

2 We'll be in Boston next week on unrelated business.

3 I'll have Jodi B. set up a place and time. I'm looking forward to a productive meeting.

Sincerely,
Bill

2 Each packet is numbered and addressed to the destination computer.

1 from: bill@oregon.edu
to: christine@aol.com

2 from: bill@oregon.edu
to: christine@aol.com

3 from: bill@oregon.edu
to: christine@aol.com

3 After reading the packet's address, the router consults a table of possible paths to the packet's destination. If more than one path exists, the router sends the packet along the path that is least congested.

Microwave towers

Phone lines

Bill in Oregon

Christine in Boston, MA

Satellite relay

4 On the receiving computer, protocols put the packets in the correct order and decode the message they contain.

Dear Christine,

Mike and I would like to meet with you.

We'll be in Boston next week on unrelated business.

I'll have Jodi B. set up a place and time. I'm looking forward to a productive meeting.

Sincerely,
Bill

The oldest packet-switching protocol for WAN usage, **X.25**, is optimized for dial-up connections over noisy telephone lines and is still in widespread use. Local connections generally offer speeds of 9.6 to 64 Kbps. X.25 is best used to create a point-to-point connection with a single computer. A point-to-point connection is a single line that connects one communications device to one computer. It is widely used with ATMs and credit card authorization devices. New protocols designed for 100 percent digital lines, such as Switched Multimegabit Data Service (SMDS) and Asynchronous Transfer Mode (ATM), enable much faster data transfer rates (up to 155 Mbps).

To learn more about WAN protocols, visit Cisco's WAN documentation site at **www.cisco.com/en/US/docs/ internetworking/technology/ handbook/Intro-to-WAN.html**.

Now that you understand how WANs work, let's explore how they are used.

WAN APPLICATIONS

WANs enable companies to use many of the same applications that you use, such as e-mail and conferencing, document exchange, and remote database access. Some WANs are created to serve the public, such as those maintained by online service providers such as AOL and MSN. Other WANs are created and maintained for the sole purpose of meeting an organization's internal needs.

LAN-to-LAN Connections In corporations and universities, WANs are often used to connect LANs at two or more geographically separate locations. This use of WANs overcomes the major limitation of a LAN—its inability to link computers separated by more than a few thousand feet. Companies can connect their LANs over their ISP connection, which often provides bandwidth that far exceeds capabilities of internal networks. With these connections, users get the impression that they're using one huge LAN that connects the entire company and all of its branch offices.

Transaction Acquisition When you make a purchase at a retail store, information about your transaction is instantly relayed to the company's central computers through its WAN. That's because the cash register the clerk uses is actually a computer, a point-of-sale (POS) terminal, that's linked to a data communications network (Figure 7.21). The acquired data is collected for accounting purposes and analyzed to see whether a store's sales patterns have changed.

As you've seen, networking is a powerful tool, allowing users to communicate, share resources, and exchange data.

Home Networks

When people hear the word *network*, they often think, "Oh, that's too technical for me." Although networks require hardware and software technology, you should simply think of a network as a way to share computing power and resources. Setting up a home network may not be as difficult as you think, and the advantages are well worth the effort. Because networking capabilities are built into all modern operating systems, it is easy to share data among computers, portable media devices, and, of course, connect to the world's biggest network—the Internet. Approximately two-thirds of all U.S. households own a computer. And more than 25 percent of those households own two or more computers. Market research indicates that multicomputer households are becoming more common because people who already own PCs are still buying new ones. It is not unusual for

FIGURE 7.21 POS terminals instantly relay information about transactions to the company's central computers through its WAN.

each parent and one or more children in a household to have their own computer or mobile device, such as a smartphone (Figure 7.22). Why is this important? People in multi-computer households want to share scanners, printers, data, music, movies, and games among multiple users using different computers. In addition, they want every member of the household to share a single Internet connection. The computers in a single household may be of different makes and models (such as a mix of Macs and PCs). How can these computers share information and resources? The answer is a home network.

FIGURE 7.22 Today it is not unusual to have several family members with media devices. In order to share data, music, and other content, a home network is needed to provide connectivity between users and devices.

By the end of 2012, it is estimated that there will be more than 160 million home networks in place worldwide, and as many as 70 percent of them will be using wireless technology. A **home network**, also referred to as a **home area network** or **HAN**, is a personal and specific use of network technology that provides connectivity between users and devices located in or near one residence. It enables users who reside at that location to quickly and conveniently share files and resources by using network connections between computers and peripheral devices. Home networks can accommodate both wired and wireless communications. Wired home networks typically use Cat-5 or Cat-6 Ethernet cable or a home's electrical wiring. Wireless home networks rely on Wi-Fi radio signals. Let's first look at wired networks.

WIRED HOME NETWORKS

The Ethernet has become the standard network of choice for home networks that are still using a wired system. Ethernet standards detail the types of wires that must be used and how fast data can travel across the network.

Home Ethernet Network Ethernet is a communications standard that uses packets to send data between physically connected computers in a network. The most popular type of Ethernet wiring is twisted-pair wire. Home networks use either Cat-5 or Cat-6 version of twisted pair wire. These wires are then connected by RJ-45 connectors, which look like large telephone jacks. Cat-5 wire transfers data at speeds of up to 100 Mbps; Cat-6 transfers data at speeds of up to 1,000 Mbps (1 Gbps).

The simplest form of Ethernet network links different computers with a connecting switch or router. Devices connected by a switch can communicate only with other devices on the same network, whereas devices connected by a router can access other networks, including the Internet. See Figure 7.23 for an example of a simple Ethernet network. In this example, the computer can send a message to the notebook or the printer by way of the router. Routers and switches are available in many configurations. Most have 4 to 12 ports. The majority of home networks use a 100Base-TX router that is capable of a transfer rate of 100 Mbps (100 million bits per second). If you have the money, you can upgrade to a 1000Base-T router with a transfer rate of 1 Gbps. Also known as gigabit Ethernet, 1000Base-T is useful when transferring large amounts of data such as digital multimedia.

With an Ethernet network, each networked computer must have an Ethernet network adapter, also called a network interface card (NIC). Most newer computers already include a NIC, but a NIC can also be installed as an expansion card on an older system.

WIRELESS HOME NETWORKS

Although several wireless network standards are currently available, Wi-Fi is the

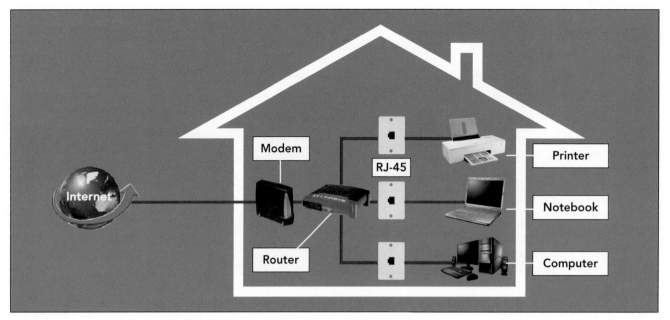

FIGURE 7.23 A Typical Ethernet Network Setup Using a Router

wireless standard used for home networking. Wireless network standards have been developed to ensure that companies that build wireless connecting devices do so in compliance with strict definitions and exchange rules. Ultimately, three factors determine which standard best suits your needs: (1) the cost of the hardware or software, (2) the speed at which data can travel over the network, and (3) the range within which you can reliably transmit between devices.

Home Wi-Fi networks are wireless networks in which each computer on the network broadcasts its information to another using radio signals. Wi-Fi networks use communications devices called network access points, also referred to as wireless access points, to send and receive data between computers that have wireless adapters. In a home network, in addition to enabling communication between networked devices and other networks, wireless routers also act as network access points. Network access points enable you to move a notebook with a wireless adapter from room to room or to place computers in different locations throughout a house (Figure 7.24).

A peer-to-peer relationship exists among all of the computers in a wireless network (Figure 7.25). This means that all the computers are equals, or peers, with no particular computer acting as the server. However, some home wireless networks can also be of the client/server type. In a client/server home network, each computer communicates with the server, and the server then communicates with other computers or peripherals. All peripherals in a wireless network must be within the router's range, which is usually 100 to 300 feet, depending on the building's construction and thickness of the walls, floors, and ceilings.

Wi-Fi networks use the 802.11 wireless transmission specifications. Although some older systems may still use the 802.11a or 802.11b standards, the most prevalent standards are 802.11g and 802.11n. The 802.11g specification operates in the 2.4 GHz radio band and is capable of data transfer rates of up to 54 Mbps. The 802.11n can operate in both the 2.4 GHz and 5 GHz radio band, and the average data transfer rate is about 300 Mbps.

Wireless networks are gaining in popularity because of their ease of setup and convenience. There are no unsightly wires to run through the home, and users are no longer limited to working in just one location. However, there are some disadvantages to wireless networks.

FIGURE 7.24 Apple's AirPort Extreme is a wireless router that is compatible with Macs and PCs.

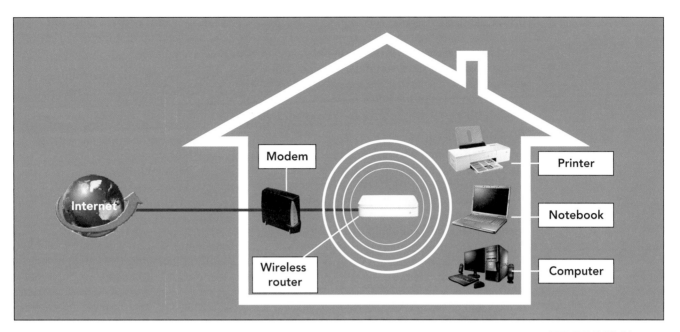

FIGURE 7.25 A home network setup using a Wi-Fi wireless network.

Newer notebook computers are usually equipped for wireless access, but older notebooks may require the addition of a wireless adapter card, which plugs into a slot on the notebook. A USB adapter can be connected to the USB port of a notebook or desktop PC. Another alternative is to install a wireless adapter expansion card in a desktop PC (Figure 7.26). Wireless networks may be affected by interference from other devices such as microwave ovens and cordless phones. And some users may find that reception can be a problem if the radio waves are unable to pass through interior walls. Conversely, because radio waves are able to pass through walls, it is important to take appropriate measures to safeguard

your privacy from passersby outside your home.

Now that we've examined the various types of home networks, let's look at the steps involved in setting one up.

SETTING UP A HOME NETWORK

Setting up any network, including one for your home, goes much more smoothly if you can follow a series of steps. The steps

FIGURE 7.26 A wireless adaptor card (**a**) can be installed in a notebook's PC card slot. A USB adapter (**b**) can be used for notebooks or desktop PCs and a PCI adapter (**c**) can be used to enable wireless access for a desktop PC.

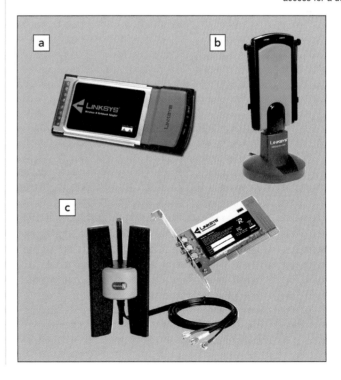

Not everyone takes the steps necessary to secure their wireless network. Do you know how to tell which wireless network you're using? Have you ever used a neighbor's network to access the Internet? In most areas, this is considered theft of services. How do you feel about that? Would you warn your neighbor about your ability—and the ability of other people—to access their unsecured network?

presented in this section correspond roughly to those followed by computer professionals who develop large-scale networks. Don't let that intimidate you though! You don't have to be a computer professional to set up a home network successfully.

Planning As with any type of project, you must first come up with a plan based on your specific home networking needs. Ask yourself realistic questions: What are you trying to accomplish with your network? Is it for a small business or just for personal use? Is it only for your computer and peripherals or will it support multiple family members? Will the hardware be concentrated in one room (such as an office or den) or be spread throughout many rooms? Based on your answers to these questions and the type of home network you choose, you should develop a needs, or requirements, checklist. You can determine your specific requirements by visiting your local home electronics store or by reading recommendations you find on the Web. Go to **http://compnetworking. about.com/od/homenetworking/a/ homeadvisor.htm** and launch the Home Network Interactive Advisor. This interactive questionaire will ask you relevant networking questions and, based on your answers, make network recommendations that will meet your needs.

When planning a home network, you will need to do two things. First, you will need to decide which network technology to use and then, based on your first choice, you will need to purchase the appropriate hardware. You may want to visit a home electronics store for advice, but many manufacturers such as Linksys and Netgear, as well as retailers such as Best Buy and Circuit City, provide tutorials on their Web sites to help you determine what type of network would best suit your needs and what equipment you will require. You may already have a NIC and a modem but will probably need a router (wired or wireless) and possibly a wireless adapter.

These sites also provide help and advice about setting up a home network:

- Microsoft (**www.microsoft.com/ athome/moredone/wirelesssetup. mspx**)
- About.com (**http://compnetworking. about.com/od/homenetworking/ Home_Networking_Setting_Up_a_ Home_Network.htm**)
- CNET Reviews (**http://reviews. cnet.com/wireless-network- buying-guide**)

You should also consider purchasing and installing personal firewall software to keep your home network safe from viruses and hackers. Visit the U.S. Computer Emergency Readiness Team Web site (**www. us-cert.gov/cas/tips/ ST04-004.html**) to find out more about firewalls and what type of firewall is the best. The site also provides hints on configuration settings (Figure 7.27).

A wired Ethernet network is best installed during home construction if you want to conceal the wires. When installing this type of network in an existing home, it is possible to route the cables through the walls by use of either attic or basement access, but it will take a lot of work. If you decide to use Ethernet, you will need to determine whether you are going to do the job yourself or whether you are going to hire someone to do it. In either case, the installer must carefully plan the routing of the cables through walls and across floors. You can find tutorials on the Web that will help you lay out the appropriate locations to drill into your walls. Search for "home network wiring" in your favorite search engine to find guides to wiring your home network.

Once you have purchased the appropriate hardware and software, you must configure the network so that all of the components function together. When your network is properly configured, you will find that a home network improves your home-computing experience.

> " Consider purchasing and installing **personal firewall** software to keep your **home** network **safe** from **viruses** and **hackers.** "

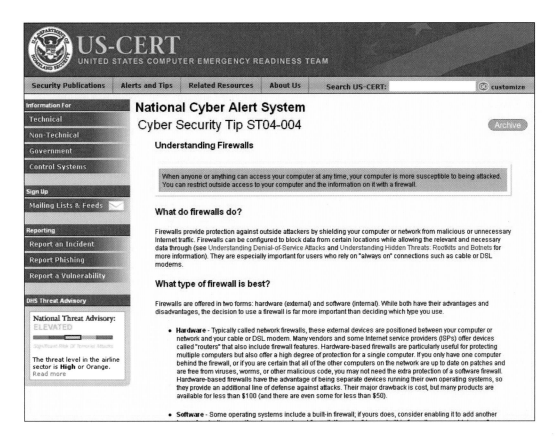

Configuring a Wired Network

Computer networks for homes and small businesses can be built using either wired or wireless technology. Wired Ethernet has been the traditional choice in homes. Every computer on the network needs a network interface that bundles data into chunks to travel across the network, as well as a connection point, or port, for the special wiring that connects all the PCs. The port is either built into the computer or provided as an add-in NIC. The NIC sends data to the network and receives data sent from other computers on the network. Wired LANs generally also require central devices like hubs, switches, or routers to accommodate more computers.

The next step is to configure the central hub, most frequently a router. In a wired network, a wire runs from the back of each computer to the router, which serves as a communications point to connect the signal to the appropriate cable that goes to the intended destination. Printers, scanners, and other peripherals are usually plugged into one of the networked computers and then shared with the others. However, many new peripherals come with network interfaces that allow them to be plugged directly into the router. The router must be placed in a convenient location so that you can string individual cables from the router to each port in each room in which you want to use the network. Wired cables, hubs, switches, and routers are relatively inexpensive and provide superior performace and high reliability.

Configuring a Wireless Network

As with a wired network, a wireless network also requires equipment. To create a wireless network, you will need a wireless router, which will act as a hub of the service. The wireless router changes the signals coming across your Internet connection into a wireless broadcast, sort of like a cordless phone base station. Today, 802.11g wireless broadband routers are usually recommended because they offer excellent performance and are compatible with almost any device. Each node that is to be connected to the wireless network will need a wireless adapter that will connect and communicate to the wireless router. Newer computers and devices may already have them embedded within the system unit. For older equipment you will have to purchase an adpater and connect it through a USB port. To make your setup easier, choose network adapters made by the same vendor that made your wireless router. Finally connect your DSL or cable modem to your wireless router. Wireless networks have some performance issues usually associated with interference from devices like microwave ovens. Careful positioning of the router and nodes is required in the planning stage. Wireless equipment can cost more than the equipment needed for a wired network. This cost, however, is often offset by the savings provided by the inclusion of security software in wireless routers. Security for wired systems requires the purchase of additional software.

The final step in configuring a wired or wireless network is to access the operating systems control panel and locate the network configuration option. Windows 7 has a Network Setup Wizard that can be accessed from the Control Panel by choosing the Network and Sharing Center, and selecting Set up a new connection or network (Figure 7.28). You can also search for "network" from the Start menu to access the Network and Sharing Center. Setup information may also be available from the store where you purchased your networking supplies or from Web searches on home networks.

MAINTENANCE AND SUPPORT

Computer and network problems can be extremely frustrating. You should set up a regular maintenance schedule for both your computer and your network. The good news is that there isn't much to maintain with today's home networking solutions. You may need to blow off dust and lint that accumulates on your router, wireless adapter, or modem. You may also need to use your operating system's network utilities to refresh your network's settings.

When something goes wrong, you should try to think of what might have caused the problem. Sometimes the solution is as simple as restarting your computer and/or unplugging the power source from your router and other peripherals and then plugging them back in. You may also need to restart each computer that is connected to your system. If these actions do not solve the problem, you have several other options. If the problem produces an error message, write down the subject of the error message and then type it into the search box on your favorite search engine site. You can also search manufacturers' Web sites. For instance, if you have a

FIGURE 7.28 The Network and Sharing option from the Control Panel will guide you though the steps to connect to a wired or wireless network.

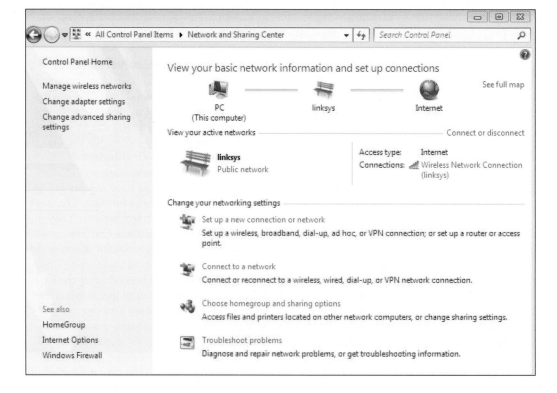

Linksys router and Netgear network cards, you could go to **www.linksys.com** and **www.netgear.com**, respectively, to see if downloads are available to update your network devices.

THE FUTURE OF HOME NETWORKING

Convergence will be the future of home networking systems. You may be skeptical, but someday you may be able to use home networks to control household appliances, prepare food, or maintain a home's appearance. Networked home security systems already help protect us from intrusion or damage from natural events.

In the near future, new houses will have a central control unit that is capable of managing home network events as well as communication, entertainment, temperature regulation, lighting, and household appliances. It is very possible that someday your refrigerator may send you an e-mail informing you of the state of its cooling coils, including a request that you vacuum out the lint that is blocking good air circulation.

In the future, your home networking system will almost certainly be wireless. It will have capabilities that will help it adapt to new technologies as they develop. Wireless technology will be able to provide the flexibility that is required to seamlessly integrate convenience, simplicity, and, hopefully, long-term cost savings.

Chapter Summary

Networks: Communicating and Sharing Resources

Computer networks link two or more computers so that they can exchange data and share resources. Networks are of two primary types: local area networks (LANs), which serve a building or a small geographic area, and wide area networks (WANs), which can span buildings, cities, states, and nations. The special components that distinguish a WAN from a LAN are a point of presence and backbones.

Computer networks can be advantageous by reducing hardware costs, enabling application and data sharing, and fostering teamwork and collaboration. Disadvantages of computer networks include loss of autonomy, threats to security and privacy, and potential productivity losses due to network outages.

A peer-to-peer LAN doesn't use a file server. It is most appropriate for small networks of fewer than 10 computers. Client/server networks include one or more file servers as well as clients such as desktops, notebooks, and handheld devices. The client/server model works with any size or physical layout of LAN and doesn't slow down with heavy use. A home network can be set up as either type of network.

The physical layout of a LAN is called its network topology. The three different LAN topologies are bus (single connections to a central line), star (all connections to a central switch), and ring (tokens carry messages around a ring).

Protocols are the rules that define how network devices can communicate with each other. Messages move through the layers of the protocol stack. When a computer sends a message over the network, the application hands the message down the protocol stack. At the receiving end, the message goes up a similar stack in reverse order.

Circuit switching creates a permanent end-to-end circuit that is optimal for voice and real-time data. Circuit switching is not as efficient or reliable as packet switching; it is also more expensive. Packet switching does not require a permanent switched circuit. A packet-switched network can funnel more data through a medium with a given data transfer capacity. However, packet switching introduces slight delays that make the technology less than optimal for voice or real-time data.

Home networks are the wave of the future. They can be wired or wireless, peer-to-peer or client/server. The first step in setting up a home network is the planning phase. After that, you must configure the network. The final step is maintenance and support. If you need assistance, call local retail stores or search for online guidance.

Key Terms and Concepts

Matching

Match each key term in the left column with the most accurate definition in the right column.

_____ 1. network topology

_____ 2. switch

_____ 3. IP

_____ 4. protocol

_____ 5. packet

_____ 6. node

_____ 7. network operating system

_____ 8. latency

_____ 9. terminator

_____ 10. hot spot

_____ 11. TCP

_____ 12. congestion

_____ 13. modulation protocol

_____ 14. backbone

_____ 15. contention

a. A unit of data transferred over a network that has a header containing the origin and destination.

b. Any device connected to a network.

c. Defines the way Internet connected computers communicate.

d. A device that filters and forwards data between nodes within a single network.

e. Enables modems to communicate with one another, regardless of the manufacturer.

f. Delay caused by the examination of a packet by multiple routers.

g. A special connector located at the end of a bus.

h. A performance interruption that is caused by a segment of a network experiencing an overload.

i. The physical layout of a network.

j. A situation caused when two or more computers try to access a network at the same time.

k. Standards or rules that enable devices on a network to communicate.

l. A high-speed, high capacity medium designed to carry large volumes of data over long distances.

m. A public wireless access point.

n. Installed on the server and managed by a network administrator.

o. A fundamental, connectionless protocol that defines the packet setup and addressing scheme.

Multiple Choice

Circle the correct choice for each of the following.

1. Which of the following statements about packet switching is *not* true?
   a. It is used by WAN protocols.
   b. Packets are examined by routers.
   c. Packets must be received in the same order in which they were sent.
   d. Missing packets must be retransmitted.

2. What is assigned to every computer on the Internet to facilitate the exchange of data?
   a. IP address
   b. Terminator
   c. Logical address
   d. Physical address

3. Which type of network topology uses a switch or hub as its central point of connection?
   a. P2P
   b. Star
   c. Bus
   d. Ring

4. Which of the following is a WAN network connection point?
   a. TCP
   b. IP
   c. NOS
   d. POP

5. Which of the following statements about peer-to-peer networks is true?
   a. They require at least one router.
   b. They require at least one server.
   c. They require a network operating sytem.
   d. They perform best when connecting 10 or fewer computers.

6. A computer that is connected to a network is known as a
   a. packet.
   b. client.
   c. token.
   d. circuit.

7. What type of network topology uses of a single conduit and terminators?
   a. Ring
   b. Star
   c. POP
   d. Bus

8. Which of the following is a common contention-management technique?
   a. Abandoning data corrupted by a collision
   b. Retransmitting unreceived packets
   c. Generating a new token
   d. Adding terminators to minimize signal loss

9. What is the name of the expansion board that enables a computer to connect to a network?
   a. Network information client
   b. Node interface circuit
   c. Network interface card
   d. Network interval circuit

10. Which computer professional installs, maintains, and supports computer networks?
    a. Client
    b. LAN
    c. Chief executive officer
    d. Network administrator

Fill-In

In the blanks provided, write the correct answer for each of the following.

1. Novell's SUSE and Windows Server 2008 are both examples of a(n) _____ _____ _____.

2. A(n) _____ is a point of presence on a WAN that transfers data at rates exceeding 1 Gbps.

3. The _____ network topology makes use of a token.

4. A(n) _____ _____ is an identifier embedded within the hardware of a network node.

5. A(n) _____ is used to move data between networks.

6. A high-speed, high-capacity computer containing the network operating system, network applications, and data files is a(n) _____ _____.

7. In a(n) _____-_____-_____ network, all users are equal and there is no file server.

8. _____ _____ is a WAN architecture, used in telephone systems, in which a direct electrical connection is made between communication devices.

9. _____ is the most popular LAN standard used by 90 percent of all LANs.

10. _____ _____ are the components of a network's architecture that each have their own functions and enable changes to be made without a redesign of the entire network.

11. A(n) _____ _____ _____ is a computer network within a single residence.

12. A(n) _____ _____ _____ is a computer network that is limited to a close geographical area like a building or set of clustered buildings.

13. A wireless LAN uses _____ _____ instead of wires to transmit data.

14. _____ _____ is a WAN architecture, used in computer transmissions, that makes no attempt to establish a single electrical connection between two computing devices.

15. _____ can be enabled on a wireless network by turning on WEP or WPA.

Short Answer

1. Explain the difference between a peer-to-peer network and a client/server network.

2. How do LANs, WANs, and HANs differ?

3. What is the difference between topology and protocol?

4. Name three types of LAN topologies and describe how each works.

5. List three advantages and three disadvantages of networking.

6. How do circuit switching and packet switching differ? What are the advantages of each method?

Teamwork

1. **Home Computing** As a team, create a survey that asks respondents whether they have a home network and if so, whether it is wired or wireless. Ask such questions as these: What devices are connected via the network? What equipment is used to operate the network? Who maintains the network? Make a list of terms and equipment relative to a home network and have the respondents check the ones that they either have in their network or are familiar with. Accumulate responses from at least 15 individuals. In a one-page, double-spaced report, summarize your findings. Are home network users really familiar with the technology they use? What can be done to make home network users more familiar with devices and services?

2. **Computer Lab Topologies** Break your team into groups. Have each group visit a different campus computer lab and determine the network topology installed. In addition to computers, what other resources are available on each network? What types of physical media are used to connect the computers and the peripherals in each lab? Are the computers within the lab capable of connecting to computers located in other labs or locations on campus? Does the lab allow Internet access? If Internet access is available, how is it connected and who is the service provider? After your investigations, regroup and arrange your findings in a table that allows you to compare the sites easily. Answer such questions as these: What do all sites have in common? Which site is the best equipped? Which site is the least equipped? Include your table and summary statements in a one-page, double-spaced paper.

3. **Designing a Network** As a team come up with a network design, list of hardware devices, and an estimate of the cost to connect equipment to be shared among four friends in a dorm suite. Assume the connection will be between four notebooks (perhaps not with the same operating system), one laser printer, and one scanner. The four friends will also connect to the wireless Internet service that the college provides. Present your design and cost analysis in a one-page, double-spaced paper.

4. **Creating Your Own Business** Assume the members of your team are going to create a small business after graduation. This business will be installing and maintaining home area networks. Come up with a company name, statement of policy, services that you will provide, a diagram of a wired and wireless HAN, and a list of fees for those services. Place all of this information into a flyer and create a 5- to 10-slide PowerPoint presentation to entice your customers.

5. **Wired versus Wireless Networks** Have each individual in the team keep track of his or her interaction with network connectivity for one week. List the device used to connect to a network, whether it was wired or wireless, the time you used the device, and where you were when you were using the device. Remember to include cell phones, Bluetooth devices, and Internet connections at school or work, including checking for e-mail. As a team, accumulate your results and compile a list of the most frequently used devices, types of connection, uses, and locations. See whether a pattern exists or whether any correlation between devices, uses, and locations can be made. Present your results in a two-page, double-spaced paper or a PowerPoint presentation.

On the Web

1. **Establishing a Wired Home Network** Visit http://compnetworking.about.com/od/homenet working/a/homeadvisor.htm, to learn more about establishing a home network. Click on the link labeled "Home Network Interactive Advisor" and answer each question. Assume that you have two computers (one tower and one notebook), a printer, and a scanner that you wish to network and that you want Internet access. After you complete the survey, accumulate the information suggested for your network by the Web site. Go one step further and use the Internet or local retail stores to create a list of the hardware you will need, how much it will cost, and the cost of Internet service with a local provider. Calculate the total cost of the network suggested by the advisor. In a one-page, double-spaced paper, present the network recommendation given by the advisor. Include your research into the estimated cost of the network. Remember to take into account monthly Internet provider fees.

2. **Identity Theft at Hot Spots** Recently two of your friends were at a local coffee shop using the shop's public Internet access (hot spot) for customers. In the weeks since that visit, both have noticed unauthorized activity on accounts accessed while using that Internet connection. Using the information in this chapter and other Web sites you locate with the help of your favorite browser, create a flyer or slide presentation with at least 5 to 10 safety precautions that individuals using technology should follow to minimize the risk of identity theft or fraud.

3. **Networking Jobs and Certifications** Use the Internet, your favorite browser, local newspapers, and trade journals to create a list of jobs that require networking skills. For each position, list the education needed, certifications desired, and salary range (if possible). Look up certifications offered in the area of networking. State the name of the certification, who offers such training or certification preparation, and the job opportunities that the certification will allow you to become qualified for. Present your findings in a one-page, double-spaced paper.

4. **A Smartphone for You** Because of their small size, smartphones are popular mobile computing devices. Do you own or have you considered buying a smartphone? Go to Tiger Direct (**www.tigerdirect.com**) and search for "smartphone" to find information on smartphones. What are the most popular methods for networking a smartphone to a desktop computer? Which of these methods requires additional PC hardware? Is the use of the word *networking* correct? In a one-page, double-spaced paper, summarize your research, including answers to the questions posed.

5. **Firewall Comparisons and Use** Users can protect their personal computers by using firewalls. A firewall can be implemented through software, hardware, or a combination of both. Two of the leading software applications, McAfee Total Protection (**www.mcafee.com**) and Norton Internet Security (**www.symantec.com**), are designed for personal computers running various operating systems. According to these and other security utility sites, why should you purchase firewall software? What are the various pricing structures available for each of these products? After reading descriptions of these products on McAfee's and Norton's Web sites, search the Web to find independent evaluations of each product. Identify the URLs of these additional review sites. Explain which firewall application you would purchase and why. Submit your findings in a one-page, double-spaced paper.

chapter 8

Wired and Wireless Communication

Chapter Objectives

- Define *bandwidth* and discuss the bandwidth needs of typical users. (p. 292)

- Discuss how modems transform digital computer signals into analog signals. (p. 293)

- List transmission media and explain several transmission methods. (p. 294)

- Explain the limitations of the public switched telephone network (PSTN) for sending and receiving computer data. (p. 298)

- Describe multiplexing and digital telephony, including their impact on line usage. (p. 298)

- Provide examples of how digitization and convergence are blurring the boundaries that distinguish popular communications devices, including phones and computers. (p. 303)

- Discuss various wired and wireless applications. (p. 309)

The excitement of using a wireless remote to change the channel of a television set seems like an emotion from the Stone Age. In the last decade, wired and wireless devices seem to have proliferated. How many wired and wireless devices do you use in a day? Do you even notice how accessible and easy communication and access to multimedia has become? Can you identify all of the chargers you have plugged into outlets? Do you ever get irritated with the constant interruption of your thoughts, activities, or relaxation time by friends, relatives, or telemarketers with what seem to be nonsense calls, harassing e-mails, and irrelevant twitters? You can try to escape, but the Telecommunication Era is upon us. The real question is: Could any of us really disconnect and go back to the quiet tranquility of one phone, one television, and one stereo?

Suppose you're on a trip and need to access your e-mail—but you left your notebook at home. No problem; you just use your Web-enabled cell phone to retrieve your messages. As for sending e-mail messages back, again, no problem; you can do this with most messaging devices. Back at home, you hop on your ultrafast FiOS connection to download and upload files. The whole time, you're experiencing the realities of **connectivity**. Defined broadly, this term refers to the ability to link various media and devices. Connectivity enhances communications and improves access to information. In this chapter, we'll examine the various technologies involved in communications, whether they're **wired** (connected by a physical medium) or **wireless** (connected through the air or space).

Moving Data: Bandwidth and Modems

Communications (data communications or telecommunications) is the process of electronically sending and receiving messages between two points. Communication can be split into two parts, the message (content) and the **communications channel** (also referred to as the **link**), the path through which the message is sent from one location to the next.

Signals in the real world, like sound and light, are **analog signals**, or continuous waves that vary in strength and quality. Before these real world signals can be used by digital equipment, like a computer, the signal passes through an analog-to-digital converter. An **analog-to-digital converter (ADC)** is simply a microchip that contains the circuitry to convert an analog signal into a digital signal. A **digital signal** is one that includes discontinuous pulses in which the presence or absence of electronic pulses represent 1s and 0s. When a computer signal has to be sent out to the real world, for example as sound, the digital signal must pass through a digital-to-analog converter. A **digital-to-analog converter (DAC)** is a microchip that contains the circuitry to convert a digital signal to analog (Figure 8.1).

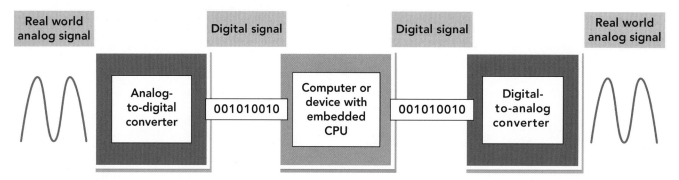

| Real world analog signal | Digital signal | Digital signal | Real world analog signal |

Analog-to-digital converter

001010010

Computer or device with embedded CPU

001010010

Digital-to-analog converter

FIGURE 8.1 An ADC (analog-to-digital converter) converts the analog signal into digital so that a computer can interpret the data. A DAC (digital-to-analog converter) converts the digital signal to real-world analog output.

In communications, both analog and digital signals move data over communications channels. The conversion from analog to digital or digital to analog is normally not something a user can detect or has to be concerned with. However, if you have ever scanned an image, recorded your voice or used VoIP on your computer, or talked on a phone, you used an analog-to-digital converter. Likewise, if you have ever listened on the phone or played back a CD, you made use of a digital-to-analog converter.

Because a digital signal is discrete, composed of 0s and 1s that are sampled from an analog signal, the data arrives in a much clearer format (Figure 8.2). As a result, the receiving end knows exactly how to reconstruct the data back into its original form. Digital signals also transfer much more data than analog and at much greater speeds. For instance, digital TV systems can now deliver more than 500 stations across digital cable, which allows not only more stations than analog cable, but also more features.

So how are the digital signals from your computer prepared for traveling over analog telephone lines? Let's look at two additional considerations for sending data over communications channels: bandwidth and modems.

BANDWIDTH: HOW MUCH DO YOU NEED?

Bandwidth refers to the theoretical maximum amount of data that can be transmitted through a given communications channel at one time (usually per second). The physical characteristics of the transmission medium and the method used to represent and transmit data via the transmission medium determine bandwidth. For analog signals, bandwidth is expressed in cycles per second, or hertz (Hz). For digital signals, bandwidth is expressed in bits per second (bps). **Throughput**, often used incorrectly as a synonym for bandwidth, is the *actual* amount of data that is transmitted. It is almost always lower than bandwidth, especially with wireless communications.

Broadband refers to any transmission medium that carries several channels at

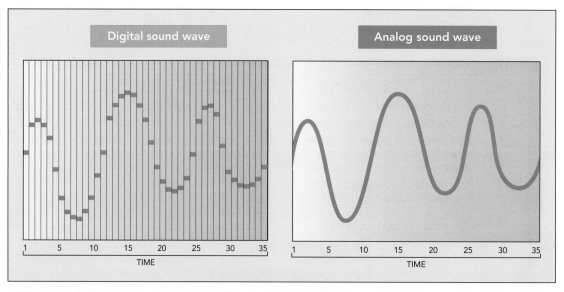

FIGURE 8.2 Digital signals are composed by sampling an analog wave at discrete points in time. The analog wave is then approximated by these discrete measurements.

once and thus transports high volumes of data at high speeds, typically greater than 1 Mbps (megabits per second, or million bits per second). Cable TV uses broadband transmission. So how much bandwidth do you need? Conventional dial-up connections to the Internet use a relatively low bandwidth of 56 Kbps (kilobits per second, or thousand bits per second) or less. Most users find this painfully slow when searching the Web. But dial-up connections are still cheaper than broadband connections, so some people sacrifice speed for low price.

Broadband digital connections are now widely available in the United States. The major cable and telephone (DSL) companies added 5.4 million new subscribers in 2008, which is considerably less than the 8.5 million they added in 2007. This slowdown is being attributed to the economic downturn. The total number of broadband subscribers for these two technologies in the United States as of the end of 2008 was close to 68 million. Over the next few years, wireless Internet and FiOS are going to figure into the continuing growth of broadband, and re-distribution of the market share should spur some fierce competition (Figure 8.3).

MODEMS: CHANGE OR ADAPT SIGNALS FROM ONE TRANSMISSION SYSTEM TO ANOTHER

The term **modem** comes from combining the words **mod**ulate and **dem**odulate. It is an appropriate compressed term because a modem is a communication device used to send and receive data from one transmission system to another. On the sending end, a modem uses a process called *modulation* to transform the computer's digital signals into signals appropriate for

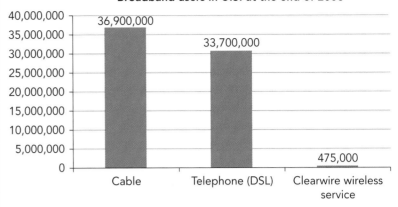

Broadband users in U.S. at the end of 2008

FIGURE 8.3 Currently it appears that cable-based Internet service is the preferred form of high speed Internet access.

the transmission system bring used. On the receiving end, the process used is *demodulation,* whereby the receiving modem transforms the signal from the transmission system back in computer understandable digital form. For systems that use telephone lines as a transmission medium, the modulator converts the computer's digital signals into analog tones that can be conveyed through the telephone system. The demodulator receives the analog signals and converts them to digital form (Figure 8.4).

Modems are available as internal or external units. An internal modem, the most common in computer systems today, is not visible. Instead, it is located within the system unit and is powered by the system unit's power supply. An external modem, located outside of the system unit, has its own case and power supply. For this reason, external modems are slightly more expensive. The types of modems available include analog, digital subscriber line (DSL), cable, and Integrated Services Digital Network (ISDN). Analog modems are used for dial-up connections. DSL and cable are

FIGURE 8.4 A modem transforms the computer's digital signals into analog signals that can be transmitted through the telephone system. Once the transmission reaches its destination, the receiving modem converts the analog signal back to a digital signal.

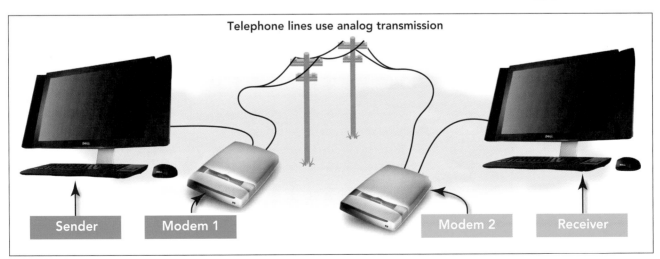

Telephone lines use analog transmission

Sender Modem 1 Modem 2 Receiver

high-speed broadband connections. ISDN modems transfer information in channels of 64 kilobits per second (Kpbs), which can be combined for higher speeds. We'll discuss Integrated Services Digital Networks in more detail later in this chapter.

The **data transfer rate**, the rate at which two modems can exchange data, is measured in bits per second and is referred to as the **bps rate**. Analog modems communicate at a maximum rate of 56 Kbps. (In practice, modems rarely achieve speeds higher than 42 Kbps.) A modem that can transfer 56 Kbps is transferring only about 7,000 bytes per second, or about five pages of text. Baud is often used incorrectly as a substitute for bps, the unit of data transfer rate. **Baud** is actually the number of signaling elements per second. At slower rates, bauds and bps may be equal, but on higher speed transmissions, more than one bit can be encoded in each signaling element. Thus a 4,800 baud rate may have a transmission rate of 9,600 bps.

Often, a single message travels over several different wired and wireless transmission media, including telephone lines, coaxial cable, fiber-optic cable, radio waves, microwaves, and satellite, before it arrives at its destination. We'll look at each of these types of wired and wireless transmission media in more detail.

Wired Transmission Media

Wired transmission media for data travel is still widely used today. Most new buildings incorporate into the original structure the appropriate wiring to support most types of data transfer that the individuals or companies that occupy the building might want to access. Let's look more closely at the various forms of wired media.

TWISTED PAIR

Twisted pair wire is a copper cable used for telephone and data communications. The term *twisted pair* refers to the interweaving of two pairs of wires that are twisted together, a practice that provides a shield that reduces interference from electrical fields generated by electric motors, power lines, and powerful radio signals (Figure 8.5). On the plus side, twisted pair is an inexpensive medium. On the negative side, the bandwidth of traditional twisted-pair telephone lines is too low to simultaneously carry video, voice, and data. Twisted pair carries data at transfer rates of less than 1 Kbps.

KEY VARIATIONS OF TWISTED PAIR

Cat-5 cable, short for **Category 5**, is the fifth generation of twisted pair data communication cable. Cat-5 cable contains four pairs of twisted copper wire and supports speeds up to 100 Mbps over a maximum distance of 100 m (328 feet). However, only two of the four pairs of wires are actually used for most fast network communications. A newer variation of the Cat-5 cable, **Cat-5e**, short for **Category 5 enhanced**, uses all four wire pairs, enabling speeds up to 1,000 Mbps (1 Gbps) over a short distance. This enhanced medium is backward compatible with ordinary Cat-5 (Figure 8.6).

Cat-6, short for **Category 6**, is the sixth generation of twisted pair cable and is

FIGURE 8.5 *Twisted pair* refers to inexpensive copper cable that's used for telephone and data communications.

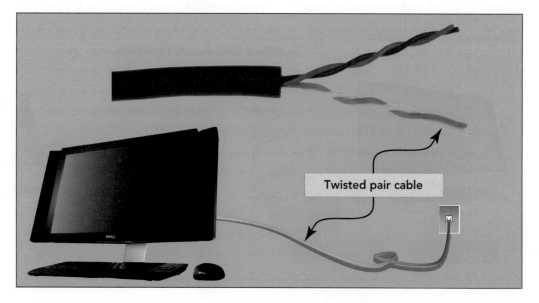

Twisted pair cable

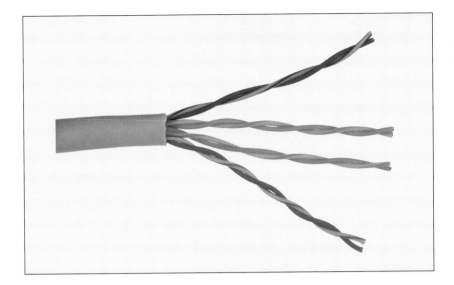

backward compatible with Cat-5 and Cat-5e. It contains four pairs of copper wire like the previous generation, utilizes all four pairs, supports speeds up to 1 gigabit per second (Gbps), expands available bandwidth from 100 MHz for Cat-5e to 200 MHz, and has superior immunity from external noise. Polls predict that 80 to 90 percent of new installations will be cabled with Cat-6.

COAXIAL CABLE

Coaxial cable, familiar to cable TV users, consists of a center copper wire surrounded by insulation, which is then surrounded by a layer of braided wire. Data travels through the center wire, and the braided wire provides a shield against electrical interference (Figure 8.7). Coaxial cable carries data at transfer rates of 10 Mbps. In contrast to twisted pair, coaxial cable allows for broadband data communications. Your home is probably already wired with coaxial cable if you subscribe to a cable TV service.

FIBER-OPTIC CABLE

Fiber-optic cable, another broadband transmission medium, consists of thin strands of glass or plastic that carry data by means of pulses of light (Figure 8.8). Fiber-optic cable carries data at transfer rates of 10 Gbps (gigabits per second) or more, without loss of signal strength, and for longer distances than twisted pair or coaxial cable.

Wireless Transmission Media

Unlike communications using wired transmission media such as twisted-pair, coaxial, and fiber-optic cables, wireless media

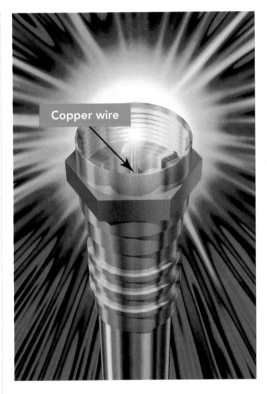

FIGURE 8.7 In coaxial cable, data travels through the center copper wire and is shielded from interference by the braided wire.

Copper wire

don't use solid substances to transmit data. Rather, wireless media send data through air or space using infrared, radio, or microwave signals. Why would you want to use wireless media instead of cables? One instance would be in situations where cables can't be installed or the costs to do so are prohibitive. The popularity of portable computing devices has led most colleges, airports, hotels, shopping malls, and coffee shops to offer wireless access to customers. This option is usually cheaper than running wires through existing buildings. Let's investigate the wireless options of data transfer and their features.

INFRARED

If you use a remote control to change television channels, you're already familiar with infrared signaling. **Infrared** is a wireless transmission medium that carries data via beams of light through the air. No wires are required, but the transmitting and receiving devices must be in line of sight or the signal is lost. When the path between the transmitting and the receiving devices is not obstructed by trees, hills, mountains, buildings, or other structures, infrared signals can work within a maximum of about 100 feet.

To use infrared technology with your computer system, you need an **IrDA port** (Figure 8.9). You may encounter an IrDA (Infrared Data Association) port on a mobile computing device or wireless peripheral such as a PDA, digital camera, notebook, mouse, printer, or keyboard. The most common use of the IrDA port is to transfer data from your PDA to your desktop or notebook computer or another PDA. To enable data transfer, the IrDA port on the transmitting device must be in line of sight (usually within a few feet) of the port on the receiving device. IrDA ports offer data transfer rates of 4 Mbps. With these restrictions of distance and speed, why would you want to use infrared? If you had a situation where hooking devices together with cables wasn't an option, such as with a wireless keyboard or mouse, infrared would be a good choice. On modern networks, however, IrDA is too slow to be of practical use for transferring large amounts of data.

FIGURE 8.9 An IrDA port allows for more flexibility in managing external devices such as a mouse, keyboard, phone, or PDA.

RADIO

Radio transmissions offer an alternative to infrared transmissions. You probably have experienced one type of radio transmission by listening to your favorite radio station. But you may not realize the impact that radio waves have on your daily life or on society in general. All kinds of gadgets—from cell and cordless phones to baby monitors—communicate via radio waves. Although humans cannot see or otherwise detect them, radio waves are everywhere.

With **radio** transmission, data in a variety of forms (music, voice conversations, and photos) travels through the air as radio frequency (RF) signals or radio waves via a transmitting device and a receiving device. Instead of separate transmitting and receiving devices, radio transmissions can also use a wireless transceiver, a combination transmitting-receiving device equipped with an antenna. Data transfer rates for wireless devices have the potential to reach up to 3 Mbps for cell phones and up to 250 Mbps for wireless networks.

A major disadvantage of radio transmission is susceptibility to noise and interference. One of radio's advantages is that radio signals are effective at both long range (between cities, regions, and countries) and short range (within a home or office).

Bluetooth **Bluetooth** is a short-range radio transmission technology that has become very popular in recent years. Named after the 10th-century Danish Viking and king Harald Blåtand ("Bluetooth" in English) who united Denmark and Norway, Bluetooth was first conceived by Swedish cell phone giant Ericsson (Figure 8.10). Bluetooth technology relies on a network called a **piconet** or a **PAN (personal area network)** that enables all kinds of devices—desktop computers, mobile phones, printers, pagers, PDAs, and more—within 30 feet of each other to communicate automatically and wirelessly.

How exactly does Bluetooth work? Bluetooth-enabled devices identify each other using identification numbers that are unique to each device. When these devices are within 30 feet of each other, they automatically "find" and link to one another. You don't have to worry about being connected to Bluetooth devices that you don't want to connect to: The device requires that you confirm a connection before making it final. Up to eight Bluetooth-enabled devices can be connected in a piconet at any one time.

Unlike infrared technologies, Bluetooth doesn't require a direct line of sight to connect devices. Because the frequency used by Bluetooth devices changes often, Bluetooth devices never use the same frequency at the same time and don't interfere with each other. The new Bluetooth 3.0 standard can accommodate data transfer rates of up to 24 Mbps, up from 3 Mbps. At Bluetooth's maximum transfer capacity, you would be able to move a document easily within just a few seconds. A testimony to the popularity of the connectivity provided by Bluetooth technology is verified by industry statistics that point to the 2 billion devices that have been shipped with Bluetooth installed. For more information on Bluetooth technology and a brief video on the differences between Bluetooth and Wi-Fi connectivity, go to **www.bluetooth.com/bluetooth**.

MICROWAVES

Microwaves are electromagnetic radio waves with short frequencies that are used to transmit data. Using relay stations similar to satellite dishes (including an antenna, transceiver, and so on), microwave signals are sent from one relay station to the next. Because microwaves must travel in a straight line with no obstructions such as buildings, hills, mountains, and so on, relay stations are built at a distance of approximately every 30 miles (the line-of-sight distance to the horizon), or closer if the terrain blocks transmission. Microwave relay stations are also often situated on the tops of buildings or mountains.

Microwave transmission eliminates the need for a wired infrastructure. It is used to transmit data across cellular telephone networks and to provide connectivity in areas where the use of physical wires is impractical or impossible. Disadvantages include the 30-mile line-of-sight restriction, sensitivity to electrical or magnetic interference, and costs of maintaining the multitude of relay stations it takes to transfer messages across long distances.

SATELLITES

Essentially microwave relay stations in space, communications satellites are positioned in geosynchronous orbit, which matches the satellite's speed to that of the Earth's rotation, and are, therefore, permanently positioned with respect to the ground below (Figure 8.11). **Satellites** transmit data by sending and receiving microwave signals to and from Earth-based stations. Devices such as handheld

FIGURE 8.10 Bluetooth-enabled devices make tasks, such as synchronizing your phone calendar with your computer calendar or keeping your hands free while talking on the phone, easier.

computers and Global Positioning System (GPS) receivers can also function as Earth-based stations.

Direct broadcast satellite (DBS) is a consumer satellite technology that uses an 18- or 21-inch reception dish to receive digital TV signals at microwave frequencies directly from geostationary satellites broadcast at a bandwidth of 12 Mbps. Increasingly, DBS operators offer Internet access as well as digital TV service, but at much lower bandwidth. A good overview of a DBS can be found at **http://electronics.howstuffworks .com/satellite-tv.htm**, where a video demonstrates the progression of an image from its initial capture by a camera to its reception and viewing on a home TV.

Currently, DIRECTV offers DirecWay 1-way and DirecWay 2-way Internet satellite systems. DirecWay 1-way offers high-speed broadband download via satellite link, with uploads requiring a telephone and modem. This is the inexpensive option for most broadband Internet users because downloading is used more frequently than uploading. No professional installation is required because you only receive the high-speed signal and don't transmit. DirecWay 2-way uses a high-speed satellite link both for uploading and downloading. The drawback of the 2-way system is its increased cost and the FCC's requirement that satellite dishes that both transmit and receive signals be installed professionally.

Broadband access is still not available in many rural or other low-population areas, thus many of these areas are prime candidates for DBS. If it is the only option available, something is better than nothing!

To use these various wireless transmission media, a computer system must also use a special communications device called a **network access point**, which sends and receives data between comput-

FIGURE 8.11 Communications satellites are often permanently positioned with respect to points on the Earth to provide specific areas of coverage.

ers that contain wireless adapters. Access points are usually built into wireless routers.

So, what is it about wireless connectivity that is so interesting? Well, one answer is that wireless technology removes place-specific restrictions, that is, the need to be in a certain place to receive a service. Some forms of wireless technology allow you to be wherever you choose and still have the ability to be connected.

Now that you know more about wired and wireless media, the next section will explore the most common wired communication system: the public switched telephone network.

Wired Communication Via the Public Switched Telephone Network

Although many components of the conventional phone system have been enhanced, until all devices have been replaced with digital equivalents, limitations still exist.

The **public switched telephone network (PSTN)** is the global telephone system, a massive network used for data as well as voice communications, comprising various transmission media ranging from twisted-pair wire to fiber-optic cable. Some computer users derisively (and somewhat unfairly) refer to the PSTN as plain old telephone service (POTS). The derision comes from most analog telephone lines being based on standards that date back more than a century. Although a few parts of the PSTN remain based on analog communications, the majority of the system has been switched over to digital communications.

Many home and business telephones in use today are analog devices. These telephones are linked to subscriber loop carriers by means of twisted-pair wires. A **subscriber loop carrier (SLC)** is a small, waist-high curbside installation that connects as many as 96 subscribers; you've probably seen one in your neighborhood. The area served by an SLC is called the **local loop**. When the analog signal reaches the SLC, it is converted to digital form and remains that way throughout the PSTN network.

From the SLC, the digital signals are routed via high-capacity fiber-optic cables to the **local exchange switch**, a digital device capable of handling thousands of calls located in the local telephone company's central office (CO). From the local phone company's CO, the call can go anywhere in the world. It continues on the digital portion of the PSTN's fiber-optic cables and can even be converted to radio waves and sent out over cellular networks (Figure 8.12).

Although analog connections still exist, **digital telephony**, a system in which the telephones and transmissions are digital, are the trend. Compared with analog devices, which are prone to noise and interference, digital phones offer noise-free transmission and high-quality audio. You might have used a digital phone at work or on campus. Typically companies and universities install their own internal digital telephone systems, called private branch exchanges (PBXs). Calls to the outside, however, must be translated into analog signals to connect to the PSTN.

Because long-distance lines must handle thousands of calls simultaneously (32 calls per second, 24 hours a day, 7 days a week in the United States), a technique called **multiplexing** is used to send more than one call over a single line. The electrical and physical characteristics of copper wire impose a limit of 24 multiplexed calls per line, whereas fiber-optic cables can carry as many as 48,384 digital voice channels simultaneously. In contrast to the analog local loop, most long-distance carriers use digital signals so that they can pack the greatest number of calls into a single circuit.

The inability of homes or businesses to access the PSTN's high-speed fiber-optic cables, along with the bottleneck of data on the last mile of twisted-pair phone lines connecting homes and businesses, is often referred to as the **last-mile problem**. Here's why. In most areas of the United States, only the local loop is still using analog technology, because nearly all existing buildings were originally constructed with built-in twisted-pair wiring. These analog lines are vulnerable to noise and can't surpass a theoretical limit of 56 Kbps. But things are starting to change. Telephone

FIGURE 8.12 Pathways on the PSTN

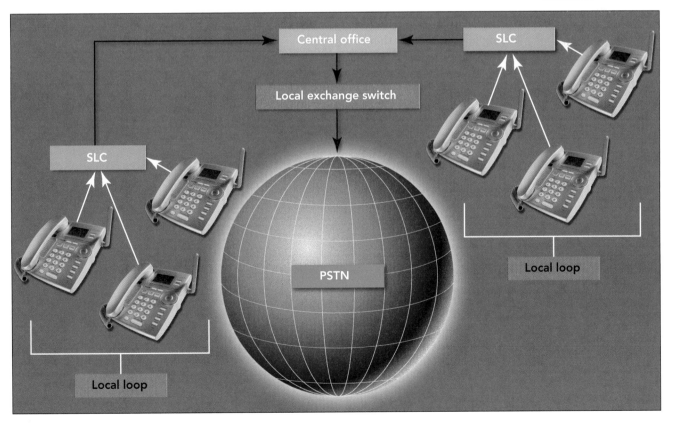

companies are getting into other businesses (such as providing Internet connectivity) and need to deliver higher bandwidth to homes. Therefore, telephone companies are now replacing analog local loop technology with digital technology (such as FiOS). The last-mile problem might soon be solved in your neighborhood!

LAST-MILE TECHNOLOGIES

Local loops are in the process of being upgraded, but until the upgrade is complete, phone companies and other providers offer a number of interim digital telephony technologies that make use of twisted-pair wiring. Sometimes called **last-mile technologies**, these solutions include digital telephone standards (such as ISDN and DSL) that use twisted-pair wiring, as well as high-speed wired services (such as coaxial cable and cable modems). To learn more about 21st-century telephone technology and trends of the future, check out **http://telecom.hellodirect.com/docs/ Tutorials/default.asp**.

Integrated Services Digital Network ISDN (integrated services digital network) is a standard that provides digital telephone and data service. ISDN offers connections ranging from 56 to 128 Kbps (basic rate ISDN) or 1.5 Mbps (primary rate ISDN) using ordinary twisted-pair telephone lines. The cost of an ISDN line is often two to three times that of an analog phone line, but there's a payoff. With a 128-Kbps ISDN service, you get two telephone numbers with one ISDN account; you can use one for computer data and the other for voice or fax. When you're using the connection for computer data only, the system automatically uses both data channels to give you the

maximum data transfer rate; if a phone call comes in, the connection automatically drops back to 64 Kbps to accommodate the incoming call. What's more, connection is nearly instantaneous. Unlike analog connections with a modem, there's no lengthy dial-in procedure and connection delay.

To connect computers to ISDN lines, you need an **ISDN adapter** (also called a **digital modem**, although it isn't actually a modem; Figure 8.13). Although ISDN has been largely supplanted by faster technologies (such as DSL and fiber optics), ISDN may be the only broadband solution in many rural areas. Keep in mind that ISDN requires that special wiring be installed from the SLC to your home.

Digital Subscriber Line DSL (digital subscriber line), also called **xDSL**, is a blanket term for a group of related technologies, including **ADSL** (asymmetric digital subscriber line), **SDSL** (symmetrical digital subscriber line), **HDSL** (high bit-rate digital subscriber line), and **VDSL** (very high bit-rate digital subscriber line), that offer high-speed Internet access. DSL technologies, in general, can deliver data transfer rates of 1.54 Mbps or higher. DSL is widely available in the United States and is akin to ISDN in that it uses existing twisted-pair wiring. But because DSL is always on, requires no call set up time, and achieves much higher throughput than ISDN, it quickly became more popular. For the difference between the four DSL technologies, refer to Figure 8.14.

To use DSL, you need a DSL phone line and a DSL service subscription. Unlike conventional telephone service, which is available to almost any home, DSL service is limited by the distance from the CO, or telephone switching station, to

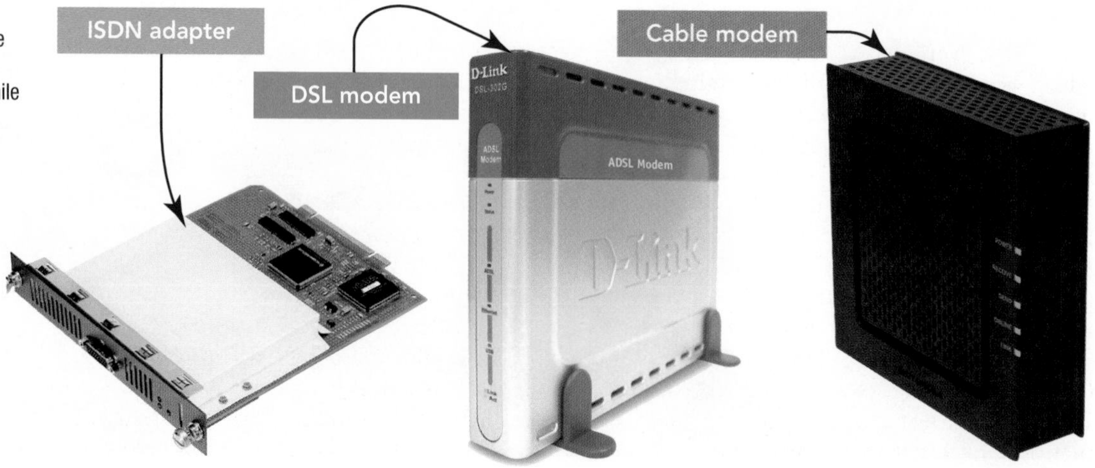

FIGURE 8.13 Various types of modems facilitate the connection between your computer and last-mile technologies.

ISDN adapter

DSL modem

Cable modem

FIGURE 8.14 The Details behind DSL Technologies

	ADSL	SDSL	HDSL	VDSL
Actual Name	Asymmetrical Digital Subscriber Line	Symmetrical Digital Subscriber Line	High Bit-Rate Digital Subscriber Line	Very High Bit-Rate Digital Subscriber Line
Technology Feature	An ADSL modem separates an ordinary copper telephone line into three separate data channels with different capacities and speeds. The lowest capacity transmits analog voice for telephones; the second, medium capacity, uploads data to the network; and the third, highest capacity, downloads data from the network. This means that uploads are slower than downloads on an ADSL connection.	A SDSL modem splits the copper telephone line channels into three channels: telephone, upload and download; but it does this so that the distributed bandwidth for each channel is equal. On SDSL connections, uploads and downloads occur at the same rate.	HDSL, the most mature DSL technology, is a form of SDSL that provides T1 connections over two or three twisted-pair copper lines. Unlike most other forms of DSL, HDSL is not a typical consumer service.	VDSL is the next generation DSL with super-accelerated rates of 52 Mbps for downloads and 12 Mbps for uploads. It will provide services like HDTV and Video-on-Demand along with Internet access.
Bandwidth	Uploads at speeds of up to 640 Kbps, downloads at speeds of up to 8.1 Mbps	Supports data exchange rates each way, up to 3 Mbps	1.544 Mbps of bandwidth each way	Uploads at speeds of up to 52 Mbps, downloads at speeds of up to 12 Mbps
Users	Popular with residential users in the United States	Popular with residents in Europe	PBX network connections, digital loop carrier systems, interexchange POPs, Internet servers, and private data networks.	VDSL is available worldwide in specific regions. Its use is growing all the time, though it's not easily found in the United States.

your home. You also need a **DSL modem**, which is similar to a traditional telephone modem in that it modulates and demodulates analog and digital signals for transmission over communications channels. However, DSL modems use signaling methods based on broadband technology for much higher transfer speeds. DSL service is now standardized so that almost any DSL modem should work with the wiring your telephone provider uses (Figure 8.15). However, it is best to buy a DSL modem that your provider recommends. Check with your provider for a list of approved modems before purchasing one. Although DSL service is more expensive than dial-up, it is usually cheaper than other broadband access options.

Cable-Based Broadband Aside from telephone companies, the leading provider of broadband is your local cable TV company. Approximately 120 million homes in the United States have accessibility to high-speed cable Internet service (Figure 8.16).

When cable and the cabling equipment were originally installed in homes, signals

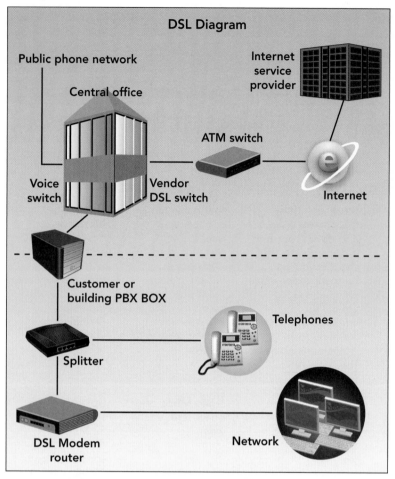

DSL Diagram

Public phone network

Central office

Internet service provider

ATM switch

Voice switch

Vendor DSL switch

Internet

Customer or building PBX BOX

Telephones

Splitter

DSL Modem router

Network

FIGURE 8.15 The Path of Data from an Internet Service Provider to a DSL Subscriber's Residence

ment. Bandwidth across a cable connection is shared among subscribers who are connected to the cable company in local groups. If you are lucky enough to have subscribers in your group who don't use much bandwidth, you can experience impressive speed while using the Internet. To help you decide which last-mile technology might be right for you, check out the "Cable or DSL" tutorial at **http://telecom.hellodirect.com/docs/ Tutorials/CableVsDSL.1.030801.asp.**

Leased Lines A **leased line** is a specially conditioned telephone line that enables continuous, end-to-end communication between two points. Larger organizations, such as ISPs, corporations, and universities, connect using leased **T1 lines**, which are fiber-optic (or specially conditioned copper) cables that can handle 24 digitized voice channels or carry computer data at a rate of up to 1.544 Mbps. If the T1 line is being used for telephone conversations, it plugs into the users' phone system. If it is carrying data, it plugs into the network's router. The price of T1 lines ranges from $1,000 to $1,500, depending on the provider, the location, and the use. Leased lines may use modems, cable modems, or other communications devices to manage the transfer of data into and out of the organization.

Other Last-Mile Technologies There are also interim technologies that make better use of existing fiber-optic cables.

were designed to run in only one direction: to the home. When the Internet became popular, the cable companies invested tremendous amounts of money in equipment and cable to enable two-way communication to capture the Internet market.

For computer users, these services offer data transfer rates that exceed the speed of DSL. **Cable modems**, devices that enable computers to access the Internet by means of a cable TV connection, now deliver data at bandwidths of 1.5 to 6 Mbps or more, depending on how many subscribers are connected to a local cable seg-

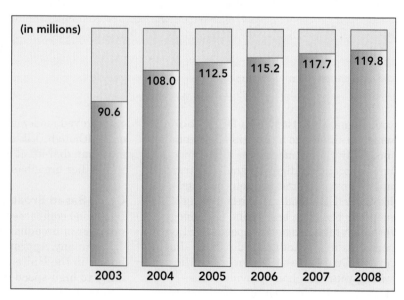

(in millions)

2003	2004	2005	2006	2007	2008
90.6	108.0	112.5	115.2	117.7	119.8

FIGURE 8.16 In five years, high-speed Internet cable has been made accessible to an additional 30 million Americans.

Fiber-optic **T3 lines** can handle 44.7 Mbps of computer data. Although T3 lines can cost approximately $3,000 per month, Internet service providers, financial institutions, and large corporations that move a large amount of data find these lines critical to their operations. Another technology that uses fiber-optic cable, **SONET (synchronous optical network)** is a standard for high-performance networks. The slowest SONET standard calls for data transfer rates of 52 Mbps; some enable rates of 1 Gbps or faster. SONET is widely used in North America, and a similar standard, synchronous digital hierarchy (SDH), is used in the rest of the world.

In addition to adapting twisted-pair wiring, broadband coaxial cable, and fiber-optic cable, wireless technologies are helping to solve the last-mile problem as well. Here's a look at two wireless solutions.

MMDS (multichannel multipoint distribution service, sometimes called multipoint microwave distribution system) can be thought of as wireless cable. MMDS was originally slated as a wireless alternative to cable television, but now its main application is Internet access. Service providers offer MMDS Internet access within a 35-mile radius of the nearest transmission point at projected speeds of 1 Gbps.

MMDS will most likely be supplanted by WiMAX (worldwide interoperability for microwave access). **WiMAX** is a wireless up-and-coming digital communication system designed to deliver high-speed access over long distances, either point to point (both sender and receiver are stationary) or through mobile access (sender or receiver is moving). WiMAX is effective for up to 30 miles for point-to-point access and 3 to 10 miles for mobile access. In mountainous areas or other places where there are obstructions, MMDS and WiMAX face challenges because they are susceptible to interference. To view a brief video on the technology behind WiMAX and an explanation of how it works, visit **www.wimax.com/ education**.

In the next section, we will explore the phenomenon of the coming together of these communications technologies.

> " In addition to adapting **twisted-pair** wiring, broadband **coaxial** cable, and **fiber-optic** cable, **wireless** technologies are helping to solve the last-mile problem... "

ETHICS

When you log on to the Internet through a wireless connection at your home, are you sure that you're logging onto your own network? Some people inadvertently connect to their neighbor's wireless network instead of their own. Using another person's network without permission is called **piggybacking**. This term can also apply to using free Internet connections designated for customers of an establishment like McDonalds or Starbucks when you are not a customer. Is it right to use services from a business that you do not frequent? Is it wrong to use your neighbor's network if you don't download or upload pirated materials? Would you like to be paying for a service and have someone else use it, without permission, for free? Piggybacking is a crime in most jurisdictions in the United States. Do you need to rethink your behavior?

Convergence: Is It a Phone or a Computer?

We've been examining technologies that carry computer data over voice lines as well as through the air. At the core of this process is **digitization**, the transformation of data such as voice, text, graphics, audio, and video into digital form. Digitization enables convergence.

Convergence refers to the merging of disparate objects or ideas (and even people) into new combinations and efficiencies. Within the IT industry, convergence means two things: (1) the combination of various industries (computers, consumer

a

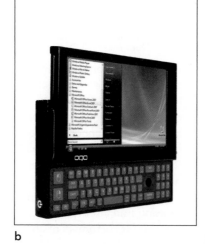

b

FIGURE 8.17
Convergence means smaller devices do more. (**a**) The BlackBerry Curve 8350i is a PDA, phone, and Internet access device all rolled into one. (**b**) The OQO model 2+ is one of the world's smallest computers at 5.6 × 3.3 inches, making it easy to take your computer with you.

electronics, and telecommunications) and (2) the coming together of products such as PCs and telephones.

Wireless devices are proliferating at a tremendous pace. Today, it is not unusual for your phone to double as a PDA or talk to your computer, or for your computer to be controlled by a wireless mouse or keyboard. Convergence has culminated in the transmission of data. With the advent of Internet telephony (the use of the Internet to transmit real-time voice data), all forms of information (voice, data, and video) now travel over the same network, the Internet (Figure 8.17).

Digitization also enables media convergence. Media convergence is the unification of all forms of media (including newspapers, TV, and radio). The Internet is already a major source of breaking news, rivaling such traditional sources as newspapers and television. Many telephone calls are now transmitted across the Internet using a technology known as Voice over IP (VoIP). This trend could be signaling the end of the traditional public switched telephone network.

Another threat to the PSTN is the November 2003 legislation on telephone number portability. Under this rule, people can keep their existing phone number when changing providers, whether from traditional land-based or cellular phone service. Despite the ongoing challenges of cell phones (battery life, spotty connectivity, dropped calls), in 2008 approximately 10 to 15 percent of U.S. households have opted to disconnect their conventional landline telephones and rely solely on cellular service. Industry professionals expect

this migration away from land-based telephones to continue. In support of this statistic, smartphones like the iPhone and BlackBerry, which can surf the Web and provide e-mail access, experienced a 75.7 percent increase in the United States in 2008.

Why should you care about convergence? Understanding convergence will help you make more informed decisions about current and future technology purchases. This section explores some of the dimensions of computer-telephony convergence, a process of technological morphing in which previously distinct devices lose their sharply defined boundaries and blend together. As you'll see, it's creating some interesting hybrids.

CELLULAR TELEPHONES

Cellular telephones are computing devices. Although cell phones started out as analog devices (**1G**, for first generation), the current generation of wireless cell phones (**3G**, for third generation) are all digital systems that provide high-speed access to transmit voice, text, images, and video data. For more information, dates, and features of each cell phone technology generation refer to Figure 8.18.

In 1971, AT&T built a network of transmitters that automatically repeat signals. This network of transmitters, which are called **cell sites**, broadcasts signals throughout specific, but limited, geographic areas called **cells**. When callers move from cell to cell, each new cell site automatically takes over the signal to maintain signal strength. But who or what monitors your cell phone's signal strength so that you have the best reception? That's the job of the **mobile switching center (MSC)**, and each cellular network contains several MSCs that handle communications within a group of cells (Figure 8.19). Each cell tower reports signal strength to the MSC, which then switches your signal to whatever cell tower will provide the clearest connection for your conversation.

MSCs route calls to the gateway mobile switching center (GMSC), which in turn sends calls to their final destination. If the call is headed for a land-based phone, the GMSC sends the call to the PSTN. Otherwise, it forwards the call directly to another cellular network.

FIGURE 8.18 Cell Phone Generations

Wireless Technologies	Year	Feature
1G	1981	Analog mobile phone service allowed callers to make their own calls without operator assistance and move seamlessly from cell to cell.
2G	1991	Digital signaling decreased interference, improved reception, and provided better protection from eavesdropping. This generation also increased security features designed to discouraging cell phone fraud.
3G	2001	These technologies enabled faster data transmission, greater network capacity, more advanced network services, and allowed transmission of voice, text, images, and video data.
4G (beyond 3G)	2012–2015 (estimated release)	The next generation promises even higher data rates as well as real-time (streamed) formatting for voice, data, and high-quality multimedia.

Terrain, interference, weather, antenna position, and battery strength can all affect signal strength. However, there may be times when you've extended your antenna, recharged your battery, have clear weather, and are standing at the top of a hill—and still cannot achieve a good signal. Cell coverage is not perfect, and cellular networks have *holes* (areas in which you can't send or receive calls).

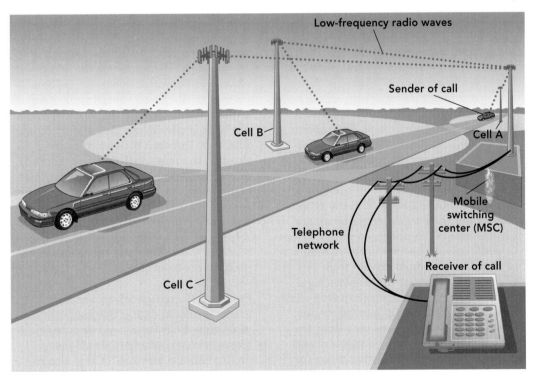

FIGURE 8.19 When callers move from cell to cell, the mobile switching center locates the cell with the strongest signal strength and that cell automatically takes over transmission.

FIGURE 8.20 In 2008, 75 billion text messages were sent, with a majority by users between the ages of 25 and 34.

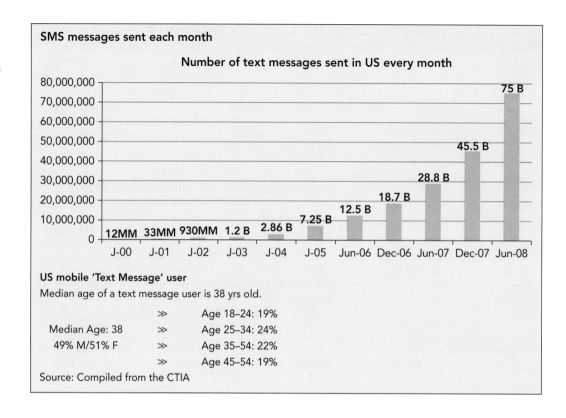

SMS messages sent each month

Number of text messages sent in US every month

US mobile 'Text Message' user
Median age of a text message user is 38 yrs old.

Median Age: 38	≫	Age 18–24: 19%
49% M/51% F	≫	Age 25–34: 24%
	≫	Age 35–54: 22%
	≫	Age 45–54: 19%

Source: Compiled from the CTIA

MSCs are also key players in another widely used cellular service, SMS (short messaging service), better known as text messaging. As of June 2008, over 75 billion text messages were sent every month compared to just 18 billion in December 2006. That number has grown by 250% each year for the last two years (Figure 8.20). The MSC forwards the message to a messaging center for storage and then locates the other cell phone that will receive the message. An appropriate signal is then sent out through the cell in which the receiving phone is located to let it know it will be receiving a message. The receiving phone sends an acknowledgment to the message center when the message is received.

Cell phone etiquette and safety are other issues to be aware of. Many people may be irritated or concerned by others' careless use of cell phones in public places or while driving motor vehicles. A number of states have banned drivers from using handheld cell phones while operating a motor vehicle. Other agencies have policies on cellular phone use in aircraft, trains, and hospitals. Businesses may limit the use of cell phones in movie theaters and restaurants. In addition, your college or university may restrict the use of cell phones in classrooms. For a list of the top

10 cell phone etiquette rules people break go to **www.bspcn.com/2008/08/14/top-10-cell-phone-etiquette-rules-people-still-break**.

Besides cell phone etiquette and safety, burgeoning cell phone use has another societal impact. Just as with old computer equipment, you need to think about the proper disposal of your cell phone when you upgrade or damage it beyond repair. The average life of a cell phone is 18 months; about 125 million phones are disposed of each year in the United States alone. Discarded cell phones are toxic waste. When they end up in landfills, they threaten the environment through the release of arsenic, lead, cadmium, and other heavy metals that can creep into the water supply and cause cancer or birth defects. AT&T, Cingular, and many other providers, as well as indirect retailers, will accept old phones. The bottom line: Recycling your old cell phone is good for the environment.

Personal Communication Service A group of related digital cellular technologies called **PCS (personal communication service)** quickly replaced most analog cellular services. PCS is also referred to as **2G**, for second-generation cellular technology, or dual-band service.

GREEN tech tips

Simply throwing away a cell phone is hazardous to the environment. With cell phones made of recycled material still in the concept stage, how you dispose of your old phone is left up to you. So, what can you do to dispose of your phone responsibly? Check out **www.nokia.com/environment/we-recycle**.

Nokia's We Recycle program will recycle your phone for no cost. Verizon's HopeLine refurbishes or recycles old phones and uses the proceeds to help prevent domestic violence. Through this program, more than 1 million phones and more than 170,000 batteries have been disposed of properly.

Visit the Shelter Alliance (Fund Raising with Accountability) Web site at **www.shelteralliance.net/index.cfm** to learn about several cell phone recycling programs offered through this organization and its nonprofit partners.

Digital 2G phones made strides toward solving many of the problems that plagued analog phones. Improvements included decreasing signal interference, increasing reception, providing better protection from eavesdropping, and increasing the difficulty of committing cell phone fraud. In short, 2G design specifications enabled the manufacturers to use convergence to make the **smartphones** we enjoy today, which are handheld devices that integrate mobile phone capability, computing power, and Web access. (Figure 8.21).

For millions of people, 2G made mobile computing a reality. Because 2G technology is digital, it's much more amenable to data communications than analog cellular services. It made it possible to access the Internet by means of a modem connected to an analog cellular phone, but data transfer rates were extremely low because of line noise and poor connections. Throughput of up to 384 Kbps for downloads was enabled by 2G standards.

Technology has marched on with the introduction of 3G technology and the planning of **4G** (fourth generation) cell phones. The main benefit of 3G is that it supports much higher numbers of data and voice customers and provides higher data transfer rates (greater than 384 Kbps while walking and up to 2 Mbps while stationary). Although still under development, 4G is expected to offer improvements in connectivity, data transfer rates, and support for the next generation of multimedia.

So, should you dump your 2G phone and opt for a 3G? If your phone is providing you with good-quality service and the feature set is sufficient for your needs, you should probably keep it. However, if you need to regularly access the Internet, you may wish to consider upgrading to a 3G phone to take advantage of the higher data transfer rates.

WEB-ENABLED DEVICES

A **Web-enabled device** is any device that can connect to the Internet and display and respond to the codes in markup languages, such as HTML (Hypertext Markup Language) or XML (Extensible Markup Language), typically used to build Web pages. Web-enabled devices include PDAs, smartphones, and notebook PCs.

PDAs are fast disappearing from the market because of convergence. Many smartphones now offer all the functionality that PDAs used to offer and also act as phones. Windows Mobile and the Palm OS are popular operating systems for smartphones that were originally developed for PDAs. BlackBerry devices (which use their own operating system called RIM) continue to be a popular choice for managing enterprise business life (which includes checking e-mail, making phone calls, and accessing the Internet). BlackBerry devices actually lead the smartphone revolution as one of the first truly convergent devices.

The market for mobile operating systems has heated up, with Apple iPhone OS and Symbian leading the way. RIM BlackBerry, Windows Mobile (based on Windows CE), and Google Android are

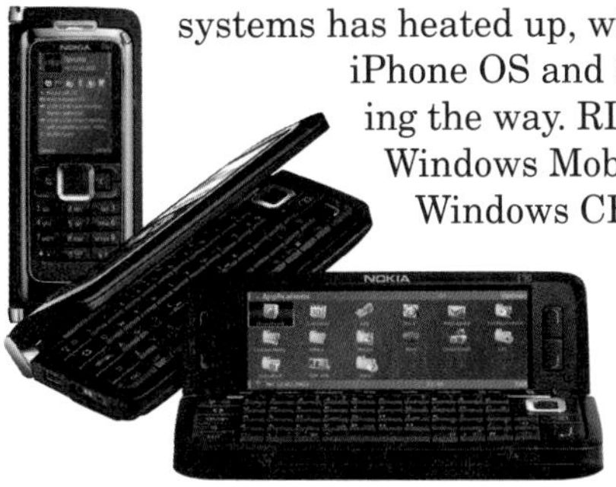

FIGURE 8.21 The Nokia E90 Communicator boasts high-speed 3G mobile broadband connections for Internet browsing and file transfer.

FIGURE 8.22 As of
August 2009, the leading
mobile OS is the Apple
iPhone 3G operating sys-
tem, which is a mobile
version of Mac OS X.

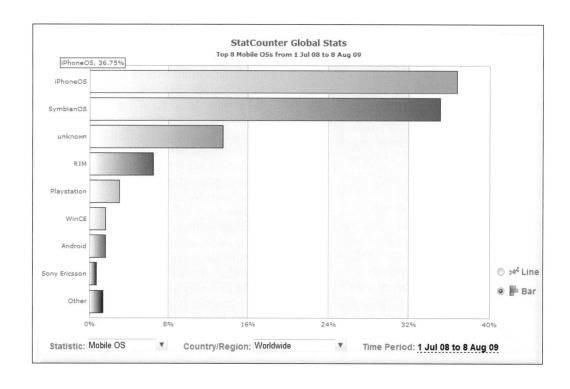

FIGURE 8.23 When
considering nine security
issues relative for business
use, the BlackBerry RIM OS
surpassed the iPhone OS
and Windows Mobile OS.

all making attempts to compete for their share of the market. For the current statistics on mobile OS popularity, see Figure 8.22.

Although the iPhone OS is the most widely used mobile operating system, a study completed in February of 2009 concluded that the most secure mobile platform for business use is the BlackBerry RIM. Refer to Figure 8.23 to view the criteria used to arrive at this assessment.

To work over wireless networks, Web-enabled devices require **WAP (Wireless Application Protocol)**. WAP is a standard that specifies how users can access the Web securely using pagers, smartphones, PDAs, and other wireless handheld devices. It doesn't matter which operating system your device uses because WAP is supported by all of them. However, WAP-enabled devices do require a **microbrowser**, a special Web browser that has all of the features of computer-based browsers but is simplified to meet handheld device limitations. These limitations include smaller screen size, smaller file sizes (due to the low memory capacities of WAP-enabled devices), and wireless networks with low bandwidth.

Now that you understand how convergence is blurring the boundaries between phone and computer devices, let's take a look at some wired and wireless applications used with these devices.

Comparative Evaluation of Secure Mobile OS Components

	BlackBerry OS	iPhone OS	Win Mobile OS
Authentication	🎧🎧🎧	🎧	🎧🎧
Data Vaulting	🎧🎧🎧	🎧	🎧🎧
Application Verification	🎧🎧	🎧	🎧
Reliability	🎧🎧🎧	🎧🎧🎧	🎧🎧
Manageability/ Policy Enforcement	🎧🎧🎧	🎧	🎧🎧
Tamper Resistance	🎧🎧	🎧	🎧
Security vs. Usability	🎧🎧	🎧🎧	🎧🎧
Meeting Security Validations	🎧🎧🎧	🎧🎧	🎧
Allowing Security Extensions	🎧🎧	🎧	🎧🎧

Wired and Wireless Applications

The world of wired and wireless applications is receiving more attention every day. You can't open a magazine, surf the Web, or watch TV without seeing ads for the latest wireless solutions. More and more businesses and home users are implementing these various applications to help them communicate, collaborate, and share text, graphics, audio, and video. You can sit in a classroom today and receive instant messages, e-mail, and stock quotes and even browse the Web—all from your cell phone! And it is happening at increasingly faster speeds, higher data transfer rates, and lower costs.

INTERNET TELEPHONY: REAL-TIME VOICE AND VIDEO

Internet telephony, more commonly known as **VoIP (Voice over Internet Protocol)**, uses the Internet for real-time voice communication. Although the Internet isn't ideal for real-time voice, you can place calls via the Internet in a variety of ways. To place free long-distance calls, you'll need a computer equipped with a microphone, speakers or headphones, an Internet connection, and a telephony-enabled program such as Skype (**www.skype.com**). With Skype, you can make free calls to other similarly equipped Skype users (Figure 8.24).

What about placing a call to an ordinary telephone? You can't do it for free. However, VoIP service providers such as Vonage are stepping into the act by offering computer-to-phone and phone-to-phone services that use the Internet for long-distance transmission (Figure 8.25). Rates are cheaper than conventional landline phones and the quality is very good.

The basic idea of Internet telephony has an enormous advantage:

Because the Internet doesn't rely on switches to route messages, like the PSTN does, it's cheaper to operate. Providers can route dozens, hundreds, or even thousands of calls over the same circuit. Many conventional phone companies already send voice calls over the Internet. You may have actually experienced VoIP without even knowing it. You can try Internet telephony by using Skype, which is the cheapest way (free!) to experience VoIP, and see how you like it.

If you and the person you're calling have a digital video camera, you can converse through real-time videoconferencing as well. **Videoconferencing** is the use of digital video technology to transmit sound and video images so that two or more people can have a face-to-face meeting even though they're geographically separated (Figure 8.26). Many notebook computers sold today come with built-in video cameras (Webcams) and Skype software to support video conferencing. However, you won't always have perfect quality; you'll hear echoes and delays in the audio, and the picture will be small, grainy, jerky, and liable to delays. But there are no long-distance charges (using Skype).

In addition to Internet voice and video calls, Internet telephony products support real-time conferencing with such features as a shared whiteboard, file-exchange capabilities, and text chatting. A **whiteboard**, generally shown as a separate area of the videoconferencing screen,

Call someone who's on Skype

Call someone in your Contact list:

1. Click the Contacts button at the top of Skype.

2. In the list, find the person you want to call.
Click on them. (Remember - anyone with one of these beside them is on Skype so it's free to call. Anyone with one of these means it's a phone or mobile number and calls will cost you a little.)

3. You will see their details in the main window.
Click the green Call button. You should hear ringing. If you don't hear the other person or they can't hear you, click the call quality icon at the top of your call window.

4. To hang up, click the red End call button.

FIGURE 8.24 Skype features a simple interface and offers free calls to other Skype users. All you need is the Skype software, a microphone, and speakers (or headphones).

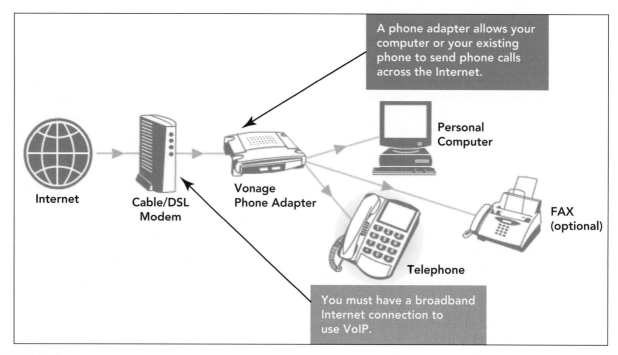

A phone adapter allows your computer or your existing phone to send phone calls across the Internet.

Internet

Cable/DSL Modem

Vonage Phone Adapter

Personal Computer

FAX (optional)

Telephone

You must have a broadband Internet connection to use VoIP.

FIGURE 8.25 VoIP installation is relatively easy. The system can be configured by a novice computer user.

enables participants to create a shared workspace. Participants can write or draw in this space as if they were using a physical whiteboard in a meeting. Combine this with live video and audio and it's like being in a conference room with your group.

A **Webcam** (Figure 8.27) is an inexpensive, low-resolution analog or digital video camera that is integrated into a notebook computer or designed to sit on top of a computer monitor. Sometimes an individual, company, or organization places a Webcam in a public location, such as a street corner, a railway station, or a museum (Figure 8.28). Often, the camera is set up to take a snapshot of the scene every 15 minutes or so. The image is then displayed on a Web page. Some sites offer streaming cams, also called live cams, which provide more frequently updated images. To learn more about Webcams and their use, and to obtain a few helpful hints, visit (**www.microsoft.com/canada/home/styleandhome/2.3.35_webcambasicshowdoesonework.aspx**).

FIGURE 8.26 In a videoconference, two or more people can see and communicate with each other even though they are not physically present in the same room.

If you want only to transmit voice over the Internet, and not video, you can use a dial-up modem and connection with transfer speeds of 56 Kbps. But for any high-bandwidth Internet application, such as streaming video, you need a broadband connection with transfer speeds of at least 1.5 Mbps. Network-based delivery of high-quality videoconferencing requires a bandwidth of at least 10 Mbps. Videoconferencing will be a much smoother experience for all participants with broadband's faster upload speeds.

Streaming video wasn't practical for home viewing before broadband and cheap, powerful computers became available for the home market. Now, streaming video sites such as YouTube are some of the most visited sites on the Internet.

Powerful, inexpensive computers and increased bandwidth offered by ISPs have made Internet telephony and videoconferencing affordable and practical for small businesses. And millions of Internet users employ Webcams and programs such as Skype to stay in touch with friends and family—often for free!

FIGURE 8.27 If your computer lacks a Webcam, you can buy one like the Logitech Quickcam Pro 9000, which is designed to be freestanding or placed on top of a monitor (or notebook).

FAXING: DOCUMENT EXCHANGE

Facsimile transmission—or **fax** as it's popularly known—enables you to send an image of a document over a telephone line or the Internet (Figure 8.29). The sending

FIGURE 8.28 The EarthCam Web site (**www.earthcam.com**) provides live satellite links to many popular locations, including the world-renowned Eiffel Tower in Paris, France.

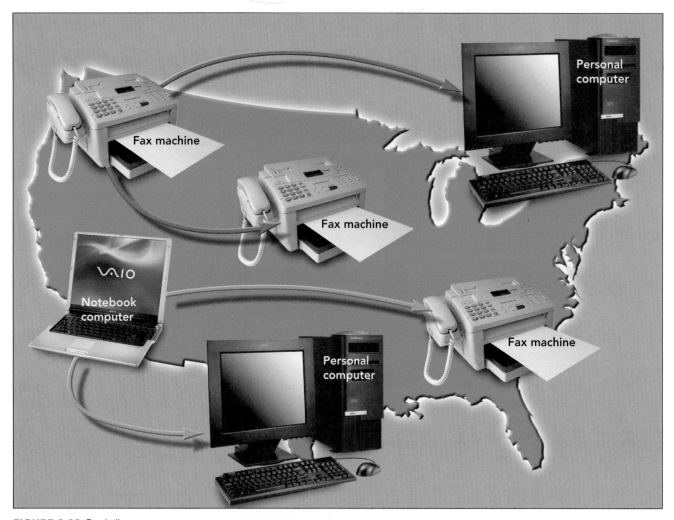

FIGURE 8.29 Facsimile transmissions can be sent over telephone lines or the Internet through the use of fax machines or computers equipped with fax modems.

fax machine makes a digital image of the document. Using a built-in modem, the sending fax machine converts the image into an analog representation so that it can be transmitted through the analog telephone system. The receiving fax machine converts the analog signals to digital signals, converts the digital signals to an image of the document, and then prints the image.

Some computer users use fax modems instead of fax machines. A **fax modem** is a computerized version of a stand-alone fax machine. This device and software allow your computer to do everything a fax machine can: send and receive documents, print documents, and store documents. The big difference between using a regular fax machine and using your computer as a fax machine is that the fax modem does everything in a digitized way. So, you may need a scanner to put a document into a digital format if you want to fax something that's printed or sketched on paper.

Traditional fax machines are quickly becoming obsolete. Some companies have chosen to use a spare computer as a fax server to handle incoming and outgoing faxes. Desktop software can convert e-mails to faxes and vice versa. This is referred to as fax-to-mail or mail-to-fax technology and reduces costs significantly because there is no need for a fax machine or an additional phone line. In addition, there is no extra charge for using your Internet connection to send a fax.

Faxes received in this way are usually converted to a PDF file and attached to an e-mail, or they may be sent to a cell phone. Similarly, sent faxes are converted to a PDF file and forwarded to a fax server, which then sends it over the Internet to its destination. If the receiving fax machine is a conventional machine attached to a phone line, the fax is forwarded to the PSTN for delivery.

Because computers can send and receive faxes, it is not a far stretch of the imagination to see that sending and receiving documents will soon be accomplished by network-enabled cell phones or Web-enabled devices, thereby making fax machines as we know them today obsolete.

SATELLITE RADIO, GPS, AND MORE

Many applications use satellite technology, including air navigation, TV and radio broadcasting, paging, and videoconferencing. **Satellite radio** broadcasts radio signals to satellites orbiting more than 22,000 miles above the Earth. The satellites then transmit the signals back to a radio receiver. Unlike ground-based radio signal transmitters, satellite radio is not affected by location, distance, or obstructions. Because of their great height, satellites can transmit signals to a radio receiver wherever it might be located.

Satellite radio is a boon for folks living in areas with limited local radio stations or where regular AM/FM reception is hampered by terrain. Sirius XM Radio Inc. is one of the largest satellite radio subscriptions companies. It is the result of the merger of satellite radio giants Sirius and XM in 2008. Satellite radio can mimic your local radio broadcasting station's style, including commercials. It can provide you with more than 100 channels offering different genres, including continuous music, sports, news, and talk programs. In contrast to music programs that are offered by some cable or satellite in-home providers, satellite radio uses portable receivers that plug into your home or car stereo, so it is totally mobile and transportable to wherever you happen to want to listen. SIRIUS now offers Backseat TV, which streams live TV broadcasts to subscribers who have video receivers in their vehicles.

Total revenue for Sirius XM Radio Inc. grew by 1 percent year-over-year to $608 million, while total subscribers, currently estimated at 19 million, continued to decline, also by 1 percent, for the second quarter of 2009. The decline in subscribers is attributed to the economy and decline in auto sales, while the boost in revenue is due to an increase in monthly charges and a decrease in operating costs since the merger.

Sirius XM is battling for subscribers. Its iPhone application has been a hit with existing users of the service, but it has failed to bring in new subscribers due to its higher cost and reduced radio content. Competition from other sources like Internet radio services, for example, Pandora, which can stream music into wireless-enabled cars such as certain Ford models, will continue to heat up as the auto industry and economy rebound.

GPS Another interesting application of satellite technology is GPS. **GPS (Global Positioning System)** is a cluster of 27 Earth-orbiting satellites (24 in operation and 3 extras in case one fails). Each of these 3,000- to 4,000-pound solar-powered satellites circles the globe at an altitude of 12,000 miles, making two complete rotations every day. The orbits are arranged so that at any time, anywhere on Earth, at least four satellites are "visible" in the sky. A GPS receiver's job is to locate four or more of these satellites, figure out the distance to each, and use this information to deduce its own location. Most systems are accurate to within 100 meters.

A GPS receiver can be either handheld or installed in a vehicle. Navigation systems in rental cars are a typical application of GPS. OnStar is a multifaceted GPS communications system that enables drivers to talk to a service representative to obtain driving directions and information on hotels, food venues, and the like. Drivers can also use OnStar to notify the police, fire department, or ambulance service in case of an emergency. Through in-vehicle sensors, it can even detect when a car has been involved in an accident. Finally, OnStar can also aid a driver with minor inconveniences such as unlocking car doors should a driver accidentally lock car keys inside (Figure 8.30).

GPS units for cars have become more mobile. Many different models can be easily attached to a dashboard and moved

> " Many applications use **satellite technology**, including **air navigation**, TV and radio broadcasting, paging, and **videoconferencing**. "

How OnStar Works

1 A GPS receiver in the vehicle picks up signals from Global Positioning System (GPS) satellites and calculates the location of the vehicle. That location information is stored in the vehicle's OnStar hardware.

2 When the driver pushes the blue OnStar button or red Emergency button, or an air bag deploys, OnStar places an embedded cellular call to the OnStar Center. Vehicle and GPS location data is sent at the beginning of the call.

3 The cellular call is received by a cellular tower and routed to the landline phone system.

4 The OnStar switch sends the call to the first available advisor, who has the location of the vehicle and the customer's information on her computer screen.

from one vehicle to another. Some units can even convert maps from road maps to walking maps that list house numbers and specific points of interest. You can update the maps on many GPS units via the Internet. Higher priced units allow you to swap media cards to provide foreign travel maps or conversion your unit into a marine GPS unit.

Other Satellite Applications Echelon is a system used by the U.S. National Security Agency to intercept and process international communications passed via satellites. The system uses ground-based listening devices and up to 120 satellites to intercept messages. It combs through the huge volume of intercepted messages, looking for words and phrases such as "bomb" and "terrorist" and other information of interest to intelligence agencies.

Satellites also bring Internet access to areas that don't have a communications infrastructure. The Navajo Nation, which straddles the borders of Arizona, New Mexico, and Utah and covers a 26,000-square-mile area, faces special challenges for connecting its residents to the Internet.

Approximately half the households don't even have phone service, and those that do, find the quality of that service sometimes lacking. For data communications, the maximum reliable data speed is often limited to 28.8 Kbps. In addition, Internet access through a private service provider is virtually always a long-distance call.

Navajo Nation school administrators purchased a system called HughesNet, which uses a small 18-inch satellite dish to receive information from the Internet and regular telephone or data lines to send information (Figure 8.31). Because Internet use in an educational environment involves massive amounts of downloaded information, the satellite solution was ideal.

TEXT, PICTURE, AND VIDEO MESSAGING AND MORE

A growing niche in cell phone use is within the K–12 age group, with experts predicting that 54 percent of 8- to 12-year-olds will have cell phones within the next three years. Cell phones give teens (and a growing number of preteens) not only a sense of community but also a sense of freedom. Cell phone ownership is being compared with the freedom and individuality of having a driver's license. And the cell phone market for teens is growing rapidly. Approximately 60 percent of teens in the United States now have cell phones. And a recent survey indicates that one-third of them would give up their radio, video games, or a trip to the mall before going without their phone!

FIGURE 8.31
HughesNet, also used in Alaska, uses orbiting satellites to retrieve and relay information, delivering Internet access to remote locations.

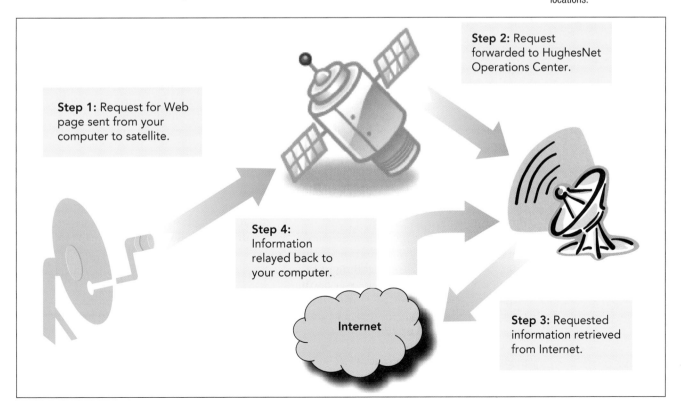

Step 1: Request for Web page sent from your computer to satellite.

Step 2: Request forwarded to HughesNet Operations Center.

Step 3: Requested information retrieved from Internet.

Step 4: Information relayed back to your computer.

Internet

More so than adults, teens and young adults use their cell phones to do things besides placing and receiving calls. Text, picture, and video messaging are the hot applications for mobile devices that e-mail and IM once were for computers. **Text messaging** is similar to using your phone for instant messaging or as a receiver and transmitter for brief e-mail messages (Figure 8.32).

Picture and video messaging are mobile services that will transform the way we electronically interact with each other. People have sent pictures by way of FTP or as e-mail attachments for more than 10 years, but the use of the telephone for such services has exploded in recent years. Today, **picture messaging** allows you to send full-color pictures, backgrounds, and even picture caller IDs on your cell phone. With picture messaging, your phone performs as a camera

FIGURE 8.32 Text messaging enables users to converse without bothering those nearby.

so that you can send pictures from your vacation or capture spontaneous moments and share them with others.

Many people want to use their phones to take pictures instead of carrying a digital camera. In order to have your phone replace your digital camera, you have to consider the resolution of the cell phone camera, which is measured in megapixels. A megapixel is 1 million pixels, or points of light, that make up an image. For pictures that will be printed out in large format (8 × 10 inches or larger), you need a camera with a resolution of at least 4 megapixels. Otherwise, the picture will not be sharp.

Images you capture with your phone can be sent by way of e-mail attachments or as a single picture when calling or talking to someone. Note that the user on the other end needs to have a picture-enabled phone as well and that there is a charge for sending pictures or video.

One cell phone application that is more popular with parents than kids is **location** (or **position**) **awareness**. This technology

uses GPS-enabled chips to pinpoint the location of a cell phone (and its user). Teens may find location awareness to be a downside of owning a cell phone because their parents can monitor their location. Teens often complain about such surveillance with statements such as "You're intruding on my privacy," "You're treading on my independence," and "I feel as though I'm always being watched." From the parents' perspective, however, they are simply keeping watch over their children in an effort to help them make better decisions.

Location awareness also has consumer and safety applications. The location-awareness feature enables your cell phone to quickly provide the location of the nearest restaurants and entertainment venues. It also can provide your location to a police station or other emergency service if needed. Law enforcement and government officials with the right credentials can access a Web site and locate a phone to within 35 feet of its actual location.

Cell phones manufactured since the end of 2004 are location aware. The benefit for society is that the 911 system can be used to determine the location of a phone, and thus the user, and then provide whatever assistance is necessary. Visit **www.ulocate.com** to learn more about location-awareness technology.

Along with all of its benefits, wireless technology also has its dark side that requires the user to be aware of evils lurking around the corner. As in the real world, predators exist and the user needs to keep a sharp eye for technology invasions.

SURFING SAFELY AT PUBLIC WIRELESS HOT SPOTS

A wireless hot spot is easy to locate today. McDonalds, Starbucks, and many other merchants offer Internet connectivity to lure customers. But when using public hot spots, especially free ones, you need to

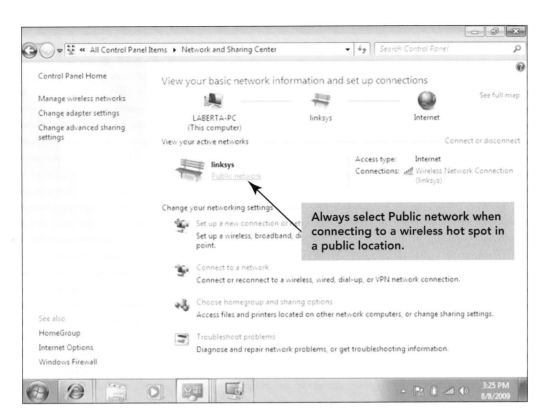

FIGURE 8.33 The screen displays the network settings available in Windows 7. Always use the Public location option when using a public wireless hot spot.

Always select Public network when connecting to a wireless hot spot in a public location.

take some extra precautions to keep you and your data safe. Here are a few issues to keep in mind at these sites: Wireless security is often not implemented on public hot spots; your shared files and directories might be accessible to others using the same wireless network; and you might be logging into a malicious network. A **malicious network** is a network set up by a hacker within the operating area of a legitimate hot spot. The hacker hopes to lure the user into the bogus network, referred to as an "evil twin," and gather sensitive information as passwords and credit card numbers.

Sounds scary, doesn't it? Well, you can't deny yourself the use of technology any more than you can deny yourself a trip to the mall for fear that something negative will happen. Here are a few precautions that you can follow to protect yourself while surfing on a public hot spot.

- Use firewalls and antivirus software.
- Ask an employee for the name of the legitimate network, to prevent connecting to an evil twin.
- Do not engage in sensitive financial transactions while connected to an unsecured hot spot.
- Select the appropriate operating system option to limit sharing of resources and discovery of your computer while connected to a public hot spot (Figure 8.33).

Chapter Summary

Wired and Wireless Communication

Bandwidth refers to the maximum data transfer capacity of a communications channel and is measured in hertz (Hz) and bits per second (bps). To transmit text, you can get by with low bandwidth (such as a 56 Kbps connection). But for viewing multimedia on the Internet, a broadband connection of at least 1.5 Mbps is preferable.

To transmit digital data over dial-up phone lines, it's necessary to use a modem. On the sending end, the modem modulates the signal (transforms it into analog form). On the receiving end, the modem demodulates the signal (transforms it back into digital form).

Communications require physical media, like twisted-pair wire, coaxial cable, and fiber-optic cable, or wireless media like infrared, radio, microwaves, and satellite. Additionally, WiMAX and MMDS are wireless technologies used to transmit signals over large geographic areas.

Digitization is the transformation of data such as voice, text, graphics, audio, and video into digital form. Convergence refers to the coming together of products such as PCs and telephones. Smartphones, PCs, and other Web-enabled devices enable all types of digital information (voice, video, and data) to travel over wireless communication systems. Along with the benefits of wired and wireless technology, be aware of the concern over the loss of privacy and rise in computer-related crimes.

Internet telephony and faxing can now be accomplished through the use of the Internet by traditional wired technology. New wireless technologies allow for text and picture messaging, satellite radio, and GPS services.

With wireless hot spots located in airports, coffee shops, and most public meeting places, it is important to use additonal safety precautions to secure your information and verify the hot spot's official name to avoid logging onto a bogus evil twin by mistake.

Key Terms and Concepts

Matching

Match each key term in the left column with the most accurate definition in the right column.

_____ 1. fiber-optic cable

_____ 2. twisted pair

_____ 3. infrared

_____ 4. throughput

_____ 5. coaxial

_____ 6. analog

_____ 7. multiplexing

_____ 8. Bluetooth

_____ 9. T1 line

_____ 10. microwave

_____ 11. bandwidth

_____ 12. modem

_____ 13. T3 line

_____ 14. digital

_____ 15. broadband

a. Short-range radio transmission technology often used in personal computing devices.

b. A broadband transmission medium in which an insulated wire runs through the middle of the cable.

c. Converts analog signals to digital signals and digital signals to analog signals.

d. Telecommunications line with a bandwidth capacity of 1.54 Mbps.

e. High bandwidth fiber optic medium capable of handling 43 Mbps of data.

f. Cabling that uses two to four intertwined pairs of wires.

g. The maximum amount of data that can sent though a specific transmission medium at one time.

h. A wireless transmission and receiving medium, used in TV remotes, that must be in the direct line of sight for the signal to be detected.

i. Signals emitted by computers or computing equipment.

j. Enabling more than one signal to be conveyed on a transmission medium.

k. Communications technologies with high bandwidth.

l. Transmission media that uses pulses of light.

m. The actual amount of data that is sent though a specific transmission medium at one time.

n. Signals emitted by real-life occurrences like light and sound.

o. An electromagnetic radio wave with a short frequency.

Multiple Choice

Circle the correct choice for each of the following.

1. What is the area served by an SLC called?
   a. Cell
   b. Local loop
   c. ISDN
   d. Network access point

2. What communication medium is capable of a data transfer speed of up to 1.544 Mbps and is often leased by organizations and businesses?
   a. T3 line
   b. Bluetooth
   c. T1 line
   d. IrDA

3. Which wireless technology is designed to deliver high-speed access over long distances?
   a. WiMAX
   b. Bluetooth
   c. DSL
   d. PSTN

4. Which component of the cellular network monitors your signal strength and switches you to the cell tower that will provide the clearest connection?
   a. Cell site
   b. Mobile switching center
   c. Subscriber loop carrier
   d. Personal communication service

5. What is the main advantage that 2G cellular devices provide over 1G devices?
   a. 2G devices never drop calls.
   b. 2G devices can stream video.
   c. 2G devices are digital, whereas 1G are analog.
   d. 2G devices have built in Bluetooth.

6. When someone makes a cellular phone call to another cellular phone, which of the following eventually handles the call?
   a. Public switched telephone network (PSTN)
   b. Mobile switching center (MSC)
   c. Global Positioning System (GPS)
   d. Synchronous optical network (SONET)

7. What is accessing a network without permission called?
   a. Telephony
   b. Malicious networking
   c. Piggybacking
   d. Throughputting

8. What is the technology used by GPS systems to pinpoint the location of a cell phone and its user?
   a. Local loop
   b. Piggybacking
   c. Mobile switching center
   d. Location awareness

9. Which is a broadband solution for rural areas?
   a. PBX
   b. ISDN
   c. SLC
   d. PSTN

10. Which of the following is true of VoIP (Internet telephony)?
    a. It is often cheaper than conventional phone service.
    b. It is of such poor quality that businesses refuse to use it.
    c. It is only usable with a dial-up Internet connection.
    d. It is too expensive to install for home use.

Fill-In

In the blanks provided, write the correct answer for each of the following.

1. The _____-_____ _____ refers to the lack of high-connectivity media (such as fiber-optic cable) extending all the way into the home.

2. _____ is the merging of technologies into a single device.

3. _____ technology facilitates conducting a meeting when participants are in different geographic locations.

4. _____ is the generation in which cellular devices became digital.

5. _____ is the process of transforming data like voice, text, and graphics into digital form.

6. Fiber-optic cable uses _____ to transmit data.

7. Another term for personal area network or PAN is _____.

8. A global positioning system (GPS) tracks locations through the use of _____.

9. Participants in a videoconference can use a(n) _____ to create a shared workspace.

10. A wireless mouse might use _____ technology to transmit data to the computer system.

11. A(n) _____ is a distinct area of coverage in a wireless phone network.

12. The nickname for a malicious network is _____ _____.

13. _____ is a broad term that describes the ability to link various media and devices to enhance communications and improve access to information.

14. Computers using wireless adapters use a special wireless communication device known as a(n) _____ _____ _____ to send and receive data.

15. A _____ is a camera designed for transmitting video over the Internet.

Short Answer

1. List three mobile operating systems. Explain the features the systems need to take into consideration for mobile device implementation.

2. List the computer equipment needed for a user to implement VoIP technology.

3. Explain the difference between bandwidth and throughput.

4. Define *convergence*. Provide at least two current examples of devices that serve as examples of technological convergence.

5. Briefly explain the features of the four different types of DSL technology available today.

6. Explain the last-mile problem. List the current technology being used to minimize this problem.

Teamwork

1. **Internet Availability and Convergence with TV and Phone Service** As a team, research the various Internet services available in your community and the surrounding regions. Using a map with the local towns labeled, color code or use some other method of designation to show the Internet services provided in each town and the names of the possible providers. Break into smaller groups and contact each provider. Investigate the cost of the service or services that each supplies. Investigate whether any of the providers offer a comprehensive package that would include data, phone, and television service. If such packages are offered, what are the monthly fees? Is there any special hardware required? Does the customer purchase or lease the hardware? What are the cancellation fees, if any? Present your map and a summary of your findings in a one-page, double-spaced report.

2. **Phone Service Evaluation** Have each team member examine his or her most recent cell phone bill. Answer the following questions and summarize the results:

   - How many monthly anytime calling minutes are included in your plan?

   - What is the per minute charge if you exceed your allotted minutes?

   - Do you have times when you can call for free (nights and weekends)?

   - Do you have a data plan (for sending text messages, digital photos, etc.)? How much does it cost per month?

   - Are you charged for roaming (that is, making calls when you are out of your local service area)?

   - Are long distance calls included in your anytime minutes or is there an additional charge for them?

   - Do you have any additional features like Internet access? If so what is the monthy cost?

   - Some plans allow each member of the plan to pick five numbers that they can call any time from any place with no charge. Are there any other special features like "favorite five?"

   - Does your plan meet your current needs?

   Accumulate your findings, and in a Word table or an Excel spreadsheet, present a summary of the features the reviewed plans include. Then identify the features your team finds to be essential. Calculate an approximate monthly cost for those features.

3. **Disposing of Your Cell Phone** With many of the current cell phone plans, an upgrade of a phone is included on a regular basis at a reduced rate. That means that every year or two a user can get a new phone at a reasonable rate. Have team members divide up to investigate local methods of cell phone disposal. Check with local cell providers, city or local disposal drop sites, college or university green disposal centers, and manufacturers such as Verizon, Nokia, T-Mobile, and BlackBerry for disposal options that they might offer. Present your findings in a one-page, double-spaced paper.

4. **Local Hot Spots** Split into smaller groups and divide your city or town into subregions. Using a map of the region, label the location of each establishment that provides a wireless hot spot. Find out whether accessibility is provided only for customers or whether they will accept a fee from nonpatrons. If the service is fee-based, what is that fee? Inquire whether they have ever detected anyone piggybacking on their service or whether anyone has claimed that a security violation occurred while using their wireless connection. Present your map and the results of your research in one-page, double-spaced report.

5. **GPS Units and Responsibility** GPS units can be attributed to locating and leading to the rescue of an experienced hiker lost in the Australian desert in January of 2009. On the flip side, a female lost in Death Valley National Park in California in August of 2009 is blaming a GPS unit for providing her with faulty directions that led her and her son to a desolate and extremely remote region of the park. After several days, she and her son depleted their water supply. Her 11-year-old son died. She places blame on the GPS provider. As a team, research cases of technology helping people and cases in which it has malfunctioned and caused someone to be injured or something to be damaged. When is the incident the fault of the provider and when is it the fault of the human operator? How does the GPS react in rural regions or in areas of new construction where streets might not be labeled? What can the technology provider do to disclaim responsibility? What can the user do to validate technology behavior or, in the case of the Death Valley hiker, navigational instructions? Present your team findings in a one-page, double-spaced report.

1. **4G Technology** The next generation of mobile communications devices will be known as 4G (fourth generation). Type "4G" into your favorite search engine to learn about this new technology. Which organizations are developing the specifications for 4G? What advantages will 4G provide over 3G devices? What are the expected data transmission rates for 4G? When are 4G devices expected to be widely available? Explain why you would or would not consider upgrading to a 4G phone. Present your findings, references, and upgrade decision in a PowerPoint presentation. Remember to cite your references.

2. **Pandora versus Sirius XM Radio** Will free music beat paid services? Using the Internet and your favorite search engine, investigate and compare Pandora and Sirius XM radio. Compare the costs, fine tuning features, iPhone app and cost, and any other features that each service offers. Summarize of your findings in a one-page, double-spaced report. Remember to cite your references.

3. **Using Bluetooth Technology** Go to the official Bluetooth site at **www.bluetooth.com** and research new products that use Bluetooth. What types of products are profiled on the site? Which products might you be interested in buying? Where can you get the best price on devices that you are interested in purchasing?

4. **Camera Cloning** Visit **www.youtube.com/watch ?v=TJxkNKtOpJ8** and view a brief video on the cell phones clones. Using the Internet and a search engine of your choice, investigate further this aspect of cell phone duplication with respect to cost, performance, and the ethical issue of purchasing an unauthentic product. In which countries are clones the most popular? Do clones of products, like BlackBerry, have access to that product's restricted user network? Present your findings, with references cited, in a one-page, double-spaced report.

5. **Location Aware Devices: Safety versus Privacy** Using the Internet and your favorite search engine, search for "location aware devices." Research such issues as these: If we are going to walk around with devices that tell the world where we are, will there be an "off" switch? Will that switch be easy to locate and use? And, perhaps most important, will the default position for the privacy switch when the devices are shipped from the factory be set for "off" or "on?" Attempt to locate references on the benefits and drawbacks of location-aware devices embedded into our cell phones, cars, and other devices. Present the pros and cons of such devices in a one-page, double-spaced paper. Remember to cite your references.

Phone with Bluetooth capability

Computer with Bluetooth capability

Bluetooth headset

Spotlight

Digital Life

Our lives continue to be ever more reliant on the use of digital devices, including smartphones, handheld devices, computers, cameras, and so on. These digital devices, also referred to as multimedia devices, have been around for a long time. Now, however, because of computer and Internet technologies, it's much easier to incorporate them into our lives. Multimedia is one of the reasons that the Web is so popular. Simply put, **multimedia** can be defined as *multisensory stimulators*, or things that stimulate our senses of sight, sound, touch, smell, or taste. For our purposes, we'll consider multimedia that stimulates the senses of sight, sound, and touch.

Just a few years ago, most personal computers needed additional equipment to run multimedia applications. Today, such equipment—sound cards, CD or DVD drives, and speakers—is standard issue. However, for advanced multimedia applications, you may still need additional equipment, such as a pen-based graphics tablet, a stereo microphone, a digital camera, or a video adapter. If you enjoy playing games, you'll want a 3D video accelerator, which is an add-on video adapter that works with your current video card. For surround sound, you'll need a sound card capable of producing the surround effect. And you'll probably want to pick up a few extra speakers and a subwoofer.

FIGURE 6A Service kiosks that use touch-screen technology can be found in many locations.

Multimedia is part of computer games of all kinds, but it is also being used more and more in computer-based education (CBE), distance learning, and computer-based training (CBT). Businesses use it in multimedia presentations using PowerPoint and other software. It's also finding its way into **information kiosks**, which are automated presentation systems used to provide information to the public or employee training (Figure 6A).

What if you want your multimedia files to travel with you? Today, a number of portable multimedia devices are available, from MP3 players and digital cameras to Web-enabled devices such as smartphones, PDAs, e-books, and portable televisions. In this Spotlight, you'll learn about a variety of multimedia devices, both mobile ones and those used with desktop computers.

Audio: MP3 Players and Voice Recorders

Unlike previous forms of push technology (products marketed by industries to consumers), such as cassette tapes and CDs, the MP3 movement has been largely fueled by music lovers' use of the Internet to compile and share libraries of digitized music files. Files are created and shared by the users—without industry involvement. An MP3 file is a compressed audio format that is usually used for music files. The term MP3 is derived from the acronym MPEG, which stands for the Motion Picture Experts Group; the *3* refers to audio layer 3.

Without losing any noticeable sound quality, the MP3 format reduces the size of sound files by eliminating frequencies and sounds the human ear cannot hear. A song on a typical music CD takes up approximately 32 MB. The same song in MP3 format takes only 3 MB.

MP3 works like this: A CD has a sample rate of 44,100 times per second. Each sample is two bytes in size, and separate samples are taken for the left and right speakers. Thus, the sample rate in bits per second is 44,100 × 8 bits per byte × 2 bytes × 2 channels, which is 1,411,200 bits per second. This equals a sample rate of 176,400 bytes per second × 180 seconds in an average song, or roughly 32 MB per song. MP3 compresses the sound file by a factor of 10 to 14 by applying a compression algorithm.

You can record, store, and play MP3 files on your computer. You can legally copy music from CDs that you own, or you can purchase files from Web sites such as **www.apple.com/itunes**, **www.zune.net**, and **www.mp3.com** (Figure 6B). Windows-based PCs come

FIGURE 6B You can use iTunes to copy, record, and play audio files plus download to a portable MP3 player.

FIGURE 6C   You can use a portable MP3 player to take your music with you.

FIGURE 6D   The iPhone provides advanced recording and playback features similar to those of a digital voice recorder.

with the Windows Media Player already installed. Other systems may have a different default player or you may need to download one, such as Winamp (**www.winmap.com**), from the Internet. You can find a list of the various MP3 players that are available at **www.superwarehouse.com/mp3_players/c2b/2387**.

MP3 files also can be stored on portable players. Portable players come in many shapes and sizes (Figure 6C). When purchasing an MP3 player, make sure to consider the battery life and storage capacity of the device. Over 3.5 million MP3 players were shipped in 2003. On April 9, 2009, Apple announced that the 100 millionth iPod had been sold, making the iPod the fastest selling music player in history.

MP3 players have several components: a data port that is used to upload files, memory, a processor, a display screen, playback controls, an audio port for output, an amplifier, and a power supply. When you select a file to listen to on your MP3 player, the device's processor pulls the file from storage and decompresses the MP3 encoding. The decompressed bytes are converted from digital to analog, amplified, and then sent to the audio port for your enjoyment. MP3 players plug into your computer by way of a USB or FireWire port. Most players have solid-state memory, but some use a microdrive (a tiny hard drive) to store files. MP3 players are usually very small, portable, and battery powered. They range in price from less than $100 to $399 for the Apple iPod Touch with 32 GB of storage designed especially for video viewing.

You can use a digital voice recorder to record voice and sound that can later be retrieved from the device or downloaded to your computer. The device captures sound through a built-in microphone and then stores it on a memory chip. Several companies make these

devices (Figure 6D). Two things to consider when purchasing a digital voice recorder are the amount of storage offered and the price. Some of the newer phones, including the Apple iPhone, also have the capability of recording voice messages, which can be stored and/or shared as an e-mail.

Visual: E-Books, Digital Cameras, and Camcorders

E-books have the potential to provide a richness that is not possible in a printed book. An **e-book** is a book that has been digitized and distributed by means of a digital storage medium (such as flash memory or a CD disc). An **e-book reader** is a book-size device that displays e-books. E-book readers may be devices that are built solely for reading e-books or they may be PDAs, handheld devices, or other computing devices that have a processor and display screen (Figure 6E). The newest e-book readers are available in a larger size, increasing the ease of reading. Some even boast an auto-rotating screen with a text-to-speech mode.

Someday you may read an e-book that provides background music for each page or scenario. You may find hot links on the page that will take you to pictures that support the scene. Or better yet, you may find a link to a video of the scene. All of this extra material can be easily stored on a flash memory card along with the text of the story. And, if you don't want to purchase an e-book reader, you can download software to use your smartphone as an e-book reader! We may also see schools use e-books, especially at the elementary level, when students need to carry more books than their book bag or little arms can handle.

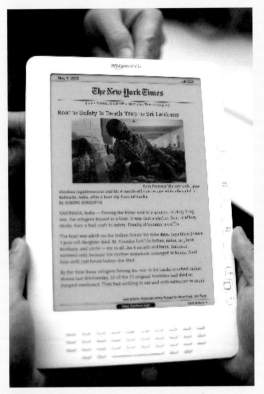

FIGURE 6E E-book readers share the market with PDAs and other computing devices.

Digital Cameras

It seems as though it was just yesterday that computer technology was so difficult to use that only computer scientists were able to use it. But today's digital technology is so easy to use that you can even digitize your family photo album!

One of the hottest products on today's consumer market is the digital camera (Figure 6F). Approximately 76 percent of households owned a digital camera by the end of 2008. A **digital camera** uses digital technology to store and display images instead of recording them on film. When you take a photo with a digital camera, the shot is stored in the camera until it is transferred to a computer for long-term storage or printing.

Like traditional cameras, digital cameras have a lens, a shutter, and an optical viewfinder. What sets digital cameras apart from traditional cameras is their inner workings—specifically, how an image is saved. With digital cameras, the captured image's light falls on a **charge-coupled device (CCD)**, a photosensitive computer chip that transforms light patterns into pixels (individual dots). A CCD consists of a grid made up of light-sensitive elements. Each element converts the incoming light into a voltage that is proportional to the light's brightness. The digital camera's picture quality is determined by how many elements the CCD has. Each CCD element corresponds to one pixel, or dot, on a computer display or printout; the more elements, the sharper the picture.

A 1-megapixel digital camera has a CCD consisting of at least 1 million elements; such a camera can produce a reasonably sharp snapshot-size image. With at least 2 million elements, 2-megapixel cameras can take higher-resolution pictures; you can expect to get near-photographic quality prints at sizes of up to 5 × 7 inches with such a camera. Three- and 4-megapixel cameras can produce images that can print at sizes of 8 × 10 inches or even 11 × 14 inches. Today's 5- to 12-megapixel cameras produce high-quality photographs that can be greatly enlarged without loss of quality.

Because digital cameras do not have film, any photos you take are stored in the camera until you transfer them to a computer for long-term storage or printing. Two popular methods of storing images in the camera are **CompactFlash** and **xD Picture Cards** (Figure 6G). Both use flash memory technologies to store anywhere from 64 MB to 8 GB of image data. About 12 MB of flash memory is the equivalent of a standard 12-exposure film roll. However, most cameras enable you to select from a variety of resolutions, so the

FIGURE 6F Digital cameras are among today's hottest products.

FIGURE 6G The xD-Picture Card is a type of flash memory card available in capacities of 16 MB up to 2 GB.

FIGURE 6H A photo printer allows you to print your pictures at your convenience in a variety of sizes directly from your camera.

number of shots you get will vary depending on the resolution you choose. If you need more "film," you need only carry more flash memory cards. Digital cameras enable you to preview the shots you've taken on a small LCD screen, so you can create more room on the flash memory cards by erasing pictures that you don't like.

In most cases, you'll need to download the image data to a computer for safekeeping and printing. Most cameras are designed to connect to a computer by means of a serial or USB cable. Others can transfer data into your computer by means of an infrared port. If you're using a digital camera that stores images on flash memory cards, you can obtain a PC card that contains a flash memory card reader. This type of PC card enables the computer to read the images from the flash memory card as if it were a disk drive. Also available are standalone flash memory readers, which serve the same purpose. Once you've transferred the images to the computer for safekeeping and printing, you can erase the flash memory card and reuse it, just as if you had purchased a fresh roll of film.

Once the images are transferred to the computer, you can use a **photo-editing program** to enhance, edit, crop, or resize the images. Photo-editing programs also can be used to print the images to a color printer. Some specially designed printers called **photo printers** have flash memory card readers that enable you to bypass the computer completely (Figure 6H).

How good are digital cameras? With the exception of a few expensive high-end digital cameras, most digital cameras are the equivalent of the point-and-shoot 35-mm cameras that have dominated the traditional (film-based) camera market. They take pictures that are good enough for family photo albums, Web publishing, and business use (such as a real estate agent's snapshots of homes for sale); however, they are not good enough for professional photography. Some professional photographers are moving to digital media and are pleased with the results. They tend to like digital cameras for the same reason the general population likes them: flexibility, ease of use, easy-to-view photos, and cost savings.

A color printer or a photo printer can make prints from digital camera images that closely resemble the

snapshots you used to get from the drugstore, but only if you choose the highest print resolution and use glossy photo paper. Getting good printout results takes time—most consumer-oriented printers will require several minutes to print an image at the printer's highest possible resolution—and can be costly when you consider the printer, ink, and special photo paper.

But printing is only one of the distribution options that are open to you when you use a digital camera—and that's exactly why so many people love digital photography. In addition to printing snapshots for the family album, you can copy the images onto CDs or DVDs, send them to friends and family via e-mail, and even display them on the Internet.

Point-and-shoot digital cameras are designed so that anyone can take good pictures (Figure 6I). Their features typically include automatic focus, automatic exposure, built-in automatic electronic flash with red-eye reduction, and optical zoom lenses with digital enhancement. Some point-and-shoot cameras come with a built-in LCD viewfinder, so you can preview the shot to make sure it comes out right.

FIGURE 6I Point-and-shoot cameras are designed for portability and for grabbing quick shots.

Single-lens reflex (SLR) digital cameras are much more expensive than point-and-shoot cameras, but they offer the features that professional photographers demand, such as interchangeable lenses, through-the-lens image previewing, and the ability to override the automatic focus and exposure settings (Figure 6J).

For reviews, comparisons, and price information for digital cameras, see the Digital Camera Buyer's Guide: Spring 2009 at **www.digitalcamerareview.com/resource/buyers_guide_spring_09/**.

DIGITAL CAMCORDERS

Just as digital cameras are revolutionizing still photography, indications are that digital video cameras are poised to do the same for full-motion images—animations, videos, and movies.

In the past, most full-motion images were captured and stored by means of analog techniques. A video-capture board (also called a video-capture card)

FIGURE 6J Leading camera maker, Nikon, features SLR digital cameras with 10 or more megapixels.

digital video camera uses digital rather than analog technologies to store recorded video images. Like digital cameras, digital video cameras can connect to a computer, often by means of a USB port. Because the signal produced by a digital video camera conforms to the computer's digital method of representing data, a video-capture board is not necessary. Most digital video cameras can take still images as well as movies (Figure 6K). Like most technologies over the years, digital video cameras have increased capabilities at a reduced price.

Communication and Entertainment Devices

Multimedia devices continue to transform ordinary devices and expand their capabilities. A phone is no longer just a device used to speak with another person. Many are sophisticated, wireless devices that enable you to surf the Web, send text messages, take photos, and listen to music—and you can still call your friends too!

is a device that inputs analog video into a computer and transforms the analog video into its digital counterpart. Because a digital video file for even a short video requires a great deal of storage space, most video-capture boards are equipped to perform on-the-fly data compression to reduce file size using one of several **codecs** (compression/decompression standards), such as MPEG, Apple's QuickTime, or Microsoft's AVI. Three-dimensional games have driven computer video card manufacturers to new feats of technical innovation; today's 3D video cards offer sophisticated, ultrafast graphics processing that only a few years ago would have required a supercomputer.

Video-capture boards enable computers to display and process full-motion video—a "movie" that gives the illusion of smooth, continuous action. Like actual movies, digitized video consists of a series of still photographs called **frames** that are flashed on the screen at a rapid rate. The frame-flashing speed—the **frame rate**—indicates how successfully a given video can create the illusion of smooth, unbroken movement. A rate of at least 24 frames per second (fps) is needed to produce an illusion of smooth, continuous action. What can you "capture" with a video-capture board? You can use just about any video source, including TV broadcasts, taped video, or live video from video cameras.

With the advent of the popular Internet site YouTube, **digital video cameras** (also known as **camcorders**) have become even more popular. A

FIGURE 6K Small, but powerful, pocket-sized camcorders provide portability, allowing you to capture HD video anytime, anywhere.

The most notable of these is the new Apple iPhone 3GS (Figure 6L). The 3G stands for the third generation of mobile technology, which provides enhanced capability allowing the transfer of both voice and nonvoice data, including full-motion video, high-speed Internet access, and videoconferencing.

The original iPhone was first sold in July 2007, and later that year it was named *Time* magazine's invention of the year. The 3GS version was released in June 2009. The iPhone 3GS combines four products in one—a phone with voice control, a widescreen iPod, a camera, and an Internet device with HTML e-mail and Web browser capability. It is a small device (4.5 × 2.4 × 0.48 inches, and weighing only 4.7 ounces) yet has a 3.5-inch display screen with a screen resolution of 480 × 320 pixels. To function as a phone, it requires a broadband connection with AT&T. Additionally, it has 802.11b/g and Bluetooth 2.0 wireless compatibilities. As with an iPod player, you can scroll through songs, artists, albums, and playlists, browse the music library by album artwork, and view song lyrics that have been added to the library in iTunes. The video feature enables you to watch TV shows and movies from the iTunes Store. When you connect your iPhone to your computer, you can use iTunes to sync the audio and video files from your computer's iTunes library to your iPhone.

FIGURE 6L Apple's newest iPhone is the 3GS, which features phone, iPod, video camera, Internet capabilities with enhanced video, and additional features.

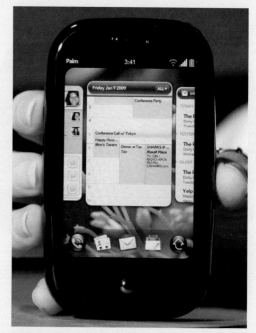

FIGURE 6M The Palm Pre is a phone designed to make your life easier with enhanced, new capabilities featuring the first Palm webOS.

A possible contender to the iPhone's popularity is the Palm Pre (Figure 6M). It was introduced on June 6, 2009, and is the first to use the new Linux-based Palm operating system. It also is a multimedia smartphone that is designed and marketed by Palm, Inc. It has a touch screen with an enhanced keyboard. Using the touch screen, it will function as a camera phone, a portable media player, a GPS navigator, and an Internet client. It also allows you to text message, e-mail, browse the Web, and connect to local Wi-Fi hot spots. Having just won recognition as CNET's Best in Show, the Pre appears to be a viable competitor for the iPhone.

The Samsung Instinct, another smartphone, was first sold in June 2008. It works with fast 3G cellular networks, but it does not support Wi-Fi. It contains GPS technology and is also controlled by a multitouch interface. The Instinct is a phone, an audio and video player, and an Internet device with e-mail capability and a Web browser. It is a small device (4.57 × 2.17 × 0.49 inches, and weighing only 4.4 ounces) yet has a 3.1-inch display screen with a screen resolution of 432 × 240 pixels. To function as a phone, it requires a broadband connection with Sprint. You can get streaming media from more than 30 channels—music, videos, sporting news—streamed to your phone. The Instinct is Sprint

TV enabled, which allows you to watch live TV and video-on-demand with full-motion video and sound. As with Apple's iTunes store, you can use Sprint's Music Store to download stereo-quality tracks to your wireless phone or PC.

DIGITAL VIDEO RECORDERS

Digital video recorders (DVRs) are similar to VCRs, but instead of using tape to store video they use a hard disk. Hard disk storage is digital, thus the user can quickly move through video data, fast-forwarding through commercials. You can use a DVR just like a VCR or you can subscribe to a DVR-management service. One service provider, TiVo, can record up to 180 hours of your favorite shows automatically to a DVR every time they're on (Figure 6N). This way, all of your entertainment is ready for you to watch whenever you are. Just buy a DVR, activate the TiVo service, and you can enjoy television viewing your way. TiVo's competitors include ReplayTV, UltimateTV, DirecTV, and others.

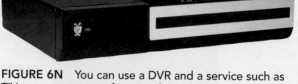

FIGURE 6N You can use a DVR and a service such as TiVo to capture your favorite shows and watch them at your convenience.

COMPUTER GAMING DEVICES

Computer game consoles such as Sony's PlayStation 3, Nintendo's Wii, and Microsoft's Xbox 360 are popular multimedia devices. You can use these devices to load and play interactive games using a television or computer screen as the display device. You also can go online and play games against a diverse population of players. Gaming accessories are available, such as game consoles, specialized backpacks, wireless support, and cable accessory packs.

Game consoles are similar to computers. A game console has a processor, a graphics driver, an audio driver, memory, and an operating system. It reads input from a storage device, such as a CD or memory card, processes that input into sounds and animation, and then stores user input for further processing as the game progresses.

Gamers can use portable handheld game consoles such as Nintendo's DS/DSi to take their games with them. Nintendo has also entered the home market with the introduction of the Nintendo Wii. This popular gaming device features many games for the entire family that are activity based. The Wii Fit is especially popular for the all members of the family as it combines yoga, balance, strength training, and aerobics (Figure 6O). Sony released the newest version of its popular PlayStation Portable product line in fall 2009. Called PSP-Go, the device is touted as the

FIGURE 6O The Nintendo Wii brings a new level of inter-activity to computer games.

smallest and mightiest of the handheld game systems. It features access to games, video, movies, and the Internet through the PlayStation Network.

HEADSETS

Perhaps the ultimate multimedia device is the headset. A **headset** (also called a **head-mounted display**) is a wearable device that includes twin LCD panels. When used with special applications that generate stereo output, headsets can create the illusion that an individual is walking through a 3D environment (Figure 6P).

Gaming enthusiasts can use the **Cave Automated Virtual Environment (CAVE)** to dispense with the headsets in favor of 3D glasses. In the CAVE, the walls, ceiling, and floor display projected 3D images. More than 50 CAVEs exist. Researchers use CAVEs to study topics as diverse as the human heart and the next generation of sports cars.

Smart Home

Home owners continue to embrace technology with small, clever, interesting digital devices that help the performance of the home in general while making it more eco-friendly. During spring 2009, the Museum of Science and Industry in Chicago opened an exhibit that features a smart home that is both green and wired (Figure 6Q). The exhibit portrays an environmentally responsible, modular home full of technology. Of course, the home's climate, lighting, and entertainment are controlled by touch-screen panels throughout the home.

FIGURE 6P Headsets are essential to many computer gaming experiences.

FIGURE 6Q Interest in smart home technologies has increased, as evidenced by the latest Museum of Science and Industry exhibit.

Some other interesting features are that the lights, television, and music turn off when no one is in the room; the home greets the owners when they arrive home, telling them what's been going on with the house while they were gone; the baby's room can be broadcast via cribcast on video screens in the master bedroom and on the first floor; and the home has a hibernation mode that lowers shades and turns down heat/air when residents are leaving for a day or longer—and adjustments can be made remotely via a cell phone. Many of these features may be incorporated into homes in the future.

Although many of the items mentioned shown in the smart home are representative of features coming in the future, there are many smart features already in our homes today. The digital photo frame is one example. It displays JPEG pictures as a slide show from a screen often measuring from 7 to 15 inches in size. Newer varieties also may display MPEG video files and play MP3 audio files from the camera's memory card or a USB drive (Figure 6R).

Technology has even advanced to help pet owners know what Fido is doing while they are gone. Dogs or cats wear a specially designed digital pet camera around their necks. The owner may set the camera to take pictures at various intervals, from 1 to 15 minutes. The photos can be uploaded to a computer via a USB cable for viewing (Figure 6T).

FIGURE 6T Pets wear this device around their neck so that worried owners can view what they are doing throughout the day.

FIGURE 6R A digital photo picture frame that also projects video and audio can be used to display family pictures.

Another home digital device is the Slingbox produced by Sling Media of San Mateo, California. This device is for TV streaming, allowing users to view their home's cable or satellite TV remotely from an Internet-enabled computer with a broadband Internet connection, which could be a cell phone (Figure 6S).

FIGURE 6S A Slingbox will allow you to view video from your home cable system while you are away from home, using a remote connection, which could be supplied by your cell phone if it has broadband Internet access.

Homeowners continue to be more aware of conserving energy in their homes. Almost every computer sold today comes with some type of a power management utility. Ideally computers should have the designation of ENERGY STAR (Figure 6U). This rating means the computer meets the federal standards for energy consumption as determined by the EPA (Environmental Protection Agency) and the U.S. Department of Energy. ENERGY STAR notebooks utilize about 15 watts of electricity compared to a desktop, which uses from 200–400 watts. Solar-powered computers and/or battery packs are beginning to arrive to our markets. Ideally, however, we want to move to zero waste with eco-friendly, biodegradable digital components.

FIGURE 6U Computers with the designated ENERGY STAR label indicate that the computer is built to be energy efficient.

Spotlight Exercises

1. There are many types of MP3 players. Visit the MP3 site at **www.mp3.com**. Explore the MP3 Players link and choose four players from this list. Be sure to include an iPod or an iTouch. Compare each of your chosen devices in terms of cost, functionality, and consumer reviews. Write a short paper describing the four players. Then choose which one you would recommend and explain why.

2. Visit the Museum of Science and Industry at **www.msichicago.org/whats-here/exhibits/ smart-home/**. Investigate the home and its many features. Write a short paper describing five features that, in your opinion, have merit and will be incorporated into our homes within the next few years. Also select three features of the home that may not be embraced by the home consumer. Describe them and explain why you don't feel they will be popular.

3. Use your favorite search engine and the World Wide Web to research digital cameras. How many pixels will suffice for your picture-taking needs? What is the price range for such cameras? What is the difference between optical zoom and digital zoom? How much optical zoom would be acceptable for your personal use? What is the storage medium of your chosen camera? How many pictures can you store on a 16-MB disk? How much storage capacity will you buy? What will it cost? Write a brief paper describing what you've learned.

4. Video recording has become even more popular recently due to the advent of YouTube. Many people use small, inexpensive video recorders to record and then upload their files to YouTube or another site. However, there are other reasons people want video recorders, for example, family events, business presentations, and so on. Investigate the types of digital video recorders that are available today. Choose three different recorders at three different price points. Write a short paper describing each, including the manufacturer, price, functionality, warranty, peripheral items needed, and intended audience for each.

5. Want to take your TV show with you? Sling Media uses "placeshifting" technology that sends your television, DVR, digital cable, satellite receiver, or DVD player signal to you anywhere in the world. Its Slingbox is a set-top box that connects to your TV and streams the signal to another machine in real time—there is no recording involved. This other machine might be your computer in your home, in which case your home network is used. If you are away from home, you can connect your notebook or cell phone using a high-speed Internet connection. Slingbox works with the SlingPlayer software you install on your computer. After installing the software, you can control the video source from your computer just as you can from the remote that came with your TV. Visit **www.slingmedia.com** to watch the videos, compare the three Slingbox versions, and check the minimum PC or Mac requirements. If you had the necessary funds, explain which model you would purchase, the reasons for your choice, and how you would use the Slingbox. Use the Internet to find the best price. Where and at what price would you buy your Slingbox?

6. E-books are becoming more popular than ever with the advent of the Kindle. Go to the Kindle Web page found at **www.amazon.com**. Explore the Web site for the newest Kindle. Configure a Kindle for yourself that includes the reader, protection case, warranty, light, two books, and two subscriptions. Write a short paper describing the Kindle model you would choose. Be sure to include how much money you would spend if you bought this device. Do you think this device is something for you, our schools, and our colleges? In your paper, list three other e-book readers that are available and compare the Kindle to them.

chapter 9

Privacy, Crime, and Security

Chapter Objectives

- Understand how technological developments are eroding privacy and anonymity. (p. 337)

- List the types of computer crime and cybercrime. (p. 346)

- List the types of computer criminals. (p. 354)

- Understand computer system security risks. (p. 358)

- Describe how to protect your computer system and yourself. (p. 361)

- Define *encryption* and explain how it makes online information secure. (p. 364)

- Describe the issues the government faces when balancing the need to access encrypted data and the public's right to privacy. (p. 366)

Do you remember when a social security number, phone number, or bank account number was private information, given out with extreme discretion? Today you can find individuals at the mall entering passwords on portable devices, totally unaware of the people next to or behind them. Users at public computers often ask the computer to remember their login and password. By eavesdropping on a cell conversation, you can gather a great deal of personal information. Have you ever been careless with the bank statement or display of important information? Have any of your accounts ever been violated and used by an unauthorized individual? Are you concerned about the use of credit cards to purchase items online? Just how far will you go to keep your personal information private and safe? Just how far will an intruder go to break your wall of protection and violate your personal integrity?

The extensive and public nature of the Internet raises privacy issues as greater numbers of corporations and private citizens increasingly rely on the Internet as a business medium. Just as brick-and-mortar businesses in your neighborhood lock their doors at night to protect merchandise and equipment, electronic businesses employ a variety of security measures to protect their interests and your privacy from cybercriminals. In this chapter, you will explore how online connectivity can threaten your privacy, personal safety, and computer system, and you will learn how to protect yourself from online threats.

Privacy in Cyberspace

Of all the social and ethical issues raised by the use of widely available Internet linked computers, threats to privacy and anonymity are among the most contentious. Sites like the Privacy Rights Clearinghouse, a nonprofit consumer information and advocacy organization, are emerging to offer practical consumer advice, display privacy alerts, and cover hot privacy issues (Figure 9.1).

Defined by U.S. Supreme Court Justice Louis Brandeis in 1928 as "the right to be left alone," **privacy** refers to an individual's ability to restrict or eliminate the collection, use, and sale of confidential personal information. Some people say that privacy isn't a concern unless you have something to hide. However, this view ignores the fact that privacy means something different to every individual, government, and corporation, and it is not just the collecting of private information that is cause for concern, but the use of this information in ways that may harm people unnecessarily.

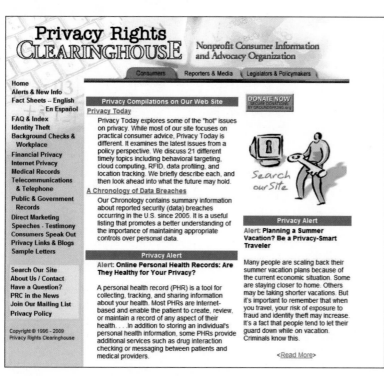

FIGURE 9.1 The Privacy Rights Clearinghouse (**www.privacyrights.org/index.htm**) acts as a source of information on privacy issues to consumers, the media, and policymakers.

THE PROBLEM: COLLECTION OF INFORMATION WITHOUT CONSENT

Many people are willing to divulge information when asked for their consent and when they see a need for doing so. When you apply for a loan, for example, the bank can reasonably ask you to list your other creditors to determine whether you'll be able to repay your loan.

Much information is collected from public agencies, many of which are under a legal obligation to make their records available to the public upon request (public institutions of higher education, departments of motor vehicles, county clerks, tax assessors, and so on). This information finds its way into computerized databases—thousands of them—that track virtually every conceivable type of information about individuals. You are probably aware of credit reporting databases that track your credit history (Figure 9.2). Other databases include information such as your current and former addresses and employers, other names you've used (and your previous name, if you're married and use a different name now), current and former spouses, bankruptcies, lawsuits, property ownership, driver's license

information, criminal records, purchasing habits, and medical prescriptions.

The **P3P** (**Platform for Privacy Preferences**) was developed by the **W3C** (**World Wide Web Consortium**), an international consortium of over 440 organizations in more than 40 countries responsible for ensuring long-term growth for the World Wide Web and promoting Web interoperability through the publication of open standards for Web languages and protocols, as a means of increasing consumer confidence in online transactions (Figure 9.3). P3P allows users and Web sites to create profiles. For users, the profile contains personal information and settings that make all or parts of the profile accessible, as the user specifies. For Web sites, the profile will contain the site's security policies. When a user requests a Web page, that Web site's P3P policy files are sent to the user's browser, which compares the files with the user's privacy settings and delivers an alert if there is a conflict between the two. This process automates user security decisions and reduces the time the user needs to take reading the privacy policies of Web sites he or she visits. The P3P platform has been published and is ready for implementation. The only problem is that it lacks widespread browser support. The W3C is continuing research and pushing browser conformity by encouraging the use of P3P as the basis of a number of research directions in the area of privacy worldwide.

Most of the companies that maintain databases today claim that they sell information only to bona fide customers such as lending institutions, prospective employers, marketing firms, and licensed private investigators. They maintain that their databases don't pose a threat to the privacy of individuals because they are highly ethical firms that would not release this information to the general public.

According to privacy activists, the problem is what happens to information after it's sold. The Internet has made it much easier and much cheaper for ordinary individuals to gain access to sensitive personal information. If you search the Web for "Social Security numbers," you'll find dozens of Web sites run by private investigators who offer to find someone's Social Security number for a small fee, which can easily be charged to your credit card. Sites such as InfoUSA

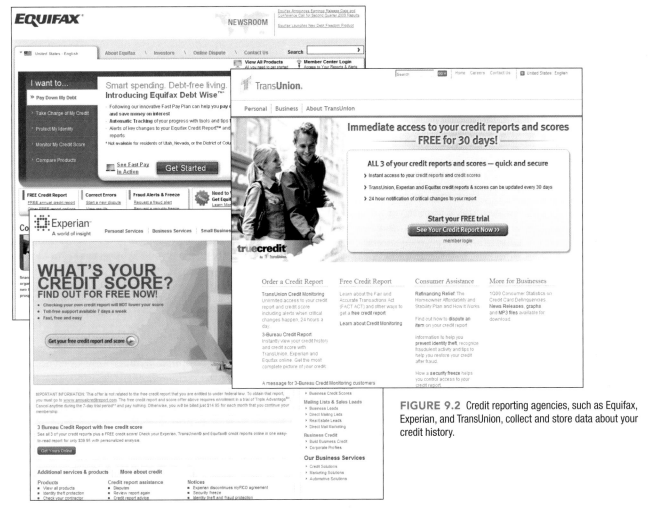

FIGURE 9.2 Credit reporting agencies, such as Equifax, Experian, and TransUnion, collect and store data about your credit history.

(**www.infousa.com**) provide sales leads and mailing lists for businesses, but the personal information they offer on more than 210 million consumers can easily be misused (Figure 9.4).

TECHNOLOGY AND ANONYMITY

Marketing firms, snoops, and government officials can use computers and the Internet to collect information in ways that are

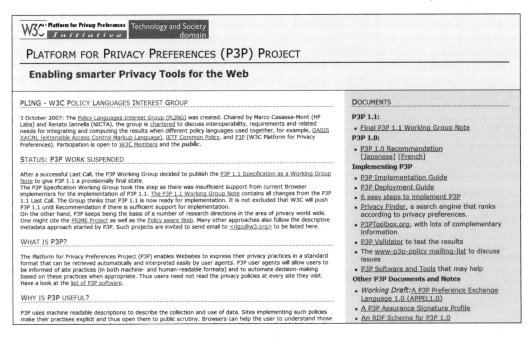

FIGURE 9.3 P3P (Platform for Privacy Preferences) is a process that compares the security settings of a user to those of a visited Web site. Only if the settings match will the profile information of the user be shared with that site.

hidden from users. The same technology also makes it increasingly difficult for citizens to engage in anonymous speech. **Anonymity** refers to the ability to convey a message without disclosing your name or identity.

Anonymity is both a curse and a blessing. On one hand, it can be seen as an abuse because it frees people from accountability. On the other hand, as supported by the U.S. Supreme Court—it must be preserved in a democracy, to ensure that citizens have access to the full range of possible ideas to make decisions for themselves. Freeing authors from accountability for anonymous works, the Court argued, raises the potential that false or misleading ideas will be brought before the public, but this risk is necessary to maintain a free society.

Anonymity with respect to Internet use is necessary to protect whistleblowers. However, the right to anonymity is being challenged on an individual case basis. Recently, the Honorable Mr. Justice Eady ruled that bloggers have no right to privacy in what is essentially the public act of publishing. Eady, a high court judge in England and Wales, overturned an injunction that had prevented *The Times* from revealing the identity of Richard Norton, the detective behind the controversial NightJack blog. Additionally, a few years earlier, a judge handed a Florida sheriff a victory in his mission to suppress what he says were inflammatory postings to an Internet message board used by law enforcement. Examples of technologies that threaten online anonymity include cookies, global unique identifiers, ubiquitous computing, and radio frequency identification.

Cookies Cookies are small text files that are written to your computer's hard disk by many of the Web sites you visit (Figure 9.5). In many cases, cookies are used for legitimate purposes. For example, online retail sites use cookies to implement "shopping carts," which enable you to make selections that will stay in your cart so that you can return later to the online store for more browsing and shopping. What troubles privacy advocates is the use of tracking cookies to gather data on Web users' browsing and shopping habits, without their consent.

Several Internet ad networks, such as DoubleClick, use cookies to track users' browsing actions across thousands of the most popular Internet sites. When you visit a Web site that has contracted with one of these ad networks, a cookie containing a unique identification number is deposited on your computer's hard drive. This cookie tracks your browsing habits and preferences as you move among the hundreds of sites that contract with the ad network. When you visit another site, the cookie is detected, read, and matched with a profile of your previous browsing activity. On this basis, the ad network selects and displays a **banner ad**, which often appears at the top of a Web page but can appear in other locations as well. A banner ad is not actually part of the Web page you are viewing but an ad supplied separately by the ad network.

In response to concerns that their tracking violates Internet users' privacy, ad network companies claim that they do not link the collected information with users' names and addresses. However, current technology would enable these firms to do so—and privacy advocates fear that some of them already have. Internet ad networks such as DoubleClick can collect the following:

- Your e-mail address
- Your full name

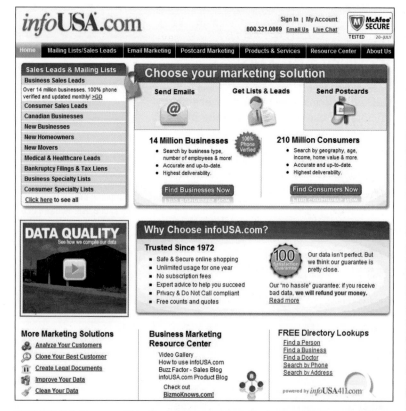

FIGURE 9.4 Numerous Web sites sell personal information to anyone they please. In the United States, you have no legal recourse against those who collect and sell sensitive personal information.

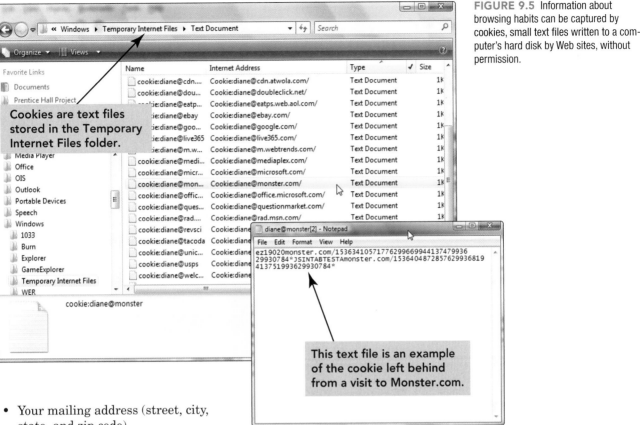

FIGURE 9.5 Information about browsing habits can be captured by cookies, small text files written to a computer's hard disk by Web sites, without permission.

Cookies are text files stored in the Temporary Internet Files folder.

This text file is an example of the cookie left behind from a visit to Monster.com.

- Your mailing address (street, city, state, and zip code)
- Your phone number
- Transactional data (names of products purchased online, details of plane ticket reservations, and search phrases used with search engines)

Internet marketing firms explain that by collecting such information, they can provide a "richer" marketing experience, one that's more closely tailored to an individual's interests. Privacy advocates reply that once collected, this information could become valuable to others. These kinds of debates ensure that cookies and the information they collect will remain on the forefront of the privacy controversy for years to come.

You can, however, prevent cookies from being placed on your hard disk. The means by which you disable cookies differs from one browser to another. Use the help feature in your browser to locate this information. To find out more on how a computer cookie works, how Web sites make use of them, and the privacy issues that surround their use, go to **http://computer.howstuffworks.com/cookie.htm**.

Global Unique Identifiers A **global unique identifier (GUID)** is an identification number that is generated by a hardware component or a program. Privacy advocates discovered GUIDs in several popular computer components and programs, such as Intel's Pentium III chip and Microsoft's Word 97 and Excel 97. The GUIDs can be read by Web servers or embedded in various documents, identifying the computer and inadvertently making it more difficult to use the Internet anonymously. Although the use of GUIDs does not seem to be as prevalent as it was earlier this decade, a similar concept has been discovered in color laser printers. The Electronic Frontier Foundation (**www.eff.org**), a civil liberties group that defends your rights in the digital world, has reported that many color laser printers embed printer tracking dots—nearly invisible yellow dots—on every page that is printed, at the urging of the U.S. government. These dots can identify the serial number and manufacturing code of the printer, as well as the time and date the document was printed. Officially, the tracking dots are designed to track counterfeiters, but privacy advocates are concerned because there is no law to prevent this information from being used by U.S. government agencies, foreign governments, or individuals to identify materials printed and distributed by private citizens.

Companies that introduce GUIDs into their products generally conceal this information from the public. When forced to admit to using GUIDs, the firms typically remove the GUID-implanting code or enable users to opt out of their data collection systems. Advocates of online anonymity insist that these companies are missing the basic point: Users, not corporations, should determine when and how personal information is divulged to third parties.

Ubiquitous Computing Ubiquitous computing, a term coined by Mark Weiser in 1988, during his tenure as Chief Technologist of the Xerox Palo Alto Research Center (PARC), describes an emerging trend in which individuals no longer interact with one computer at a time but instead with multiple devices connected through an omnipresent network, enabling technology to become virtually embedded and invisible in our lives. The concept is to make technology implicit, built into the things we use. The proponents of this technology hold that this type of computing will be a more natural tool and envision a system where billions of miniature, ubiquitous intercommunication devices will be spread worldwide. An example of the use of ubiquitous computing would be the automatic adjustment of environmental setting, like heat or light, in your office or home based on the signals sent to these environmental devices by monitors built into the clothing of individuals in the setting.

Imagine your movements being tracked by an **active badge**, a small device worn by an individual that transmits a unique infrared signal every 5 to 10 seconds. Networked sensors detect these transmissions and the location of the badge and, hence, the location of its wearer, allowing e-mail, phone calls, or messages to be forwarded to wherever you are. Also imagine "electronic trails" left by you or others as they pass through the neighborhood, office, or conference.

> **"Users**, not **corporations**, should determine when and how personal information is **divulged** to third parties. **"**

You already accept the idea of receiving e-mail anywhere; after all, that is already a feature of portable communication devices, the early ubiquitous computing tools. However, the concept of electronic trails probably made you a little uncomfortable. Proponents of ubiquitous computing say that a user can dissent and not wear a badge. Some experts argue that not being tracked, or not wearing a badge, should be the default. How do you feel about being tracked, having your movements monitored and recorded as you move about your daily routine?

Today, the closest devices to ubiquitous computing tools are digital music players, smartphones, and PCs that act as a media center for your entire home. These devices transmit data about us; they also search for data via Internet connections. Privacy can be compromised when smaller devices are lost or stolen. Most devices

ETHICS

Technology has provided a means of surveillance that is invisible and ever present. Even devices that are installed for protection can be manipulated and become mechanisms of surveillance. Recently the FBI served OnStar with a court order to give the agency access to the passive listening feature embedded within OnStar devices. Such access would enable the FBI to record conversations held in a vehicle. OnStar filed a suit and won, after a two-year court battle. The ruling in OnStar's favor, however, was not on the grounds of invasion of privacy. Instead, the court ruled that the fact that the use of the passive listening feature would disable the emergency calling feature and thus constitute a breach of the consumers' contract. How do you feel about the use of such devices for surveillance? When do such actions become a violation of privacy? How private are your private conversations?

maintain some form of log, such as a playlist, records of incoming or outgoing calls, or a list of recently viewed media, which can be retrieved and exploited. As users become accustomed to using such technology, privacy advocates are concerned that society has become more willing to tolerate lower levels of privacy in favor of convenience.

Radio Frequency Identification Radio frequency identification (RFID) uses radio waves to track a chip or tag placed in or on an object (Figure 9.6). RFID tags are often used, as an alternative to bar codes, for inventory control in the retail environment. RFID does not require direct contact or line-of-sight scanning. Instead, an antenna using radio frequency waves transmits a signal that activates the transponder, or tag. When activated, the tag transmits data back to the antenna. However, if the tag is not deactivated, the object's movements can continue to be tracked indefinitely. This technology is also used when microchips are inserted in pets and other livestock, and has even been used for people. The RFID chip can include contact information and health records for the individual or animal, or other personal details.

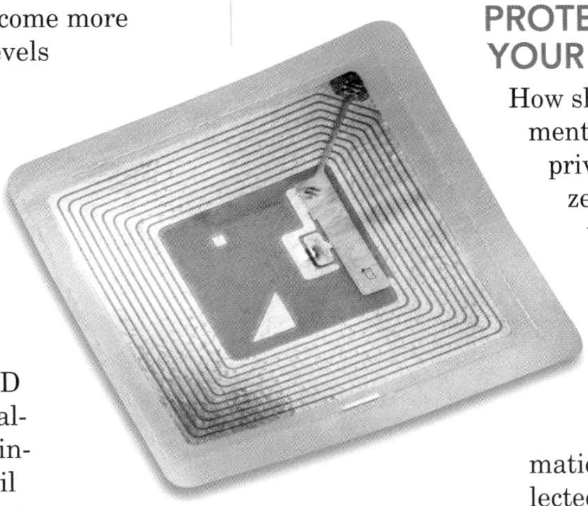

Privacy advocates have been concerned about the use of encrypted, passive RFID tags in U.S. passports for several years. The tag contains the same information included on the actual passport—name, nationality, gender, date of birth, and place of birth of the passport holder, as well as a digitized signature and photograph of that person. The government asserts that the RFID tag does not broadcast a signal and can only be read within close proximity of special scanning devices. However, a new passport card approved in 2008 as part of the Western Hemisphere Travel Initiative for travel to Mexico, Canada, Bermuda, and the Caribbean will use an unencrypted chip that can be read from up to 30 feet away, raising serious concerns that a passport holder's identity could easily be stolen or their location tracked without their consent or awareness. So far, these scenarios remain hypothetical, but the concept is disturbing to many.

Now that you've read about some of the privacy threats posed by the Internet, let's discuss how you can protect your privacy.

FIGURE 9.6 RFID tags are often used as antitheft devices or to track merchandise, but concerns arise when we use the same technology for personal items or individuals.

PROTECTING YOUR PRIVACY

How should governments protect the privacy of their citizens? Privacy advocates agree that the key lies in giving citizens the right to be informed when personal information is being collected as well as the right to refuse to provide this information. In the European Union (EU), a basic human rights declaration gives all citizens the following privacy rights:

- Consumers must be informed of exactly what information is being collected and how it will be used.
- Consumers must be allowed to choose whether they want to divulge the requested information and how collected information will be used.
- Consumers must be allowed to request that information about themselves be removed from marketing and other databases.

Protecting the privacy rights of U.S. citizens has been a controversial area for years. Most of us agree that our rights should be protected, but our definition of acceptable levels of protection varies widely. Some of the legislation currently in place includes the Fair Credit Reporting Act, which provides limited privacy protection for credit information; the Health Insurance Portability and Privacy Act (HIPAA), which establishes standards for the transmission of electronic health care data and the security and privacy of this information; and the Family Educational Rights and Privacy Act (FERPA), which protects the privacy of student education records. However, there is no comprehensive federal law governing the overall privacy rights of U.S. citizens. Instead,

FIGURE 9.7 Web sites can collect information without your knowledge or consent. To learn more about this and other privacy issues, visit the Federal Trade Commission's Consumer Information site at **www.ftc.gov/bcp/ consumer.shtm**.

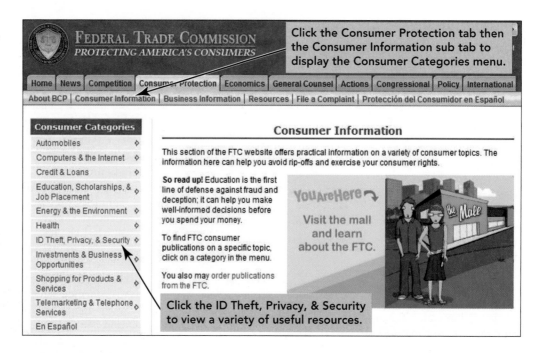

privacy is protected by a patchwork of limited federal and state laws and regulations. Most of these laws regulate what government agencies can do. Except in limited areas covered by these laws, little exists to stop people and companies from acquiring and selling your personal information (Figure 9.7).

Marketing industry spokespeople and lobbyists argue that the U.S. government should not impose laws or regulations to protect consumers' privacy. They argue that the industry should regulate itself. Privacy advocates counter that technology has outpaced the industry's capability to regulate itself, as evidenced by the widespread availability of highly personal information on the Internet.

The Direct Marketing Association (DMA) claims to enforce a basic code of ethics among its member organizations. The organization takes steps to ensure that confidential information doesn't fall into the wrong hands and that consumers can opt out of marketing campaigns if they wish. For more information, visit the DMA Web site at **www.the-dma.org/index.php**.

Be aware that many of the most aggressive Internet-based marketing firms have no ties to or previous experience with the DMA, and several opt-out systems on the Internet are already used for fraudulent purposes. For example, e-mail spammers typically claim that recipients can opt out of mass e-mail marketing campaigns. But recipients who respond to such messages succeed only in validating their e-mail addresses, and the result is often a

major increase in the volume of unsolicited e-mail. A report from the TRACElabs team at M86 Security for the week ending July 19, 2009, revealed that Brazil and the United States (Figure 9.8) were the leaders in relaying spam and that health and product-related messages accounted for 88 percent of all spam sent (Figure 9.9).

In the United States, the CAN-SPAM Act of 2004 gave ISPs the tools to combat spammers. The Federal Trade Commission (FTC) and the Department of Justice have primary jurisdiction over spammers, but other agencies, including states and ISPs, can also prosecute them. The legislation has been criticized because it prevents states from enacting tougher laws, prevents individuals from suing spammers, and does not require e-mailers to request permission before sending messages. Additionally, it may be ineffective against foreign spammers who are outside U.S. jurisdiction. Although many contend that the act is just a drop in the bucket, the monetary threat the CAN-SPAM Act poses can't hurt. In 2008, MySpace successfully sued the so-called "Spam King" Sanford Wallace and a business partner for violations of the CAN-SPAM Act. A federal judge awarded MySpace close to $230 million, although it is doubtful the money will ever be collected. At one time, a National Do Not Email Registry (similar to the National Do Not Call list to combat telemarketers) was considered but discarded because of the potential for misuse and the inability to provide effective enforcement. States are also enacting their own laws,

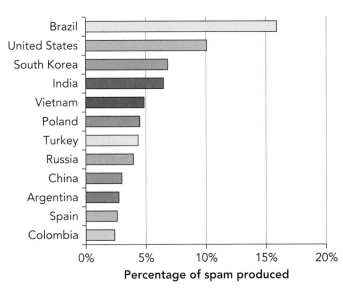

This week		Last week	
1	–	1	Brazil
2	–	2	United States
3	–	3	South Korea
4	–	4	India
5	≫	8	Vietnam
6	–	6	Poland
7	≪	5	Turkey
8	≪	7	Russia
9	–	9	China
10	≫	11	Argentina
11	≪	10	Spain
12	–	12	Colombia

Spam Sources by Country

This chart measures spam by country of origin as a percentage of all spam. The top 12 countries are ranked in order of the volume of spam they contribute from highest to lowest.

FIGURE 9.8 As of the week ending July 19, 2009, Brazil was the top spam-relaying country.

within the parameters of the CAN-SPAM Act, and other types of legislation, such as the Anti-Phishing Consumer Protection Act of 2008. Such laws are being debated across the country. Private lawsuits have not been effective yet, but they may be a bright spot on the horizon. The threat of monetary penalties may be the only thing that can thwart the growth of the spam industry.

Although some individuals may be discouraged from participating in e-commerce activities because of privacy concerns and fears regarding the use of information collected by Web sites, the Internet retail sector continues to thrive. The Census Bureau records show that, despite economic issues, the estimate of U.S. retail e-commerce sales for the first quarter of 2009 was $31.7 billion, an increase of 0.7 percent from the fourth quarter of 2008.

According to a 2008 survey by the Pew Internet and American Life Project, 66 percent of Americans who use the Internet have made purchases online, despite the fact that 75 percent of online users are concerned about providing personal and financial information online. The survey results also indicate that if privacy concerns are addressed, Internet sales would increase by at least 7 percent. Most popular commercial Web sites have attempted to allay these fears by creating "privacy policy" pages that explain how they collect and use personal information about site visitors. Many also display privacy seals from third-party vendors such as TRUSTe, WebTrust, or the Better Business Bureau as a sign that they comply with the vendor's privacy standards and regulations (Figure 9.10).

Privacy Online Internet users overwhelmingly agree—by a ratio of three to one—that the U.S. government should adopt laws that will safeguard basic privacy rights. Until then, it's up to you to safeguard your privacy on the Internet. To do so, follow these suggestions:

• Surf the Web anonymously by using software products such as Anonymizer's Anonymous Surfing (**www.anonymizer. com**)

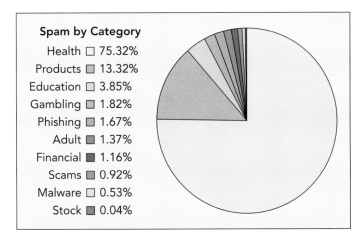

FIGURE 9.9 Health and products-related messages accounted for a majority of spam during the week ending July 19, 2009.

or devices such as the IronKey Secure USB flash drive (**www.ironkey.com**), which includes special security software to protect your data and encrypt your online communications (Figure 9.11).

- Use a "throwaway" e-mail address from a free Web-based service such as Google's Gmail (**www.google.com**) for the e-mail address you place on Web pages, mailing lists, chat rooms, or other public Internet spaces that are scanned by e-mail spammers.

- Tell children not to divulge any personal information online without first asking a parent or teacher for permission.

- Don't fill out site registration forms unless you see a privacy policy statement indicating that the information you supply won't be sold to third parties.

- Turn off cookies in order to prevent the activity of **Web beacons**, transparent graphic images, usually no larger than 1 pixel × 1 pixel, that are placed on a Web site or in an e-mail and used to monitor the behavior of the user visiting the Web site or sending the e-mail. Web beacons are typically used by a third-party to monitor the activity of a site. Turning off the browser's cookies will prevent Web beacons from tracking the user's activity.

Privacy at Home Are you aware that all new cell phones in the United States must have GPS awareness? This means that your phone can be located, usually within 30 feet, by law enforcement and emergency services personnel when you dial 911. Some services, such as uLocate and BrickHouse child locator, provide the exact location of a cell phone. This can come in handy when a parent is trying to keep track of a child, but it can be intrusive when an employer uses it to track an employee using a company cell phone.

Some software is so powerful that it will send a notification to the home unit whenever the cell phone leaves a designated geographic area. MIT students recently developed programs using GPS capabilities for the upcoming Android mobile OS by Google. One program lets you change your phone's settings as your location changes, so it will be silent in the movie theater or classroom but will ring

FIGURE 9.11 Devices like the IronKey Secure USB flash drive include special security software to allow you to surf the Web privately and securely while protecting your identity and data.

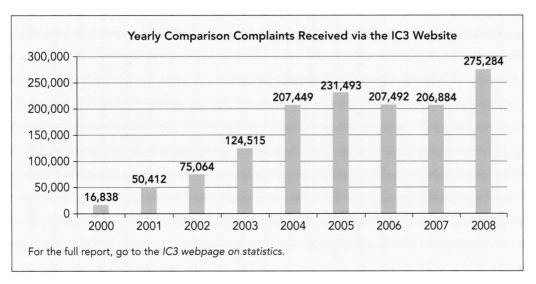

FIGURE 9.12 Complaints of Web crimes have been on a constant rise, with a 31 percent increase occurring between 2007 and 2008.

For the full report, go to the *IC3 webpage on statistics.*

when you're outdoors. Another program will remind you that you need to pick up milk as you pass by the store! This location-aware tracking software is already in use by the criminal justice system to keep track of offenders who are sentenced to home detention. The subject is fitted with an ankle or wrist bracelet, and then the software is set to trigger an alarm if the wearer strays from the designated area. These bracelets also are being used to keep track of Alzheimer's patients.

As it has evolved, home computing is subject to a decrease in security caused by sharing computing devices and using portable devices in public. A lot of credit card fraud and unauthorized banking access can be traced back to Internet and e-mail use. Some of the security measures you can use on home and portable devices to deter unauthorized access to your accounts include these:

- Create logins and passwords for each individual using a system to provide each user with a section to store documents that no other user can see or utilize when logged in.
- Do not save account numbers or passwords for access to secured sites such as bank accounts and personal e-mail on a shared system.
- Do not leave a secured account active on the monitor and walk away. A passer-by can easily brush a key and enter a transaction that could be critical.
- Do not leave devices like cell phones and PDAs on tables at restaurants and college facilities. Information left on the screen can easily be read, remembered, and reused.

- Turn off services that are not in use, especially Bluetooth.
- Ensure that devices are configured securely and, if necessary, require authentication.

Statistics from the Internet Crime Complaint Center (IC3), a partnership between the FBI, National White Color Crime Center, and the Bureau of Justice Assistance, substantiate that complaints registered on their Web site, **www.ic3.gov**, for Web-related crimes have increased significantly between 2007 and 2008 (Figure 9.12). E-mail and Web pages were the two primary mechanisms by which the fraudulent contact took place. Financial losses for complaints in 2008 reached an all-time high of $264.59 million, with males losing more than females and those between the ages of 30 and 50 as the primary victims (Figure 9.13).

FIGURE 9.13 Financial losses due to Web crimes reached an all-time high in 2008.

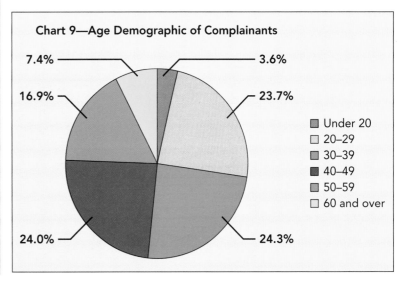

Privacy, Crime, and Security **345**

Privacy at Work In the United States, more than three-quarters of large employers routinely engage in **employee monitoring**, observing employees' phone calls, e-mails, Web browsing habits, and computer files. One program, Spector, provides employers with a report of everything employees do online by taking hundreds of screen snapshots per hour (Figure 9.14). About one company in four has fired an employee based on what it has found.

Such monitoring is direct and invasive, but it will continue until laws are passed against it. Why do companies monitor their employees? Companies are concerned about employees who may offer trade secrets to competitors in hopes of landing an attractive job offer. Another concern is sexual harassment lawsuits. Employees who access pornographic Web sites or circulate offensive jokes via e-mail may be creating a hostile environment for other employees—and that could result in a huge lawsuit against the company.

To protect your privacy at work, remember the following rules:

- Unless you have specific permission, don't use your employer's telephone system for personal calls. Make all such calls from a pay phone or from your personal cell phone.
- Never use your e-mail account at work for personal purposes. Send and receive all personal mail from your home computer.
- Assume that everything you do while you're at work—whether it's talking on the phone, using your computer, taking a break, or chatting with coworkers—may be monitored and recorded.

Now that you've learned about some important privacy issues, let's take a look at some intentional invasions of your privacy—computer crime.

> " Assume that **everything** you do while you're at **work** may be monitored and recorded. "

Computer Crime and Cybercrime

Privacy issues, such as collecting personal information and employee monitoring, should be distinguished from **computer crimes**, computer-based activities that violate state, federal laws, or international laws. **Cybercrime** describes crimes carried out by means of the Internet. A new legal field—**cyberlaw**—is emerging to track and combat computer-related crime.

In 2006, the United States ratified the Convention on Cybercrime. Developed by the Council of Europe, this is the first international treaty to address the issues and concerns surrounding cybercrime. Its goal is to provide guidelines for consistent cybercrime legislation that is compatible with other member countries and to encourage international cooperation in these areas. Many government agencies,

FIGURE 9.14 Employers can use Spector, an employee-monitoring program from SpectorSoft, to track everything employees do online.

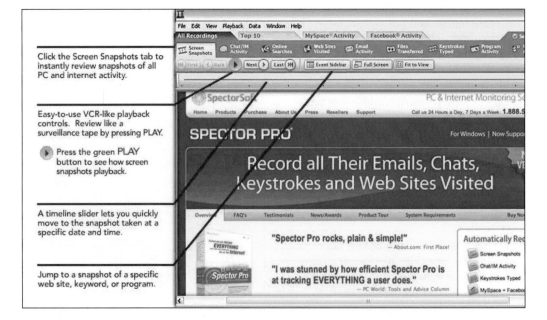

such as the Department of Justice (**www.cybercrime.gov**) and the FBI (**www.fbi.gov/cyberinvest/cyberhome. htm**) have set up special sites to provide information and assistance to help combat cybercrime. The FTC's OnGuard Online site (**http://onguardonline.gov**) has collaborated with government agencies and technology organizations to provide tutorials and activities to educate consumers about the threats and risks posed by cybercriminals (Figure 9.15).

TYPES OF COMPUTER CRIME

Anyone who wants to invade or harm a computer system can use a variety of tools and tricks. Pay close attention; you'll learn several facts that could help you avoid becoming a victim.

Identity Theft The phone rings and it's a collection agency demanding immediate payment for a bill for a $5,000 stereo system that's past due. You can't believe what you're hearing—you always pay your bills on time, and you haven't purchased any stereo equipment lately. What's going on?

It's identity theft, one of the fastest growing crimes in the United States and Canada. With **identity theft**, a criminal obtains enough personal information to impersonate you. With a few key pieces of information, such as your address and Social Security number, and possibly a credit card or bank account number, an identity thief can open a credit account, access your bank account, open accounts for utilities or cell phones, or apply for a loan or mortgage—all in your name! Although some laws may limit your liability for fraudulent charges, victims of identity theft have found themselves saddled with years of agony. The bad marks on their credit reports can prevent them from buying homes, obtaining telephone service, and even getting jobs. Although some reports show a slight decline in identity theft in the United States, according to a Javelin Strategy and Research report in 2009, there were 10 million victims of identity theft in 2008 in the United States. Consider the following interesting identity theft statistics:

- Approximately 1.6 million households had their bank accounts or debit cards compromised.
- It can take up to 5,840 hours (the equivalent of working a full-time job for two years) to correct the damage from ID theft, depending on the severity of the case.

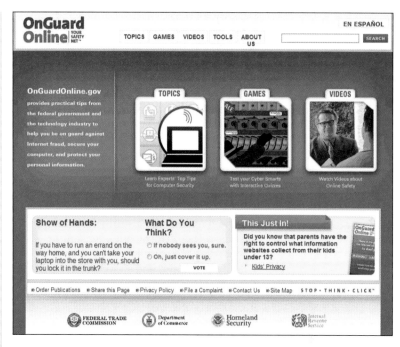

- Businesses across the world lose $221 billion a year due to identity theft.
- On average, victims lose between $851 and $1,378 out-of-pocket trying to resolve identity theft.
- Approximately 70 percent of victims have difficulty removing negative information that resulted from identity theft from their credit reports.
- About 43 percent of victims know the perpetrator.
- In cases of child identity theft, the most common perpetrator is the child's parent.

How do criminals get this information? Most identity theft doesn't even involve computers. Disgruntled employees may steal information from their company, thieves may steal your mail or wallet, or they may go through your trash or a company's trash. But, information can also be stolen by criminals if computer data is not properly secured, if you respond to spam or phishing attacks, or if you have malware on your computer. And unfortunately, many Web sites and spammers sell such data to others.

In a **phishing** attack, a "phisher" poses as a legitimate company in an e-mail or on a Web site in an attempt to obtain personal information such as your Social Security number, user name, password, and account numbers. For example, you might receive an e-mail that appears to come from XYZ Company asking you to confirm your e-identity (user name and

FIGURE 9.15 The FTC's OnGuard Online site provides many resources to help educate the public about various types of cybercrime. Visitors can view tutorials, explore topics, or file a complaint if they've been victims.

password). Because the communication looks legitimate, you comply. The phisher can now gain access to your accounts. **Spear phishing**, which is similar to phishing, also uses fake e-mails and social engineering to trick recipients into providing personal information to enable identity theft. But rather than being sent randomly, spear phishing attempts are targeted to specific people, such as senior executives or members of a particular organization.

Malware The term **malware** is short for *malicious software* and describes software designed to damage or infiltrate a computer system without the owner's consent or knowledge. Malware is used to commit fraud, send spam, and steal your personal data. It includes spyware and computer viruses, as well as other rogue programs like worms and Trojan horses. For the period of January 1, 2008, to March 31, 2008, US CERT, an agency that interacts with federal agencies, industry, the research community, state and local governments, and others to collect cyber-security information and to identify emerging cybersecurity threats, reported the main threat to be scans, probes, and attempted access. A study by McAfee and the National Cyber Security Alliance (**http://staysafeonline.org**) indicates that fewer than one in four Americans is fully protected against malware. This Web site offers a list tips to keep you safe online.

- Know who you're dealing with online.
- Keep your Web browsers and operating system up to date.
- Back up important files.
- Protect your children online.
- Use security software tools as your first line of defense.
- Use strong passwords or strong authentication technology to help protect your personal information.
- Learn what to do if something goes wrong.

Malware takes many different forms, the most common of which are discussed in this chapter. While the United States is not the biggest source of malware activity (Figure 9.16), the exploits of those in other countries can have equally devastating consequences. Malware, by its nature, has no boundaries.

Spyware is software that collects your personal information, monitors your Web surfing habits, and distributes this information to a third party, often leading to identity theft. Some spyware, such as **adware**, generates pop-up ads and targeted banner ads, and is usually considered a nuisance rather than malicious. However, **keyloggers**, which can record all the keystrokes you type—such as passwords, account numbers, or conversations—and relay them to others, pose a more dangerous security threat.

Spyware is often distributed when you download free software or infected files. File-sharing sites are notorious for this. However, clicking on a pop-up ad can also install spyware, and visiting an infected Web site can trigger a "drive-by" download.

Most spyware is not designed to disable your computer, but you might find that your computer seems sluggish or crashes more frequently. Other signs of infection include an increase in pop-up ads, unauthorized changes to your home or search pages, and the appearance of new browser toolbars.

Your best defense is to install antispyware software and update it frequently. Many experts recommend using at least two products, because one may catch something the other missed. Other safe practices include using a firewall, avoiding questionable Web sites, never clicking on pop-up ads, and downloading software only from reputable sources.

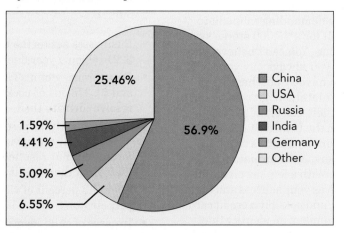

FIGURE 9.16 Just a few countries were responsible for most of the attempts to infect computers via the Web in July 2009.

Today Internet Explorer (IE) and Mozilla Firefox include pop-up blocking features. Although some pop-ups may be able to evade the browsers, most are blocked and a yellow information bar will appear at the top of the browser. It's important to read the message on the information bar. It usually gives you options about how to handle the incident it is reporting. Both browsers also offer built-in antiphishing features to help protect you from a list of known phishing sites that is updated regularly. Firefox will display a warning dialog box when you attempt to access a phishing site, and IE uses a color-coded Security Status bar. IE uses the familiar stoplight color code—green indicates a site that is using a new High Assurance identity verification certificate; yellow indicates a site that may be suspicious; and red is used for known phishing sites or sites whose identification does not match their encryption certificate. A white status bar simply means that no identity information is available. However, the lack of a warning color or dialog box does not guarantee that a site is safe. No matter how efficient these built-in browser features are, it is still important to practice safe surfing methods.

A **computer virus** is hidden code within a program, designed as a prank or sabotage, that replicates itself by attaching to other programs. It often performs dangerous actions like damaging or destroying the infected files. Like living viruses, computer viruses require a host (such as a program file) and are designed to make copies of themselves.

Typically, virus infections spread when an infected file or program is downloaded onto a computer. Opening the file or running the program executes the virus, allowing it to perform its designated tasks. Most viruses act as **file infectors** by attaching themselves to a program file. When the program is executed, the virus spreads to other programs on the user's hard disk. If you copy a file on your computer to a USB drive, CD, or DVD and give it to someone, the infection spreads even further (Figure 9.17).

Many computer viruses are spread by e-mail attachments. When you open an e-mail, you may see a dialog box asking whether you want to open an attachment. Don't open it unless you're sure the attachment is safe.

Consider the following scenario. A professor with a large lecture section of

FIGURE 9.17 Computer viruses can be passed from one computer to another by network connections or portable media such as USB drives, CDs, and DVDs.

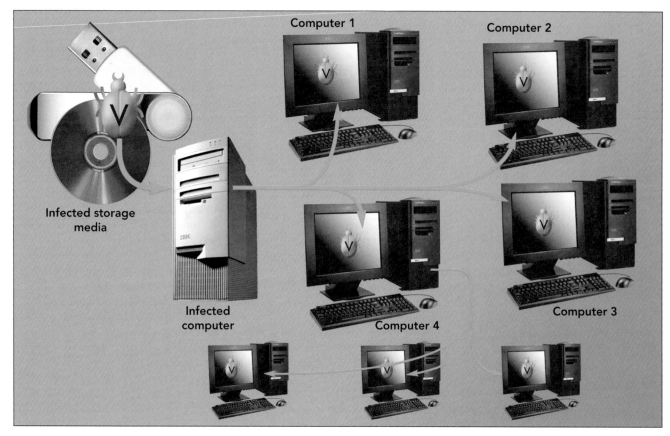

Infected storage media

Infected computer

Computer 1

Computer 2

Computer 3

Computer 4

100 students receives an e-mail from a former student with an attachment named "Spring Break" that apparently contains a picture from the student's spring break. The professor opens the attachment, which appears to do nothing, and the professor moves on to the next e-mail. The attachment, however, is doing something. It is sending a copy of itself to everyone in the professor's e-mail address box—including each of the 100 students in the class. As students open the attachment, the virus will continue to propagate to the addresses in each of their contact lists. The attachment is received by parents, friends, other professors, and fellow students. Many open the attachment, and the process accelerates very rapidly.

Executable file attachments pose the most serious risk. You can tell an executable file by its extension. In Microsoft Windows, the extension is .exe, but executable files also can be named .vbs, .com, .bin, or .bat. However, you can't be sure that a file is executable by its extension alone. You should also be wary of opening Microsoft Office documents, such as Microsoft Word and Microsoft Excel files. The best policy is to always check attachment files with an antivirus program before you open them.

> "The best policy is to always **check** attachment **files** with an **antivirus** program before you open them."

Although some viruses are best categorized as nuisances or pranks, others can corrupt or erase data or completely disable a computer. All of them consume system memory and slow the computer's processing speed. In the prank category is the Wazzu virus, which randomly relocates a word in a Microsoft Word document and sometimes inserts "wazzu" into the text. Still others, such as Disk Killer, are far more malicious: Disk Killer wipes out all of the data on your hard drive.

A far more serious type of virus is a boot sector virus. A **boot sector virus** also propagates by an infected program, but it installs itself on the beginning tracks of a hard drive where code is stored that automatically executes every time you start the computer. Unlike file infectors, boot sector viruses don't require you to start a specific program to infect your computer; starting your system is sufficient. Boot sector viruses also may lead to the destruction of all the data stored on your hard drive.

A **macro virus** takes advantage of the automatic command execution capabilities found in some productivity software called **macros,** A macro, in a word processing or spreadsheet program, is a saved sequence of commands or keyboard strokes that get recalled when needed with a single command or keyboard stroke. Macro viruses infect the data file that contains the macro. When these files are shared with others, the virus infects their computers. By default, macros are disabled in newer versions of Microsoft Office, but users can adjust security settings to allow them. Files containing macros should always be scanned by antivirus software.

The number of viruses sent by e-mail increased by almost 300 percent in July 2009 and was at its highest level of the year, with approximately 12 viruses per customer per hour. The leading sources of these viruses are India (5.2%), Korea (6.2%), Brazil (14.11%), and the U.S. (16.59%).

Malware has spread beyond computers. During the 2007 holiday season, many shoppers found that their new digital photo frames came from the factory with a preinstalled virus. Fortunately, it was an old virus and consumers using up-to-date antivirus software were protected. However, other devices, such as GPS units and digital music players, have had similar experiences. Mobile devices are also at risk. A spam text message, known as **spim**, was sent to more than 200 million mobile phone users in China during just one day in March 2008. Luckily, the spim did not include any malicious code, but it's a very real possibility. And contrary to popular belief, Mac and Linux computers are also vulnerable. Although not as prevalent, malware designed for these systems can also infect them, with the same negative results.

Computer virus authors are trying to "improve" their programs. Some new viruses are self-modifying; each new copy, known as a **variant**, is slightly different from the previous one, making it difficult to protect your computer. Sites such as Snopes.com and Vmyths.com can help you determine whether the latest news about a virus is real or a hoax.

More Rogue Programs Spyware and viruses aren't the only types of rogue programs. Other destructive programs include time bombs, worms, zombies, Trojan horses, and botnets.

A **time bomb**, also called a **logic bomb**, is a virus that sits harmlessly on a system until a certain event or set of circumstances causes the program to become active. For example, before leaving a Texas firm, a fired programmer planted a time bomb program that ran two days after he was fired and wiped out 168,000 critical financial records.

A **worm** is a program that resembles a computer virus in that it can spread from one computer to another. Unlike a virus, however, a worm can propagate over a computer network and doesn't require an unsuspecting user to execute a program or macro file. It takes control of affected computers and uses their resources to attack other network-connected systems. Some worms such as Sasser and Slammer exploit vulnerabilities found in Microsoft Windows and quickly propagate. Newer worms have begun infecting social networking sites such as MySpace and Facebook, retrieving user information and passwords, and directing users to phishing sites. Although patches are usually released quickly, if your computer isn't updated, it remains vulnerable. Even if you don't think your personal information is worth protecting, worms compromise the security of a computer, making it accessible to cybercriminals who can then use it for their own purposes.

Another type of threat is a denial of service attack. With a **denial of service (DoS) attack**, a form of network vandalism, an attacker attempts to make a service unavailable to other users, generally by bombarding the service with meaningless data. Because network administrators can easily block data from specific IP addresses, hackers must commandeer as many computers as possible to launch

> "A **worm** can propagate over a **computer network** and doesn't require an unsuspecting user to **execute** a **program** or **macro** file."

their attack. When multiple computer systems are involved, it becomes a **distributed denial of service (DDoS) attack**. The commandeered computers form a **botnet**, and the individual computers are called **zombies** because they simply do what the DoS program tells them to do. **Syn flooding** is a form of denial of service attack in which a hostile client repeatedly sends SYN (synchronization) packets to every port on the server, using fake IP addresses, which uses up all the available network connections and locks them up until they time out. This results in a denial of service for legitimate users.

According to a quarterly report from antivirus firm McAfee, botnet criminals have taken control of almost 12 million new IP addresses since January 2009. The number of zombie machines represents a 50 percent increase over last year, with the largest concentration of botnet-controlled machines in the United States.

A **Trojan horse** is a rogue program disguised as a useful program, but it contains hidden instructions to perform a malicious task instead. Sometimes a Trojan horse is disguised as a game or a utility program that users will find appealing. Then, when users begin running the game, they discover that they have loaded another program entirely. A Trojan horse may erase the data on your hard disk or cause other irreparable damage. More frequently, Trojan horses are used to install malware or to open a port for easy access by hackers. The Storm Trojan, which is frequently delivered via holiday-themed or weather-related e-mails, has more than 50,000 variants and has infected millions of computers. These infected computers then send out more Storm-infected spam in an endless cycle. At one point, it was responsible for one in every six e-mails that were sent.

Fraud, Theft, and Piracy When computer intruders make off with sensitive personal information, the potential for fraud multiplies. For example, the Hannaford supermarket chain experienced a data breach that exposed credit and debit card numbers for more than 4 million customers, resulting in more than 2,000 cases of fraud.

Physical theft of computer equipment is a growing problem as well (Figure 9.18). An estimated 85 percent of computer thefts are inside jobs, leaving no signs of forced physical entry. In addition, it's difficult to trace components after they've been taken out of a computer and reassembled. Particularly valuable are the microprocessor chips that drive computers. **Memory shaving**, in which knowledgeable thieves remove some of a computer's RAM chips but leave enough to start the computer, is harder to detect. Such a crime might go unnoticed for weeks.

Software piracy is the unauthorized copying or distribution of copyrighted software. This can be done by copying, downloading, sharing, selling, or installing multiple copies onto personal or work computers. What a lot of people don't realize—or don't think about—is that when you purchase software, you are actually purchasing a license to use it, not the actual software. That license is what tells you how many times you can install the software; so, be sure you read it. If you make more copies of the software than the license permits, you are pirating software.

Piracy can be intentional or unintentional. Regardless of intention, the Business Software Alliance, an antipiracy industry group, stated that the worldwide piracy rate rose between 2007 and 2008 (Figure 9.19) in their report issued in May of 2009. Losses grew by 11 percent, to $53 billion in nonadjusted dollars (not accounting for changes in exchange rate), although half of that growth was the result of the falling U.S. dollar. Excluding the effect of exchange rates, losses grew by 5 percent, to $50.2 billion.

Software piracy affects much more than just the global software industry. A 2008 IDC study predicted that lowering PC software piracy by 10 points over four years would create 600,000 additional new jobs worldwide and would generate $24 billion in higher government revenues, without a tax increase. Software piracy also increases the risk of cybercrime and security problems. For example, the recent global spread of the Conficker virus has been attributed in part to the lack of automatic security updates for unlicensed software. And in a 2006 study, IDC found that 29 percent of Web sites and 61 percent of peer-to-peer sites offering pirated software tried to infect test computers with Trojans, spyware, keyloggers, and other tools of identity theft. Software piracy also *lowers tax revenues* at a time of increased fiscal pressures on governments worldwide.

Much software piracy takes place on file-sharing sites like LimeWire or BitTorrent or on online auction sites. It's difficult, but not impossible, to trace the actions of individuals. And when software

FIGURE 9.18 To prevent theft, users should lock their doors and turn off their computers. In some cases, it may be wise to secure hardware to desks.

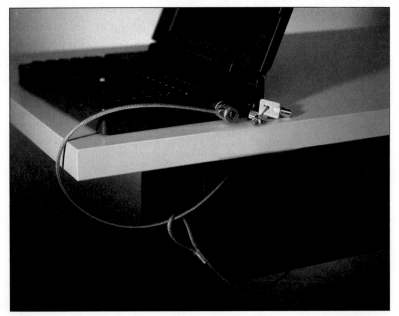

pirates are found, it is becoming more likely that they will be prosecuted. In fact, the first criminal lawsuit against a member of a piracy group has resulted in a guilty verdict in federal court. Barry Gitarts hosted and maintained a server for the Apocalypse Production Crew that traded hundreds of thousands of pirated copies of movies, music, games, and software. He is facing up to five years in prison for conspiracy to commit criminal copyright infringement, a $250,000 fine, and three years of supervised release—and he must make full restitution. Gitarts may be the first person to go to jail for illegally uploading files to the Internet.

New legislation is being debated that would make piracy penalties even tougher. If passed, the Prioritizing Resources and Organization for Intellectual Property (Pro-IP) Act will strengthen civil and criminal penalties for copyright and trademark infringement, substantially increasing fines and allowing officials to confiscate equipment. What about sharing programs without money changing hands? That's illegal too—and subject to similar penalties: Under the No Electronic Theft (NET) Act, profit does not have to be a motive in cases of criminal copyright infringement.

Cybergaming Crime A large portion of the population today play some sort of computer-based game. Some choose *Tetris,* others choose *Counter Strike,* and many choose the more virtual and global world of MMORPGs (Massive Multiplayer Online Role Playing Games). In these global battlefields, players can meet other players, become friends, engage in battle, fight shoulder to shoulder against evil, find their virtual destiny—and play, play, play. . . . However, for as much as online virtual gaming is a method of entertainment, virtual evil can become greedy reality. Online games are played by real people, including thieves and con artists who make real money by stealing other people's "virtual" property. The stolen items are put up

for auction (on sites such as ebay.com and other forums), and can be sold to others for virtual or real money. Cybergaming criminals have been known to demand a ransom for the stolen items. Malicious game users can really rake in the money.

Tricks for Obtaining Passwords The most publicized computer crimes involve unauthorized access, in which an intruder gains entry to a supposedly secure computer system. Typically, computer systems use some type of authentication technique—usually plaintext passwords—to protect the system from uninvited guests. Many techniques are used to guess or obtain a password (Figure 9.20). Another widely used technique involves exploiting well-known holes in obsolete e-mail programs, which can be manipulated to disclose a user's password.

Salami Shaving and Data Diddling With **salami shaving**, a programmer alters a program to subtract a very small amount of money from an account—say, two cents—and diverts the funds to the embezzler's account. Ideally, the sum is so small that it's never noticed. In a business that handles thousands of accounts, an insider could skim tens of thousands of dollars per year using this method.

With **data diddling**, insiders modify data by altering accounts or database records so that it's difficult or impossible to tell that they've stolen funds or equipment. A Colorado supermarket chain recently discovered it was the victim of data

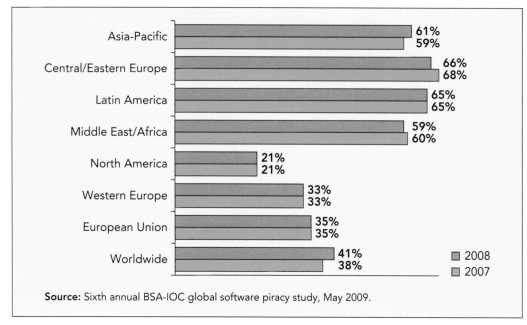

Source: Sixth annual BSA-IOC global software piracy study, May 2009.

FIGURE 9.19 The rates of software piracy are significantly higher in underdeveloped nations.

FIGURE 9.20 Techniques Used to Obtain Passwords

Password guessing	Computer users too often choose a password that is easily guessed, such as "password." Other popular passwords are "qwerty" (the first six letters of the keyboard), obscene words, personal names, birthdays, celebrity names, movie characters such as Frodo or Gandalf, and cartoon characters such as Garfield.
Shoulder surfing	In a crowded computer lab, it's easy to peek over someone's shoulder, look at the keyboard, and obtain his or her password. Watch out for shoulder surfing when using an ATM machine too.
Packet sniffing	A program called a packet sniffer examines all of the traffic on a section of a network and looks for passwords, credit card numbers, and other valuable information.
Dumpster diving	Intruders go through an organization's trash hoping to find documents that contain lists of user IDs and even passwords. It's wise to use a shredder!
Social engineering	This is a form of deception to get people to divulge sensitive information. You might get a call or an e-mail from a person who claims, "We have a problem and need your password right now to save your e-mail." If you comply, you might give an intruder entry to a secure system.
Superuser status	This enables system administrators to access and modify virtually any file on a network. If intruders gain superuser status, they can obtain the passwords of everyone using the system.

diddling when it found nearly $2 million in unaccounted losses.

Forgery Knowledgeable users can make Internet data appear to come from one place when it's really coming from another. This action is referred to as **forgery**; third-party remailer sites and programs strip the sender's tracking data from a message and then resend the message.

Forged messages and Web pages can cause embarrassment and worse. A university professor in Texas was attacked with thousands of e-mail messages and Usenet postings after someone forged a racist Usenet article in his name. In Beijing, a student almost lost an $18,000 scholarship when a jealous rival forged an e-mail message to the University of Michigan turning down the scholarship. Fortunately, the forgery was discovered and the scholarship was reinstated, but only after a lengthy delay.

MEET THE ATTACKERS

A surprising variety of people can cause security problems, ranging from pranksters to hardened criminals, such as the Russian intruders who recently made off with $10 million from Citibank. Motives vary too. Some attackers are out for ego gratification and don't intend any harm. Others are out for money or on a misguided crusade; some are just plain malicious.

Hackers, Crackers, Cybergangs, and Virus Authors To the general public, a hacker is a criminal who illegally accesses computer systems. Within the computing community, several terms are used to describe various types of hacking. However, it is important to note that accessing someone's computer without authorization is illegal, no matter what the motivation might be. The most celebrated intruders are computer hobbyists and computer experts for whom unauthorized access is something of an irresistible intellectual game. **Hackers** are computer hobbyists who enjoy pushing computer systems (and themselves) to their limits. They experiment with programs to try to discover capabilities that aren't mentioned in the software manuals.

They modify systems to obtain the maximum possible performance. And sometimes they try to track down all of the weaknesses and loopholes in a system's security. When hackers attempt unauthorized access, they rarely damage data or steal assets. Hackers generally subscribe to an unwritten code of conduct, called the **hacker ethic**, which forbids the destruction of data. Hackers form communities. Such communities have a pecking order that is defined in terms of an individual's reputation for hacking prowess. **Cybergangs** are groups of hackers or crackers working together to coordinate attacks, post online graffiti, or engage in other malicious conduct. **IP spoofing**, one activity usually associated with hackers, is done by sending a message with an IP address disguised as an incoming message from a trusted source to a computer. The hacker must first locate and modify the message packet headers of a trusted source (called a port) and then manipulate the hacker's own communication so that it appears to come from the trusted port.

Hacking goes beyond public sites. A few years ago, a 23-year-old hacker known as "RaFa" downloaded about 43 MB of data from a top-security NASA server, including a 15-slide PowerPoint presentation of a future shuttle design. He then sent the plans to a *Computerworld* reporter as proof that the NASA system was not secure. Although NASA didn't experience any direct financial loss from RaFa's activities, many companies do lose money because of hacker attacks—as much as $1 million can be lost from a single security incident.

However, a lot more is at stake than just money. What if terrorists or foreign agents could hack the U.S. government's computers and read, change, or steal sensitive documents? What if hackers could disrupt the networks that support vital national infrastructures such as finance, energy, and transportation? Recognizing the danger, the federal government, through US-CERT, has emergency-response teams ready to fend off attacks on critical systems. Internationally, a group of security specialists is using **honeypots**— computers baited with fake data and purposely left vulnerable—to study how intruders operate in order to prepare stronger defenses (Figure 9.21).

Crackers (also called **black hats**) are hackers who become obsessed (often uncontrollably) with gaining entry to highly secure computer systems. The frequency and sophistication of their attacks can cause major headaches for system administrators. Many U.S. government sites are constant targets for hackers, but they are usually able to divert them. However, in June 2007, Chinese hackers were able to breach an unclassified e-mail system in the Department of Defense, affecting more than 1,500 users and shutting down the network for more than a week. A recent attack on the Epilepsy Foundation's forums caused actual headaches, and much worse, for their viewers. Hackers posted hundreds of pictures and links to flashing animations that caused severe migraines and seizures in some visitors.

Like hackers, crackers are often obsessed with their reputations in the hacking and cracking communities. To document their feats, they often leave calling cards, such as a prank message, on the systems they penetrate. Sometimes these traces enable law enforcement personnel to track them down.

Hackers and crackers should be distinguished from criminals who seek to use unauthorized access to steal money or valuable data. Keep in mind, however, that anyone who tries to gain unauthorized access to a computer system is probably breaking

FIGURE 9.21 US-CERT provides defense support against cyberattacks and disseminates cybersecurity information to the public.

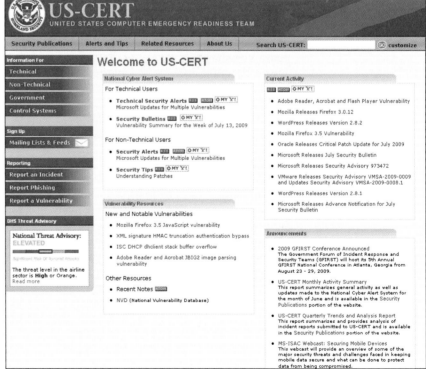

one or more laws. However, more than a few hackers and crackers have turned pro, offering their services to companies hoping to use hacker expertise to shore up their computer systems' defenses. Those who undertake this type of hacking are called **ethical hackers**, or **white hats**.

Computer virus authors create viruses and other types of malware to vandalize computer systems. Originally, authors were usually teenage boys, interested in pushing the boundaries of antivirus software and seeking to prove their authoring skills over those of their competitors. These days, virus authoring has become big business, and many authors are involved with organized crime. If caught and convicted, virus authors face prison and heavy fines. David L. Smith, the 33-year-old programmer who created the Melissa virus, was sentenced to 20 months in jail and a $5,000 fine in 2002, and in 2004 a 19-year-old female hacker known as Gigabyte faced up to three years in jail and almost $200,000 in fines. More recently, Li Jun, the 25-year-old creator of the Fujacks, or Panda, worm, was sentenced by a Chinese court to four years in prison. Hackers and other cybercriminals can no longer be stereotyped—their members include all ages, both sexes, and many nationalities. For more information on hackers, including the history of hacking, the types of vulnerabilities hackers look for, and what motivates them, check out Kaspersky Lab's Viruslist site at **www.viruslist.com**.

Swindlers Swindlers typically perpetuate bogus work-at-home opportunities, illegal pyramid schemes, chain letters, risky business opportunities, bogus franchises, phony goods that won't be delivered, overpriced scholarship searches, and get-rich-quick scams. Today, the distribution media of choice include e-mail, Internet chat rooms, and Web sites.

Estimates of the scope of the problem vary, especially because many cases of fraud are never reported. According to the 2008 Internet Crime Report, consumers reported losses of more than $264 million on a variety of Internet scams—and the

figure is growing by leaps and bounds (Figure 9.22).

Shills Internet auction sites such as eBay attract online versions of the same scams long perpetrated at live auctions. A **shill** is a secret operative who bids on another seller's item to drive up the price. In a recent case, an online jewelry store was charged with illegally bidding on its own merchandise. The store allegedly made more than 200,000 bids totaling more than $5 million and drove up auction prices by as much as 20 percent. In a settlement with the New York attorney general's office, the jeweler has agreed to pay $400,000 in restitution and is banned from online auctions for four years.

> " **... consumers** reported losses of more then **$264 million** on a variety of Internet scams—and the figure is growing by leaps and bounds. "

Cyberstalkers, Sexual Predators, and Cyberbullying One of the newest and fastest growing of all crimes is **cyberstalking**, or using the Internet, social networking sites, e-mail, or other electronic communications to repeatedly harass or threaten a person. Cyberstalking, like real-world stalking, is a repeated, unwanted, and disruptive break into the life-world of the victim.

For example, one San Diego university student terrorized five female classmates for more than a year, sending them

FIGURE 9.22 Internet Scams

Rip and tear	A Seattle man posted ads for Barbie dolls and other goods on eBay, collected more than $32,000 in orders, and never delivered any goods. Swindlers move to a new state once their activities are uncovered. The perpetrators believe that law enforcement won't be concerned with the relatively small amounts involved in each transaction.
Pumping and dumping	Crooks use Internet stock trading sites, chat rooms, and e-mail to sing the praises of worthless companies in which they hold stock. Then, after the share prices go up, they dump the stocks and make a hefty profit.
Bogus goods	Two Miami residents were indicted on charges of mail and wire fraud after selling hundreds of "Go-boxes," which purported to turn red traffic lights to green. The boxes, which were actually nothing more than strobe lights, sold for between $69 and $150.

hundreds of violent and threatening e-mail messages. Kathy Sierra was a well-known technology blogger and author who began receiving offensive comments on her blog, Creating Passionate Users. These comments included disturbingly edited images of Sierra and violent, sexual threats that finally escalated to death threats from several sources. The posts also appeared on other blogs. Because of their seriousness, Sierra cancelled plans to make a presentation at a technology conference, claiming she feared for her life, and she eventually suspended her blog. Although several people were linked to the comments, no one was ever prosecuted.

Cyberstalking has one thing in common with traditional stalking: Most perpetrators are men, and most victims are women, particularly women in college. One in every eight women attending college has been followed, watched, phoned, written, or e-mailed in ways that they found obsessive and frightening.

Concerns about online sexual predators and the risk they pose to children have continued to grow. The Crimes Against Children Research Center (CCRC) reports that 1 in 25 children has received an aggressive sexual solicitation that included an attempt to contact the child offline. Additionally, 1 in 25 youths was asked to take sexual photos of himself or herself, and 1 in 25 reported being extremely upset or distressed because of these solicitations. Some online predators may pose as children, but the CCRC reports that many predators admit that they are older and manipulate their victims by appealing to them in other ways. They attempt to develop friendships and often flatter or seduce their victims. Although there have been situations that have ended in kidnapping or murder, violence has occurred in only 5 percent of reported cases. In the majority of cases, the victims have gone with the predator willingly, expected to have a sexual relationship, and often met with the predator on multiple occasions.

Online predators also look for new victims on cyberdating sites. Most cyberdating sites use profiling to match potential mates. The downside is that it is difficult to check someone's cyberidentity against his or her actual identity. Although some sites indicate that they perform background checks, it's doubtful that they are as comprehensive as necessary (Figure 9.23). Most are based on user-provided information—usually a credit card and birth date. An effective background check would require more detailed information, such as a Social Security number, home address, and possibly fingerprints. And this information would apply only to paying customers—it would not apply to free social networking sites.

Cyberbullying involves situations in which one or more individuals harass or threaten another individual less capable of defending himself or herself, using the Internet or other forms of digital technology. Cyberbullying can include sending threatening e-mail or text messages or assuming someone else's online identity for the purpose of humiliating or

FIGURE 9.23 To protect site users from unscrupulous predators, True.com conducts criminal and marital status checks on its communicating members and requires all site users to agree to a member code of ethics.

misrepresenting him or her. In a weird twist of fate, the woman who created a fake MySpace profile of a 16-year-old boy to start an Internet relationship with Megan Meier, the Missouri teen who hanged herself after receiving hurtful messages, is now believed to be the victim of a cyberbullying impersonator herself. The online harassment laws that were passed after Meier's death last year now may be used to help the middle-aged woman, who many believe was responsible for the 13-year-old girl's suicide. Preventing cyberbullying can be just as difficult as preventing real-time bullying. In cases that involve school-age children, both the parents and schools need to make students aware of the dangers and provide them with the knowledge and confidence they need to stand up to bullies.

Now that you understand the types of perpetrators who pose a risk to your online privacy and safety, let's look more closely at the growing risks to equipment and data security.

Security

As our entire economy and infrastructure move to networked computer systems, breaches of computer security can be costly. Even when no actual harm has

occurred, fixing the breach and checking to ensure that no damage has occurred require time, resources, and money. It's no wonder that security currently accounts for an estimated 10 to 20 percent of all corporate expenditures on computer systems.

SECURITY RISKS

Not all of the dangers posed to computer systems are caused by malicious, conscious intent. A **computer security risk** is any event, action, or situation—intentional or not—that could lead to the loss or destruction of computer systems or the data they contain. Some research indicates that security breaches may cost individuals and industry billions of dollars per year because of their impact on customer service, worker productivity, and so on.

Wireless Networks Wireless LANs pose challenges to security, especially hotspots that are designed for open access. Unlike wired networks, which send traffic over private dedicated lines, wireless LANs send their traffic across shared space—airwaves. Because no one owns the space that airwaves travel across, the opportunity for interference from other traffic is great, and the need for additional security is paramount.

To break into a wireless network, you must be within the proximity limits of the wireless signal. In a process called **wardriving**, an individual drives around with a wireless device, such as a notebook computer or smartphone, to look for wireless networks. Some people do this as a hobby and map out different wireless networks, whereas hackers look for wireless networks to break into. It is fairly easy to break into an unsecured wireless network and obtain confidential information. Wardriving applications carry names such as NetStumbler, MiniStumbler, Kismet, and MacStumbler and are readily available for download from the Internet (Figure 9.24).

Security methods for wireless networks include **WEP (Wired Equivalent Privacy)**, **WPA (Wi-Fi Protected Access)**, and **WPA2**. WEP was the earliest of the three and has several well-known weaknesses, but it may be the only option for some devices or older equipment. WPA was developed to provide a stronger level of security, and WPA2 improves on WPA's abilities. WPA2 provides confidentiality and data integrity and is

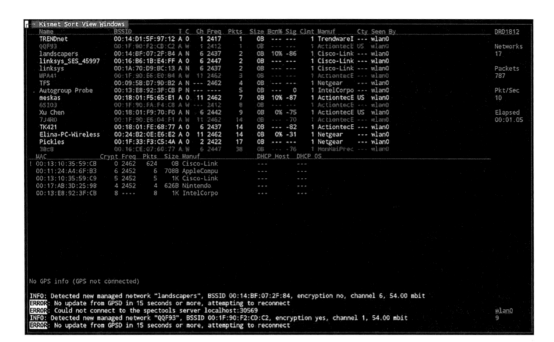

FIGURE 9.24 Wireless network detectors, sniffers, and intrusion detection systems like Kismet will work with any wireless card and are available at no cost.

far superior to WEP, because it uses AES (Advanced Encryption Standard) to provide government-grade security. The need for wireless security is great, and more powerful security systems continue to be developed. Wireless network owners should implement the security that is currently available so their systems are at least protected from the casual hacker.

The newest trend in Internet fraud is **vacation hacking**. Travelers are being targeting by cybercriminals who create phony Wi-Fi hot spots, called **evil twins**, whose names make users believe they are legitimately connected to the airport, hotel, or airline. Users believe that they are using a valid Wi-Fi access point; instead, they're signing onto a fraudulent network. The information being entered is not reaching the desired destination, but is being captured by criminals.

Corporate Espionage Corporate computer systems contain a great deal of information that could be valuable to competitors, including product development plans and specifications, customer contact lists, manufacturing process knowledge, cost data, and strategic plans. According to computer security experts, **corporate espionage**, the unauthorized access of corporate information, usually to the benefit of a competitor, is on the rise—so sharply that it may soon eclipse all other sources of unauthorized access. The perpetrators are often ex-employees who have been hired by a competing firm pre-

cisely because of their knowledge of the computer system at their previous place of employment.

According to one estimate, 80 percent of all data loss is caused by company insiders. Unlike intruders, employees have many opportunities to sabotage a company's computer system, often in ways that are difficult to trace. Although incoming e-mail is routinely scanned for threats, outgoing mail is often overlooked, allowing employees to easily transfer data. Similarly, employees can use USB drives, iPods, or other removable storage media to create an unauthorized copy of confidential data, an activity known as **podslurping**. They may discover or deliberately create security holes called **trap doors** that they can exploit after leaving the firm. They can then divulge the former employer's trade secrets to a competitor or destroy crucial data.

Companies can take a variety of steps to hinder corporate espionage:

- Identify and label sensitive information.
- Protect against data deletion and loss by write and password protecting documents and creating regular backups.
- Make employees aware of security policies and the consequences of violating them.
- Reassess security policies annually or more frequently if needed.
- Perform regular auditing, and random and regular monitoring.

- Install necessary hardware and software to protect systems and data from violations both from inside and outside sources.
- Force password changes every five days or less if data within the organization is highly secure.

The espionage threat goes beyond national borders. Nations bent on acquiring trade secrets and new technologies also are trying to break into corporate computer systems. According to a recent estimate, the governments of more than 125 countries are actively involved in industrial espionage.

In 2006, U.S. security experts estimated that industrial spying costs global businesses more than $200 billion a year. Congress has attempted to help companies protect themselves with the Economic Espionage Act of 1996. The Act permits legal action regarding "financial, business, scientific, engineering, technical and economic information," if a company can demonstrate it has attempted to keep this information classified and protected. But many companies don't take advantage of the Act except as a last resort. They feel that news of the theft may damage the company's reputation.

> 66 According to a recent estimate, the **governments** of more than **125 countries** are actively involved in **industrial espionage.** 99

Information Warfare **Information warfare** is the use of information technologies to corrupt or destroy an enemy's information and industrial infrastructure. A concerted enemy attack would include electronic warfare (using electronic devices to destroy or damage computer systems), network warfare (hacker-like attacks on a nation's network infrastructure, including the electronic banking system), and structural sabotage (attacks on computer systems that support transportation, finance, energy, and telecommunications). However, we shouldn't overlook old-fashioned explosives directed at computer centers. According to one expert, a well-coordinated bombing of only 100 key computer installations could bring the U.S. economy to a grinding halt.

According to experts, defenses against such attacks are sorely lacking, as the country of Estonia learned in the spring of 2007. Estonia is a small country, but it is on the leading edge of technology, with most of its population relying on the Internet for news, communication, and finance. When a Soviet-era war monument was relocated, against the wishes of the Russian government, several days of civil unrest ensued. Once the rioting ended, the cyberattacks began. Estonian sites, including government agencies, ISPs, financial networks, and media outlets, suffered massive DoS attacks originating from botnets controlling nearly 1 million computers. Incoming Internet traffic, primarily from Russia but also from other countries, rose to thousands of times above normal, disrupting commerce and communications for several weeks. Although allegations were made against the Russian government, nothing was ever proven. Many believe the attacks were conducted by activist hackers rather than by a specific government agency. Many also fear that the attack against Estonia was just a test—a way of demonstrating the power of those who control the botnets and a warning to other countries.

The U.S. Department of Homeland Security (DHS) reports that in 2007 there was an 81 percent increase in hacking attacks on banks. The U.S. Computer Emergency Readiness Team (US-CERT) is a national cyberwatch and warning center that coordinates activities with the private sector and handled more than 37,000 incidents in 2007. It also oversees EINSTEIN, an early-warning system that looks for malicious or irregular activity on the Internet. Once every two years, the DHS and US-CERT coordinate a national simulation known as Cyber Storm to assess the ability of the United States to identify and respond to a critical cyberattack. Cyber Storm II, held in March 2008, involved 18 government agencies, 5 countries, 9 states, 40 companies, and 10 information-sharing and analysis centers. The exercise simulated an attack on telecommunication centers, the Internet, and control systems. Preliminary results emphasize the need for improved communications between the public and the private sectors before, during, and after an attack (Figure 9.25).

Even if no enemy nation mounts an all-out information war on the United States, information terrorism is increasingly likely. Thanks to the worldwide distribution of powerful but inexpensive microprocessors, virtually anyone can construct electronic warfare weapons from widely available materials. These weapons include high-energy radio frequency (HERF) guns and electromagnetic pulse transformer (EMPT) bombs, which can damage or destroy computer systems up to a quarter mile away.

If this scenario sounds frightening, remember that information technology is a double-edged sword. Information technology gives despots a potent weapon of war, but it also undermines their power by giving citizens a way to organize democratic resistance. In Russia, for example, e-mail and fax machines played a major role in the failure of the 1989 military coup. In the United States, we have learned more about the importance of redundant data backup systems and the resiliency of the U.S. monetary system since the September 11 attacks, but we're still vulnerable and must develop ways to protect our computer systems and infrastructure.

Security Loophole Detection Programs

Intruders can use a variety of programs that automatically search for unprotected or poorly protected computer systems and notify them when a target is found. Such programs include Nessus, a security loophole detection program used by system administrators. In the wrong hands, the program can help an intruder figure out how to get into a poorly secured system.

Public Safety

Perhaps the greatest threat posed by security breaches is the threat to human life; computers are increasingly part of safety-critical systems, such as air-traffic control. By paralyzing transportation and power infrastructures, attackers could completely disrupt the distribution of electricity, food, water, and medical supplies.

This threat nearly became a reality when a 14-year-old hacker knocked out phone and radio service to a regional airport's communications tower. Although the hacker didn't realize he had accessed an airport computer and meant no harm, his actions paralyzed the airport's computer system and forced air-traffic controllers to rely on cellular phones and battery-powered radios to direct airplanes until the system was back up and running.

Terrorism

Perhaps the brightest spot in the war on terror is the identification of persons of interest by using special security software programs. One program that attempts to find such people is IBM's Real-Time Collaborative Criminal Investigation and Analysis tool. It quickly analyzes data to discover similarities and links between individuals to determine whether they are connected with unsavory characters. The SOMA Terror Organization Portal (STOP) permits analysts to network with other analysts to pool their knowledge and resources about the behavior of terrorist organizations and to forecast potential terrorist behavior. The downside of these methods is the potential for violating individual privacy rights and mistakenly targeting innocent people.

PROTECTING YOUR COMPUTER SYSTEM

Several measures can safeguard computer systems, but none of them can make a computer system 100 percent secure. A trade-off exists between security and

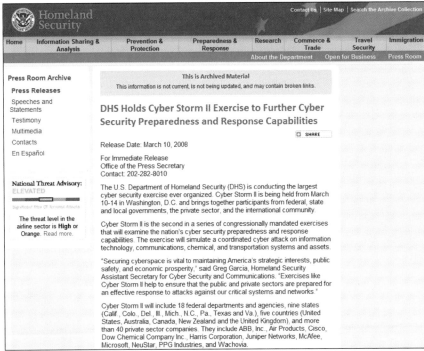

FIGURE 9.25 Cyber Storm II was the second in a series of congressionally mandated exercises that examined the nation's cybersecurity preparedness and response capabilities.

usability: The more restrictions imposed by security tools, the less useful the system becomes.

Power-Related Problems Power surges, which are often caused by lightning storms or fluctuations in electrical currents, and power outages can destroy sensitive electronic components and carry the threat of data loss. To safeguard your equipment and data, you should always use a surge protector. Additionally, some applications offer an autosave feature that backs up your work at a specified interval (such as every 10 minutes). You can also equip your system with an **uninterruptible power supply (UPS)**, a battery-powered device that provides power to your computer for a limited time when it detects an outage or critical voltage drop (Figure 9.26). Many companies have electric generators to run large-scale computer systems when the power fails.

Controlling Access
Because many security problems originate with purloined passwords, password authentication is crucial to controlling authorized access to computer systems. Typically, users select their own passwords—and that is the source of a serious computer security risk. If an intruder can guess your password, the intruder can gain access to the computer system. Any damage that results will appear to have been perpetrated by you, not the intruder. What's a good password? The best passwords, often referred to as strong passwords, contain at least eight characters, combine upper- and lowercase letters, include one or more numbers, and one or more symbols. Xa98Mso#Z is an example of a good password.

In addition to password authentication, **know-and-have authentication** requires using tokens, which are handheld electronic devices that generate a logon code. Increasingly popular are smart cards, devices the size of a credit card with their own internal memories. In tandem

FIGURE 9.26 A UPS is a battery-powered device that provides power to your computer for a limited time during a power outage.

with a supplied personal identification number (PIN), a smart card can reliably establish that the person trying to gain access has the authorization to do so.

However, when used with digital cash systems, smart cards pose a significant threat to personal privacy. Because every smart card transaction is recorded, regardless of how small a transaction it is, a person's purchases can be assembled and scrutinized. An investigator could put together a list of the magazines and newspapers you purchase and read, where and when you paid bridge tolls and subway fares, and what you had for lunch.

The most secure authentication approach is **biometric authentication**, which uses a variety of techniques, including voice recognition, retinal scans, fingerprint scans, and face and hand recognition (Figure 9.27). For example, Gateway now offers a built-in biometric fingerprint sensor on its latest notebook that locks access to the computer unless the correct fingerprint is matched. In an experiment in Barcelona, Spain, a soccer club used a database of ticket barcodes matched with fans' photographs to verify the tickets of more than 100,000 ticket holders as they entered the stadium. If the ticket holder's face did not match the face in the database, the person was not admitted to the stadium.

Firewalls A **firewall** is a computer program or device that permits an organization's internal computer users to access the external Internet but severely limits the ability of outsiders to access internal data (Figure 9.28). A firewall can be implemented through software, hardware, or a combination of both. Firewalls are a necessity, but they provide no protection against insider pilferage. Home users opting for "always on" broadband connections, such as those offered by cable modems or DSL, face a number of computer security risks. **Personal firewalls** are programs or devices that protect home computers from

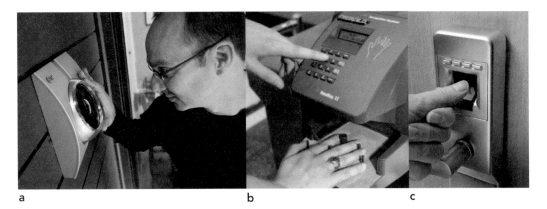

FIGURE 9.27 Biometric authentication devices such as (**a**) retinal scanners, (**b**) hand-geometry readers, and (**c**) fingerprint scanners are often used to provide access to restricted locations.

a   b   c

unauthorized access. For information and additional diagrams on how a firewall works or how to choose a firewall for your system, visit **http://computer.howstuffworks. com/firewall.htm** or **www.microsoft. com/protect/computer/firewall/ choosing.mspx**. To find out whether your firewall is configured properly, use the free ShieldsUP! service found at **www.grc.com**.

PROTECTING YOURSELF

In addition to protecting your system from intrusion or attack, it has become increasingly important to protect your personal data from theft and yourself from a cyberattack. Following the old clichés of the real world such as User beware; Don't talk to strangers; and If something is too good to be true, it usually is, will keep you out of trouble in the cyberworld.

Avoiding Scams To avoid being scammed on the Internet, follow these tips:

- Do business with established companies that you know and trust.
- Read the fine print. If you're ordering something, make sure it's in stock and that the company promises to deliver within 30 days.
- Don't provide financial or other personal information or passwords to anyone, even if the request sounds legitimate.
- Be skeptical when somebody in an

Internet chat room tells you about a great new company or stock.

Preventing Cyberstalking To protect yourself against cyberstalking, follow these tips:

- Don't share any personal information, such as your real name, in chat rooms. Use a name that is gender- and age-neutral. Do not post a user profile.
- Be extremely cautious about meeting anyone you've contacted online. If you do, meet in a public place and bring friends along.
- If a situation you've encountered online makes you uncomfortable or afraid, contact the police immediately. Save all the communications you've received.

Now that you've learned some ways to protect your security, let's discuss one of the

FIGURE 9.28 A firewall permits an organization's internal computer users to access the Internet but limits the ability of outsiders to access internal data.

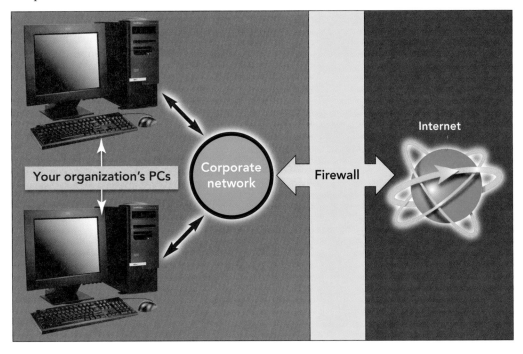

Your organization's PCs

Corporate network

Firewall

Internet

FIGURE 9.29
Decoding Key for "I Love You"

A	1
B	2
C	3
D	4
E	5
F	6
G	7
H	8
I	9
J	10
K	11
L	12
M	13
N	14
O	15
P	16
Q	17
R	18
S	19
T	20
U	21
V	22
W	23
X	24
Y	25
Z	26

major security measures used to keep information safe on the Internet: encryption.

The Encryption Debate

Cryptography is the study of transforming information into an encoded or scrambled format. Individuals who practice in this field are known as **cryptographers**. **Encryption** refers to a coding or scrambling process that renders a message unreadable by anyone except the intended recipient. Until recently, encryption was used only by intelligence services, banks, and the military.

E-commerce requires strong, unbreakable encryption; otherwise, money could not be safely exchanged over the Internet. But now, powerful encryption software is available to the public, and U.S. law enforcement officials and defense agencies aren't happy about it. Criminals, including drug dealers and terrorists, can use encryption to hide their activities. In the aftermath of the September 11 terrorist attacks, U.S. officials revealed that the terrorist network had used encrypted e-mail to keep their plans and activities secret.

ENCRYPTION BASICS

To understand encryption, try this simple exercise: Consider a short message such as "I love you." Before it is encrypted, a readable message such as this one is in **plaintext**. To encrypt the message, for each character substitute the letter that is 13 positions to the right in the 26-letter alphabet. (When you reach the end of the alphabet, start counting from the beginning.) This is an example of an **encryption key**, a formula that makes a plaintext message unreadable. After applying the key, you get the coded message, which is now in **ciphertext**. The ciphertext version of the original message looks like this:

```
V YBIR LBH
```

It looks like gibberish, doesn't it? That's the idea. No one who intercepts this message will know what it means. Your intended recipient, however, can tell what the message means if you give him or her the decoding key: in this case, counting 13 characters down (Figure 9.29). When your recipient gets the message and decrypts it, your message reappears:

```
I LOVE YOU
```

With **symmetric key encryption**, the same key is used for encryption and decryption. Some of the keys used by banks and military agencies are so complex that the world's most powerful computer would have to analyze the ciphertext for several hundred years to discover the key. However, there is one way to defeat symmetric key encryption: stealing the key, or **key interception**. Banks deliver decryption keys using trusted courier services; the military uses trusted personnel or agents. These methods provide opportunities for key theft.

PUBLIC KEY ENCRYPTION

Public key encryption is considered one of the greatest (and most troubling) scientific achievements of the twentieth century. In brief, **public key encryption** is a computer security process, also referred to as **asymmetric key encryption**, in which two different keys—an encryption key (the **public key**) and a decryption key (the **private key**)—are used. The use of two different keys safeguards data and thus provides confidentiality. Additionally it allows a digital signature to be verified by anyone who has access to the sender's public key, thereby proving that the sender is authentic and has access to the private key. The way it works is that people who want to receive secret messages publish their public key, for example, by placing it on a Web page or sending it to those with whom they wish to communicate. When the public key is used to encrypt a message, the message becomes unreadable. The message becomes readable only when the recipient applies his or her private key, which nobody else knows, guaranteeing confidentiality (Figure 9.30).

Public key encryption is essential for e-commerce. When you visit a secure site on the Web, for example, your Web browser provides your public key to the Web server; in turn, the Web server provides the site's public key to your Web browser. Once a secure communication channel has been created, your browser displays a distinctive icon, such as a lock in the address bar, or the address bar may turn green. You can now supply confidential information, such as your credit card number, with a reasonable degree of confidence that this information will not be intercepted while it is traveling across the Internet.

Digital Signatures and Certificates

Public key encryption can be used to implement **digital signatures**, a technique that guarantees a message has not been tampered with. Digital signatures are important to e-commerce because they enable computers to determine whether a received message or document is authentic and in its original form. A digital signature can be compared to the sealing of an envelope with a personal wax seal. Anyone can open the envelope, but the seal authenticates the sender. So, a digital signature would provide an assurance that an order was authentic and not the result of a hacker who was trying to disrupt a business transaction.

Public key encryption also enables **digital certificates**, a method of validating a user, server, or Web site. For a user, a digital certificate validates identity in a manner similar to showing a driver's license when you cash a check. For example, to protect both merchants and customers from online credit card fraud, Visa, MasterCard, and American Express collaborated to create an online shopping security standard for merchants and customers called **Secure Electronic Transaction (SET)** that uses digital certificates. They enable parties engaged in Internet-mediated transactions to confirm each other's identity. For a server or Web site, a digital certificate, validates that the Web server or Web site is authentic, and the user can feel secure that his or her interaction with the Web site has no eavesdrop-

pers and that the Web site is who it claims to be. This security is important for electronic commerce sites, especially ones that accept credit cards as a form of payment.

Toward a Public Key Infrastructure A **public key infrastructure (PKI)** is a uniform set of encryption standards that specify how public key encryption, digital signatures, and digital certificates should be implemented in computer systems and on the Internet. Although there are numerous contenders, no dominant PKI has emerged.

One reason for the slow development of a PKI involves the fear, shared by many private citizens and businesses alike, that a single, dominant firm will monopolize the PKI and impose unreasonable fees on the public. This was a concern when Microsoft introduced their Windows Live ID system, which implements a Microsoft-developed PKI (Figure 9.31). Originally devised as a single sign-on service for e-commerce sites, consumers and businesses feared it might be used to drive Microsoft's competitors out of business and impose artificially high costs on e-commerce, but Live ID has failed to gain popular acceptance in the marketplace and those fears have proved unfounded. Another concern involving the implementation of a PKI is that governments may step in to regulate

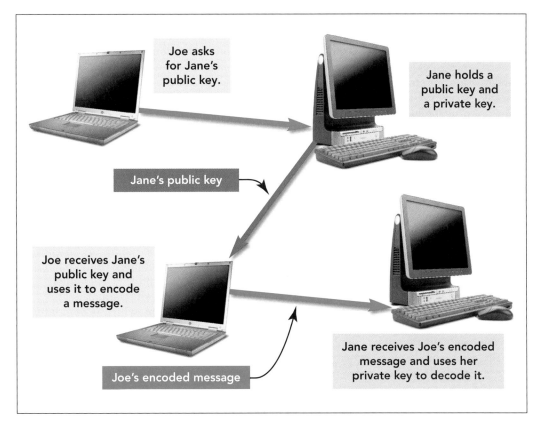

FIGURE 9.30 Jane's private key ensures that no one else can decipher Joe's message.

Joe asks for Jane's public key.

Jane holds a public key and a private key.

Jane's public key

Joe receives Jane's public key and uses it to encode a message.

Jane receives Joe's encoded message and uses her private key to decode it.

Joe's encoded message

public key encryption—or at the extreme, outlaw its use entirely.

ENCRYPTION AND PUBLIC SECURITY ISSUES

Just one year before the September 11 terrorist attacks on the World Trade Center and Pentagon, FBI Director Louis Freeh told the U.S. Congress that "the widespread use of robust unbreakable encryption ultimately will devastate our ability to fight crime and prevent terrorism. Unbreakable encryption will allow drug lords, spies, terrorists, and even violent gangs to communicate about their crimes and their conspiracies with impunity." In light of the terrorists' use of public key encryption—specifically, Pretty Good Privacy (PGP)—Freeh's warning now seems prophetic. Soon after the attacks, there were calls in the U.S. Congress to outlaw public key encryption.

However, recognizing that public key encryption is vital to the electronic economy, U.S. law enforcement and security agencies have not recommended that public key encryption be outlawed entirely. Instead, they advise that the U.S. Congress pass laws requiring a public key algorithm or a PKI that would enable investigators to eavesdrop on encrypted communications. U.S. government agencies have proposed some possibilities.

The government's need to know often conflicts with the public's right to privacy. Recently, the government released a new random-number standard, a critical component of encryption methods. It consisted of four random-number generators, one of which was included at the request of the National Security Agency (NSA). Upon examination, it was discovered that the NSA's random-number generator included a **backdoor**, a method of bypassing normal authentication to secure access to a computer, a vulnerability that could enable someone to crack the code, compromising the security of this encryption tool. Experts are still debating the ramifications of this discovery. In another instance, Sebastian Boucher was arrested at the U.S.–Canada border when his notebook computer was found to contain child pornography. When authorities tried to examine his computer several days later, they found his data was encrypted by PGP and they were unable to access it without the password. The government has tried to force Boucher to reveal the password, but his attorneys successfully argued that this was in violation of his Fifth Amendment rights, which protect him against self-incrimination. Further appeals are expected and privacy experts are carefully watching the outcome.

The government doesn't dispute the importance of encrypting data. The theft of a government employee's notebook computer containing the names and Social Security numbers of more than 26.5 million veterans and military personnel resulted in the federal Data at Rest Encryption program, which is mandatory for all military agencies and optional for civilian agencies. The software is available for all notebooks and other portable or handheld devices. It's obvious that there is a fine line between security and privacy, and the debate is far from resolved.

Prosecuting Violators

How is evidence obtained in cases of electronic fraud, cyberstalking, cyberbullying, phishing, or hacking? Likewise, how is data collected electronically in a noncomputer-related crime like hit-and-run or murder? There are two relatively recent areas of study that address these questions: e-discovery and computer forensics.

E-DISCOVERY

E-discovery, an abbreviated term for **electronic discovery**, is the obligation of parties to a lawsuit to exchange documents that exist only in electronic form, including e-mails, voicemails, instant messages, e-calendars, audio files, data on handheld devices, animation, metadata, graphics, photographs, spreadsheets, Web sites, drawings, and other types of digital data. Advances in technology have created an ever-expanding universe of such documents, making e-discovery more expensive, time-consuming, and burdensome than ever before. Consider this: The world sends over 60 billion e-mails daily, and 90 percent of all documents generated today are electronic. A single hard drive can store the equivalent of 40 million pages.

E-discovery is a $2 billion industry, and qualified professionals are in demand. E-discovery professionals use technology to discovery and manage electronic data. The e-discovery professional's knowledge of information technology and legal processes is invaluable to technology-challenged attorneys and clients. E-discovery professionals help identify, collect, process, review, and produce the electronic evidence in court cases.

COMPUTER FORENSICS

Computer forensics, a complex branch of forensic science, pertains to legal evidence found in computers and digital storage meda. It is a field that requires careful preparation and procedural strictness. Because of the scope and technical requirements of this field, there are many subsections such as firewall forensics and mobile device forensics. However, all have the same purposes: to analyze computer systems related to court cases, evaluate a computer after a break in, recover lost data, gather evidence against an employee by an employer, and reverse engineer. Taking the correct actions—in the right order—and recording evidence properly are often as important as having underlying knowledge of the issue being examined. Software developers have fortunately developed several forensic tool kits to help in the logical and procedural components of this field (Figure 9.32). These kits spell out proper procedure and contain forms to properly document every action and event involving a piece of digital evidence, guaranteeing its authenticity, accuracy, and thus, its reliability as evidence. This is a current and growing industry that is going to require individuals with an organized and logical mind, sharp perception skills, and a strong math and science focus.

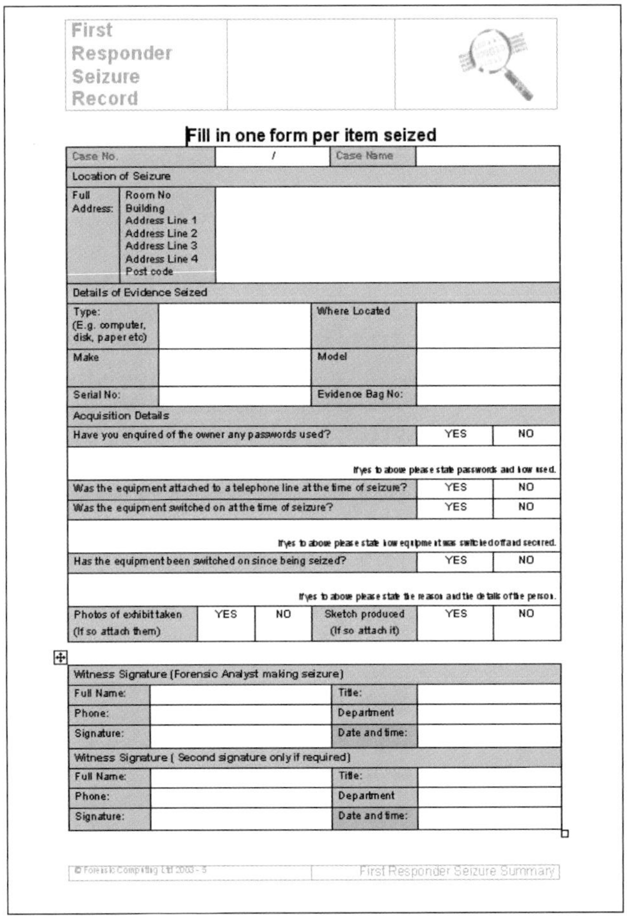

First Responder Seizure Record

Fill in one form per item seized

Case No.	/	Case Name	
Location of Seizure			
Full Address:	Room No Building Address Line 1 Address Line 2 Address Line 3 Address Line 4 Post code		
Details of Evidence Seized			
Type: (E.g. computer, disk, paper etc)		Where Located	
Make		Model	
Serial No:		Evidence Bag No:	
Acquisition Details			
Have you enquired of the owner any passwords used?		YES	NO
If yes to above please state passwords and how used.			
Was the equipment attached to a telephone line at the time of seizure?		YES	NO
Was the equipment switched on at the time of seizure?		YES	NO
If yes to above please state how equipment was switched off and secured.			
Has the equipment been switched on since being seized?		YES	NO
If yes to above please state the reason and the details of the person.			

Photos of exhibit taken (If so attach them)	YES	NO	Sketch produced (If so attach it)	YES	NO

Witness Signature (Forensic Analyst making seizure)			
Full Name:		Title:	
Phone:		Department	
Signature:		Date and time:	
Witness Signature (Second signature only if required)			
Full Name:		Title:	
Phone:		Department	
Signature:		Date and time:	

© Forensic Computing Ltd 2003 - 5 | First Responder Seizure Summary

FIGURE 9.32 One of many forms in the Computer Forensics Toolkit designed to record actions and observations made on a digital client.

Chapter Summary

Privacy, Crime, and Security

Web sites collect and store highly sensitive personal information, such as Social Security numbers, without informing their visitors. Public agencies and online merchants use computerized databases to track information about individuals. Other personal information, such as browsing habits, is often captured in cookies and by global unique identifiers (GUIDs) in hardware components and programs.

Computer crime and cybercrime include identity theft; malware, including spyware and viruses; other rogue programs such as time bombs, worms, zombies, and Trojan horses; fraud and theft; password theft; salami shaving and data diddling; forgery; and blackmail. These actions are performed by computer criminals that include hackers, crackers, cybergangs, virus authors, swindlers, shills, cyberstalkers, and sexual predators.

A computer security risk is any event, action, or situation—intentional or not—that could lead to the loss or destruction of computer systems or the data they contain. No computer system is totally secure, but you can do several things to cut down on security risks. Safe surfing guides should always be followed in addition to utilizing some software and hardware deterrents including an uninterruptible power supply (UPS), strong passwords, know-and-have authentication, biometric authentication, encryption of sensitive data, and an installed firewall.

The U.S. government continues to look for ways to balance the government's need to know with the public's right to privacy. The inclusion of backdoors in encryption standards creates unacceptable vulnerabilities, and legal issues surround attempts to force people to divulge their passwords.

Key Terms and Concepts

Matching

Match each key term in the left column with the most accurate definition in the right column.

_____ 1. cookie

_____ 2. phishing

_____ 3. spim

_____ 4. Trojan horse

_____ 5. worm

_____ 6. spyware

_____ 7. podslurping

_____ 8. memory shaving

_____ 9. digital signature

_____ 10. adware

_____ 11. botnet

_____ 12. trap door

_____ 13. wardriving

_____ 14. backdoor

_____ 15. salami shaving

a. A spam text message.

b. A nonmalicious program that generates pop-up ads and targeted banner ads.

c. A type of physical theft involving RAM chips.

d. A deliberately created security hole exploited at a later time.

e. Illegitimate e-mail or Web sites that look and act authentic in order to obtain personal information from a user.

f. A collection of zombies used to launch DoS attacks and distribute spam or malware.

g. A virus that spreads over networks.

h. A method of bypassing normal authentication to securing access to a computer.

i. A program disguised as useful but containing instructions to perform malicious tasks.

j. The process of searching for an unsecured wireless network.

k. The act of copying sensitive data to a small, removable storage device.

l. Embezzling technique in which small amounts of money are diverted into another account by altering a program.

m. A text file deposited by a Web site on a Web user's computer system, without consent, that is used to gather data on browsing and shopping habits.

n. Used to determine the authenticity of a message or document.

o. Software that collects personal information, monitors surfing habits, and distributes this information to a third party.

Multiple Choice

Circle the correct choice for each of the following.

1. What is the act of harassing or threatening an individual less capable of defending himself or herself repeatedly through the use of electronic communications?
   a. Phishing
   b. Cracking
   c. Cyberbullying
   d. Hacking

2. What is the substitute for the barcodes that are often used for inventory tracking, which can also pose privacy risks if it is not deactivated?
   a. RFID
   b. SET
   c. WEP
   d. WPA

3. What is the name for text that has been encrypted and converted to a coded message format?
   a. DoS
   b. Ciphertext
   c. GUID
   d. Spim

4. What is the term for flooding a service with meaningless data in an attempt to make a service unavailable to other users?
   a. Salami shaving
   b. Spam
   c. Spim
   d. A denial of service (DoS) attack

5. In an auction, which of the following refers to an accomplice of the seller who drives up prices by bidding for an item he has no intention of buying?
   a. Shill
   b. Phish
   c. Spim
   d. Variant

6. Which of the following is an example of malware?
   a. Zombie
   b. Evil twin
   c. Macro virus
   d. Active badge

7. What is malware that sits harmlessly on your system until a certain event or set of circumstances makes the program active?
   a. A macro virus
   b. A worm
   c. A Trojan horse
   d. A time bomb

8. What is the name for an identification number that is generated by a hardware component or a program that can be read by Web servers or embedded in various documents, making anonymity difficult?
   a. Global Unique Identifier (GUID)
   b. File infector
   c. Key interception
   d. Zombie

9. What method of user validation uses a variety of techniques such as voice recognition, retina scans, and fingerprints?
   a. Digital signature
   b. Digital certificate
   c. Biometric authentication
   d. Global unique identifier

10. Which of the following is one of the earliest wireless security standards that may be the only option for older devices, despite known weaknesses?
    a. 802.11n
    b. WPA
    c. GUID
    d. WEP

Fill-In

In the blanks provided, write the correct answer for each of the following.

1. _____ _____ _____ uses a single key to encrypt and decrypt.

2. Applications such as NetStumbler or Kismet are often used in _____ to locate wireless networks.

3. A(n) _____ _____ is a transparent graphic image, usually no larger than 1 pixel × 1 pixel, that is placed on a Web site or in an e-mail and is used to monitor the behavior of the user visiting the Web site or sending the e-mail.

4. A(n) _____ is an individual who studies the process of transforming information into an encoded state.

5. _____ refers to a coding or scrambling process that renders a message unreadable by anyone except the intended recipient.

6. _____ is the ability to convey a message without disclosing your name or identity.

7. _____ _____ makes use of fake e-mails and social engineering to trick specific people, such as senior executives or members of a particular organization, into providing personal information, to enable identity theft.

8. _____ _____ is a computing scenario that foresees individuals interacting with multiple devices in every aspect of our lives connected through an omnipresent network.

9. A(n) _____ is a type of software program that records all the keystrokes a user enters—such as passwords, account numbers, or conversations—and relays them to others.

10. A(n) _____ _____ _____ is a form of malware that installs itself on the beginning tracks of a hard drive, where stored code is automatically executed every time you start the computer. Thus the infection is spread by simply starting your system.

11. _____ _____ _____ makes use of an encryption and decryption key.

12. Commandeered computers known as _____ are often used by botnets to distribute spam and malware.

13. A(n) _____ is a group of computer users that are obsessed with gaining entry into highly secure computer systems.

14. A(n) _____ is a program that permits an organization's computers to use the Internet but places severe limits on the ability of outsiders to access internal data.

15. _____ _____ _____ is an online shopping and security standard for merchants and customers.

Short Answer

1. Define and explain the difference between the two different types of phishing.

2. List the five actions an organization can take to deter corporate espionage.

3. List the three types of viruses and explain how they differ.

4. What are some of the signs that might indicate that spyware is on a system?

5. List three actions users can take to prevent inadvertently having spyware or malware attached to their systems.

Teamwork

1. **Computer and Internet Security** Investigate the computer and Internet security procedures at your school or place of employment. One key area of interest might be physical security. Check whether the computers are physically locked against theft. If so, what is the mechanism and how secure is it? Another important consideration is antivirus and antispyware protection. Check with the IT department and find out the names of the antispyware and antivirus software that is installed on the systems and how often they are updated. Contact campus or corporate security and find out if any theft of products or accounts has occurred recently. If any theft has occurred, what actions have been taken to beef up security and prevent further incidents? Do not limit your research to these questions, but include ones of your own. Consolidate your findings and present the results of your investigations in a one-page, double-spaced summary paper.

2. **Password Requirements** As a team create a survey that will attempt to collect information on the use, frequency, minimum length, and security aspects of passwords. Include such questions as these: What actions online or at home are accessed by the use of a password? Approximately how many different passwords do you have for your various accounts? Do any accounts require you to change a password frequently; if so, how often? Are your passwords strong passwords? Do you have any of your portable devices password protected? Does your computer at home, which is used by others, have individual user accounts with passwords? Have any of your accounts ever been violated? Distribute the survey to 25 individuals. Consolidate the data and use a table, spreadsheet, or series of graphs to present the accumulation of your data.

3. **Browser Security Indicators** Have each member of your group identify which browser and version of that browser he or she uses most often. Explain how your browser indicates that you have connected to a secure site. This is especially important when making an online purchase with a credit card. Have you ever made purchases online? Were they always at secure sites? Collaborate on a paper that summarizes your findings and discusses the necessity of using secure sites for online purchases.

4. **Using Internet History, Search Engines, and Cell Phone Records for Evidence** Several high-profile criminal cases have recently convicted individuals of horrific acts without anyone seeing them commit the crime. Prosecutors have used technology and technology records to re-create scenes and actions that led to the final act. As a team, use local sources or the Internet and locate at least three cases in which technology has been

used to prove guilt when there were no witnesses or the witness was unable to defend himself or herself due to injury or loss of life. In a collaborative effort, accumulate the data on these cases, and in a one-page, double-spaced paper defend a pro or con stance on the use of electronic evidence in criminal cases.

5. **Big Brother Is Watching** A recent newspaper article reported that a customer was fined by a car rental company for speeding. Although he was not cited for a speeding violation by any police agencies, his credit card was charged a penalty. His rental car was equipped with a GPS system that reports the location of the vehicle. This feature allowed the company to determine the speed at which the driver was traveling. This type of system is also used by some long-distance trucking companies to monitor the movements of their trucks. Divide your group into two, and have one subgroup take the company viewpoint and the other the consumer viewpoint. Debate the following: Should this type of monitoring be allowed? From a privacy standpoint, what are your feelings about these systems? What are the advantages of using these systems? Disadvantages? Write two papers: one that affirms the use of such systems and one that argues against their use.

On the Web

1. **BitTorrents** Using a search engine locate several Web sites that explain and provide uses for BitTorrent, a peer-to-peer file sharing protocol used for distributing large amounts of data. Using the information from those sites, provide a detailed definition of bittorrent along with its uses, both legal and illegal. In a table, state the URL of each site you visited, the type of information or data available for download, and the fee associated with joining the site. Then, with additional online research or using the content of this chapter substantiate your answer to the question: Is the use of BitTorrent technology legal when applied to copyright protected materials, like movies, video games, and music? Submit your reply to this question and the table of your Internet research results in a one-page, double-spaced paper.

2. **Virtual Crime** They say that crime doesn't pay, and that seems to hold true for virtual crimes too. A Chinese man has been sentenced to three years in jail for stealing virtual goods. In this latest virtual theft, an individual actually assaulted another man with the aid of three others and demanded the victim hand over virtual goods and currency. The victim transferred an estimated $14,700 to the assailant. The main attacker got three years in jail, while his helpers all received a fine of around $735.

Online currency is a growing trend with Xbox Live and Wii, which use points to replace money for buying virtual goods. Facebook is building a virtual currency service. Virtual crimes could explode over the coming years.

Use the Internet and locate any other article on virtual theft. Check ebay or any other online or sales forum for virtual merchandise associated with several MMORPGs (Massive Multiplayer Online Role Playing Games). Create a table with the name of the MMORPG, the virtual product, the forum on which it was located, and the asking or bid price. Using a search engine, attempt to locate statistics on the marketing and sale of virtual MMORPG products. Include the table and cite the sources of your statistics in a one-page, double-spaced report.

3. **Keyloggers: Protectors or Spies?** Using the Internet and a search engine, find several sites that sell keyloggers. From your research, compile a definition of keylogging. Examine the pros and cons of such software. Read testimonials on the benefits of using a keylogger to make sure that data is secure and no unauthorized files have been tampered with or Web sites visited. Then read the violations to confidentiality and individual privacy tenets that keylogging software seems to overlook. In a one-page, double-spaced paper, take a stand on this controversy and support your viewpoint using your collected research.

4. **Web Beacons** Web beacons, defined in this chapter, are also sometimes referred to as Web bugs. Like adware detectors and pop-up blockers, browsers like the Internet Explorer and Firefox are beginning to include Web bug detectors. Using the Internet and your favorite search engine, determine whether both of these browsers include a Web bug detector in their current versions or as add-ons. If one exists, state the name of the program, describe exactly what this add-on will do, and provide the URL for the download site. If detectors are not included in these browsers, locate at least two Web bug detectors from other sources. For each program, locate the URL of the product; its cost, if any;

the features provided; and any testimonial statements as to its effectiveness. Present your accumulated research in a one-page, double-spaced paper.

5. **Social Networks and Security** Visit **www.itsecurity.com/features/malware-new-frontier-021408/**, to view a recent article on security violations of a social network. Use the Internet to locate at least one other article on the insecure nature of social network sites and two on the benefits and security of social networks. After reading the four articles, take a stand on the security of social network sites, substantiate it with references from the researched articles, and present your stand in a one-page, double-spaced paper.

Spotlight

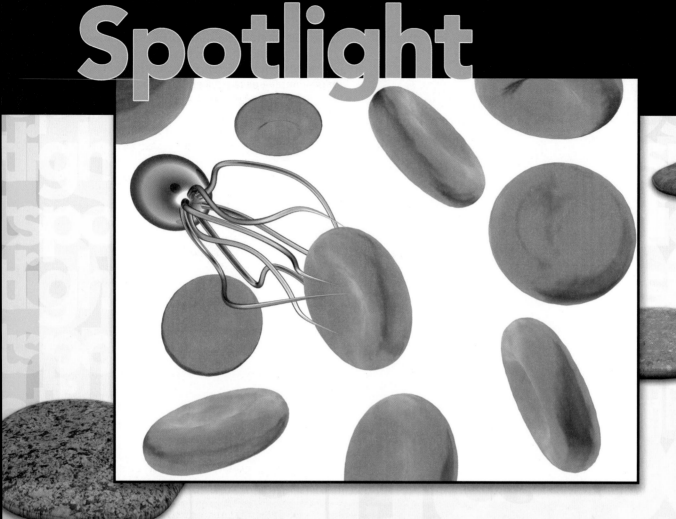

Emerging Technologies

It's easy to predict the future; the hard part is getting it right, particularly where technology is concerned. Past attempts offer examples of just how difficult it can be to predict technology. For example, in 1876, a Western Union official said, "The telephone has too many shortcomings to be seriously considered as a means of communication. The device is inherently of no value." A century later, the chairman of IBM stated that there was no reason why anyone would want a computer in his or her home.

No one can accurately predict the future of technology. If you plan on living by a crystal ball, you must be prepared to eat crushed glass; the future is unpredictable. However, you can keep abreast of news and learn to recognize emerging technology trends. This Spotlight looks at the trends driving contemporary computing and the potential impact of artificial intelligence as computer designers work toward creating a truly intelligent machine.

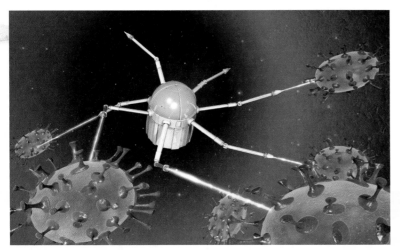

FIGURE 7A Some day medical nanobots in the bloodstream will fight diseases like the H1N1 virus with laser beams.

Tomorrow's Hardware: Smaller, Faster, Cheaper, and Connected

In the early days of computing, room-size noisy machines read punched cards to perform their calculations. Today, many computers are smaller than the palm of your hand and can accomplish a wide array of tasks. But what will computers be like in the future?

NANOTECHNOLOGY AND BIOCHIPS

What would you say if someone told you that someday various products will be able to manufacture themselves or that computers will work billions of times faster than they do now? And that it will be possible to use computers to end famine and disease or to bring extinct animals and plants back to life? Or that computers will be used to make distant, uninhabitable planets more Earth-like? All of these things and more may one day be possible with nanotechnology (Figure 7A).

Merriam-Webster's Collegiate Dictionary, 11th edition, defines **nanotechnology** as "the art of manipulating materials on an atomic or molecular scale, especially to build microscopic devices." Nanotechnology is based on a unit of measure called a nanometer, which is a billionth of a meter. Today, nanotechnologists manipulate atoms and molecules to perform certain limited tasks, but someday nanotechnology will be used to perform an array of tasks. And because of the small size of atoms and molecules, we'll be able to use them to do things we never before thought possible.

The tie between medical and corporate research in nanotechnology is already strong (Figure 7B). In fact, the first breakthroughs in nanotechnology will probably be in nanomedicine and the use of medical nanorobots. For instance, medical nanorobots may one day be able to destroy fatty deposits in the bloodstream or organize cells to restore artery walls, thereby preventing heart attacks. Nanorobots may also one day improve our immune system by disabling or ridding viruses from our bodies. Someday, doctors may use nanorobots to deliver cancer-treatment drugs to specific areas of the body.

Meanwhile, NASA has funded research to create nanoparticles and nanocapsules. Although this research will be invaluable to medical researchers, NASA hopes to use nanotechnology applications for space travel and for long-term space habitation. One of NASA's concerns is the effect of radiation on astronauts. NASA thinks that nanomedicine could perhaps be used to provide radiation protection to astronauts, to enable the self-diagnosis of disease while in space, and to deliver medication during long space missions, among other things. Nanotechnology may also be able to alter the properties of known materials, making them lighter and stronger for lengthy space flights.

FIGURE 7B The National Nanotechnology Initiative (NNI) is a U.S. government program that coordinates research and development in nanotechnology.

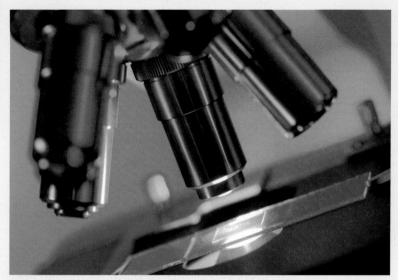

FIGURE 7C   Researchers at Argonne National Laboratory are using biochip technology to study and identify infectious diseases.

Moore's Law, formulated more than 40 years ago by Intel Corporation chairman Gordon Moore (Figure 7D), states that microprocessors and other miniature circuits double in circuit density (and therefore in processing power) every 18 to 24 months. If Moore's Law remains true until the middle of this century, computers will be 10 billion times more powerful than today's fastest machines. Storage technology shows a similar trend: steep increases in capacity and steep declines in cost.

Moore's Law predicts that by 2020 all of the components of unbelievably powerful computers will be accommodated on just one tiny mass-produced silicon chip. These chips will hold superfast processors (capable of performing a trillion instructions per second), huge amounts of RAM, video circuitry—the works. And they could cost less than $500!

However, today some people question whether Moore's Law is still relevant. In the past, the personal computer industry was driven by the consumer who desired the latest and greatest hardware on the market. Today some people wonder about the Moore's Law philosophy because many individuals simply use their computer to browse the Internet or send e-mail. There is a new phenomenon called **cloud computing** with which users access their applications and information over the Internet. As a result, users don't need a powerful machine. Consumers are also embracing cloud computing devices like netbooks and smartphones that don't have and don't need the processing power of the latest desktop and notebook computers. These devices allow users to access the applications and data they need without using a powerful computer.

Could it be that Moore's Law may need a small revision or new direction based upon new technologies coming to market?

Metcalfe's Law, formulated by Ethernet inventor Bob Metcalfe, states that the value of a computer network grows in proportion to the square of the number of people connected to it. A telephone line that connects two people is of limited value, but a telephone system that connects an entire city becomes an indispensable resource. Using Metcalfe's Law, a network connecting two people has a value of 4, and a network connecting

Perhaps the most interesting practical use of nanotechnology is the development of the **biochip** (Figure 7C). Think of a biochip as being similar to a microprocessor, or a computer chip, with one main difference. A computer chip processes millions of computer instructions per second, whereas a biochip processes biological instructions, such as determining the number of genes in a strand of DNA.

Because the silicon-based microprocessors we know today are limited as to how fast and small they can become, researchers are looking at biochips to produce faster computing speeds. Chip makers are hoping that they will be able to integrate DNA into a computer chip to create a so-called DNA computer that will be capable of storing billions of times more data than your personal computer. Scientists are using genetic material to create nanocomputers that may someday take the place of silicon-based computers.

Nanotechnology sounds complex, and it is, but its possibilities and implications are truly endless. In fact, some say that nanotechnology is the most important technological breakthrough since steam power. With corporate and medical research and development on parallel "nanopaths," there may be high demand for nanotechnicians in your lifetime.

FIGURE 7D   Gordon Moore created Moore's Law in 1965.

Besides shrinking components through the use of nanotechnology and biochips, tomorrow's computers are affected by two laws of technology and economics: Moore's Law and Metcalfe's Law.

FIGURE 7E As computers become smaller, faster, cheaper, and more interconnected, new technology will encourage the trend toward the digitization of all of the world's information and knowledge.

storehouse of accumulated human experience (Figure 7E).

COMPUTERS EVERYWHERE

In light of these trends toward lower cost and miniaturization, some computer scientists are beginning to speak of ubiquitous computing (*ubiquitous* means "everywhere"). With **ubiquitous computing**, computers are everywhere, even in the background, providing computer-based intelligence all around us. The realms of business, industry, science, and entertainment are employing ubiquitous computing in a number of ways.

Smart Cars, Smart Drivers, and Smart Highways IntelliDrive was launched in January 2009 by the U.S. Department of Transportation (USDOT), enabling a surface transportation system in which vehicles do not crash and travelers have the information they need about travel conditions. This system promises to alleviate the social and economic impacts of the U.S. crash fatality and injury rates, which in 2007 amounted to 41,000 fatalities and 2.49 million injuries. Experts estimate that up to 15 percent of crashes in the United States might be avoided if drivers were made aware of unexpected conditions (see Figure 7F). IntelliDrive safety alerts

four people has a value of 16. According to some predictions, the Internet will ultimately connect 1 billion users worldwide.

Over the next several years, you'll see both Moore's and Metcalfe's Laws at work. If you put these two laws together, you get a potent mixture: The computer industry is now giving us *networked* machines that double in power every 18 to 24 months.

As computers become smaller, faster, cheaper, and more interconnected, new technology will encourage the trend toward the digitization of all of the world's information and knowledge—the entire

FIGURE 7F The IntelliDrive system would rely on an active safety system that involves sensing and messaging not only among vehicles, but between vehicles and outside elements.

allowing drivers enough time to brake include warning if a driver is at risk of running a red light, warning a driver to slow down for a curve, and warning if a driver is approaching a slow or stopped object.

Japan has a similar system, SmartWay, which provides drivers with timely alerts about hazards. Since implementation, the system has been up to 80 percent effective in reducing traffic crashes at certain traffic safety hot spots in Japan.

These vehicle on-board technologies are all based upon Dedicated Short-Range Communications (DSRC). This technology allows for extremely fast transmission and meets security requirements. Although this infrastructure integration continues, there is a parallel effort to deliver mobility benefits using market-ready wireless consumer electronics. The U.S. DOT launched SafeTrip-21, an emerging mobile communication and navigation technology that was tested in 2009 in the San Francisco Bay area. This networked traveler system delivers information directly to consumers in practical and personalized formats using cell phones, desktop computers, notebooks, handheld computers, and in-vehicle Internet devices. Using the system, drivers will be able to choose their route to avoid traffic and decrease travel times with updated road conditions. Public transportation information is also integrated into this GPS-based transit system.

Other innovative uses of this technology can be found at Tyson's Corner shopping mall in Northern Virginia and at Interstate welcome centers in Virginia, where large-screen displays of travel time help travelers plan their trips. The future of travel promises to change as the IntelliDrive system establishes an information backbone for transportation that will enhance safety and mobility, enabling a crashless, information-rich surface transportation system.

Digital Forensics Because computers are everywhere, they are often used to commit crimes. A new science called **digital forensics** has emerged that uses computers to uncover evidence that can be used to fight cybercrime and computer crime. After a network or other type of attack, investigators use digital tools to determine what occurred, what resources were affected, and who was responsible (Figure 7G).

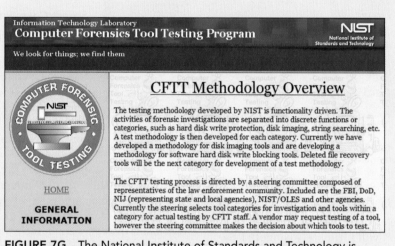

FIGURE 7G The National Institute of Standards and Technology is attempting to bring proven methods and standards to digital forensics with its Computer Forensics Tool Testing program.

In fact, digital forensics is such a hot area that a number of colleges and universities offer courses, programs, and degrees in the field. Students who are working toward a degree in digital forensics study computer and networking technology, criminal justice, and other related fields.

Biological Feedback Devices **Biological feedback devices** translate eye movements, body movements, and even brain waves into computer input. Using **eye-gaze response systems** (also called **vision technology**), quadriplegics can control a computer by focusing their eyes on different parts of the screen. A special camera tracks the person's eye movements and moves the cursor in response.

Microsoft researchers are working on vision technology computer programs that enable computers to "see" and respond to a user's physical presence, gestures, and even certain facial expressions. Of course, Microsoft is not the only company working on this technology. Research labs around the world are trying to develop new ways for people to interact with computers that do not rely on standard input devices, such as keyboards.

In fact, vision technology is part of a larger category of research (called *perceptual user interfaces* at Microsoft) that focuses not just on vision technology, but also on speech recognition, gesture recognition, and machines that "learn."

Gesture-recognition research focuses on enabling computers to understand hand movements. As you might imagine, gesture recognition would have an obvious benefit if it could be used with American Sign Language. It will also one day play a large role in making entertainment applications, including games, more animated and exciting. Many hope that perceptual user interfaces will one day help physically challenged computer users control their computers with facial expressions and eye gazes. Already on the market, VisualMouse translates a user's head motions into mouse movements, allowing users to control a mouse without using their hands.

Virtual Reality **Virtual reality (VR)** refers to immersive, 3D environments that are generated by a computer. With virtual reality, you can actually go in and explore a virtual environment (see Figure 7H).

FIGURE 7H This virtual reality environment allows the user to experience the thrill of evading traffic at high speeds.

Helmets and sensor-equipped gloves enable users to experience virtual reality programs. The helmet or **head-mounted display (HMD)**, which is a helmet-like contraption or a pair of goggles, contains two miniature television screens that display the world in what appears to be three dimensions (Figure 7I). In addition to the dual monitors that display three-dimensional images, a head tracker adjusts images when you move your head to the left or right. If you turn your head, your view of the world moves accordingly. Users can use **data gloves** to touch and manipulate simulated objects. You can also use navigation controls to walk around—or fly, if you prefer—in the simulated world. You can physically explore what appears to be a complex virtual environment, even though you're really walking around a big, empty room.

The most advanced (and expensive) immersive technology to date is the **Cave Automated Virtual Environment (CAVE)**, which projects stereoscopic images onto walls to give the illusion of a virtual environment. To create the illusion of objects in the virtual environment, users wear special shutter glasses that alternately block the left and right eyes in synchrony with the projection sequence, which similarly alternates between the left and right stereo vision seen from the person's location. The resulting effect is so realistic that users can't tell the difference between real

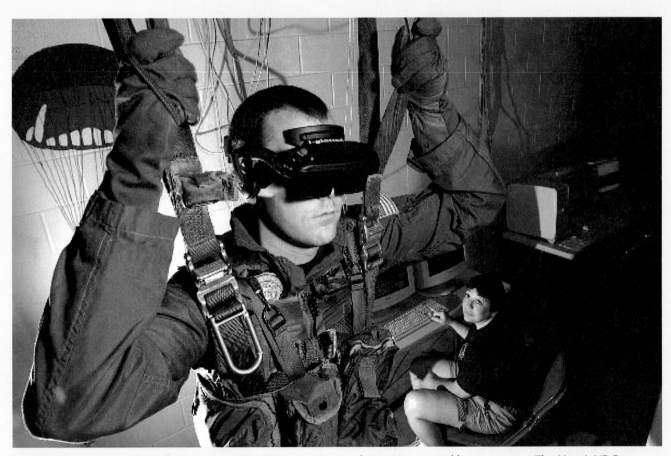

FIGURE 7I Virtual reality refers to immersive, 3D environments that are generated by computers. The Navy's VR Parachute Trainer teaches aircraft personnel how to handle a parachute in different weather conditions and during equipment malfunctions.

and simulated objects in the room unless they touch them.

On the Web, **Virtual Reality Modeling Language** (**VRML**, pronounced "vir-mal") can be used to create virtual environments online. Programmers can use VRML to define the characteristics of Web-accessible, 3D worlds. To visit a VRML site on the Web, you'll need to equip your Web browser with a VRML plug-in (see **http://cic.nist.gov/vrml/vbdetect.html**), such as the Microsoft VRML Viewer for Internet Explorer or the Cosmo Player, a VRML plug-in for Firefox, Opera, Safari, and Chrome. After installing the plug-in and accessing a VRML "world" (a Web site with a .wrl extension), you can walk or fly through the 3D construct.

What's the point of virtual reality? For many consumers, the answer is simple: games. Almost all of the top-selling computer games offer 3D virtual realities. But virtual reality isn't all fun and games. The military uses virtual reality systems to train fighter pilots and combat soldiers. Architects use virtual reality simulations to enable clients to preview and walk through a design. Surgeons can use virtual reality to learn and practice delicate and dangerous surgical techniques (Figure 7J). Manufacturers use virtual reality to analyze the manufacturing costs and design of complex, 3D structures.

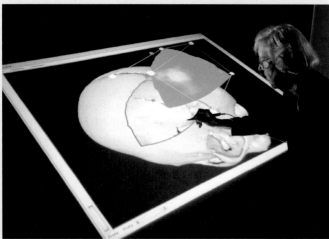

FIGURE 7J In medicine, surgeons can use virtual reality to learn and practice new techniques.

Wearable virtual reality devices could even affect the lives of maintenance workers. A computer on a belt could easily be connected with a display monitor concealed in an ordinary pair of eyeglasses. As the worker looks at the inside of a piece of equipment, the computer could supply a schematic. The schematic, shown on the inside of the eyeglass lens, could then be positioned over the piece of equipment. This would enable the worker to quickly pinpoint the name, purpose, and condition of each of the item's components.

This blending of virtual reality with the real world, known as **augmented reality**, is not science fiction. It's already being used by some large corporations. Taken to the next level, the schematics shown in the worker's field of vision could be interfaced with motion and position sensors so that when the worker moves his or her head, the schematics projected by the computer change to reflect the worker's field of view.

New uses for augmented reality are being discovered all the time. For instance, agents for U.S. Customs and Border Protection have special wearable computers that use voice-recognition software and full-color monitors. When looking for stolen vehicles, the agents can use the computers to recall the license number of any vehicle in the United States as they stroll through parking lots or drive through traffic.

Chemical Detectors The human nose can detect remarkably minute traces of airborne chemicals. And increasingly, so can computers. If you've visited an airport recently, you may already have been "sniffed" by a computer device designed to detect minute traces of explosives. Some travelers are asked to step into special booths that use air jets to dislodge chemicals from clothes and hands. The air is then sucked through a chemical sensor that can identify many types of explosives. A computer screen displays the results of the test and tells the operator whether explosives are detected.

Tactile Displays You've seen how computers engage our eyes and ears. What about our sense of touch? If researchers in a new field called **haptics** have their way, you'll soon be able to feel with computers as well. (The term *haptics* refers to the sense of touch.) Haptics researchers are developing a variety of technologies, including **tactile displays** that stimulate the skin to generate a sensation of contact. Stimulation techniques include vibration, pressure, and temperature changes. When used in virtual reality environments, these technologies enhance the sense of "being there" and physically interacting with displayed virtual objects. Scientists are quickly investigating the use of tactile simulations via the computer. In the game world, it might be simulating the impact of a golf club hitting the ball; in the medical training field, it could be feeling the springiness of a kidney under forceps; or in the Internet consumer experience, it would be feeling the texture of clothing for sale before ordering.

It's unclear when perceptual interfaces will hit computer store shelves. But one thing is clear: Someday it will be possible for people to interact with electronic devices using every one of their senses.

What if we put all of these capabilities together to develop a machine endowed with human intelligence, giving it the ability to reason, to converse in natural language (ordinary human speech), and to formulate a plan or strategy? One branch of technology is moving in that direction—artificial intelligence.

Artificial Intelligence: Toward the Smart Machine?

The goal of **artificial intelligence (AI)** is to endow computers with humanlike intelligence. AI specialists have succeeded in creating special-purpose programs that exhibit some aspects of human intelligence, but these programs are still unable to function intelligently outside the context for which they were designed. Computer scientists are sharply divided between optimists who believe that these problems will be overcome and pessimists who believe that the underlying problems are so difficult that they're impossible to solve. So let's start with an easy question: Just what *is* intelligence?

Intelligence has many components:

- Learning and retaining knowledge
- Reasoning on the basis of this knowledge
- Adapting to new circumstances
- Planning (developing strategies)
- Communicating
- Recognizing patterns

However, there's no scientific consensus as to what constitutes intelligence. So how do we answer the question of whether a computer is more intelligent than the human brain?

THE COMPUTER VERSUS THE HUMAN BRAIN

How does the human brain compare with a computer? Some speculative estimates are shown in Figure 7K. Compared with computers, the human brain accepts voluminous amounts of input and stores an unbelievable amount of data. In terms of processing, the human brain excels at pattern recognition (for example, recognizing faces and understanding speech), but it's a slow calculator. In contrast, computers accept much smaller amounts of input and do a poor job of recognizing patterns, but they can calculate rapidly and produce output much faster than humans can.

So how can we tell whether a computer is intelligent? British computer scientist Alan Turing created the Turing Test to measure artificial intelligence (Figure 7L). During a Turing Test, a person sits at a computer and types questions. The computer is connected to two hidden computers. At one of the hidden computers, a person reads the questions and types responses. The other hidden computer runs a program that also gives answers. If the person typing the questions can't tell the difference between the person's answers and the computer's answers, Turing says that the computer is intelligent.

By Turing's standard, computers have already passed the test of artificial intelligence. In the mid-1960s, Joseph Weizenbaum, a computer scientist at the Massachusetts Institute of Technology (MIT), wrote a simple program called ELIZA. This program mimics a human therapist. If you type "I'm worried about my girlfriend," the program responds with "Tell me more

FIGURE 7L British computer scientist Alan Turing. According to most psychologists, the Turing test's type-and-response method is too simplistic.

FIGURE 7K The Human Brain as a CPU (Speculative Estimates)	
Operation	**Estimated Speed or Capacity**
Input	Fast (1 gigabit per second); the human retina can achieve a resolution of approximately 127 million "pixels"
Processing	Fast for pattern recognition (10 billion instructions per second); slow for calculations (2 to 100 per second)
Output	Slow (speech: 100 bits per second)
Storage	Very large (10 terabytes), but retrieval can be uncertain

about your girlfriend." The program is actually very simple. If the user types a word that matches one on the program's list, such as *girlfriend, father, guilt,* or *problem,* the program copies this word and puts it into the response. Even so, some people were fooled into thinking that they were conversing with a real therapist.

ELIZA doesn't fool many people for long, but today's programs are much larger and more resourceful. Many of these programs have been displayed at the Loebner Prize Competition, an annual event designed to implement the Turing Test and award a prize to the most "human" computer. In 2000, 2002, and 2004 Richard Wallace won the prize for his work on ALICE. Short for Artificial Linguistic Internet Computer Entity, ALICE uses AI case-based reasoning to formulate replies to comments. However, the program is unable to pass the Turing Test.

Neural Networks Neuroscientists know that the brain contains billions of interconnected brain cells called neurons (Figure 7M). One type of AI involves creating computers that mimic the structure of the human brain. Called **neural networks** (or neural nets), these computers are composed of hundreds of thousands of tiny processors that are interconnected, just like the neurons in the human brain.

Neural nets aren't programmed; they're trained. A neural net learns by trial and error, just as humans do. An incorrect guess weakens a particular pattern of connections; a correct guess reinforces a pattern. After the training is finished, the neural net knows how to do something, such as operate a robot.

Neural nets behave much the way that brains do. In fact, neural nets exhibit electromagnetic waves that are surprisingly similar to human brain waves. None of today's neural nets approach the complexity of even a farm animal's brain, but more complex neural nets are being developed.

Ordinary computers are good at solving problems that require linear thinking, logical rules, and step-by-step instructions. Neural nets are good at recognizing patterns, dealing with complexity, and learning from experience. As a result of these abilities, neural nets are emerging from laboratories and finding their way into commercial applications. Right now, banks are using neural nets to compare a customer's signature made at the bank counter with a stored signature. Neural nets can also be used to monitor aircraft engines and to predict stock market trends.

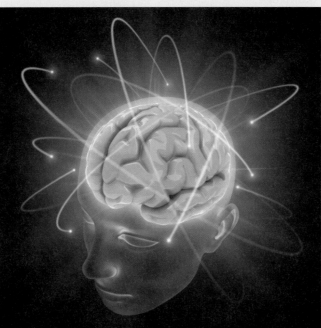

FIGURE 7M The brain contains billions of neurons. Just as the brain connects these neurons, a neural net connects thousands of computer processing units in multiple ways.

PATTERN RECOGNITION

Imagine a computer that can see beyond the digitized image that it's recording. Computers equipped with digital cameras and **pattern-recognition software** can process digital images and draw connections between the patterns they perceive and patterns stored in a database. Pattern-recognizing computers are already used for security. For example, a new type of video surveillance camera can detect shoppers with suspicious patterns of movement and alert security personnel. The U.S. Department of State operates one of the largest face recognition systems in the world, with over 75 million photographs, which it uses for processing travel visas. Pattern-recognition software is also playing an important role in data mining, discovering previously unnoticed trends in massive amounts of transaction data.

INTELLIGENT AGENTS

You may not realize it, but you already have a helper inside your computer, one that can converse with you, understand your needs, and offer assistance. These helpers, called **intelligent agents**, can monitor conversations in newsgroups and recommend items of interest, locate human experts who can solve specific problems, help you negotiate the best price for a purchase, or scout ahead for Web pages based on your interests.

If you used Microsoft Office before the release of Office 2007, you may have been familiar with an intelligent agent: the Office Assistant. The Office Assistant was linked to Office's Help feature, so the Office Assistant could suggest formatting options and shortcuts or help find topics in the Help library. The online Help feature in Office 2007 has been completely redesigned and does not include the Office Assistant. You

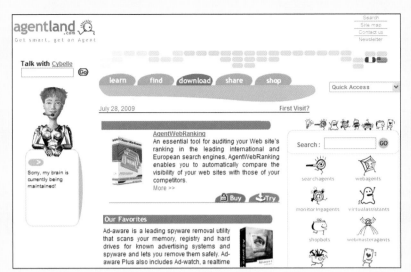

FIGURE 7N Agentland (**www.agentland.com**) has a variety of agents and shopbots that you can download.

can download agents to help your Web ventures. One source of such agents is Agentland (**www.agentland.com**; Figure 7N).

TRANSLATION TECHNOLOGY

In the 1960s, experts confidently predicted that **machine translation**—the use of computers to translate foreign language text automatically—could be achieved quite easily. However, many problems emerged, including how to resolve ambiguity. For example, compare the word *pen* in the following two sentences: "My pen is in my pocket" and "Charlie is doing 25 to life in the pen." After many years of work, automatic translation software is coming closer to the dream of machine translation. The software is fast—one program can translate 300,000 words per hour—but the results can be riddled with errors. Still, the results are good enough to provide a working draft to human translators; some systems make only three to five errors for every 100 words translated.

Today, computer-aided translation (CAT) software can be used to translate text from one language to another. CAT technology is being used in international business to stand in when a human translator is not available. Even professional translators can use CAT tools to improve their skills.

Three major categories of CAT tools are currently available: terminology managers to handle basic word translations, automatic or machine translation (MT) tools to provide computer-aided translations, and machine-

FIGURE 7O Lingo Translator Model TTV5 translates an amazing 20 languages and speaks over 400,000 words

assisted human translation (MAHT) to aid professional translators. In addition to these programs, portable handheld translation devices, some as small as a credit card, help international travelers translate conversations from English to French, Spanish, German, Russian, Chinese, Japanese, and many more languages (Figure 7O). As more-sophisticated translation technology emerges, someday people may be able to use CAT tools to communicate with anyone using any language.

GENETIC ALGORITHMS

Intelligence is a product of evolution through natural selection. So why not try to create artificial intelligence by creating laboratory conditions in which the most intelligent programs survive? That's the object of research on **genetic algorithms**, defined as automated program development environments in which various approaches compete to solve a problem.

According to evolutionary theory, an organism's goal is to survive and reproduce. Occasional errors in the genetic code introduce mutations, which lead to changes. Sometimes these changes are advantageous and give the organism a better chance of surviving and reproducing. Organisms with an advantageous genetic code dominate because they have more opportunities to reproduce.

Genetic algorithm research mimics nature by imitating this competition for survival. For example, researchers place a number of algorithms into a computer environment and allow them to mutate in random ways. All of the algorithms compete to try to solve a problem. Over time, one algorithm emerges as the best at tackling the problem. Where's the AI connection here? AI requires the creation of algorithms that can mimic the behavior of intelligent beings, and genetic algorithm techniques offer a new way to discover these algorithms.

STRONG AI

Although these piecemeal advances in artificial intelligence are transforming the computers and software we use every day, the decades-old dream of creating a truly intelligent computer seems as far away as ever. What's been achieved so far is a semblance of intelligence within only highly restricted areas of knowledge, such as routing parts through a factory or making airline reservations. Is the dream of true machine intelligence still alive? Proponents of **strong AI**, an area of research based on the conviction that computers will achieve an intelligence equal to that of humans, believe that it is, and that the achievement of true artificial intelligence is only decades away.

What is needed to achieve true artificial intelligence? Everyone agrees that an intelligent computer would need a high proportion of the knowledge that people carry around in their heads every day, such as that Philadelphia is a city on the East Coast, and that East Coast cities can be almost unbearably hot in the summer. You use this type of knowledge constantly. If someone tells you, "My friend went to work in Philadelphia for the summer," you can respond, "She must not mind the heat!" But there's considerable disagreement about how this knowledge can be provided to a computer. Should humans provide such knowledge or should computers learn it on their own? One AI project, Cyc, illustrates the first approach to knowledge acquisition.

Cyc In Austin, Texas, computer scientist Douglas B. Lenat and the Cycorp company are programming a computer called Cyc (pronounced "sike," from *encyclopedia*) with basic facts about the world that everyone knows, such as "mountain climbing is dangerous" and "birds have feathers." The goal is to create a computer that knows as much as a 12-year-old. The challenge is that 12-year-olds know a great deal. Lenat's staff has spent more than 20 years feeding basic knowledge into Cyc—the computer now stores

nearly 200,000 terms and hundreds of thousands of rules, and they're still many years away from achieving their goal. Eventual goals for Cyc are to provide text and speech understanding, translation, expert systems, training simulations, games, and online advice. It will also be capable of integrating databases and spreadsheets, providing an encyclopedia, and answering questions as well as searching for documents and photos (Figure 7P).

Cyc's designers say that someday the computer will be able to learn on its own, reading material from the Internet and asking questions when it can't understand something. Already, companies are using Cyc in various capacities, and the U.S. military has invested millions of dollars in Cyc in hopes of using the computer as a military intelligence tool.

Cog, Kismet, and Nexi MIT professor Rodney A. Brooks takes a different approach to computer learning, one that is based on the natural world. For example, in the natural world, intelligence evolved as organisms needed information to survive and reproduce. The path to artificial intelligence, Brooks argues, lies in creating robots that have minimal preprogrammed knowledge. The robots will then gather information on their own using massive sensory input (sight, hearing, and touch) and have artificially programmed "desires." For Brooks, intelligence isn't reasoning but rather a set of behaviors acquired as organisms interact with their environment.

Brooks and his students constructed a series of robots that learned how to crawl across fields strewn with boulders. Their projects were Cog, a humanoid robot that has a torso, a head, and two arms, and Kismet, a "sociable humanoid robot" that elicited

FIGURE 7P The objective of the Cyc project is to program a computer with basic common-sense facts.

emotional responses and was able to learn from and interact with humans. A current project of MIT's Personal Robots Group is Nexi, a mobile-dexterous-social (MDS) robot. The purpose of this group is "to support research and education goals in human-robot interaction, teaming, and social learning." Visit the Personal Robots Group's Web site **http://robotic.media.mit.edu/projects/robots/mds/ overview/overview.html** for information and videos about Nexi.

ROBOTS

Late at night, Dottie cleans the floors in a Richmond, Virginia, office building. The work is dull and repetitive, but she doesn't mind. She's never late to work, doesn't call in sick, and doesn't even receive a salary. Dottie is a robot, created by CyberClean, a company that's going after a $50 billion industrial cleaning market. A **robot** is a computer-based device programmed to perform motions that can accomplish useful tasks. But can robots function safely? Using video sensors, Dottie observes simple rules to avoid doing any damage, such as stopping and waiting if somebody walks in front of her. When her work is finished, she returns to her charging station.

Dottie and robots like her are at the cutting edge of **robotics**, a division of the computer science field that is devoted to improving the performance and capabilities of robots. Robots are taking the place of humans in industry in many ways. In 2001, IBM conducted an experiment in which robots participated in simulated trading of commodities such as pork bellies and gold. By using specially designed algorithms, the robots performed the same tasks as human commodity brokers—and made 7 percent more money than their human counterparts!

More than 1 million industrial robots are in operation throughout the world. The United States is second only to Japan in robot use. Increasingly, robots are performing tasks such as assembly, welding, material handling, and material transport (Figure 7Q). Once found only in scientific labs, today robots paint cars for auto manufacturers, help surgeons conduct surgery, and make trips to outer space. Rock-steady surgical robots are saving lives where natural hand tremors in human surgeons could lead to fatal consequences. Robots are also exploring hazardous environments, such as the radioactive ruins of the Chernobyl Unit 4 nuclear power plant.

Need help at home or at work? Honda's ASIMO (Advanced Step in Innovative Mobility) humanoid robot may be able to assist you. Launched in 2000, ASIMO remains the world's most advanced bipedal humanoid robot. It can run 4 miles per hour, climb stairs, grasp objects, carry trays, and evade moving obstacles. With its AI capabilities for improved human interaction, it can comprehend simple voice commands, recognize a familiar face, and even direct an orchestra

FIGURE 7Q Increasingly, robots are performing tasks such as assembly, welding, material handling, and material transport.

(Figure 7R). ASIMO visited children who had experienced the Sichuan earthquake and entertained them with games such as rock, paper, scissors and balancing on one foot.

Another robot is the Japanese-made PaPeRo (short for **pa**rtner-type **pe**rsonal **ro**bot). PaPeRo's colorful, rounded canister shape may not look huggable at first, but when treated with kindness, it's irresistible. PaPeRo can welcome you home after a long day, and when you're away, it wanders around looking for human companionship. If it doesn't find any, it takes a nap. PaPeRo even has the ability to recognize voice patterns; if these patterns are unfriendly, it runs away.

So where's the all-in-one personal robot that will someday mow the lawn, clean the house, and shampoo the carpets? Most experts agree that such personal robots are a decade or so away. These robots are just too expensive for consumers right now, but that will change as technology advances and market demand grows.

Researchers are also working on a robot that changes its shape to accomplish a specific task. The

FIGURE 7R ASIMO has performed with the Detroit Symphony Orchestra.

shape-changing robot has pieces that are moved around by a computer-managed algorithm. Such shape-changing robots will one day walk, crawl, carry tools, and fit into tight spaces where humans cannot.

The Future of Emerging Technology

What will the computers of the future be like? We know that they'll be fast and will have tremendous storage capacity. We are at the very beginning of an age: the information age. The one distinguishing feature about this age is that we know we're in it. Just think of what might have happened if people had known that they were at the beginning of the Industrial Revolution and could envision the fantastic advances to come. Think what they could have accomplished had they only known what was to happen!

Today, we know we are at the dawn of a new age. So *think*. Think about the new possibilities *every day*. Computers are your future, and they'll provide you with the means for a successful and satisfying life. Enjoy the ride!

Spotlight Exercises

1. There are many new technologies rapidly coming to our consumer market. Visit **www.gizmag. com**. Explore the new, innovative items found there. Choose three items related to the topics covered in this Spotlight that you think will be successful in today's market. Describe them, their function, and why you think these items might actually be successfully sold to consumers. Be sure to mention where they can be purchased and the price. Submit your findings in a one- to three-page report.

2. Thanks to a breakthrough surgical technology, there is a new robot specially designed for the medical community. It was designed as an alternative to both open surgery and laparoscopy. Through the use of the da Vinci Surgical System (**www.davincisurgery.com**), surgeons are now able to offer this minimally invasive option for complex surgical procedures. Is this something which might interest you personally if needed? Please explain your concerns and the potential benefits of robotic surgery in a one- to two-page paper.

3. Nanotechnology is making many medical improvements and advancements possible. Investigate the cancer treatment option described at **http://news.ucf.edu/UCFnews/index?page= article&id=0024004103738142901 2136c33d 79005996&subject_id=0024004102975ad83011b 2b83251c0a02**. Briefly describe this cancer treatment method. Then find an equally interesting use of nanotechnology and describe it in detail. Your report should not exceed four pages.

4. Virtual reality is a hot topic. Search the Web to learn more about virtual reality games. Is any special hardware needed? Describe your recommendations for computer components that would provide an optimal gaming experience (monitor size, video memory requirements, processor speed, and so on). Write a one-page paper that describes a virtual reality game and the ideal computer system for playing it.

5. Visit iRobot's Web site (**www.irobot.com**) to learn about the home and tactical robotic products. Check out the home products and watch the videos. Choose one product you might use. Briefly describe the product, features, and price. Check out the government industrial products, watch the videos, and briefly describe one of the products and its features. Finally, visit **www.sciencedaily. com/releases/2009/06/090612115531.htm**. Describe this product and explain your thoughts on whether there is a need for it. Submit your findings in a one-page report.

6. Artificial intelligence was once only thought of as science fiction, but today it is getting much more attention. It is now appropriate to ask the question: Where is artificial intelligence technology headed? You might also ask whether computer intelligence will surpass our own, and how quickly. Using your favorite search engine, find three articles or Web sites that provide some insight into the future of artificial intelligence. Based on your research, write a one-page, double-spaced essay describing what you think the future will be for AI. List your references in the paper.

chapter 10

Careers and Certification

Chapter Objectives

- Describe traditional information technology (IT) career paths and how these paths are changing. (p. 391)

- Describe two settings in which most IT workers find employment and list at least three typical job titles. (p. 391)

- Compare and contrast computer science (CS) and management information system (MIS) curricula in colleges and universities. (p. 394)

- Identify the business skills information system (IS) managers want in new IT workers. (p. 399)

- List the technical skills currently in high demand. (p. 400)

- Discuss both the positive and negative aspects of certification. (p. 401)

Take a look around: Careers are changing. Yes, there are still the doctors, dentists, lawyers, and teachers—along with a few other standard career choices. However, now information technology professional can be added to the list of stable careers. An individual entering the workforce can make a conscientious choice to be an Information Technology (IT) professional. The opportunities, pay, and excitement of a constantly changing and challenging career that promises to be on the cutting edge of technology is moving IT careers to the top of the list. Are you interested in technology? Do you like to solve problems? Do computers and their processes intrigue you? Is a career in IT a good choice for you?

Today, almost all companies, regardless of their size, use computers and information technology (IT). But just because they use IT doesn't make them part of the IT industry. The **IT industry** is made up of organizations that are focused on the development and implementation of technology and applications. This includes well-known companies such as Microsoft, Dell, and Intel as well as companies from the telecommunications sector such as Verizon, resellers such as Best Buy, vendors like AMD, and suppliers of parts like TigerDirect.com.

Even employers that are not part of the IT industry are demanding higher levels of computer literacy than ever before. It does not matter whether your future career is in health care, retail, finance, or any other industry. Such fields use computers to access medical records and perform procedures, ring up sales using POS terminals, research stock market or other financial information, and so on. According to a recent study, employers described computer literacy as "important" or "very important" in their hiring decisions. Particularly attractive to employers were the following skills: word processing, e-mail, spreadsheet analysis, database entry and editing, use of presentation software, and Web searching. This demand by employers for current computer skills makes computer knowledge a component of lifelong learning and a skill that will require constant updating and retraining as technology progresses.

Is a career in IT for you? How can you investigate the careers or jobs available to you? With regard to job searches, how would you like to send your resume to more than 52 million potential readers? You can accomplish this very easily by using online services that post your resume on the World Wide Web for potential employers to view (Figure 10.1). Perhaps the most widely known of these sites for IT careers is

Dice.com (**www.dice.com**). The Dice.com database is searchable by keyword, industry, company, or geographic location. The site lists hundreds of thousands of jobs as well as company information with hyperlinks to corporate Web sites. Companies that have joined Dice.com can place recruitment ads, post company profiles, and gain access to a database of resumes that grows in number daily.

FIGURE 10.1 Popular Job Search Sites

Web Site	URL
General Job Search Sites	
CareerBuilder.com	www.careerbuilder.com
Indeed	www.indeed.com
Monster	www.monster.com
Yahoo! HotJobs	http://hotjobs.yahoo.com
Federal Job Search Sites	
Studentjobs.gov	www.studentjobs.gov
USAJOBS	www.usajobs.gov
IT Job Search Sites	
CareerBuilder.com—IT Jobs	http://information-technology.careerbuilder.com
code-jobs.com	www.code-jobs.com
ComputerJobs.com	www.computerJobs.com
ComputerWork.com	www.computerwork.com
Dev Bistro	www.devbistro.com
Dice	http://dice.com
JustTechJobs.com	www.justtechjobs.com
Quintessential Careers	www.quintcareers.com/computer_jobs.html
Tech-centric.net	www.tech-centric.net
Tech-Engine	www.techengine.com

This chapter looks at the traditional educational path to an IT career, alternative IT career paths, and IT careers of the future. Before reading further, see whether a career in information technology is a fit for your skills, abilities, and personality. Try one of the free online career assessment tools from Assessment.com (**www.assessment.com**) or ProjectCareer (**www.projectcareer.com**). Be aware that these sites will ask you personal information to formulate an assessment of your strengths, likes, and motivations. They may include ads, want an e-mail address for follow-up, or offer additional services for a fee. An approximate 15-minute investment can help you make a life-changing decision.

Traditional Information Technology Career Paths

In the world of technology, nobody knows what the future will bring. That can be a little troubling for future job seekers attempting to acquire today the skills they'll apply tomorrow. Will the job of your dreams be around when you're ready for employment? Does it even exist yet? How do you prepare for an uncertain career landscape?

Learning about computers and getting a bachelor's degree is a step in the right direction, as is keeping up with emerging technologies. Nobody wants to head down a path toward an occupation that won't exist in five years. Staying abreast of job trends is an excellent way to ensure you're heading in the right direction. Where do you find such information? The *Occupational Outlook Handbook* for 2008–2009, found on the U.S. Department of Labor's Bureau of Labor Statistics site (**www.bls.gov/oco/home.htm**), is a good place to start (Figure 10.2).

As we look to the year 2016, reports from the Bureau of Labor Statistics indicate that information technology (IT) professionals will continue to be in high demand. These reports foresee employment in professional, scientific, and technical services growing by 28.8 percent and adding 2.1 million new jobs by 2016. Employment in computer systems design and related services are predicted to grow by 38.3 percent and add nearly one-fourth of all new jobs in professional, scientific, and technical services. The information sector is expected to increase by 6.9 percent, adding 212,000 jobs by 2016. This subcategory of IT jobs includes some of the newer and fast-growing computer-related industries such as software publishing; Internet publishing and broadcasting; wireless telecommunication; motion picture production; radio and television broadcasting; and newspaper, book, periodical, and directory publishing.

Information technology (IT) professionals work with information technology in all its various forms (hardware, software,

FIGURE 10.2 The Bureau of Labor Statistics Web site contains useful information about a wide array of IT-related occupations.

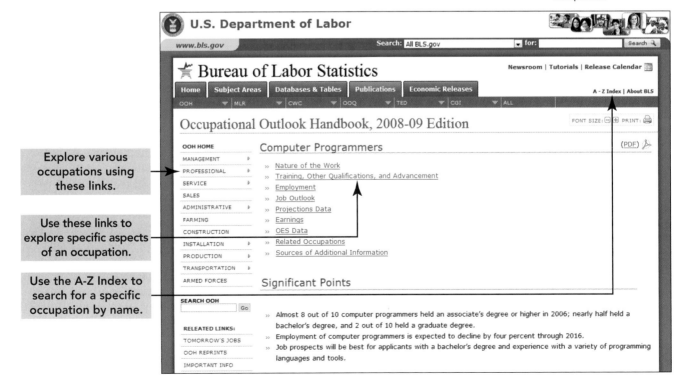

Explore various occupations using these links.

Use these links to explore specific aspects of an occupation.

Use the A-Z Index to search for a specific occupation by name.

networks) and functions (management, development, maintenance). Both small and large companies will need computer specialists and administrators who can keep up with the fast-changing technologies that keep them growing and competitive. This is especially important when integrating emerging sophisticated technologies.

In the coming years, companies will need many more skilled IT professionals than they're likely to find. Currently, not enough students are graduating from U.S. colleges and universities with degrees in computer science, systems engineering, or management information systems to meet the forecasted employment needs. Students who do have these degrees will be in high demand. The IT Professionals Association of America sees a continuing decline of students pursuing degrees in computer science. Scott Kirwin, founder of the group, cites two reasons for this decline. The first is **outsourcing**, the act of one company contracting with another to provide services that might otherwise be performed by in-house employees. Examples include such activities as call center services, e-mail services, and payroll. The second reason cited is **labor dumping**, a term coined by Kirwin to describe the flooding of a labor market with foreign workers. Both actions are driven by the search for cheap labor, and this search is the main reason that graduates in this field are still declining both in the United States and abroad.

What this means for you is opportunity. If you have the right background, skills, and motivation you can find a job as an IT professional.

The average Computer Programmer salary in the United States is around $60,000, with the bottom and top ranges stretching from $35,000 to $97,000. For recent college graduates with a Bachelor's degree in Computer Science, starting salaries are somewhere in the range of $46,000 per year.

Ten years ago, most people got into IT careers by obtaining a computer-related bachelor's degree and landing a job with a corporate **information systems (IS) department**, the functional area within companies or universities responsible for managing information technology and systems (Figure 10.3), or a software development firm (Figure 10.4), also called a

> **" Individuals** that team **technology** with communication **skills** will be the **most effective** job seekers. **"**

vendor. The four-year college degree was, and still is, a prerequisite for the best jobs. In a recent survey, 83 percent of surveyed U.S. corporations stated that they require a four-year college degree for entry-level programming jobs.

The U.S. Bureau of Labor Statistics report on network systems and data communication analysts, cites that analysts, data communications analysts, and computer software engineers are expected to be the fastest-growing occupations in the U.S. economy. Jobs for network systems and data communications analysts are projected to increase 53 percent between 2006 and 2016. In addition, more than 500,000 jobs in computer systems design and related fields will be created between 2006 and 2016. IT professionals (versus less-skilled workers) continue to have the best prospects because of demand for higher-level skills needed to keep up with changes in technology. Individuals that team technology with communication skills will be the most effective job seekers.

Of course, as with any career, computer-related jobs aren't for everyone. Change, not

FIGURE 10.3 Typical Job Titles and Responsibilities in a Corporate IS Department

Job Title	Responsibilities	Salary Range	Preferred Educational Level
Chief Information Officer (CIO)	*Senior-level management position* Defines the IS department's mission, objectives, and budgets and creates a strategic plan for the company's information systems	$149,000 to $329,000	Master's, Ph.D.
Director of Computer Operations	*Middle management position* Ensures overall system reliability	$66,000 to $135,000	Master's, Ph.D.
Director of Network Services	*Middle management position* Ensures overall network reliability	$70,000 to $148,000	Master's
Network Engineer	Installs, maintains, and supports computer networks; interacts with users; and troubleshoots problems	$45,000 to $117,000	Master's
Systems Administrator	Installs, maintains, and supports the operating system	$60,000 to $122,000	Master's, Ph.D.
Client/Server Manager	Installs, maintains, and supports client/server applications	$42,000 to $122,000	Master's
Systems Analyst	Interacts with users and application developers to design information systems	$46,000 to $130,000	Bachelor's, Master's
Programmer Analyst	Designs, codes, and tests software according to specifications	$46,000 to $134,000	Bachelor's, Master's
Programmer	Writes code according to specifications	$46,000 to $75,000	Bachelor's

FIGURE 10.4 Typical Job Titles and Responsibilities in a Software Development Firm

Job Title	Responsibilities	Salary Range	Preferred Educational Level
Director of Research and Development	Senior-level management position in charge of all product development activities	$122,000 to $278,000	Master's, Ph.D.
Software Architect	Computer scientist who is challenged to create new, cutting-edge technologies	$116,000 to $235,000	Master's, Ph.D.
Software Engineer	Manages the details of software development projects	$50,000 to 144,000	Master's, Ph.D.
Systems Engineer	Assists the sales staff by working with current and prospective customers; gives technical presentations and supports products on-site	$55,000 to 100,000	Master's, Ph.D.
Software Developer	Develops new programs under the direction of the software architect	$50,000 to $114,000	Bachelor's, Master's
Customer Support Technician	Provides assistance to customers who need help with products	$39,000 to $76,000	Bachelor's

continuity, is the norm in IT careers. Jobs are changed or eliminated and new ones created as technology forces a continuous shifting and updating of priorities and skills. Flexibility is essential because individuals must be comfortable adapting to change and willing to learn new skills and update existing ones frequently. And today's job market offers no such thing as job security. In a computer-related field, you'll probably work at as many as eight or nine different jobs before you retire. This trend is due, in part, to today's global environment in which work is often outsourced or off-shored.

Offshoring is the transfer of labor from workers in one country to workers in other countries. Two examples of job categories that have seen work transferred from the United States to other countries, such as India, China, and the Philippines, are call center work and computer programming. Some companies are learning, though, that the transfer of labor has its costs—particularly in the case of call center workers who don't always meet customer expectations. Forrester Research has predicted that 3.3 million service jobs will move overseas between 2000 and 2015. What is not clear is the total economic and social benefit to U.S. companies. Lehman Brothers and Dell Computer are returning jobs to the U.S. because of the ineffectiveness of foreign workers in computer services and technical support. Actual cost savings may be misleading because of the importance of communication and cultural consistency in project development that makes companies use higher-priced but more reliable expertise based in the United States.

BusinessWeek rated countries based on their appropriateness for handling outsourced jobs, taking into account such factors as cost, language skills, and infrastructure. The results are listed in Figure 10.5.

Before the era of corporate downsizing and offshoring, IT workers could remain with a firm for many years, perhaps until retirement. Workers with business savvy and good communication skills could move into management. If employees needed to acquire additional skills, the employer might arrange and pay for additional training.

The traditional IT career path still exists, but it's changing. Let's look first at the components of a traditional IT career.

FIGURE 10.5 Best Outsourcing Countries

Country	Ranking
Canada	1
Australia	2
Ireland	2
Singapore	4
India	5
New Zealand	5
Spain	7
Israel	8
Mexico	9
Czech Republic	10

EDUCATION FOR TRADITIONAL IT CAREERS

Reflecting the long-standing split in computing between science and business, education for traditional IT careers has been divided between four very different majors: computer science, management information systems, systems and software engineering, and electrical engineering (Figure 10.6).

Computer Science Computer science (CS) is the study of the storage, change, and transfer of information. It includes both the theoretical study of algorithms and the practical problems to which they can be applied. For students, the emphasis is typically on learning a programming language or running a computer, with little attention paid to the usefulness or practical application of the program outcome. In general, CS programs focus on cutting-edge technologies, fundamental principles, and theories. Computer scientists use their honed analytical and technical skills to develop solutions to problems and determine how to best use computing resources. CS typically involves various high-level programming languages and a considerable amount of mathematical ability. At most colleges and universities, CS programs grew out of mathematics programs and are often housed in the engineering school.

Qualified CS graduates find that their theoretical and analytical skills make them good candidates for jobs in cutting-edge software development firms; as researchers for government funded programs with computer simulators; and in IS departments

interpersonal skills required for effective teamwork and leadership. With their business savvy and communication skills, MIS graduates can find jobs in almost any department of a corporation. All departments need people with IT skills to interface with the employees in the IT department—and MIS graduates fill this demand very well.

Systems and Software Engineering The engineering discipline called **systems engineering** applies an interdisciplinary

FIGURE 10.6 Information Technology-Related College Degrees

Degree Field	Description	Course Focus
Computer Science	Theoretical study of algorithms and the problems they can be applied to	Programming languages and mathematics
Management Information Systems	Combines information technology with business skills	Programming languages, application software, and business processes
System and Software Engineering	Reviews the whole IT picture, including the people and the organization as well as the technologies	Analysis and problem solving using engineering and math applications, business processes, and project management skills
Electrical Engineering	Focuses on digital circuit design and cutting-edge communication technologies	Engineering concepts and mathematics

that are working with advanced technologies or developing software in-house.

Management Information Systems

Generally located in business schools, management information systems (MIS) departments are often the flip side of CS departments. Some schools may still refer to this program as computer information systems (CIS), but *MIS* is becoming more commonplace and helps to clearly differentiate the program from CS. **Management information systems (MIS)** focuses on the practical application of information systems and technology to provide the skills businesses need right now to successfully compete in the marketplace. In addition to work in programming and systems analysis, MIS departments strongly emphasize important business topics such as finance and marketing, communication skills, and

approach to creating and maintaining quality systems. Unlike other engineering disciplines, systems engineering looks at the whole picture, including the people and the organization as well as the technologies. The principles of systems engineering are useful for software development, systems analysis, and program development. Systems engineering students learn strong project management skills, and graduates are in high demand.

Computer software engineering is projected to be one of the fastest-growing occupations over the next five years,

"Computer software **engineering** is **projected** to be one of the fastest-growing occupations over the next **five years**, **especially** in the computer and data-processing services industry."

especially in the computer and data-processing services industry. **Software engineering** involves upgrading, managing, and modifying computer programs. Software engineers will continue to develop applications for the ever evolving Internet and a whole new age of Web applications. Software engineers with strong programming, systems analysis, interpersonal, and business skills are those most likely to succeed. Of course, the future will bring with it many new problems for software engineers to solve—problems we can't even think of because they don't exist yet.

Electrical Engineering The engineering discipline called **electrical engineering** (**EE**) offers a strong focus on digital circuit design as well as cutting-edge communication technologies. It's the primary choice for those whose interests lean more toward hardware design, including computer chips, integrated circuits, robotics, and devices that include solid-state, mobile, and embedded technology.

FIGURE 10.7 Training seminars are often offered by hardware or software developers or by established IT training companies.

CONTINUING EDUCATION FOR TRADITIONAL IT CAREERS

In traditional IT careers, professionals keep up with new technologies by attending seminars and continuing education courses, subscribing to computer-related periodicals, attending conferences and shows, and actively participating in professional associations.

Training Seminars Computer-related **training seminars** are typically presented by the developer of a new hardware or software product or by a company specializing in training IT professionals in a new technology (Figure 10.7). These seminars usually last from one day to a week and are often advertised in the local paper's technology or business section as well as in trade magazines such as *PC World* or *Wired*.

Due to the challenging financial times, many companies have slashed their training programs. One side effect of this cut in training is the decrease in employee job mobility. Today, employees may need to foot the bill to attend training seminars to bolster their own skill levels and improve their opportunities for advancement.

Computer Magazines, Newspapers, and Journals Computer-related trade journals are an indispensable resource for IT professionals. Some, such as *Computerworld*, *PC Magazine*, or *Wired*, cover a wide range of computer issues. Others are aimed at a specific section of the IT industry, such as networking (*Network World*), technology management (*InformationWeek*), or security (*SC Magazine*). More than 100 of these types of periodicals are in print. If you have a particular area of interest, you can probably find a periodical that reports late-breaking developments in your field. Most of these periodicals also are published on the Web. A quick search using the magazine's title in your favorite search engine should lead you to such sites as Techweb (**www.techweb.com**) IDG (**www.idg.net**), and Ziff Davis PCMag Network (**www.pcmagnetwork.com**).

Computer Career–Related Web Sites Besides online journals and magazines, there are Web sites dedicated to the computer professionals that provide training information, instructional guides, and forums to exchange information. The InformIT (**www.InformIT.com**) and SANS (**www.sans.org**) sites are two valuable sources of information. InformIT is a true learning site with courses, videos, and relevant articles, while the SANS site is a resource for security information and certification.

Conferences and Shows One way to keep in touch with others in your profession and learn about the latest trends is to attend conferences and trade shows. A **trade**

> " Today, **employees** may need to foot the **bill** to attend training seminars to **bolster** their own skill levels and **improve** their **opportunities** for advancement. "

FIGURE 10.8 The International Consumer Electronics Show in Las Vegas is the largest show of its kind.

show is typically an annual meeting at which computer product manufacturers, designers, and dealers showcase their products. Some shows are held nationally, while others are regional. Job fairs offering on-the-spot interviews provide incentives for job seekers.

Every year the International Consumer Electronics Show (CES), sponsored by the Consumer Electronics Association and the world's largest technology trade show, draws representatives from many facets of the technology industry. Exhibitors at the show include representatives from music, broadcasting, motion picture, cable, and engineering industries, in addition to well-known technology companies. Held yearly in January in Las Vegas, Nevada, the show attracts at least 140,000 attendees from more than 130 countries (Figure 10.8).

Many of the 2,700 exhibitors provide seminars on topics such as cutting edge audio developments, digital imaging, gaming, home theater and video, home networking, in-vehicle technology, wireless connectivity, mobile devices, and emerging technologies. Many of the latest technology innovations are launched at CES. The show is not open to the general public and is considered a must-see for those involved in the technology industry.

Professional Organizations Joining one of the many IT **professional organizations** or **professional associations** can help you keep up with your area of interest as well as provide valuable career contacts. Some associations have local chapters, and most offer publications, training seminars, and conferences for members. Figure 10.9 provides a listing of some of the most important IT organizations and related resources.

Two of the best resources on the Web for familiarizing yourself with the myriad issues and legislation related to technology are the Association for Computing Machinery (ACM, **www.acm.org**) and the Electronic Frontier Foundation (EFF, **www.eff.org**). One major goal of the ACM is to educate its members about important legal, technical, and ethical issues. Whether you're an IT professional or a savvy consumer, the ACM's computing and public policy page at **www.acm.org/public-policy** is a great place to start. You'll be able to research everything from the "legal regulation of technology" to copyright policy.

Although not a professional organization like ACM, the EFF shares some similar objectives, such as protecting fundamental rights regardless of technology; educating the media, policy makers, and the public about technology-related civil liberties issues; and defending those liberties. The EFF has done an excellent job of aggregating a large list of important ethical and legislative issues on a single page, which can be found by clicking on the "Our Work" link at the top of their home page (Figure 10.10).

FIGURE 10.9 Professional Associations and IT Resources

Organization Name	Description
American Society for Information Science and Technology (ASIS&T) www.asis.org	This organization supports information professionals in the advancement of information sciences and related fields, uniting researchers, developers, and end users.
Association for Computing Machinery (ACM) www.acm.org	ACM is the oldest and largest scientific computing society, providing access to computing literature, publications, conferences, and special interest groups.
Association for Women in Computing (AWC) www.awc-hq.org	A nonprofit organization, the AWC promotes the advancement of women in the IT field.
Computer Professionals for Social Responsibility (CPSR) http://cpsr.org	This global organization promotes the responsible use of computer technology and seeks to educate the public and policy makers on technology-related issues.
Diversity/Careers in Engineering & Information Technology www.diversitycareers.com	Devoted to diversity issues in the IT field, this site is a resource for people with disabilities, women, and other minority groups who are traditionally underrepresented in the fields of engineering and information technology.
Gamasutra www.gamasutra.com	Gamasutra is a comprehensive resource for the game development community.
Guild of Accessible Web Designers (GAWDS) www.gawds.org	This global organization provides networking opportunities and information for Web designers and developers interested in promoting Web accessibility standards.
IEEE www.ieee.org	The IEEE, formerly known as the Institute of Electrical and Electronics Engineers, Inc., is a professional society dedicated to promoting the growth of technology.
International Game Developers Association (IGDA) www.igda.org	The largest nonprofit organization for game developers, IGDA promotes professional development and advocates for issues affecting the gaming community.
Network Professional Association (NPA) www.npanet.org	This vendor-neutral, nonprofit organization provides programs and services for network computing professionals and students.
Association of Information Technology Professionals (AITP) www.aitp.org	This professional organization partners with businesses, government, and academia to provide IT leadership and educational opportunities to its members.
The Center for Women and Information Technology (CWIT) www.umbc.edu/cwit	CWIT encourages women and girls to enter the IT field, fosters research on the subject of gender and IT, and provides resources to support this initiative.
Women in Technology International (WITI) www.witi.com	This global organization empowers women in business and technology by providing information, networking opportunities, and career development advice.
World Organization of Webmasters (WOW) www.webprofessionals.org	A professional association, WOW provides education and certification opportunities, as well as technical and employment services, to Web professionals.

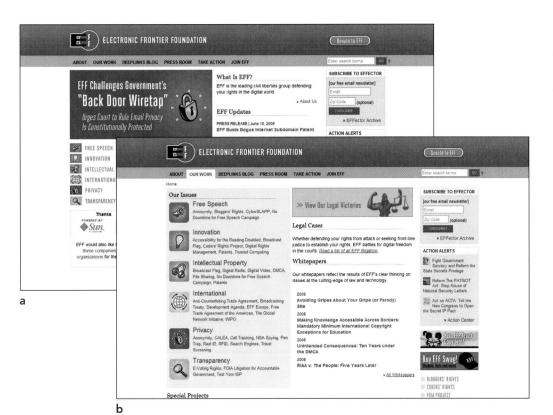

a

b

FIGURE 10.10 The Electronic Frontier Foundation (EFF) Web site includes a large list of important ethical and legislative issues. You can find the link by clicking on the "Our Work" link at the top of the EFF home page.

Now that you're familiar with how to prepare for a more traditional IT career path, let's take a look at new career paths in IT.

Alternative Information Technology Career Paths

IT careers are changing, driven both by rapid technological change and by shifts in the nature of today's businesses. Increasingly, a four-year college degree isn't sufficient to convince prospective employers that would-be employees possess needed skills, because many of these skills aren't yet taught in many colleges and universities.

As you'll see in this section, good communication skills, business savvy, and technical skills are necessary for success in fast-emerging areas such as Web 2.0, virtualization, and mobile technology. For this reason, IT workers must learn how to manage their careers. You may change jobs often, or you may forsake the job market altogether, preferring—as do increasing numbers of IT professionals—to work as an independent contractor or consultant.

Whichever path you choose, it's increasingly becoming the worker's, responsibility to develop the skills needed to keep up with fast-changing technology and manage his or her career in an ever-changing job market. For information, including videos, about various IT careers go to **www.careertv.com**. For podcasts and blogs provided by employers describing their companies, job requirements, and ideal employee go to **http://jobsinpods.com**.

SOUGHT-AFTER BUSINESS SKILLS

Ten years ago, most IT jobs were internally focused: IT professionals worked inside companies. They created and supported computer services, such as payroll and inventory systems. But this picture is changing—and it's changing radically.

Today, driven by new network-based information systems, IT jobs increasingly combine both an internal and an external focus. IT professionals are expected to work with a company's external partners and customers. They'll work in teams that include people from different divisions of the enterprise. Rather than performing a specific function, IT professionals are much more likely to work on a series of projects on which they'll use different skills. For all of these reasons, today's businesses are looking for workers that possess "soft" business skills in addition to "hard" business skills or technical knowledge. **Soft business skills** are people-related skills. Some of the soft skills that businesses are seeking in IT employees are:

- **Communication.** Today, every employee needs communication skills, even those who formerly worked internally and seldom had contact with people outside their departments. Employers are looking for excellent written, verbal, and interpersonal skills. Good presentation skills and the ability to convey technical ideas to nontechnical audiences are also highly valued.

- **Teamwork.** Increasingly, IT personnel are working in teams with workers from finance, marketing, and other corporate divisions. IT professionals need to appreciate varying intellectual styles, work effectively in a team environment, and understand business perspectives.

- **Project management.** The ability to plan and budget a project, itemize the resources needed for completion, and determine the availability and cost of those resources, especially with project management software, is a plus for job hunters.

- **Business acumen.** Information technology is now part of most companies' strategic planning, and IT employees are expected to possess some basic business knowledge. In the past, you could focus on technology and ignore business and communication skills, but that's no longer true. Older, experienced IT workers who suffer job losses due to downsizing may have difficulty finding employment if they don't possess these skills. As a result, the wise IT student also takes courses in general business subjects, including finance and marketing.

Hard business skills are more process related with emphasis on technological expertise in areas as networking, Web development, knowledge of UNIX, C++, and firewall administration. In addition, familiarity with the processes involved in content areas as accounting, finance, and logistics are essential, depending on the professional's focus and concentration in the industry.

ETHICS

As an IT professional, you will often have access to the data residing on other people's computers. Although deliberate snooping is probably not part of your job description, it is possible that you could happen upon information of a sensitive or even illegal nature. Some companies have policies governing how such a situation should be handled, and the Electronic Communications Act of 1986 prohibits unlawful access and certain disclosures of communication content. But what would you do if your company didn't have a policy? What types of information would you report? Who would you report it to—someone within your company or an outside agency? Would you act differently depending on whose computer the information was discovered?

SOUGHT-AFTER TECHNICAL SKILLS

Businesses are also demanding new **technical skills**. Here's what's hot as of this writing:

- **Networking.** Skills related to the process of interconnecting computers are in high demand. Experience with Ethernet, TCP/IP (Internet protocols), and LAN administration are key qualifications.

- **Microsoft Product Skills.** Expertise in managing Microsoft Office applications, working with operating systems, and being able to handle the .NET environment continues to pay big rewards within organizations.

- **Linux.** There is a strong demand for IT workers skilled in Linux operating system configuration and maintenance, networking, and systems programming.

- **TCP/IP.** Knowledge of the protocols underlying the Internet, such as TCP/IP, are needed to manage both external Web servers and internal intranets.

- **Oracle.** Experience with products, especially relational database and client/server application tools are skills always sought by companies.

- **AJAX.** Knowledge of **AJAX,** a group of interrelated Web development techniques used on the client-side that combine HTML/XHTML and JavaScript to provide interactive Web pages, and other Web 2.0 development techniques, is in high demand.

- **Enterprise Resource Planning systems (ERP systems).** Experience with company-wide computer software systems, such as SAP, that are used to manage and coordinate all the resources, information, and functions of a business from shared data stores is a real advantage. Today such ERP systems are used by most large corporations and many smaller ones.

Although a four-year degree in CS or MIS may fail to give you some of these desirable skills, the best preparation for a successful IT career still involves the invaluable theoretical background you get from a four-year college degree.

Now that you understand both traditional and alternative IT career paths, let's examine how IT professionals can adapt to further change.

Web Technologies, New Jobs

New technology brings not just more jobs but new *types* of jobs. Many of these new jobs are inherently cross-disciplinary, involving artistic or communication skills as well as top-notch technical capabilities. Existing CS and MIS programs may produce graduates who lack creativity, marketing knowledge, graphic design experience, or communication skills. For this reason, many companies are hiring students who have taken many computer courses but possess degrees in other fields, such as design, marketing, or English.

For example, Web design involves technical skills and knowledge in areas such as HTML/XHTML, XML, CSS, AJAX, Flash, JavaScript, and server configuration. But in many cases, that's not enough to keep a Web site up and running. Increasingly, companies are looking for Web administrators and content developers who understand marketing, advertising, and graphic design. These jobs require not only technical skills and business smarts, but also artistic sensitivity, including some background in the aesthetics of design and color, coupled with a good deal of creativity (Figure 10.11).

Some future jobs might seem to be somewhat removed from the CS or MIS fields; however, do not let an initial overview fool you. **Telemedicine**, for one, is on the rise and seems to be catching on. This field combines computers and medical expertise to create the equivalent of a long-distance house call. Through the use of computers and telecommunication devices, a physician can consult on a case literally from continents away.

CERTIFICATION

Rapid changes in IT have created a demand for new ways to ensure that job applicants possess the skills they claim. Certification is increasingly seen as a way

FIGURE 10.11 Jobs in Web Technologies	
Job Title	Responsibilities
Interactive Digital Media Specialist	Uses multimedia software to create engaging presentations, including animation and video
Web Database Engineer	Designs and maintains databases deployed on the Web and their related database servers
Web Application Engineer	Designs, develops, tests, and documents new Web-based services for Web sites
Web Designer	Works with internal and external customers to create attractive and usable Web sites
Network/Internet Security Specialist	Installs and maintains firewalls, antivirus software, and other security software; maintains network security

FIGURE 10.12 Selected Certification Programs

Certification Program	Description
Microsoft Certified Systems Administrator (MCSA)	Microsoft Windows Server 2003 implementation, management, and maintenance, as well as LAN-based client/server administration (Microsoft Corporation)
Microsoft Certified Systems Engineer (MCSE)	Microsoft Windows 2000 and Windows Server 2003; operating system and network planning, design, and implementation, as well as LAN-based client/server development (Microsoft Corporation)
Microsoft Certified Technology Specialist (MCTS)	New generation of Microsoft certification; indicates expertise within a specific technology (Microsoft Corporation)
Microsoft Certified IT Professional (MCITP)	New generation of Microsoft certification; builds on core technology expertise to demonstrate key IT professional job and role skills (Microsoft Corporation)
Systems Security Certified Practitioner (SSCP)	To demonstrate vendor-neutral skills and competency for information security practitioners [(ISC)2]
Red Hat Certified Engineer (RHCE)	Performance-based certification for Linux network design, deployment, and administration (Red Hat)
Novell Certified Linux Administrator (CLA)	Administration of installed SUSE Linux Enterprise Server networks (Novell)
Sun Certified Java Programmer (SCJP)	Programming in Java (Sun Microsystems)
Sun Certified Java Developer (SCJD)	Programming and application development in Java (Sun Microsystems)
A+	To validate vendor-neutral skills for entry-level computer technicians (Computing Technology Industry Association [CompTIA])
Network+	To validate vendor-neutral skills for network technicians (CompTIA)
Cisco Certified Network Associate/Cisco Certified Internetwork Expert (CCNA/CCIE)	Installation, configuration, and operation of LAN, WAN, and dial-up access services for small networks (Cisco Systems)

that employers can assure themselves that newly hired workers can do necessary tasks.

In brief, **certification** is a skills and knowledge assessment process organized by computer industry vendors (and sometimes by professional associations). To obtain a certificate, you choose your preferred method of training. You can take courses at a college or at a private training center, or study on your own using vendor-approved books, CD/DVD materials, or the Web. When you're ready, you take a comprehensive examination. If you pass, you receive the certificate (Figure 10.12). But unlike a college degree, the certificate isn't good for life. To retain certification, you may need to take refresher courses and exams periodically, sometimes as often as every six months.

The Institute for Certification of Computing Professionals (ICCP) offers credentials for the highest level of computer professionals. The institute certifies competency for a variety of computer professionals, including computer scientists, system analysts, and computer programmers. Visit the ICCP Web site at **www.iccp.org/iccpnew/index.html**.

Benefits of Certification How does certification pay off for job applicants? A certificate won't guarantee a job or even higher pay, but it does provide a benchmark that enables prospective employers to assess an applicant's skills. In areas of high demand, certification can translate into salary offers that are 10 to 15 percent higher than the norm.

How does certification benefit employers? Although the effects of certification haven't been rigorously studied by independent investigators, vendors and trainers claim that employers who hire certified employees have less downtime and lower IT costs. This makes sense, because certification sets a standard that helps guarantee that new employees will have a certain skill set. When an employee's skill set is matched with the employer's job requirements, everyone wins.

Risks of Certification Certification entails some risks for employees and employers alike. The reason lies in the nature of the certification process, which emphasizes a form of learning that is both narrow (focused on a specific technology) and deep (rigorous and thorough).

For employees, certification requires that they devote a great deal of time and effort to a specific vendor's technology. But changing technology may make vendor-specific skills less marketable. If you're certified as a Novell Linux administrator, for example, you won't impress a prospective employer who's running a Windows network. If you make a bad bet on which certificate to pursue, you could wind up with excellent skills in a technology or application that's losing market share (Figure 10.13).

For employers, hiring people with narrow training is a risk. People with narrow training may not be able to adjust to rapidly changing technologies. In addition, having just one skill isn't enough. Some companies expect employees to possess strong skills in as many as four or five areas. That's why it's a good idea to take as many CS and MIS courses as you can. With a solid theoretical foundation, you can learn new skills throughout your career. You'll prove most attractive to employers if you combine certification with a solid college transcript, communication skills, and business-related courses.

FIGURE 10.13 To find out which certification will benefit you the most, visit sites such as Certification Magazine (www.certmag.com), which contains current information about technical certification programs from a variety of vendors.

Chapter Summary

Careers and Certification

Traditional information technology (IT) career paths require a four-year college degree in computer science (CS) or management information systems (MIS). This path is changing today because of corporate downsizing, outsourcing, labor dumping, and the use of offshore labor.

Training in computer science emphasizes the theoretical and cutting-edge aspects of computing. Training in MIS emphasizes more practical aspects of computing in business settings. IT careers today usually look for skills in both fields, are constantly changing, and require lifelong learning through seminars, trade shows, and certification programs. Other traditional training tracks include systems and software engineering, as well as electrical engineering.

IT professionals today need both soft business skills, like good verbal and written communication skills, project management experience, and business perspectives, as well as hard business skills, which in the IT field are the technology skills in areas like networking, database, and Web development. In addition to possessing this combination of skills IT professionals need to keep up these skills, stay ahead of the times, and be adaptive and ready to pursue alternative career paths.

Key Terms and Concepts

Matching

Match each key term in the left column with the most accurate definition in the right column.

_____ 1. outsourcing

_____ 2. software engineer

_____ 3. hard business skills

_____ 4. labor dumping

_____ 5. computer science

_____ 6. certification

_____ 7. trade shows

_____ 8. professional organizations

_____ 9. electrical engineering

_____ 10. offshoring

_____ 11. management information systems

a. Competency discipline that has a strong focus on digital circuit design and cutting-edge communication technologies.

b. A skill and knowledge assessment process.

c. The transfer of labor from workers in one country to workers in another.

d. Computer-related instructional sessions presented by the developer of a new hardware or software product.

e. A company supplying materials or services, such as a software development firm.

f. One company contracting with another company to provide services that might otherwise be performed in-house.

g. Organizations that help you keep up with your area of interest as well as provide valuable career contacts.

_____ 12. training seminars

_____ 13. InformIt

_____ 14. vendor

_____ 15. soft business skills

h. Skills that refer to the knowledge of processes mostly with reference to technological expertise in areas as networking, Web development, knowledge of UNIX, C++, and firewall administration as well as some of the processes in accounting, finance, and logistics.

i. A source of courses, videos, and relevant articles for IT professionals.

j. Involves upgrading, managing, and modifying computer programs.

k. The practical application of information systems and technology to provide the skills a business needs to compete successfully.

l. Periodic meetings in which computer product manufacturers, developers, and dealers display their products.

m. Skills associated with human resources, relationships, learning, personal development, and ethics.

n. The study of the theoretical foundations of information and computation.

o. The flooding of a labor market with foreign workers.

Multiple Choice

Circle the correct choice for each of the following.

1. Which is a resource for certification, and information for IT professionals in the area of security?
   a. Sans.org
   b. Techtalk.com
   c. InformIt.com
   d. Dice.com

2. Which of the following jobs in the Web technology industry designs, develops, tests, and documents new Web-based services for Web sites?
   a. Web Database Engineer
   b. Web Designer
   c. Network/Internet Security Specialist
   d. Web Application Engineer

3. Which of the following is a valid certification?
   a. Digital Media Specialist (DMS)
   b. Microsoft Certified IT Professional (MCITP)
   c. Microsoft Certified Application User (MCAU)
   d. System Maintenance Director

4. Which of the following statements about management information systems is true?
   a. The theoretical aspects of computing are emphasized.
   b. Finance, marketing, communication skills, and interpersonal skills are required for effective teamwork and leadership.
   c. Training usually includes several semesters of higher math.
   d. Topics such as artificial intelligence and programming language structure are required.

5. Which of the following is the oldest and largest scientific computing society?
   a. Association for Computing Machinery (ACM)
   b. Computer Professionals for Social Responsibility (CPSR)
   c. IEEE
   d. Association of Information Technology Professionals (AITP)

6. Which statement is true about a career in the IT field?
   a. A graduate with a B.S. in computer science will never need any retraining.
   b. IT professionals usually stay at the same job doing the same tasks for their entire career.
   c. IT professionals usually change jobs several times during their career and are dedicated to lifelong learning.
   d. IT professionals today do not need strong interpersonal skills.

7. Which of the following provides resources for the game development community?
   a. World Organization of Webmasters (WOW)
   b. United Gaming Professionals
   c. Network Professional Association (NPA)
   d. Gamasutra

8. Which of the following is used in developing interactive Web pages?
   a. Oracle
   b. ERP systems
   c. Project management software
   d. AJAX

9. Who defines the IS department's mission, budget, and strategic plan?
   a. Chief Executive Officer
   b. Chief Information Officer
   c. Chief Financial Officer
   d. Chief Operations Officer

10. Which position in an IS corporate department interacts with users and application developers to design information systems?
    a. Systems Administrator
    b. Programmer Analyst
    c. Network Engineer
    d. Systems Analyst

Fill-In

In the blanks provided, write the correct answer for each of the following.

1. _____ _____ skills involve the ability to organize a project and the project resources as well as budget for its completion.

2. A _____ _____ department is the functional area responsible for managing information technology and systems at a business or university.

3. Information about job trends can be found in the Occupational Outlook Handbook located on the _____ _____ _____ _____ Web site.

4. The use of computers and medical expertise to provide the equivalent of a long-distance house call is called _____.

5. Knowledge of Ethernet, and LAN administration fall within the technical skill of _____.

6. Many large companies use a(n) _____ _____ _____ system, such as SAP.

7. Communication, teamwork, and project management are known as nontechnical or _____ business skills.

8. The largest technology trade show, which is held annually in Las Vegas, is the _____ _____ _____.

9. _____ is ranked as the number one outsourcing country.

10. _____ is a soft business skill that encourages individuals from different departments to work together to better understand business perspectives.

11. _____ _____ are excellent opportunities to learn more about technologies and network with other professionals; however, employees must often pay their own way to attend such functions.

12. HTML, XHTML, CSS, Flash, and JavaScript are areas of knowledge in the field of _____ _____.

13. The certification need for an entry-level computer technician position is _____.

14. The functional area within an organization responsible for managing systems and technologies is known as the _____ _____ _____ department.

15. The International Game Developers Association (IGDA) and the Computer Professionals for Social Responsibility (CPSR) are examples of _____ _____.

Short Answer

1. Name three soft business skills and three hard business skills that IT professionals should possess.

2. What are three of the basic differences between computer science and management information systems departments?

3. What is the difference between outsourcing and offshoring?

4. Describe three jobs associated with Web technology.

5. Describe three ways an IT professional can continue his/her lifetime learning.

Teamwork

1. **IT Jobs and Certifications** Locate IT jobs in your community using local newspapers, the college placement office, and local Web sites. Using a table or spreadsheet, list the job title and the certifications that may be valuable for the position. Using your educational institution, others in the community, or professional training centers, locate the nearest facility that offers those certifications and, if possible, the cost for training and testing.

Present your findings in a logical method using either a table, spreadsheet, or Web page.

2. **MIS Departments versus CS Departments** In this exercise, divide your team into two groups and explore MIS department courses and content and Computer Science courses and content. Does your school have an MIS and CS department? If so, look at a school catalog (printed or online) to find information about the program. If you can't find answers

to some of the following questions in the catalog, you'll have to contact the department directly. If your school does not have a department, go to another institution's Web site for the type of department your school doesn't have, and base your answers on the information provided there.

What are the job titles for which graduates are prepared? If courses in the areas of interpersonal communication, business knowledge, or the Internet are required, identify them by title. Is there an elective or a required course that enables students to intern with an IT company for credit? Write a report based on your findings.

3. **IT Professional Associations** Select five IT associations from the list in Figure 10.9. Using traditional research techniques or search engines, find their mission statements and issues of focus. Present your findings in a one-page double-spaced report.

4. **Offshoring and Outsourcing** Create a survey to learn more about individuals' satisfaction with their experiences in having to talk to someone outside of their company or out of their country to resolve a service question, repair question, or billing error. First create the survey, and then have each team member administer it to approximately five individuals. Collect, combine, and summarize the data. Present your findings in a consolidated and informational manner. Were consumers generally satisfied with the service from an offshore or outsourced provider?

5. **Certification—Help Yourself?** IT professionals do not have to attend certification training sessions to learn new skills. They can study at home and then take a certification examination. As a team, visit a bookstore and look for books that help professionals study for certification examinations. For each book, list the name of the certification program that is covered, the title, the author, and the price. Select one of these texts and examine the table of contents and several pages. Does the book appear to provide IT professionals with background knowledge and content depth or does it just focus on passing the examination? Prepare a group presentation based on your findings.

On the Web

1. **IT Jobs on Campus** Using online resources for job descriptions and your own school as a reference, try to determine the number and titles of IT and IT-related jobs on campus. Do some research and determine which of these jobs did not exist 10 years ago. Which of these jobs do you see continuing and increasing in demand? Do you see a need for a position that does not exist as of yet? If so describe the position and its function. Present your findings and insight in a one-page double-spaced paper.

2. **IT Jobs Today and Tomorrow** Go to the U.S. Department of Labor's Bureau of Labor Statistics site (**www.bls.gov/oco/home.htm**). At the bottom of the screen is an alphabetical link to job categories. Locate five jobs posted in such categories as computer science and information technology. Make a list of these jobs and using the Web, find a description of each along with the business and technical qualifications each requires. Present your findings in a one-page double-spaced report.

3. **IT Jobs and Salaries** Use the **www.salary.com** Web site as a start to locate IT jobs and their salaries. Salary.com has a link on its home page for "Jobs by Salary Range." Use this section and any other Web sites to locate various IT jobs and their average salaries. Then, using search engines, obtain a job description for each position. Try to locate at least five jobs that are not listed in the text. Provide a description of the position, the education requirements, and the area of country in which they are in demand. Arrange and present your findings in a table or spreadsheet.

4. **Technical Skills Training** The text identifies the following as sought-after technical skills: networking, Microsoft product skills, Linux, TCP/IP, Oracle, AJAX, and ERP systems. Visit the following training Web sites:

www.learningtree.com

www.nextecinc.com (watch the video)

www.cbtplanet.com (review the offerings)

Each company provides training—online, onsite, or both—to IT professionals. From the information on their Web sites, identify the methods of training each provides, the type of professionals they are trying to attract, the certification tests they administer, and the cost range of their training. Present the results of your research in a one-page report.

5. **Web Technology Jobs** Jobs in Web technology are a more recent addition to the list of IT professions. Research the credentials that Web technology IT professionals need for the positions listed in Figure 10.10 and any others your research uncovers. Indicate whether a four-year degree is needed, what software programs professionals use as their tools of the trade, and any certifications that they can obtain. Present your results in a one-page report or on a Web page.

chapter 11

Programming Languages and Program Development

Scroll and click . . . and you can access a library of contemporary music, a listing of e-books, your address book, a calendar, and any number of other applications. When you work in Word, by making a few selections you can change the look of your entire document. Have you ever wondered how such things are possible? They are possible because of the advances that have been made in programming languages—the languages through which programmers create the applications we have all come to enjoy. It all seems so instant and magical. How is it done?

Programming is the process used to create the software applications you use every day. These applications are the result of the efforts of programmers, trained experts who work individually or in groups to design, write, and test software applications for everything from word processing to virus protection. Knowing the basics of the history and practices of the programming industry will help you better understand what goes on inside your computer.

Programmers use programming languages to create software (Figure 11.1). Unlike the natural languages that people speak, a **programming language** is an artificial language, one that is deliberately created to tell the computer what to do in a step-by-step manner. Typically, each programming language consists of a vocabulary and a set of rules called **syntax**. A **programmer** must learn these rules because they govern the structure of the instructions, commands, and statements of the language he or she uses to write a program. Usually it refers to the proper use of commas, parentheses, braces, semicolons, and other punctuation, symbols, or keywords that are used to accurately construct a segment of code. In most cases the language used by a programmer, **source code**, needs to be translated from its original form into a form recognized by the internal hardware before a computer can actually run it. In general, the written computer instructions that programmers create are called **code** (Figure 11.2). The term *code* can be a noun or a verb. For example, a programmer might say, "I wrote most of the code for this project" or "I must code a new program." Code comes in many forms. We'll discuss another form of code, called object code, in subsequent sections.

Every programming language has its advantages and disadvantages. What's the best programming language? If you ask 10 IT professionals, chances are you'll get five different answers. The truth is that there isn't any one language that's best for all programming purposes. The question is, which language is the right one for the job?

step closer to the languages that humans use. The five generations of programming languages are

- Machine language
- Assembly language
- Procedural languages
- Nonprocedural languages
- Natural languages

This section discusses the development of these languages and how they've evolved to keep up with changing technology.

In this chapter, you'll learn about several programming languages, how these languages have developed, the applications that each support, and which languages are the most popular today. You'll also learn how programs are developed using the program development life cycle (PDLC), a step-by-step method of software development.

Even if you don't plan to study programming, this chapter will expose you to some of the basic languages and their uses. If you decide to give programming a try, this chapter will provide background information, examples, and a solid look at what programming involves.

Development of Programming Languages

Programming languages are classified by levels, or generations. Each generation is a

FIRST-GENERATION LANGUAGES (1GL): 0S AND 1S

Because the earliest computers predated programming languages, computers had to be programmed in the computer's language, also known as **machine language**. Machine language consists of binary numbers—0s and 1s—that directly correspond to the computer's electrical states. Though tedious for humans to work with, machine language is the only programming language that a computer can understand directly without translation. Each type or family of processor requires its own machine language with instructions that conform to the processor's special characteristics. For this reason, machine language is said to be **machine dependent** (or **hardware dependent**).

During the first generation of computing, programmers had to use machine language because no other option was available. Programmers had to know a great deal about the processor's design and

```
Basic
10 REM Hello World in BASIC
20 PRINT "Hello World!"
```

```
Visual Basic .NET
'Hello World in Visual Basic .NET (VB.NET)

Imports System.Console

Class HelloWorld

    Public Shared Sub Main()
        WriteLine("Hello World!")
    End Sub

End Class
```

how it functioned. As a result, programs were few in number and lacked complex functionality. Today, programmers almost never write programs directly in machine code, because it requires attention to numerous details and memorizing numerical codes for every instruction that is used. It also locks the code to a specific platform.

More recent programming languages, which look like natural language, make it easier for programmers to write programs, but all of the code they write, no matter what language is used, must still be translated into machine language by special utility programs before the processor can execute the program on a system.

SECOND-GENERATION LANGUAGES (2GL): USING MNEMONICS

The first programming language to break programmers' dependence on machine language was assembly language. In **assembly language**, each program statement corresponds to an instruction that the microprocessor can carry out. Assembly language closely resembles machine language in that it's processor dependent and closely tied to the hardware inside the system unit. For this reason, assembly and machine languages are called **low-level languages**. The word *low* refers to the small or nonexistent amount of difference between the language and machine language; because of this, low-level languages are sometimes described as being "close to the hardware."

To program in assembly language, programmers still need to know how the computer's internal hardware works. However, assembly language doesn't force programmers to program in binary. Instead, it enables them to use familiar base-10 (decimal) numbers as well as brief abbreviations for program instructions called **mnemonics** (pronounced "nih-MON-icks") (Figure 11.3). For example, the mnemonic MOV tells the processor to move a value, while ADD instructs it to add one value to another, SUB to subtract, MUL to multiply, DIV to divide, and JMP to jump to an instruction in the code.

Before an assembly language program can be run on a computer, it must be translated into machine language. The source code is translated into machine language by a utility program called an **assembler**.

Assembly language is still used occasionally to write short programs, such as a **device driver** (a program that controls

```
title          Hello World      (hello.asm)
               Program
; This program will display "Hello, World!"
dosseg
.model         small
.stack         100h
.data
     hello_message db 'Hello, World!',0dh,0ah,'$'
.code
main           proc
               mov          ax,@data
               mov          ds,ax
               mov          ah,9
               mov          dx, offset hello_message
               int          21h
               mov          ax,4C00h
               int          21h
main           endp
end            main
```

FIGURE 11.3 Assembly language for the IBM-PC to output "Hello, World!"

a device attached to a computer), and in game console programming.

THIRD-GENERATION LANGUAGES (3GL): PROGRAMMING COMES OF AGE

Because of the difficulties of writing code in machine and assembly languages, third-generation languages were developed with the goal of making programming languages more user-friendly, modular, and reusable. Third-generation languages are considered high-level languages. Unlike machine and assembly languages, **high-level languages** eliminate the need for programmers to understand the intimate details of how the hardware, specifically the processor, handles data. The programmer can write an instruction using familiar English words such as PRINT or DISPLAY. Such an instruction sums up many lines of assembly or machine language code. As a result, third-generation languages are much easier to read, write, and maintain than machine and assembly languages.

Compilers and Interpreters Just as they do when writing in assembly language, programmers create source code in third-generation languages. For the source code to run on a specific type of computer system, it must be translated by a compiler or an interpreter, also referred to as a *language translator* (Figure 11.4).

A **compiler** is a utility program that translates all of the source code into **object code**, which is a set of instructions in (or close to) a specific computer's machine language. With some compilers, it's necessary to use a program called a linker or an assembler to transform the object code into an **executable program**—one that is ready to run and does not need to be altered in any way. In most operating system environments, these files have an .exe file extension and run by simply double-clicking an icon. Applications such as word processing programs are executable programs. When the compiler translates the code, from source to object form, it checks the code for syntax errors. If any syntax errors are found, the program identifies the likely location of the error.

Another translation program, an **interpreter**, doesn't produce object code. Instead, it translates one line of the source code at a time and executes the translated instruction. Interpreters are helpful tools for learning and ridding a program of errors; because the program executes line by line, the programmer can see exactly what each line does.

Spaghetti Code and the Great Software Crisis Early third-generation languages represented a major improvement over assembly and machine languages. However, early third-generation languages used GOTO statements to enable programs to branch or jump to new locations if a specified condition were met. This wasn't a problem for simple, short programs, but for lengthier programs, the use of many GOTO statements resulted in code that was difficult to follow, messy in design, and prone to errors, earning it the label **spaghetti code**.

> " A **compiler** is a **utility program** that translates all of the source code into object code . . . an **interpreter** doesn't produce object code. Instead, it **translates** one line of source code at a time and **executes** the translated instruction. "

The attempt to create larger and more complex programs led to the software crisis of the 1960s. Programs were not ready on time, exceeded their budgets, contained too many errors, and didn't satisfy customers.

Structured Programming Languages
One response to spaghetti code problems focused on improving the management of software development. Another response focused on improving the languages themselves. The earliest product of such efforts (in the late 1960s) was the concept of structured programming and languages that reflected structured programming concepts. **Structured programming**, also referred to as top-down program design, is a set of quality standards that makes programs more verbose but more readable, reliable, and maintainable. With structured programming, GOTO statements are forbidden, which results in code that is better logically developed. Examples of structured languages include Algol, Pascal, and Ada.

Modular Programming Languages By the 1970s, it was clear that structured programming languages, although better than their predecessors, weren't able to solve the problems encountered in the even larger development projects underway. As a result, programmers developed the modular programming concept. With **modular programming**, larger programs are divided into separate modules, each of which takes care of a specific function that the program has to carry out. Each module

FIGURE 11.4 A compiler and an interpreter both translate source code.

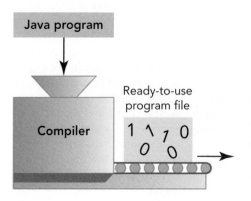

Java program

Compiler

Ready-to-use program file

1 1 1 0
0 0

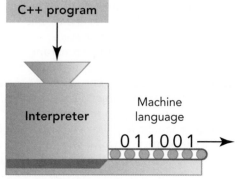

C++ program

Interpreter

Machine language

0 1 1 0 0 1 →

requires a specified input and produces a specified output, so the programming job can be easily divided among members of the programming team. Modular languages include Fortran and C. As programs became more and more complex and the applications more sensitive in nature, the need for more modularity coupled with **information hiding** increased. This approach of hiding details and developing individual modules led to the creation of object-oriented programming languages like C++ and Java. These languages further encapsulate information and increase code security by defining objects, their components, and actions. Once an object is defined, it can be reused or become a subcomponent within another object definition. Object-oriented languages are discussed in detail later in this chapter.

FOURTH-GENERATION LANGUAGES (4GL): GETTING AWAY FROM PROCEDURE

Procedural languages provide detailed instructions that are designed to carry out a specific action, for example printing information in a tabular format. **Nonprocedural languages**, on the other hand, aren't tied down to step-by-step procedures that force the programmer to consider the procedure that must be followed to obtain the desired result. The 4GLs are designed to reduce programming effort, the time it takes to develop software, and the cost of software development—while generating the equivalent of very complicated 3GL instructions with fewer errors. In general, 3GL focused on software engineering, while 4GL and 5GL focus on problem solving and system engineering. Various types of programming languages have claimed to be "fourth-generation," including **report generators** (languages for printing database reports that provide a user-friendly interface and enable a user to design and generate high-quality reports and graphs) and **query languages** (languages with instructions designed to

retrieve and edit information included in databases). FoxPro, Agile, ColdFusion, Mathematica, and SPSS are nonprocedural languages. A specialized query language known as **structured query language**, or **SQL** (pronounced "sequel"), enables users to phrase simple or complex requests for data. For example, in SQL you can ask the following question of the data in a database:

```
SELECT employee-name
FROM employee-salary-table
WHERE salary > 50000
AND position = 'Engineer'
```

In everyday terms, this request is to "Get the names of all engineers who make more than $50,000 from the employee-salary-table." Note that this question isn't totally nonprocedural; you still have to know quite a bit about how the database is structured. (For example, you have to specify which table the information should come from.)

FIFTH-GENERATION LANGUAGES: NATURAL LANGUAGE

The ultimate nonprocedural language would be **natural language**, the everyday language that people speak. Computers would be much easier to use if they could understand natural language, whether the input was spoken or typed. For example, instead of looking through folder after folder in search of a missing file, imagine asking the computer, "Where's that file I created a couple of days ago—the one I wrote about those two paintings we saw in my art history class?"

Despite years of effort to create natural language interfaces, computers are still not very good at understanding what they hear and acting on this understanding. Much of what passes for a natural language interface amounts to word matching; for example, you can navigate the folders on a Mac by speaking their names and giving a few simple commands, such as "Open" or "Close." Combined with software that can parse (decode) a sentence's

"Computers are still not very good at understanding what they hear and acting on this understanding. Much of what passes for a natural language interface amounts to word matching."

FIGURE 11.5 The chat robot ALICE (Artificial Linguistic Internet Computer Entity) uses speech recognition and natural language programming to converse with visitors at *http://alice.pandorabots. com.*

Human: *Hello!*
ALICE: *Hi there!*
Human: *How are you tonight?*
ALICE: *My logic and cognitive functions are normal.*
Human: *Are you a computer?*
ALICE: *Would it matter to you if I were metal instead of flesh?*
Human: *No.*
ALICE: *I am glad that you don't discriminate against robots.*
You say: |

grammatical structure, word-matching programs can work well in areas with highly specialized vocabularies of a few thousand words.

Attempts to create natural language systems with more general capabilities have run into profound problems. One such problem is the ambiguity of human language. The term *intelligence*, for instance, has at least four other meanings. In the military, for example, *intelligence* means knowledge about the enemy. A program capable of understanding the various contexts of a word would have to know a great deal about the world. For example, natural language software should be able to understand that "the day before Christmas" is December 24. The underlying problems presented by these ambiguities are exceedingly complex and will require many more years of research to solve.

Natural language understanding may be a part of computing's future, but this trend toward natural language in programming is currently being assisted by major advances in **speech recognition software**, programs that translate the spoken word into text. Previously, speech-recognition software worked only if the speaker paused between words. New software is much better at continuous speech recognition. Users generally complete a brief (10-minute) tutorial provided with the software. In addition to learning the various commands, they'll have to interact with the software; with most speech recognition applications, users speak several designated sentences to help the computer adjust to their speaking style. However, that is changing. Using the speech recognition component of Windows 7 and the newest release of Dragon NaturallySpeaking, no voice training is required. In any instance, the user will encounter some errors in the application's interpretation of his or her spoken word initially; but the software continues to improve its accuracy with repeated use.

Continuous speech recognition is the first step toward a true natural language interface, because such an interface would require the computer to recognize anyone's natural speech. With reliable speech recognition technology developing rapidly, the day is approaching when you'll be able to control a computer solely by talking to it in ordinary speech (Figure 11.5).

In the next section, you'll learn how expanding a language to work with objects may be a close approximation of a natural language.

OBJECT-ORIENTED PROGRAMMING

Object-oriented programming (OOP) is a programming technique based on defining data as objects. These objects are assigned attributes and methods, which are used to define the object, identify its components, and set the limits of its behavior. Multiple objects can be assembled into one program to create a solution for a specific problem.

Objects An **object** in object-oriented programming (OOP) is a unit of computer information that defines a data element. It contains **attributes** (members) that define the data's features and **methods** (actions) that can process or manipulate the attributes. The object can also contain information that defines its **interface**, or its means of exchanging messages with other objects. For example, one object can ask another object, in effect, "What methods do you have available?" and the object will describe them. With object-oriented programming, information hiding, or **encapsulation**, becomes a reality. Users (or other objects) don't have to know the specifics of how the object was implemented internally; the object is simply acted on by the program and provides whatever information it is asked for.

Suppose you're running a bike shop and you have a specific type of racing bike in stock called the DASHER. Dasher is an object in your shop, and your books or records on DASHER contain all of the data attributes about a Dasher bicycle (including inventory ID number, unit price, and quantity in stock). You can also perform

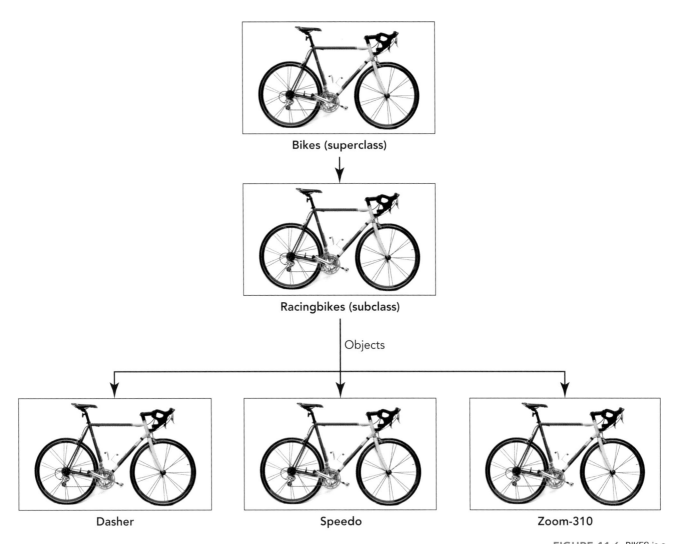

Bikes (superclass)

Racingbikes (subclass)

Objects

Dasher   Speedo   Zoom-310

actions (methods) on the DASHER's data. For example, you can increase or decrease its price, update the quantity, and calculate the total inventory value of the DASHER bike in your shop.

Classes An important feature of object-oriented programming is the concept of a **class**, a category of objects. In the DASHER example, the DASHER object is part of a broader, more abstract category of objects called BIKES. In other words, it's an object within the BIKES class. Suppose, however, that you carry several racing bikes besides DASHER, like the SPEEDO and ZOOM-310. It would make sense to group these three bikes and create a RACINGBIKES class. You can add additional attributes to this class that apply just for racing bikes. By doing so, you make it a **subclass**, a more specialized class, of the BIKES class. BIKES then becomes the base class, superclass, or parent of RACINGBIKES because it is the more abstract and generic category.

RACINGBIKES is referred to as the subclass or child of BIKES. DASHER, SPEEDO, and ZOOM-310 are then objects of the RACINGBIKES subclass of the BIKES base class (Figure 11.6).

The benefit of creating this structure of subclasses, which might seem complex at the moment, is the feature of inheritance and the invisible passing of features from a parent class to a child class.

Inheritance One of the major objectives of object-oriented programming is reusability, the capability to create an object and then reuse it whenever it's needed. With inheritance, possibilities for object reuse are multiplied.

Inheritance refers to the capability of a class to "pass on" its characteristics or properties to its "children," or subclasses. To create objects for the bike shop, a programmer begins by creating the BIKES class and defining in it all the features possessed by all bikes in the shop. Another class, called RACINGBIKES, is created

FIGURE 11.6 BIKES is a superclass, RACINGBIKES is a subclass of BIKES, and DASHER, SPEEDO, and ZOOM-310 are objects of the RACINGBIKES subclass.

as a subclass of BIKES. The features defined in BIKES are not repeated in RACINGBIKES as they are invisibly inherited by the subclass. The subclass will only include the more specific features that are associated only with racing bikes (as number of speeds and tire type). DASHER, SPEEDO, and ZOOM-310, objects of this RACINGBIKES subclass each possess all of the features of the RACINGBIKES class plus the inherited features of the more general BIKE superclass.

Program Development Because objects can be easily reused, object-oriented programming enables a fast method of program development called **rapid application development (RAD)**. With RAD, which was developed to respond to the need to deliver systems very quickly, a programmer works with a library of prebuilt objects that have been created for a huge variety of applications. For instance, a text box is an object that contains a label and the contents of a field object. Using RAD, a programmer does not have to write code that describes the object, but instead simply inserts the prebuilt text box and then modifies it to suit the program's needs. Project scope, size, and circumstances all determine the success of a RAD approach.

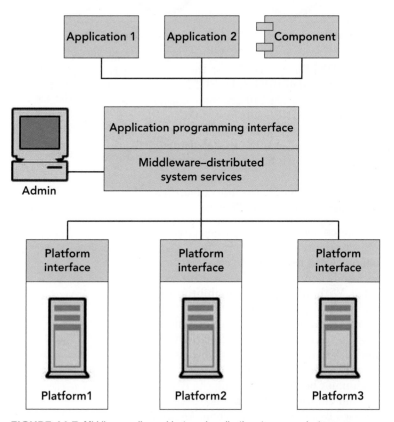

FIGURE 11.7 Middleware allows objects and applications to communicate across a network, regardless of the programming language used.

Joint application development (JAD) is another program development method, which uses a team approach and involves end users throughout the planning and development stages. The objective is to better design objects that suit end user needs. **Agile** software development, a term coined in 2001, refers to a group of software development techniques with which solutions are created through collaboration between teams. Agile methods follow a project management process that aligns development with customer needs and company goals. It encourages frequent inspection and adaptation as well as teamwork, self-organization, and accountability; and it uses a set of engineering practices that allow for rapid delivery of high-quality software that was developed by following a business approach to solution development.

Middleware (Accessing Objects across Networks) One of the most appealing possibilities of object-oriented programming lies in its suitability for use in computer networks. Stimulated by the growth of network-based applications, middleware technologies are becoming more important. They cover a wide range of software systems, including distributed objects and components, message-oriented communication, and mobile application support. Suppose you have hundreds, or even thousands, of objects with processes being performed on them accessible on a network, and each one contains data, as well as the knowledge of how to use that data. To access these objects on the network, you need middleware. **Middleware** is software that does what its name implies, it sits "in the middle" making the connection between varied applications working on multiple networks being supported by different operating systems. Middleware is especially integral to modern information technology based on XML, Web services, and service-oriented architecture (Figure 11.7).

In this category of software, Microsoft offers the .NET standard. IBM and Oracle provide middleware services; and the OW2 Consortium develops and distributes reliable open source middleware.

Other Advantages of Object-Oriented Programming In traditional programming, the program and data are kept separate. If the data must change—because, for example, a company needs to start tracking the exact time of orders as well as the date—all programs that access that data also must be changed. That's an expensive, time-consuming process.

With object-oriented programming, however, the data is stored along with all the program methods needed to access and use the data. If another program accesses the data, it immediately learns which methods are available, including any new ones. This eliminates the need to change many programs just because of a minor change in the data, which saves both time and money.

Object-oriented programming encourages the programmer to start thinking *from the beginning* about the real-world environment in which the program will function, because each object contains the methods for manipulating the object. Proponents of object-oriented programming believe that this focus leads to more usable software.

Now that you understand how programming methods have developed, let's take a look at some of the specific languages that programmers use today.

A Guide to Programming Languages: One Size Doesn't Fit All

This section provides a guide to programming languages found in the various generations with emphasis on the five most popular languages today: Java, C, C++, Visual Basic, and PHP. As you'll see, each program has its pros and cons. Successful programming involves choosing the right language for the job.

COBOL AND FORTRAN: HISTORICALLY IMPORTANT

Imagine it's 1959. Cars have big fins. Dwight Eisenhower is president of the United States. Hawaii becomes a state. And computer programmers are using COBOL and Fortran. Thanks to these early languages for being the springboard of user-friendly language development.

COBOL One of the earliest high-level programming languages, **COBOL**, short for Common Business-Oriented Language, was the most widely used 3GL business programming language for decades. COBOL's success was due to the simple fact that it was a proven way to handle a large organization's accounting information, including inventory control, billing, and payroll. Today it is not a popular language, and its current use is attributed to the survival of legacy (obsolete) mainframe computer systems, where COBOL programming dominates. Employment opportunities for programmers with COBOL skills usually focus on editing and fixing aged code (Figure 11.8).

Fortran **Fortran**, short for "formula translator," is a 3GL language well suited for scientific, mathematical, and engineering

```
000100 IDENTIFICATION DIVISION.
000200 PROGRAM-ID.      HELLOWORLD.
000300
000400*
000500 ENVIRONMENT DIVISION.
000600 CONFIGURATION SECTION.
000700 SOURCE-COMPUTER. RM-COBOL.
000800 OBJECT-COMPUTER. RM-COBOL.
000900
001000 DATA DIVISION.
001100 FILE SECTION.
001200
100000 PROCEDURE DIVISION.
100100
100200 MAIN-LOGIC SECTION.
100300 BEGIN.
100400     DISPLAY " " LINE 1 POSITION 1 ERASE EOS.
100500     DISPLAY "Hello world!" LINE 15 POSITION 10.
100600     STOP RUN.
100700 MAIN-LOGIC-EXIT.
100800     EXIT.
```

FIGURE 11.8 The COBOL program displays Hello world! on the screen.

applications. In its time, if you needed to solve a complex engineering equation, no other programming language came close to Fortran's simplicity, economy, and ease of use (Figure 11.9). Currently, it is being replaced by more object-oriented programming languages like C++ and Java, or by formula-solving programs such as Wolfram Research's Mathematica, which can transform equations into complex (and often beautiful) graphics that reveal underlying mathematical patterns.

Mathematica is a single system that can handle all the various aspects of technical computing in a coherent and unified way. The key to this system was the invention of a new kind of symbolic computer language that could, for the first time, manipulate the very wide range of objects using only a fairly small number of basic elements.

```
! Hello World in Fortran 90 and 95

PROGRAM HelloWorld
 WRITE(*,*)"Hello World!"
END PROGRAM
```

FIGURE 11.9 Example of a Fortran 90 or 95 program that will display Hello World! on the screen.

STRUCTURED AND MODULAR LANGUAGES

COBOL and Fortran may still be used with some legacy systems, but large-scale program development requires structured and modular languages. The following languages are in widespread use among professional developers and software firms.

```
— Hello World in Ada

with Text_IO;
procedure Hello_World is

begin
 Text_IO.Put_Line("Hello World!");
end Hello_World;
```

FIGURE 11.10 Example of an Ada program that will display Hello World! on the screen.

Ada Ada, a programming language (Figure 11.10) that incorporates modular programming principles, is named after Augusta Ada Byron (1815–1852), who helped 19th-century inventor Charles Babbage conceptualize what may have been the world's first digital computer. Part of this language's popularity lies in the fact that it was the required language for most U.S. Department of Defense projects until 1996. Major advantages of Ada include its suitability for the reliable control of real-time systems (such as missiles). For example, the U.S. Navy's Seawolf submarine uses more than 5 million lines of Ada code running on more than 100 Motorola processors.

BASIC Short for Beginner's All-Purpose Symbolic Instruction Code, **BASIC** is an easy-to-use, high-level programming language that was available on many older personal computers. Developed at Dartmouth College in the mid-1960s to teach programming basics to beginners, BASIC has been used by many hobbyists to create simple programs. Some high schools and colleges still teach BASIC in beginning programming courses. Many educators, however, believe that the original versions of BASIC taught flawed programming skills because of BASIC's reliance on GOTO statements. More recent versions of BASIC incorporate the principles of structured, modular, and object-oriented programming.

Visual Basic Developed in the early 1990s and based on the BASIC programming language, Microsoft's **Visual Basic (VB)** is an event-driven programming language. With an **event-driven programming language**, the program's code (Figure 11.11) is not written to execute in any specific sequence. Instead, the code executes in response to user actions, such as the clicking of a mouse button. The newest version of VB enables a programmer to develop an application quickly by designing the graphical user interface on the screen as the *first* step in program development (Figure 11.12). The behavior in which the program looks for events (mouse click, keyboard, etc.) and performs operations in response is also referred to as an event loop.

Each on-screen control, such as a text box or a radio button, can then be linked to a brief BASIC program that performs an action. The programmer doesn't have to worry about any of the code that generates the user interface because it's all handled automatically by the VB compiler, which creates an executable program capable of running on its own. Using VB, even a novice programmer can develop an impressive application in short order.

BASIC	Visual Basic 2.0	Visual Basic 6

```
10 REM Hello World in
   BASIC
20 PRINT "Hello World!"
```

```
REM Hello World VB
for Windows

VERSION 2.00
Begin Form Form1
  Caption = "Form1"
  ClientHeight = 6096
  ClientLeft = 936
  ClientTop = 1572
  ClientWidth = 6468
  Height = 6540
  Left = 876
  LinkTopic = "Form1"
  ScaleHeight = 6096
  ScaleWidth = 6468
  Top = 1188
  Width = 6588
  Begin Label Label1
  Caption = "Hello World!"
  Height = 372
  Left = 2760
  TabIndex = 0
  Top = 2880
  Width = 972
  End
  End
Option Explicit
```

```
Hello World in Visual Basic 6

Private Sub Form_Load()
Print "Hello World"
End Sub
```

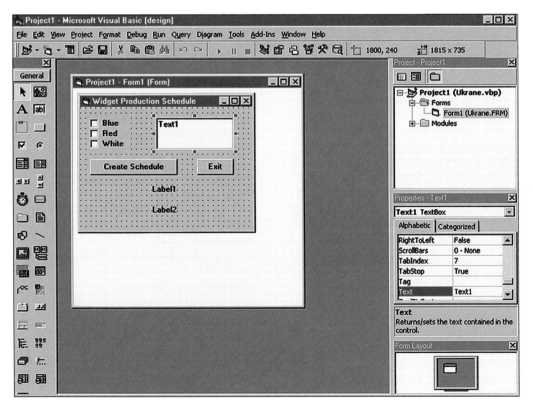

FIGURE 11.12 The Visual Basic 2008 graphical user interface greatly simplifies program development.

```
// Hello World in C++

#include <iostream>

int main()
{
    std::cout << "Hello World!\n";
}
```

FIGURE 11.13 This simple C++ program displays "Hello World!" on the screen.

Although VB was a widely used program development package, it has been replaced by Visual Basic.NET an object-oriented language. Microsoft ended support for VB in 2008.

C A high-level programming language developed by AT&T's Bell Labs in the 1970s, **C** combines the virtues of high-level programming languages with the efficiency of an assembly language. Using C, programmers can directly manipulate bits of data inside the processing unit. As a result, well-written C programs run significantly faster than programs written in other high-level programming languages. However, C is difficult to learn, and programming in C is a time-consuming activity.

OBJECT-ORIENTED LANGUAGES

Structured and modular languages are the workhorses of software development, but the honor of being cutting edge goes to object-oriented (OO) languages.

Smalltalk **Smalltalk** is considered by many to be the only "100 percent pure" object-oriented programming language. It was developed in the early 1970s at Xerox Corporation's Palo Alto Research Center (PARC), home of the graphical user interface (GUI) and many other key computing innovations. Smalltalk, a prototype for a computation model, is not

FIGURE 11.14 Java has gained acceptance faster than any programming language in computing history. Here is an example of Java code.

```
// Hello World in Java

class HelloWorld {
  public static void main(String[] args) {
    System.out.println("Hello World!");
  }
}
```

often chosen for professional software development.

C++ A more recent version of C, **C++**, was developed at Bell Labs in the 1980s and incorporates object-oriented features—but doesn't force a programmer to adhere to the object-oriented model (Figure 11.13). Thanks to this flexibility and the fast execution speed of compiled C++ programs, C++ is in widespread use for professional program development. For more specific information on C++, examples of source code, virtual courses, and tutorials go to **www.desy.de/user/projects/C++.html**.

Java Developed by Sun Microsystems in 1995 for consumer electronic devices, **Java** is an object-oriented, high-level programming language (Figure 11.14). According to Java backers, it's the world's first truly **cross-platform programming language**, a programming language capable of running on many different types of computers, including those using the Windows, Mac OS, or Linux operating systems. Java enables programmers to create programs that "write once, run anywhere."

How is it possible to write one program and run it on any computer? The secret to this remarkable capability is the Java Virtual Machine, which must be installed on any computer that runs Java. The **Java Virtual Machine (VM)** is a Java interpreter and runtime environment for Java applets and applications that provides a "home away from home" for Java, no matter what type of computer it's running on. It is called a "virtual machine" because it creates a simulated computer that provides the correct platform for executing Java programs.

Javabeans are the programming specifications that are created in Java and used to create reusable, platform-independent Java components. You can combine these components into **applets** (miniprograms embedded in a Web document), applications, or composite components (Figure 11.15). Javabean components are known as **beans**. Beans can be changed or customized. For more information on this powerful platform-independent language, visit **http://java.sun.com**. For tutorials and specific applets use the Java Boutique at **www.javaboutique.internet.com**.

Java is ranked by many as the number one programming language today. Many believe Java is one of the best RAD tools available, but it does face some competition from Microsoft's Visual Basic .NET.

However, despite Java's considerable advantages, the language has many of the weaknesses of a programming language that's still evolving. For example, downloaded applets pose a security risk, so they're limited to actions that don't involve storage devices. Another concern involves speed. Java programs aren't as slow as interpreted programs, but they're considerably slower than compiled programs.

An article in InfoWorld cites Java's competition as formidable. It suggests that Java may be losing ground to newer languages, such as Ruby on Rails, PHP, and AJAX, when it comes to developing rich Internet applications. For this reason, it is often recommended that Java programmers learn these languages.

Ruby Ruby is an open-source (free-of-charge) object-oriented programming language. It was released in 1995 and described by its developer, Yukihiro "Matz" Matsumoto, as simple in appearance (see Figure 11.16) but very complex inside, just like the human body. The TIOBE index, which measures the growth of programming languages, ranks Ruby as ninth among programming languages worldwide. Much of the growth is attributed to the popularity of software written in Ruby, particularly Ruby on Rails, a Web

```
# Hello World in Ruby
puts "Hello World!"
```

FIGURE 11.16 Hello World! program written in Ruby.

framework that allows applications that took months to create to be developed in days. Ruby is a pure object-oriented approach in which even primitive data types like numbers are treated as objects.

Visual Basic .NET In 2001, Microsoft introduced **Visual Basic .NET** (**VB .NET**) as the next evolution of VB, moving from an object-based language to an object-oriented language. This news was greeted with a great deal of controversy. Many programmers felt the changes to VB .NET were so significant that it was essentially a different language. Microsoft's refusal to continue supporting VB—at one time considered the world's most popular programming language—disappointed

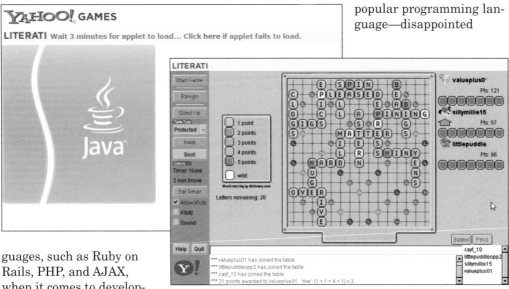

FIGURE 11.15 Some Web-based games need to download a Java applet before they will run.

many developers. VB .NET is used for building powerful applications for Microsoft Windows and for the Web. It competes with Java but has been unable to attain the same market share that VB once held.

Some major trends in program usage are changing the languages of choice and might make some of those languages cited here obsolete in the future. One critical trend is the exploding use of the Internet, where the browser becomes the interface of choice. A second trend is the continuing migration to packaged software starting with the Office Suites, but extending into every corner of work, including software designed for document management and accounting.

Visual Studio .NET Microsoft's answer to Java and JavaScript, **Visual Studio. NET**, is a suite of products that contains Visual Basic .NET, which enables programmers to work with complex objects; Visual C++, which is based on C; and Visual C# (pronounced "C sharp"), which is a .NET aware language for .NET development. C# allows C and C++ coders to use their existing knowledge of C to create .NET applications and services quickly.

The .NET Framework is a software framework that can be installed on computers running Microsoft Windows operating systems. It includes a large library of coded solutions to common programming problems and a virtual machine that manages the execution of programs written specifically for the framework. The .NET Framework is a key Microsoft offering and is intended to be used by most new applications created for the Windows platform.

WEB-BASED LANGUAGES

Strictly speaking, Web-based languages are not considered programming languages. Whereas programming languages tell the computer what to do and how to do it, **Web-based languages** tell a browser how to interpret text and objects. Web-based languages include markup languages and scripting languages.

Markup Languages A **markup language** is a set of codes, or **elements**, used to define the structure of text, such as a title or a heading, that a Web browser reads. Elements are identified by markers, known as **tags**, which usually come in pairs. The actual text to be displayed, known as **content**, is enclosed by an opening and closing tag. By using this method, markup languages indicate to a browser how text or an object is to be rendered on the screen. The following are examples of today's most commonly used markup languages.

To create a Web page, programmers use a markup language called **HTML (Hypertext Markup Language)**. HTML supports links to other documents as well as graphics, audio, and video files. This means that you can jump from one document to another simply by clicking a link. HTML enables hypertext and describes the structure of Web pages. For example, using the b tag (which stands for bold) as follows, This text is bold., will cause this line, when viewed with a Web browser, to produce the following sentence:

This text is bold.

The following illustrates HTML for a level 1 (major) heading, a paragraph of text, and an ordered list, a list whose elements are preceded by numbers as opposed to bullets:

```
<h1> This is the text of a
major heading.</h1>
<p>This is a paragraph of
text. Most browsers display
paragraph text with a blank
line before the paragraph and
flush left alignment.</p>
<ol>This is the line above the
start of the list items. It
will not be numbered.
<li>first item labelled as
1</li>
<li>second item labelled as
2</li>
<li>third item labelled as
3</li></ol>
```

To see how simple it is to create a marked-up document, type a few lines into your word processor and apply bolding or other attributes to different words or phrases. Save the file as a Web page using the "Save as type" feature. Use your Web browser to open the saved file, then right-click the page and choose View Source (for Internet Explorer) or View Page Source (for Firefox) to view the tags that have been added.

A document marked up with HTML contains plain text (ASCII text). When browsers access the document, they read the markup and position the various portions of the document in accordance with the markup language's format settings.

HTML's simplicity is an important reason for the Web's popularity—nearly anyone can learn how to create a simple Web page using HTML. As a result, it's possible for millions of people to contribute content to the Web. In fact, it may be easier than you imagine; Microsoft Word, Excel, and PowerPoint allow you to save documents as Web pages using HTML.

XML (Extensible Markup Language) is a set of rules for creating markup languages that enable programmers to capture specific types of data by creating their own elements. XML is to data what HTML is to text. XML is used for sharing data and complex forms and objects in a Web-based environment. It provides a standardized format that is readable on many different devices, such as PDAs, notebooks, and desktops. A newer version of HTML, **XHTML (eXtensible Hypertext Markup Language)**, uses XML to produce Web pages that are easily accessible by these devices.

Documents created with Microsoft Office 2007 are saved in a file format based on XML standards. Files saved in this new XML format may be up to 75 percent smaller than files saved in the old format.

Here's an example of XML that can be used to define part of a bibliographic citation:

```
<citation><last>Smith</last>
<first>Janet</first><pubdate>
2002</pubdate>
<title>Easy Guide to XML</title>
<publisher>Xdirections
</publisher><place>
Charlottesville,
VA</place></citation>
```

The bibliographic citation tags, such as <last> and <place>, are contained within <citation> tags. An XML-savvy browser doesn't know anything about what these tags mean, but it does know that <last> and <place> (and the other tags) go within the <citation> element. An XML-capable browser, such as Microsoft Internet Explorer (versions 5 and later) and Mozilla Firefox (versions 0.9 and later), can detect the nested structure of XML tags and display the structure in a navigation panel.

What's so great about a browser being able to detect the structure of XML tags? Simple: It means that it's possible for Web authors to invent all the tags they want and still have them displayed in a meaningful fashion. Suddenly, the information presented on a Web page becomes *meaningful*. To understand why this is an advantage, suppose you're running an online art gallery and you're exhibiting and selling works by Tom Smith—a great artist, but one with a very common name. Entering "Tom Smith" in a popular search engine might result in millions of Web pages, however on your Web page, the artist's name is coded with XML as follows: <artist>Smith, Tom (1956–) </artist>. Thanks to XML, people can now search effectively for the very few Tom Smiths who are artists.

Although XML enables anyone to create new tags, efforts are going on in virtually every type of business and profession to develop common XML **vocabularies**, which are sets of elements and tags for a particular field or discipline. For example, architectural associations are developing XML coding schemes for special architectural documents.

XML will be a big part of your computing future as more documents are encoded and placed online. Wireless devices use a specialized form of XML called **WML (Wireless Markup Language)**. This language enables developers to create pages specifically designed for wireless devices.

Standardizing HTML and XHTML and forcing the separation of content from formatting is the responsibility of **World Wide Web Consortium (W3C)**, an international consortium in which member organizations, a full-time staff, and the public work together to develop Web standards. W3C's mission is to lead the World Wide Web to its full potential by developing protocols and guidelines that ensure long-term growth for the Web. Recently the organization has developed an Education Alliance Incubator Group to promote the inclusion of high standards and "best" coding practices in the education of future generations of Web professionals. You can learn more about the W3C at the organization's Web site (**www.w3c.org**).

Scripting Languages **Scripting languages** enable users to quickly create useful **scripts**, simple programs that control any action or feedback on a Web page. A script might control an action that takes place when you roll the mouse over a particular part of a Web page or check the data you enter into a form. In fact, a script isn't compiled; it's interpreted by the Web browser, line by line. **VBScript** and JavaScript are examples of client-side scripting languages; their scripts run on a user's computer. Other scripting languages are server-side scripting languages that manipulate the data, usually in a database, on the server (Figure 11.17).

```
<html>
<body>
<script language="JavaScript"
type="text/javascript">
// Hello World in JavaScript
document.write('Hello World');
</script>
</body>
</html>
```

FIGURE 11.17 The code for the JavaScript Hello World! program is embedded within HTML tags.

ActiveX controls are miniprograms (mainly written in VB) that can be downloaded from Web pages and used to add functionality to Web browsers. However, VBScript and ActiveX controls require users to be running Microsoft Windows and Microsoft Internet Explorer.

Like VBScript, **JavaScript** is a simple, easy-to-learn scripting language designed for writing scripts on Web pages. Despite including "Java" in its name, JavaScript isn't based on Java. Rather, JavaScript was created by Netscape Communications. Although still called JavaScript, it was recently standardized by the European Computer Manufacturers Association (ECMA), and is now properly known as **ECMAScript**.

AJAX, shorthand for asynchronous JavaScript and XML (sometimes written as Ajax), is a group of client-side, interrelated Web development techniques used to create interactive Web applications. AJAX is not a technology in itself, but a term that refers to the use of a group of technologies. AJAX uses a combination of HTML and CSS for marking up and styling information; JavaScript to dynamically display and interact with the information presented; the XMLHttpRequest object to exchange data between the browser and the server; and some common formats such as XML plain text, and JSON. The use of AJAX has led to an increase in interactive animation on Web pages and better quality of Web services.

JSON (short for JavaScript Object Notation), is a text-based, human-readable technique for representing simple data structures and objects. The JSON format is often used for **serialization**, transmitting structured data over a network connection. Its main application is in AJAX Web application programming, where it serves as an alternative to the use of the XML format. Although JSON was based on a subset of the JavaScript programming language and is commonly used with that language, it is considered to be a language-independent data format.

Another very popular scripting language is PHP. **PHP** is a general purpose, server-side, open source, cross-platform scripting language used primarily to make dynamic Web sites. So what is PHP really? PHP is a language located on the server, unlike JavaScript, which is a component of the user's browser; it is open source, unlike ASP or ColdFusion (its competitors), which means it is a free download

over the Internet; it will run on any server running any operating system, and thus it is cross-platform and similar to coding C or C++; and its coding makes pages interactive so the user can manipulate the page content, thus making it dynamic.

Let's take a Web page created with HTML, JavaScript, and PHP and see how it works. When a user opens the page, the HTML and any embedded JavaScript are interpreted by the browser. If PHP is within the page, those instructions are sent to the computer that is hosting the Web page (the server). The server processes the PHP elements and the results are sent back over the Internet. Sound complicated? Well, if you have ever had a Web page display a pop-up box and ask you for data, or filled in a form online and received a Web page back with a personalized thank you after you submitted it, or had a cookie (a small string of text that holds information about the user) placed on your computer, or had a password authenticated, or made an online purchase in which the products were located in an inventory database, then you have encountered the PHP language.

You now know enough about programming methods and languages to appreciate the next section, which covers program development.

The Program Development Life Cycle

At the dawn of the modern computer era, no one thought about managing the software development process. Programs were written for specific, well-defined purposes such as calculating missile trajectories. If a program didn't work, the programmer corrected it. As a result, this approach came to be known as code-and-fix (or "cut-and-run," as detractors put it).

When businesses began using computers for more complex purposes, problems arose. Often, programmers didn't really understand what managers wanted a program to do, and correcting problems became expensive and time-consuming. In addition, programmers didn't document their programs well (if at all), and some developed idiosyncratic programming styles that assured their continued employment because no one else could figure out what their code did! These early programs were almost impossible to maintain (especially if the original programmer left the company).

To address these problems, the program development life cycle was introduced in the 1970s, and it is still in widespread use today. The **program development life cycle (PDLC)** provides an organized plan for breaking down the task of program development into manageable chunks, each of which must be successfully completed before programmers move on to the next phase (Figure 11.18). Let's look at each of these six phases in detail.

PHASE 1: DEFINING THE PROBLEM

The first step in developing a program is to define the problem that the program is to solve. This is the job of systems analysts, who provide the results of their work to programmers in the form of a program specification.

The **program specification**, or spec, precisely defines the input data, the processing that should occur, what the output should look like, and how the user interface should look. Depending on the size of the job, program development might be handled by an individual or by a team of analysts.

PHASE 2: DESIGNING THE PROGRAM

After an analyst has determined the program's specs, the next step is for programmers to create a **program design**—a plan drawn on paper that can be reviewed and discussed until everything's right. The program design specifies the components that make the program work.

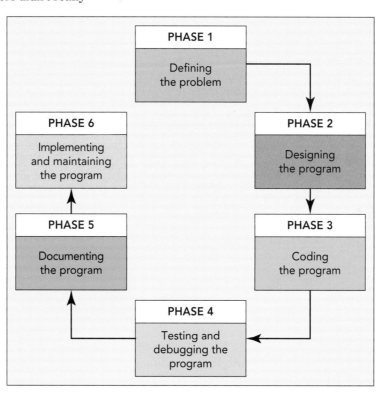

FIGURE 11.18 The program development life cycle has six phases.

Top-Down Program Design Program design begins by focusing on the main goal that the program is trying to achieve and then breaking up the program into manageable components. This approach is called **top-down program design**. The first step involves identifying the main routine. A **routine** (also referred to as a procedure, function, or subroutine) is a section of code that executes a specific task in a program. Multiple routines grouped together are called **modules**; modules grouped together make up programs. After identifying the main routine, programmers try to break down the various components of the main routine into smaller subroutines until each subroutine is highly focused and accomplishes only one major task. Experience shows that this is the best way to ensure program quality. For example, if an error appears in a program designed in this way, it's relatively easy to identify the module causing the error.

Structured Design Within each subroutine, the programmer draws on control structures to envision how the subroutine will do its job. **Control structures** are logical elements grouped in a block with an END statement that specify how the instructions in a program are to be executed. This section discusses the three basic control structures.

In a **sequence control structure**, instructions to the computer are executed, or performed, by the computer in the order, or sequence, in which they appear. Sequence control structures provide the basic building blocks for computer programs. If you can imagine yourself as a computer, here's an example of a sequence of instructions you'd follow to obtain a pizza:

```
Go to the phone.
Dial the pizza place.
Order the pizza.
Hang up.
```

In a **selection control structure** (also called a conditional, or branch, control structure), the program branches to different instructions depending on whether a condition is met. A condition is an expression that compares instructions. Most conditions are based on IF . . . THEN . . . ELSE logic. If a condition is true, one set of instructions is executed. If the condition is not true, a different set of instructions is executed. Here's an example of a selection control structure that includes a *very* important test—making sure you have enough money to order a pizza.

```
Open your wallet.
IF you have enough money,
THEN Go to the phone.
Dial the pizza place.
Order the pizza.
Hang up.
ELSE    Forget the whole thing.
```

A variant of the selection control structure is the case control structure. In a **case control structure**, the condition is fundamental, and each branch leads

to its own lengthy series of instructions. For example, the IRS processes tax returns differently depending on five categories of marital status. A coded field indicates whether the taxpayer is married filing a joint return, married filing separately, single, head of household, or widowed. A case control structure can be used so that the computer can determine which of those five categories a taxpayer belongs to and then use the correct set of instructions to process the return.

In a **repetition control structure** (also called a looping, or iteration, control structure), the program repeats the same instructions over and over. The set of instructions that is repeated is called a loop. The two types of repetition structures are DO-WHILE and DO-UNTIL. In a DO-WHILE structure, the program tests a condition at the beginning of the loop and executes the specified instructions only if the condition is true. The following example illustrates a DO-WHILE structure:

```
DO gobble down pizza,
WHILE there is still more pizza.
```

Note that a DO-WHILE structure doesn't guarantee that the action will be performed even once. If the initial test condition is false, the action doesn't occur. In a DO-UNTIL structure, the program executes the instructions and then tests to see whether a specified condition is true. If not, the loop repeats. Here's a DO-UNTIL structure:

```
DO gobble down pizza,
UNTIL none remains.
```

Developing an Algorithm Control structures are combined to create an algorithm. An **algorithm** is a step-by-step description of how to arrive at a solution. You can think of an algorithm as a recipe or as a how-to sheet. But algorithms aren't restricted to computers. In fact, we use them every day. Most people do long division by following an algorithm. Here's another example: Suppose that you want to determine your car's gas mileage. You probably do this by filling the tank and noting your mileage. The next time you get gas, you note the mileage again, determine the number of miles you drove, and then divide the miles driven by the amount of gas you put in. The result tells you your car's gas mileage, which you generated by using a simple algorithm.

In programming, coming up with an algorithm involves figuring out how to get the desired result by assembling control structures. To get programs to do useful things, programmers use **nesting**, a process of embedding control structures within one another. Here's an example that remedies some of the unhealthy implications of the examples in the previous section:

```
DO check to see whether you're
  still hungry,
  IF you are still hungry,
  THEN gobble down a piece
    of pizza
  ELSE Put the rest in the
    fridge.
WHILE there is still more
  pizza, repeat the loop
  starting with the
  DO statement.
```

Program Design Tools A variety of design tools are available to help programmers develop well-structured programs.

Structure charts (also called **hierarchy charts**) show the top-down design of a program. Each box, or module, in the chart indicates a task that the program must accomplish (Figure 11.19). The top module, called the **control module**, oversees the transfer of control to the other modules.

A **flowchart** is a diagram that shows the logic of a program. Programmers create flowcharts either by hand, using a flowcharting template, or on the computer. Each flowchart symbol has a meaning. A diamond, for example, indicates a condition; a rectangle is used for a process; and a parallelogram indicates an input or output procedure (Figure 11.20). A variation on flowcharting is the **Unified Modeling Language (UML)**, an open method used to illustrate and document the components of an object-oriented software system under development. UML offers a standard way to visualize conceptual components such as business processes, system components and activities, programming language statements, and database schemas.

Visit the SmartDraw Web site at **www.smartdraw.com/specials/ flowchart.asp** to find tutorials for drawing flowcharts as well as examples of professional flowcharts and flowcharting templates that can be downloaded for free.

Pseudocode, which was created in the 1970s as an alternative to flowcharts, is a stylized form of writing used to describe the logic of a program. Pseudocode can't be compiled or executed—it doesn't follow any formatting or syntax rules. Instead, pseudocode enables programmers to focus on basic algorithms without having to worry about the details of a programming language. Programmers are even able to write pseudocode without knowing what programming language they're going to use upon implementation.

PHASE 3: CODING THE PROGRAM

Creating the code involves translating the algorithm into specific programming language instructions. The programming team must choose an appropriate programming language and then create the program by writing the code. The

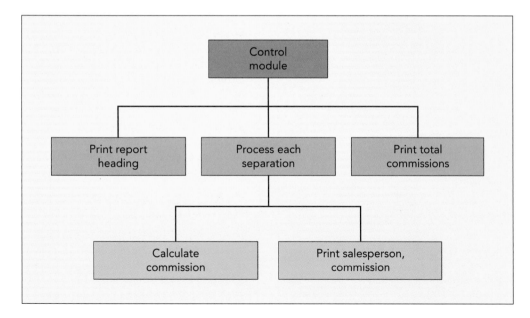

FIGURE 11.19 Each box, or module, in a structure chart indicates a task that the program must accomplish.

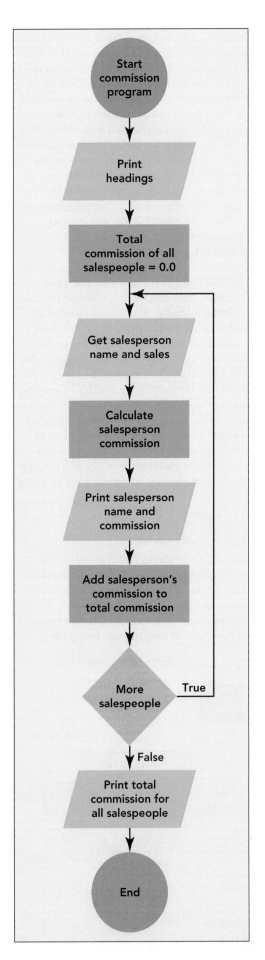

Start commission program

Print headings

Total commission of all salespeople = 0.0

Get salesperson name and sales

Calculate salesperson commission

Print salesperson name and commission

Add salesperson's commission to total commission

More salespeople — True

False

Print total commission for all salespeople

End

programmers must carefully follow the language's rules of syntax, which specify precisely how to express certain operations. For example, different programming languages specify basic arithmetic operations in different ways. Program development tools can check for **syntax errors**, or flaws in the structure of commands, while the program is being written. Syntax errors must be eliminated before the program will run.

PHASE 4: TESTING AND DEBUGGING THE PROGRAM

The fourth step in a programming project is to eliminate all errors. After the syntax errors are eliminated, the program will execute. The output may still not be correct, however, because the language translator can't detect logic errors. A **logic error** is a mistake the programmer made in designing the solution to the problem, for example, telling the computer to calculate net pay by adding deductions to gross pay instead of subtracting them. The programmer must find and correct logic errors by carefully examining the program output. Syntax errors and logic errors are collectively known as **bugs**. The process of eliminating these errors is known as **debugging**.

After the visible logic errors have been eliminated, the programming team must test the program to find hidden errors. However, it's not always possible to examine every outcome for each program condition. Inevitably, some errors will surface only when the program is put into use.

After suffering from a 22-hour outage in 1999, eBay is an example of a company that changed its way of thinking and has established one of the most thorough methods of testing and debugging its software. After the outage, eBay switched from one server and one massive database to a series of 2,500 servers (plus 2,500 backup servers) and 20 databases (plus 6 backups). Any new software feature is tested on one server; if successful, it is expanded to 25 percent of the servers, tested again, and then expanded to all 5,000 servers. As a result, eBay counts only 325 bugs among its 5 million lines of code, a tremendous improvement over the 3,000 bugs it had in 2003.

PHASE 5: DOCUMENTING THE PROGRAM

The job isn't finished until the program is thoroughly documented. This requires writing a manual that provides an overview of the program's functionality, tutorials for beginning users, in-depth

FIGURE 11.21 Users are often encouraged to assist with the documentation process for open source software such as Mozilla Firefox.

explanations of major program features, reference documentation of all program commands, and a thorough description of the error messages generated by the program. These manuals, along with the program design work, are known as **documentation**.

For example, the structure chart and pseudocode or flowchart developed during the design phase become documentation for others who will modify the program in the future. In addition, other documentation should have been created as the program was coded: lists of variable names and definitions, descriptions of files that the program needs to work with, and layouts of output that the program produces. All of this documentation must be gathered and saved for future reference (Figure 11.21).

PHASE 6: IMPLEMENTING AND MAINTAINING THE PROGRAM

All that is left is the sixth and final step: implementation and maintenance. Even if the program has been developed by in-house programmers, the program will still need to be tested by the users. Even the best-written program is useless if the user does not understand how to work with it. What's more, no matter how exhaustively the program was tested, users will discover program errors.

As a result, even after a program is complete, it needs to be maintained and evaluated. Maintenance is by far the most expensive part of the software development process, so good design and documentation are crucial to keep costs in

check. During **program maintenance**, the programming team fixes program errors discovered by users. The team conducts periodic evaluations asking users whether the program is fulfilling its objectives. The evaluation may lead to modifications to update the program or to add features for the users. It may even lead to a decision to abandon the current program and develop a new one, and so the program development life cycle begins anew.

GREEN tech tips

You may be wondering how programmers can help the environment. One way is by creating online documentation materials rather than printed materials. It is estimated that the energy used to create the average software manual creates approximately 6.5 pounds of CO_2 emissions. Another way to be more ecofriendly is to develop well-designed Web sites. Poorly designed sites often generate more network traffic due to frequent requests to the server—each request requires additional power. Creating more efficient Web pages can help reduce power consumption. Taken individually, these may seem like small steps, but they do add up! ●

Chapter Summary

Programming Languages and Program Development

A programming language is an artificial language consisting of a vocabulary and a set of rules used to create instructions for a computer to follow. The earliest (and lowest-level) programming language is machine language, which consists of instructions using binary numbers—0s and 1s. Assembly language is easier to use because the programmer can use symbols to sum up program instructions. High-level languages (third-generation) free the programmer from having to know processor details, but these languages still require the programmer to specify the procedure to be followed to solve the problem. Fourth-generation languages free programmers from having to worry about the problem-solving procedure, but most of these languages, like SQL, are restricted to accessing databases. Natural language and understanding (fifth-generation) is the language of the future.

Languages can be categorized by the design used within their code. Early languages like Basic were called structured and were followed by Fortran and Pascal, which were modular in design. Object-oriented, 3GL programming languages, like C++, Java, Ruby, and the .NET suite, work with prebuilt objects and focus more on encapsulating and hiding data. They also allow for inheritance.

The six phases of the program development life cycle (PDLC) are (1) defining the problem, (2) designing the program, (3) coding the program, (4) testing and debugging the program, (5) documenting the program, and (6) implementing and maintaining the program. The PDLC is needed because earlier ad hoc programming techniques produced software that was riddled with errors and virtually impossible to debug or maintain.

Key Terms and Concepts

Matching

Match each key term in the left column with the most accurate definition in the right column.

_____ 1. compiler

_____ 2. tags

_____ 3. module

_____ 4. routine

_____ 5. pseudocode

_____ 6. flowchart

_____ 7. syntax

_____ 8. inheritance

_____ 9. source code

_____ 10. encapsulation

_____ 11. spaghetti code

_____ 12. interpreter

_____ 13. algorithm

_____ 14. executable program

_____ 15. class

a. An artificial language used as an alternative to flowcharts to describe a program's logic.

b. A program that is ready to run and does not need to be altered in any way.

c. A translation program that executes a program line by line.

d. The capacity of an object to pass on characteristics or properties to a subclass.

e. Code that contains numerous GOTO statements, is difficult to follow, messy in design, and prone to errors.

f. Code markers that come in pairs and identify elements in a markup language like HTML.

g. A step-by-step description for solving a problem.

h. The set of rules governing the structure of instructions, commands, or statements.

i. A diagram that shows the logic of a program.

j. A section of code that executes a specific task in a program.

k. Program instructions in their original form as written by a programmer.

l. A category of objects in object oriented programming.

m. An independently created code component that is combined with others to create a final program.

n. Utility program that translates source code into object code.

o. Information hiding within object-oriented programming.

Multiple Choice

Circle the correct choice for each of the following.

1. Which is the only language a computer understands without having to be translated?
   a. BASIC
   b. Machine language
   c. Ada
   d. Visual Basic .NET

2. Which is a fourth-generation language used to obtain data from a database?
   a. Java
   b. C++
   c. SQL
   d. ActiveX

3. Which is not an Assembly language mnemonic?
   a. JUMP   b. MOV
   c. ADD   d. DIV

4. Eliminating syntax and logical errors occurs during which phase of the PDLC?
   a. Documentation phase
   b. Testing and debugging phase
   c. Implementation phase
   d. Problem definition phase

5. Which is the proper name for the popular scripting language JavaScript?
   a. JScript   b. VBScript
   c. XHTML   d. ECMAScript

6. Which is a Java miniprogram made available over a network?
   a. Applet   b. Module
   c. Class   d. Javabean

7. Which programming language is well suited to scientific, mathematical, and engineering applications?
   a. C++   b. Java
   c. Fortran   d. JavaScript

8. What are brief abbreviations for assembly language program instructions called?
   a. Mnemonics   b. Scripts
   c. Beans   d. Applets

9. What is a simple program that controls an action or feedback on a Web page known as?
   a. Script   b. Syntax
   c. Compiler   d. Element

10. Which language is used to produce Web pages that can be read on many different types of devices, including mobile devices?
    a. ECMAScript   b. Visual Studio .NET
    c. Visual C#   d. XHTML

Fill-In

In the blanks provided, write the correct answer for each of the following.

1. Syntax errors and logic errors are known as _____.

2. _____ is an open source, object-oriented language recently ranked as the ninth most popular programming language.

3. The most expensive part of software development is _____ _____.

4. _____ is a group of software development methodologies based on an iterative project management process that aligns development with customer needs.

5. _____ _____ _____ is a program development method that involves the end user in the planning stage.

6. The construction of a program through the use of a library of prebuilt objects is called _____ _____ _____.

7. The _____ _____ _____ _____ is an international organization working to develop Web standards.

8. _____ _____ is an example of an event-driven programming language that enables a programmer to design a graphical user interface.

9. _____ _____ _____ is a language that enables developers to create Web pages for wireless devices.

10. IF-THEN-ELSE is an example of a _____ control structure.

11. Report generators and query languages are examples of _____ languages.

12. _____ is the collection of all recorded design, development, and production information pertinent to a programming project's completion.

13. _____ is a cross-platform programming language capable of running on many different types of computers with different operating systems.

14. A program will fail to compile due to _____ errors.

15. DO-WHILE and DO-UNTIL are examples of _____ control structures.

Short Answer

1. State two ways that the first and second generation of programming languages are similar.

2. List and explain the six phases of the PDLC.

3. What are the two developments in the programming and computer usage that might lead to the demise of the currently popular Java?

4. Explain the difference between syntax errors and logic errors. Identify the errors below as either a syntax or logical error.

- Calculating the average of four numbers by adding the four numbers and dividing by three
- Missing a semicolon at the end of a programming line of code
- Missing a set of parenthesis

- Figuring out the total cost of an item including an 8 percent sales tax by multiplying the cost of the item by 0.08
- Misspelling a keyword in a program like print as pint or move as mov

5. The translation of a high-level program to a machine language is done by applications known as compilers and interpreters. Distinguish between a compiler and an interpreter. Give an example of a compiled language and an interpreted language.

Teamwork

1. **Documentation** Your team is to research the documentation practices followed by computer programmers and then answer the following questions. Documentation is created primarily for what two groups? Describe the types of documentation that would be supplied to each group. What constitutes good documentation? (*Hint:* Do a Web search on "documentation practices.") Write a one-page paper that answers these questions. Be sure to cite your sources.

2. **Programming Courses** Does your school have a computer science (CS), computer information systems (CIS), or management information systems (MIS) department? If so, look at a school catalog to see what programming language is covered in the beginning programming courses. If a language is not specified in the course catalog, then contact the department directly to find out. What are the prerequisites, if any, for the programming courses? Are additional computer languages taught in subsequent courses? What additional languages are taught? Prepare a group presentation based on your findings.

3. **Classes and Inheritance** Using the example in the text of the BIKES superclass and RACING-BIKES subclass (or create your own original superclass and subclass), define two additional subclasses of the BIKES class, one for dirt bikes and another for recreational bikes (or any category of bikes your team agrees on). You do not have to

define the subclasses in actual programming code. You can use natural language or a drawing. Represent your two new classes in any way you choose, then state the class names, their specific features, and the methods that apply to that class. Submit the original BIKES and RACINGBIKES class definitions from this chapter with the two additional subclasses created by your group.

4. **Algorithms** Algorithms are not used just for writing programs. They also can be used to describe processes. As a team, design an algorithm that lists the correct steps to change a light bulb in a ceiling fixture. Include at least one selection control structure, either branch or conditional. Create a flowchart to show the logical flow of your process. Submit both your algorithm and flowchart.

5. **A BASIC Program** Just as it is easier to read a report than it is to write one, it is easier to read a program than it is to write one. One of the simplest computer languages is BASIC. As a team, write a report that explains the purpose of the three lines of code that follow. Why was it necessary to divide by 3? If the input is 80, 70, 90, what is the resulting output? Are the parentheses necessary in the formula? Explain why they are or are not needed.

Input Grade1, Grade2, Grade3, Average

Average = (Grade1 + Grade2 + Grade3) / 3

Print Average

On the Web

1. **Learning Programming Languages** Being a programmer requires learning new languages as the times and programming needs change. Most programmers learn these new languages by returning to school, taking seminars, attending workshops, or by reading and experimenting themselves. Using a

search engine and the Web, locate sites that help or give pointers on the best ways to learn new programming languages. After your research is complete, compose a list of what you consider to be the best five strategies.

2. **Hello World!** Using a search engine, locate Web sites that show the code that displays the words "Hello World!" on a computer screen in several programming languages. Locate the programming code for this display in seven different languages of your choice. Include the name of the language, the actual code, and which language you consider the easiest to read, the hardest to read, and which languages look similar. Cite reasons for your choices. Present, in a double-spaced paper, your seven code examples and responses to the questions above.

3. **Looking for Alice** Visit the Web site for Alice (**www.alice.org**), a 3D authoring system first developed by the Stage 3 Research Group at Carnegie Mellon University with the goal to "provide the best possible first exposure to programming for students ranging from middle school to college." From the menu at the top of the homepage click the "About Alice" link and the sublink "What is Alice?" Read the description of this program and watch the videos. Use the other navigation links to obtain more information. In a one-page, double-spaced paper, provide a description of the Alice program, its features and uses. See whether any schools in your state are using Alice.

4. **Discovering Mathematica** Mathematica is a relatively new programming language that was briefly mentioned in the text. Visit the Web site **www.wolfram.com/products/mathematica/history.html** to answer the following questions. What company produces Mathematica? On which platforms does it run? How much does it cost? Is Mathematica used in any of your school's mathematics classes? If so, identify the course in which it is used. Have you taken one of these courses and used Mathematica?

5. **Creating a Web Page with HTML and Notepad** You can make a Web page using Word. All you have to do is open Word, enter your content, and use the File > Save As a Web Page option from the Menu or Save As dialog box. Open Word and create a simple Web page using this method. In the document that will become a Web page, include your name, course number, and instructor's name as content. Add some formatting, perhaps bold a few words, underline others, and maybe make a few words a different color. When you open the file in a browser, look at the HTML code that Word created for you by using the View > Source option from the menu in the browser's window. You will be surprised at the amount of code generated by Word for such a simple page. Print this source code.

Now, using a search engine, enter "basic html page" and locate a Web site that displays the code for a basic HTML page. Open Notepad (from the Start menu, select All Programs, then the Accessories folder, and finally Notepad) and using the Web site you located as a guide, enter the HTML tags and your own content between the tags to create another simple HTML page in Notepad. Save this page from Notepad with the html file extension. Open the page in a browser and again view the source code by using the View > Source option from the menu in the browser's window. Print this code. It should look the same as what you entered in Notepad. Notice, it has a lot less code than the page created with Word. Can you think of any reasons for the different amount of code? Turn in both printouts and your reasons for the difference in code.

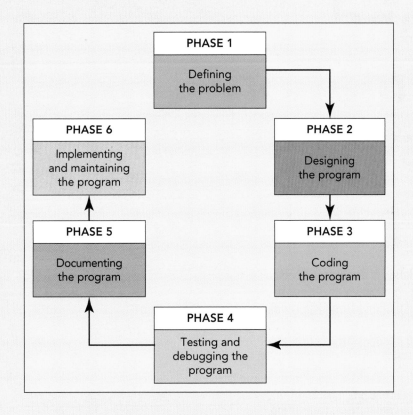

chapter 12

Databases and Information Systems

Wake up, check banking account balance, log in to the college or university and check any assignments or recent postings from professors, verify season ticket renewal for local theater production company, and make an appointment for six-month check up with physician. Does this sound like your normal or seminormal daily routine? Within one regular day, have you ever thought about the number of databases in which your name and personal data reside? How is the information in them secured? How is the information retrieved and accessed so quickly? How is a collection of the information from the many entries in these databases used to provide information to the host company or organization so that it can study trends— and make decisions based on those trends?

Data refers to unorganized text, graphics, sound, or video. Information is data that has been processed and organized in a way that people find meaningful and useful. But information isn't useful if it is overwhelming, difficult to sift through, or tedious to interpret. Databases and database management programs are used to cut the amount of information down to a more manageable size so that people can cope with it more efficiently.

You can use databases and database management software to input, edit, sort, organize, and store data and turn it into information. Computer users set up personal databases to organize music libraries, names and addresses of friends and relatives, research notes, and more. Databases are typically a main component of the overall set of systems used to coordinate, monitor, and interrelate the components of an organization. Information systems make information manageable. In businesses, they work to assemble key information for employees, managers, executives, and customers. An example of one such system is the program developed by OpenTable.com (**www.opentable.com**). The company's software helps restaurant owners and managers book reservations, manage staff, and track customer orders. Other areas such as law enforcement, university research centers, government agencies, and even religious groups find information systems, and the programs that are incorporated into them, invaluable to their operation. Other examples of information systems that you might personally use include library reference systems, ATMs, and airline reservations systems.

As you'll learn in this chapter, information systems and the programs that they incorporate are essential in today's fast-paced, wired world. Many of your daily activities—from grocery shopping, to renewing your driver's license, to registering for classes—are supported by information systems that include databases and database programs. They can even save lives. The field of traffic safety provides useful examples of the benefits of detailed data collection systems. Since 1975, the National Highway Traffic Safety Administration has collected details on fatal motor vehicle crashes in all 50 states through the Fatality Analysis

Reporting System (FARS). Policymakers and others have used these findings to assess the impact of specific interventions—from child restraint laws to anti-drunk driving campaigns—and to develop policies that make our roads safer. Those policies have contributed to a dramatic decline in the rate of motor vehicle-related fatalities over the past 25 years.

Learning about information systems and database concepts is a prerequisite for understanding the importance of managing data and information in businesses and society. In almost everything you do—making online reservations, performing Internet searches, or completing a project at work or school—you will encounter information system strategies and the databases they use (Figure 12.1).

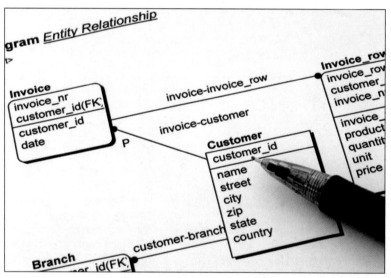

FIGURE 12.1 Understanding database and information systems concepts is a must for many careers and in daily life in this digital world. Before we can understand the true impact of databases on our lives, we need to understand exactly what a database is and how data is organized within it.

The Levels of Data in a Database

A **database** is a collection of related data that is organized in a manner that makes it easy to access, manage, update, group, and summarize. In a database, data is constructed from the bottom up, like the layers of a cake (Figure 12.2). At the lowest level, or layer, is the **bit**, a 1 or a 0, which is the smallest unit of data that the computer can store and understand. The next level up, the smallest unit of data that an individual can work with, is made up of bytes that represent **characters**, including letters, numbers, and special symbols produced by keyboard keys or key combinations. When

FIGURE 12.2 The Levels, or Layers, of Data in a Database

Bit	0 or 1
Character	8 bits (the letter *M* = 01001101)
Field	A unit of relative information of a specific data type
Record	All the combined fields about a person, place, thing, or event
Data file (or table)	A collection of records
Database	One or more data files

you enter characters, the computer translates them into bits. For example, the letter *M* or the number *4* represents the character level of the database. (*M* in a particular binary code is represented by the bit string 01001101; *4* is represented by 00110100.)

The next layer in this development is a field. In a database, a **field** is single unit of relative information; it must be of a specific defined **data type**. In a computerized database, data types are defined by the overall purpose of the database coupled with the specific data being entered. Common data types include text, numbers, currency, and dates. One data type called **Yes/No**, **Logical**, or **Boolean**, depending on the program, allows a yes or no, true or false, or 1 or 0 value. The **memo** data type is used for large units of text, while the **object** data type is used for nontextual data. Examples of objects include pictures, sounds, and videos. Modern databases include a data type for very large objects up to several gigabytes in size, such as an entire spreadsheet file or a picture file, called a **BLOB**, or **binary large object**.

Except for fields containing memo and object data types, each field has a specified field size. For example, a field for U.S. states (such as Minnesota) would have a text data type and a field size of two characters (such as MN). Field size along with format, input mask, caption, default value, and validation rule are the field properties. These properties are set and changed by the database creator or user and are based on the specific data to be entered into a field.

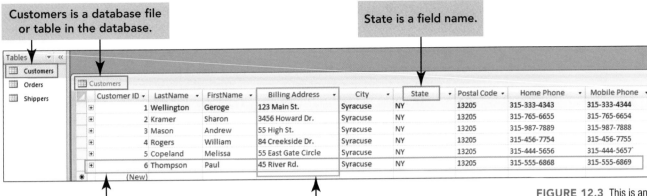

Customers is a database file or table in the database.

State is a field name.

Customer ID	LastName	FirstName	Billing Address	City	State	Postal Code	Home Phone	Mobile Phone
1	Wellington	Geroge	123 Main St.	Syracuse	NY	13205	315-333-4343	315-333-4344
2	Kramer	Sharon	3456 Howard Dr.	Syracuse	NY	13205	315-765-6655	315-765-6654
3	Mason	Andrew	55 High St.	Syracuse	NY	13205	315-987-7889	315-987-7888
4	Rogers	William	84 Creekside Dr.	Syracuse	NY	13205	315-456-7754	315-456-7755
5	Copeland	Melissa	55 East Gate Circle	Syracuse	NY	13205	315-444-5656	315-444-5657
6	Thompson	Paul	45 River Rd.	Syracuse	NY	13205	315-555-6868	315-555-6869

A row containing all the information on one customer is a record.

The column BillingAddress is one field in the database.

FIGURE 12.3 This is an example of a table containing several records similar to information found in a customer database.

Each field has a name, called a **field name**, a descriptive label that helps identify the type of content to be entered into a field. Fields contain items that are all of the same type. For example, in a database of customers, a field named "Credit Limit" would have a data type of currency and hold the maximum credit limit allowed for each customer. Some fields have a **default value** specified in their properties, which is an automatic entry placed into a field when no other value is provided. For a credit limit field, that default value might be $100.00. So if no other value were entered for the credit limit of a customer, then $100.00 would be entered by default.

The next level up from a field is a **record**, which contains a group of one or more related fields. In a database of customer information, a record would be the group of all fields containing information on one customer. A typical customer record might include a customer ID number, the last name of the customer, the first name of the customer, billing address, city, state, zip code, home phone, and mobile phone (Figure 12.3).

Within a record, one of the fields is identified as the **primary key** (also called the **key field**). This field contains a code, a number, a name, or some other piece of information that uniquely identifies the record. In other words, no two records can have the same value or information in the primary key. In your school record, for example, chances are you're identified by your student identification number. When you register for courses or request transcripts, you must supply this number so that the registrar's computer system can find your data. Your student identification number would be the unique value in the

primary key field in your school record. In the customer example, the Customer ID is the unique value in the primary key field for each customer's record.

Near the top of the layers in a database is the data file. A database consists of one or more related data files. A **data file**, also called a **table**, is a collection of related records. In the customer database, in order to keep the information grouped in a meaningful way, there are three tables, Customers, Orders, and Shippers. To summarize, as shown in Figure 12.4, the database (file cabinet) contains data files (tables) made up of records (customers) organized into fields (CompanyID, CompanyName, LastName, and so on).

Now that you understand the levels that make up a database, let's look at some of the programs you can use to create one.

FIGURE 12.4 A database consists of one or more data files. A data file is made up of records, and within a record, information is organized into distinct fields.

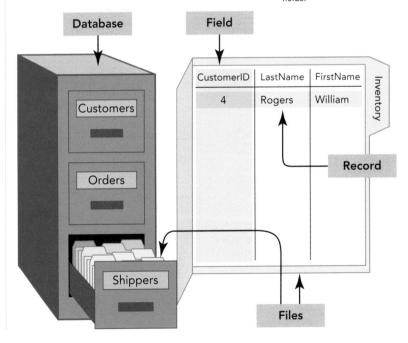

Types of Database Programs

Database programs are software applications that are used to create databases or to work with the data in existing databases. Two types of database programs enable you to create or work with database files: file management programs and database management systems.

FILE MANAGEMENT PROGRAMS

A **file management program** enables users to create, edit, and manage databases in which files or tables are independent of each other, with no link between the data stored in each. A **flat file** refers to the type of file generated by a file management program. Flat files, sometimes called lists, are independent structures. That means that there is no relation between fields in one flat file and fields in another. Examples of flat files include a list of addresses, appointments, or items, such as favorite music CDs or books. Flat-file databases can be accessed randomly to retrieve a specific record or sorted so that the records can be accessed sequentially in a different order. You can create a flat-file database with Microsoft Excel or any other spreadsheet program.

File management programs come in handy when an individual or small business needs to set up a simple computerized information storage and retrieval system. The owner of a baseball card store, for example, could create a flat-file database of available baseball cards for customer reference. This simple database would consist of one file, or table, containing all of the information related to the available baseball cards. The file would contain a record for each baseball card, including fields for player name, teams played for, and statistics concerning that player.

Because file management programs are less complex than database management systems, they're also less expensive and easier to use. The ease of use comes at a price, though. The data stored in a flat-file database cannot be joined with or related to data in another flat file. For example, if that same baseball card store owner had another database that contained information on customers, the data in the baseball card file and the data in the customer file would be independent data with no relation or connection between any of the data in the two tables.

DATABASE MANAGEMENT SYSTEMS

In contrast to file management programs, which manage only a single flat file at a time, a **database management system (DBMS)** is a database program that can join or connect several files or tables to manage, access, store, and edit data in a structured manner. DBMSs come in many types and sizes, from smaller programs for PCs to very large programs for mainframes. DBMSs aren't usually platform specific, but some are. For example, popular DBMSs for PCs include Microsoft Access and MySQL. A popular DBMS for Macs is FileMaker Pro, which also runs on Microsoft Windows. See the list of popular database management systems in Figure 12.5. View a video on Alpha Five, an easy-to-use relational database management system designed by Alpha Software at **http://databases. about.com/b/2007/07/19/creating-a-database-with-alpha-five.htm**. The software received the Computer Reseller News Database of the Year and *PC Magazine*'s Editors' Choice awards.

Information from a database can be presented in many different formats,

FIGURE 12.5 Popular Database Management System Software

Software	Company
Access 2007	Microsoft
DB2	IBM
FileMaker Pro	FileMaker, Inc.
MySQL	Open source
Oracle Database 11g	Oracle, Inc.
Paradox	Corel
R:BASE 7.6	R:BASE Technologies, Inc.
SQL Server 2008	Microsoft
Visual FoxPro	Microsoft

including reports, graphs, or charts. DBMSs enable a user to create these items, with little effort, through the use of built-in components, referred to as wizards. A wizard acts like an assistant guiding a user through the steps toward the final creation. DBMSs are categorized as flat, relational, hierarchical, network, and object-oriented based on the way they organize information internally. Using a DBMS to organizing data in a database in flat form, with disconnected and unlinked files, is treating the management system like a file management program and not using it to its true capacity. The most widely used type of DBMS is called a relational database management system (RDBMS). Microsoft Access is a popular RDBMS for casual users, whereas Oracle has the largest market share for business database applications.

In a **relational database management system (RDBMS)**, data in several files is related by a common primary key. The RDBMS uses the primary key field as an index to locate records without having to read all the records in the files, and to make connections between files. This connection is often made between a primary and a foreign key. As mentioned earlier, in the customer example the Customer ID is the unique value in the primary key field for each record in the Customers table. The Orders table also contains a Customer ID; however, in the Orders table it is a **foreign key** field, a field that is a primary key in another file.

A relational database is best envisioned as a collection of two-dimensional tables, where each table corresponds to a data file. Each row in the table corresponds to a record, and each column corresponds to a field. A relational database structure can link a Customers table and an Orders table, for example, by a common field, such as Customer ID (Figure 12.6). To keep track of the tables that make up the database, the DBMS uses a data dictionary. The **data dictionary** holds a list of the tables the database contains along with details concerning each table, including field names, field lengths, data types, and validation settings.

An RDBMS is usually more expensive and more difficult to learn than a file management program. What's the advantage of using a relational DBMS instead of a file management program? Before DBMS software came along, it was not unusual for companies to have dozens of database files with incompatible formats. Because some of the same data appeared in different files, data would be typed into the database in two or more places, which multiplied the possibility for errors. With relational database programs, it's possible to design the database using two or more tables so that data duplication is eliminated.

Hierarchical database management systems organize data in the shape of a pyramid, with each row of data items linked to items directly beneath it, creating a pyramid or parent/child type of alignment. An example of this arrangement is the connection between an employee and data on his or her children. The employee data represents the parent segment and the children data represents the

FIGURE 12.6 In this Microsoft Access database, three tables are related by common fields.

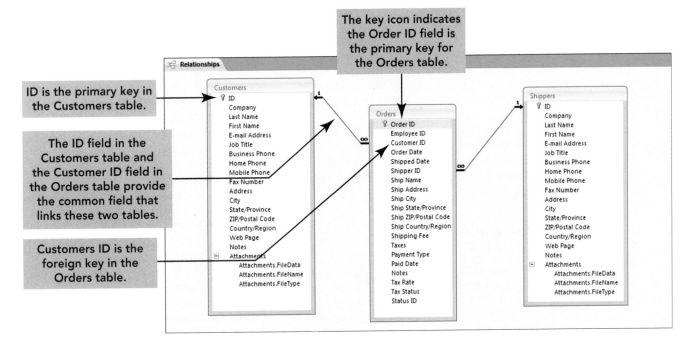

The key icon indicates the Order ID field is the primary key for the Orders table.

ID is the primary key in the Customers table.

The ID field in the Customers table and the Customer ID field in the Orders table provide the common field that links these two tables.

Customers ID is the foreign key in the Orders table.

child segment. If an employee has three children, then there would be three child segments associated with one employee segment. In a hierarchical database, the parent/child relationship is one parent to many children. This organization was popular from the 1960s through the 1970s.

During this time period, **network database management systems** were also in use. This software makes use of the mathematical concept of sets and allows for each record to have multiple parent and child records, forming a lattice structure. This database management system was replaced by the currently popular relational database structure.

Object-oriented database management systems (ODBMS) are the newest type of database structure and are well suited for multimedia applications in which data is represented as objects. In an object-oriented database, the result of a retrieval operation is an object of some kind, such as a document. Within this object are miniprograms that enable the object to perform tasks, such as display a graphic. Object-oriented databases can incorporate sound, video, text, and graphics into a single database record, making them suitable for supporting such applications as financial portfolio risk analysis, design and manufacturing systems, and hospital patient record systems. The Federal Aviation Bureau uses an object-oriented database to simulate passenger and baggage traffic, and the French National Center for Space Studies uses one as a multimedia database to model complex and integrated aircraft systems.

Now that you know about the basic types of database programs and management systems, let's look more closely at some advanced database programs and applications.

DATA WAREHOUSES AND DATA MINING

In large corporations, a trend has emerged toward ever-larger databases called **data warehouses**, a central location capable of storing all the information that a corporation possesses and making this data available for analysis. These data warehouses can contain more than 1 petabyte, or a million gigabytes, of data and are typically the result of combining several smaller databases from different areas within an organization.

The collection of data in data warehouses helps managers make decisions by representing what business conditions look like at a particular point in time. Using a technique called **drill down**, managers are able to view information in a data warehouse and focus their attention on a specific data element. They accomplish this by starting at the summary level of information and narrowing their search at each progressive level of data (department, region, office, individual employee). Smaller-scale data warehouse projects that support one division rather than the entire organization are called **data marts**.

The payoff from data warehouses can be huge. Fraudulent returns cost retailers an estimated $16 billion annually. The Canadian retailer Hudson's Bay Company (Hbc) stores more than 10 terabytes of data in its data warehouse. This allows Hbc to update sales, returns, voids, and exchanges almost instantaneously, making it almost impossible for someone to return merchandise illegally. Hbc saved $26,000 in the first week this fraud control system was implemented and more than $2 million in the first year.

For more information on data warehousing, including articles and new developments, see The Data Warehousing Institute (TDWI) Web site at **www.tdwi .org**. You can read articles on such topics as data mining and business intelligence in *DM Review*, an online magazine, at **www.dmreview.com**.

Using a data exploration and analysis technique called **data mining**, managers can explore data in an attempt to discover previously unknown patterns (Figure 12.7). The resulting information can be used to increase revenue, cut costs, or both. Data mining uncovers information through statistical analysis and modeling, and its results help managers better understand their customers and market and predict

> "Data mining uncovers information through statistical analysis and modeling, and its results help managers better understand their customers and market and predict future trends."

future trends. Retail leader Wal-Mart takes full advantage of data mining. Its 136,000 point-of-sale (POS) terminals worldwide and its Web site send the data warehouse precise records of what each day's 200 million customers have purchased, at what price, where, and when. Wal-Mart then slices and dices the data to turn up nuggets of information. Wal-Mart's data warehouse was designed with no particular purpose in mind, but that's the point: Data warehouses are intended to support data mining's exploration and discovery of data patterns that aren't obvious even to experienced managers and executives.

Another company that uses data mining is Delta Air Lines. In the past, Delta had difficulty making sense of all the data it had collected. Because Delta's old data was not housed in one central database, it used to take days or weeks for users to get answers to information requests. Now, with the help of technologies and solutions supplied by Teradata, a hardware and software vendor specializing in data warehousing and analytic applications, businesses and organizations can get more specific and accurate results in just minutes.

Data mining can be used in other sectors besides the business world. The Pentagon's Total Information Awareness program was a massive data mining project designed to identify terrorists and protect against terrorist acts. Developed as a surveillance system that would link a number of different databases storing public and private information, it met with high levels of opposition because of privacy issues and was deactivated by Congress in 2003.

CLIENT/SERVER DATABASE SYSTEMS

Database server software runs on a LAN and responds to remote users' requests for information. Database server software is difficult to use because users never interact with the database server software directly. To access the data in the server database, users run a database client program, a user-friendly program that enables them to add data to the database, maintain existing records, perform queries, and generate reports. Because these database systems draw a distinction between the database server and client, they are often called **client/server database systems**. Many users—hundreds or even thousands—can access the database simultaneously. The front end of the

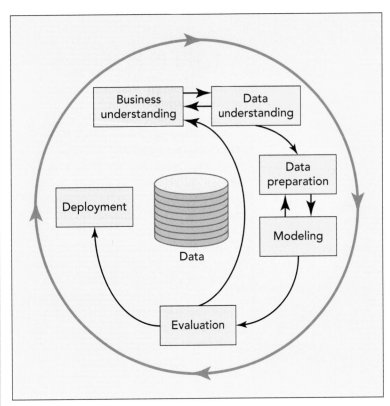

database server software consists of the part of the program that the user manipulates. The back end of the software refers to the server and program code. You probably work with the front end of database server software fairly often, for example, whenever you use an ATM or use a computer for online banking. Examples of database server software include the market-leading Oracle from Oracle Corporation, DB2 from IBM, and SQL Server from Microsoft. A Web site that focuses on server software is **www.serverfiles.com**. The site is a hardware directory for network administrators and IT professionals and does not focus on single-user software.

To request information from a client/server database, remote users formulate the request as a query. A **query** is a specially phrased question used to locate data in a database. A college administrator using a client program might query your school's database to provide the names and addresses of students with junior standing who have a GPA greater than 3.5. A query language uses distinct rules to build a query.

Many DBMSs rely on the query language SQL (Structured Query Language) to request data in a way that the server can understand. SQL isn't difficult to learn. However, most users prefer to use client software that provides more user-friendly tools for constructing SQL

FIGURE 12.7 The CRISP-DM (CRoss Industry Standard Process for Data Mining) diagram provides an overview of the life cycle of a data mining project.

queries. One such client is Microsoft Access. With Access, you can build queries by inserting fields and conditions into a table, which are transformed into SQL queries that can be sent to a database server and applied to the database.

THE INTERNET CONNECTION: GOING PUBLIC WITH DATA

The latest trend in database software is **Web-database integration**, a name for techniques that make information stored in databases available through Internet connections. Web-database integration enables UPS customers to access shipping information through the UPS Web site (Figure 12.8). You don't have to learn SQL or any other query language to use this or similar sites. The Web server uses a form to accept your input and translates it into a query that is then sent to the database. The database responds with the requested information, and the server generates a new Web page on the fly that contains the information you've requested.

Web databases are everywhere—and whether you know it or not, you use them every day. Search engines such as Google and Yahoo! use large database systems to store all of the information they collect about the Web. When you search the Web, you are actually making use of Web-based integration software to search the huge database of information that has been collected and stored by the company providing the Web-searching service. If a Web page has not been cataloged in a search engine's database, it will not appear in your search results. Search engines are reluctant to reveal the exact number of sites they index, but experts estimate at least 30 billion Web pages are available on the Internet. Even though Google's database does not contain every page on the Web, the company catalogs more Web pages than any other search engine.

You can use many online databases to explore topics ranging from obscure computer terminology to pop culture. If you love movies, you may already know

FIGURE 12.8 The UPS Web site's tracking system uses Web-database integration to track a shipment from pickup to delivery. All the customer has to do is enter the label/receipt tracking number and hit *Go*.

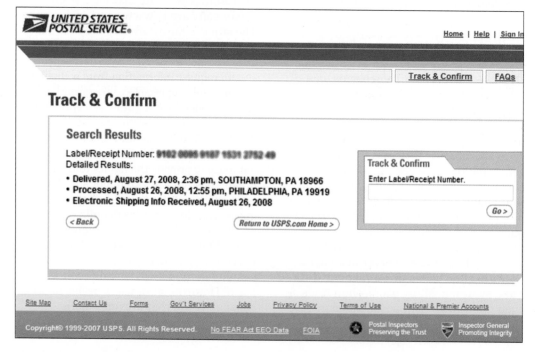

FIGURE 12.9 The Web has many databases, such as Wikipedia, that you can use to explore topics ranging from technical terminology to pop culture.

about the Internet Movie Database (IMDB) at **www.imdb.com**. Do you want to know all of the movies and television appearances that your favorite star has made? Will there be more *Star Wars* movies? Who did the special effects for *The Matrix*? The IMDB has more information about television shows and movies than you can imagine, including cast and crew listings, plot summaries, ratings, dates, interesting tidbits, and user comments.

If movies aren't your thing, take a look at **www.wikipedia.org** (Figure 12.9). Wikipedia claims to be "a free content encyclopedia being written collaboratively by contributors from all around the world." As of this writing, Wikipedia contains approximately 10 million articles in more than 250 languages. You can use Wikipedia as you would any traditional encyclopedia, with the exception that you can add new articles as well as correct inaccuracies in articles you find during your research. The site allows any Web user to edit articles by clicking the "Edit this page" link that appears at the top of each page. In the constantly evolving Wikipedia, you won't find an article that discusses how humans may someday walk on the moon. The down side of this constant updating by multiple sources is that Wikipedia should not be used as an authoritative source for academic research and may contain inaccuracies and self-serving content.

Web-database integration is a key factor in the success of online retailers such as Amazon. Amazon's catalog includes millions of new and used products that are made available to customers through Web servers linked to Amazon's databases. Amazon's Web-database integration capabilities have become so successful that they now offer database storage and solutions, such as Amazon SimpleDB, to a number of companies, including photo-sharing site SmugMug, blog-hosting site WordPress, and social networking site Facebook.

Employees with knowledge of Web-database integration skills are in high demand. Such skills include knowing how to configure and maintain a Web server such

Web-database integration is a powerful technological advancement. One of the benefits of such integration is the ability to pay bills online. Not only is it easier and safer, but eliminating all that paper also saves trees, fuel, and water.

A recent study indicates that if all U.S. households received and paid their bills online, we'd save 16.5 million trees each year, reduce solid waste by 1.6 billion pounds, and reduce carbon emissions by 3.9 billion tons—the equivalent of removing more than 355,000 cars from the roads for a year.

Consider joining the growing number of people who have taken advantage of Web-database integration and have, in the process, helped save our environment. ●

as Apache (the market leader) or Microsoft's Internet Information Services (IIS); knowing how to write scripts that tell the server how to interact with the database software; and knowing how to design and maintain the database.

If you would like to learn more about databases, you may want to download and explore some of the free open source DBMSs such as MySQL (**www.mysql.com**) or PostgreSQL (**www.postgresql.com**). Both Web sites provide you with the necessary information to get started. Books on both of these database management systems are also available at most bookstores. You can also find details about getting certified as a DBA in either Oracle or Microsoft SQL Server by visiting their respective Web sites at **www.oracle.com/education/chooser/selectcountry_new.html** and **www.microsoft.com/learning/mcp**.

You're now familiar with database programs and applications that you might encounter in the real world. Let's take a look at the benefits of using DBMSs and the qualities of a well-built database.

Advantages of Database Management Systems

A DBMS helps people work with all aspects of data in a database. But a database wouldn't be of much use if it contained errors or made confidential data available to people who weren't authorized to access it. In this section, you'll learn the advantages of DBMSs and five characteristics of quality databases (Figure 12.10).

DATA INTEGRITY

Data integrity refers to the validity of the data contained in a database. Data integrity can be compromised in many ways, including typing errors during input, hardware malfunctions, and data transmission errors. To avoid data integrity errors (such as typing mistakes), database programs use **data validation** procedures, which define acceptable input ranges for each field in a record. If the user tries to input data that is out of this range, an error message is displayed.

Database programs use several different types of data validation (Figure 12.11). An **alphabetic check** ensures that only alphabetic data (the letters of the alphabet) are entered into a field, for instance, state abbreviations. Similarly, a **numeric check** ensures that only numbers are entered. A **range check** verifies that the entered data falls within an acceptable range. For example, a U.S. ZIP code must not exceed 99999 (or 99999-9999). A **consistency check** examines the data typed into two different fields to determine identical entries. For example, a Web page that asks you to create a user name and a password for yourself typically asks you to type your password twice. If there is a discrepancy between the two typed passwords, you will be asked to type them again. This ensures that you've typed the password

FIGURE 12.10 The Five Characteristics of a Good Database	
Characteristic	Result
Data integrity	Ensures data is valid.
Data independence	Input data is kept separate from program data.
Avoiding data redundancy	Data is only entered one time.
Data security	Data is not accessible to unauthorized users.
Data maintenance	Set procedures for adding, updating, and deleting records are in place.

correctly. A **completeness check** determines whether a required field has been left empty. If it has, the database program prompts the user to fill in the needed data.

DATA INDEPENDENCE

Data independence means that the data is separate from the applications, and changes in data do not require changes in the structure of forms, reports, or programs accessing the database. If a user changes data in an Access database, data independence makes further changes to any other applications within the program unnecessary. In older database programs, the database and the applications that access the database were

adds to the overall size of the database. Will the data be typed the same way twice? If the data is entered differently, some of it will be unavailable upon retrieval. Data redundancy can be avoided by proper database design.

DATA SECURITY

Data security means that the data stored in a database shouldn't be accessible to people who might misuse it, particularly when the collected data is sensitive. Sensitive data includes personal data such as medical records and data about an organization's finances. Protection can be as simple as a password locking the database or setting permissions for users on a network to prohibit access by unauthorized individuals. Creating an audit

FIGURE 12.11 Data Validation Techniques

Technique	Result
Alphabetic check	Ensures that a field contains only letters of the alphabet.
Numeric check	Ensures that a field contains only numbers.
Range check	Verifies that entered data falls within a certain range.
Consistency check	Determines whether incorrect data has been entered.
Completeness check	Determines whether a required field has been left empty.

closely connected, so any changes to data in the database required changing the program's code. DBMSs with data independence are much more flexible, allow other programs to access data, and make it easier to modify data.

AVOIDING DATA REDUNDANCY

Data should be entered once—and only once. **Data redundancy** (repetition of data) is a characteristic of poorly designed systems and can cause peculiar query and report results. For example, in many companies customer names and addresses may appear in two different, unrelated databases. This not only doubles the amount of work needed to update the customer's records if the customer moves, it increases the chance of an error and

trail, a report of who accesses what data on a system, is an additional security measure. Audit trails help with maintaining security and recovering lost transactions. Most accounting systems and database management systems include an audit trail component. Besides monitoring who accesses the database, it is equally important to protect against the loss of data due to equipment failure or power outages. Regular backup procedures are needed so that data can be restored after an equipment failure.

DATA MAINTENANCE

Good database management also involves having a system in place for data maintenance. **Data maintenance** includes procedures for adding, updating, and deleting records for the purpose of keeping the database in optimal shape. Always create a backup copy of the database before performing maintenance and be particularly careful when deleting an entire field. Field referencing, especially fields that have been designated as primary keys, is an integral part of a relational database. Do not delete a field unless you are certain that it is not a primary or foreign key and that the deleted data is never going to be needed again.

Visit **www.geekgirls.com/menu_databases.htm** and explore the step-by-step guides and tutorials on creating and using databases. The site displays eight steps with easy-to-follow instructions and directions. Screen captures act as visual aids.

Now that you understand databases, let's explore how information systems are used.

Information Systems: Tools for Global Competitiveness

An **information system** is a purposefully designed system that includes the collection of people, hardware, software, data records, and activities that process the data and information in an organization. Information systems, which include both the organization's manual and automated processes, are constantly changing and evolving as the business changes, grows, and alters its mission (Figure 12.12).

An information system's main functions include accepting input in the form of mission-critical data, processing this data to produce information, storing the data, and disseminating information throughout the organization. Information systems help organizations achieve their goals by providing essential information services, including recording and keeping track of transactions, assisting decision makers by providing them with needed facts and figures, and providing documentation needed by customers and suppliers.

Smart businesses know that information systems aren't merely a cost to the business. Viewed properly, an information system adds more value than its cost and can be considered a wealth-producing asset that enables a firm to compete more effectively on a global scale.

Even with all of these benefits, a company needs to be aware that information systems create a deluge of information, sometimes more than employees and managers can handle. The next section discusses how to combat this problem.

TECHNIQUES FOR REDUCING INFORMATION OVERLOAD

It's important that you understand a few things about information in general. For one, not all information is valuable, a fact you'll appreciate after doing some research on the Internet. Figure 12.13 describes the characteristics of valuable information.

Computers are indispensable, but they also pose the threat of **information overload**, providing too much information, which makes processing, absorbing, and validating it difficult (Figure 12.14). It's important to control information to keep it from overwhelming people and reducing productivity in an organization. With an information system, the following control methods are possible:

- Route information only to those people who really need to see it.

- Summarize information so that decision makers do not drown in the details.

- Enable selectivity so that people with specific information needs can get that information (and ignore the rest).

- Eliminate unnecessary information (exclusion) so that it doesn't take up time and resources.

FIGURE 12.12 The Components of an Information System

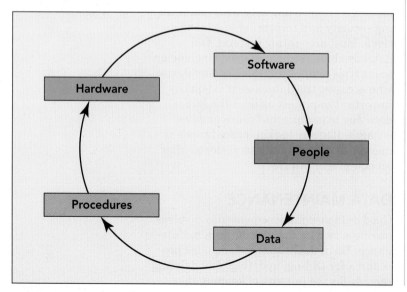

FIGURE 12.13 The Characteristics of Valuable Information

Characteristic	Result
Accessible	It can be found quickly and easily.
Accurate	It doesn't contain errors.
Complete	It doesn't omit anything important.
Economical	The benefit exceeds the cost of producing the information.
Relevant	It is related to the task you're trying to perform.
Reliable	It is available every time you need it.
Secure	Unauthorized people can't access the information.
Simple	It doesn't overwhelm you.
Timely	It is up to date.
Verifiable	It can be confirmed or double-checked.

Now that you understand what makes information valuable and why organizations need to control the flow of information, let's examine how information systems fit into existing organizational structures.

FUNCTIONAL DIVISIONS OF AN ORGANIZATION

An organization is composed of **functional divisions** (also referred to as **functional areas** or **functional units**)

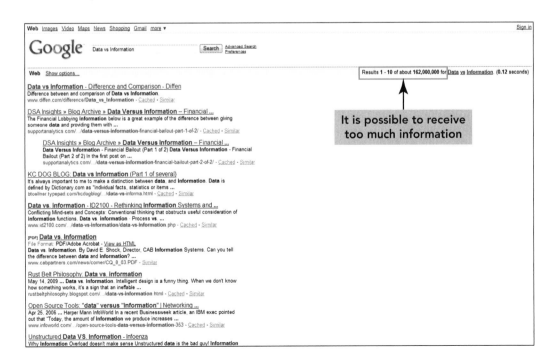

It is possible to receive too much information

FIGURE 12.14 Not all information is valuable. All too often, people are overwhelmed with more information than they can use.

FIGURE 12.15 In an organization, specialized divisions handle each of the organization's core functions.

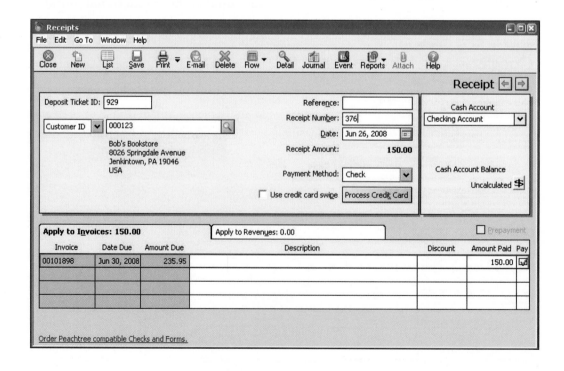

Information Systems

Accounting & Finance

Management

Marketing & Sales

Manufacturing

Human Resources

accounting, sales information, and accounting reports for management and the government. The finance function is responsible for forecasting, budgeting, cash management, budget analysis, and financial reports. Both accounting and finance use spreadsheet software as well as proprietary software packages such as Peachtree Accounting (Figure 12.16). These functional areas mainly use PCs in a client/server networked environment.

Marketing and Sales The marketing function is responsible for maintaining the company's public image and for generating sales. Marketing professionals use database, spreadsheet, and proprietary software packages to manage sales figures and customers.

Salespeople rely heavily on computers and technology to do their jobs (Figure 12.17). In addition to desktop computers, they often use mobile devices, such as notebooks, tablet PCs, and smartphones, to interact with mainframes and client/server networks.

Human Resources The human resources function uses technology to keep track of employees and to service employee queries. Tracked information includes

that handle each of the organization's core functions (Figure 12.15). No matter which functional unit an information system supports, it still includes hardware, software, data, people, and procedures. Let's look at each of the functional units typically found in an organization and the information systems that support them.

Accounting and Finance The accounting function is responsible for accounts payable, accounts receivable, cost

FIGURE 12.16 Accounting software packages such as Peachtree enable companies to manage their finances.

Receipts

File   Edit   Go To   Window   Help

Close   New   List   Save   Print   E-mail   Delete   Row   Detail   Journal   Event   Reports   Attach   Help

Receipt

Deposit Ticket ID: 929

Customer ID   000123
Bob's Bookstore
8026 Springdale Avenue
Jenkintown, PA 19046
USA

Reference:

Receipt Number: 376

Date: Jun 26, 2008

Receipt Amount: 150.00

Payment Method: Check

Use credit card swipe   Process Credit Card

Cash Account

Checking Account

Cash Account Balance

Uncalculated

Apply to Invoices: 150.00   Apply to Revenues: 0.00   Prepayment

Invoice	Date Due	Amount Due	Description	Discount	Amount Paid	Pay
00101898	Jun 30, 2008	235.95			150.00	✓

Order Peachtree compatible Checks and Forms.

date of hire, position, rank, salary, and benefits (Figure 12.18). Employees often have questions about health and retirement benefits. Human resources (HR) managers and staff use workstations to interact with mainframes, and PCs to interact with client/server networks. The HR function often uses spreadsheets, databases, and in the case of a large organization, an employee relationship management (ERM) system. An ERM system can help an employee gather information regarding his or her retirement account. Most ERM software applications include a Web interface.

At Charles Schwab & Co., employees use a client/server network to access detailed information about benefits,

training, technical support, and other company information. Instead of contacting the company's HR department, employees obtain information about themselves, their responsibilities, and the company itself.

Management The management function plans, organizes, leads, and controls the organization. Management professionals use workstations and PCs, respectively connected to mainframes and client/server networks, to make decisions about running the business. They use databases, spreadsheets, and proprietary software packages to keep track of what the company has done and to plan for what the company will do.

FIGURE 12.18
Companies often work with financial services firms to provide their employees with information about retirement and health care benefits.

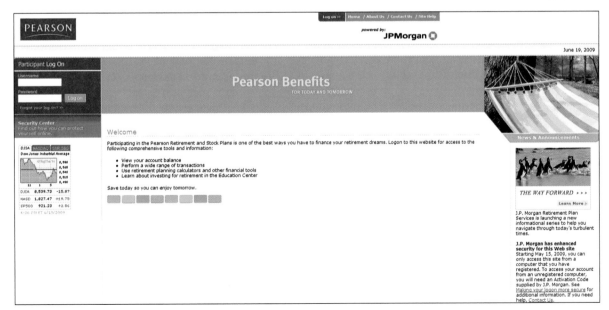

Manufacturing The manufacturing function plans and controls processes that produce goods and services (Figure 12.19). Information systems in this function help monitor and maintain inventories and purchases, and track the flow of goods and services. Transportation companies, wholesalers, retailers, banks and brokerage firms, and utility companies use production/operations information systems to plan and control their operations. Manufacturing systems typically exist on mainframe computers that are accessed by highly specialized control stations.

Information Systems Information systems refer to the system of people, data records, hardware, and software that process the data and information in an organization, including the organization's manual and automated processes. Besides managing existing systems in an organization, information systems can include the planning and purchasing of new systems, establishing the level of user training required to stay current, and dealing with day-to-day operational problems. All organizations, including nonprofit organizations and government agencies, tend to develop a functionally differentiated structure, a method of distributing the core functions of an organization into divisions such as finance, human resources, and operations. This subdivision of functions is called the **traditional organizational structure**.

Now that you understand how an organization is structured, let's move on to the various ways information systems are used in organizations.

Information Systems in Organizations: A Survey

Many different systems have been developed to meet the information needs of an organization's employees. In a very small business, a single computer might meet all of the business's information needs. Larger organizations supplement single-user systems with desktop, notebook, and handheld computers; mainframe computers; LANs; and WANs. Some of these larger systems are used by teams of two or more people working on the same project; others are available throughout an organization, including all of the organization's branch offices.

TRANSACTION PROCESSING SYSTEMS

A **transaction processing system** (**TPS**; also called an **operational system** or a **data processing system**) handles an organization's day-to-day accounting needs. It keeps a verifiable record of every transaction involving money, including purchases, sales, and payroll

Customers			Monday, June 29, 2009 7:03:16 AM			
Customer ID LastName		FirstName	Billing Address	City	State	Postal Code
1 Wellington		Geroge	123 Main St.	Syracuse	NY	13205
2 Kramer		Sharon	3456 Howard Dr.	Syracuse	NY	13205
3 Mason		Andrew	55 High St.	Syracuse	NY	13205
4 Rogers		William	84 Creekside Dr.	Syracuse	NY	13205
5 Copeland		Melissa	55 East Gate Circle	Syracuse	NY	13205
6 Thompson		Paul	45 River Rd.	Syracuse	NY	13205
6						

Page 1 of 1

FIGURE 12.20 A management information system (MIS) produces easy to read reports that provide a valuable snapshot of information.

payments. In businesses that sell products, a TPS is often linked with an inventory control system so that sales personnel will know whether an item is in stock. TPSs date to the earliest years of business computing, and the cost savings they introduced created a huge market for business computers. A TPS saves money by automating routine, labor-intensive recordkeeping.

Early TPSs used **batch processing**, whereby the data was gathered and processed at periodic intervals, such as once a week. Batch processing uses computer resources efficiently but is less convenient than **online** or **interactive processing**, in which you see the results of your commands on-screen so that you can correct errors and make necessary adjustments before completing the operation. In the 1970s, TPSs began to use online processing to enter transaction data and see totals and other results immediately.

TPSs provide useful tools for employees, such as sales and human resources personnel, but they're useful for managers, too. Operational managers focus on supervision and control, and they make **operational decisions** concerning localized issues (such as an inventory shortage) that need immediate action. A well-designed TPS can produce periodic **summary reports** that provide managers with a quick overview of the organization's performance. They also can provide **exception reports** that alert managers to unexpected developments (such as high demand for a new product).

TPSs are only as good as the integrity of the data they contain and only as useful as the information they provide to users. Using the example of an inventory control system, you can imagine the problems that would be caused by a TPS that didn't accurately reflect the volume of inventory on hand. Likewise, managers need reports that will help them make good decisions—inaccurate data or unsophisticated reports are not valued.

MANAGEMENT INFORMATION SYSTEMS

TPSs work with management information systems. A **management information system (MIS)** is a computer-based system that supports the information needs of various levels of management. This type of system helps management make informed decisions. Middle managers must make **tactical decisions** about how to best organize resources to achieve their division's goals. MISs can produce reports that display resource usage of all or selected resources, where they were allocated, and the percentage of the assigned project completed. In short, the reports can tell middle managers whether they are meeting their goals (Figure 12.20).

Although MISs continue to play an important role in organizations, they do have drawbacks. They generate predefined reports that may not contain the information a manager wants. The information may not be available when it's needed, and it might be buried within reams of printouts.

DECISION SUPPORT SYSTEMS

A **decision support system (DSS)** is a computer-based system that addresses the deficiencies of MISs by enabling managers to retrieve information that cannot be supplied by fixed, predefined MIS reports. For example, a retail chain manager can find information on how an advertising campaign affected sales of advertised versus nonadvertised items. Many DSS applications enable managers to create simulations that begin with real data and ask what-if questions, such as "What would happen to profits if we used a shipper who could cut our packaging costs by 2 percent, but who would sometimes cause slight delivery delays?"

Some DSSs include **online analytical processing (OLAP)** applications, which provide decision support by enabling managers to import rich, up-to-the-minute data from transaction databases. For example, managers at Pizzeria Uno, a chain of more than 100 pizza stores, obtain and analyze all of the sales information from each of the firm's stores every morning using OLAP. As a result, they can quickly spot trends that may be emerging in customer preferences and employee performance. Visit Decision Support Systems Resources at **www.dssresources.com** for information, articles, and case studies on various types of decision support systems.

EXECUTIVE INFORMATION SYSTEMS

An **executive information system (EIS)**, also known as an **executive support system (ESS)**, supports management's strategic-planning function. Executives in senior management (including the CEO) are concerned with high-level planning and leadership. They make **strategic decisions** concerning the organization's overall goals and direction. Though similar to a DSS, an EIS supports decisions made by top-level management that will affect the entire company.

An EIS filters critical information (including information about the firm's external environment) so that overall trends are apparent and presents this information in an easy-to-use graphical interface. For instance, an executive might create a report that compares the company's inventory levels with the industry average. Little training is required to use these systems.

An executive information system that is gaining in popularity is referred to as the **dashboard**. This system has a user interface, similar to an automobile's dashboard, that is designed to be easy to read. The information provided to the dashboard units might be obtained from the local operating system in a computer, from one or more applications that may be running, and from one or more remote sites on the

> " An **EIS** filters critical information (including information about the firm's external environment) so that **overall trends** are apparent and presents this information in an easy-to-use graphical interface. "

Web. Nonetheless, it appears as though it all came from the same source. A dashboard provides decision makers with the input necessary to "drive" the business and make effective up-to-the-minute decisions. Thus, a graphical user interface on a dashboard may be designed to display summaries, graphics (e.g., bar charts, pie charts, bullet graphs, and so on), and gauges (with colors similar to traffic lights) in a portal-like framework to highlight important information on a designated component of an organization, like sales or production, or the organization as a whole.

KNOWLEDGE MANAGEMENT SYSTEMS

Organizations are increasingly aware not only that information is crucial but also that knowledge is a valuable asset. As you've already learned, information is data that is organized in a way that has meaning to us. But knowledge is more than just information found in documents, reports, and spreadsheets stored on computers. Knowledge is information in context, including the processes, procedures, best practices, and other information employees create. How can organizations capture the knowledge employees create? A variety of information technologies are being used to create **knowledge management systems (KMSs)**, which capture knowledge from books and experienced individuals and make it available where it is needed. This process doesn't have to be high tech. Organizations can document successful business processes, also known as best practices, by meeting with employees and recording useful procedures; by engaging a consulting firm specializing in standardizing best practices procedures; or by investing in a KMS. The resulting information is then made available to others within the organization.

EXPERT SYSTEMS

An **expert system (ES)** is an information system that deals with detailed and in-depth knowledge in a specific area supplied by experts in that field. An expert system formulates a decision in the way that a human expert in the field might. Research in expert systems attempts to formulate the knowledge of human experts (such as doctors) according to if-then rules ("if you have a temperature, then you might have an infection"). These rules formally express the knowledge used by human experts as they reason their way to a conclusion. The process of eliciting these rules from human experts is called *knowledge representation*. When elicited, the rules are programmed into expert systems. Expert systems use these rules to reach a conclusion the same way that a human expert does.

An expert system relies on a **knowledge base**, a database of knowledge designed to meet the complex storage and retrieval needs of computerized expert systems. To use an expert system, the user supplies information to the program. On the basis of the information supplied, the program consults its knowledge base and draws a conclusion, if possible.

Expert systems work best when they are limited to sharply defined subjects, such as jet engine maintenance, planning and scheduling, diagnosis and troubleshooting of a specific device, or financial decision making. However, expert system technology is making its appearance in application software too. Microsoft Word uses rule-based reasoning to check documents for grammatical errors. Similarly, spam filtering software often uses a combination of preset and user-defined rules to determine whether an e-mail should be sent to the junk mail folder or to your Inbox.

Expert systems are improving service in one area in which organizations sometimes perform an unsatisfactory job: providing technical support for customers. Expert systems also can provide expert knowledge in areas outside the business arena, such as medicine and health care. To better understand the various types of decisions made by the various stages of management and the information systems they use to make them, see Figure 12.21.

COMPUTERS AND DATABASES IN THE RETAIL SECTOR

In the retail sector, computers are indispensable for traditional applications, such as automating the checkout process. But some companies have also figured out how to use computers and databases for strategic purposes, enabling them to get an edge on their competitors. Such companies have grown rapidly and have made fortunes for their shareholders.

At the Checkout Stand Today's cash registers are really computers—referred to as POS terminals (Figure 12.22). Clerks check out items by passing them over an optical scanner, which reads the universal product code (UPC) encoded on the item's label or tag. The UPC code is located in a database of product codes. When the

---

FIGURE 12.21 Types of Decisions and Information Systems for Managers			
Managers	Decisions	Type	Information System
Senior managers	Strategic	Determining the organization's goals and direction	Executive information systems (EISs) and expert systems
Middle managers	Tactical	Deciding how to organize resources to achieve their division's goals	Management information systems (MISs) and decision support systems (DSSs)
Operational managers	Operational	Deciding how to handle localized issues requiring immediate action	Knowledge management systems (KMSs) and transaction processing systems (TPSs)

FIGURE 12.22 The latest POS terminals are fully integrated with credit card authorization systems.

matching code is located in the database, the associated price is displayed and charged to the customer. The first live use of the UPC was in a Marsh Supermarkets Store in Troy, Ohio, June 26, 1974. The product: a pack of Wrigley's gum. The use of POS terminals and UPCs has resulted in faster checkout times and fewer price errors.

The latest POS terminals are fully integrated with credit card authorization systems that automatically send calls to call centers. A **call center** is a centralized computer-based routing system used for the purpose of receiving and transmitting a large volume of requests by telephone.

Because POS terminals produce digitized data, they're useful for more purposes than just determining the customer's bill. POS terminals also are linked to the store's inventory database. When a customer buys an item, the database is automatically updated to reflect the lowered stock level. When the inventory gets too low, a reorder is auto-generated.

POS terminals also are used as marketing devices. If a customer buys a particular brand of coffee, the terminal may produce a coupon for a discount on a competing brand. Another POS feature is to list the total of the discounts a customer received on his or her purchase. Marketers believe that creating a sense of well-being at the point of sale will subliminally influence the customer to associate the store with good feelings, causing the customer to come back in the future.

Chain stores such as Wal-Mart link their POS terminals to central computer systems using public data networks (PDNs). Disney, however, is taking POS data to the airwaves. At Walt Disney World, POS terminals at hundreds of retail carts supply data to company computers using wireless communications. As a result, the Lion King cart never runs out of those cute stuffed animals, which means bigger profits for Disney.

POS terminals also can reduce losses due to bad checks and credit card fraud. According to one estimate, banks and retailers lose a staggering $58 billion annually because of bounced checks and check fraud. A **check-screening system** reads a check's account number, accesses a database containing delinquent accounts, and compares the account numbers. Such systems allow vendors to catch problem transactions before they become losses. Check-screening systems have reduced bad check losses by as much as 25 percent, translating into big savings for retail firms.

Stores can use **signature capture systems** to capture a customer's digital signature by having the customer sign the receipt on a pressure-sensitive pad, using a special stylus. What's the point? The system cuts down on credit card disputes. With a receipt signed by the customer, the store can prove that the purchase was made. This system isn't popular with consumers, however, because of fears that a dishonest employee could use the captured signatures for fraudulent purposes. **Photo checkout systems** access a database of customer photos and display the customer's picture when a credit card is used. In a New York test, this system cut credit card fraud by 94 percent.

The Future of Shopping Imagine that you're standing in the supermarket, deciding which type of candy to buy. Would you want to know whether one of the sweets had just been recalled or whether the parent company of another candy had recently paid a big fine to settle charges of unethical behavior? In the not-so-distant future, you may be able to research nearly anything and everything about a product before you buy it—without leaving your shopping cart.

In such a scenario, shoppers would use a wireless Internet connection to send a product's bar code to an online database and retrieve information about the product and its manufacturer. You could use the Internet to obtain other details too. You might find that a product contains an ingredient you're trying to avoid because of allergy or diet. Or you might learn that a manufacturer has just been honored for its environmentally friendly practices. Digging deeper, you might examine a company's product safety record or trace its global operations. Of course, such research takes time, so you probably wouldn't investigate every product on every shopping trip. But if you did a quick scan before buying at least some items, you would still be a better-informed consumer.

The MediaCart computerized shopping cart is putting some of these concepts into action (**www.mediacart.com**). It uses Microsoft technologies, including SQL Server, and has already been piloted at selected ShopRite supermarkets (Figure 12.23). Shoppers slide their store loyalty card through a scanner. Once identified, shoppers receive ads and special promotions on the basis of their shopping history—displayed on the cart monitor. It is expected that shoppers will also be able to upload their shopping lists from their home PCs and sort them by aisle location, check prices, view in-store specials, and obtain recipes and nutritional information. Users will also be able to tally their grocery orders as they shop and use a cart-level checkout feature designed to speed up the checkout process. Now if only they could fix that wobbly wheel!

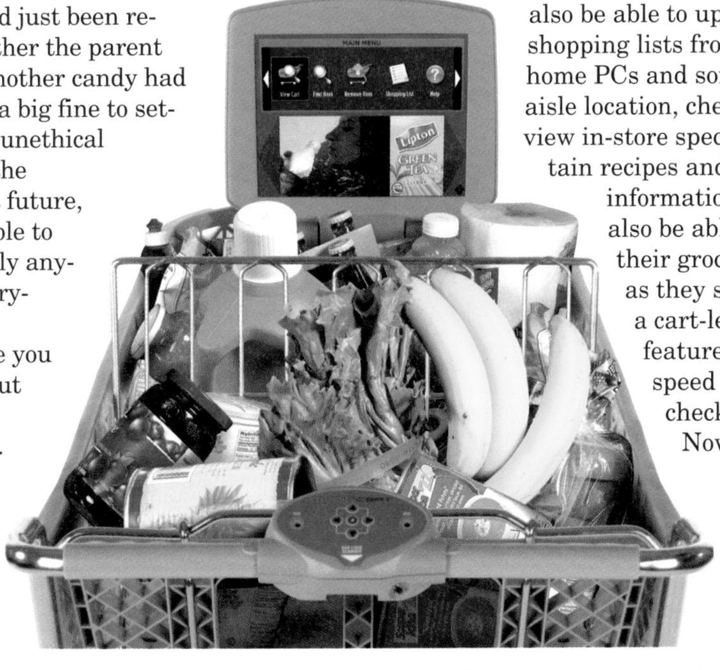

FIGURE 12.23 The MediaCart, powered by Microsoft technologies, may change the way you shop.

Chapter Summary

Databases and Information Systems

A database is a collection of data stored in an organized way. A data file is made up of records, which are units of information about a person, place, thing, or event. Each record has one or more fields. Each field stores a certain type of data and has a specific field name.

File management programs work with only one data file, called a flat file, at a time. Database management systems (DBMSs) work with two or more data files, called tables, at a time. The data in the various tables can be related by common fields. The five types of database management systems are flat, relational, hierarchical, network, and object-oriented.

Data warehouses bring data together from many smaller databases in different areas of an organization into a massive database that managers can use to make decisions. Data mining is a data exploration and analysis technique that managers use to explore data in an attempt to discover previously unknown patterns. Client/server database systems enable many users to access the database simultaneously, usually over a LAN. Web-database integration refers to techniques that make information stored in databases available through Internet connections.

A good database ensures data integrity (validity of the data), promotes data independence (separation of data from applications), avoids data redundancy (entry of the same data in two or more places), ensures data security (protection from loss of confidentiality), and provides procedures for data maintenance (adding, updating, and deleting records). These features prevent incorrect and redundant results in queries and reports.

An information system includes data, hardware, software, people, and procedures. An information system's main functions are accepting input in the form of mission-critical data, processing this data to produce information, storing the data, and disseminating information throughout functional divisions of an organization. These divisions typically include accounting and finance, marketing and sales, human resources, management, manufacturing, and information systems.

Information systems used in organizations today include transaction processing systems (TPSs), management information systems (MISs), decision support system (DSSs), executive information system (EISs), knowledge management systems (KMSs), and expert systems. These systems help managers at different levels make operations, tactical, and strategic decisions for the organization.

Key Terms and Concepts

Matching

Match each key term in the left column with the most accurate definition in the right column.

_____ 1. logical

_____ 2. query

_____ 3. knowledge system

_____ 4. dashboard

_____ 5. online processing

_____ 6. check-screening system

_____ 7. data file or table

_____ 8. primary key

_____ 9. completeness check

_____ 10. expert system

_____ 11. batch processing

_____ 12. range check

_____ 13. default value

_____ 14. numeric check

_____ 15. data redundancy

a. Processing data as it is entered.

b. A collection of records.

c. Verifying that entered data falls within a range.

d. A repetition of data.

e. The data type that allows only a "yes" or "no" value.

f. An information system that works with data in an area that was obtained from books or individuals who are not specialists in the area.

g. A specifically phrased question used to locate data in a database.

h. Used to determine whether a field has been left empty.

i. Gathering and processing data at periodic intervals.

j. Ensures that a field contains only numbers.

k. A system that accesses a database of delinquent accounts.

l. Field containing information that uniquely identifies a record.

m. An information system whose user-friendly desktop interface is the key to the collection and consolidation of information from multiple sources.

n. Information system that works with knowledge in a specific area supplied by a qualified individual in that area.

o. A setting that is automatically selected unless another is provided.

Multiple Choice

Circle the correct choice for each of the following.

1. Which is *not* an example of an object?
   a. A sound
   b. A video
   c. An e-mail address
   d. A picture

2. Which system supports management's strategic planning functions?
   a. Executive information system
   b. Management information system
   c. Expert system
   d. Check-screening system

3. Which of the following is used to ensure the integrity of entered data?
   a. Data validation
   b. Data independence
   c. Data redundancy
   d. Data authorization

4. Which is a technique used by managers to obtain more detailed information in a database warehouse?
   a. Data validation
   b. Data authorization
   c. Data inspection
   d. Drill down

5. Which TPS report provides information on the overall performance of an organization?
   a. Summary
   b. Tactical
   c. Operational
   d. Exception

6. Which system enables managers to create simulations beginning with real data and to ask what-if questions?
   a. Executive information system
   b. Expert system
   c. Knowledge management system
   d. Decision support system

7. Which of the following is an example of a DBMS?
   a. Microsoft Access
   b. Excel
   c. Word 2007
   d. MySQL

8. Which of the following is *not* an acceptable data type?
   a. Number
   b. Character
   c. Text
   d. Memo

9. Which of the following statements about data warehouses is true?
   a. They can store information for only one division.
   b. They are composed of flat files.
   c. They help managers make decisions using a drill-down technique.
   d. Batch processing is used to generate reports rapidly.

10. What type of database would contain information *only* for a single department of a specific organization?
    a. Data mine
    b. Data warehouse
    c. Data mart
    d. Blob

In the blanks provided, write the correct answer for each of the following.

1. _____-_____ _____ is a technique that makes information stored in databases available via Internet.

2. Middle managers make _____ decisions about how to manage resources to achieve goals.

3. A(n) _____ _____ system identifies customers through the use of a pressure-sensitive pad and stylus.

4. _____ _____ is the analysis of data in a database to search for previously unknown patterns.

5. A(n) _____ _____ is a transaction report that alerts someone to unexpected developments.

6. A(n) _____ _____ is a field in one table of a relational database that is a primary key in another.

7. Managers make _____ decisions, which focus on supervision and control of local issues that need immediate attention.

8. A(n) _____ _____ _____ system provides decision support by enabling managers to import up-to-the-minute data from transaction databases.

9. A(n) _____ _____ is a central computer routing system that receives and transmits large volumes of requests by telephone.

10. The _____ _____ contains a list of the tables in a database and the details for each table.

11. _____ _____ is the providing of too much information, which makes processing, absorbing, and validating it difficult.

12. _____ _____ is the process by which a database determines whether incorrect data has been entered.

13. Executive decisions concerning the overall goals and direction of an organization are called _____ decisions.

14. A(n) _____ _____ is the collection of people, hardware, software, data records, and activities that process the data and information in an organization.

15. An expert system consults its _____ _____ of information to draw a conclusion or provide a possible solution.

Short Answer

1. Define the three main components of a relational database: data file, field, and record. Give examples of each.

2. What is a primary key? What is a foreign key? How are these used in a relational database?

3. List the five components of an information system.

4. What is the advantage of a relational database system over a file management program?

5. Explain the difference between a knowledge management system and an expert system.

Teamwork

1. **Erroneous Data** Preventing erroneous data from being entered into a database is extremely important. As a team, work together to explain the validation rules below that are being defined from an Access database. Brainstorm and discuss at least five consequences of entering erroneous data into a database. Write a group report that answers these questions and that summarizes your brainstorming.

Validation Rule Setting	Meaning
<>0	
0 Or >100	
Like "P???"	
<#1/1/99#	
>=#1/1/98# And <#1/1/99#	
>=Date()	
"M" Or "F"	

2. **Backup, Backup, Backup!!** As a team, make up a form containing questions on data backup. Include questions like these: Do you have a backup policy? How frequently do you back up data? How frequently do you back up applications? Did you ever have a data disaster (if so explain)? Break into groups and, using this form, interview several local businesses on their data backup policies and problems. After the interviews, regroup and brainstorm to come up with at least five backup strategies that can prevent data disasters. Present your findings and strategies in a one-page, double-spaced paper.

3. **Database Tutorials** As a team, research normalizing a database. Define the term *normalization* with respect to a database and explain the rules that a database needs to follow in order to be normalized. Present your definition and rules in a one-page, double-spaced paper or in a PowerPoint presentation.

4. **Database Templates** Have each team member launch Microsoft Access or a similar database management program and open one of the sample database templates that are located within the General Templates choice in the Task Pane or wherever the program's templates are stored. Have each team member write a brief summary of a different template: How many tables are there? How many forms? Are there any queries or reports? Print one of the tables and draw callouts to a field and to a record. Write a short collaborative paper that describes the value of database templates.

5. **How Many Databases Are You In?** Make a list of 10 to 15 databases that members of your team might be a part of. Try to determine what might be the primary key field of each database file, and define five other fields that are likely to appear in each database. Create an organized presentation of your results.

On the Web

1. **Database Design Help** Visit **www.geekgirls. com/menu_databases.htm**, a Web site that provides step-by-step guides for using databases. On this site, step 2 is a guide on creating your first database. Review the contents of this guide and use the information along with that in your text to create the structure of a relational database, with at least two tables, for a coffee shop (or any other concept that is approved by your instructor). State the purpose of the database; define the tables and fields you will need; and provide the names that you would assign to the fields and the type of data to be inserted into each. Identify which field in each table would be a primary key (if one is needed). Create a visual representation of your developed database or actually create it in a database program. Submit your concept and final design.

2. **Expert Systems** Complete the expert system introduction tutorial at **www.expertise2go.com**. It is located under the tutorial section on the left side of the home page. What is an expert system? What are the three methods for delivering advice without the expert's presence? What are the two parts of a rule? Define forward and backward chaining. What three components does a typical rule-based expert system integrate? What kinds of problems are good candidates for expert systems? In what area were some of the first expert systems developed? Present your findings in a one-page, double-spaced paper.

3. **Executive Dashboards** Use a search engine and query dashboards. List at least three companies that produce, sell, or customize data dashboards. Locate screen captures or videos that display or demonstrate the capabilities of these new executive decision tools. Present your findings in either a one-page, double-spaced paper or a spreadsheet. Include the name of the company, a description of the data dashboard and its contents, a screen capture (if possible), and any additional features that make the product unique.

4. **Data Disasters** Data disasters can occur at all levels of business and personal computer usage. For some humorous, and not so humorous, episodes of lost data go to **www.ontrackdatarecovery.com/ data-disaster-2008/** (change the year to view previous year's top 10). After reading the crazy, humorous disasters from this cite or any others that a search might target, locate five that relate to business. In a one-page, double-spaced report or a PowerPoint presentation, describe each of the five disasters, the year it occurred, and what action could have prevented its occurrence.

5. **Database Templates, So Many to Choose From** There are many database templates already developed to help new users get started in the right direction. Visit **www.databaseanswers.org/data_ models/index.htm** and select any three templates from the list of templates on the site. List the database files (tables) located in each database model selected. For each database file, name the primary key, foreign key(s), and fields. See whether you can come up with any additional fields for any of the database files. Display your three choices and their components in a visual manner, using a table, spreadsheet, or PowerPoint presentation.

chapter 13

Systems Analysis and Design

You may be wondering what systems analysis and design has to do with computers. Well, actually, quite a bit. You see, it's in the analysis and design of information systems that we can create new, innovative ways of doing things. This is particularly pertinent today because we constantly interact with information systems. Those who understand the capabilities of information systems and their structure will be better able to capitalize on the systematic management of information. This chapter explores information systems development, or the analysis and design of systems that help us manage all of the information with which we are constantly inundated.

An information system includes the people, hardware, software, data records, and activities that process an organization's data and information into a usable form. Creating the computerized component of an information system isn't something to take lightly. The benefits are great, but so are the risks. A poorly planned information system can eat up profits, anger customers, and even cause a company to go bankrupt. Unfortunately, poor results are all too common.

Is it too much to ask that computerized information systems be finished on time and within budget and that they perform their intended job? Admittedly, information systems development is a difficult challenge, and the unique requirements of many businesses don't make it any easier. Whether it's how they track customers and sales or inventory and expenses, most businesses need something a little different. (For example, a pizza delivery company needs a different type of information system than a pharmaceutical firm or an automaker.) In addition, users and clients may have difficulty communicating their needs clearly, leading to the development of systems that don't satisfy them. And too frequently, time estimates for developing information systems are overly optimistic, typically by as much as 20 to 30 percent. Just like any construction project, such as building a new home, building an information system takes longer than most people care to admit.

In the face of such chaos, it makes good sense to try to get organized. **Systems analysis** is the field concerned with the planning, development, and implementation of artificial systems, including information systems. The systems analysis discipline learns from previous development efforts and formulates strategies for improved planning, organization, control, and execution of information systems development projects.

Modern information systems are all about managing data to provide information, entertainment, and systems to support society's many activities. With that said, let's now turn our attention to all of the procedures and people involved with information systems development.

Systems Analysts: Communication Counts

The human component of an information system includes users as well as trained personnel, such as systems analysts. **Systems analysts** are problem-solving computer professionals who work with users and management to determine an organization's information system needs (Figure 13.1). Systems analysts determine the requirements needed to modify an existing system or to develop a new one. They don't ordinarily do the development; the development is reserved for other trained computer professionals such as computer programmers or systems developers. Rather, systems analysts identify and evaluate alternative solutions, make formal presentations to management, and assist in the development of the system after an option has been chosen.

Much of a systems analyst's job involves communication, including listening skills. Systems analysts must understand the organization's mission, including its strategic goals. A strategic goal might be to ensure that each of a company's customers receives accurate, timely, and personalized correspondence at least once a month—thereby building customer loyalty. Analysts also must talk to users and understand their needs. They must involve users in the project so that they feel some element of ownership. They must keep in close contact with project team members so that they know how the project is progressing. They must write voluminous documentation that explains, at every step, what was performed, why and how it was performed, and who did it. They must know who (the user, the project team, or the vendor) is supposed to do what during the systems development process. To stay organized and keep track of these various tasks, systems analysts follow an organized procedure for planning and building information systems called the systems development life cycle.

The Systems Development Life Cycle: A Problem-Solving Approach

In the early years of business computing, information systems development was a disorganized, ad hoc process that frequently produced discouraging results. Systems typically were delivered late, went over their budgets, and didn't provide the services users expected. The **systems development life cycle (SDLC)** is an approach or model used in the development of information systems. Its intent is to provide a structure or systematic guide to development with the goal of improving system quality. The

FIGURE 13.1 Systems analysts must talk to a variety of users and understand their needs. They must involve users in the project so that they feel a sense of ownership.

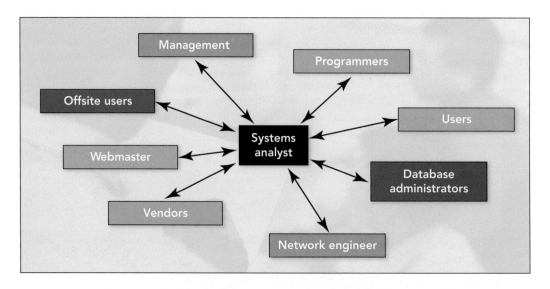

SDLC is better understood if it's broken down into digestible pieces. Let's begin with what the "systems" part means.

A **system** is a collection of components purposefully organized into a functioning whole to accomplish a goal. Systems occur in nature, but what we're talking about here are **artificial systems**, systems deliberately constructed by people to serve some purpose. Systems are all around us. The commercial airline transportation system, for example, is a complex system that does a remarkably good job of safely delivering millions of people to their destinations every day.

At the core of the systems concept lies the recognition that various parts of a system need to be modified or adapted to function together smoothly. (After all, you wouldn't want to fly on an airplane that had the wrong type of wing installed.) A second important concept about systems is that they have a **life cycle**: They are born, go through a process of maturation, live an adult life, and become obsolete to the point that they have to be modified or abandoned. This sequence of life is also referred to as "cradle to grave." Figure 13.2 displays the key tasks associated with each phase of a system's life cycle. If you think about yesterday's transportation systems, such as canals or covered wagons, you'll see it's obvious that systems outlive their usefulness.

At this point, we could be talking about any kind of system, including a manufacturing system such as an assembly line. No organization, not even a small one, can function without an information system of some kind, even if it doesn't have a computer-based component. But developing the right information system for the right purpose takes patience, time, and the right plan. That's exactly the function of the SDLC and its steps, or phases.

THE PHASES OF THE SDLC

At the core of the SDLC model is a simple idea: You shouldn't go on to the next step until you're certain that the current one has been performed properly. Several models of the SDLC exist. Interestingly, they vary in depth from 5 to 14 steps. The five basic phases (steps or stages) of the SDLC are (1) planning or investigation, (2) analysis, (3) design or development, (4) implementation and testing, and (5) maintenance or support. Each phase is intended to address key issues and to produce **deliverables**, which are outcomes or tangible output such as reports or other documents. Figure 13.3 displays each of the five basic phases with the deliverable each phase produces. These deliverables often form the input for the next phase.

Note that different organizations and systems development teams may use modified or slightly different versions of the SDLC; some versions identify more phases than others, and some use different names for the individual phases. The five-part process described here represents what is common practice. Visit the Startvbdotnet Web site at **www.startvbdotnet.com/ sdlc/sdlc.aspx** to see how one version of the basic system development life cycle works.

AVOIDING MISTAKES

Systems analysts have learned, often through bitter experience, to avoid the classic mistakes of failed projects. Consequently, the information systems development process looks at an organization's overall

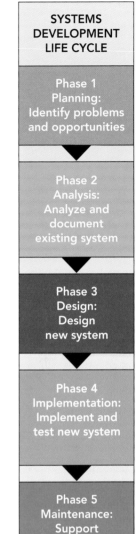

SYSTEMS DEVELOPMENT LIFE CYCLE

Phase 1 Planning: Identify problems and opportunities

Phase 2 Analysis: Analyze and document existing system

Phase 3 Design: Design new system

Phase 4 Implementation: Implement and test new system

Phase 5 Maintenance: Support new system

FIGURE 13.3 The Five Basic Phases of the Systems Development Life Cycle

FIGURE 13.2 The System Life Cycle

Life Cycle Phase	Key Tasks
Planning Phase	Identifying systems development goals
Analysis Phase	Designing specific components
Design Phase	Putting it all together
Implementation Phase	Using the system
Maintenance Phase	Maintaining, and eventually terminating and retiring the system

goals and objectives and identifies the various systems and subsystems that the organization uses to achieve its goals and objectives. The following essentials of systems development wisdom are built into the SDLC:

- **User involvement is crucial.** Users include any person for whom the system is built, and that may include customers. Users are the ultimate judges of the system's usability, although they may not know how to express their needs clearly. Without user involvement, the system may not meet users' needs, and they may then resist or even sabotage efforts to use the new system.

- **A problem-solving approach works best.** To create an effective system, you must identify the problem, place the problem in context, define the solution, examine alternative solutions, and choose the best one. Without this approach, the new system may not fully address the underlying shortcomings of the existing system.

- **Good project management skills are needed.** Many failed systems development projects are characterized by unrealistic expectations, overly optimistic schedules, lack of solid backing from management, people's inability to make decisions and stick with them, lack of control over insertion of new but unnecessary features, and interference from problem personnel. A poorly managed project may become so chaotic that it must be cancelled.

- **Documentation is required.** The term **documentation** refers to the recording of all information pertinent to the project, for instance, manuals, tutorials, start-up procedures, and installation instructions. A **project notebook**, which is frequently a digital file that is maintained online, is often used to store the documentation for a project. The documentation enables everyone connected with the project to understand all the decisions that have been made. Documentation should be an ongoing process; it shouldn't be put off until the end of the project, at which time important information or key personnel might not be available. Without documentation, the system can't be properly supported or modified (especially after key development personnel have left).

- **Checkpoints should be used to make sure the project is on track.** At the end of each phase, the project must be critically and independently evaluated to make sure that it's on track. An organization shouldn't be afraid to cancel the project (or repeat a phase) if results aren't satisfactory. Some of the worst development disasters occur when the project team conceals the fact that the system couldn't possibly work.

- **Systems should be designed for growth and change.** A system should be designed so that it won't break down or require a major redesign in the event of change (including unanticipated increases in usage). Failure to anticipate change and growth could make the entire system useless in short order.

Avoiding mistakes doesn't guarantee success. On the other hand, making mistakes may very well guarantee failure!

THE WATERFALL MODEL

Although the SDLC calls for a step-by-step process, it's not always wise to keep going if work in a later stage turns up problems with work performed in an earlier one. For example, in the analysis phase, the team may discover that the problem hasn't been formulated correctly. The **waterfall model** is a systems development method that builds correction pathways into the process so that analysts can return to a previous phase (Figure 13.4). It's a widely used implementation of the SDLC.

> " The information systems **development process** looks at an organization's overall **goals** and **objectives** and identifies the various **systems** and **subsystems** that the **organization** uses to achieve its **goals** and **objectives.** "

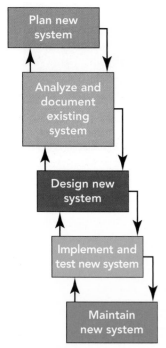

FIGURE 13.4 The waterfall model demonstrates the two-way flow of progress through the SDLC. Progress can advance to the next stage or return to the previous one if results do not measure up.

Plan new system

Analyze and document existing system

Design new system

Implement and test new system

Maintain new system

MODERN APPROACHES TO SOFTWARE DEVELOPMENT

Although the traditional waterfall model is still used by many organizations, the fast pace of change in information technology today sometimes requires more responsive techniques. The waterfall approach, which requires sequentially progressing from phase to phase, has been criticized as time-consuming and lacking in flexibility. To address these issues, new methods have developed.

Prototyping (or **rapid application development**) became popular for a while. This is a process in which a small scale mock-up of the system is shown to the users. Although prototyping increases user involvement, the approach has several drawbacks, including the following:

1. **Incomplete analysis of the problem and solution:** Developers can get distracted while developing prototypes and neglect to fully analyze the problem and develop comprehensive solutions.
2. **User confusion:** Users may begin to think of the prototype as the finished system. This can lead to resentment if revisions to later prototypes change the functionality of the original prototype.
3. **Too much time spent on developing prototypes:** If not properly managed, prototype development can take up too much time, leaving insufficient time for development of the final system.

To combat some of the issues surrounding prototyping and the traditional waterfall model of software development, **joint application development (JAD)** was born. This process attempts to speed up the overall development process by collecting the requirements of the new (or modified) system while the new system is being developed. This means that the first four phases of the traditional SDLC are conducted simultaneously. Emphasis is placed on the critical tasks of identifying the problem and developing solutions.

Sound impossible? It isn't if it is properly coordinated by a skilled project leader. The leader develops workshops for participants and regularly brings them together to identify problems, develop solutions, create prototypes, and test and evaluate solutions. JAD is a complex process and requires an intense amount of face-to-face interaction among all team members

FIGURE 13.5 JAD development requires superior project management skills and more face-to-face interaction than other strategies to communicate and interweave four steps of the SDLC into one smoothly.

(Figure 13.5). However, this level of interaction tends to increase communication and the likelihood of a positive project outcome. It also tends to significantly speed up the development process because problems and solutions tend to be more accurately identified and mapped out. JAD still uses the phases of the SDLC but conducts the first four simultaneously. Again, several arrangements and combinations of the SDLC phases exist, but the basic steps are still usually embedded somewhere within each variation.

Let's look at phase 1 of the traditional SDLC.

Phase 1: Planning the System

Phase 1 is the planning or investigation phase. In phase 1 of the SDLC, an organization recognizes the need for an information system, defines the problem, examines alternative solutions, develops a plan, and determines the project's feasibility. The result is a project proposal submitted to senior management. If this phase is performed well, it can assure the foundation for the appropriate information system to be built, and just as important, it can assure that the wrong system won't be built.

RECOGNIZING THE NEED FOR THE SYSTEM

New information systems (or modified ones) result from recognition of deficiencies in performance, information quality,

FIGURE 13.6   Recognizing the Need for a New or Modified System

Deficiency in:	Example
Performance	Slow response time
Information quality	Out-of-date or inaccurate information
Economics	High operating costs
Security	Vulnerability to break-ins
Efficiency	Wasting resources (employee time, printer paper, toner, etc.)
Service	Difficult, awkward to use

economics, security, efficiency, or service (Figure 13.6). If the current system demonstrates poor response time, users might experience delays when they attempt to process data or transfer files. If the existing system lacks information quality, a sales or customer service representative may give a customer an incorrect stock number on an item being ordered or report that an item is out of stock when there are actually plenty in stock. Economic deficiencies need to be addressed if the existing system generates high bills from ISPs or other vendors. If the existing system lacks security, hackers or competitors can steal or destroy valuable company data. An inefficient system might automatically print customer statements even when their account balance is zero, wasting employee time, paper, toner, and other resources. A system demonstrates deficient service when employees must go through unnecessary or repetitive steps to perform a task.

Even if the current system doesn't have obvious deficiencies, it might still be worthwhile to replace it if a redesigned system could generate new business opportunities. For example, a new or redesigned airline reservation system could generate better customer profiles that would identify the need for additional services, such as providing more first-class seats, arranging car rentals, making hotel reservations, and so on, thus creating increased revenue and customer satisfaction by offering related services.

To get the project going, someone makes a formal project request to the organization's **information technology steering committee**, which generally includes representatives from senior management, information systems personnel, users, and middle managers. The steering committee reviews requests and decides which ones to address. If a project request is approved, the steering committee appoints a project team and phase 1 continues.

DEFINING THE PROBLEM

To solve a problem, you must first understand it. But that's not always as easy as it might seem. Problems are often confused with symptoms. A **symptom** is an unacceptable or undesirable result, whereas a **problem** is the underlying cause of the symptom. Another way to differentiate a symptom from a problem is that a symptom is an indication or a sign of something, whereas a problem is a state of difficulty that needs to be resolved. For example, someone might say that a headache is a symptom of the wrong eyeglass prescription. Although the headache may seem like the problem, the incorrect prescription is actually the problem. In an information system, users might complain about a symptom, such as slow response time when entering a transaction into their computers. Users may think the solution is to demand more powerful computers, because they think the problem is with the computers. But the slow response time is just a symptom. The problem could be any number of different things, such as the slow speed of network transmissions. If this is the case, then it's a waste of money to buy faster computers! If a symptom is confused with a problem, the wrong solution might be implemented.

Determining the exact problem often is a difficult task. Ideally, the problem definition stage identifies the features that need to be added to or built into the information system to make it acceptable to users. Although users must be involved in defining the problem, they're not accustomed to looking at information systems in a structured, unbiased way. The systems analyst talks to as many users as possible, and slowly a picture emerges of what these people do, when they do it, how they do it, and why they do it (Figure 13.7). From these facts, the analyst then derives recommendations for new system features (if an existing system will be modified) or proposes that a new system be built from scratch.

EXAMINING ALTERNATIVE SOLUTIONS

After the problem has been identified, system requirements need to be specified. A process called **requirements analysis** determines the requirements of the system by analyzing how the system will meet the needs of end users. The requirements analysis is extremely important because errors or omissions could lead to expensive missteps or modifications later in the development process or after users express dissatisfaction with the new or modified system. It also is important for the project team to focus the requirements analysis primarily on user needs and not get caught up in the technical details.

After system requirements have been determined, the project team then looks at a range of possible solutions. The range of solutions that the project team examines often includes internally developed systems, off-the-shelf software, and outsourcing. The project team should consider the advantages and disadvantages of each potential solution. For example, an internally developed system offers the project team control over each phase of development. However, this control has a price—internally developed systems are usually the most expensive to build and maintain. Purchasing off-the-shelf software would obviously save the project team the hassle of creating its own software or hiring programmers if none exist in-house. However, some companies require specialized software features that aren't available in off-the-shelf software packages. Outsourcing

FIGURE 13.7 The systems analyst interacts with a variety of users to understand their roles and how they work with the system. Armed with this knowledge, the analyst can make better, more accurate recommendations for new system features or a complete overhaul.

the development of the system offers a range of additional options: A project team may outsource one part of the project for which there is no in-house expertise (such as programming software) or choose to outsource the entire project. Obviously, as more portions of the project are outsourced, the expense of the potential solution increases. When the project team agrees on a solution, the project proceeds.

One business adept at solving organizational problems is a company called EDS, which was recently acquired by Hewlett-Packard. Visit the EDS Web site at **www.eds.com** to view examples of their successes.

DEVELOPING A PLAN

When an appropriate solution has been identified, the project leader (who may or may not be the systems analyst) formulates a project plan. The project leader also handles project budgets and schedules. The **project plan** identifies the project's goal and specifies all of the activities that must be completed for the project to succeed. For each activity, the plan specifies the estimated time that the project will require as well as the estimated costs. The plan also identifies activities that must be completed before new ones can begin and indicates which activities can occur simultaneously.

Before developing a system, it is imperative that system specifications be

Project management software, such as Microsoft Office Project, provides an excellent means of developing and modifying project plans.

DETERMINING FEASIBILITY

A feasible project is one that can be successfully completed. To determine whether a project is feasible, three types of feasibility must be examined: technical, operational, and economic.

Technical feasibility means that a project can be accomplished with existing, proven technology. For example, consider a project that requires speech recognition. Although computers are getting much better at recognizing and transcribing human speech, they do make errors. If the error rate is unacceptable, the project isn't technically feasible until speech recognition technology improves.

Operational feasibility refers to a project that can be accomplished with the organization's available resources. If some of the project's goals include changes beyond the organization's control (such as regulations in a foreign country), the project isn't operationally feasible.

When a project demonstrates **economic feasibility**, it can be accomplished with available financial resources. The question of whether a project is economically feasible is usually answered by a **cost-benefit analysis**, an examination of the losses and gains related to a project. The costs are the expected costs to develop and run the new system.

A cost-benefit analysis examines both tangible and intangible benefits. You can easily measure **tangible benefits**, such as increased sales, faster response time, and decreased complaints. **Intangible benefits**, such as improved employee morale and customer satisfaction, may be difficult or impossible to measure. Bank managers, for example, may decide to install an ATM because they believe that many people won't deal with a bank that

created. Think of system specifications in the same vein as blueprints for a building or a house. These specifications act as benchmarks to evaluate as well as implement the system while it is being developed. System specifications also assist in answering tough questions, such as whether the correct system solution is being implemented, whether it meets user requirements, and whether it matches the project plan.

Project plans are often graphically summarized with a **Gantt chart**, a type of bar chart that indicates task due dates and project milestones (Figure 13.8).

FIGURE 13.8 A Gantt chart is a graphical summary of project plans that indicates activities performed over a period of time.

ID	Task name	Duration	Jan	Feb	Mar	Apr	May	Jun	Jul	Aug
1	Planning	3w	1/26 ▬ 2/13							
2	Analysis	10w		2/9 ▬▬▬▬ 4/17						
3	Design	11w			3/23 ▬▬▬▬ 6/5					
4	Implementation	4w						6/5 ▬ 7/3		

doesn't have one. The improved customer satisfaction that would occur as a result of installing the new system is an intangible benefit.

In many companies, managers will request a study of the proposed system's **return on investment (ROI)**, its overall financial yield at the end of its lifetime. The money invested in the system should produce a return that is greater than alternative investments, such as putting the money in the bank.

PREPARING THE PROJECT PROPOSAL

At the conclusion of phase 1, the project leader writes a **project proposal**, a document that introduces the nature of the existing system's problem, explains the proposed solution and its benefits, details the proposed project plan, and concludes with a recommendation. A good project proposal will include the **scope**, the sum total of all project elements and features, as well as some

> "An unexpected but valuable **benefit** of the **systems analysis phase** is that it often points out **problems** that weren't fully **identified** in **phase 1**."

funds to cover **scope creep**, the uncontrolled changes or bumps that arise during a project that lead to increased costs and a longer development schedule. In response, management decides whether to continue the project. The project proposal is the deliverable from phase 1.

Phase 2: Analyzing and Documenting the Existing Information System

In phase 2 of the SDLC, the systems analyst or the systems development team determines precisely what the new system should accomplish. Here, the emphasis is placed on what the system should do, not how. (That comes next, in phase 3.) This phase includes two steps: analyzing the existing system and determining the needs of the new system. Phase 2 is often referred to as the systems analysis (or just analysis) phase.

ANALYZING THE EXISTING SYSTEM

A study of the existing system (whether computerized or manual) determines which activities currently being performed should be continued in the new system. This step can be simple if the current system is well documented. Unfortunately, most systems are not well documented, and that's especially true of updates to an original system. Thus, a major part of the analysis of the existing system is to document it. If the existing system is computerized, the current hardware needs to be examined to see whether it's adequate to do the job.

An unexpected but valuable benefit of the systems analysis phase is that it often points out problems that weren't fully identified in phase 1. This analysis may be the first time a group of people has sat down in the same room and talked about the existing system. The discussion can result in new insights, and problems that were not uncovered in the preliminary investigation can be brought to light and resolved.

DETERMINING THE NEW SYSTEM'S REQUIREMENTS

After the existing system has been exhaustively documented, the new system's requirements are precisely stated. This listing of the new system's requirements is the deliverable for phase 2. The requirements state the innovations that need to occur for the system to be acceptable to users. Again, user involvement is crucial because systems analysts often obtain information about system requirements through interviews, surveys, and observations of how the system is currently used.

Phase 3: Designing the System

Phase 3, the design phase of the SDLC, is concerned with how the new information system will work. This phase isn't concerned with the nitty-gritty details of how the software will be coded. Instead, this phase's deliverable is a logical design that provides an overall picture of how the new system will work. The goal of this phase of the project is to specify in exact terms the type of data that flows into the system, where the data goes, how the data is processed, who uses the data, how the data is stored, what data entry forms are involved, and what procedures people follow. To do this, the project team can use graphical tools, such as entity-relationship diagrams, data flow diagrams, project dictionaries, and data dictionaries.

DESIGN TOOLS

To describe the new information system, analysts use methods of graphical analysis to convey their findings to managers, programmers, and users. An **entity-relationship diagram (ERD)** shows all of the entities (organizations, departments, users, programs, and data) that play a role in the system as well as the relationships among those entities (Figure 13.9). A **data flow diagram (DFD)** uses a set of graphical symbols to show how data moves through the existing system (Figure 13.10).

FIGURE 13.9 An entity-relationship diagram depicts all of the entities that play a role in the system.

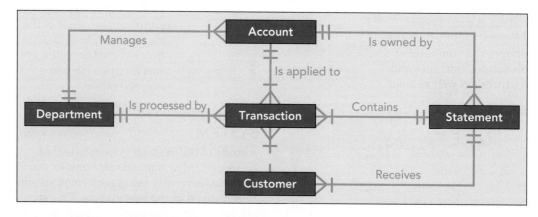

FIGURE 13.10 A data flow diagram shows how data moves through the existing system.

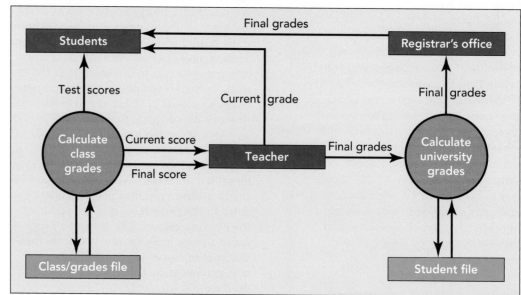

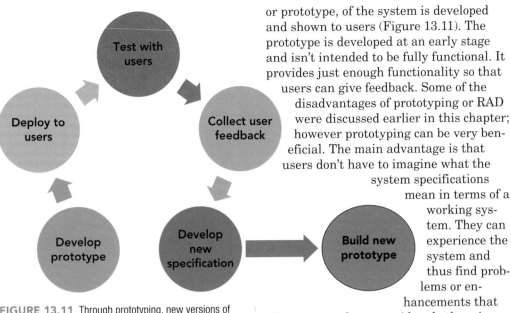

FIGURE 13.11 Through prototyping, new versions of the system are constantly deployed and tested to gather appropriate user feedback. After enough feedback is gathered, the final system can be built.

or prototype, of the system is developed and shown to users (Figure 13.11). The prototype is developed at an early stage and isn't intended to be fully functional. It provides just enough functionality so that users can give feedback. Some of the disadvantages of prototyping or RAD were discussed earlier in this chapter; however prototyping can be very beneficial. The main advantage is that users don't have to imagine what the system specifications mean in terms of a working system. They can experience the system and thus find problems or enhancements that they may not have considered otherwise.

The DFD also specifies the details of how the data is processed.

ERD and DFD software are available from several sources. Visit **www.smartdraw.com/tutorials/ software/dfd/tutorial_01.htm**, **http://office.microsoft.com/ en-us/visio/default.aspx**, and **www.conceptdraw.com/en/products/ cd5/ap_data_flow.php** to learn about several different products.

Team members create a **project dictionary**, which explains all the terminology relevant to the project; they also develop a data dictionary, which defines the types of data that are inputted into the system.

Two recent approaches, prototyping and computer-aided software engineering, are helping to improve the design phase. Recall that with prototyping, also called rapid application development (RAD), a small-scale mock-up,

The second approach, **computer-aided software engineering (CASE)**, automates the often tedious task of documenting entity relationships and data flows in a complex new system. Most CASE tools include project management features, data dictionaries, documentation support, and graphical output support; some even automatically generate prototype code (Figure 13.12).

During this phase, it's important that analysts think about the system's logical requirements and not think about what

FIGURE 13.12
PowerBuilder is an example of a CASE tool that can be used to build powerful Web applications such as Google Maps.

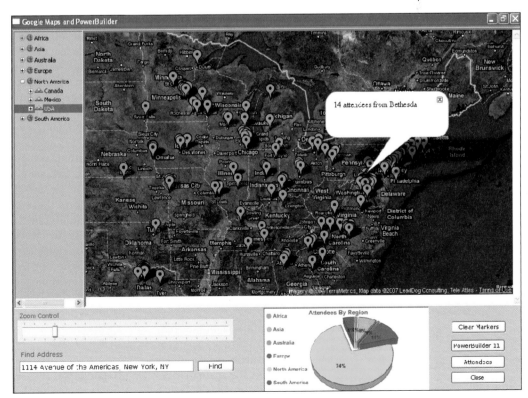

can be accomplished (and what can't) with existing information systems and software. Such thinking might prevent them from realizing that they may need to create an entirely new type of system, one that's never been developed before. This is the reason phase 3 is clearly separated from phase 4, in which attention turns to the system's physical implementation. These two phases must be rigorously kept separate.

Phase 4: Implementing the System

In phase 4 of the SDLC, the system implementation phase, the project team and management decide whether to create the physical system using internal expertise or to purchase it from outside vendors. If the project team decides to build the system in-house, hardware must be purchased and installed, and programs must be written. The system must be exhaustively tested, and users must be trained. When the team is confident that the new system is ready for use, the conversion to the new system takes place.

DECIDING WHETHER TO BUILD OR BUY

After the new system's requirements and logical design have been specified, the project team faces the **build-or-buy decision**: Should the new system be developed in-house or purchased from an outside vendor?

In-house development provides the opportunity for detailed customization, but it often carries with it the high costs of programmer salaries, testing, and time. Most organizations cannot afford to have programmers on staff and don't have the time that is required to properly develop an application. For these reasons, an organization will often purchase an off-the-shelf product and then customize it for its specific needs. Another option is to outsource the project to a company that specializes in creating systems applications.

If the decision is made to outsource the project, the project team sends out either a request for quotation or a request for proposal. A **request for quotation (RFQ)** is a request for a vendor to quote a

price for specific components of the information system. A **request for proposal (RFP)** is a request for a vendor to write a proposal for the design, installation, and configuration of the information system. RFQs and RFPs are often sent to vendors called **value-added resellers (VARs)**, independent companies that combine and install equipment and software from several sources.

DEVELOPING THE SOFTWARE

Developing the software can be considered a separate subset of the information systems development process. However, in most cases, developing the software amounts to less than 15 percent of the time involved in the entire project. To develop the software required for the new system, programmers use the program development life cycle (PDLC). Recall that the PDLC separates the task of software program development into six manageable phases. Programmers must define the problem, design the program, code the program, and then test and debug, document, and implement it.

Software development can affect an organization's cost-benefit analysis according to whether the new software will be used as a replacement for a manual procedure or simply to enhance an already automated process.

TESTING

Thorough testing is essential. The two basic types of testing are application testing and acceptance testing. With application testing, programs are tested individually and then tested together. With **acceptance testing**, users evaluate the system to see whether it meets their needs and whether it functions correctly. It's essential that errors or problems be detected before the system is released for use in the organization.

TRAINING

A computerized information system includes not only computer hardware and software but also knowledgeable users and procedures. A successful conclusion to the project requires training the users of the new system. The best training methods involve sitting users down with the new system in one-on-one training sessions. Users also will need manuals that include tutorials as well as reference information.

CONVERTING SYSTEMS

After the new system has been tested and the users have been trained, conversion to the new system occurs. System conversion can be performed in any of the following ways:

- A **parallel conversion** involves running both the new and the old systems for a while to check that the new system produces answers at least as good as those of the old system. This type of conversion is the safest; the old system can carry the load until any problems with the new system are cleared up. This conversion is also the most expensive, however, because the work is duplicated.
- With a **pilot conversion**, one part of the organization converts to the new system while the rest of the organization continues to run the old system. When the pilot group is satisfied with the new system, the rest of the organization can start using it.

- A **phased conversion** occurs when the new system is implemented over different time periods, one part at a time. After one part of the new system is running, another piece is implemented.
- A **direct conversion**, sometimes called a **crash conversion** or **plunge**, requires stopping the old system and then starting the new system. A direct conversion is the most risky type of conversion, but it may be necessary in some situations.

Phase 5: Maintaining the System

In the final phase of the SDLC, the new system is evaluated to ensure that it has met its intended needs and works correctly. A **postimplementation system review** is a process of ongoing evaluation that determines whether the system has met its goals. After conversion, widespread use may reveal errors that were not detected during testing that must be corrected. In addition, changes will be needed as the business environment changes. For example, changes may be needed in data entry forms to deal with an expanded product line.

In addition to the postimplementation review, the system must be maintained. Maintenance includes such tasks as making adjustments to the system as the organization changes; adding, deleting, and adjusting records; making backup copies of files; and providing security for the system. Most organizations spend much more time and money on maintenance than any other component of the SDLC.

In time, the system may be found to be so deficient that a new round of systems development must take place—and the systems development life cycle begins anew.

"A successful conclusion to the project requires training the users of the new system."

Chapter Summary

Systems Analysis and Design

Systems analysts determine an organization's information system needs by working closely with both users and management. Systems analysts determine the requirements needed to modify an existing system or to develop a new one. They identify and evaluate alternative solutions, make formal presentations to management, and assist in the development of the system after an option has been chosen. To stay organized and keep track of these various tasks, systems analysts follow an organized procedure for planning and building information systems called the systems development life cycle (SDLC).

A system is a collection of components purposefully organized into a functioning whole to accomplish a goal. Systems occur in nature, but artificial systems are deliberately constructed by people to serve a specific purpose. Although many models of the SDLC exist, the five traditional phases are (1) planning or investigation, (2) analysis, (3) design, (4) implementation, and (5) maintenance or support. The SDLC was developed to impose order on earlier, haphazard development processes and to improve the quality of information systems.

The three classic mistakes of failed information systems development projects are lack of user involvement, poor project management, and lack of documentation. Systems analysts can avoid mistakes by involving users, using a problem-solving approach, applying project management skills, keeping thorough documentation, using checkpoints to make sure the project is on track, and designing the system with room for growth and change.

In phase 1 of the SDLC, the organization recognizes the need for an information system, defines the problem, examines alternative solutions, and determines the project's feasibility. In phase 2 of the SDLC, the systems analyst determines what the new system should accomplish by analyzing the existing system and determining the needs of the new system. In phase 3 of the SDLC, the systems analyst determines how the new system will work. In phase 4 of the SDLC, the management team decides whether to build or buy a new system, develops the software, tests the system, trains users, and converts to the new system. In phase 5 of the SDLC, the new system receives ongoing evaluation and maintenance to ensure that it meets the organization's needs and works properly.

Key Terms and Concepts

Matching

Match each key term in the left column with the most accurate definition in the right column.

_____ 1. system

_____ 2. prototyping

_____ 3. pilot conversion

_____ 4. acceptance testing

_____ 5. VAR

_____ 6. application testing

_____ 7. parallel conversion

_____ 8. waterfall model

_____ 9. artificial system

_____ 10. phased conversion

_____ 11. deliverable

_____ 12. CASE

_____ 13. project dictionary

_____ 14. postimplementation system review

_____ 15. direct conversion

a. Type of vendor that combines and installs equipment and software from multiple sources.

b. Occurs when a new system is implemented one part at a time, until the complete system is functional.

c. A design tool used to automate documentation.

d. Stopping an old system and starting a new system.

e. A systems development method that builds in correction pathways that return to a prior phase.

f. A collection of components purposefully organized into a functioning whole to accomplish a goal.

g. An ongoing evaluation process to determine whether a system has met its goals.

h. An outcome or tangible output such as a report.

i. Users evaluate a system to see whether it meets their needs and functions.

j. Occurs when one part of an organization begins using a new system, while the rest of the organization continues to use the old system.

k. Uses a small-scale mock-up of a system.

l. A document that includes all the terminology relevant to a project.

m. A plan deliberately constructed by people to serve a purpose.

n. The process of testing applications individually and then in connection with other components.

o. Running both new and old systems at the same time for a time.

Multiple Choice

Circle the correct choice for each of the following.

1. What document highlights the current system's problems and then proposes solutions and makes recommendations?
   a. Project plan
   b. Project dictionary
   c. Project proposal
   d. Project notebook

2. How is operational feasibility determined?
   a. The project has sufficient fiscal resources.
   b. The project has measurable tangible benefits.
   c. The project can be accomplished using existing technology.
   d. The project can be accomplished with the organization's available resources.

3. What is the name of a type of graphic that displays all of the interested parties and the relationship between them that is used to create the process under consideration?
   a. Entity-relationship diagram
   b. Gantt Chart
   c. CASE diagram
   d. Data flow diagram

4. Which type of conversion method presents the most risk?
   a. Phased
   b. Parallel
   c. Direct
   d. Pilot

5. What is a Gantt chart?
   a. A bar chart that shows different activities over time
   b. A pie chart that shows allocation of resources
   c. A bar chart that shows return on investment
   d. A column chart that shows RFQ status

6. What is the deliverable for phase 1 of the SDLC?
   a. The decision to buy or build a new system
   b. The project proposal
   c. A logical design providing an overall picture of how the system will work
   d. A listing of the new system's requirements

7. What is another term for prototyping?
   a. Computer-aided software engineering
   b. Joint application development
   c. Operational feasibility
   d. Rapid application development

8. Which of the following is an example of an intangible benefit?
   a. Increased sales
   b. Improved customer satisfaction
   c. Faster response time
   d. Decreased complaints

9. Which of the following statements about joint application development is true?
   a. It is also known as rapid application development.
   b. It produces a fully functional model.
   c. It produces a small-scale mock-up of the system.
   d. It combines the first four phases of the traditional SDLC.

10. What are the two basic types of software testing that take place during phase 4?
    a. Application and acceptance
    b. User and application
    c. Parallel and crash
    d. Prototype and data flow

Fill-In

In the blanks provided, write the correct answer for each of the following.

1. The logical design that will provide an overall picture of how the new system will work is a deliverable for phase _____.

2. A request for _____ is sent to a vendor to obtain pricing for information system components.

3. The process of ongoing evaluation, referred to as postimplementation system review, occurs in the _____ phase.

4. The project _____ is an online reference containing all of the documentation associated with a project.

5. The _____ _____ process determines the system's needs by examining how the system will meet end-user needs.

6. _____ conversion is the most expensive type of conversion but presents the least risk.

7. A project's gains and losses are examined by creating a(n) _____-_____ analysis.

8. A(n) _____ is an unacceptable or undesirable result.

9. A request for _____ is sent to a vendor to obtain a quote for the design, configuration, and installation information for a system.

10. A _____ _____ works with both users and management to determine a project's requirements.

11. _____ feasibility determines whether a project can be accomplished with existing technology.

12. _____ _____ _____ is the overall financial yield of a system over its lifetime.

13. A(n) _____ _____ diagram uses graphical symbols to show the flow of data through a system.

14. Increased sales figures and faster response time are examples of _____ benefits.

15. A listing of the system requirements is the deliverable for the _____ phase.

Short Answer

1. What are the five phases of the SDLC?

2. What is the purpose of an information technology steering committee?

3. What are the three classic mistakes of failed information systems development projects?

4. What advantages does the joint application development method have over the waterfall and prototyping methods?

5. Identify the four ways a system conversion can be performed.

Teamwork

1. **System Conversion** As a team, determine the answers to the following questions and then write a group report based on your findings. What are the four types of system conversions? Which is the most expensive? Which is the most risky? If your school were going to change its student accounts, registration, and financial aid systems, which method of conversion would you want it to use? Explain why. Does your campus have an information technology steering committee? If it does, who are its members? If it doesn't, then inquire how information technology decisions are made on campus? As a team, merge your findings and present your results in a one-page, double-spaced paper.

2. **Systems Analysis** Work together to research and answer the following questions. Does your school have a computer studies department? Typically these departments are identified as computer science (CS) or management information systems (MIS). If it does, what is the actual title of the department? Look

at a school catalog to see whether the department offers any systems analysis courses. What, if any, are the prerequisites for the systems analysis courses? Which courses do you think would best prepare you for studies in systems analysis? Find the name of an instructor and contact him or her to find out what software tools are used in the course. If your institution does not have the necessary resources, then use the Web to locate an institution that does and consult its online catalog. Write a one-page, double-spaced summary of your team's findings.

3. **Systems Analyst Job Description** Using your college placement center or other employment references, including the Internet, locate systems analyst job descriptions. As a team, collaborate and create a comprehensive definition of the job title. Include a list of the responsibilities the job entails as well as the knowledge and skill level required. Present your definition, list of responsibilities, and knowledge/skill requirements in a one-page, double-spaced paper.

4. **Library Systems** As a team, take a tour of the school library. Describe the current process used by your school's library for finding, reading, and checking out a book or periodical. Can this system be improved? What improvements would you suggest? What would be the tangible and intangible benefits of implementing your system changes? Be sure to use key terms from this chapter in your answer. Write a one- or two-page, double-spaced paper that describes your group's findings and provides a recommendation.

5. **Using the SDLC to Plan a Business System** As a team, make plans to start a business that will post and sell items on eBay for customers. Using the SDLC, create a chart of the problems, opportunities, business design, hardware requirements, and employee and customer components to be considered in each phase of the development process for your business. Keep in mind the information-processing component of the business and such questions as these: How will you track inventory. How will you keep track of customers? How will you keep track of expenses and income? Remember, this does not have to be complete, but you do need to demonstrate that you can use the phases of the SDLC to develop your business. Present your detailed chart and answers to the questions in a one- to two-page, double-spaced paper.

On the Web

1. **Investigate the V-Shaped Model of Software Development** The waterfall model is only one implementation of the software development life cycle; there are others. Using the Internet and a search engine of your choice, research the V-shaped model of software development. Locate a diagram that displays the relationship among the phases of this model. In a one-page, double-spaced paper, summarize the model, state its advantages and disadvantages over other models, and include the diagram.

2. **PowerBuilder** One of the CASE tools illustrated in this textbook is PowerBuilder. Visit the PowerBuilder Web site at **www.sybase.com/products/development/powerbuilder**. In a one-page, double-spaced paper or short PowerPoint presentation, provide the answers to the following questions and any other related information that you locate during your research. What company created this tool? What is the current version of PowerBuilder? In what environments can PowerBuilder be used to develop applications? As with many software applications, a trial version of PowerBuilder is available. After how many days does the trial version expire? Identify a city, a state, a U.S. government organization, and a college or university that has used PowerBuilder. What are the upgrade and purchase prices for this development tool?

3. **Green Systems** Using the Internet and a search engine of your choice, search for green information technology sources. You can go to **www.eds.com** (a source cited in this chapter) and use the search window in this site to locate green solutions proposed by this vendor. Accumulate your research, and in a one-page, double-spaced paper present your findings on green information technology solutions as well as their goals. Be sure to note any implementation concerns. Remember to cite your references.

4. **Using Gantt Charts** Search the Web to locate three software applications that create Gantt charts. Identify the manufacturer, the specific product name, and the cost of each application. Identify the products that offer free trial versions and the length of the trial periods. Based on the product descriptions, do you think you could learn how to use one of these applications? Explain why or why not. Answer these questions, citing references, in a one-page, double-spaced paper.

5. **Dream Green Jobs** Use the Internet and a search engine of your choice to locate employment sites that focus on green information technology jobs. Create a list of the green jobs you find, along with a description of the type of job (analyst, management, supervisory, educational, or assistant), the required level of education, pay rate (if posted), and location. Make sure to include the part of the job description that substantiates these posted jobs as "green" jobs. Present your list and the related information either in a Word table or an Excel spreadsheet. Remember to cite your references.

chapter 14

Enterprise Computing

"Hey you, get off of my cloud!" You might not remember that song; it was sung back in the day by The Rolling Stones. However, today the song might be referring to a crowded, shared computing service called a cloud. Are you familiar with cloud computing? How about blade servers, Web portals, and RAID? It is hard to keep up with the technology that is developed by the driving need for companies to keep data and users connected and updated at all times. Enterprise services and technology are always changing, being reinvented, and being renamed with catchy labels—all with the goal of increasing accessibility and decreasing cost. Do you see the need to keep up with the changes in enterprise technology? Do you think you might want to get on that cloud, use that blade, jump through that portal, and join that RAID?

Until now, you've been learning primarily about the various technologies involved in personal computing. **Personal computing** refers to any situation or setup where one person controls and uses a computer or handheld device for personal or business activities. You've learned about what goes on inside a computer with system and application software as well as the various input/output and storage devices. Along with these basic computing concepts, you've also been introduced to how networks, the Internet, wireless applications, and databases work and are used. Now that you have a solid foundation in the hardware and software associated with personal computing, let's turn our attention to computing within an enterprise.

An **enterprise** is simply a business or organization, which can include universities, government agencies, and not-for-profit groups or charities. **Enterprise computing** is information technology on a large scale, encompassing all aspects of technology and information resources, including problems or malfunctions, within an organization or a business. It includes understanding the use of computers in the networks that span the organization, as well as the software needed to process and monitor activities involved in daily business operations (Figure 14.1).

A short list of enterprise computing issues includes ensuring the security of passwords and corporate data while providing employees access to such data; creating network connectivity between LANs, mainframes, microcomputers, and handheld devices; handling multiple hardware and software configurations; maintaining an effective e-mail system; maintaining licenses, repair contracts, and backups; software development and testing; and providing support and training for employees.

In this chapter, you will explore various enterprise computing solutions and learn how technology is used to manage the flow of data and information within an enterprise.

FIGURE 14.1
Enterprise computing en-
compasses all aspects of
technology and information
in an organization.

Business Processes and Activities

Companies use information systems, the collection of people, hardware, software, data records, and activities that process the data and information, to support business processes for internal operations such as manufacturing, order processing, and human resources management. **Business processes** are activities that have an identifiable output and value to the organization's customers. A business process begins with a customer's need and ends with that need being fulfilled. The activities that compose this progression from need to fulfillment can be viewed as a series of links in a chain along which information flows within the organization. At each link, value is added in the form of the work performed by people associated with that process, and new, useful information is generated. Information begins to accumulate at the point of entry (for example, a customer sends an order to the company) and flows through the various links, or processes, within the organization. New, useful information is added every step of the way (Figure 14.2).

Information systems can be used to support or streamline business activities for a competitive advantage. A **competitive advantage** is a condition that gives an organization a superior position over the companies it competes with. For example, an enterprise might use an information system to support a billing process that reduces the use of paper and, more

FIGURE 14.2 At each link in a business process, value is added to products to make them more desirable to the consumer.

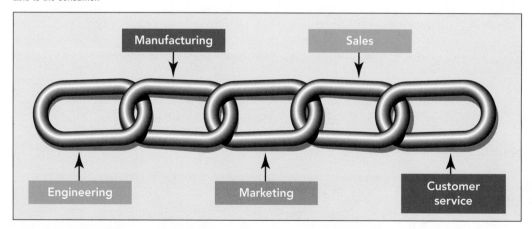

important, the handling of paper, thus reducing material and labor costs. This same system can help managers keep track of the billing process more effectively because they will have more accurate, up-to-date information about it, enabling them to make smart, timely business decisions.

Information systems can support either internally or externally focused business processes. Internally focused systems work to smooth communication among the functional areas (such as accounting, finance, human resources, and so on) or activities within the organization. For instance, Visa International's accounting system automatically compares outgoing payments with invoices and sends e-mail requests to managers to review any discrepancies.

Externally focused systems coordinate business activities with customers, suppliers, business partners, and others who operate outside the organization's boundaries. The Nordstrom retail chain is noted for its exceptional customer service, including its easy-return policy and soft touches such as thank-you notes from employees. In 2008, in response to customer requests, it began offering a "buy online, pick up in store" option. Other companies have been doing this for some time but often face complaints about long waits and poor customer service. To avoid similar problems, Nordstrom implemented policies to ensure customers receive the same level of customer service they've come to expect. The initial program was limited to specific departments on a trial basis, transactions are confirmed via e-mail within one hour, and additional gift services are available at the time of pickup.

Businesses have used information systems to support business processes for decades, beginning with the installation of applications for specific business tasks such as issuing paychecks. Often these systems were built on different computing platforms. Each platform often operated in a unique hardware and software environment. Applications running on different computing platforms are difficult to integrate because customized interfaces are required for one system to communicate with another.

When systems get too complex and productivity suffers, businesses reevaluate the way departments and individuals interact and reassess their roles and positions in the overall business life cycle. Two methods of reevaluation are business process reengineering and business process management.

BUSINESS PROCESS REENGINEERING

Business process reengineering (BPR) refers to the use of information technology to bring about major organizational changes and cost savings. At the core of BPR is the principle that information technology doesn't bring big payoffs if you simply automate existing business processes. Success results when information technology is used to change existing processes, improve customer service, and hopefully reduce overall cost.

The structure of a typical organization is shown in Figure 14.3. Each business area has its own information systems and business processes. In BPR, designers ignore an organization's functional divisions and focus instead on business processes, sometimes completely redesigning them from the ground up. For example, in a traditional organization, the product development process involves many functional divisions, each of which works on the product's development separately before passing it on to the next division. BPR attempts to improve efficiency by restructuring how, where, and when activities are performed. After reengineering, cross-functional teams work together as a unit on a single activity, rather than working on it separately at different stages.

BPR can lead to big payoffs, but a high proportion of early BPR projects failed. Many companies came to see BPR as a means of downsizing, and employees learned to fear and resist these efforts. The Prosci Web site at **www.prosci.com/howto.htm** provides more information and free tutorials on BPR.

FIGURE 14.3 The Flow of Information Technology across the Functional Areas of an Organization

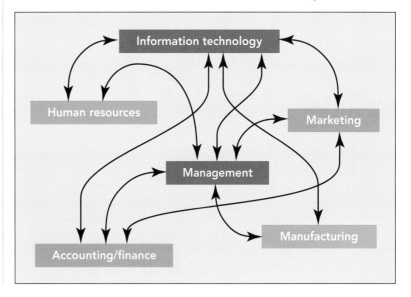

FIGURE 14.4 The BMP-basics Web site is an excellent source of real BMP examples, Webinar information, and updates to the current BMP software applications.

FIGURE 14.5 Enterprise systems enable users to share information and applications though a common interface.

BUSINESS PROCESS MANAGEMENT

Business process management (BPM) evolved from BPR. BPM's goal is to improve existing processes and optimize assets by effectively and efficiently managing the entire life cycle of these business processes.

BPM also uses a cross-functional approach and information technology. However, BPM examines the person-to-person interactions within a process, as well as the communications that

take place among various systems. By doing so, BPM can enhance the effectiveness and integration of these processes while increasing their flexibility and providing opportunities for innovation. BPM is often applied to discrete parts of an organization rather than to the entire enterprise.

The BPM philosophy encourages employees to suggest and implement changes within their areas of expertise. Various BPM systems have been developed to technologically manage this process. Typically, a business analyst or process architect from the business area with a strong IT background is selected to lead the BPM initiative and manage the underlying technology used to assess and automate the various business processes. To view industry resources and examples of successful BPM implementations, visit the BPMbasics site at **www.bpmbasics.com** (Figure 14.4).

During business process reengineering and business process management, the overall connectivity and efficiency of systems within the enterprise is evaluated. The next section will look at some of these systems, their purpose, and effectiveness in detail.

Enterprise Systems

Enterprise systems are information systems that integrate an organization's information and applications across all of the organization's functional divisions. Rather than storing information in separate places throughout the organization, enterprise systems provide an **enterprise data center**, a secure common repository, for **enterprise data**, the centralized data shared throughout an organization, and a common user interface to all corporate users. Enterprise systems enable personnel to share data, **enterprise software** (software designed to solve problems at the enterprise level of an organization rather that at the departmental level), and departmental level applications seamlessly, no matter where they originated, the platform they originated from, or who is using the application (Figure 14.5).

With the launching of its **e-business (electronic business)** campaign in 1997, IBM began to use the Internet to buy, sell, provide customer service, and collaborate with business partners.

To continue to compete in global markets, competitors realized that they also had to provide quality customer service, buy materials more economically, and develop products faster and more efficiently. The emergence of the Internet and the World Wide Web resulted in the globalization of supplier networks, opening up new opportunities and methods of conducting business. **Globalization** refers to conducting business internationally where the goods and services are identical (or nearly identical) in all locations (Figure 14.6). This means that a McDonald's in Singapore is almost exactly the same as a McDonald's in Chicago.

Customers have increasing numbers of options available to them, and they are demanding products that are more sophisticated and customized to their unique needs. Enterprise systems can help companies find innovative ways to increase accurate and on-time shipments, minimize costs, and ultimately increase customer satisfaction and the overall profitability of the company.

Enterprise systems come in many shapes and sizes, each providing a unique set of features and functionality. Remember that an enterprise system is an information system; therefore, it is composed of data, hardware, software, people, and procedures. It can include network servers, database management systems, desktop and notebook computers, and handheld devices. When deciding whether to implement enterprise solutions, managers need to consider a number of different issues. One of the most important is selecting and implementing applications that meet the requirements of the business as well as its customers and suppliers. Let's start by examining how enterprise systems are categorized and managed.

CENTRALIZED VERSUS DISTRIBUTED STRUCTURES

Enterprise networking, the technology infrastructure within an enterprise, requires an enormous amount of planning, integration, managing, and flexibility to continually adapt to the new interfaces, technology, and market demands that constantly change the ground rules. Enterprise networks are managed in one of two ways: They are either centralized or

FIGURE 14.6
McDonald's recently opened Quarter Pounder stores in Tokyo without any brand marketing—no arches on the building, but the pictures identify the product.

distributed (Figure 14.7). In a **centralized structure**, technology management is centered in the IT department, and everyone within the organization works with standardized technology solutions in their everyday work. In a **distributed structure**, users are able to customize their technology tools to suit their individual needs and wants. Typically, an enterprise will start with one structure; but rarely does it use that structure exclusively.

For example, the computer labs at your school are most likely managed in a centralized way. Each time a student begins a work session, the computer operating environment, desktop, and applications are always the same. It doesn't matter which computer in the lab you use—they all look and function the same way. Conversely, your instructor's computer is most likely managed in a distributed way. Some things, such as applications, are the same on all faculty computers, but by and large, your instructor is able to customize the operating environment, desktop, and application configurations to suit his or her individual needs and wants. The structure a company chooses depends on a variety of factors including cost, applications being used, security, and objectives.

Now that you know how information systems can be structured within an enterprise, let's take a closer look at the ongoing process involved in maintaining and upgrading enterprise technology.

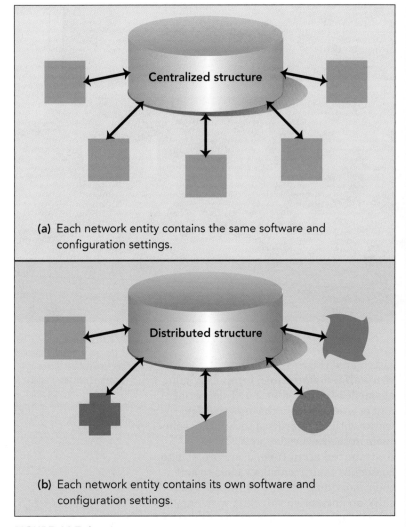

(a) Each network entity contains the same software and configuration settings.

(b) Each network entity contains its own software and configuration settings.

FIGURE 14.7 An enterprise has two options for managing its technology infrastructure: **(a)** centralized structure or **(b)** distributed structure.

APPLYING TECHNOLOGY IN THE ENTERPRISE

In this section, you'll learn about the day-to-day concerns an enterprise encounters as it manages its technology assets. The process is ongoing and active because technology changes every day. The enterprise must respond by staying current with both its internal and external constituents.

Currency At any given moment, all of the technology used by an organization is more or less current with the marketplace. As time moves on, one would expect that administrators and end users would become more comfortable with the existing technology in the organization because they have used it for a period of time. However, as technology improves and programs update, a tension eventually develops between the current status of the system and the most current technology available. The tradeoff is that implementing the most current technology and

software often means a lower comfort level among users.

For instance, let's say that an organization is using Microsoft Office 2003, but the current version in the marketplace is Microsoft Office 2007. This would mean that there are several years of tension between the organization's software and what is available in the current marketplace. However, upgrading to Office 2007 means that users will have to adapt to the changes that have been made to the software since the last release (Figure 14.8). Therefore, being current has the benefit of having the latest tools, but it carries the risk of a reduced comfort level among users and reduced employee productivity.

Upgrading When an organization decides to upgrade its technology, it should consider several things. First and foremost is the impact on the users. How difficult will it be for the users to adapt to the new hardware and applications? How much training will they need? What influence will the upgrade have on the organization's business constituents? Is the organization leading with this change or responding to market pressures?

The second consideration is whether hardware upgrades are required. Software applications upgrades may require minimum or no changes in hardware, or they might necessitate major hardware changes to accommodate new applications. Additionally, changes in the structure of the network or changes in communication pathways may be costly when new hardware must be purchased for these changes to be implemented.

The third consideration is the cost of the upgrade. Obviously, there are costs to changes in hardware. But even if no new hardware will be required, upgrades can be costly. Not only does the organization need to purchase the requisite number of licenses for the software, but it needs to account for the time necessary to install and customize the software. This is where centralized versus distributed management structures are important. In a centralized structure, upgrading may be relatively easy and less expensive, because all of the computers are managed from one location. As a result, an IT staff member can install and release new software from one location. In a distributed environment, upgrading might involve sending IT personnel to many different locations to install the upgrade on user-managed machines.

Additional expenses might be incurred for user training during the transition from one version to another. File compatibility issues also may arise. For example, if external users are not using Office 2007, they may not be able to read documents created using the Office 2007 suite unless those documents are saved in a compatible format.

Maintenance Maintenance is another important consideration in managing technology within an organization. It too depends on whether IT structures are centralized or distributed. As with upgrading, maintenance may be easier and less expensive in a centralized environment. With a distributed infrastructure, maintenance and training might require IT personnel to travel to multiple sites for scheduled visits and training sessions.

Scalability
Another important consideration is **scalability**, a hardware or software system's ability to continue functioning effectively as demands and use increase (Figure 14.9). For example, a network is scalable if an organization can easily expand it from a few nodes to hundreds or thousands of nodes. Scalability ensures that an organization's systems won't become obsolete as user needs and demands grow. Scalability does not depend on whether the system is centralized or distributed, although adding nodes to a centralized system is somewhat easier because the software installation is centralized and standardized.

Interoperability The ability to connect and exchange data with another computer, even one that is a different brand or model,

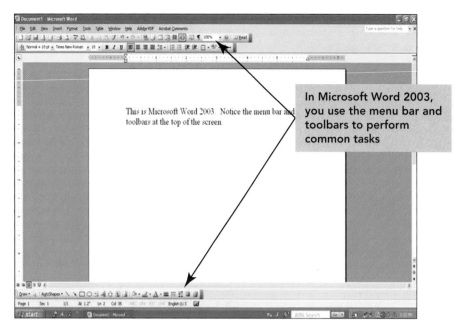

In Microsoft Word 2003, you use the menu bar and toolbars to perform common tasks

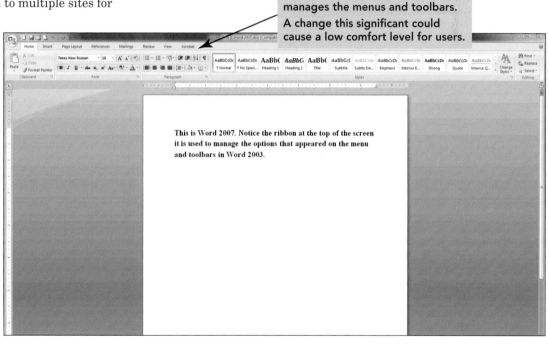

In Microsoft Word 2007 the Ribbon manages the menus and toolbars. A change this significant could cause a low comfort level for users.

is known as **interoperability**. Most enterprise systems have computers that run a variety of different platforms. For example, the enterprise may use Macs, Windows PCs, Linux machines, servers, and mainframes. Interoperability enables all of these computers to interact seamlessly on a network, regardless of whether the technology structure is centralized or distributed.

Adding Workstations and Applications
What do enterprises do when new employees are hired and need a computer

FIGURE 14.8 The change from one software version to another can require some time for learning new elements such as the Ribbon in Microsoft Office 2007, which did not exist in Microsoft Office 2003.

FIGURE 14.9 A computer infrastructure is scalable when technicians can easily add new users to the system—even if there are hundreds of new users.

for their work? What if they want to implement a new application on a network? Adding a new user's workstation or installing a new application on a network increases the number of locations where problems can occur. One common problem is a single point of failure. A **single point of failure (SPOF)** refers to any system component, such as hardware or software, that causes the entire system to malfunction when it fails.

SPOF problems can be minimized by using a centralized technology management structure because it gives network administrators more control over the software that is installed and managed on the computers throughout the enterprise.

Adding a Network How can enterprises create networks on the fly, such as those that connect devices in a conference or at a meeting? **Zero configuration (Zeroconf)** is a method for networking devices via an Ethernet cable that does not require configuration and administration. Zeroconf is best used in small networking situations where the need for security is low. It also can be used to form a functional network in a home or a small business.

Disaster Recovery = Business Continuity
Another important application of technology in large enterprises is disaster planning, also referred to as business continuity planning (BCP). A **disaster recovery plan**, also referred to as a **business continuity plan (BCP)**, is a written plan with detailed instructions

that specifies alternative computing facilities to be used for emergency processing until nonoperational computers can be repaired or replaced. It is important to remember that there is no single approach to disaster recovery and no one way to protect your business operations. Strategies and procedures established by one company may be inappropriate for another. Disaster recovery starts with a sound plan and design. Important essentials in that plan are:

- For backup protection, be sure to place a copy of your backup in a different physical location.
- To recover the business from the backup, there must be enough data in a protected location backup to continue normal business operations.
- The recovery process must be completed in the time specified in the backup plan. If the physical building has been compromised, a secondary location for set up and providing business continuity should be established.
- A constant and ongoing evaluation of the recovery process by supervisors and recovery personnel is required so that no disruption is perceived by customers or business associates.

Once a plan is developed, business leaders must take additional steps to ensure it will function appropriately when it is called into action.

- Test the backup system regularly.
- Update backup software when needed.
- Protect backup servers from accidental or deliberate damage.
- Check regularly for security breaches.
- Distribute the disaster recovery or business continuity plan to essential personnel.

Disasters can be created by humans, such as the September 11 terrorist attacks on the World Trade Center and the Pentagon, or due to natural forces like Hurricane Katrina in the Gulf Coast states, and they can have far-reaching consequences. However, smaller-scale disasters, such as a fire, theft, or security breach, can also be detrimental to a company. A distributed technology structure is extremely important in disaster recovery plans. Enterprises have begun to see the importance of a backup system in a different geographical region. In the aftermath of September 11, many enterprises are moving their backup centers to suburban areas with independent utility and transportation systems.

Some backup centers are dedicated to functioning during emergencies and serve only as backup facilities, complete with their own electrical generators and telecommunications grids. These sites can be either hot disaster recovery sites or cold disaster recovery sites. A **hot site** is the more expensive as it is kept in a state of readiness at all times. A **cold site** only becomes operational once a disaster has occurred. Other backup centers have a dual purpose. They are fully functioning business facilities that act as satellite offices with the additional duty of duplicating all enterprise data. The backup portion of these dual purpose sites can function as either a hot or cold site. Because such "mirroring" of data needs to be performed in an organized fashion, professional backup and security companies can be hired to ensure that the job is done efficiently, effectively, and without compromising data integrity. The National Security Agency provides some guidelines and assistance with respect to information security (Figure 14.10). The Disaster Recovery World Web site at **www.disasterrecoveryworld.com** is an excellent location providing a continuity and recovery directory along with software to help with business analysis and risk impact.

Now that you understand the issues that enterprises must consider when applying technology solutions, let's look at some of the specific software tools that enterprises use.

Tools for Enterprise Computing

Enterprises have many opportunities to apply technology to different situations, whether to improve internal business processes or external interactions with customers and vendors. Software tools help the various areas of the enterprise manage their responsibilities.

ENTERPRISE RESOURCE PLANNING

Enterprise resource planning (ERP) software brings together various enterprise functions, such as manufacturing, sales, marketing, and finance, into a single computer system. Managers implement ERP applications from vendors such as SAP, Oracle, and Sage to support activities in functional areas such as finance and human resources, as well as business processes such as order tracking and inventory, accounts payable, accounts receivable, and customer support (Figure 14.11).

Let's take a closer look at the order-tracking process in an enterprise that does not use ERP software. When a customer places an order with the sales division or customer service, the order travels to the individuals and departments that need to handle it. Errors and delays can be introduced along the way, or the order could be misplaced or lost. At any given time, few people in the enterprise can pinpoint the order's status should the customer inquire about it. For example, a salesperson may not have access to the manufacturing department's computer system to see whether manufacturing has even begun to fulfill the order.

With ERP software, one software program with separate modules for each functional unit replaces the separate,

FIGURE 14.10 The National Security Agency (**www.nsa.gov**) provides information, programs, products, and guidelines to help business and other organizations keep their information systems secure.

FIGURE 14.11 SAP is the leading ERP software company, providing solutions for companies of all sizes.

FIGURE 14.12 The survey supports the concern over user adoption problems in an ERP software rollout.

independent systems that sales and marketing, manufacturing, and other divisions use. The ERP software modules are linked so that a salesperson can access manufacturing's module to see whether an order has been processed. ERP improves the order process; provides customers with up-to-date, accurate information on the status of an order; and, in the end, accomplishes order fulfillment faster and with fewer errors.

Organizations undertake ERP projects to integrate financial, human resources, customer, and order information; speed up

manufacturing processes; and reduce inventory. ERP systems have been implemented in many Fortune 500 companies but have been slower to catch on with small and mid-size companies. Although ERP sounds like an ideal solution, it does have some drawbacks. With ERP, customer service representatives' job duties are no longer confined to merely keying in orders. With ERP, their duties are associated with every department in the organization. They must make decisions and respond to situations that they never had to before, such as whether customers pay on time or whether the warehouse can ship orders in a timely manner.

Some ERP projects fail because employees are resistant to change. If an organization simply installs ERP software without providing sufficient staff training and transition time to change processes, it won't experience the benefits of ERP. In fact, it may cause a chain reaction of negative effects. Replacing old software that everyone knows how to use with new software that no one knows how to use can slow business processes, causing delays in production, shipping, and billing. End user adoption problems are cited as the primary concern in most ERP software changes (Figure 14.12). However, when done properly with planning and training, an organization that switches to ERP software improves its order fulfillment, manufacturing, shipping, and billing processes.

Finally, the cost and time involved with ERP implementation sometimes blindsides organizations. For a large organization, the total cost of implementing ERP, including hardware, software, retraining, service, and support costs, might be $15 million and can easily exceed $100 million. Hidden costs for implementing an ERP system include integration and testing, customization, and data analysis and conversion. ERP vendors often estimate an implementation time of three to six months. More realistic time lines are usually between one and three years. It may take companies up to eight months before they begin to see any benefits from the new system. However, companies do see as much as $1.6 million in average annual savings from a new ERP system. Multimillion-dollar ERP projects can fail when the software chosen or developed does not support an

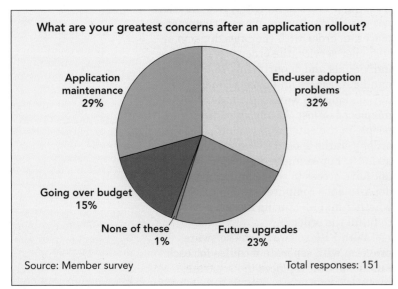

What are your greatest concerns after an application rollout?

Application maintenance 29%

End-user adoption problems 32%

Going over budget 15%

None of these 1%

Future upgrades 23%

Source: Member survey   Total responses: 151

Customer acquisition	• Locate leads, track prospects and proposals, achieve initial sale
Customer retention	• Monitor customer satisfaction, gain repeat business
Customer enhancement	• Continued customer contact, expand sales to new or extended products or services

FIGURE 14.13 CRM software enables organizations to track and communicate with customers from the original lead development phase through the established relationship phase.

organization's most important business process. When this occurs, organizations can either change business processes to fit the software or change the software to fit the processes. Both of these options have serious disadvantages and the potential to truly cripple an organization.

CUSTOMER RELATIONSHIP MANAGEMENT

Customer relationship management (CRM) software keeps track of an organization's interactions with its customers and focuses on retaining those customers. Salespeople can use CRM software to match company resources with customer wants and needs (Figure 14.13). A recent survey found that it can cost five to seven times more to replace a current customer than it does to keep one. Additionally, a 2 percent increase in keeping current customers has the same effect on overall profits as cutting costs by 10 percent, and retaining just 5 percent of the current customer base can cause profits to rise by 25 to 125 percent, depending on the industry. With statistics like these, CRM has become a leading enterprise focus.

Due to new advances in technology, companies are changing their approach to customer relationship management. In the 21st century, most organizations manage their customer relationships electronically. Today, consumers can access self-service applications and technical support via the Web with not only computers but also Web-enabled devices such as smartphones.

Organizations must find ways to personalize customers' online experiences using tools such as help-desk software, e-mail organizers, and Web development applications. A current CRM trend in e-commerce is the use of an invisible timer on when the user last viewed or placed an item in an online shopping cart. If a customer exceeds that time, an instant message pops up and asks whether the user needs the help of a sales representative. A live chat can follow, and the shopper's questions can be answered. Hesitation is removed, and the cart can progress to check out.

Just as with ERP, an organization must consider its business processes along with its existing IT infrastructure before considering CRM solutions. CRM vendors include FrontRange Solutions, Oracle, SAP, and Salesforce.com Inc.

SALES FORCE AUTOMATION

Often used interchangeably with CRM, **sales force automation (SFA) software** automates many of the business processes involved with sales, including processing and tracking orders, managing customers and other contacts, monitoring and controlling inventory, and analyzing sales forecasts (Figure 14.14).

EXTENSIBLE BUSINESS REPORTING LANGUAGE

Public and private enterprises use **Extensible Business Reporting Language (XBRL)** to publish and share financial information with each other and

FIGURE 14.14
Relatively large enterprises
sometimes use sales force
automation software and
services such as provided
by Salesforce.com
(**www.salesforce.com**).

industry analysts across all computer platforms and the Internet. XBRL makes use
of XML syntax and related technologies to
standardize formatting to present various
types of financial information, including
net revenue, annual and quarterly reports,
and U.S. Securities and Exchange Commission (SEC) filings. XBRL is a Web
protocol developed and promoted by an international not-for-profit consortium. It is
free, but has some regulatory guidelines
that the user must adhere to. Because of
XBRL's broad usage and financial implications, the consortium that guides its use
consists of more than 480 major international companies, organizations, and government agencies. Current users of XBRL
include the Tokyo Stock Exchange; the U.S.
Federal Financial Institutions Examination Council (FFIEC), including the Federal Reserve System and Federal Deposit
Insurance Corporation (FDIC); Microsoft;
IBM; and EDGAR Online. For more information on the language, its users, and current developments, visit **www.xbrl.org**.

SOFTWARE AS A SERVICE

Software as a service (SaaS) provides
software-based services and solutions to
companies that want to outsource some
of their information technology needs.
Rather than purchasing and installing
software, businesses can access software
that is hosted on the provider's site, or
on the site of a third party known as an
application service provider (ASP),

and deployed over the Internet to the
provider's customers. Unlike an ERP solution, which takes time and often considerable amounts of money to implement,
SaaS customers typically pay an initial
fee based on the number of users and a
monthly service fee. Because the software
is Web based, companies can begin using
the software with little or no setup time.
The lower start-up costs and faster deploy-
ment times for SaaS have made it attractive to small and medium-size companies,
where it is most often used in CRM, HR,
and procurement. The SaaS market
reached $6.3 billion in 2006 and is forecast
to grow to $19.3 billion by the end of 2011.

OPERATIONAL SUPPORT SYSTEMS

An **operational support system (OSS)**
is a suite of programs that support an enterprise's network operations. OSS originally referred to a system that controlled
telephone and computer networks for
telecommunications service providers.
However, a modern OSS enables any enterprise to monitor, analyze, and manage
its network system.

ENTERPRISE APPLICATION INTEGRATION

**Enterprise application integration
(EAI)** is a combination of processes, software, standards, and hardware that results in the integration of two or more

enterprise systems. This integration enables multiple systems to operate as one and share data and business processes throughout an organization. In the past, enterprises used custom-built, proprietary software and systems for such functions as inventory control, human resources, sales automation, and database management that ran independently and didn't interact with each other. Enterprises now recognize the need to share information and applications between systems, so many companies are investing in EAI.

Organizations can choose from a range of EAI categories, from database and application linking to data warehousing. When enterprises want all aspects of their computing integrated into one application, it is referred to as a *common virtual system*.

As wonderful as EAI sounds, it is very complex, and a high percentage of such projects fail due to management issues. EAI incorporates every level of the enterprise system: architecture, hardware, software, and processes. EAI vendors include IBM, Microsoft, and Oracle.

Now that you are familiar with various enterprise computing software solutions, let's examine storage systems commonly used in an enterprise.

Enterprise Storage Systems

According to a recent estimate, the amount of information an enterprise must store doubles each year. Add to that the increased demand created by employees, managers, executives, and customers expecting this information to be readily available when and where it's needed—and to be kept safe from prying eyes if it's confidential. It is not surprising that corporate demand for fast, secure, and reliable storage systems is skyrocketing.

New technologies are being developed to meet the unique needs of large organizations. To cope with their information storage needs, many corporations are developing enterprise storage systems. Enterprises invest in enterprise storage systems not necessarily to gain a competitive advantage but to protect and back up their mission-critical data.

RAID

A group of two or more hard drives that contain the same data is called **RAID (redundant array of independent disks)**. The key word in this phrase is *redundant*, which means "extra copy." Everything that is recorded on the original drive is instantaneously recorded on the second disk. No matter how many disks a RAID 1 (or mirrored) device contains, the computer "thinks" it's dealing with just one disk. All of the disks contain an exact copy of all the data. If one of the disks fails, service is not interrupted. This helps to ensure against data loss if something happens to the original, or working, drive (Figure 14.15). If the original disk fails, one of the other disks kicks in and delivers the requested data.

There are several types of RAID devices, such as RAID 0 and RAID 5. The process of using the array of disks differs in each RAID system, but the goal of each is the same: to improve storage speed and protect against data loss.

RAID devices offer a high degree of **fault tolerance**; that is, they keep working even if one or more components fail. For this reason, RAID devices are widely used wherever a service interruption could prove costly, hazardous, or inconvenient to customers. Most of the major Web sites use RAID devices to ensure that their Web pages are always available.

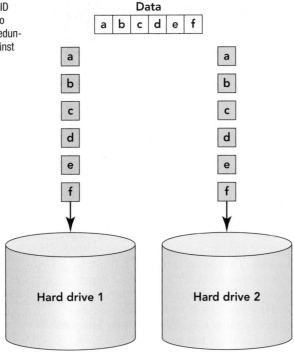

FIGURE 14.15 RAID devices are essential to mission-critical data redundancy and protect against data loss.

Data

| a | b | c | d | e | f |

Hard drive 1

Hard drive 2

RAID is used primarily in medium to large enterprises. Most personal computer users don't need (and couldn't afford) RAID devices. RAID disk drives can be purchased from most computer manufacturers and are installed and maintained by network management personnel. RAID devices run constantly—24 hours a day, 7 days a week, 365 days a year.

CD AND DVD JUKEBOXES AND BLU-RAY OPTICAL LIBRARIES

Digital content can be one of an enterprise's most valuable assets. But an enterprise loses time and money if employees are constantly searching for, repurchasing, or re-creating files. Enterprise storage systems should allow for quick and simple access, management, and organization of data. Jukeboxes and libraries are enterprise storage devices used to store or backup an enterprise's digital content and give users network access to it. The terms *jukebox* and *library* are sometimes used interchangeably—incorrectly. **Jukebox** is used when referring to enterprise storage units that use DVD and CD discs as the storage medium. The term **library** refers to enterprise storage units that use Blu-ray optical media for storage. A double-sided, dual-layer DVD can hold approximately 17 GB per disc, while Blu-ray, the newest type of optical disc, supports up to 50 GB per disc.

STORAGE AREA NETWORKS

Another type of storage device available to all servers on a LAN or WAN is a **storage area network (SAN)**. A SAN is a network of high-capacity storage devices that link all of the organization's servers. In this way, any of the storage devices are accessible from any of the servers. In a SAN, servers provide only pathways between end users and stored data, keeping servers available for processing activities. A SAN contains nothing but disks that store data. SANs often make use of network attached storage (Figure 14.16).

NETWORK ATTACHED STORAGE

Network attached storage (NAS) refers to high-performance devices that offer little more than data and file sharing to clients and other servers on a network. Unlike a file server in a client/server network, which typically handles all processing activities, such as e-mail, authentication, and file management, NAS merely supplies data to users. NAS can be installed anywhere in a LAN, not just within or near a server. When a network uses NAS, more hard disk storage space can be added to the network without shutting down the file servers for upgrading or maintenance. Storage capacities range from 1 terabyte (TB) to as much as 12 petabytes (PB).

We've now examined the software and hardware solutions often employed in enterprise systems. Let's turn our attention to some of the technologies that pull both of these areas together within an enterprise.

Enterprise-Wide Technologies

Enterprise computing solutions don't exist in a vacuum. If an organization has no overall strategy for implementing CRM, RAID, or any of the other software and hardware solutions previously discussed, there's not much sense in spending hundreds of thousands or millions of dollars to install them. In this section, we will examine many of the enterprise-wide technologies being used for competitive advantage.

GRID COMPUTING

Grid computing is applying the abilities of many computers in a network to a single problem at the same time. This amount of concentrated power is usually directed at scientific or technical problems that require a high level of processing power and access to large amounts of data. A well-known example of grid computing in the public domain is the ongoing SETI (Search for Extraterrestrial Intelligence) @Home project in which thousands of people are sharing the unused processor cycles of their PCs in the vast search for signs of "rational" signals from outer space. If you are interested in joining the search for ET, go to **www.seti.org** (Figure 14.17).

CLOUD COMPUTING

Cloud computing is a subscription-based or pay-per-use service that provides scalable resources and IT services over the Internet. The name comes from the use of the cloud symbol to represent the Internet in flowcharts and diagrams. A cloud service can be public, and sell its services to anyone on the Internet, or private and sell only to a limited number of users. The

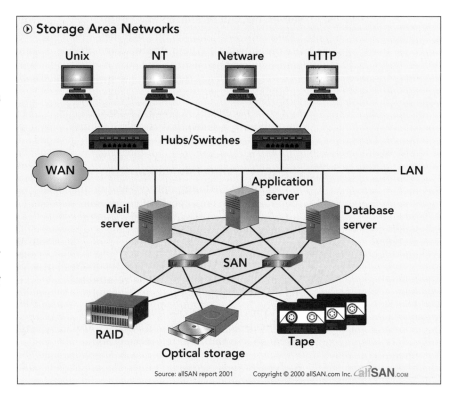

FIGURE 14.16 A storage area network (SAN) is an enterprise network that transfers data between servers and multiple storage devices.

power of cloud computing is the admission of users to a shared data center containing multi-tenancy applications. What does this actually mean? **Multi-tenancy** means that the application is installed only once in the cloud, on the cloud's

FIGURE 14.17 The search for extraterrestrials is global, with data being collected by thousands of people constantly. Grid computing provides the network infrastructure for this massive connectivity.

server, but can be shared and customized with individual options for each user. So, instead of running your applications on your own system, using your own resources, you access the cloud, log into the application, customize it, and start using it. That's the power of cloud computing. You can view a video that clearly explains the power of cloud computing and its benefits for enterprise users at **www. salesforce.com/cloudcomputing**.

Again as with any new development, there are negative aspects of cloud computing, security issues being the most prominent. Before subscribing to a cloud service, obtain detailed information on the security aspects and safeguards the service has in place. Ask questions related to the qualifications and integrity of the employees of the service and the testing that has been done to verify security and response to unanticipated intrusions.

BLADE SERVERS

With data centers growing and becoming more complex, **blade servers**, stripped-down, energy-efficient, low-cost modular computers with server software installed, seem to be a solution. These space-saving units provide a powerful platform to fulfill the requirements of data centers and enterprise demands, enabling the reduction of power consumption without

compromising performance. Blade servers are designed to get the most out of your power and space-constrained data center with a potential 90 percent reduction in energy costs.

THIN CLIENTS

A **thin client** can refer to either a software program or to an actual computer that relies heavily on another computer to do most of its work. It is usually part of a network, and the client software or computer acts as an interface, while the network server computer does all the real work. In the case of a computer, a thin client is unable to perform many functions on its own. It is usually designed only for online use, sending and receiving e-mail, and surfing the net.

WEB PORTALS

Web portals (or **portals**) are Web sites that provide multiple online services. A portal is a jumping-off place—a place that provides an organized way to go to other places on the Web. AOL, MSN, Yahoo! and Google are all examples of sites that have become Web portals to draw more traffic and dedicated users to their sites (Figure 14.18).

Organizations implement portals for different reasons. Merrill Lynch created an enterprise-wide portal to cut expenses and consolidate all of the Web sites and portal sites that had been built throughout the company. To avoid the expense of training its retail associates and partners on how to use many of its standard applications, Guess Jeans installed a portal that provides access to Web-based training materials. When Chevron acquired Texaco, merging the various Web applications from both companies would have been time-consuming and expensive. Instead, the newly merged company implemented a portal. Business portals offer centralized knowledge and content management, helping to ensure consistent business processes across different functional units.

ELECTRONIC DATA INTERCHANGE

Electronic data interchange (EDI) is a set of standards that specifies how to transfer data and documents between enterprises using the Internet and other networks without

FIGURE 14.18 Visitors to portals such as Yahoo!'s can check their e-mail, get the latest news and weather forecasts, and shop all in one place.

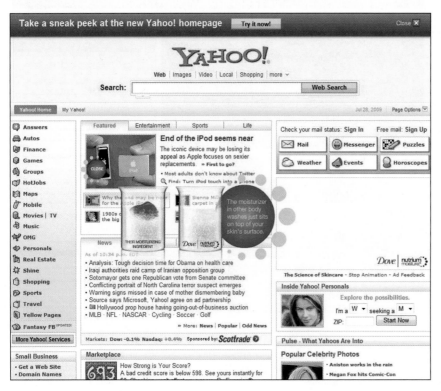

human intervention. EDI is emerging as a popular way for companies to exchange information and to conduct business transactions. For instance, if two companies have compatible systems, they can establish a connection through which purchase orders, shipping notices, and invoices can be sent by EDI—computer to computer. The entire operation occurs without any paper changing hands. EDI can make many business processes more efficient. For example, buyers can use EDI to order parts from suppliers that will be delivered just in time to be used. This capability reduces inventory costs and the time between the buying of the parts and the sale of the finished product.

To get an idea of the widespread use of EDI standards, view the list of companies that use EDI standards in their business transactions at **www.covalentworks. com/companies-and-edi.asp** Statistics indicate that there are 160,000 EDI partners in North America constituting 99% of companies in the United States, Canada, and Mexico (Figure 14.19).

Business-to-business e-commerce enterprises sometimes lease network capacity from a value-added network. A **value-added network (VAN)** is a public data network offered by a service provider that an enterprise uses for EDI or other services. Such a network offers end-to-end dedicated lines with guaranteed security. Enterprises can electronically exchange documents and data over a VAN, including shipping orders, tracking requests, and invoices as well as e-mail, management reports, and payments.

But those services come with a hefty per-byte fee for handling an enterprise's data and transactions. To take advantage of cost efficiencies from doing business over the Internet, many VANs offer additional services such as EDI translation, encryption, and other security measures.

INTRANETS AND EXTRANETS

Many companies are building internal networks, known as intranets, which are based on TCP/IP protocols. An **intranet** is a network that belongs to an enterprise and is accessible only by that enterprise's employees or authorized users. Intranets offer users the same familiar tools, such as browsers, that they use on the Internet. However, intranets are intended only for internal use and aren't accessible from the external Internet unless the user has a registered user name and password. Jakob Nielsen, an expert in Web site usability,

rates the quality of Intranets annually. Figure 14.20 lists the best sites by his standards.

Intranets are transforming the way organizations produce and share information with employees, vendors, and other select outside partners. Web sites on an

FIGURE 14.19 The use of EDI standards is becoming the way to conduct secure online business transactions within and between companies.

FIGURE 14.20 The 10 Best Intranets of 2009 as Rated by Jakob Nielsen (in Alphabetical Order)
Altran, France
Advanced Micro Devices (AMD), United States
Basf SE, Germany
COWI Group A/S, Denmark
Deloitte Touche Tohmatsu (DDT), United States
Environmental Resource Management (ERM), Global
HSBC Bank, Brazil
Kaupthing Bank, Iceland
L.L. Bean, United States
McKesson Corporation, United States

intranet are similar to Internet Web sites, except that firewalls protect the enterprise content from unauthorized access. Because it's so easy to create a Web page, companies can distribute Web publishing duties throughout the enterprise. Every department can maintain its own internal Web page, making its resources available to everyone. By moving expensive print-based publications, such as employee manuals and telephone directories, to the intranet, companies can realize enormous savings and significantly reduce the amount of trash that goes to local landfills.

Some companies allow authorized outsiders, such as research labs, suppliers, or key customers, to access their intranets. Called **extranets**, these networks are connected over the Internet, and data traverses the Internet in encrypted form, safe from prying eyes. Access to an extranet is limited to those provided with valid user names and passwords. These security measures determine the extranet content that outsiders are allowed to view. Extranets have become a viable conduit for sharing information between business partners.

Intranets continue to be one of the fastest-growing enterprise applications in IT. They cost much less to build and maintain than public and private data networks such as VANs and virtual private networks.

FIGURE 14.21 A virtual private network (VPN) allows authorized individuals to access a company's network using a secure connection.

VIRTUAL PRIVATE NETWORKS

Enterprises use virtual private networks to connect distributed LANs over the Internet. A **virtual private network (VPN)** consists of lines that are leased to a single company, thus ensuring excellent security. VPNs transport data over the Internet but offer encryption and additional security measures to ensure that only authorized users have access to the network and its data (Figure 14.21).

Potomac Hospital in Virginia has more than 1,200 employees and medical professionals. The hospital uses a VPN to provide safe, secure access to hospital records and patient data for more than 250 medical professionals and vendors who frequently work off-site, including an Australian vendor who reads X-rays over the VPN.

COMPUTER-BASED AND WEB-BASED TRAINING

Computer-based training (CBT) is a form of education that uses multimedia, animation, and programmed learning to teach new skills with a computer. CBT has typically been used to train people how to use computer applications, because it enables students to learn by actually using the application. The tutorials included with many software applications are a form of CBT.

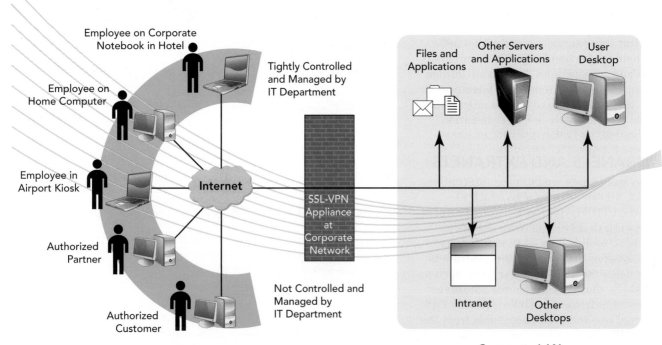

When new software is deployed within an enterprise, employee training is critical to its success. Traditional classroom-style training can be expensive and often requires employees to go off-site. CBT programs can be more convenient and affordable because they are typically not time or place dependent. Training is available whenever an employee has the time to access the tutorials.

Web-based training (WBT) is basically CBT implemented via the Internet or an intranet. Web-based training methods often include instant messaging, discussion forums, and chat tools, in addition to more advanced applications, such as live Web broadcasts with streaming audio or video and videoconferencing.

Enterprises often use Web-based training to educate employees about a new application, program, or system. WBT is often run by a facilitator or trainer; however, it can also be self-paced and involve only the trainee.

TELECONFERENCING

Teleconferencing is when two or more people, separated by distance, use telecommunications and computer equipment to conduct business activities. Enterprises use teleconferencing to gain a competitive advantage by cutting costs and facilitating enterprise-wide communications.

Large enterprises or small office–home office (SOHO) businesses seeking to employ teleconferencing should consider professional-grade or PC-based teleconferencing systems. Professional-grade teleconferencing requires enterprises to own, purchase, or rent dedicated conferencing equipment or to contract with a company or service provider that offers these services (Figure 14.22). One type of teleconferencing service is when each caller dials the teleconference number, provides a pass code, and is then connected with the other callers. Teleconferencing isn't limited to just voice communications, however.

PC-based solutions offer a number of benefits over professional-grade systems, such as lower cost and easier installation and maintenance. Many enterprises find it well worth the time and money to implement PC-based systems. Most companies immediately begin to reap the rewards of lower long-distance phone bills and higher productivity. They also can cut travel budgets because participants don't need to be physically present at meetings. The

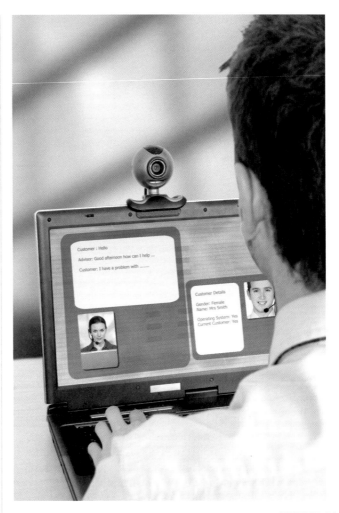

biggest drawback to the successful implementation of teleconferencing is that the video portion requires lots of bandwidth. Other concerns include poor video quality, real-time transmission delays, lack of access to facilities or equipment, and potential threats to privacy.

TELECOMMUTING

Because of the burgeoning home network market, many large and small enterprises are giving their employees the option of telecommuting. **Telecommuting**, sometimes referred to as **teleworking**, refers to using telecommunications and computer equipment to work from home while still being connected to the office (Figure 14.23). The home system must be able to connect to the company computer system to communicate with and transfer data to and from other employees.

In 2000, an estimated 6 million Americans telecommuted to work at least part time. Between 2006 and 2008, there was a 39 percent increase in the number of Americans who worked from home, or

FIGURE 14.22
Teleconferencing allows many people in many locations to share the convenience of a common connection.

remotely, at least one day per month for their employers, amounting to an additional 4.8 million "employee telecommuters." Going back one more year to 2005, the statistics show a surprising 74 percent increase in the number of telecommuters. This trend is expected to continue. However, not all jobs lend themselves to telecommuting. Enterprises whose employees must serve or greet the public (bank tellers, waitstaff, office receptionists, and so on) are not candidates for telecommuting.

Studies have shown that enterprises experience various benefits by allowing employees to telecommute, including productivity gains, lower employee turnover, and reduced costs for office space. One major disadvantage of telecommuting is the enterprise's lack of direct supervision over a telecommuting employee's workload.

Teleworkers experience a variety of benefits, including little or no commuting, flexible hours, more family time, and savings on car expenses (gas, tolls, parking, and so on) and work clothes. Disadvantages include the lack of social interaction and the difficulties of keeping the work and home environments separate. Societal benefits from telecommuting include fuel conservation and less air pollution.

A vital technology for enterprises with telecommuters is teleconferencing. Thanks to inexpensive software and Webcams, telecommuters can attend important meetings they may otherwise have missed. Programs such as Office Live

Meeting enable teleworkers to communicate, interact, and share applications with coworkers. Skype and iVisit are Web-based services that provide simultaneous chat and video capabilities for multiple users (Figure 14.24). To use these services, you must first download and install their software. Many videoconferencing services also offer additional functions, such as file transfer, application sharing, or online whiteboards.

Telecommuting would be nearly impossible without broadband Internet service. With a high-speed Internet connection, telecommuters can talk with others in real time or record video messages to attach to e-mails.

WORKGROUP COMPUTING

Another technology that enterprises are using for competitive advantage is workgroup computing. **Workgroup computing** occurs when all of the members of a *workgroup*—a collection of individuals working together on a task—have specific hardware, software, and networking equipment that enables them to connect, communicate, and collaborate. **Groupware**, also known as **teamware**, is software that provides computerized support for the information needs of these workgroups. Most groupware applications include e-mail, videoconferencing tools, group-scheduling systems, customizable electronic forms, real-time shared applications, and shared information databases.

The first successful groupware product, Lotus Notes, was designed to run on

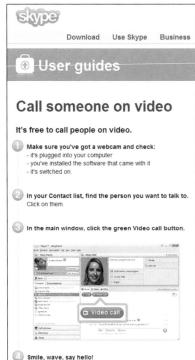

a

b

FIGURE 14.24
Web-based services such as (a) Skype can provide telecommuters with (b) simultaneous chat and video capabilities.

client/server systems. Newer groupware products, such as Microsoft Exchange Server and new versions of Lotus Notes, run on intranets and extranets. These groupware applications enable collaboration between geographically separated workgroups and even between group members who work for other organizations, such as affiliated research labs.

A groupware application such as Microsoft Exchange Server can quickly determine the optimum time for a meeting, locate an open room, send a notice asking for the meeting, and then coordinate responses to show who has confirmed that they will be at the meeting (Figure 14.25). Groupware also facilitates workflow automation. **Workflow automation** is the process of sending documents and data to the next person who needs to see them. For example, a master document may be

shared among a group, and then all of the group's comments can be collectively edited by the author of the document. Consider the case of an engineer at a firm who prepares a proposal for an external

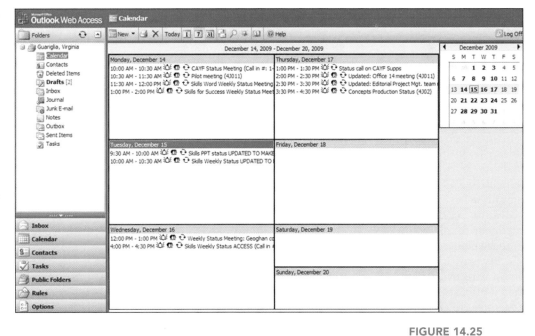

FIGURE 14.25
Microsoft Exchange Server provides remote access to e-mail, contacts, and calendars through the Outlook Web Access client.

contract. The proposal goes to the engineer's supervisor for review and approval. The document may have to be seen by several other people before it's finally approved and sent.

Chapter Summary

Enterprise Computing

Enterprise computing is the use of technology, information systems, and computers within an organization or business. Personal computing is the use of technology by an individual for business or personal activities.

A business process begins with a customer's need and ends with the fulfillment of that need. The activities that compose this progression from need to fulfillment can be viewed as a series of links in a chain along which information flows within the organization. At each link, value is added in the form of the work performed by people associated with that process, and new, useful information is generated.

In a centralized structure, the management of technology is centered in the IT department, and everyone within the organization works with standardized technology solutions in their everyday work. In a distributed structure, users are able to customize their technology tools to suit their individual needs and wants.

Tools commonly used in enterprise computing include enterprise resource planning (ERP), customer relationship management (CRM), sales force automation (SFA), Extensible Business Reporting Language (XBRL), Software as a Service (SaaS), operational support systems (OSSs), and enterprise application integration (EAI).

Enterprise storage systems include RAID, CD and DVD jukeboxes, Blu-ray optical libraries, storage area networks (SAN), and network attached storage (NAS). Enterprise-wide technologies that provide a competitive edge in today's business environment include, grid computing, cloud computing, blade servers, thin clients, Web portals, electronic data interchange, intranets, extranets, virtual private networks, computer-based and Web-based training, teleconferencing, telecommuting, and workgroup computing.

Key Terms and Concepts

Matching

Match each key term in the left column with the most accurate definition in the right column.

____ 1. zero configuration

____ 2. hot site

____ 3. fault tolerance

____ 4. business process reengineering

____ 5. intranet

____ 6. distributed structure

____ 7. scalability

____ 8. e-business

____ 9. cold site

____ 10. interoperability

____ 11. extranet

____ 12. multi-tenancy

____ 13. competitive edge

____ 14. centralized structure

____ 15. enterprise resource planning

a. Refers to the ability of a system to continue working even if one or more components fail.

b. Technology infrastructure in which all users work with standardized technology solutions.

c. Provides secure access to an organization's data for employees of that organization.

d. Disaster recovery site that becomes operational after a disaster occurs.

e. An organization's superior position over its competitors.

f. Uses the Internet to buy, sell, collaborate with partners, and provide customer service.

g. Provides secure access to an organization's data for authorized outsiders.

h. The ability to exchange data with another computer of any model or one running on any platform.

i. The installation of an application once with the ability for it to be shared and customized by each user.

j. Often used to set up an Ethernet network for a home or small business.

k. Integrates various functions into a single computer system.

l. Use of information technology to bring about major organizational changes and cost savings.

m. A disaster recovery site always in a state of readiness.

n. The ability of a system to keep functioning as demands and use increase.

o. Technology infrastructure that allows users to customize their own tools.

Multiple Choice

Circle the correct choice for each of the following.

1. What device copies data to one or more hard drives as the data is being written to the original drive?
   a. SAN
   b. Jukebox
   c. NAS
   d. RAID

2. Which enterprise computing tool enables companies to use Web-based software for a fee and avoid expensive and time-consuming installations?
   a. SaaS
   b. OSS
   c. XBRL
   d. ERP

3. Which of the following statements about enterprise application integration (EAI) is *not* true?
   a. EAI combines processes, software, standards, and hardware to integrate multiple enterprise systems.
   b. EAI is complex, and management issues have caused a high failure rate.
   c. EAI enables custom-built proprietary software to run independently from other programs.
   d. A wide range of EAI categories is available.

4. What is one of the advantages of a value-added network?
   a. It establishes a set of standards to specify how data is transferred.
   b. It provides end-to-end dedicated lines with guaranteed security.
   c. It belongs to an enterprise and can be accessed only by its employees and authorized users.
   d. It links all of the servers in an enterprise to increase storage capacity.

5. Because they continue working even if one or more components fail, RAID devices have a high degree of _____.
   a. scalability
   b. interoperability
   c. electronic data interchange
   d. fault tolerance

6. _____ is when documents are sent without request to individuals that need them.
   a. Zero configuration
   b. Workflow automation
   c. Grid computing
   d. Electronic data interchange

7. What is a subscription-based or pay-per-use service that provides scalable services and IT services over the Internet?
   a. Grid computing
   b. Web portal
   c. Cloud computing
   d. Enterprise application integration

8. A common location used to house computer systems and centralize data, telecommunication devices, and storage systems is a(n) _____.
   a. enterprise data center
   b. Web portal
   c. electronic data integration
   d. blade server

9. The use of IT to improve business processes and optimize assets by managing the entire life cycle of these processes is _____.
   a. business process reengineering
   b. customer relationship management
   c. business process management
   d. customer resource planning

10. Which of the following is *not* a drawback of ERP projects?
    a. The job duties for customer service representatives may be expanded.
    b. Employees may resist change.
    c. Implementation times and costs may be underestimated.
    d. Separate ERP modules replace established systems.

Fill-In

In the blanks provided, write the correct answer for each of the following.

1. _____ _____ describes the overall use of technology, information systems, and computers within an organization.

2. A(n) _____ _____ _____ uses the Internet to connect two physically separate local area networks.

3. _____ _____ _____ software is an enterprise resource tool that allows salespeople to match company resources with customer wants and needs.

4. A system component that causes the entire system to malfunction when it stops working properly is called a(n) _____ _____ _____ _____.

5. A(n) _____ _____ _____ system links all of an organization's servers to provide pathways between end users and stored data.

6. _____, also called teleworking, uses telecommunications and computer equipment to conduct business activities between two or more people at different locations.

7. _____ _____ are stripped-down, energy-efficient, low-cost modular computers.

8. _____ - _____ _____ is an education style that uses multimedia, animation, and programmed learning to teach new skills with a computer.

9. The tradeoff for _____ is that using the latest tools may result in a low comfort level for users.

10. XBRL, also known as _____ _____ _____ _____, is used by enterprises to share financial information across all computer platforms and over the Internet.

11. E-mail, videoconferencing, and calendar tools that enable individuals to work together collaboratively are called _____ applications.

12. A(n) _____ _____ is a Web site that provides an organized way to access other Web locations and businesses.

13. A(n) _____ _____ _____ is a detailed plan shared throughout an enterprise that is

followed when a system or component of a system becomes nonfunctional.

14. A(n) _____ _____ _____ supplies software-based services and solutions to companies that want to outsource some or all of their IT needs.

15. Activities that have an identifiable output and provide value to an organization's customers are known as business _____.

Short Answer

1. Describe the difference between the centralized and distributed technology structures.

2. Explain the difference between an intranet and an extranet.

3. List three enterprise storage systems. Provide a brief description of each.

4. What is cloud computing? What is one of its benefits?

5. What are three components of a disaster recovery plan?

6. List three benefits of telecommuting.

Teamwork

1. **Telecommuting Survey** As a team, create a survey with questions on telecommuting for work. Include questions as to the amount of days a month an individual telecommutes, the equipment a telecommuter needs in a home office to perform his or her job and stay connected with fellow employees and managers, the amount the company reimburses for home services to be able to telecommute, the estimated individual savings obtained by telecommuting (gas, child care, lunch), the number of other employees in the respondent's workgroup that telecommute, and any other such related questions that the group might develop. Include questions about the respondent's gender, job title, salary range, and education level so you can analyze your results to see whether any correlations exist. Distribute the survey to at least 15 individuals who are employed by enterprises. Accumulate the data obtained from the survey, analyze it, and present your results in a one-page, double-spaced report. An Excel spreadsheet can be used to display the accumulated statistics and graphs to demonstrate your findings in a more visual style.

2. **Enterprise Storage Systems and Backup** Have team members each interview one IT employee at your school. Come up with a standard list of questions to ask. Focus on the type of enterprise storage system the school uses, the frequency of backups, the backup medium used, and whether any loss of data has ever occurred. Regroup, combine, and

present your research in a one-page, double-spaced paper.

3. **Cloud Computing Concerns** As a team, research cloud computing. Locate at least three cloud computing services and investigate their security policies, encryption methods, location of data storage, segregation of data from other users, and data recovery plans. Use Word to present the results of your research in a table that allows for an easy comparison between the services and their policies.

4. **E-Business and You** Many companies conduct e-business through digital storefronts. As a team, list the online e-business companies that you or one of your family members have used. Provide the name of the company; what products were purchased; how the product was distributed; whether the company has brick-and-mortar stores as well as a digital presence; what the payment options were; how your was payment made; and how shipping was handled. Indicate whether team members would consider purchasing more products from this company? Why or why not? Accumulate your findings in a one-page, double-spaced report. Try to draw some summary conclusions on the success of the experience, the types of products purchased, and prevailing methods of payment.

5. **Enterprise Support: AT&T Versus Verizon** Divide your team into two groups and research the

enterprise services offered by AT&T and Verizon. Visit the Web sites of each company and obtain information from local branches. Regroup and compose either a one-page, double-spaced report or a PowerPoint presentation to present the results of your investigation. Include a list of the enterprise services offered by each company, the cost of such services, and any restrictions that apply to usage. Remember to cite your references.

On the Web

1. **Wal-Mart and CRM** Wal-Mart is currently one of the largest retail chains in the world. Its use of technology and the Internet to service customers and suppliers has set industry benchmarks. Using the Internet and your choice of search engines, locate statistics and information on the enterprise systems and customer relationship management strategies (CRM) employed by Wal-Mart. Present your research, citing references, in a one-page, double-spaced paper.

2. **Enterprise Career Choices** Using the Internet, a search engine of your choice, and job listing Web sites, locate at least three careers that relate to enterprise technology and security management. Present your results in a table. Make sure to include the three career titles, the minimum amount of education each requires, the salary range, job description, job location (city and state), whether your school offers a degree in this area, and any other related and relevant data. Be sure to include your references.

3. **XBRL: The New King of Reports** Use the Internet and your favorite search engine to research XBRL, an XML-based reporting technology that is quickly becoming the most widely accepted format for publishing financial information. State the type of reports this language can generate; the benefits of creating the reports with this language; the security features associated with it; and the companies,
agencies, and governments that currently use it. Present your research in a one-page, double-spaced report or a PowerPoint presentation. Remember to cite your references.

4. **Data Disasters** Use the Internet and search engine of your choice to locate at least three data disasters due to equipment failure, technological malfunction, or environmental interference. Briefly describe each disaster and its effects on the business or government involved. Continue your research to locate articles or other journals on avoiding data disasters or data center disasters. From your research, compose a list of the five steps to take to avoid data disasters. Present your disaster descriptions, their effects on the business or government, and your list of five steps to take to avoid such disasters in either a one-page, double-spaced paper or a PowerPoint presentation.

5. **Thin Clients** Using the Internet or other research options, look up thin clients. In a table, list at least four manufacturers, the name or number of at least one system from each manufacturer, the hardware specifications, accessories, and price. Note whether the company's Web site has links to other services that can be connected to for a price. If such services exist, name the service and price. Present your comparative shopping experience in a table, with each unit and feature clearly listed.

Acronym Finder

Note: see Glossary for definitions

ADSL asymmetric digital subscriber line

ADC analog-to-digital converter

AGP Accelerated Graphics Port

AI artificial intelligence

AJAX asynchronous JavaScript and XML

ALU arithmetic-logic unit

ASCII American Standard Code for Information Interchange

ASP application service provider

B2B business-to-business

B2C business-to-consumer

BCP business continuity plan

BD Blu-ray disc

BD-R Blu-ray disc-recordable

BD-RE Blu-ray disc-rewritable

BD-ROM Blu-ray disc ROM

BIOS basic input/output system

BLOB binary large object

BPM business process management

BPR business process reengineering

bps bits per second

C2C consumer-to-consumer business

CASE computer-aided software engineering

cat-5 category 5

cat-5e category 5 enhanced

cat-6 category 6

CAVE Cave Automated Virtual Environment

CBT computer-based training

CD-R compact disc-recordable

CD-ROM compact disc ROM

CD-RW compact disc-rewritable

CPU central processing unit

CRM customer relationship management

CRT cathode ray tube

CS computer science

DAC digital-to-analog converter

DBMS database management system

DBS direct broadcast satellite

DDoS distributed denial of service attack

DFD data flow diagram

DLP digital light processing

DNS domain name system

DoS denial of service attack

DSL digital subscriber line

DSS decision support system

DVD digital video disc

DVD-R digital video disc-recordable

DVD-RW digital video disc-rewritable

DVD-RAM digital video disc-RAM

DVD-ROM digital video disc-ROM

DVI digital video interface port

EAI enterprise application integration

EBCDIC Extended Binary Coded Decimal Interchange Code

EDI electronic data interchange

EE electrical engineering

EEPROM electrically erasable programmable ROM

EIS executive information system

EPROM electrically programmable ROM

ERD entity-relationship diagram

ERP enterprise resource planning

ESS executive support system

FAT file allocation table

FTP File Transfer Protocol

FiOS fiber-optic service

GB gigabyte

GHz gigahertz

GPL General Public License

GPS Global Positioning System

GUI graphical user interface

GUID global unique identifier

HAN home area network

HDSL high bit-rate DSL

HDTV high definition television

HHD hybrid hard drive

HMD head-mounted display

HTML Hypertext Markup Language

HTTP Hypertext Transfer Protocol

IC integrated circuit

ICC integrated circuit card

IM instant messaging

I/O input/output

IP Internet Protocol

IRC Internet Relay Chat

IS information systems

ISDN Integrated Services Digital Network

ISP Internet service provider

IT information technology

JAD joint application development

JSON JavaScript Object Notation

KB kilobyte

KMS knowledge management system

LAN local area network

LCD liquid crystal display

MAC Media Access Control

MB megabyte

MIDI Musical Instrument Digital Interface

MIS management information system

MMPORG massively multiplayer online role-playing game

MSC mobile switching center

MUD multiuser dungeon

NAS network attached storage

NIC network interface card

NTFS new technology file system

NSP network service provider

OCR optical character recognition

OLAP online analytical processing

OMR optical mark reader

OOP object-oriented programming

OS operating system

OSS operational support system

P2P peer-to-peer network

P3P Platform for Privacy Protection

PAN Personal Area Network

PC personal computer

PCI peripheral component interconnect

PCS personal communication service

PDA personal digital assistant

PDLC program development life cycle

PKI public key infrastructure

PNG Portable Network Graphics

PnP plug-and-play

PoP point of presence

POST power-on self-test

PROM programmable ROM

PSTN public switched telephone network

RAD rapid application development

RAID redundant array of independent disks

RAM random access memory

RDBMS relational database management system

RFID radio frequency identification device

RFP request for proposal

RFQ request for quotation

ROI return on investment

ROM read-only memory

RSS Really Simple Syndication (or Rich Site Summary)

SaaS software as a service

SAN storage area network

SATA serial advance technology attachment

SCSI Small Computer System Interface

SDLC systems development life cycle

SET secure electronic transfer

SFA sales force automation

SLC subscriber loop carrier

SMIL Synchronized Multimedia Integration Language

SONET Synchronous Optical Network

SSD solid state drive

SVGA Super Video Graphics Array

SXGA Super Extended Graphics Array

TB terabyte

TCP Transmission Control Protocol

TCP/IP Transmission Control Protocol/Internet Protocol

TFT active matrix (Thin Film Transistor)

TLD top-level domain

TPS transaction processing system

UML Unified Modeling Language

UPS uninterruptible power supply

USB universal serial bus

VAN value-added network

VAR value-added reseller

VB Visual Basic

VDSL very high rate DSL

VGA video graphics array

VM Java Virtual Machine

VoIP Voice over Internet Protocol

VPN virtual private network

VR virtual reality

VRML Virtual Reality Modeling Language

W3C World Wide Web Consortium

WAN wide area network

WAP Wireless Application Protocol

WBT Web-based training

WEP Wired Equivalent Privacy

WML Wireless Markup Language

WPA Wi-Fi Protected Access

WSXGA+ Widescreen Super Extended Graphics Array +

WUXGA Widescreen Ultra Extended Graphics Array

WWW World Wide Web

XBRL Extensible Business Reporting Language

XGA Extended Graphics Array

XHTML eXtensible Hypertext Markup Language

XML Extensible Markup Language

Glossary

1394 port An interface that offers high-speed connection for dozens of peripherals. This port is ideal for use with real-time devices such as digital video cameras. FireWire is Apple Computer's name for 1394 port technology.

1G First generation of cellular technology, it used analog signals and allowed callers to make their own calls without operator assistance as they move seamlessly from cell to cell.

2G Second-generation cellular technology that quickly replaced most analog cellular services due to its use of digital signaling. Features of this generation were decreased signal interference, increased reception, better protection from eavesdropping, and increased security features that decreased cell phone fraud.

3G Third-generation cellular technology offers faster data transmission that enables transmission of voice, text, images, and video data.

4G Fourth-generation cellular technology, due to be released between 2012 and 2015, promises even higher data transfer rates, as well as providing voice, data, and high-quality multimedia in real-time (streamed) format all the time from anywhere.

A

Accelerated Graphics Port (AGP) A port specification developed by Intel Corporation to support high-speed, high-resolution graphics, including 3D graphics, which is being phased out.

acceptable use policy (AUP) An Internet service provider (ISP) policy that indicates which types of uses are permissible; also used by universities and public entities.

acceptance testing Testing in which users evaluate a system to see whether it meets their needs and functions correctly.

access time In secondary storage devices, the amount of time that lapses between a request for information from the device and the delivery of the information.

account A record on multiuser systems that consists of a user's name, password, and storage space location, which is called the user's folder or user's directory. Accounts are usually set up and managed by a server/computer administrator.

active badge A small device worn by an individual that transmits a unique infrared signal every 5 to 10 seconds. Networked sensors detect these transmissions and thus the location of the badge and, hence, the location of its wearer.

active matrix (Thin Film Transistor) A form of LCD display in which electric current drives the display by charging each pixel individually as needed.

ActiveX control A miniprogram that can be downloaded from a Web page and used to add functionality to a Web browser. ActiveX controls require Microsoft Windows and Microsoft Internet Explorer and are written in Visual Basic (VB).

Ada A programming language, named after Augusta Ada Byron, that incorporates modular programming principles. It was the required language for most U.S. Department of Defense projects until 1996 because of its suitability for the reliable control of real-time systems (such as missiles).

address bar Used for navigation, the address bar displays the route you've taken to get to the current location.

adware Software similar to spyware, that is usually installed on your computer through the Internet without your knowledge or consent. Adware however, is created specifically by an advertising agency to collect information about your Internet habits or encourage you to purchase a product. It is usually considered a nuisance rather than malicious.

aggregators Web sites where headlines are collected, either manually, as the Drudge Report, or through the use of algorithms as in Google News.

agile Refers to a group of software development methodologies based on an iterative project management process that aligns development with customer needs and company goals. It describes the development of solutions through collaboration between functional teams.

AJAX Sometimes written as Ajax (shorthand for asynchronous JavaScript and XML). A group of interrelated Web development techniques used on the client-side to create interactive Web applications. AJAX is not a technology in itself, but a term that refers to the use of a group of technologies.

algorithm A mathematical or logical step-by-step procedure for solving a problem.

all-in-one computer A compact version of a desktop that combines the system unit and monitor into one component. Its smaller size reduces the surface space needed to hold the system.

alphabetic check A data validation procedure that ensures that only alphabetic data (the letters of the alphabet) are entered into a field.

analog signal Real-world signals, like sound and light, sent via continuous waves that vary in frequency and amplitude. It is the signal sent and received over phone lines. See digital signal.

analog-to-digital converter (ADC) A microchip that contains the circuitry to convert an analog signal into a digital signal.

anonymity The ability to convey a message without disclosing your name or identity.

anonymous FTP An Internet service that enables you to contact a distant computer system to which you have no access rights, log on to its public directories, and transfer files from that computer to your own. These sites lack security and should never be used to send sensitive data like financial information.

antivirus software Software that protects a computer from computer viruses by using a pattern-matching technique that examines all of the files on a disk, looking for telltale virus code "signatures."

applet 1. A small- to medium-sized computer program that provides a specific function, such as emulating a calculator. 2. In Java, a miniprogram embedded in a Web document that, when downloaded, is executed by the browser. Most major browsers can execute Java applets.

application service provider (ASP) Provides software-based services and solutions to companies that want to outsource some or almost all of their information technology needs.

application software Programs that sit on top of the operating system and enable you to do something useful with the computer, such as writing or accounting (as opposed to utilities, which are programs that help you maintain the computer). Examples include word processing, spreadsheet, database, presentation, e-mail, and Web browser software.

application testing Testing programs individually and then together.

application window The area on-screen that encloses and displays a launched application and work in progress.

application workspace The on-screen area that displays the document you are currently working on.

archive A single file that contains two or more files stored in a compressed format, which is handy for storage as well as file-exchange purposes because as many as several hundred separate files can be stored in a single, easily handled unit.

argument set In spreadsheet programs such as Microsoft Excel, the part of a mathematical function that contains its passable parameters or variables.

arithmetic logic unit (ALU) The portion of the central processing unit (CPU) that makes all the decisions for the microprocessor based on the mathematical computations and logic functions that it performs.

arithmetic operations One of the two groups of operations performed by the arithmetic logic unit (ALU). The arithmetic operations are addition, subtraction, multiplication, and division.

arrow keys See cursor movement keys.

artificial intelligence (AI) A computer science field that tries to improve computers by endowing them with some of the characteristics associated with human intelligence, such as the capability to understand natural language and to reason under conditions of uncertainty.

artificial system A system deliberately constructed by people to serve some purpose.

ASCII (American Standard Code for Information Interchange) A standard computer character set that uses seven bits and can represent 128 different characters. It is used on minicomputers, personal computers, and computers that make information available on the Internet.

assembler A program that transforms source code written in assembly language into machine language, which is readable by a microprocessor.

assembly language A low-level programming language, one level up from machine language, in which each program statement uses mnemonics and decimal values to create instructions that the microprocessor can carry out.

asymmetric key encryption See public key encryption.

asymmetrical digital subscriber line (ADSL) A transmission technology that separates an ordinary copper telephone line into three separate data channels with different capacities and speeds. The lowest capacity transmits analog voice for telephones; the second, medium capacity, uploads data to the network; and the third, highest capacity, downloads data from the network. This means that ADSL connections upload more slowly than they download.

asynchronous communication Communication in which both parties are not necessarily online at the same time, for example, e-mail.

attribute In programming, a characteristic, trait, or feature of an object in an object-oriented language.

augmented reality (AR) The blending of virtual reality with the real world.

authentication The process, usually involving a dialog box, that requests a user to enter a user name and password, thereby verifying that the user is indeed the person authorized to use the computer; also called login.

automation The replacement of human workers by machines.

autorecover See autosave.

autosave A software feature that backs up open documents at a default or user-specified interval; also called autorecover.

avatar A virtual representation of a player in a game or a person on a social networking site.

B

back door A method of bypassing normal authentication to secure access to a computer.

backbone In a wide area network (WAN), such as the Internet, a high-speed, high-capacity medium that transfers data over hundreds or thousands of miles. A variety of physical media are used for backbone services, including microwave relay, satellites, and dedicated telephone lines.

background application From the user's perspective, the application that appears inactive, as indicated by how the application appears on the desktop, when more than one application is running.

backside cache Secondary cache (L2) that is packaged with the microprocessor but is not on the same circuit as the microprocessor or primary cache (L1).

backup A copy of programs, data, and information created from one secondary storage media and stored in another.

backup procedures Routines created to make copies of data files to protect them against data loss, change, or damage from natural or other disasters.

backup software Programs that copy data from the computer's hard disk to backup devices, such as CDs or DVDs, an external hard drive, or an online storage location.

bad sector In magnetic storage media such as hard drives, a sector of the disk's surface that is physically damaged to the point that it can no longer store data reliably.

bandwidth The amount of data that can be transmitted through a given communications channel, such as a computer network.

banner ad On a Web page, an ad that is not actually part of the Web page itself, but is supplied separately by an ad network based on analysis of cookies.

bar code reader An input device that scans bar codes and, with special software, converts the bar code into readable data.

BASIC (Beginner's All-Purpose Symbolic Instruction Code) An easy-to-use high-level programming language developed in 1964 for instruction and still used in beginning programming classes and by many hobbyists to create simple programs.

batch processing An early transaction processing system whereby data was gathered and processed at periodic intervals, such as once a week.

baud The number of signaling elements per second. At slower rates, bauds and bps may be equal, but on higher speed transmissions, more than one bit can be encoded in each signaling element; thus a 4,800 baud may have a transmission rate of 9,600 bps.

BD-R An optical storage medium that can record high-definition video or PC data storage.

BD-RE An optical storage medium that can record and erase high-definition video or PC data storage.

BD-ROM A standard for storing read-only high-definition computer data on optical discs. It is a format used for video or data distribution.

beans The components of Javabean programming specifications.

beta version In software testing, a preliminary version of a program that is widely distributed before commercial release to users who test the program by operating it under realistic conditions.

binary number A number system with a base of 2 that represents numbers as sequences of 0s and 1s.

biochip A biochip is similar to a microprocessor, but rather than processing millions of computer instructions per second, it processes biological instructions, such as determining the number of genes in a strand of DNA.

biological feedback device A device that translates eye movements, body movements, and even brain waves into computer input.

biometric authentication A method of authentication that requires a biological scan of some sort, such as a fingerprint, retinal scan, or voice recognition.

BIOS (basic input/output system) The part of the system software, permanently encoded on the computer's ROM memory, that equips the computer with the instructions needed to accept keyboard input and display information on the screen.

bit Short for binary digit, the basic unit of information in a binary numbering system. The lowest level of data in a database, a 1 or a 0, which is the smallest unit of data that the computer can store and understand.

bitmapped graphic Image formed by a pattern of tiny dots, each of which corresponds to a pixel on the computer's display; also called raster graphic.

bitmapped image A representation of an image as a matrix of dots called picture elements (pixels).

black hat See cracker.

blade server Stripped-down, energy-efficient, low-cost modular computers with server software installed.

BLOB (binary large object) A data type for very large objects up to several gigabytes in size, such as an entire spreadsheet file or a picture file.

block A unit of memory on a flash drive.

blog Short for Web log. A Web site that contains an online, personal journal with reflections, comments, and often hyperlinks provided by the writer. Individuals, called bloggers, post their thoughts and opinions, along with photos or links to interesting Web sites, for the entire world to see.

Bluetooth A trademarked personal area network (PAN) technology, conceived by cell phone giant Ericsson and named after a 10th-century Viking. It uses short-range radio transmission technology to provide automatic and wireless communication between computers, mobile phones, printers, and other devices located within 30 feet of each other.

Blu-ray Disc (BD) One of the newest forms of optical storage, Blu-ray technology was developed for the management of high-definition video and for storing large amounts of data. The name is derived from the blue-violet laser beams (blue rays) used to read and write data.

Boolean data type A data type that, depending on the program, allows a yes or no, true or false, or 1 or 0 value.

Boolean search A database or Web search that uses the logical operators AND, OR, and NOT to specify the logical relationship between search words or phrases.

boot disk A storage device, like a USB drive, CD, DVD, or network device that, in case of an emergency or boot failure, can load a reduced version of the operating system that can be used for troubleshooting purposes; also called an emergency disk.

boot sector virus A computer virus that copies itself to the beginning tracks of a hard drive where code is stored that automatically executes every time you start the computer. Unlike file infectors, boot sector viruses don't require you to start a specific program to infect your computer; starting your system is sufficient.

booting The process of loading the operating system into RAM memory.

bot herder An individual that controls a botnet.

botnet A set of computers infected with a malicious program that places the computers under the control of a bot herder. Such computers are typically used during a distributed denial of service (DDoS) attack.

bps (bits per second) rate The rate used to measure data exchange.

branch prediction A technique used by advanced CPUs to prevent a pipeline stall. The processor tries to predict what is likely to happen with surprising accuracy.

broadband Refers to any transmission medium that carries several channels at once and thus transports high volumes of data at high speeds, typically greater than 1 Mbps.

broken link See dead link.

buffer An area that temporarily holds data and instructions.

bug A programming error that causes a program or a computer system to perform erratically, produce incorrect results, or crash.

build-or-buy decision A decision project teams face when they must determine whether a new system should be developed in-house or purchased from an outside vendor.

business continuity plan (BCP) See disaster recovery plan.

business process An activity that has an identifiable output and value to an organization's customers.

business process management (BPM) Evolved from BPR, BPM's goal is to improve existing processes and optimize assets by effectively and efficiently managing the entire life cycle of these business processes.

business process reengineering (BPR) The use of information technology to bring about major organizational changes and cost savings.

business-to-business e-commerce (B2B) The online exchange or trade of goods, services, or information in which one business provides another business with the materials, services, and/or supplies it needs to conduct its operations.

business-to-consumer e-commerce (B2C) A business supplies consumers with services, information, or products online. B2C is essentially the same as shopping at a physical store—you have a need or want, and the online marketplace offers products and solutions.

bus topology The physical layout of a local area network in which the network cable is a single conduit that forms a bus, or line; every node, whether it is a computer or peripheral device, is attached to that bus. At the ends of the bus, connectors called terminators signify the end of the circuit.

byte Eight bits grouped to represent a character (a letter, a number, or a symbol) and used as a unit of capacity for storage devices.

C

C A high-level programming language developed by Bell Labs in the 1970s. C combines the virtues of high-level programming with the efficiency of assembly language but is somewhat difficult to learn.

C++ A flexible high-level programming language derived from C that supports object-oriented programming but does not require programmers to adhere to the object-oriented model.

cable modem A device that enables a computer to access the Internet by means of a cable TV connection. Cable modems enable two-way communications through the cable system and do not require a phone line. Cable modems enable Internet access speeds from 1.5 Mbps to 6 Mbps, although most users typically experience slower speeds due to network congestion.

cache memory A small unit of ultrafast memory used to store recently accessed or frequently accessed data, increasing a computer system's overall performance.

call center A centralized computer-based routing system used for the purpose of receiving and transmitting a large volume of requests by telephone.

carpal tunnel syndrome A painful swelling of the tendons and the sheaths around them in the wrist due to injury caused by motions repeated thousands of times daily (such as mouse movements or keystrokes).

case control structure In structured programming, a variant of the selection control structure in which the condition is fundamental. Each branch leads to its own lengthy series of instructions.

Cat-5 Short for Category 5, it's the fifth generation of twisted pair data communication cable. Cat-5 cable contains four pairs of copper wire and supports speeds up to 100 Mbps over a maximum distance of 100 m (328 feet).

Cat-5e Short for Category 5 enhanced, it uses all four wire pairs, enabling speeds up to 1,000 Mbps (1 Gbps) over a short distance. This enhanced medium is backward compatible with ordinary Cat-5.

Cat-6 Short for Category 6, is the sixth generation of twisted pair cable and is backward compatible with Cat-5 and Cat-5e. It contains four pairs of copper wire like that of the previous generation, utilizes all four pairs, supports speeds up to 1 gigabit per second (Gbps), expands available bandwidth from 100 MHz for Cat-5e to 200MHz, and has superior immunity from external noise.

Cave Automated Virtual Environment (CAVE) A virtual reality environment that replaces headsets with 3D glasses and uses the walls, ceiling, and floor to display projected three-dimensional images.

CD drive A read-only storage device that reads data encoded on CD-ROM media discs and transfers the data to a computer.

CD-R (compact disc-recordable) Optical storage media that cannot be erased or written over once data has been saved; they're relatively inexpensive.

CD-ROM (compact disc–read-only memory) A standard for storing read-only computer data on optical compact discs (CDs), which can be read by CD-ROM drives and DVD-ROM drives. CD-ROM discs can hold up to 700 MB of data.

CD-RW (compact disc–rewritable) An optical storage media that allows data that has been saved to be erased or written over.

CD-RW drive (burner or CD burner) A compact disc–rewritable storage device that provides full read/write capabilities using erasable CD-RWs.

cell 1. In a spreadsheet, a rectangle formed by the intersection of a row and a column in which you enter information in the form of text (a label) or numbers (a value). 2. In telecommunications, a limited geographical area in which a signal can be broadcast.

cell address The column letter and row number that identifies a cell.

cell site In a cellular telephone network, an area in which a transmitting station repeats the system's broadcast signals so that the signal remains strong even though the user may move from one cell site to another.

cellular telephone A radio-based wireless telephone system that provides widespread coverage through the use of repeating transmitters placed in zones (called cells). The zones are close enough so that signal strength is maintained throughout the calling area.

central processing unit (CPU; microprocessor or **processor)** The computer's processing and control circuitry, including the arithmetic logic unit (ALU) and the control unit; referred to as the "brain" of the computer.

centralized structure An infrastructure where technology management is centered in the IT department, and everyone within the organization works with standardized technology solutions in their everyday work.

certification A skills and knowledge assessment process organized by computer industry vendors (and sometimes by professional associations).

channel In Internet Relay Chat (IRC), a chat group in which as many as several dozen people carry on a text-based conversation on a specific topic. This is dated technology that has been replaced by instant messaging, blogging, wikis, and tweeting.

character 1. The smallest unit of data that an individual can work with, made up of bytes that represent letters, numbers, and special symbols produced by keyboard keys or key combinations. 2. A letter, number, punctuation mark, or symbol produced onscreen by the press of a key or a key combination.

character code An algorithm used to translate between the numerical language of the computer and characters readable by humans.

character map A comparison chart or lookup table located in a computer's read-only memory (ROM) on the motherboard. The system uses this table to locate the key that was struck on the keyboard and then notifies the processor of the character corresponding to that matrix location. The character map lets the processor know that pressing the a key by itself corresponds to a small letter a, but the Shift and a keys pressed together correspond to a capital A.

charge-coupled device (CCD) A photosensitive computer chip that transforms light patterns into pixels (individual dots). A CCD consists of a grid made up of light-sensitive elements. Each element converts the incoming light into a voltage that is proportional to the light's brightness. The digital camera's picture quality is determined by how many elements the CCD has.

chart A graphical representation of numbers that makes it easier to interpret data.

check-screening system A system that reads a check's account number, accesses a database containing delinquent accounts, and compares the account numbers, allowing vendors to catch problem transactions before they become losses.

chipset A collection of chips that are designed to work together smoothly on a computer motherboard and move data throughout the computer system.

ciphertext The coded message that results from applying an encryption key to a message.

circuit switching One of two fundamental architectures for a wide area network (WAN), in which high-speed electronic switches create a direct connection between two communicating devices. The telephone system is a circuit-switching network.

class A category of objects in object-oriented programming.

clickstream The trail of Web links that you have followed to get to a particular site.

client In a client/server network, any type of computer—PC, Mac, desktop, notebook, or even handheld device—that is connected to a network and contains the software that enables it to send requests to the server.

client/server database system A system that incorporates a database server that is accessed through queries input through a client program.

client/server network A network in which a client makes a request to a central server by sending messages, and the server responds to the client by acting on each request and returning results.

Clip Organizer In Microsoft Office, a repository of clip art and images that can be inserted into a document or presentation.

clock speed The speed of the internal clock of a microprocessor that sets the pace at which operations proceed in the computer's internal processing circuitry.

cloud computing A relatively new subscription-based or pay-per-use service that provides scalable resources and IT services over the Internet; its power lies in the admission of users to a shared data center containing multi-tenancy applications.

cluster On a magnetic disk, a storage unit that consists of two or more sectors.

coaxial cable A broadband transmission medium that consists of a center copper wire surrounded by insulation, which is then surrounded by a layer of braided wire. Data travels through the center wire, and the braided wire provides a shield against electrical interference.

COBOL (Common Business-Oriented Language) An early, high-level programming language primarily used for business applications.

code The written computer instructions that programmers create.

code of conduct A set of ethical principles developed by a professional association, such as the Association for Computing Machinery (ACM).

codec Short for compression/decompression standard. A standard for compressing and decompressing video information to reduce the size of digitized multimedia files. Popular codecs include MPEG (an acronym for Motion Picture Experts Group), Apple's QuickTime, and Microsoft's AVI.

cold boot Starting a computer that is not already on.

cold site A less expensive disaster recovery site than a hot site because it only becomes operational once a disaster has occurred.

collaboration tools Applications that help you work in partnership with team members online.

collision In local area networks (LANs), a garbled transmission that results when two or more workstations transmit to the same network cable at exactly the same time. Networks have means of detecting and preventing collisions.

column In Microsoft Excel and Word, a block of data presented vertically across the screen.

command-line user interface Requires the user to type commands using keywords and specific syntax (rules for entering commands) that tell the OS what to do (such as *format* or *copy*) one line at a time.

commerce The selling of goods and services with the expectation of making a reasonable profit.

commercial software Copyrighted software that must be purchased. The current trend is to make them available as an online download or to give the potential customer a trial period. Once the trial period is over, the user can pay for the program directly on the Web site and download their official copy.

communications The process of electronically sending and receiving messages between two points.

communications channel In communications, the path through which messages are passed from one location to the next; also referred to as links.

communications device Any hardware device that is capable of moving data into or out of the computer including modems, routers, switches, wireless access points, network interface cards, and other computers.

CompactFlash A popular flash memory storage device that can store up to 128 MB of digital camera images.

competitive advantage A condition that gives an organization a superior position over the companies it competes with.

compiler A program that translates source code in a third-generation programming language into instructions in (or close to) a specific computer's machine language.

completeness check A data validation procedure that determines whether a required field has been left empty and, if so, prompts the user to fill in the needed data.

computer A machine that can physically represent data, process the data by following a set of instructions, display the results so people can use them, and store the results for future use.

computer-aided software engineering (CASE) Software that automates the often tedious task of documenting entity relationships and data flows in a complex new system.

computer-based training A form of education that uses multimedia, animation, and programmed learning to teach new skills with a computer.

computer crime A computer-based activity that violates state, federal, or international laws.

computer ethics A branch of philosophy dealing with computing-related moral dilemmas.

computer forensics A complex branch of forensic science pertaining to legal evidence found on computers and digital storage media.

computer science (CS) The study of storage, change, and transfer of information. It includes both the theoretical study of algorithms and the practical problems to which they can be applied.

computer security risk Any event, action, or situation—intentional or not—that could lead to the loss or destruction of computer systems or the data they contain.

computer system A collection of related computer components that have been designed to work smoothly together.

computer virus A program, designed as a prank or as sabotage, that replicates itself by attaching to other programs and carrying out unwanted and sometimes dangerous operations.

congestion In a packet-switching network, a performance interruption that occurs when a segment of the network experiences an overload, too much traffic flooding the same network path.

connectivity The ability to link various media and devices, thereby enhancing communication and improving access to information.

connector A physical receptor that enables users or technicians to connect a cable securely to the computer's case. A male connector contains extended pins or plugs that fit into the corresponding female connector.

consistency check A data validation procedure that examines the data typed into two different fields to determine identical entries.

consumer-to-consumer e-commerce (C2C) The online exchange or trade of goods, services, or information between individual consumers. Often C2C e-commerce involves the use of an intermediate site, such as the popular online auction destination eBay.

content pane Displayed on the right side in a Windows Explorer. It displays subfolders and files located within the selected folder; also called a file list.

contention In a computer network, a problem that arises when two or more computers try to access the network at the same time. Contention can result in collisions, which can destroy data or require frequent and costly retransmissions.

contention management In a computer network, the use of one of several techniques for managing contention and preventing collisions.

contextual tab In Microsoft Office, a tab that is displayed when additional tools are needed.

control module In a program design tool called a structure chart, the top module or box that oversees the transfer of control to the other modules.

control structure In structured programming, logical elements grouped in a block that specify how the instructions in a program are to be executed.

control unit A component of the central processing unit (CPU) that obtains program instructions and sends signals to carry out those instructions.

convergence The merging of disparate objects or ideas (and even people) into new combinations and efficiencies. Within the IT industry, convergence means two things: the combination of various industries (computers, consumer electronics, and telecommunications) and the coming together of products such as PCs and telephones.

cookie A text file that is deposited by a Web site on a Web user's computer system, without the user's knowledge or consent. Mostly used for legitimate purposes, such as implementing "shopping carts," they can also be used to gather data on Web users' browsing and shopping habits.

cooling fan A fan designed to keep the system unit cool. The fan is usually built into the power supply, although some high-powered systems include auxiliary fans to provide additional cooling.

copy-protected software Computer programs that include some mechanism to prevent users from making or running unauthorized copies.

copyright infringement The act of plagiarizing or using material from a copyrighted source without getting permission to do so.

copyright protection scheme A method used by software manufacturers to ensure that users cannot produce unauthorized copies of copyrighted software.

corporate espionage The unauthorized accessing of corporate information, usually to the benefit of one of the corporation's competitors.

cost-benefit analysis An examination of the losses and gains related to a project.

cracker A computer user obsessed with gaining entry into highly secure computer systems; also called a black hat.

crash conversion See direct conversion.

cross-platform programming language A programming language that can create programs capable of running on many different types of computers supported by different operating systems.

CRT (cathode-ray tube) monitor A monitor that displays data through a vacuum tube that uses an electron gun that repeatedly sweeps across the screen to emit a beam of electrons that illuminates red, green, and blue phosphorus to produce viewable images and colors. Considered legacy technology.

cryptographer An individual who specializes in encoding information.

cryptography The study of transforming information into an encoded or scrambled format.

cursor (insertion point) A blinking vertical bar, a horizontal underline character, or a highlighted box located on the monitor that indicates the location in which keystrokes will appear when typed.

cursor-movement keys (arrow keys) A set of keys on the keyboard that moves the location of the cursor on the screen. The numeric keypad can also move the cursor when in the appropriate mode.

custom software Application software designed for a company by a professional programmer or programming team. Custom software is usually very expensive.

customer relationship management (CRM) software Keeps track of an organization's interactions with its customers and focuses on retaining those customers.

cyberbullying A cybercrime that involves situations in which one or more individuals harass or threaten another individual who is less capable of defending himself or herself, using the Internet or other forms of digital technology. Cyberbullying can include sending threatening e-mail or text messages or assuming someone else's online identity for the purpose of humiliating or misrepresenting him or her.

cybercrime Crime carried out by means of the Internet.

cybergang A group of computer users obsessed with gaining entry into highly secure computer systems.

cyberlaw A new legal field designed to track developments in cybercrime and combat occurrences of such abuses.

cyberspace Territory that isn't an actual, physical place, but is the unlimited span of worldwide networks of computer networks that use the same method to facilitate data transmission and exchange.

cyberstalking A form of harassment in which an individual uses the Internet, social networking sites, e-mail, or other electronic communications to repeatedly harass or threaten a person. Cyberstalking, like real-world stalking, is a repeated, unwanted, and disruptive break into the life-world of the victim.

D

dashboard An executive information system with a user interface, similar to an automobile's dashboard, that is, designed to be easy to read.

data The raw material of computing: words, numbers, images, sounds, or a combination of these. The data from the input phase of the information processing cycle is passed to the processing phase.

database A collection of related data that is organized in a manner that makes the data easy to access, manage, update, group, and summarize.

database management system (DBMS) A database program that can join or connect several files or tables to manage, access, store, and edit data in a structured manner.

database program Software application that is used to create databases or to work with the data in existing databases.

database server software Software that runs on a network and responds to information requests from remote users.

data bus A set of parallel wires that acts as an electronic highway on which data travels between computer components. It is the medium by which the entire system communicates with the CPU.

data dependency A microprocessor performance problem in which a CPU is slowed in its functioning by the need to wait for the results of one set of instructions before moving on to process the next set.

data dictionary A list of the tables the database contains along with details concerning each table, including field names, field lengths, data types, and validation settings.

data diddling A computer crime in which data is modified in accounts or databases to conceal theft or embezzlement.

data file A collection of related records; also called a table.

data flow diagram (DFD) A diagram that uses a set of graphical symbols to show how data moves through the existing system.

data glove A wired glove-like input device for virtual reality environments.

data independence Data is separate from the applications, and changes in data do not require changes in the structure of forms, reports, or programs accessing the database.

data integrity The validity of the data contained in a database.

data maintenance Procedures for adding, updating, and deleting records for the purpose of keeping the database in optimal shape.

data mart A smaller-scale data warehouse project that supports one division rather than the entire organization.

data mining A data exploration and analysis technique that uncovers information through statistical analysis and modeling in an attempt to discover previously unknown patterns.

data redundancy Repetition of data characteristic of poorly designed systems, which can cause peculiar query and report results.

data security Ensures that the data stored in a database is not accessible to people who might misuse it, particularly when the collected data is sensitive.

data set The contents of a table in Access.

data transfer rate 1. In secondary storage devices, the maximum number of bits per second that can be sent from the hard disk to the computer. The rate is determined by the drive interface. 2. The speed, expressed in bits per second (bps), at which a modem can transfer, or is transferring, data over a telephone line.

data type In a computerized database, a data type is defined by the overall purpose of the database coupled with the specific data being entered.

data validation Procedures that define acceptable input ranges for each field in a record.

data warehouse A central location capable of storing all the information that a corporation possesses and making this data available for analysis.

dead link On the World Wide Web, a hyperlink that refers to a resource (such as a sound or a Web page) that has been moved or deleted; also called broken link.

debugging In programming, the process of finding and correcting errors, or bugs, in the source code of a computer program.

decision support system (DSS) A computer-based system that addresses the deficiencies of management of information systems (MIS) by enabling managers to retrieve information that cannot be supplied by fixed, predefined MIS reports.

default In a computer program, a fallback setting or configuration value that is used unless the user specifically chooses a different one.

default value An automatic entry placed into a field when no other value is provided.

deliverable An outcome or tangible output such as a report or another document.

denial of service (DoS) attack A form of network vandalism that attempts to make a service unavailable to other users, generally by flooding the service with meaningless data.

design template A professionally created slide design that can be applied to a presentation.

desktop The screen image that appears after an operating system finishes loading into memory (RAM), displaying pictures (icons) representing files, folders, and windows in the file system. The desktop image can change with the operating system or version.

desktop computer A personal computer designed for an individual's use at a desk or in a fixed location.

details pane Located at the bottom of the window, it provides a thumbnail view and information about the selected file or folder; the details vary depending on the object that has been selected.

device driver A program that controls a device attached to a computer.

dialog box Within computer programs, a display in which a user can supply additional information that the program needs.

digital camera A camera that takes video or still photographs, or both, using digital technology and recording images via an electronic image sensor.

digital cash system A method for using smart cards and prepaid amounts of electronically stored money to pay for small charges such as parking and tolls.

digital certificate A form of digital identification enabled by public key encryption that serves as a method of validating a user, server, or Web site. For a user, a digital certificate validates identity in a manner similar to showing a driver's license. For a server or Web site, a digital certificate validates that a Web server or Web site is authentic, so that the user can feel secure in his or her interaction.

digital divide The racial and/or income disparity in computer ownership and Internet access.

digital forensics A branch of forensic science pertaining to legal evidence found on computers and digital storage media.

digital modem See ISDN adapter.

digital piracy Unauthorized reproduction and distribution of computer-based media.

digital signal A signal used by digital equipment, like computers, sent via discontinuous pulses, in which the presence or absence of electronic pulses represents 1s and 0s. See analog signal.

digital signature A technique enabled by public key encryption that is used to guarantee that a message is authentic, not sent by a hacker, and has not been tampered with.

digital telephony Telephone systems using all-digital protocols and transmission, offering the advantage over analog telephony of noise-free transmission and high-quality audio.

digital-to-analog converter (DAC) A microchip that contains the circuitry to convert a digital signal to analog.

digital video camera Camera that uses digital rather than analog technologies to store recorded video images.

digitization The transformation of data such as voice, text, graphics, audio, and video into digital form, thereby allowing various technologies to transmit computer data through telephone lines, cables, or air and space. Digitization also allows the data to be shared as files, something difficult to do with analog technologies.

direct broadcast Satellite (DBS) A consumer satellite technology that offers television channels and Internet access.

direct conversion (crash conversion or plunge) Stopping an old system and then the starting the new system; sometimes called a crash conversion or plunge.

directory See folder.

directory structure See folder structure.

disaster recovery plan A written plan with detailed instructions that specifies alternative computing facilities to be used for emergency processing until nonoperational computers can be repaired or replaced. Also referred to as a business continuity plan (BCP).

disk cache A small amount of RAM that stores the program instructions and data you are working with. When the CPU needs to get information, it looks in the disk cache first. If it doesn't find the information it needs, it retrieves the information from the hard disk.

disk cleanup utility A program that can save disk space by removing files you no longer need.

disk defragmentation program A utility program used to reorganize data on the disk so that file pieces are reassembled as one chunk of disk space (decreasing disk search time); storage is made more efficient (by clustering files into structures more efficiently searched), and the time needed to access files is decreased.

disk scanning program An error checking program that can detect and resolve a number of physical and logical problems that may occur when your computer stores files on a disk.

distributed denial of service (DDoS) attack A computer attack on multiple systems by a hacker who bombards an Internet server with a huge number of requests so that the server becomes overloaded and unable to function.

distributed hypermedia system A network-based content development system in which individuals connected to the network can each make a small contribution by developing content related to their area of expertise. The Web is a distributed hypermedia system.

distributed structure A technology infrastructure where users are able to customize their technology tools to suit their individual needs and wants.

DLP (digital light-processing) projector An output device that projects a computer's display on a screen by projecting light into a chip made of millions of microscopic mirrors to produce a brilliant, sharp image.

document A file created with an application program, such as a word processing or spreadsheet program.

documentation 1. Brief tutorials, Read Me files, help files, and printed manuals that contain information the software manufacturer thinks the user will find helpful. 2. In software development, the collection of all recorded design, development, and production information pertinent to a project's completion, such as manuals, tutorials, start-up procedures, and installation instructions.

domain name On the Internet, a readable computer address (such as **www.microsoft.com**) that gets translated into an IP address and identifies a computer on the network.

domain name registration On the Internet, a process by which individuals and companies can obtain a domain name (such as **www.c34.org**) and link this name to a specific Internet address (IP address).

Domain Name System (DNS) A system used by the Internet to link domain names with their numeric IP address. It functions like a telephone directory for the Internet.

dot-matrix printer (impact printer) Once the most popular, this type of printer creates characters by striking pins against an ink ribbon. Each pin makes a dot, and combinations of dots form characters and illustrations.

dot pitch (aperture grill) A physical characteristic that determines the smallest dot the screen can display. The space (measured in millimeters) between each physical dot on the screen.

downloading To transfer a file from another computer to your computer by means of a computer network.

drill-down A technique that enables managers to view information in a data warehouse and focus their attention on a specific data element by starting at the summary level of information and narrowing their search at each progressive level of data.

drive A storage device in which files and folders reside. Drives can be internal (installed within the system unit) or external (attached to the system unit by a cable connected to a port).

driver A utility program that contains instructions to make a peripheral device addressable or usable by an operating system.

drive activity light A light on the front panel of most computers that signals when the hard disk is accessing data.

drive bay A receptacle or opening into which you can install a CD-ROM or DVD-ROM drive, or a removable drive.

drive imaging software Backup software that creates a mirror image of the entire hard disk—including the operating system and applications, as well as all files and data.

drive letter A letter of the alphabet followed by a colon and a backslash character that identifies the drive.

DSL (digital subscriber line or xDSL) A general term for several technologies that enable high-speed Internet access through twisted-pair telephone lines. Also called xDSL.

DSL modem Similar to a traditional telephone modem in that it modulates and demodulates analog and digital signals for transmission over communications channels, but it does so using signaling methods based on broadband technology for much higher transfer speeds.

DVD drive A read-only storage device that reads the data encoded on a DVD-ROM disc and transfers this data to a computer.

DVD+R A recordable optical storage media that enables the disc to be written to one time and read many times.

DVD-R Digital video disc—recordable optical storage medium that, like CD-R discs, cannot be erased or written over once data has been saved.

DVD-ROM (digital video, or versatile disc–read-only memory) A digital video optical disc format capable of storing up to 17 GB on a single disc, enough for a feature-length movie. DVD is designed to be used with a video player and a television. DVD discs are read by DVD-ROM drives.

DVD+RW A recordable optical storage media on which you can write, erase, and read from the disc many times.

DVD-RW Digital video disc—recordable optical storage medium on which you can write, erase, and read from the disc many times.

DVI (digital video interface) port A port that enables LCD monitors to use digital signals.

dye sublimation printer A type of thermal-wax transfer printer that uses a heat process to transfer an impression onto paper. Although thermal-transfer printers are the best color printers currently available, they are very expensive.

dynamic (search) A term used to describe searches in Windows Explorer, which are automatically refreshed every time you open up a saved search. New files are added and old files that no longer meet the criteria are deleted.

E

EBCDIC (Extended Binary Code Decimal Interchange Code) An eight-bit character code used by IBM mainframe computers and some midrange systems.

e-book Short for electronic book. A book that has been digitized and is distributed by means of a digital storage medium.

e-book reader A device that can read electronic books on a personal computer, smartphone, or special device, such as Amazon's Kindle 2. The main advantages of these devices are portability, readability of the screen in bright sunlight, and long battery life.

e-business (electronic business) Use of the Internet to buy, sell, provide customer service, and collaborate with business partners.

e-commerce (electronic commerce) The use of networks or the Internet to carry out business of any type.

economic feasibility The capability of a project being accomplished with available financial resources.

ECMAScript (formerly JavaScript) A vendor-neutral standard created by the European Computer Manufacturers Association (ECMA) for what was originally Netscape's JavaScript. It is a client-side scripting language for Web publishing.

e-discovery (electronic discovery) The obligation of parties to a lawsuit to exchange documents that exist only in electronic form, including e-mails, voicemails, instant messages, e-calendars, audio files, data on handheld devices, graphics, photographs, spreadsheets, Web sites, drawings, and other types of digital data.

EEPROM Electrically erasable programmable read-only memory is a type of read-only memory that can be rewritten many times while the chip is in the computer. An EEPROM can be erased using an electric field instead of a UV light source, eliminating the need for an erasing window.

e-learning The use of computers and computer programs to replace teachers and the time–place specificity of learning.

electrical engineering (EE) An engineering discipline that has a strong focus on digital circuit design as well as cutting-edge communication technologies.

electronic data interchange (EDI) A set of standards that specifies how to transfer data and documents between enterprises using the Internet and other networks without human intervention.

electronic mailing lists Lists of e-mail addresses that automatically broadcast messages to all individuals on the list. Because the messages are transmitted as e-mail, only individuals who are subscribers to the mailing list receive and view the messages.

element In HTML, a distinctive component of a document's structure, such as a title, heading, or list. HTML divides elements into two categories: head elements (such as the document's title) and body elements (headings, paragraphs, links, and text).

e-mail (electronic mail) An Internet service requiring a software application that enables you to send and receive messages though the use of computer networks.

e-mail address A series of characters that precisely identifies the location of a person's electronic mailbox. On the Internet, e-mail addresses consist of a mailbox name (such as jsmith) followed by an at sign (@) and the computer's domain name (as in jsmith@fictitiousschool.edu).

e-mail attachment Any type of computer file—document, photo, audio, or video—that is included with an e-mail message.

embedded operating system A specialized operating system designed for specific applications. Such a system is usually very compact and efficient. An embedded operating system often eliminates many features that nonembedded computer operating systems provide.

emergency disk See boot disk.

employee monitoring When large employers routinely engage in observing employees' phone calls, e-mails, Web browsing habits, and computer files.

encapsulation In object-oriented programming, the hiding of all internal information of an object from another object and/or the user.

encryption A coding or scrambling process that renders a message unreadable by anyone except the intended recipient.

encryption key A formula that is used to make a plaintext message unreadable.

enterprise A business or organization, which can include universities, government agencies, and not-for-profit groups or charities.

enterprise application integration (EAI) A combination of processes, software, standards, and hardware that results in the integration of two or more enterprise systems, thus enabling multiple systems to operate as one and share data and business processes throughout an organization.

enterprise computing Information technology on a large scale, encompassing all aspects of technology and information resources, including problems or malfunctions, within an organization or a business. It also includes understanding the use of computers in the networks that span the organization as well as the software needed to processes and monitor activities involved in daily business operations.

enterprise data The centralized data shared throughout an organization.

enterprise data center A secure common repository for enterprise data.

enterprise networking The technology infrastructure within an enterprise.

enterprise resource planning (ERP) software Software that brings together various enterprise functions, such as manufacturing, sales, marketing, and finance, into a single computer system.

enterprise software Software designed to solve problems at the enterprise level of an organization rather that at the departmental level.

enterprise system An information system that integrates an organization's information and applications across all of the organization's functional divisions.

entity-relationship diagram (ERD) A graphic that shows all of the organizations, departments, users, programs, and data that play a role in the system as well as the relationships among those entities.

EPROM Electrically programmable read-only memory is erasable read-only memory that can be reused many times. It can be erased using an UV (ultraviolet) light source that shines through a quartz erasing window in the EPROM package.

ergonomics The field of study that is concerned with the fit between people, their equipment, and their work. It takes into account worker limitations and capabilities in attempting to ensure that the tasks, equipment, and overall environment suit each worker.

e-tailer A Web-based retailer.

Ethernet A set of standards that defines local area networks (LANs) capable of operating at data transfer rates of 10 Mbps to 6 Gbps. About 90 percent of all LANs use one of several Ethernet standards.

ethical hacker Hackers and crackers who have turned pro, offering their services to companies hoping to use hacker expertise to shore up their computer systems' defenses; also called a white hat.

ethical principle A principle that defines the justification for considering an act or a rule to be morally right or wrong. Ethical principles can help people find their way through moral dilemmas.

event-driven programming language A program design method in which the programming code is not written to execute in any specific sequence. Instead, it executes in response to user actions such as the clicking of the mouse.

evil twin A phony Wi-Fi hot spot whose name makes users believe it is a legitimate spot. Typical situated in hotels and airports, an evil twin is usually connected to a fraudulent network.

e-waste Obsolete computer equipment.

exabyte A unit of measurement approximately equal to 1 quintillion bytes.

exception report A report that alerts managers to unexpected developments (such as high demand for a new product).

exclusion operator In database and Internet searching, a symbol or a word that tells the software to exclude records or documents containing a certain word or phrase. It is usually denoted as a minus sign (–) in the search statement.

executable program A program that is ready to run and does not need to be altered in any way.

execution cycle (execute, store) In a machine cycle, a phase consisting of the execute and write-back (or store) operations.

executive information system (EIS) A system that supports management's strategic-planning function; also known as an executive support system (ESS).

exiting Quitting or closing down an application or program.

expansion card (expansion board, adapter card, or **adapter)** A circuit board that fits into slots on the motherboard and is used to connect the computer with various peripherals.

expansion slot A receptacle usually on the motherboard that is connected to the computer's expansion bus and accepts an expansion board and connects it to the rest of the system.

expert system (ES) An information system that deals with detailed and in-depth knowledge in a specific area supplied by experts in that field and formulates a decision in the way that a human expert in the field might.

ExpressCard The newest standard for the PC card, originally known as the PCMCIA card (short for Personal Computer Memory Card International Association). It is a credit-card-size adapter that fits into a designated slot to provide expanded capabilities such as wireless communication, additional memory, multimedia, or security features.

Extended ASCII A character coding system that uses eight bits and allows representation of 256 characters.

Extensible Business Reporting Language (XBRL) Used by businesses to publish and share financial information with each other and industry analysts across all computer platforms and the Internet.

Extensible Hypertext Markup Language (XHTML) A language that combines the flexibility of HTML with the extensibility of XML by allowing the user to define a tag for clarity across different browsers or create a new markup tag by simply defining it in an XHTML module and using it in a Web page as you would any other HTML tag. This feature makes a page truly compatible with all browsers.

Extensible Markup Language (XML) A language designed to reduce the complexity of HTML.

extension A suffix added to a filename (after the dot). The extension is often supplied by the application and indicates the type of application that created the file.

extranet A network connected over the Internet in such a way that data traverses the Internet in encrypted form, safe from prying eyes.

eye-gaze response system (vision technology) A biological feedback device that enables quadriplegics to control computers by moving their eyes around the screen.

F

facsimile transmission (fax) The sending and receiving of printed pages between two locations using a telephone line and fax devices that digitize the page's image.

fair use An exception to copyright laws made to facilitate education, commentary, analysis, and scholarly research.

fat client A computer that accesses a server but processes most of the data on its own system.

fault tolerance The ability of a device to keep working even if one or more components fail.

fax modem A modem that also functions as a fax machine, giving the computer user the capability of sending word-processing documents and other files as faxes.

fiber-optic cable A broadband transmission medium that consists of thin strands of glass or plastic that carry data by means of pulses of light. Fiber-optic cable carries data at transfer rates of 10 Gbps (gigabits per second) or more, without loss of signal strength, and for longer distances than twisted pair or coaxial cable.

Fiber-optic service (FiOS) Fiber-optic lines that run directly to the home and provide users with incredibly fast Internet access, easily surpassing other methods.

field A single unit of relative information in a database. Each field has a specific, defined data type.

field name A descriptive label that helps identify the type of content to be entered into a field.

file A named unit of related data stored in a computer system.

file allocation table (FAT) A table created during formatting and hidden on the disk that keeps vital records concerning the exact storage location of a file. This table was used by older operating systems and has been replaced by a system called new technology file system (NTFS).

file compression utility A program that can reduce the size of a file by as much as 80 percent without harming the data, by substituting short codes for lengthy data patterns. The resulting smaller files can be shared more efficiently, particularly over the Internet. Compressed files need to be decompressed, converted back to their lengthy form, prior to use.

file infector A computer virus that attaches to a program file and, when that program is executed, spreads to other program files.

file list See content pane.

file management program A program that enables users to create, edit, and

manage databases in which files or tables are independent of each other, with no link between the data stored in each.

file manager A program that helps you organize and manage the data stored on your disk.

file name The name that the storage device uses to identify each unique file.

file server In client/server computing, a computer that has been set aside (dedicated) to make program and data files available to users on a network that have been granted access.

File Transfer Protocol (FTP) An Internet standard for the exchange of files between two computers connected to the Internet. With an FTP client, you can upload or download files from a computer that is running an FTP server. Normally, you need a user name and password to upload or download files from an FTP server, but some FTP servers provide a service called anonymous FTP, which enables anyone to download files made available for public use.

filter 1. In Microsoft Access, a process that requires one or more conditions to be met to pass through a query. 2. In e-mail, a rule that specifies the destination folder of messages conforming to certain criteria.

firewall A program or device that permits an organization's internal computer users to access the Internet but places severe limits on the ability of outsiders to access internal data.

FireWire (1394 port) An input/output port that combines high-speed performance (up to 400 Mbps) with the ability to guarantee data delivery at a specified speed, making the port ideal for use with real-time devices such as digital video cameras. FireWire is Apple Computer's name for 1394 port technology.

flame In Usenet and e-mail, a message that contains abusive, threatening, obscene, or inflammatory language.

flash drive (solid state drive) A type of storage device that uses solid-state circuitry and has no moving parts.

flash EPROM A type of PROM that is similar to an EEPROM except that flash EPROMs are erased all at once whereas regular EEPROMs can erase one byte at a time.

flash memory Nonvolatile memory found on flash drives and memory cards that can be electronically erased and reprogrammed.

flash memory card Wafer-thin, highly portable solid-state storage system that is capable of storing as much as 64 gigabytes of data. Used with some digital cameras, the card stores digitized photographs without requiring electrical power to maintain the data.

flash memory reader A slot or compartment in digital cameras and other devices into which a flash memory card is inserted.

flat file The type of file generated by a file management program.

flexible keyboard A very adaptable foldable keyboard that weighs just 250 grams, making it perfect for travel. It is completely sealed, so it is spill- and dust–resistant, making it the perfect choice for use in factories, wet areas, and retail environments.

floating-point notation A method for storing and calculating numbers so that the location of the decimal point isn't fixed, but floats. This allows the computer to work with very small and very large numbers.

flowchart In structured programming, a diagram that shows the logic of a program.

folder An organizational tool for grouping files that have something in common; also called a directory.

folder structure An organized set of folders in which to save your files; also called a directory structure.

footprint The amount of physical space taken up by a device or the amount of RAM a program uses while it is operational.

foreground application From the user's perspective, the application that is active, as indicated by how the application appears on the screen when more than one application is running.

foreign key A field that is a primary key in another file.

forgery The making of Internet data appear to come from one place when it's really coming from another.

form In the Microsoft Access database management system, a template used to enter data into the database in place of the Table entry method.

form factor A specification for mounting internal components, such as the motherboard.

Form object In the Microsoft Access database management system, the object used to collect data.

formula In a spreadsheet program such as Microsoft Excel, a mathematical expression embedded in a cell that can include cell references. The cell displays the formula's result.

Fortran Short for formula translator. An early third-generation language that enabled scientists and engineers to write simple programs for solving complex mathematical equations in an easy to use environment.

fragmented A disk that has been used to the point that it becomes a patchwork of files, with portions of files scattered here and there. This placement of sectors slows disk access because the system must look in several locations to find all of a file's segments.

frame rate In a video or animation, a measurement of the number of still images shown per second.

frames In a video or animation, the series of still images flashed on-screen at a rapid rate.

freeware Copyrighted software that can be freely copied but not sold for profit.

full backup Backing up all files and data on the entire hard disk.

function In spreadsheet programs such as Microsoft Excel, one of the two basic types of formulas (along with mathematic expressions). In a function, operations can be performed on multiple inputs.

function key A row of keys positioned along the top of the keyboard, labeled F1 through F12. The action they perform depends on the program in use.

functional division Parts of an organization that handle each of the organization's core functions, for example, accounting and finance, marketing and sales, human resources, and management.

G

gadget An application that appears as an active icon in the Windows sidebar. Gadgets are selected or downloaded by the user and display photos, current weather conditions, control a multimedia player, or monitor the CPU's performance.

Gantt chart A type of bar chart that indicates task due dates and project milestones.

General Public License (GPL) A freeware software license, devised by the Open Software Foundation (OSF), stipulating that a given program can be obtained, used, and even modified, as long as the user agrees to not sell the software and to make the source code for any modifications available.

general-purpose application A software program used by many people to accomplish frequently performed tasks such as writing (word processing), working with numbers (spreadsheets), and keeping track of information (databases).

genetic algorithm An automated program development environment in which various alternative approaches to solving a problem are introduced; each is allowed to mutate periodically through the introduction of random changes. The various approaches compete in an effort to solve a specific problem. After a period of time, one approach may prove to be clearly superior to the others.

gigabits per second (Gbps) A data transfer measurement equivalent to 1 billion bits per second.

gigabyte (GB) A unit of measurement approximately equal to 1 billion bits.

gigahertz A unit used to measure a processor's speed in billions of cycles per second.

gigaPoP (gigabits per second points of presence) A point of presence (POP) that provides access to a backbone service

capable of data transfer rates exceeding 1 Gbps (1 billion bits per second).

global unique identifier (GUID) An identification number that is generated by a hardware component or a program. The GUIDs can be read by Web servers or embedded in various documents, detecting which computer is accessing a site and inadvertently making it more difficult to use the Internet anonymously.

globalization Conducting business internationally where the goods and services are identical (or nearly identical) in all locations.

Google Docs A free Web-based word processor and spreadsheet that allow project members to share and edit documents online.

Google Groups A free Web editor that makes it easy for anyone to create and manage simple group Web sites.

GPS (Global Positioning System) A satellite-based system that enables portable GPS receivers to determine their location with an accuracy of 100 meters or less.

graphical MUD (gMUD) A multiuser dungeon (MUD) that uses graphics instead of text to represent the interaction of characters in a virtual environment.

graphical user interface (GUI) The most popular user interface, which takes advantage of the computer's graphics capabilities to make the operating system and programs easier to use.

grid computing Applying the abilities of many computers in a network to a single problem at the same time. This amount of concentrated power is usually directed at scientific or technical problems that require a high level of processing power and access to large amounts of data.

grounding bracelet A device that is worn around the wrist with the other end attached to a grounded object. It is worn to avoid discharging static electricity into a system under repair.

grounding strap See grounding bracelet.

group In Microsoft Office, a collection of buttons and commands that appear on tabs within the Ribbon.

groupware Software that provides computerized support for the information needs of these workgroups. Most groupware applications include e-mail, videoconferencing tools, group-scheduling systems, customizable electronic forms, real-time shared applications, and shared information databases. Also called teamware.

H

hacker Traditionally, a computer user who enjoys pushing his or her computer capabilities to the limit, especially by using clever or novel approaches to solving problems. In the press, the term *hacker* has become synonymous with criminals who attempt unauthorized access to computer systems for criminal purposes, such as sabotage or theft. The computing community considers this usage inaccurate.

hacker ethic A set of moral principles common to the hacker community. According to the hacker ethic, all technical information should, in principle, be freely available to all. Therefore, gaining entry to a system to explore data and increase knowledge is never unethical. Destroying, altering, or moving data in such a way that could cause injury or expense to others, however, is always unethical. In more and more localities, any unauthorized computer access is against the law; see also cracker.

handheld computer A small, handheld computer that receives input entered with a stylus, virtual keyboard, or external corded keyboard. Most include built-in software for appointments, scheduling, and e-mail.

haptics A field of research in developing output devices that stimulate the sense of touch.

hard business skill A process-related skill. In the IT world, this type of skill refers to the knowledge of process mostly with reference to technological expertise in such areas as networking, Web development, knowledge of UNIX and C++, and firewall administration.

hard copy Output viewed in printed form.

hard disk controller An electronic circuit that provides an interface between a hard disk and the computer's CPU.

hard disk drive (hard disk, fixed disk, online disk) A secondary storage, random access, magnetic medium that uses several rigid disks (platters) coated with a magnetically sensitive material and housed in a sealed mechanism. In almost all modern computers, the hard disk is by far the easiest to access and most important storage medium.

hardware The physical components, such as circuit boards, disk drives, displays, and printers, that make up a computer system.

head-mounted display (HMD) A display device, worn on the head or as part of a helmet, that has a miniature optic in front of each eye that enables the wearer to experience a three-dimensional virtual reality environment.

headset (head-mounted display) A wearable output device with twin LCD panels for creating the illusion that an individual is experiencing a three-dimensional, simulated environment.

heat sink A heat-dissipating component that drains heat away from microprocessors, which can generate enough heat while operating to destroy themselves. Heat sinks are often used in combination with cooling fans.

hexadecimal (hex) number A number that uses a base 16 number system rather than a decimal (base 10) or binary (base 2) number system. Computer systems use this system to represent data in a shorter, faster, and more compact form using the digits 0 through 9 and the letters A through F.

hierarchical database management system Data organized in the shape of a pyramid, with each row of data items linked to items directly beneath it, creating a pyramid or parent/child type of alignment.

high bit-rate digital subscriber line (HDSL) The most mature DSL technology, it is a form of SDSL that provides T1 connections over two or three twisted-pair copper lines. Unlike most other forms of DSL, HDSL is not a typical consumer service.

high-definition television (HDTV) A digital television standard that provides extremely high-quality video and audio. HDTV displays include, plasma, rear screen, and front screen projection. HDTV requires an HDTV tuner to view. The highest resolution for the HDTV format is 1080i.

high-level language A programming language that eliminates the need for programmers to understand the intimate details of how the hardware, specifically the microprocessor, handles data.

history list In a Web browser, a window or list that shows all the Web sites that the browser has accessed during a given period, such as the last 30 days.

holographic storage A type of storage that uses two laser beams to create a pattern on photosensitive media, resulting in a three-dimensional image, similar to the holograms you can buy in a novelty shop. This 3-D approach will enable much higher-density storage capacities and is being promoted for its archiving capabilities.

home and educational program A general-purpose software program for personal finance, home design and landscaping, encyclopedias and other computerized reference information, and games.

home network (home area network or HAN) A personal and specific use of network technology that provides connectivity between users and devices located in or near one residence.

home page The start page that is automatically displayed when you enter a site its top level; also called an index page.

honeypot A computer baited with fake data and purposely left vulnerable to study how intruders operate in order to prepare stronger defenses to thwart attacks.

host name The name of the group or institution hosting a Web site. It is the first part of the domain portion of a URL. In the URL **www.microsoft.com/windows/default.aspx** the host portion is Microsoft.

hot site The most expensive disaster recovery site as it is kept is a state of readiness at all times.

hot spot A public wireless access location.

hot swapping Connecting and disconnecting peripherals while the computer is running.

HTML (Hypertext Markup Language) A markup language used for marking Web pages. It divides elements (or tags) into two categories: head elements (such as the documents title) and body elements (headings, paragraphs, links, and text). The agency responsible for standardizing HTML is the World Wide Web Consortium (W3C).

hub A simple broadcast device used as the central wiring mechanism in a star topology network layout. It does not manage traffic and usually results in frequent collisions.

hybrid hard drive (HDD) A hard drive that uses solid state flash memory to speed up the boot process in a hard disk drive.

hyperlink (link) In a hypertext system, an element in an electronic document that acts as the connector to another place in the same document or to an entirely different document. Typically, you click on the hyperlink to get to the related object. Hyperlinks are the most essential ingredient of the World Wide Web.

hypertext A system in which objects (text, pictures, music, programs, and so on) can be creatively linked to each other.

Hypertext Markup Language (HTML) A language that uses a tag system of code to create Web pages. This language is interpreted by browsers, which display the page according to the directions specified by the HTML language. HTML includes capabilities that enable authors to insert hyperlinks, which when clicked display another HTML document. The agency responsible for standardizing HTML is the World Wide Web Consortium (W3C).

Hypertext Transfer Protocol (HTTP) The Internet standard that supports the exchange of information on the Web by the use of uniform resource locators (URLs).

I

icon A small image that represents a computer resource (such as a program, data file, or network connection).

identity theft A form of fraud in which a thief obtains someone's personal information, and then uses this information to impersonate the owner and fraudulently obtain and use credit.

image editor A sophisticated paint program for editing and transforming complex bitmapped images, such as photographs.

inclusion operator In database or Web searching, a symbol or keyword that instructs the search software to make sure that any retrieved records or documents contain a certain word or phrase; it usually is a plus sign (+) in the search statement.

incremental backup Backing up only those files that have been created or changed since the last backup occurred.

index page Also called home page.

information Data that has been converted into meaningful form in the processing phase of the information processing cycle.

information hiding A modular programming term that refers to the ability of a programmer to write the code of one module without knowing or having to be concerned with the details of another module.

information kiosk An automated presentation system used for public information or employee training.

information overload The feeling of anxiety and incapacity experienced when people are presented with more information than they can process or absorb.

information processing cycle A complete sequence of operations involving data input, processing, output, and storage.

information system A purposefully designed system that includes the collection of people, hardware, software, data records, and activities that process the data and information in an organization.

information systems (IS) department The functional area within companies or universities responsible for managing information technology and systems.

information technology (IT) professional An individual who works with information technology in all its various forms (hardware, software, networks) and functions (management, development, maintenance).

information technology steering committee An organizational group, generally including representatives from senior management, information systems personnel, users, and middle managers, that reviews new project requests and decides which ones to address.

information warfare A military-like strategy that targets an opponent's information systems to corrupt or destroy information and infrastructure.

infrared A wireless data transmission medium, used in TV remote controls, that carries data via beams of light through the air. Transmitting and receiving devices must be in line of sight or the signal is lost.

inheritance In object-oriented programming (OOP), the capacity of an object to pass its characteristics to a subclass or child.

inkjet printer A nonimpact printer that sprays ionized ink from a series of small jets onto a sheet of paper, creating the desired character shapes.

input 1. The process by which data (raw facts) is received by the computer for

processing. 2. Inserting data or commands into the computer for processing.

input device A hardware component through which data is entered into the computer for processing.

input/output (I/O) bus An electrical pathway that connects the microprocessor to input and output devices via expansion slots.

insertion point See cursor.

installing To load and set up a program so that it is ready to function on a given computer system. The installation process may involve creating additional directories, making changes to system files, and other technical tasks. For this reason, most programs come with setup programs that handle the installation process automatically.

instant messaging (IM) A real-time, synchronous connection between two or more parties that uses a buddy list to identify the users a person wishes to connect with.

instant messaging (IM) system A software program that lets you know when a friend or business associate is online. You can then contact this person and exchange messages and attachments.

instruction cycle (fetch, decode) In the machine cycle, a phase consisting of the fetch (retrieve) and decode (determine action required) operations.

instruction set A list of specific instructions that a given brand and model of processor can perform.

intangible benefit A benefit that is difficult or impossible to measure, such as improved employee morale and customer satisfaction.

integrated circuit (IC or chip) A semiconductor circuit containing more than one transistor and other electronic components; often referred to as a chip.

integrated peripherals The devices embedded within a computer's plastic or metal case, which generally include the power supply, cooling fans, memory, CD drive, DVD drive, and internal hard drive.

integrated program A single program that manages an entire business or set of related tasks. It combines the most commonly used functions of many productivity software programs, like word processing, database management, spreadsheet, accounting, and customer service into one application.

intelligent agent An automatic program that is designed to operate on the user's behalf, performing a specific function in the background. When the agent has achieved its goal, it reports to the user.

interface In programming, the means of exchanging messages between objects.

internal speaker One of the components inside a computer's system unit, typically useful only for emitting beeps and other low-fidelity sounds.

Internet An enormous and rapidly growing system of linked computer

networks, worldwide in scope, which facilitates data communication services such as remote logon, file transfer, electronic mail, the World Wide Web, and newsgroups. Relying on TCP/IP, the Internet assigns every connected computer a unique Internet address (called an IP address) so that any two connected computers can locate each other on the network and exchange data.

Internet address (IP address) The unique, 32-bit address assigned to a computer that is connected to the Internet. It is represented in four parts, which are separated by periods (such as 128.254.108.7).

Internet backbone The main high-speed routes for Internet data traffic.

Internet hard drive Storage space on a server that is accessible from the Internet.

Internet Protocol (IP) One of the two core Internet standards (the other is the Transmission Control Protocol, TCP). IP defines the standard that describes how an Internet-connected computer should break data down into packets for transmission across the network and how those packets should be addressed so that they arrive at their destination. IP is the connectionless part of the TCP/IP protocols.

Internet Protocol Address (IP Address) A numerical identification and logical address that is assigned to devices participating in a computer network. See Internet address.

Internet Relay Chat (IRC) A real-time, Internet text-based chat service, in which one can find "live" participants from the world over. Today it is mostly the province of specialized communities, such as gamers or programmers.

Internet service A set of communication standards (protocols) and software (clients and servers) that defines how to access and exchange a certain type of information on the Internet. Examples of Internet services are e-mail, FTP, Gopher, IRC, and Web.

Internet service provider (ISP) A company that provides Internet accounts and connections to individuals and businesses. Access may be provided via telephone lines, cable, satellite, or fiber-optic technologies. Most ISPs today provided additional features, including e-mail, virus protection, and Web hosting.

Internet telephony The use of the Internet (or of nonpublic networks based on Internet technology) for the transmission of real-time voice data.

interoperability The ability to connect and exchange data with another computer, even one that is a different brand or model.

interpreter In programming, a translator program that converts one line of source code at a time into machine-readable code and executes the translated instruction. Interpreters are often used for learning, debugging, and more recently, production.

interrupt A signal that informs the operating system that some hardware or software event has occurred (for example, the user has pressed a key, the mouse has moved to a new position, or a document has finished printing).

interrupt handler A miniprogram that immediately responds when an interrupt occurs; also called interrupt service routine.

interrupt request (IRQ) The interrupting of an event by an interrupt signal.

interrupt request (IRQ) line A line that handles interrupt communication from input or output devices.

interrupt service routine See interrupt handler.

intranet A network that belongs to an enterprise and is accessible only by that enterprise's employees or authorized users.

IP spoofing The sending of a message with an IP address disguised as an incoming message from a trusted source to a computer. It is an activity usually associated with hackers.

IrDA port A wireless communication device that uses infrared technology to transfer data from your PDA to your desktop or notebook computer or another PDA. The transmitting device must be in line of sight (usually within a few feet) of the port on the receiving device. IrDA ports offer data transfer rates of 4 Mbps.

IRQ conflict A serious system failure that occurs when two devices are configured to use the same IRQ line but aren't designed to share that IRQ line. Often such conflicts cause significant instability and the system will cease to function.

ISDN (Integrated Services Digital Network) A worldwide standard for the delivery of digital telephone and data services to homes, schools, and offices using ordinary existing twisted-pair wiring.

ISDN adapter (digital modem) An internal or external accessory that enables a computer to connect to remote computer networks or the Internet by means of ISDN. (Inaccurately called an ISDN modem.)

IT industry The industry that consists of organizations focused on the development and implementation of technology and applications.

J

Java A cross-platform programming language created by Sun Microsystems that enables programmers to write a program that will execute on any computer capable of running a Java interpreter. Java is an object-oriented programming (OOP) language similar to C++, except that it eliminates some features of C++ that programmers find tedious and time-consuming.

Javabeans Programming specifications created in Java that are used to create reuseable, platform-independent Java components.

JavaScript Now known as ECMAScript. A client-side scripting language designed for writing scripts on Web pages.

Java Virtual Machine (VM) A Java interpreter and runtime environment for Java applets and Java applications. This environment is called a virtual machine because, no matter what kind of computer it is running on, it creates a simulated computer that provides the correct platform for executing Java programs. Java VMs are available for most computers.

joint application development (JAD) A program development process, used primarily in the construction of information systems. It uses a team approach and involves the end user throughout the planning and development stages in order to speed up the system development process.

joystick A pointing device used to move an object on screen in any direction. It employs a vertical rod mounted on a base with one or two buttons. An input device commonly used for games.

JSON Short for JavaScript Object Notation, a text-based, human-readable technique for representing simple data structures and objects.

jukebox Enterprise storage units that use DVD and CD discs as the storage medium.

jump drive Another name for a USB drive.

K

kernel The central part of the operating system that controls the actions that the OS uses most frequently, for example starting applications and managing hardware devices and memory.

key interception The act of stealing an encryption key.

key matrix A grid of circuits located under the keys of a keypad. When a key is pressed is completes a circuit on the matrix that provides the identity of the associated character to the system.

keyboard An input device that uses switches and circuits to translate keystrokes into a signal a computer can understand. It makes use of alphabetic, numeric, punctuation, symbolic, function, arrow, and control keys.

keylogger Spyware that can record all the keystrokes you type—such as passwords, account numbers, or conversations—and relay them to others.

kilobits per second (Kbps) A data transfer rate of approximately a thousand bits of computer data per second.

kilobyte (KB) The basic unit of measurement for computer memory and disk capacity, equal to 1,024 bytes or characters.

Kindle 2 A portable, wireless, paperback-size device, known as an e-book reader, onto which a user can download books

from an immense library of digitized titles. The user can either read the files on the reader, adjusting font size and type, or use the text-to-speech feature to hear the book read out loud.

know-and-have authentication A type of computer security that requires using tokens, which are handheld electronic devices that generate a logon code.

knowledge base A database of knowledge designed to meet the complex storage and retrieval needs of computerized expert systems.

knowledge management system (KMS) A system that captures knowledge from books and experienced individuals and makes it available where it is needed.

L

label In Microsoft Excel, a text entry used to identify or group numeric entries.

labor dumping The flooding of a labor market with foreign workers.

land A flat reflective area on an optical disc that bounces the light back to a light-sensing device, corresponding to a 1 in the computer's binary number system.

laser printer A popular nonimpact, high-resolution printer that uses a version of the electrostatic reproduction technology of copying machines.

last-mile problem The lack of local network systems for high-bandwidth multimedia communications that can accommodate the Information Superhighway.

last-mile technologies Digital telecommunications services and standards, such as coaxial cable and ISDN, that serve as interim solutions to the limitations associated with the twisted-pair analog phone wiring still common in many homes and businesses.

latency In a packet-switching network, a signal delay that is introduced by the time network routers consume as they route packets to their destination.

launching To start an application program.

LCD projector An output device that projects a computer's monitor display on a screen by passing light through three colored panels—red, green, and blue. LCD projectors produce sharp, accurate color images; however, they are subject to pixilation and low contrast.

leased line A permanently connected and conditioned telephone line that provides continuous, end-to-end communication between two points, usually used for connectivity between branches of an organization, business, or university.

legacy technology Older technology devices, or applications that are being phased out and replaced by new products. Examples include floppy disk drives or Zip drives.

level 1 cache (L1) See primary cache.

level 2 cache (L2) See secondary cache.

libel A form of defamation that occurs in writing. It is publication of a false statement that injures someone's business or personal reputation.

library Enterprise storage units that use Blu-ray optical media for storage.

life cycle The stages through which systems pass: They are born, go through a process of maturation, live an adult life, and become obsolete to the point that they have to be modified or abandoned.

link See communications channel.

link rot The of "out-of-datedness" that occurs in a search due to the amount of time it takes for spiders to accumulate data from the Web.

Linux A freeware operating system for personal computers introduced by Linus Torvalds and developed and maintained by volunteer programmers, who have willingly donated their time to make sure that Linux brings many features similar to those found in commercial versions of UNIX to the PC.

liquid crystal display (LCD; flat-panel display) A, flat-screen monitor that uses electrical current to control the positioning of tiny crystals to either block or allow the current to pass through and form the viewable on-screen image and color.

load To transfer something from a storage device, such as the hard disk, to RAM memory.

local area network (LAN) A computer network that connects computers in a limited geographic area, such as a building or group of clustered buildings.

local exchange switch A telephone system device, based on digital technology and capable of handling thousands of calls, located in the local telephone company's central office.

local loop In the public switched telephone network (PSTN), the region serviced by a subscriber loop carrier (SLC) where analog connections from neighborhood distribution points are converted to digital signals.

location (position) awareness A technology that uses GPS-enabled chips to pinpoint the location of a cell phone (and its user).

logic bomb See time bomb.

logic error In programming, a mistake made by the programmer in designing the program. Logic errors will not surface by themselves during program execution because they are not errors in the structure of the statements and commands.

logical address An identifier assigned to a network node by the software in use.

Logical data type See Boolean data type.

logical operations One of two groups of operations performed by the arithmetic logic unit (ALU). The logical operations involve comparing data items to see which one is larger or smaller, and return a true or false response.

login See authentication.

lossless compression In data compression, a method used to reduce the size of a file so it can be restored to its original size without introducing errors. Most lossless compression techniques reduce file size by replacing lengthy but frequently occurring data sequences with short codes; to decompress the file, the compression software reverses this process and restores the lengthy data sequences to their original form.

lossy compression In data compression, a method of reducing the size of multimedia files by eliminating information that is not normally perceived by human beings.

low-level language A language, like assembly or machine language, that is processor dependent and has a small or nonexistent amount of difference between the language and machine language; because of this, low-level languages are sometimes described as being "close to the hardware."

M

Mac OS An operating system released for the Apple Mac in 1984. It was the first OS to successful implement the GUI (graphical user interface).

Mac OS X Snow Leopard The current version of Mac OS X. It has a smaller footprint (taking up to 50 percent less storage space than the previous version) and includes a more responsive and snappier Finder, a Put Back option to return deleted items to their original location, more reliable ejection of external drives, faster shut down and wake up, four new fonts, 80 percent faster Time Machine backup, increased Airport signal strength for wireless networks, and built-in support for Microsoft Exchange Server 2007.

machine cycle (processing cycle) A four-step process followed by the control unit that involves the fetch, decode, execute, and store operations.

machine dependent (hardware dependent) The dependence of a given computer program or component on a specific brand or type of computer equipment. With new security options, some applications are also linked to one specific computer via a machine ID and will not function on any other computer.

machine language The native binary language consisting of 0s and 1s that is recognized and executed by a computer's central processing unit.

machine translation A language translation performed by the computer without human aid.

macro In a word processing or spreadsheet program, a macro is a saved sequence of commands or keyboard strokes that get recalled later with a single command or keyboard stroke.

macro virus A computer virus that uses the automatic command execution capabilities of macros stored within productivity software, like word processing or spreadsheet programs, to spread itself and often to cause harm to computer data.

magnetic storage device In computer storage systems, any storage device that retains data using a magnetically sensitive material, such as the magnetic coating found on floppy and hard disks.

mainframe (enterprise server) A multiuser computer system that meets the computing needs of a large organization.

maintenance release A minor revision to a software program that corrects bugs or adds minor features. Indicated by a decimal in the version number.

malicious network A network set up by a hacker within the operating area of a legitimate hotspot. The hacker hopes to lure the user into the bogus network, referred to as an "evil twin," and gather sensitive information such as passwords and credit card numbers.

malware Short for *malicious software,* it describes software designed to damage or infiltrate a computer system without the owner's consent or knowledge. This type of software can wreak havoc on a user's system by deleting files and directory entries; it can also act as spyware, gathering data from a user's system without the user knowing it.

management information system (MIS) 1. The practical application of information systems and technology to provide the skills businesses need to compete successfully. 2. A computer-based system that supports the information needs of various levels of management.

markup language A set of codes, or elements, used to define the structure of text, such as a title or a heading, that a Web browser reads and interprets. HTML is a markup language.

massively multiplayer online role-playing game (MMORPG) An online game that permits increasingly larger numbers of players to interact with one another in virtual worlds. These virtual worlds are often hosted and maintained by the software publisher, unlike other environments that end when the game is over.

Mathematica A single system that can handle all the various aspects of technical computing in a coherent and unified way. The key to this system was the invention of a new kind of symbolic computer language that could, for the first time, manipulate the very wide range of objects using only a fairly small number of basic elements.

mathematical formula In spreadsheet programs such as Microsoft Excel, one of the two basic types of formulas (along with functions). In a mathematic formula, or expression, the mathematic order of operation is followed.

maximize To enlarge a window so that it fits the entire screen.

media center PC An all-in-one entertainment device that provides easy access to photos, TV, movies, and the latest in online media all from the comfort of the couch by using a remote control.

megabits per second (Mbps) In networking, a data transfer rate of approximately 1 million bits per second.

megabyte (MB) A measurement of storage capacity equal to 1,024 kilobytes, or approximately 1 million bytes or characters.

memo A data type used for large units of text.

memory Circuitry that retains information temporarily so that it is readily available to the central processing unit (CPU).

memory address A binary number that specifies a specific location in memory.

memory footprint The amount of RAM a program uses in operation.

memory shaving A type of computer crime in which knowledgeable thieves remove some of a computer's RAM chips but leave enough to start the computers.

memory stick Another name for a USB drive.

menu-driven user interface A user interface that enables the user to avoid memorizing keywords (such as *copy* and *paste*) and syntax (a set of rules for entering commands) by displaying on-screen, text-based menus that show all the options available at a given point.

Metcalfe's Law Formulated by Ethernet inventor Bob Metcalfe, it states that the value of a computer network grows in proportion to the square of the number of people connected to it.

method In object-oriented programming, a procedure or operation that processes or manipulates data.

microbrowser A special Web browser that has all of the features of computer-based browsers but is simplified to meet handheld device limitations.

microcomputer Another word for personal computer.

microphone An input device that converts sound into electrical signals that can be processed by a computer.

microprocessor (processor) The computer's processing and control circuitry, including the arithmetic logic unit (ALU) and the control unit. Also called the central processing unit. See also central processing unit.

Microsoft Windows The most popular operating system, available in several iterations, and installed on almost all of the personal computers made today.

Microsoft Windows 7 The newest version of Windows operating system released in 2009. It is more efficient than its predecessor, often performing better on the same hardware, and has resolved the compatibility issues that existed between

applications. There are six versions and many new features, including jump list, snap, pin, and Windows Search.

Microsoft Windows Mobile The version of Windows operating system designed for smartphones and PDAs. It includes a simplified user interface and quicker synchronization of mobile devices with corresponding programs on the user's desktop computer.

Microsoft Windows Server 2008 A sophisticated operating system specifically designed to support client/server computing systems in a corporate environment.

Microsoft Windows Vista The version of Windows operating system released in 2007 that was available in five different versions. Its main improvements included a slick new interface, mobile support, and increased security features.

microwave An electromagnetic radio wave with a very short frequency.

middleware Software that does what its name implies: It sits "in the middle," making the connection between varied applications working on multiple networks being supported by different operating systems.

minicomputer A midsized server with the hardware and software to handle the computing needs of 4 to 200 client computers in a small corporation or organization.

minimize To reduce the size of a window so that it appears only as an icon or an item on the taskbar.

minitower case A smaller version of a system unit tower case designed to sit on the floor next to a desk.

mnemonic In programming, a brief abbreviation or short word for an instruction.

mobile switching center (MSC) The part of a cellular network that handles communications within a group of cells. Each cell tower reports signal strength to the MSC, which then switches your signal to whatever cell tower will provide the clearest connection for your conversation.

modeling A method by which spreadsheet programs are able to predict future outcomes; also called what-if analysis.

modem Short for **mod**ulator/**dem**odulator, a device that converts (modulates) the generated digital signal to a signal appropriate for the transmission medium and, likewise, transforms (demodulates) the incoming transmission signal to its digital equivalent. It enables the computer, a digital device, to access data through nondigital media such as telephone lines or cable, satellite, and cellular connections. The speed at which a modem transmits data is measured in units called bits per second, or bps.

modifier key A key, like Shift, Alt, or Ctrl, that is pressed to modify the meaning of the next key that is pressed.

modular programming A programming style that breaks down programs into independent modules, each of which accomplishes one function.

modulation protocol In modems, the communications standard or rules that governs how the modem translates between the computer's digital signals and the analog tones used to convey computer data over the Internet so that is the message is received and understood by the destination modem.

module A part of a software program; independently developed modules are combined to compile the final program.

monitor (display) A television-like screen that displays an image of data and processed information.

Moore's Law A prediction by Intel Corp. cofounder Gordon Moore that integrated circuit technology advancements would enable the semiconductor industry to double the number of components on a chip every 18 to 24 months.

motherboard A large circuit board containing the computer's central processing unit, support chips, random access memory, and expansion slots. Also called a main board, the motherboard provides connectivity between the central processing unit(s) and other system components.

mouse A palm-size pointing device designed to move about on a clean, flat surface. As you move the mouse, its movements are mirrored by the on-screen pointer. Actions are initiated by using the mouse buttons.

MS-DOS (DOS) Short for *disk operating system*, an operating system for IBM-compatible PCs that uses a command-line user interface.

MUD (multiuser dungeon or dimension) The early name for a genre of role-playing games in which multiple players could assume other persona. Players interacted in a text-based environment through text chatting.

multifunction device A device that combines printing, scanning, faxing, and copying.

multimedia 1. An application that involves two or more media, such as audio, graphics, or video. 2. Multisensory stimulators that stimulate our senses of sight, sound, touch, smell, or taste.

multimedia and graphics software General-purpose software programs for professional desktop publishing, image editing, three-dimensional rendering, and video editing.

multiplexing A technique that enables more than one signal to be conveyed on a physical transmission medium.

multitasking operating system A descriptive phrase applied to personal computer operating systems that enable multiple applications to run at the same time.

multi-tenancy An application is installed only once in a cloud, on the cloud's server, but can be shared and customized with individual options for each user.

N

name The first part of a filename.

nanotechnology Manipulating materials on an atomic or molecular scale in order to build microscopic devices.

native application A program that is compatible with a microprocessor and, therefore, capable of running on that processor.

natural language In programming, a language that would provide instruction to a computer in normal human language, such as English or Japanese.

navigation pane Located on the left in Windows Explorer, it allows you to navigate directly to specific folders listed in the Favorite Links area or access a prior search that you have saved by clicking on a desired folder.

nesting 1. Using parentheses in a Boolean search to place one expressing within another. The search engine evaluates the expression from left to right and searches for the content within the parentheses first. 2. In structured programming, embedding one control structure inside another.

netbook A portable computer designed for wireless Internet access and used primarily for Web browsing and e-mail. The device typically weighs two to three pounds and is between 5 and 13 inches in size.

netiquette Short for network etiquette. A set of rules that reflect long-standing experience about getting along harmoniously in the electronic environment (e-mail and newsgroups).

network A group of two or more computer systems connected by communications devices to enable exchanging data and sharing resources.

network access point 1. A special communications device that sends and receives data between computers that contain wireless adapters. 2. The location where equipment from one network service provider connects with equipment from another provider.

network administrator Computer professionals who install, maintain, and support computer networks, interact with users, handle security, and troubleshoot problems. Also called a network engineer.

network architecture The overall design of a computer network that specifies its functionality at every level by means of protocols.

network attached storage (NAS) Storage devices and their associated media, comprised primarily of hard drives, that are attached directly to a network. The network connection permits each computer on the network to access the NAS to save or retrieve data, enabling data and file sharing.

network database management system Software that makes use of the mathematical concept of sets and allows for each record to have multiple parent and child records, forming a lattice structure.

network interface card (NIC) An expansion board that fits into a computer's expansion slots, or an adapter built into the motherboard, that provides the electronic components to make the connection between a computer and a network. This can be either wired or wireless.

network layers Separate divisions within a network architecture with specific functions and protocols, allowing engineers to make changes within a layer without having to redesign the entire network.

network operating system (NOS) An operating system needed to enable data transfer and application usage over a local area network (LAN).

network service provider (NSP) A company or organization that maintains the Internet backbone.

network topology The physical layout of a local area network (LAN), such as a bus, star, or ring topology, that determines what happens when, for example, two clients try to access the LAN or transmit data simultaneously.

neural network In artificial intelligence, a computer architecture that attempts to mimic the structure of the human brain. Neural nets "learn" by trial and error and are good at recognizing patterns and dealing with complexity.

new technology file system (NTFS) A file allocation table for Windows NT, 2000, XP and Vista that is more advanced and powerful than the FAT system. It improves performance and is required in order to implement numerous security and administrative features in the operating system. NTFS supports file encryption, sets permissions at the file level rather than by folder, and allows individual disk space allocation.

newsgroup In Usenet, a discussion group devoted to a single topic. Users post messages to the group, and those reading the discussion send reply messages to the author individually or post replies that can be read by the group as a whole.

node Any device connected to a network. A node can be any computer, peripheral (such as a printer or scanner), or communication device (such as a modem).

nonprocedural language A language not tied down to step-by-step procedures. In programming, a nonprocedural programming language does not force the programmer to consider the procedure that must be followed to obtain the desired result.

nonvolatile memory Memory that is permanent and unchanging; see ROM.

notebook computer A portable computer that is small enough to fit into an average briefcase and includes nearly all

peripherals commonly found on desktop computers.

numeric check A data validation procedure that ensures that only numbers are entered into a field.

O

object 1. In object-oriented programming (OOP), a unit of computer information that contains data and all the procedures or operations that can process or manipulate the data. 2. A data type used for nontextual data. Examples of objects include pictures, sounds, or videos. 3. In Microsoft Access, a subprogram that manages data.

object code In programming, the instructions in (or close to) a specific computer's machine language that are created by a compiler from source code.

object-oriented database management system (ODBMS) The newest type of database structure in which the retrieved object incorporates miniprograms that enable the object to perform tasks, such as display a graphic.

object-oriented programming (OOP) A programming technique based on defining data as objects. The user then assembles different sets of objects as needed to solve specific problems.

Office button The button at the top left of a Microsoft Office application. It contains choices for creating new documents; opening existing documents; and printing, saving, and closing documents.

Office Clipboard In Microsoft Office, a feature that temporarily stores in memory whatever has been cut or copied from a document, allowing for those items to be used within any Office application.

office suite See software suite.

offshoring The transfer of labor from workers in one country to workers in other countries.

onboard video Video circuitry that comes built into a computer's motherboard.

online analytical processing (OLAP) An application included in some decision support systems that provides decision support by enabling managers to import rich, up-to-the-minute data from transaction databases.

online processing A transaction processing system in which you see the results of your commands on-screen so that you can correct errors and make necessary adjustments immediately, before completing an operation; also called interactive processing.

online service provider A for-profit firm that provides a proprietary network offering special services that are available only to subscribers. Members may participate in chat rooms and discussions and take advantage of fee-based content, such as magazines and newspapers.

open To transfer an existing document from storage to memory.

open source software Software whose source code (the code of the program itself) is available for all to see and use. Linux is an open source operating system.

operating system (OS) The most important and recognized type of system software, which integrates and controls the computer's internal functions and provides a way for the user to interact with the computer.

operational decision A decision on a localized issue, such as inventory level, that requires immediate attention.

operational feasibility A project's capability of being accomplished with the organization's available resources.

operational support system (OSS) A suite of programs that support an enterprise's network operations.

optical character recognition (OCR) Software that automatically decodes imaged content into text. Most scanners come with OCR software.

optical mark reader (OMR) A reader that scans the magnetized marks from your #2 pencil, or other device that produces such marks, to determine which responses were marked.

optical storage device A computer storage device that retains data in microscopic patterns, detectable by a laser beam, encoded on the surface of plastic discs.

options Choices within an application that allow users to change defaults and to specify how they want the program to operate.

output 1. Data and processed information that the computer displays on an output device. 2. The process of displaying the results of the processing operation.

output device A monitor, printer, or other machine that enables people to see, hear, or even feel the results of processing operations.

outsourcing One company contracting with another company to provide services that might otherwise be performed by in-house employees, such as call center services, e-mail services, and payroll. Often associated with offshoring.

P

P3P (Platform for Privacy Preferences) A process that compares the security settings of a user to those of a visited Web site. Only if the settings match will the profile information of the user be shared with that site.

packaged software Ready-to-use software that is sold through mass-market channels and contains features useful to the largest possible user base. Synonymous with commercial off-the-shelf software (COTS) and shrink-wrapped software.

packet In a packet-switching network, a unit of data of a fixed size—not exceeding the network's maximum transmission unit (MTU) size—that has been prepared for network transmission. Each packet contains a header that indicates its origin and its destination.

packet switching One of two fundamental architectures for a wide area network (WAN); the other is a circuit-switching network. In a packet-switching network, such as the Internet, no effort is made to establish a single electrical circuit between two computing devices; for this reason, packet-switching networks are often called connectionless. Instead, the sending computer divides a message into packets, each of which contains the address of the destination computer, and dumps them onto the network. They are intercepted by devices called routers, which send the packets in the appropriate direction. The receiving computer assembles the packets, puts them in order, and delivers the received message to the appropriate application. Packet-switching networks are highly reliable and efficient, but they are not suited to the delivery of real-time voice and video.

page In virtual memory, a unit of fixed size into which program instructions and data are divided.

paging Transferring of files from the hard disk to RAM and back, as needed.

PAN (Personal Area Network) A network that enables all kinds of devices—desktop computers, mobile phones, printers, pagers, PDAs, and more—within 30 feet of each other to communicate. Also known as a piconet.

parallel conversion Running both the new and the old systems for a while to check that the new system produces answers at least as good as those of the old system.

parallel port An interface that uses several side-by-side wires so that one or more bytes of computer data can travel in unison and arrive simultaneously. Considered legacy technology, parallel ports, which were often used to connect printers, offer faster performance than serial ports, in which each bit of data must travel in a line, one after the other.

parallel processing The use of more than one processor to run two or more portions of a program simultaneously.

partition A section of a hard disk set aside as if it were a physically separate disk. Partitions are required if a system is going to give the user an option of running more than one operating system.

passive-matrix (dual scan) A form of LCD display in which electrical current drives the display by charging groups of pixels, either in a row or column, at once.

path The sequence of directories that the computer must follow to locate a file.

pattern-recognition software In artificial intelligence, software that enables a computer system to recognize patterns, such as thumbprints, and associate these patterns with stored data or instructions.

PC card (PCMCIA card) A computer accessory (such as a modem or network interface card) that is designed to fit into a compatible PC card slot mounted on the computer's case. PC cards and slots are commonly used on notebook computers because they offer system expandability while consuming a small fraction of the space required for expansion cards.

PCI (peripheral component interconnect) bus A type of expansion bus used with Macs and PCs to communicate with input and output devices that contains expansion slots to accommodate plug-in expansion cards.

PCI Express A faster interface than AGP, used to support high-speed, high-resolution graphics, including 3D graphics.

PCI Express Base 2.0 The most current, second generation PCI Express.

PCS (personal communication service) A digital cellular phone service that is rapidly replacing analog cellular phones.

peer-to-peer network (P2P network) A computer network design in which all the computers on the network are equals or peers. There is no file server. File sharing is decided by each computer user. A user may choose to share a few files, an entire directory, or even an entire disk. They also can choose to share peripherals, such as printers and scanners. P2P is best used when connecting 10 or fewer computers.

peripheral device Components connected physically or wirelessly to the system unit, such as keyboards, monitors, speakers, and external storage devices.

personal computing Any situation or setup where one person controls and uses a computer or handheld device for personal or business activities.

personal computer (PC) A computer system that meets the computing needs of an individual. The term PC usually refers to an IBM-compatible personal computer.

personal digital assistant (PDA) A small, handheld computer that receives input entered with a stylus, virtual keyboard, or external corded keyboard. Most include built-in software for appointments, scheduling, and e-mail.

personal firewall A program or device that is designed to protect home computer users from unauthorized access.

personal productivity programs Application software, such as word-processing software or a spreadsheet program, that assists individuals in doing their work more effectively and efficiently.

petabyte A unit of measurement approximately equal to 1 quadrillion bytes.

petaflop A unit referring to over 1 million billion calculations per second.

phased conversion Implementing a new system over different time periods, one part at a time.

phishing Posing as a legitimate company in an e-mail or on a Web site in an attempt to learn personal information such as your Social Security number, user name, password, and account numbers.

photo checkout system A system that accesses a database of customer photos and displays the customer's picture when a credit card is used.

photo-editing program (image editing software) A program that enables a person to enhance, edit, crop, or resize the images.

photo printer An inkjet or laser printer with six or more ink colors used to print photos with high-quality results.

PHP A general purpose, server-side, open source, cross-platform scripting language used primarily to make dynamic Web sites.

phrase searching In database and Web searching, the placing of a phrase between quotation marks so the search retrieves only documents that contain the entire phrase.

physical address An identifier embedded in the hardware of a network node.

piconet See PAN.

picture messaging A mobile service that allows you to send full-color pictures, backgrounds, and even picture caller IDs on your cell phone.

piggybacking The use of a network without permission.

pilot conversion One part of the organization converts to a new system while the rest of the organization continues to run the old system.

pipelining A processing technique that provides up to four processing pathways that can be used simultaneously.

pit A microscopic indentation in the surface of an optical disc that absorbs the light of the optical drive's laser, corresponding to a 0 in the computer's binary number system.

plagiarism The presentation of somebody else's work as one's own.

plaintext A readable message before it is encrypted.

platform The combination of microprocessor chip and operating system used by a distinct type of computer, such as a Mac or a PC.

platter The fixed, rapidly rotating, storage medium in a hard drive that is coated with a magnetically sensitive material. High-capacity hard drives typically have two or more platters.

plotter A printer that produces high-quality output by moving ink pens over the surface of the paper.

plug-and-play (PnP) A set of standards jointly developed by Intel Corporation and Microsoft that enables users of Microsoft Windows-based PCs to configure new hardware devices automatically. Operating systems equipped with plug-and-play capabilities can automatically detect new PnP-compatible peripherals on startup that may have been installed while the power was switched off.

plug-in A software programs that allows you to derive the full benefits of a Web site, such as sound or video.

plunge See direct conversion

podcast A blend of the words *iPod* and *broadcast*. It has come to mean a program (of music or talk) that is made available in digital format for automatic download over the Internet. Such files contain audio, images, and videos and are released periodically by means of Web syndication.

podcatchers Applications, such as Apple Inc.'s iTunes or Nullsoft's Winamp, that can automatically identify and retrieve new files in a given series and make them available through a centrally maintained Web site.

podslurping An activity in which employees use USB drives, iPods, or other removable storage media to create an unauthorized copy of confidential data.

point of presence (POP) A wired or wireless access connection point in a wide area network. ISPs that provide connectivity to the largest WAN, the Internet, are likely to have POPs in many cities and towns, however rural areas may not be so lucky.

point-and-shoot digital camera A camera that includes automatic focus, automatic exposure, built-in automatic electronic flash with red-eye reduction, and optical zoom lenses with digital enhancement. Sometimes called a compact camera.

pointer An on-screen symbol, usually an arrow, that shows the current position of the mouse.

pointing device An input device that allows the user to control the movements of the on-screen pointer.

pointing stick A pointing device that looks like a pencil eraser between the G, H and B keys. It is pressure sensitive and is pressed and moved with the forefinger in various directions, while the thumb is used to press related keys located in front of the space bar.

pop-up A small window, that suddenly appears ("pops up") in the foreground of the current window.

port An interface that controls the flow of data between the central processing unit and external devices such as printers and monitors.

portable (or removable) storage A popular, removable, small type of storage that is easy to carry around and use, and can be easily plugged into any computer. Examples are USB flash drives, also known as memory sticks, thumb drives, or jump drives.

portal On the Web, a page that attempts to provide an attractive starting point for Web sessions. Typically included are links to breaking news, weather forecasts, stock quotes, free e-mail service, sports scores, and a subject guide to information available on the Web. Leading portals include MSN (**www.msn.com**), Yahoo! (**www.yahoo.com**), and Snap! (**www.snap.com**).

positioning performance A measure of how much time elapses from the initiation of drive activity until the hard disk has positioned the read/write head so that it can begin transferring data.

postimplementation system review A process of ongoing evaluation that determines whether a system has met its goals.

power-on light A light on the front panel of most computers that signals whether the power is on.

power-on self-test (POST) A series of tests conducted during a system boot, after the BIOS instructions are loaded into memory, to make sure that the computer and associated peripherals are operating correctly.

power supply A device that supplies power to a computer system by converting AC current to DC current and lowering the voltage.

power switch A switch that turns the computer on and off; typically located on the front of the system unit.

preemptive multitasking An environment in which programs that are running receive a recurring slice of time from the CPU. Depending on the operating system, the time slice may be the same for all programs or it may be adjustable to meet the various program and user demands. This method of multitasking ensures that all applications have fair access to the CPU and prevents one program from monopolizing it at the expense of the others.

primary cache (level 1 or L1 cache) A small unit (8 KB to 64 KB) of ultrafast memory included with a microprocessor that runs at the same speed as the microprocessor. It is used to store frequently accessed data and improve overall system performance.

primary key A field that contains a code, a number, a name, or some other piece of information that uniquely identifies a record; also called the key field.

printer An output device that prints computer-generated text or graphics onto paper or another physical medium.

privacy An individual's ability to restrict or eliminate the collection, use, and sale of confidential personal information.

private key A decryption key associated with a public key in a public key encryption scheme.

problem The underlying cause of a symptom.

procedural language A programming language that directs the computer to perform an action by grouping together instructions in a very specific step-by-step manner. Procedural languages are known for their modularity and reusability.

processing The actions taken on data to transform them into information.

processor See central processing unit.

professional organization (associations) An IT organization that can help you keep up with your area of interest as well as provide valuable career contacts.

professional workstation A high-end desktop computer with a system unit designed for technical or scientific applications requiring exceptionally powerful processing and output capabilities. Used by engineers, financial analysts, and other high-tech professionals who need powerful processing and output capabilities, professional workstations are expensive.

profile A record of a specific user's preferences for the desktop theme, icons, and menu styles.

program A set of instructions telling the computer what to do.

program design The result of phase 2 of the program development life cycle (PDLC) in which a written plan that specifies the components that make the program work is created, reviewed, and discussed.

program development life cycle (PDLC) A six-phase, organized plan for breaking down the task of program development into manageable chunks, each of which must be successfully completed before programmers move on to the next phase.

program maintenance In phase 6 of the PDLC, the process in which the programming team fixes program errors discovered by users.

program specification Part of the first phase of the program development life cycle (PDLC) in which the systems analyst precisely defines the input data, the processing that should occur, the output format, and the user interface.

programmer A trained expert who works individually or in a group to design, write, and test software applications for everything from word processing to virus protection.

programming The process used to create the software applications you use every day.

programming language An artificial language composed of a fixed vocabulary and a set of rules used to create instructions, commands, or statements for a computer to follow.

project dictionary A document that explains all the terminology relevant to a project.

project notebook Frequently a digital file maintained online, it is often used to store the documentation for a project, thus enabling everyone connected with the project to understand all the decisions that have been made.

project plan Identifies the project's goal and specifies all the activities that must be completed for the project to succeed.

project proposal A document that introduces the nature of the existing system's problem, explains the proposed solution and its benefits, details the proposed project plan, and concludes with a recommendation.

PROM Programmable read-only memory that can be written on only once and requires a special writing device.

property A setting that provides information such as the file's date of creation, its size, and the date it was last modified.

proprietary file A file whose format is patented or copyright protected and controlled by a single company. The extent of restriction depends on the company and its policies.

protocol In data communications and networking, the standard or set of rules that enable network-connected devices to communicate with each other.

protocol stack In a computer network, a means of conceptualizing network architecture as vertical layers, connected by protocols that move the data down the stack from its initial level, or transmitting node, to the lowest, physical hardware level that sends it over the network. When the data arrives at its destination it moves back up the stack through the layers in reverse order eventually arriving at the receiving node.

protocol suite In a computer network, the collection of network protocols, or rules, that define the network's functionality.

prototyping Developing and showing users a small-scale mock-up of a system; also called rapid application development (RAD).

PS/2 port A type of port that was typically used for mice and keyboards but was not interchangeable. Only one of these ports could be used by each device, and these ports were often color-coded to prevent users from plugging in the wrong device.

pseudocode In structured programming, a stylized form of writing used as an alternative to flowcharts to describe the logic of a program.

public domain software Noncopyrighted software that anyone may copy and use without charge and without acknowledging the source.

public key In public key cryptography, the encoding key, which you make public so that others can send you encrypted messages. The message can be encoded with the public key, but it cannot be decoded without the private key, which you alone possess.

public key encryption A computer security process in which an encryption (or public) key and a decryption (or private) key are used to safeguard data and thus provide confidentiality. This system allows a digital signature to be verified by anyone who has access to the sender's public key, thereby proving that the sender is authentic and has access to the private key; also called asymmetric key encryption.

public key infrastructure (PKI) A uniform set of encryption standards that specify how public key encryption, digital signatures, and digital certificates should be implemented in computer systems and on the Internet.

public switched telephone network (PSTN) The world telephone system, a massive network used for data communication as well as voice, consisting of various transmission media from twisted pair to fiber-optic-cable.

Q

query A specially phrased question used to locate data in a database.

query language A language designed to extract and edit information in a database.

Query object In the Microsoft Access database management system, the object used to ask questions of the database.

Quick Access Toolbar Located just to the right of the Office button. This customizable toolbar displays a series of buttons used to perform common tasks, such as saving a document and undoing or redoing the last action.

quoted size The front surface measured diagonally on a cathode-ray tube monitor, a figure that is greater than the viewable area, since some of the surface is hidden and unavailable for display purposes. See viewable area.

R

racetrack memory A type of memory under development that uses the spin of electrons to store information.

radio A wireless signaling technology that sends data by means of electromagnetic waves that travel through air and space between separate or combined transmitting and receiving devices.

radio frequency identification device (RFID) A tracking device, replacing bar codes, which does not require direct contact or line-of-sight scanning. Instead, an antenna using radio frequency waves transmits a signal that activates the transponder, or tag. When activated, the tag transmits data back to the antenna.

RAID (redundant array of independent disks) A group of two or more hard drives that contain the same data.

random access memory (RAM) Another name for the computer's main working memory, where program instructions and data are stored to be easily accessed by the central processing unit through the processor's high-speed data bus. When a computer is turned off, all data in RAM is lost.

random access storage device A storage device that can begin reading data without having to go through a lengthy linear search.

range In Microsoft Excel, a range consists of two or more cells selected at the same time, and is identified by the addresses of the top left and bottom right cells separated by a colon. For example, the range from cell A1 to cell D5 would be represented as A1:D5.

range check A data validation procedure that verifies that the entered data fall within an acceptable range.

rapid application development (RAD) In object-oriented programming, a method of program development, not suitable for all applications, in which programmers work with a library of prebuilt objects, allowing them to build and piece together programs more quickly. See prototyping.

raster graphic See bitmapped graphic.

ray tracing A 3D rendering technique in which color intensity on a graphic object is varied to simulate light falling on the object from multiple directions.

read-only memory (ROM) The part of a computer's primary storage that contains essential computer start-up instructions and doesn't lose its contents when the power is turned off. Information in read-only memory cannot be erased by the computer.

read/write head In a hard or floppy disk, an electromagnet that moves across the surface of a disk and records information by transforming electrical impulses into a varying magnetic field. When reading, the read/write head senses the recorded pattern and transforms this pattern into electrical impulses that are decoded into text characters.

record A group of one or more related fields.

recording media Any hardware component of a system on which data is held for future use, including hard disks, floppy disks, flash memory, CDs, and DVDs, on which data is held for future use.

refresh rate The frequency with which a CRT screen is refreshed. The refresh frequency determines whether the display appears to flicker.

register Located in a microprocessor, it is a temporary memory location used to store values and external memory addresses while the microprocessor performs logical and arithmetic operations on them.

registration fee An amount of money that must be paid to the author of a piece of shareware to continue using it beyond the duration of the evaluation period.

registry In Microsoft Windows, the name of the database in which configuration information about installed peripherals and software is stored.

relational database management system (RDBMS) A method by which a common primary key relating data in several files is used as an index to locate records, without having to read all the records in the files, and to make connections between files; this connection is often made between a primary and a foreign key.

remote storage Sometimes referred to as an Internet hard drive, this is a type of storage space on a server that is accessible from the Internet.

repetition control structure In structured programming, a control structure that repeats the same instructions over and over. Two examples of repetition structures are DO-WHILE and DO-UNTIL; also called a looping or iteration control structure.

report generator In programming, a programming language for printing database reports. It provides a user-friendly interface enabling a user to design and generate high-quality reports and graphs.

Report object In the Microsoft Access database management system, the object used to present data.

request for proposal (RFP) A request for a vendor to write a proposal for the design, installation, and configuration of an information system.

request for quotation (RFQ) A request for a vendor to quote a price for specific components of the information system.

requirements analysis A process to determine the requirements of a system by analyzing how the system will meet the needs of end users.

resolution A measurement that describes the sharpness of an image generated by an output device such as a monitor or a printer. Written in notation as 1,024 × 786, this expression is interpreted to mean 1,024 distinct dots on each of 768 lines.

restore down A mode in which, if the window is full screen, clicking the Restore Down button will cause the window to revert to a smaller size.

return on investment (ROI) A system's overall financial yield at the end of its lifetime.

Ribbon A feature of all applications in Office 2007. Includes the tabs containing groups and is positioned beneath the title bar.

ring topology The physical layout of a local network in which all nodes are attached in a circle, without a central host computer. This topology, which is no longer used frequently, employs a unit of data called a *token* that travels around the ring. A node can transmit only when it possesses the token thus avoiding collisions.

robot A computer-based device programmed to perform motions that can accomplish useful tasks.

robotics A division of the computer science field that is devoted to improving the performance and capabilities of robots.

ROM (read-only memory) Memory that is permanent and unchanging (nonvolatile). It holds programs, like BIOS, that are meant to be reliably used over and over again; see nonvolatile memory.

router A complex device, or in some cases software, used to connect two or more networks. Routers have the capability to determine the best path to route data and locate alternative pathways so that the data reaches its destination.

routine A section of code that executes a specific task in a program; also referred to as a procedure, function, or subroutine

row In a spreadsheet, a block of cells going horizontally across the screen.

RSS (Really Simple Syndication or Rich Site Summary) A technology that publishes content to you and lets you know when Web content has been updated or news events are taking place.

Ruby An open-source (free-of-charge) object-oriented programming language released in 1995.

S

safe mode An operating mode in which Windows loads a minimal set of drivers that are known to function correctly; within safe mode, the user can use the Control Panel to determine which devices are causing a configuration problem that may occur after adding a new peripheral device such as an external hard drive or new printer to the system.

salami shaving A computer crime in which a program is altered so that it transfers a small amount of money from a large number of accounts to make a large profit.

sales force automation (SFA) software Software that automates many of the business processes involved with sales, including processing and tracking orders, managing customers and other contacts, monitoring and controlling inventory, and analyzing sales forecasts.

SATA (Serial Advance Technology Attachment) An interface that provides greater speed, simpler upgradable storage devices, and easier configuration. It greatly increases the transfer rate of data between the motherboard and hard drive.

satellite In data communications, a communication device placed in a geosynchronous (stationary) orbit that transmits data by sending and receiving microwave signals to and from Earth-based stations.

satellite radio A type of communications technology that broadcasts radio signals back and forth between satellites orbiting more than 22,000 miles above the Earth and radio receivers on Earth.

saving The process of transferring a file from the computer's temporary memory, or RAM, to a permanent storage device, such as a hard disk.

scalability A hardware or software system's ability to continue functioning effectively as demands and use increase.

scanner A device that copies anything that is printed on a sheet of paper, including artwork, handwriting, and typed or printed documents, and converts the input into a graphics image for the computer. The scanner does not recognize or differentiate the type of material it is scanning and converts everything into a graphic bitmapped image.

scope The sum total of all project elements and features.

scope creep The uncontrolled changes or bumps that arise during a project that lead to increased costs and a longer development schedule.

script A program, written in a scripting language like VBScript or JavaScript, that controls any action or feedback on a Web page.

scripting language A language that enables users to create useful programs, called scripts, to control actions or feedback on a Web page. VBScript and JavaScript are examples of client-side scripting languages; their scripts run on a user's computer. Other scripting languages are server-side scripting languages that manipulate the data, usually in a database, on the server.

scroll arrows An arrow appearing within the scroll bar that enables the user to scroll up or down (or, in a horizontal scroll bar, left and right) by small increments.

scroll bar A vertical or horizontal bar that contains scroll arrows and a scroll box. The scroll bar enables the user to bring hidden portions of a document into view within the application workspace.

Scrolling TrackPad A trackpad pending patent by Apple Inc. This pointing device enables users to scroll in an arbitrary direction by touching the pad with two fingers instead of one, and then moving their fingers across the pad in the direction they wish to scroll.

SCSI (Small Computer System Interface) port A type of parallel interface that can connect up to eight compatible peripheral devices to personal computers, including hard disks, CD-ROM drives, and scanners. Considered a legacy technology.

Search box A box in a Windows Explorer window that allows you to find files. Select one of the main folders, such as Documents and begin typing a search term in the box. As you type, Windows Explorer searches the contents of the folder and subfolders, immediately filtering the view to display any files that match the search term.

search engine Any program that locates needed information in a database, but especially an Internet-accessible search service (such as Google or Ask) that enables you to search for information on the Internet.

search operator In a database or a Web search engine, a word or a symbol that enables you to specify your search with precision.

search utility A program that enables you to search an entire hard disk and any indexed network storage device for a file by querying single or multiple specifics about the file such as the name, date, and/or size.

secondary cache (level 2 or L2 cache) A small unit (256 K to 2 MB) of ultrafast memory used to store frequently accessed data and improve overall system performance. The secondary cache is usually located on a separate circuit board from the microprocessor, although backside cache memory is located on the processor.

secondary storage (fixed storage) Storage devices and their associated media that provide a means of permanently storing programs, data, and processed information.

sector A pie-shaped wedge of the concentric tracks encoded on a disk during formatting (set up). Two or more sectors combine to form a cluster.

Secure Electronic Transaction (SET) An online shopping security standard for merchants and customers that uses digital certificates.

seek time In a secondary storage device, the time it takes for the read/write head to locate the information on the disk.

selection control structure In structured programming, a control structure that branches in different directions depending on whether a condition is met. An efficient selection control statement is an IF-THEN-ELSE structure. This control is also called a conditional or branch control structure.

sequence control structure In structured programming, a control structure in which instructions are executed in the order, or sequence, in which they appear.

serial ATA See SATA.

serial port An input/output (I/O) interface that is designed to convey data in a bit-by-bit stream. Compare with *parallel port*. Considered a legacy technology.

serialization The transmission of structured data over a network connection.

server A computer that uses hardware and software to make programs and data available to people who are connected via a network. Servers also provide information in response to external requests. Common servers manage files, e-mail, printers, and databases.

setup program A program located in the computer system's BIOS that contains settings that control the computer's hardware.

sexting A combination of sex and texting. Sending sexually explicit messages or photos electronically, primarily between cell phones.

shareware Copyrighted software that may be tried without expense but requires the payment of a registration fee if you decide to use it after a specified trial period.

shill In an auction, an accomplice of the seller who drives up prices by bidding for an item that the shill has no intention of buying.

signature capture system A system that captures a customer's digital signature by having the customer sign the receipt on a pressure-sensitive pad, using a special stylus.

single-lens reflex camera (digital SLR) A digital camera that uses a mechanical mirror system to direct light from the lens to an optical viewfinder on the back of the camera. Such cameras offer the features that professional photographers demand, such as interchangeable lenses, through-the-lens image previewing, and the ability to override the automatic focus and exposure settings.

single point of failure (SPOF) Any system component, such as hardware or software, that causes the entire system to malfunction when it fails.

single-tasking operating system A descriptive phrase applied to early personal computer operating systems that could run only one application at a time.

site license An agreement with a software publisher that allows multiple copies of the software to be made for use within an organization.

sleep An alternative to shutting down a computer completely, this low-power state enables the user to restore the system to full power quickly without going through the lengthy boot process.

slide In a presentation graphics program, an on-screen image sized in proportion to a 35 mm slide.

Smalltalk An early object-oriented programming language that many OOP promoters believe is still the only pure OOP language. It was a prototype for a model of computation called message passing.

smart card Also known as a chip card or integrated circuit card (ICC). A card that resembles a credit card but has a microprocessor and memory chip, enabling the card to process as well as store information.

smart tag In Microsoft Office, icons attached to items, allowing various choices for how text is treated when pasted within an application or between applications.

smartphone A handheld device that integrates mobile phone capability, computing power, and Web access.

social network A web location like Facebook, MySpace, LinkedIn, or Twitter where users can join groups set up by region, job, or school and communicate with group members.

social networking A method of creating and expanding online communities. For example, sites such as Facebook or MySpace allow users to create online profiles, invite friends and acquaintances to join their network, and invite their friends to join too.

soft business skill A skill in business that is a people-related skill associated with human resources, relationships, learning, personal development, and ethics.

soft copy Output displayed on a monitor or played through speakers.

soft keyboard Also known as a virtual keyboard. A keyboard that appears on a touch-sensitive screen. Tapping the key on the screen with a stylus or finger is the same as pressing a key on a traditional keyboard.

software One of two basic components of a computer system (the other is hardware). It is a collection of programs that direct the operation of a computer and documentation that gives instructions on how to use them. Two major types of software include system software and application software.

software as a service (SaaS) Provides software-based services and solutions to companies that want to outsource some of their information technology needs.

software engineering An occupation that involves upgrading, managing, and modifying of computer programs.

software license An agreement included with most commercial software that stipulates what the user may and may not do with the software.

software piracy The unauthorized copying or distribution of copyrighted software.

software suite A collection individual, full-featured, standalone programs, usually possessing a similar interface, that are packaged together in order to share a common command structure; sometimes called office suite.

software upgrading The process of keeping a version of an application current with the marketplace, whether through patches, service releases, or new versions.

solid-state storage device This device consists of nonvolatile memory chips, which retain the data stored in them even if the chips are disconnected from their current source. See flash drives.

SONET (Synchronous Optical Network) A standard for high-performance networks using optical fiber with data transfer rates of 52 Mbps to approximately 1 Gbps.

sound file A file containing digitized sound that can be played back if a computer is equipped with multimedia.

source code Program instructions in their original form as written by the programmer. A source program is translated into machine instructions that the computer can execute.

spaghetti code In programming, source code that contains numerous GOTO statements and is consequently difficult to follow, messy in design, and prone to errors.

spam Unsolicited e-mail or newsgroup advertising.

speaker A device that outputs computer-generated sound, such as music and synthesized speech.

spear phishing Behavior similar to phishing, in that it uses fake e-mails and social engineering to trick recipients into providing personal information to enable identity theft. But rather than being sent randomly, spear phishing attempts are targeted to specific people, such as senior executives or members of a particular organization.

specialized search engines Web location programs, like Infoplease, that index particular types of information, such as job advertisements, newspaper articles, or quotations.

speculative execution A technique used by advanced CPUs to prevent a pipeline stall. The processor executes and temporarily stores the next instruction in case it proves useful.

speech recognition (voice recognition) The conversion of spoken words into computer text. The spoken word is first digitized and then matched against a dictionary of coded voice waves. The matches are converted into text as if the words were typed on the keyboard.

speech recognition software A program that translates the spoken word into text.

spider A computer program used by search engines to roam the World Wide Web via the Internet, visit sites and databases, and keep the search engine's database of Web pages up to date. They obtain new pages, update known pages, and delete obsolete ones. Their findings are then integrated into the search engine's database.

spim A spam text message.

spimming Sending unsolicited messages (spam) as an instant message.

spyware A form of malicious software (malware) usually installed on a user's computer through the Internet that gathers data from a user's system without the user knowing it. This can be anything from Web sites visited to bank account numbers and passwords. Such information is sometimes used by third parties to commit identity theft. Alternatively some spyware allows others to take control of the user's computer.

standalone program An application sold individually.

star topology The physical layout of a local network in which a central wiring device, which can be a hub, switch, or computer, manages the network. A new user is added by simply running a cable to the hub or switch and plugging the new user into a vacant connector.

status bar An area within a typical application's window that is reserved for the program's messages to the user.

storage 1. Also known as mass storage, auxiliary storage, or secondary storage, a general term for computer components that offer nonvolatile retention of computer data and program instructions for future use. 2. The process by which output is saved for future use on a hard disk, CD, DVD, or media card.

storage area network (SAN) A network of high-capacity storage devices that link all of the organization's servers so that any of the storage devices are accessible from any of the servers.

storage device A hardware component of a system that facilitates the embedding of the data onto recording media. In other words, the actual drives (hard drive, floppy drive, USB flash drive, and so on) that contain the tools to place the data on the recording media.

strategic decision A decision by management concerning an organization's overall goals and direction.

strong AI In artificial intelligence, a research focus based on the conviction that computers will achieve the ultimate goal of artificial intelligence, namely, rivaling the intelligence of humans.

structural unemployment Unemployment caused by advancing technology that makes an entire job category obsolete.

structure chart (hierarchy chart) In structured programming, a program planning chart that shows the top-down design of the program and the relationship between program modules.

structured programming A set of quality standards that makes programs more verbose but more readable, reliable, and maintainable. GOTO statements are forbidden, resulting in more logically developed code; also referred to as top-down program design.

structured query language (SQL) SQL is a standardized query language used to make simple or complex requests for information from a database.

stylus A device that looks like an ordinary pen except that the tip is dry and semi-blunt. It is commonly used as an alternative to fingers on touch screen devices.

subclass In programming, a more specialized class than its parent or superclass.

subfolders Folders within folders that enable you to organize your files even further.

subject guide On the World Wide Web, a search site that contains hyperlinks classified by subjects in broad categories like business, news, or travel and multiple levels of subcategories.

subnotebook A portable computer that omits some components (such as a CD or DVD drive) and usually has a smaller screen to reduce size and weight.

subscriber loop carrier (SLC) A small, waist-high curbside installation of the public switched telephone network that transforms local home and business analog calls into digital signals and routes them through high-capacity cables to the local exchange switch.

summary report A report that provides managers with a quick overview of an organization's performance.

Super Extended Graphics Array (SXGA) A resolution of 1280 × 1024, typically found on standard 17- and 19-inch monitors.

Super VGA An enhancement of the VGA display standard that can display as many as 800 pixels by 600 lines.

supercomputer A sophisticated, expensive computer that executes complex calculations at the maximum speed permitted by state-of-the-art technology. Supercomputers are used mostly by the government and for scientific research.

superscalar architecture A design that lets the microprocessor take a sequential instruction and send several instructions at a time to separate execution units so that the processor can execute multiple instructions per cycle.

swap file A hard disk file that serves as a temporary storage space for pages, the bits and bytes that the operating system will access as the user works.

swindler An individual that perpetrates bogus work-at-home opportunities, illegal pyramid schemes, chain letters, risky business opportunities, bogus franchises, phony goods that won't be delivered, overpriced scholarship searches, and get-rich-quick scams.

switch A device that filters and forwards data between computers, printers, and other network nodes, enabling them to talk to each other. A switch is used only to move data between nodes within a single network.

symmetric key encryption Encryption technique that uses the same key for encryption and decryption.

symmetrical digital subscriber line (SDSL) A transmission technology that splits the copper telephone line channels into three channels: telephone, upload, and download. The bandwidth is distributed equally among the channels. On SDSL connections, uploads and downloads occur at the same rate.

symptom An unacceptable or undesirable result.

syn flooding A form of denial of service attack in which a hostile client repeatedly sends SYN (synchronization) packets to every port on the server using fake IP addresses, which uses up all the available network connections and locks them up until they time out. This results in a denial of service.

Synchronized Multimedia Integration Language (SMIL) A simple multimedia scripting language designed for Web pages. SMIL enables Internet users to view multimedia without having to download plug-ins.

synchronous communication Communication in which both parties to the communication are online at the time and have a coherent conversation, as in instant messaging.

syntax The set of rules governing the structure of instructions, commands, and statements of a programming language.

syntax error In programming, a flaw in the structure of instructions, commands, and statements. Syntax errors must be eliminated before the program will run.

synthesizer An audio component that uses FM (frequency modulation), wavetable, or waveguide technology to create sounds imitative of actual musical instruments.

system A collection of components purposefully organized into a functioning whole to accomplish a goal.

system clock An electronic circuit in the computer that emits pulses at regular intervals, enabling the computer's internal components to operate in synchrony.

system requirements The minimum level of equipment that a program needs to run.

system software All the programs that provide the infrastructure and hardware control needed for a computer, its peripheral devices, and other programs to function smoothly. It includes the operating system and utility programs.

system unit The base unit of the computer that includes the plastic or metal enclosure, motherboard, and integrated peripherals. It provides a sturdy frame for mounting and protecting internal devices, connectors, and drives.

system utilities Programs that work in tandem with the operating system and are considered essential to the effective management of a computer system. They perform such functions as system backup, antivirus protection, file search and management, system scans, disk and file defragmentation, and file compression; also called utility programs.

systems analysis The field concerned with the planning, development, and implementation of artificial systems, including information systems.

systems analyst A problem-solving computer professional who works with users and management to determine an organization's information system needs.

systems development life cycle (SDLC) An approach or model used in the development of information systems. Its intent is to provide a structure or systematic guide to development with the goal of improving system quality.

systems engineering An interdisciplinary engineering approach to creating and maintaining quality systems.

T

T1 line A high-bandwidth telephone trunk line capable of transferring 1.544 megabits per second (Mbps) of data.

T3 line A high-bandwidth fiber-optic line capable of handling 43 megabits per second (Mbps) of computer data.

tab Located on the Ribbon, it contains categories of tasks you can accomplish within an application.

tabbed browsing A type of Internet browsing that enables a user to quickly switch between Web sites. You can customize your home page by adding tabs for sites that you frequently access.

Table object In the Microsoft Access database management system, the object used to store data.

tablet PC A type of notebook computer that has an LCD screen on which the user can write using a special pen or stylus.

tactical decision A middle management decision about how to best organize resources to achieve a division's goals.

tactile display A display that stimulates the sense of touch using vibration, pressure, and temperature changes. Such a display enhances the virtual reality experience because the user can make contact with the environment.

tag 1. A marker that identifies various elements within markup language codes. Tags usually come in pairs. The actual text to be displayed is enclosed by an opening tag and a closing tag. 2. Any user-generated word or phrase that helps organize Web content and label it in a more human way.

tailor-made application A piece of software designed for specialized fields or the consumer market, such as a program to handle the billing needs of medical offices, manage restaurants, and track occupational injuries.

tangible benefit A material benefit such as increased sales, faster response time, and decreased complaints that can be easily assessed.

TCP/IP (Transmission Control Protocol/Internet Protocol) The standard suite of methods used to package and transmit information on the Internet. TCP/IP employs a two-layer communication design. The TCP layer, Transmission Control Protocol, manages the assembling of a message or file into smaller packets that are transmitted over the Internet and received by a TCP layer on the destination computer that reassembles the packets into the original message. The lower layer, the Internet Protocol, handles the address part of each packet so that it gets to the right destination.

teamware See groupware.

technical feasibility A project's capability of being accomplished with existing, proven technology.

technical skill A practice in businesses that is about working with specific tools. In the IT field, technical skills include such skills as knowledge and experience in networking, Microsoft Windows products, UNIX, C++, and Internet-related technologies.

telecommuting Using telecommunications and computer equipment to work from home while still being connected to the office; also called teleworking.

teleconferencing When two or more people, separated by distance, use telecommunications and computer equipment to conduct business activities.

telemedicine The use of computers and medical expertise to provide the equivalent of the long-distance house call.

teleworking See telecommuting.

template A document framework that is created once and then used many times. For example, word processing programs typically include templates for faxes, letters, memos, reports, resumes, brochures, and many more types of documents.

terabyte (TB) A unit of measurement commonly used to state the capacity of memory or storage devices; equal to 1,024 gigabytes, or approximately 1 trillion bytes or characters.

terminal An input/output device consisting of a keyboard and a video display, used as an inexpensive means to connect to a server.

terminator A special connector that signifies the end of a circuit in the bus topology.

text messaging A mobile service, similar to using your phone for instant messaging or as a receiver and transmitter for brief e-mail messages.

texting A quick communication that might include text, images, video, and/or sound content that is generally delivered using a cell phone.

thermal-transfer printer A printer that uses a heat process to transfer colored dyes or inks to the paper's surface. Although thermal-transfer printers are the best color printers currently available, they are very expensive.

thin client Either a software program or to an actual computer that relies heavily on another computer to do most of its work.

thread In Usenet, a series of articles that offer a continuing commentary on the same specific subject.

throughput The actual amount of data that can be sent through a specific transmission medium at one time (usually per second). Throughput is almost always lower than bandwidth, especially with wireless communications.

thumb drive Another name for a USB drive.

thumbscrew A small screw (usually found in pairs) that is attached to a plug and used to secure the plug to the system unit or expansion card extender to prevent an accidental disconnect.

time bomb A destructive program that sits harmlessly until a certain event or set of circumstances makes the program active; also called logic bomb.

time-limited trial version A commercial program offered over the Internet that can be used on a trial basis for a period of time, after which the software is unusable.

title bar In a graphical user interface (GUI), the top bar of an application window. The title bar typically contains the name of the application, the name of the document, and window controls.

toggle key A key on a keyboard that has two states: on and off. When pressed, the function is turned on, and when pressed again, the function is turned off.

token A special unit of data that travels around the ring in a ring topology layout of a network. A node can transmit only when it possesses the token thus preventing collisions.

top-down program design Sometimes used to describe structured programming. A design strategy that starts by focusing on the main goal that the program is trying to achieve and then breaks up the program into manageable components.

top-level domain (TLD) name The last part of the domain portion of a URL. For computers located in the United States, it indicates the type of organization in which the computer is located, such as commercial businesses (com), educational institutions (edu), and government agencies (gov).

top-level folder Used to organize groups of files that have something in common. These are at the top of the folder structure.

touch pad (trackpad) A stationary, pressure sensitive, pointing device that provides a small, flat surface on which you slide your finger using the same movements as you would a mouse. You issue commands through one of the touchpad keys located near the edge of the pad or by tapping on the pad's surface.

touch screen A touch-sensitive display that enables users to input choices by touching a region of the screen.

tower case A tall and deep system unit case designed to sit on the floor next to a desk and easily accommodate add-on components.

track One of several concentric circular bands on computer disks where data is recorded, similar to the grooves on a phonographic record. Tracks are created during formatting (set up) and are divided into sectors.

trackball A stationary pointing device that contains a movable ball held in a cradle. The on-screen cursor is moved by rotating the ball with the fingers or palm.

trade show Typically, an annual meeting in which computer product manufacturers, designers, and dealers display their products.

traditional organizational structure A method of distributing the core functions of an organization into divisions such as finance, human resources, and operations.

training seminar A computer-related training session, typically presented by the developer of a new hardware or software product or by a company specializing in training IT professionals in a new technology.

transaction processing system (TPS) A system for handling an organization's day-to-day accounting needs by keeping a verifiable record of every transaction involving money, including purchases, sales, and payroll payments; also called an operational system or a data processing system.

transfer performance A measure of how quickly read/write heads are able to transfer data from a hard disk to RAM.

transistor A device invented in 1947 by Bell Laboratories that controls the flow of electricity. Due to their small size, reduced power consumption, and lower heat output, transistors replaced vacuum tubes in the second generation of computers.

Transmission Control Protocol (TCP) Part of the TCP/IP suite of protocols that regulate packaging and transmitting information over the Internet. TCP is the higher layer of the standard of transmission that permits two Internet-connected computers to establish a reliable connection. It is responsible for managing the assembling of a message or file into smaller packets that are transmitted over the Internet and received by a TCP layer on the destination computer that reassembles the packets into the original message.

trap door In computer security, a security hole created on purpose that can be exploited at a later time.

travel mouse A pointing device half the size of a normal mouse but with all of the same capabilities.

Trojan horse A rogue program that contains instructions to perform a malicious task that is disguised as a useful program.

truncation In using a search engine, the action of inserting wildcard symbols such as ? and *, also called truncation symbols, to search for various word endings and spellings simultaneously.

truncation symbol See wildcard.

tweet A posting on Twitter.

twisted pair An inexpensive copper cable used for telephone and data communications. The term *twisted pair* refers to the interweaving of the paired wires, a practice that reduces interference from electrical fields.

Twitter A free, real-time social messaging utility that allows postings of up to 140 characters. The exchanges are short and usually in a question and answer mode.

U

ubiquitous computing A scenario for future computing that foresees an emerging trend in which individuals no longer interact with one computer at a time but instead with multiple devices connected through an omnipresent network, enabling technology to become virtually embedded and invisible in every aspect of our lives.

ultraportable See subnotebook.

Unicode A character coding system that uses 16 bits and can represent over 65,000 characters, allowing it to represent most of the world's languages.

Unified Modeling Language (UML) An open method used to illustrate and document the components of an object-oriented software system under development.

uninstalling The act of removing a program from a computer system by using a special utility.

uninterruptible power supply (UPS) A device that provides power to a computer system for a short time if electrical power is lost.

UNIX An operating system developed by Bell Laboratories in 1969. It was the first operating system written in the C language. It is a free OS installed primarily on workstations and features preemptive multitasking.

uploading Transferring a file from your computer to another computer by means of a computer network.

URL (uniform resource locator) On the World Wide Web, a string of characters that precisely identifies an Internet resource's type and location. For example, the fictitious URL **http://www.wolverine. virginia.edu/~toros/winerefs/merlot. html** identifies a World Wide Web document (http://), indicates the domain name of the computer on which it is stored (**www.wolverine.virginia.edu**), fully describes the document's location in the directory structure (~toros/winerefs/), and includes the document's name and extension (merlot.html).

USB (universal serial bus) port An external bus architecture that connects peripherals such as keyboards, mice, and digital cameras. USB offers many benefits over older serial architectures, such as support for 127 devices on a single port, plug-and-play, and higher transfer rates.

USB flash drive A portable, easy-to-use, rewritable, and inexpensive external storage device, about the size of an adult thumb, that can hold up to 64 GB of data (approximately 180 CDs). Memory sticks, thumb drives, and jump drives are popular USB flash drives. USB flash drives work with both the PC and the Mac, and no device driver is required. Just plug the device into a USB port and it's ready to read and write.

USB hub A device that plugs into an existing USB port and contains four or more additional ports.

Usenet A worldwide computer-based discussion system that uses the Internet and other networks for transmission media. Discussion is channeled into more than 50,000 topically named newsgroups, which contain original contributions called articles, as well as commentaries on these articles called follow-up posts. As follow-up posts continue to appear on a given subject, a thread of discussion emerges; a threaded newsreader collates these articles together so readers can see the flow of the discussion.

user interface The part of the operating system that the user sees, interacts with, and uses to communicate with programs.

utility programs See system utilities.

V

vacation hacking Usually occurs in hotels, and airports where an unsuspected traveler accesses a rogue Wi-Fi access point, called an evil twin, on a fraudulent network. The information the traveler enters is not reaching the desired destination but is being captured by criminals running the fraudulent network.

validate After purchasing a software program, it is the process of providing a special code or product key before you can use it. Validation proves that you are using a legal copy, not a pirated version.

value-added network (VAN) A public data network offered by a service provider that an enterprise uses for EDI or other services.

value-added reseller (VAR) An independent company that combines and installs equipment and software from several sources.

variant A copy of a self-modifying virus. Each new copy is slightly different from the previous one, making it difficult to protect your computer.

VBScript A client-side scripting language used to write short programs (scripts) that can be embedded in Web pages.

vector graphic An image composed of distinct objects, such as lines, shapes, or any element created by a mathematical equation. Thus, the final image is described by a complex mathematical formula that can be edited quite easily to accommodate a change in size, location, or shape.

vendor A company that sells goods or services. In this context, it refers to a company that develops software and sells it to other firms.

very high bit-rate digital subscriber line (VDSL) The next generation DSL with super-accelerated rates of 52 Mbps for downloads and 12 Mbps for uploads. It will provide services like HDTV and Video-on-Demand along with Internet access.

VGA (video graphics array) connector A 15-pin male connector that works with standard monitor cables. VGA connectors transmit analog video signals and are traditionally used for legacy technology cathode ray tube (CRT) monitors.

video card Video circuitry that fits into an expansion bus and determines the quality of the display and resolution of your monitor. Also called video adapter or display adapter.

video editor A program that enables you to view, edit, and save a digitized video file in several video file formats.

Video Graphics Array (VGA) A display standard that can display 16 colors at a maximum resolution of 640 pixels by 480 pixels.

videoconferencing A technology enabling two or more people to have a face-to-face meeting even though they're geographically separated.

viewable area The front surface on a cathode-ray tube monitor actually available for viewing, which is less than the quoted size. See quoted size.

virtual keyboard An onscreen touch-activated keyboard. See soft keyboard.

virtual laser keyboard A keyboard image generated by a device about the size of a small cellular phone that displays a light projection of a full-sized computer keyboard on almost any surface. Its adaptable technology studies the user's finger movements to interpret and record keystrokes.

virtual memory A term used to refer to a portion of a hard drive that the operating system uses as an extension of RAM when RAM is full.

virtual private network (VPN) A network that operates as a private network over the Internet, using exclusive leased lines, making data accessible to authorized users in remote locations through the use of secure, encrypted connections and special software.

virtual reality (VR) A computer-generated illusion of three-dimensional space. On the Web, virtual reality sites enable Web users to explore three-dimensional virtual reality worlds by means of VR plug-in programs. These programs enable you to walk or "fly" through the three-dimensional space that these worlds offer.

Virtual Reality Modeling Language (VRML) A scripting language that enables programmers to specify the characteristics of a three-dimensional world that is accessible on the Internet. VRML worlds can contain sounds, hyperlinks, videos, and animations as well as three-dimensional spaces, which can be explored by using a VRML plug-in.

Visual Basic (VB) An event-driven programming language that responds to user actions, like the click of a mouse. It was developed by Microsoft and based on the BASIC programming language. Visual Basic, which was one of the world's most widely used program development packages, has been largely replaced by Visual Basic.NET.

Visual Basic. NET (VB. NET) Microsoft's next evolution of Visual Basic (VB) released in 2001, which uses an object-oriented language.

Visual Studio .NET A suite of products that contains Visual Basic .NET, which enables programmers to work with complex objects; Visual C++, which is based upon C++; and Visual C# (pronounced "C sharp").

vlog Short for video log. A series of personal reflective videos that are usually made simply by talking to a Webcam and uploading the video.

vocabulary A set of elements or tags for a particular field or discipline.

vodcast Short for video podcast. A term used for the online delivery of video clips on demand.

VoIP (voice over Internet Protocol) A type of Internet telephony that uses the Internet for real-time voice communication.

volatile memory Storage that is very fast but that is erased when the power goes off. RAM is volatile memory.

W

W3C (World Wide Web Consortium) An international consortium of over 440 organizations in more than 40 countries responsible for ensuring long-term growth for the World Wide Web and promoting Web interoperability through the publication of open standards for Web languages and protocols.

WAP (Wireless Application Protocol) A standard that specifies how users can access the Web securely using pagers, smartphones, PDAs, and other wireless handheld devices.

wardriving A process in which an individual drives around with a wireless device, such as a notebook or smartphone, to look for wireless networks to break into.

warm boot Restarting a computer that is already on.

waterfall model A systems development method that builds correction pathways into the process so that analysts can return to a previous phase.

Web 1.0 A set of techniques that were used in the early years of the Web for developing static Web pages that included no interactivity other than hyperlinks.

Web 2.0 A set of techninques currently in use that collectively provide an upgraded presentation and usefulness for the World Wide Web. It provides even more opportunities for individuals to collaborate, interact with one another, and create new content by using applications such as blogs, wikis, and podcasts.

Web 3.0 The next generation of the Web. Many experts believe that the Web 3.0 browser will act like a personal assistant, learning what you are interested in as you browse.

Web beacon A transparent graphic image, usually no larger than 1 pixel × 1 pixel, that is placed on a Web site or in an e-mail and used to monitor the behavior of the user visiting the Web site or sending the e-mail. One common use is to alert a sender when a message has been opened.

Web browser A program on the user's computer that displays a Web document by interpreting the HTML or XHTML format, enabling the user to access Web pages and linked documents.

Web page A document or resource of information on a Web site suitable for the World Wide Web that is accessed by a browser. The information on the page is in HTML or XHTML format and can include text, graphics, sound, animation, video, and hypertext links to other Web pages.

Web portals (portals) Web sites that provide multiple online services.

Web server A computer on the Web running server software that accepts requests for information, processes those requests, and sends the requested documents.

Web-based language A language that tells a browser how to interpret text and objects, as compared to a programming language that tells a computer (specifically the microprocessor) what to do and how to do it. Markup and scripting languages are examples.

Web-based training (WBT) Computer-based training implemented via the Internet or an intranet. Web-based training methods often include instant messaging, discussion forums, and chat tools, in addition to more advanced applications, such as live Web broadcasts with streaming audio or video and videoconferencing.

Webcam A low-cost video camera used for low-resolution videoconferencing on the Internet.

Web-database integration A name for techniques that make information stored in databases available through Internet connections.

Web-enabled device Any device that can connect to the Internet and display and respond to the codes in markup languages, such as HTML (Hypertext Markup Language) or XML (Extensible Markup Language), typically used to build Web pages.

Web-hosted technology A new wave in online office suites that offers the capability to upload files to an online site so they can be viewed and edited from another location. It is also possible to share files with others, making group collaboration easier. Google Docs and Windows Office Live are two examples.

Web site A collection of related Web pages.

WEP (Wired Equivalent Privacy) One of the earliest security methods for wireless networks, WEP has several well-known weaknesses, but it may be the only option for some devices or older equipment.

what-if analysis See modeling.

wheel mouse A type of mouse that has a rotating wheel that is used to scroll text vertically within a document or on a Web page.

whistle-blowing Reporting illegal or unethical actions of a company to a regulatory agency or the press.

white hat See ethical hacker.

whiteboard A separate area of a videoconferencing screen enabling participants to create a shared workspace. Participants can write or draw in this space as if they were using a chalkboard in a meeting.

wide area network (WAN) A data network that uses long-distance transmission media to link computers separated by a few miles or even thousands of miles. The Internet is the largest WAN—it connects millions of LANs all over the globe using a variety of physical media, such as microwave relay, satellites, and phone lines.

Widescreen Extended Graphics Array plus (WXGA+) A resolution of 1440 × 900, typically found in 19-inch monitors.

Widescreen Super Extended Graphics Array plus (WSXGA+) A resolution of 1680 × 1050, typically found in 20-inch monitors.

Widescreen Ultra Extended Graphics Array (WUXGA) A resolution of 1920 × 1200, typically found in 24-inch monitors.

Wi-Fi A wireless LAN standard that offers Ethernet speeds through the use of radio waves instead of wires.

wiki A simple Web page or collection of Web pages on which any visitor can post text or images, read previous posts, change posted information, and track earlier changes.

wildcard A symbol that stands for any character or any group of characters. Common wildcards are the ? for a single character and * for multiple characters; also called a truncation symbol.

WiMAX A wireless up-and-coming digital communication system designed to deliver high-speed access over long distances, either point to point (both sender and receiver are stationary) or through mobile access (sender or receiver is moving).

window border A thick line the encloses the window and allows the area to become larger or smaller; however, it is only effective if the window is not maximized.

window control In a graphical user interface (GUI), a group of window management tools that enable the user to minimize, maximize, restore, or close the window.

Windows Update An operating system update service designed to keep your Windows operating system up to date with fixes (service patches) or protections against external environment changes.

wired Connected by a physical medium.

wireless Connected through the air or space.

wireless access point (AP or WAP) A node on a network that acts as a receiver and transmitter of wireless radio signals between other nodes on a network. A WAP can also act as a join or bridge connecting wireless clients to a wired network.

wireless keyboard A keyboard that connects to the computer through infrared (IR), radio frequency (RF) or Bluetooth connections instead of a cable.

wireless LAN A local area network that connects its nodes though the use of radio signals spread over a seemingly random series of frequencies for greater security.

Wireless Markup Language (WML) A specialized form of XML that enables developers to create pages specifically for wireless devices.

wireless memory card A card that has all the storage features of a regular flash memory card and combines it with wireless circuitry. It can connect with your PC via a wireless network or send pictures directly from your digital camera to your favorite online photo site.

wireless mouse A mouse with no cord that transmits infrared or radio signals

(RF) to a base station receiver. Wireless mice eliminate the cord tangling associated with the corded variety. The infrared type requires line of sight to the receiver, whereas the RF variety uses radio waves that transmit in a wider pattern.

word size The number of bits a computer can work with at one time.

workbook In a spreadsheet program such as Microsoft Excel, a file that can contain two or more spreadsheets, each of which has its own page in the workbook.

workflow automation The process of sending documents and data to the next person who needs to see them.

workgroup computing A situation in which all of the members of a *workgroup*—a collection of individuals working together on a task—have specific hardware, software, and networking equipment that enables them to connect, communicate, and collaborate.

worksheet In a spreadsheet program such as Microsoft Excel, a single tab of a workbook.

World Wide Web (Web or WWW) The portion of the Internet that contains billions of documents. The Web uses the Internet as its transport mechanism but is a separate entity. The Web is an information resource that enables millions of Internet users to research products, get medical advice, read about current events, and much more.

World Wide Web Consortium (W3C) An international consortium in which member organizations, a full-time staff, and the public work together to develop Web standards. W3C's mission is to lead the World Wide Web to its full potential by developing protocols and guidelines that ensure long-term growth for the Web.

worm A program resembling a computer virus that can spread over networks without the user executing an infected file.

WPA (Wi-Fi Protected Access) A security method for wireless networks that was developed to provide stronger security than WEP.

WPA2 A security method for wireless networks that improves on WPA's abilities. WPA2 provides confidentiality and data integrity and is far superior to WEP, because it uses AES (Advanced Encryption Standard) to provide government-grade security.

X

X.25 A packet-switching network protocol optimized for use on noisy analog telephone lines.

xD Picture Card A type of flash memory card used in digital cameras. It is available in capacities of 16 MB up to 2 GB.

xDLS See DSL (Digital Subscriber Line).

XHTML (eXtensible Hypertext Markup Language) A newer version of HTML, it uses XML to produce Web pages that are easily accessible by PDAs, notebooks, and desktops. See Extensible Hypertext Markup Language.

XML (eXtensible Markup Language) A set of rules for creating markup languages that enables programmers to capture specific types of data by creating their own elements. It is used for sharing data and complex forms and objects in a Web-based environment. See Extensible Markup Language.

Y

Yes/No data type See Boolean data type.

yottabyte A unit of measurement approximately equal to 1 septillion bytes.

Z

zero configuration (Zeroconf) A method for networking devices via an Ethernet cable that does not require configuration and administration.

zettabyte A unit of measurement approximately equal to 1 sextillion bytes.

zombie A single computer commandeered during a denial of service (DoS) attack.

Illustration Credits

Chapter 1

Figure CO-01 Getty Images **Figure 01-01** Corepics\Shutterstock **Figure 01-03a** Michael Jarrett\Gateway Inc. **Figure 01-03b** jossnat\Shutterstock **Figure 01-03c** Courtesy of Apple **Figure 01-03d** Courtesy of Research In Motion (RIM). Research In Motion, the RIM logo, BlackBerry, the BlackBerry logo and Sure-Type are registered with the U.S. Patent and Trademark Office and may be pending or registered in other countries - these and other marks of Research In Motion Limited are used under license. **Figure 01-04a** Jellyhead360\Shutterstock **Figure 01-04b** © Dell, Inc. All Rights Reserved. The Dell logo is a trademark of Dell Inc. **Figure 01-04c** **Figure 01-05b** Courtesy of Cisco **Figure 01-05c** Motorola, Inc. **Figure 01-05d** Susan Van Etten\PhotoEdit Inc. **Figure 01-05e** © Greg Nicholas / Courtesy of **www.istockphoto.com** **Figure 01-06** Photographer's Choice\Superstock Royalty Free **Figure 01-07a** Reprinted with permission from Microsoft Corporation. **Figure 01-07b** Reprinted with permission from Microsoft Corporation. **Figure 01-08** Courtesy of Intel Corporation **Figure 01-09** Murat Baysan\Shutterstock **Figure 01-10a** Alan Klehr\Churchill & Klehr Photography **Figure 01-10b** Getty Images, Inc.-Photodisc./Royalty Free **Figure 01-10c** Eyewire, Inc./Getty Images **Figure 01-11a** Zefa Collection\CORBIS- NY **Figure 01-11d** Nick Koudis\Getty Images, Inc.- Photodisc./Royalty Free **Figure 1-12** Michael Jarrett\Gateway Inc. **Figure 01-13** © Dell, Inc. All Rights Reserved. The Dell logo is a trademark of Dell Inc. **Figure 01-14** Courtesy of Apple **Figure 01-15** Toshiba America Information Systems, Inc. **Figure 01-16a** francesco riccardo iacomino\Shutterstock **Figure 01-16b** Anatoliy Samara\Shutterstock **Figure 01-16c** Henrik Andersen\ Shutterstock **Figure 01-17** Psycho\Shutterstock **Figure 01-18** Albo\Shutterstock **Figure 01-19** iStockphoto **Figure 01-20** iStockphoto **Figure 01-21** Jupiter Unlimited **Figure 1-22** **Figure 01-24** Photodisc/Getty Images **Figure 01-27** Jupiter Unlimited **Figure 01-28** Gravitonus, Inc. **Figure 01-29** iStockphoto **Figure 01-30** michael ledray\Shutterstock

Spotlight 1

Figure SP01-CO iStockphoto **Figure SP01-A** Knumina\Shutterstock **Figure SP01-C** Mikael Damkier\Shutterstock **Figure SP01-D** Raquel Ramirez\PhotoEdit Inc. **Figure SP01-E** Amy Walters\ Shutterstock **Figure Spot-01G** © Jim Criagmyle / CORBIS All Rights Reserved **Figure Spot-01I** The Software & Information Industry Association

Chapter 2

Figure CO-02 Brad Mitchell\Alamy Images **Figure 02-02** Imageclub Royalty Free\Inmagine Corporation LLC **Figure 02-07a** Lenovo, Inc. **Figure 02-08** Lenovo, Inc. **Figure 02-09b** Courtesy of Intel Corporation **Figure 02-10a** Kingston Technology Co., Inc. **Figure 02-10b** © Creative Technology Ltd. **Figure 02-10c** © US Robotics **Figure 02-10e** Manic Photos\ Alamy Images **Figure 02-11** Antony Nettle **Figure 02-17a** Courtesy of Intel Corporation **Figure 02-20** © Carolina K. Smith, M.D. / Courtesy of www.istockphoto.com **Figure 02-21a** Mitja Mladkovic\ Alamy.com **Figure 02-22** Phil Burton \Alamy.com **Figure 02-23** Lewis - Global Public Relations **Figure 02-24** Goodshot\Corbis RF

Chapter 3

Figure CO-03 Borderlands\Alamy Images **Figure 03-01a** Photoshot Archive Creative **Figure 03-01b** Reprinted with permission from Microsoft Corporation. **Figure 03-01c** mediacolor's\Alamy Images **Figure 03-01d** Getty Images, Inc - Stockbyte Royalty Free **Figure 03-04** Steve Marcus\CORBIS- NY **Figure 03-05** ilian studio\Alamy.com **Figure 03-06** © 2008 Logitech. All rights reserved. Used with permission from Logitech. **Figure 03-07b** Logitech Inc. **Figure 03-07c** Courtesy of IBM Archives. Unauthorized use not permitted. **Figure 03-07e** Courtesy of IBM Archives. Unauthorized use not permitted. **Figure 03-07f** © Kim Kulish / CORBIS All Rights Reserved **Figure 03-07g** © Hank Drew / Stock this Way / CORBIS All Rights Reserved **Figure 03-08** Reprinted with permission from Microsoft Corporation. **Figure 03-12a** Courtesy of Canon USA. The Canon logo is a trademark of Canon Inc. All rights reserved. **Figure 03-12b** Visioneer Inc. **Figure 03-13a** Courtesy of IBM Archives. Unauthorized use not permitted. **Figure 03-13b** AP Wide World Photos **Figure 03-13c** iStockphoto **Figure 03-14b** ViewSonic Corporation **Figure 03-14c** ViewSonic Corporation **Figure 03-17** Brother International Corporation **Figure 03-18** Photo courtesy of XEROX Corporate Public Relations. **Figure 03-20a** ViewSonic Corporation **Figure 03-20b** Panasonic Corporation of North America **Figure 03-23a** Courtesy of Intel Corporation **Figure 03-23b** Courtesy of IBM Archives. Unauthorized use not permitted. **Figure 03-24** Samsung

Electronics America, Inc. **Figure 03-25a** Imation Corp. **Figure 03-25b** Copyright 2008 Mimoco. COURTESY OF LUCAS-FILM LTD. TM & © Lucasfilm Ltd. All rights reserved. Used under authorization. Unauthorized duplication is a violation of applicable law. **Figure 03-26** PhotoDisc\Getty Images, Inc.- Photodisc./Royalty Free **Figure 03-28** ExpressCard - PCMCIA **Figure 03-29a** SanDisk Corporation **Figure 03-29b** SanDisk Corporation **Figure 03-29c** Lexar Media, USA **Figure 03-30** SanDisk Corporation **Figure 03-31** © William Whitehurst / CORBIS All Rights Reserved **Figure 03-32** Seagate Technology, Inc.

Spotlight 2

Figure SP02-CO iStockphoto

Chapter 4

Figure CO-04 David Muenker\Alamy Images **Figure 04-01a** © 2004 with express permission from Adobe Systems Incorporated **Figure 4-01b** Reprinted with permission from Microsoft Corporation. **Figure 4-03** **Figure 04-10e** Sun Microsystems, Inc. **Figure 04-16** HTC America. **Figure 04-20** Palm, Inc. **Figure 04-22a** One Laptop Per Child **Figure 04-22b** Everex, Inc.

Spotlight 3

Figure SP03-CO gibsons\Shutterstock **Figure SP03-A2** goory\Shutterstock **Figure SP03-A3** Dmitry Melnikov\Shutterstock **Figure SP03-B1** Targus, Inc. **Figure SP03-B2** jossnat\Shutterstock **Figure SP03-B3** Targus, Inc. **Figure SP03-** Photoalto Royalty-free\Inmagine Corporation LLC **Figure SP03-C1** Shutterstock **Figure SP03-E** Pioneer Electronics (USA) Inc. **Figure SP03-F** Advanced Micro Devices **Figure SP03-G** Reprinted with permission from Microsoft Corporation. **Figure SP03-G1** Ximagination\Shutterstock **Figure SP03-H** American Power Conversion Corporation **Figure SP03-I** Targus, Inc. **Figure SP03-J** Peter Cade/Image Bank/Getty Images **Figure SP03-L** Falk Kienas\Shutterstock **Figure SP03-M** Mark Scott/Taxi/Getty Images

Chapter 5

Figure CO-05 © B.S.P.I. / CORBIS All Rights Reserved **Figure 05-06** cloki\Shutterstock **Figure 05-07** iStockphoto **Figure 05-09** Gilles Tran \Wikipedia, The Free Encyclopedia **Figure 05-15** Apple Computer, Inc. **Figure 05-18a** Intuit, Inc. **Figure 05-18b** Chief Architect

Index

terabyte (TB), 45
terminals, 14
terrorism
    data mining, 443
    information, 361
    9/11, 361, 366
    public key encryption, 366
texting, 33, 252–254, 316
theft, 351–352
thermal-transfer printers, 81
thin client, 14, 498
Thin Film Transistor (TFT). *See* active-matrix
third generation (3G) cell phones, 304,
       305, 307
Thomas, Eric, 229
threads, 229
three-dimensional rendering programs, 162
throughput, 292
thumb drives. *See* flash drives
thumbscrews, 59
time bombs, 351
time-limited trial versions, 173
title bar, 185
TiVo, 129
toggle keys, 71
tokens, 268
top-down program design. *See* structured programming
top-level domain (TLD), 213
top-level folder, 100
topologies (network), 266–268
Torvalds, Linus, 125
touch screens, 74, 75
touchpads, 74, 75
tower case, 48
trackballs, 74, 75
trackpads. *See* touchpads
tracks, 84
trade shows, 396–397
training seminars, 396
transaction acquisition, 278
transaction processing system (TPS), 452–453
transfer performance, 85
transistors, 50
translation, machine, 383
Transmission Control Protocol (TCP), 204, 276
trap doors, 359
travel mouse, 74
trial versions, 173
Trillian, 252
Trojan horses, 351
troubleshooting, 135–136
truncation symbols. *See* wildcards
Turing, Alan, 381
Turing Test, 381, 382
TV. *See* televisions
tweets, 17
twisted pair wiring, 294–295, 300
Twitter, 17, 248, 249–250, 255

U

ubiquitous computing, 340–341, 377
Ubuntu, 126. *See also* Linux

ultraportables. *See* subnotebooks
Unicode, 47
Unified Modeling Language (UML), 427
uninstalling software, 177, 178
uninterruptible power supply (UPS), 149, 362
UNIX, 124–125
update services, 135
upgrading
    enterprise computing, 488–489
    software, 25, 173–174
    your computer, 152–153
uploading, 215
URL (Uniform Resource Locator), 213–214
USB (universal serial bus)
    flash drives, 9, 86–87, 147, 344
    hubs, 61
    ports, 7, 60–61, 70
    SuperSpeed (3.0), 61
Usenet, 228–229
user interfaces, 118–120
user names, 114–115
utility programs. *See* system utilities

V

vacation hacking, 359
validation, 175, 446–447
value-added networks (VANs), 499
value-added retailers (VARs), 476
variants, 350
VBScript, 423, 424
VDSL (very high bit-rate digital subscriber line),
      300, 301
vector graphics, 161
vendors, 392
Verizon, 307
VGA (video graphics array) connector,
      60, 61
video cards, 49, 50, 61, 147
video connectors, 60, 61
video editors, 164–165
Video for Windows, 165
Video Graphics Array (VGA), 79
video logs. *See* vlogs
video podcasts. *See* vodcasts
videoconferencing, 309–311
View tab, 187
viewable area, 79
virtual keyboards, 13, 71–73
virtual laser keyboards, 73
virtual memory, 57–58, 116–117
virtual private networks (VPNs), 266, 500
Virtual Reality Modeling Language (VRML), 380
virtual reality (VR), 378–380
viruses, 25, 130–131, 349–351
Visa International, 485
vision technology. *See* eye-gaze response systems
Vista. *See* Windows Vista
Visual Basic .NET (VB .NET), 421
Visual Basic (VB), 418–420
Visual Studio .NET, 421–422
vlogs, 246
Vmyths.com, 350

wireless access points (WAPs), 261
Wireless Application Protocol (WAP). *See* WAP
    (Wireless Application Protocol)
wireless communication, 295–298
    home networks, 279–281, 283–284
    infrared, 296
    microwave transmission, 297
    radio transmission, 296–297
    satellites, 297–298
    security issues, 264, 272, 316–317, 358–359
wireless keyboards, 70–71
wireless LANs, 264. *See also* Wi-Fi
Wireless Markup Language (WML). *See* WML
    (Wireless Markup Language)
wireless memory cards, 90–91
wireless mouse, 74
wireless network detectors, 358, 359
wireless printers, 148
wizards, 441
WML (Wireless Markup Language), 423
Women in Technology International (WITI), 398
Woods, Tiger, 250
Word, 158, 159, 171, 190–191, 198
word processing programs, 172. *See also specific
    programs*
word size, 52, 53
workbooks, 191
workflow automation, 503
workgroup computing, 502
worksheets, 191

World Organization of Webmasters (WOW), 398
World Wide Web. *See* Web
worms, 351
WPA2, 358–359
WPA (Wi-Fi Protected Access), 358–359

X

X.25, 278
XBRL. *See* Extensible Business Reporting
    Language (XBRL)
xD Picture Cards, 327
xDSL. *See* DSL (digital subscriber line)
    Internet access
XHTML. *See* Extensible Hypertext Markup Language
    (XHTML)
XML. *See* Extensible Markup Language (XML)

Y

Yahoo!, 217, 218, 219, 498
Yahoo! Messenger, 252
yottabyte, 46
YouTube, 247–248, 255, 329

Z

zero configuration (Zeroconf), 490
zettabyte, 46
Zip disks, 86
zipped files, 134
zune.net, 325